Microsoft® Virtual Server 2005 R2 Resource Kit

Janique Carbone and Robert Larson
with the Windows Virtualization Team

PUBLISHED BY
Microsoft Press
A Division of Microsoft Corporation
One Microsoft Way
Redmond, Washington 98052-6399

Library of Congress Control Number: 2007930350

Printed and bound in the United States of America.

1 2 3 4 5 6 7 8 9   QWT   2 1 0 9 8 7

Distributed in Canada by H.B. Fenn and Company Ltd.

A CIP catalogue record for this book is available from the British Library.

Microsoft Press books are available through booksellers and distributors worldwide. For further information about international editions, contact your local Microsoft Corporation office or contact Microsoft Press International directly at fax (425) 936-7329. Visit our Web site at www.microsoft.com/mspress. Send comments to rkinput@microsoft.com.

Acquisitions Editor: Martin DelRe
Developmental Editor: Karen Szall
Project Editor: Melissa von Tschudi-Sutton
Editorial Production Services: Custom Editorial Productions, Inc.
Technical Reviewer: Ronald Beekelaar; Technical Review services provided by Content Master, a member of CM Group, Ltd.
Cover Illustration: Todd Daman

Body Part No. X13-91396

Contents at a Glance

Part I Getting Started with Microsoft Virtual Server 2005 R2 SP1

1 Introducing Virtual Server 2005 R2 SP1 3
2 Virtual Server 2005 R2 SP1 Product Overview 29
3 Virtual Server Architecture 55

Part II Installing and Managing Virtual Server 2005

4 Installing Virtual Server 2005 R2 SP1 73
5 Virtual Server 2005 R2 Advanced Features 109
6 Security in Depth 145
7 Best Practices for Configuration and Performance Tuning 167
8 Virtual Machine Creation Process 195
9 Developing Scripts with the Virtual Server COM API 227
10 Virtual Machine Migration Process 281
11 Troubleshooting Common Virtual Server Issues 313

Part III Virtualization Project Methodology

12 Virtualization Project: Envisioning Phase 333
13 Virtualization Project: Discovery Phase 347
14 Virtualization Project: Assessment Phase 361
15 Virtualization Project: Planning and Design Phase 373
16 Virtualization Project: Pilot Phase 389

Part IV Virtual Server Infrastructure Management

17 Managing a Virtual Server Infrastructure 403
18 Using the MOM 2005 Virtual Server 2005 R2 Management Pack . . . 427
19 Microsoft System Center Virtual Machine Manager 2007 451
20 Additional Management Tools 481

Part V Appendices

A Virtual Server 2005 R2 Event Codes 503
B Virtual Server 2005 R2 Management Pack Rules 521

Table of Contents

Dedication xix

Acknowledgments. xxi

Introduction xxiii

Part I   Getting Started with Microsoft Virtual Server 2005 R2 SP1

1   Introducing Virtual Server 2005 R2 SP1 3

    Understanding Virtualization 4

    What Is Software Virtualization? 4

        Machine-Level Virtualization 5

        Operating System–Level Virtualization. 8

        Application-Level Virtualization. 9

    Making a Business Case for Virtualization 11

        Reducing Capital and Operating Costs. 11

        Implementing a Simple, Flexible, and Dynamic Infrastructure 12

        Increasing the Availability of Computing Resources. 13

        Decreasing Time to Provision or Distribute Services 13

        Decreasing Management Complexity. 14

    Defining Virtualization Scenarios. 15

        Consolidating the Data Center. 15

        Consolidating the Branch Office 15

        Virtualizing the Test and Development Infrastructure 16

        Implementing Business Continuity and Recovery. 16

    Virtual Server 2005 R2 SP1 Benefits 17

    What's New in Virtual Server 2005 R2 SP1. 19

        Intel VT and AMD-V Support. 20

        Volume Shadow Copy Service Support 20

        Virtual Server Host Clustering 21

What do you think of this book? We want to hear from you!

Microsoft is interested in hearing your feedback so we can continually improve our books and learning resources for you. To participate in a brief online survey, please visit:

www.microsoft.com/learning/booksurvey/

VHDMount Command-Line Tool 21

Virtual Machine Server Publication Using Active Directory Service
Connection Points 21

Host Operating System Support 21

Guest Operating System Support 23

Guest Virtual Machine Capacity 24

Default Size for a Dynamic VHD 24

Linux Guest Virtual Machine SCSI Emulation Fix 24

Microsoft Virtual Server 2005 R2 SP1 Support Policies 24

Product Support Policy 25

Application Support Policy 25

Microsoft Virtualization Product Roadmap 25

Summary 27

Additional Resources 27

2   Virtual Server 2005 R2 SP1 Product Overview 29

Reviewing Virtual Server 2005 R2 29

Virtual Machine Hardware Environment 30

Virtual Hard Disks 31

Virtual IDE Interface 32

Virtual SCSI Interface 32

Virtual Networks 33

Virtual Network Adapters 34

Virtual Machine Additions 34

Virtual Machine Remote Control 35

Managing with the Administration Website 35

Managing Multiple Virtual Server Hosts 36

Managing Virtual Machines 37

Managing Virtual Hard Disks 40

Managing Virtual Networks 42

Managing Virtual Server Properties 44

Managing Website Properties 49

Managing Virtual Machine Resource Allocation 51

Inspecting the Virtual Server Event Viewer 52

Outlining the Virtual Server 2005 R2 COM API 53

Summary 53

Additional Resources 53

3   Virtual Server Architecture **55**

Product Architecture 55

Virtual Machine Monitor Architecture 57

Virtual Server Service 58

Virtual Machine Helper Service 58

Virtual Machine Additions 58

Virtual Processors 59

Virtual Server Memory 61

Virtual Networking 61

Virtual Hard Disks 64

How Is a Virtual Hard Disk Structured? 65

Block Allocation Table 68

Virtual Floppy Disks 69

A Save State File 69

Summary 69

Additional Resources 70

Part II   Installing and Managing Virtual Server 2005

4   Installing Virtual Server 2005 R2 SP1 . . . . **73**

What Are the Prerequisites? 73

Hardware Requirements 74

Operating System Requirements 74

Active Directory Requirements 75

What Are the Installation Scenarios? 76

Configuring Constrained Delegation 78

Installing Microsoft Internet Information Services 6.0 80

Windows XP 81

Windows Vista 82

Windows Server 2003 85

Installing Virtual Server 2005 R2 SP1 87

Single-Server Configuration 89

Local Administration Website and Remote Resources 91

Server Farm with Central Administration Website and Remote Resources . . 93

Documentation and Developer Resources Only 97

Virtual Machine Remote Control Client Tool Only 98

VHD Mount Tool Only 99

Uninstalling Virtual Server 2005 R2 SP1 101
Performing a Command-Line Installation 102
    Command-Line Options 103
    Command-Line Syntax 105
    Command-Line Examples 106
    Performing the Installation Scenarios Using the Command Line 107
Summary 107
Additional Resources 108

5 **Virtual Server 2005 R2 Advanced Features** **109**
Using Virtual Hard Disk Advanced Features 109
    Differencing Disks 110
    Undo Disks 116
    Linked Disks 118
    VHDMount Command-Line Tool 120
    VHD Compaction 123
Using Virtual Network Advanced Features 126
    Using the Microsoft Loopback Adapter 126
    Implementing Host-to-Guest Networking 128
    Configuring Internet Connection Sharing and Network
    Address Translation 129
Using Clustering Advanced Features 130
    Implementing a Virtual Machine Cluster Using iSCSI 131
    Implementing a Virtual Server Host Cluster Using iSCSI 135
Summary 142
Additional Resources 143

6 **Security in Depth** **145**
Securing Virtual Server 2005 R2 145
    Configuring a Virtual Server View Only Role 152
    Configuring a Virtual Server Security Manager Role 153
    Configuring a Virtual Machine Manager Role 154
    Configuring a Virtual Network Manager Role 156
    Configuring a Virtual Server Manager Role 157
    Configuring a VMRC Client Role 158
Securing Virtual Machine Access 159
    Configuring Centrally Managed Virtual Machine Security 159
    Configuring Organizationally Managed Virtual Machine Security 160
    Configuring Project-Managed Virtual Machine Security 161

Enabling Constrained Delegation 163
Configuring a Virtual Machine User Account 163
Securing Remote Administration Sessions 164
Virtual Server Services Security 164
Virtual Server Network Ports 165
Summary 165
Additional Resources 166

7   Best Practices for Configuration and Performance Tuning 167
Configuring the Administration Website 167
Configuring Search Paths 167
Configuring the Default Virtual Machine Configuration Folder 169
Enabling Virtual Machine Remote Control 170
How to Obtain the Best Host Performance 173
Maximizing Processor Performance 173
Maximizing Memory Performance 174
Increasing Display Graphics Performance 177
Increasing VMRC Performance 178
Optimizing Hard Disk Performance 179
Evaluating Virtual Server Host Applications that Are Affecting
Disk Performance 180
Understanding Disk Hardware Performance 180
Understanding How Disk Types Affect Performance 181
Understanding Disk Drive Configuration 182
Optimizing Network Performance 183
Understanding Virtual Networks and Adapters 183
Optimizing Virtual Machine Performance 184
Virtual Machine Additions 184
Understanding Processor Resource Allocation 185
Understanding the Resource Allocation Management Page 185
Understanding Virtual Machine Graphics Performance 187
Virtual Hard Disk Performance 188
Operational Considerations 189
Establishing Standards 189
Library of Virtual Machines 192
System Backup 193
Summary 194
Additional Resources 194

8   Virtual Machine Creation Process **195**

Defining Basic Virtual Machine Configuration Parameters 196

Creating a New Virtual Machine 197

Tuning Virtual Machine Key Configuration Settings 198

Changing the Virtual Machine Name 199

Automating Virtual Machine Startup and Shutdown 200

Changing the Memory Setting 201

Changing the Virtual Hard Disk Settings 201

Changing the Virtual CD/DVD Settings 203

Changing the Virtual Network Adapter Settings 204

Changing the Virtual Machine Script Settings 205

Changing the Virtual Floppy Drive Settings 206

Changing the Virtual COM Port Settings 207

Changing the Virtual LPT Port Settings 209

Adding a Virtual Machine 209

Removing a Virtual Machine 211

Configuring Virtual Machine BIOS Settings 211

Installing a Guest Operating System. 213

Installing Virtual Machine Additions 215

Controlling Virtual Machine State 217

Understanding the Benefits of a Virtual Machine Library 218

Creating a Virtual Machine Library 219

Components of a Virtual Machine Library 220

Centralized Storage 220

Structured Roles 221

Effective Security 222

Managing a Virtual Machine Library 223

Capacity Planning 223

Patch Management 224

Security 224

Content Refresh 225

Summary 225

Additional Resources 226

9   Developing Scripts with the Virtual Server COM API. **227**

Scripting with the COM API 227

Connecting to the Virtual Server Object 228

Retrieving and Displaying Information 229

Error Handling 230
Connecting to Remote Virtual Server 233
What's New in SP1 235
VHDMount Functions 235
VMTask Properties 235
VMGuestOS Properties and Methods 235
VMRCClientControl Property 236
Advanced Scripting Concepts 236
File and Folder Management 237
Logging Events 238
Using Tasks 240
Using the Virtual Server WMI Namespace 242
Managing Virtual Hard Disks 245
Obtaining Virtual Hard Disk Information 246
Creating Virtual Hard Disks 248
Adding VHDs to a Virtual Machine 250
Managing Virtual Machines 253
Creating a Virtual Machine 253
Deleting a Virtual Machine 257
Registering a Virtual Machine 259
Unregistering a Virtual Machine 261
Managing Virtual Networks 262
Creating Virtual Networks 263
Registering Existing Virtual Networks 265
Managing a Virtual Server Configuration 267
Reporting Host Information 270
Security Entries 272
Advanced Example 274
Summary 279
Additional Resources 280

10   Virtual Machine Migration Process 281
Assessing Physical Workload Virtualization Potential 281
Defining the Workload Memory Requirement 282
Defining the Workload Processor Requirement 283
Defining the Workload Network Requirement 285
Defining the Workload Storage Requirements 287

Defining the Workload Hardware Limitations 288

Defining the Workload Operational Limitations 289

Understanding the Physical to Virtual Workload Migration Process 289

System Preparation Phase 290

Workload Image Capture Phase 292

Virtual Machine Creation and Deployment 298

Using Automated Deployment Services and the Virtual Server
Migration Toolkit 299

Installing Automated Deployment Services 299

Installing the Virtual Server Migration Toolkit 302

Performing a Physical to Virtual Machine Migration 303

Performing a Virtual Machine to Virtual Machine Migration 309

Summary 310

Additional Resources 311

11   Troubleshooting Common Virtual Server Issues 313

Common Setup and Installation Issues 313

Missing or Incompatible IIS Configuration 313

Service Principal Name Registration Failures 314

Stop Error on x64 Windows Operating System with AMD-V 316

Common Administration Website Issues 316

Blank Screen Display 316

Always Prompted for Credentials 317

Access Is Denied Using Virtual Server Manager 319

Common Virtual Hard Disk Issues 320

Stop 0x7B Error Booting from a Virtual SCSI Disk 320

Broken Differencing Disk After Parent VHD Is Moved or Renamed 321

Common Virtual Network Issues 323

Problems Connecting a Virtual Network to a Physical
Network Adapter 323

Duplicate MAC Addresses 324

Common Virtual Machine Issues 326

Guest Operating System Installation Is Slow 326

Virtual Machine in Saved State Fails to Restart After a Change in
Hardware-Assisted Virtualization State 327

Virtual Machine in Saved State Fails During Start Up on a
Different Virtual Server Host 328

Virtual Machine Registration Fails After Previous Removal 328

Disabling Virtual Machine Hardware-Assisted Virtualization 329

Summary 329

Additional Resources 330

Part III   Virtualization Project Methodology

12   Virtualization Project: Envisioning Phase **333**

What Is Envisioning? 333

Defining the Problem Statements 334

Process for Defining Problem Statements 335

Setting Priorities 335

Establishing a Vision 336

Assembling a Project Team 336

Defining the Required Project Teams and Roles 336

Identifying Team Roles 337

Determining Project Scope 341

Approach to Defining Scope 341

Defining What Is Out of Scope 341

Determining Project Phases 342

Identifying Risks 342

Creating a Project Budget 344

Summary 344

Additional Resources 345

13   Virtualization Project: Discovery Phase **347**

Collecting Active Directory Information 348

Collecting Domain Information 348

Collecting Active Directory Site Information 348

Collecting Subnets-Per-Site Information 349

Collecting Server Information 349

Inventory 350

Hardware Inventory 350

Software Inventory 353

Services 354

Performance Monitoring 355

Environmental Information 357

Tools 358

Summary 358

Additional Resources 359

14   Virtualization Project: Assessment Phase........................ 361

    Identifying a Virtualization Candidate 361

        Virtual Machine Hardware Limits 362

        Setting Performance Thresholds 362

        Assessing Hardware Limits 363

        Assessing Performance Limits 365

        Assessing Application Support Limits 367

    Capital Cost Savings 368

    Environmental Savings 369

        Rack Space Savings 370

        Power Consumption 370

        Cooling Costs 371

    Summary 372

    Additional Resources 372

15   Virtualization Project: Planning and Design Phase................. 373

    Defining Virtual Server Host Configurations 374

        Physical Requirements 375

        High-Availability Hardware Requirements 375

    Consolidation Planning 377

        Grouping the Candidates 377

        Performing Workload Analysis 379

        Equipment Reuse 385

    Solution Planning 385

        Management 385

        Monitoring 386

        Patch Management 386

        Backup Requirements 386

    Summary 388

    Additional Resources 388

16   Virtualization Project: Pilot Phase.............................. 389

    Pilot Objectives 389

    Pilot Scope 390

        Selecting Pilot Locations 390

        Selecting Virtualization Candidates 391

    Pilot Architecture 391

Planning the Pilot 392

    Creating a Deployment Plan 392

    Creating a Support Plan 393

    Creating an Issue Tracking Plan 393

    Developing a Migration Plan 395

    Developing an Operations Plan. 395

    Developing a Training Plan. 395

    Creating a Communications Plan 396

    Documenting Risks 397

    Establishing Project Milestones 398

    Establishing Success Criteria. 399

Implementing the Pilot 399

Measuring Project Success 399

Incorporating Lessons Learned 400

Summary 400

Additional Resources 400

Part IV Virtual Server Infrastructure Management

17 Managing a Virtual Server Infrastructure. 403

Configuring a Centralized Administration Website 403

    Choosing a Deployment Topology 404

    Configuring Constrained Delegation 406

    Configuring the Virtual Server Manager Search Paths. 409

Managing Virtual Server and Virtual Machine Backups. 410

    Understanding the Virtual Server VSS Writer 410

    Using VSS to Back Up Virtual Server and Virtual Machines 412

    Using Traditional Methods to Back Up Virtual Server and
Virtual Machines. 415

    Backing Up an Active Directory Domain Controller Virtual Machine 417

Managing Virtual Server and Virtual Machine Patch Management 418

    Extending a Patch Management Strategy for Virtualized
Environments 419

    Identifying Key Issues and Challenges 419

    Defining Patch Management Procedures. 421

Monitoring Virtual Server and Virtual Machines. 423

Summary 425

Additional Resources 426

18   Using the MOM 2005 Virtual Server 2005 R2 Management Pack . . . 427

Understanding the Virtual Server 2005 R2 Management Pack 427

Microsoft Virtual Server 2005 R2 Management Pack Features 429

MOM Agent Requirements 432

Installing the Virtual Server 2005 R2 Management Pack 433

Executing the Microsoft Virtual Server 2005 R2 Management
Pack Installer Package. 433

Importing the Microsoft Virtual Server 2005 R2 Management Pack 434

Verifying the Microsoft Virtual Server 2005 R2 Management
Pack Version 435

Installing a MOM Agent. 435

Monitoring Virtual Server Hosts and Virtual Machines. 436

Virtual Server Service Discovery 437

Operator Console Views. 438

Virtual Server and Virtual Machine State. 439

Virtual Server and Virtual Machine Rules 443

Virtual Server and Virtual Machine Tasks. 444

Virtual Server and Virtual Machine Reports 446

Summary. 450

Additional Resources. 450

19   Microsoft System Center Virtual Machine Manager 2007. 451

Understanding System Center Virtual Machine Manager 2007. 451

Virtual Machine Manager Server 454

Virtual Machine Manager Agent. 454

Virtual Machine Manager Library. 455

Virtual Machine Manager Administrator Console 457

Windows PowerShell Command-Line Interface 469

Virtual Machine Manager Self-Provisioning Web Portal. 469

Deploying System Center Virtual Machine Manager 2007. 470

Hardware Requirements. 470

Software Requirements. 471

Single-Server Configuration. 473

Multiple-Server Configuration. 473

Using System Center Virtual Machine Manager 2007. 473

Physical-to-Virtual Machine Conversion 474

Virtual-to-Virtual Machine Conversion 475

Virtual Machine Templates. 475

Virtual Machine Provisioning. 476

　　　　Virtual Machine Placement. 477

　　　Summary 479

　　　Additional Resources 480

20　Additional Management Tools. **481**

　　　Analysis and Planning Tools 481

　　　　Microsoft Active Directory Topology Diagrammer. 481

　　　　Microsoft Windows Server System Virtualization Calculators. 483

　　　　PlateSpin PowerRecon. 485

　　　　SystemTools Exporter Pro 487

　　　Conversion Tools. 488

　　　　Invirtus Enterprise VM Converter 2007. 489

　　　　Leostream P>V Direct 3.0 490

　　　　PlateSpin PowerConvert 491

　　　VHD Tools 493

　　　　Invirtus VM Optimizer 3.0. 493

　　　　xcarab VHD Resizer 495

　　　　Xtralogic VHD Utility 495

　　　Administration Tools 495

　　　　HyperAdmin 496

　　　　Microsoft Virtual Machine Remote Control Plus. 497

　　　Summary 498

　　　Additional Resources 498

Part V　Appendices

A　Virtual Server 2005 R2 Event Codes **503**

B　Virtual Server 2005 R2 Management Pack Rules **521**

　　　Glossary. **525**

　　　About the Authors **533**

　　　Index **535**

What do you think of this book? We want to hear from you!

Microsoft is interested in hearing your feedback so we can continually improve our books and learning resources for you. To participate in a brief online survey, please visit:

www.microsoft.com/learning/booksurvey/

This book is dedicated to my parents, John and Andree Carbone, whom opened the door to many opportunities for me and provided support at every turn.

– JSC

I dedicate this book to my two children, Alex and Xavier. They have inspired me in every aspect of my life.

– REL

Principal Authors: Janique Carbone, Robert Larson

Contributing Authors: Vinod Atal, Ben Armstrong, Joseph Conway, Tony Donno, Ken Durigan, Dave Hamilton, Rob Hefner, John Howard, Michael Michael, Will Martin, Jyotiswarup Raiturkar, Allen Stewart, Bryon Surace, Eric Winner, Mike Williams, Jeff Woolsey

Microsoft Press

Acquisitions Editor: Martin DelRe
Developmental Editor: Karen Szall
Project Editor: Melissa von Tschudi-Sutton
Technical Editor: Ronald Beekelaar
Copy Editor: Roger LeBlanc
Contract Specialist: Heather Stafford
Microsoft Product Team Reviewers: Phani Chiruvolu, Tony Donno, Peter Fitzsimon, John Howard, Murtuza Naguthanawala, Mike Neil, Arvind Padole, Mike Sterling, Allen Stewart, Bryon Surace, Eric Winner, Jeff Woolsey, Edwin Yuen
Microsoft Consulting Services Reviewers: Ken Durigan, David Hitchen, Carsten Kinder, Alexander Ortha, Mike Williams,
Microsoft Customer Support Services Reviewers: Tom Acker, Tim Cerling, Joseph Conway, Ken Grainger, Ron Hefner
Microsoft Technical Specialist Reviewers: Tim Cerling, Jason Fulenchek
Microsoft Tool Contributors: Ken Durigan, Lutz Mueller, Matthijs ten Seldam

Acknowledgments

Books are generally developed through the collective effort of many individuals, and the one that you hold in your hands is not an exception. A resource kit book, especially, requires a broad range of individuals to shape, write, review, and prepare the content so that it is useful, accurate, and worth the investment that you make in it. Therefore, we have many individuals to thank, as without their help, this book would not have been possible.

We would like to thank Martin DelRe from Microsoft Press, with whom we had conversations over the last few years about doing this book project. He has worked and encouraged us throughout the Microsoft Press approval and production process, even going to bat for us with last-hour changes and getting positive results. Martin, we thank you for the opportunity that you provided to us and your assistance throughout this project. Without you, this book would not have become reality.

A thank you also goes to Heather Stafford, who helped us through the contracts maze.

Several Microsoft Press editors helped to guide our efforts and make certain that the book content was of high-quality and completed on schedule. Many thanks go to Karen Szall for getting us started on the right track. Roger LeBlanc was a wonderful copy editor. He did a terrific job in making the text clearer and more concise. Finally, we want to thank Ronald Beekelaer, the technical editor, for doing a thorough job, providing his experience and perspective, and keeping us honest.

Melissa von Tschudi-Sutton was our main project editor and a pleasure to work with throughout the process. She was instrumental in keeping us on track, and her suggestions were invaluable. Melissa, we appreciate your commitment to this book project and very much enjoyed working with you.

We would like to thank the product team for joining us in the effort to create a Virtual Server 2005 R2 Resource Kit book. Many members of the product team reviewed and contributed significant input to the book outline and content. They answered many e-mails and questions, even though they were all immersed in creating the next generation of Microsoft virtualization tools. We thank each and every one of you for your cooperation and support during these many months.

In particular, we owe a special thanks to Bryon Surace, our main point of contact in the product team, for bringing key individuals into our conversations. Bryon enlisted the help of several developers to ensure that we could get code-level questions answered. These developers were also crucial in helping us document information concerning Virtual Server 2005 R2 SP1 that will be of great interest and assistance to the readers of this book. Thank you one and all for the extra effort!

In addition to the product team, we wanted to ensure that each chapter in this book was reviewed by Microsoft team members "in the field." We received an overwhelming response to our request for reviewers from the Microsoft Consulting Services and Customer Support Services teams. Each individual that participated in chapter reviews worked above and beyond their daily responsibilities to provide feedback and suggestions that greatly improved the book content. Thank you again for giving up some of your own time to help us and adding significant value to the resultant product.

Thank you to the Microsoft team members whom contributed tools for the companion media. They were exceptionally responsive and quick to provide us all the information that we asked of them.

Several virtualization software vendors also contributed information and tools for inclusion on the companion media. Thank you so much for working with us under tight deadlines. We appreciate your cooperation!

And last, but not least, thank you for purchasing this book. We have worked hard to compile and organize the content of this book such that it might be a valuable resource to help you deploy successful solutions based on Microsoft Virtual Server 2005 R2. We are very interested in your comments, suggestions, and questions. Please send book-related e-mails to vs2005r2rk@hotmail.com. We will generally respond to you within 24 hours. For additional information regarding Microsoft virtualization technology, join the Virtual Server Community at *http://vscommunity.com* and keep up with the Virtual Server Journal blog at *http://vscommunity.com/blogs/virtualzone*.

Best Regards,

Janique S. Carbone
Managing Member, Infrastructor Group
http://www.infrastructor.com

Robert E. Larson
Architect, Microsoft Consulting Services
http://blogs.technet.com/roblarson

Introduction

Welcome to the *Microsoft Virtual Server 2005 R2 Resource Kit!*

The *Microsoft Windows Virtual Server 2005 R2 Resource Kit* is a comprehensive technical resource for planning, deploying, managing, and troubleshooting virtualization infrastructures based on Microsoft Virtual Server 2005 R2, including Service Pack 1.

Virtualization technology is quickly changing the way and speed at which IT departments can react to changing business needs by offering a more flexible and adaptable computing environment. Many organizations can draw benefits from the implementation of Virtual Server 2005 R2 SP1, including potential cost savings that can result from virtualizing multiple workloads. Therefore, our purpose for this book was to provide information and tools that could be useful to a broad spectrum of IT professionals and organizations.

Within this Resource Kit, you will find in-depth information and procedures to help you manage all aspects of Virtual Server 2005 R2 including manual and automated installation, security configuration, virtual machine and host clustering, virtual machine creation and migration processes, patch management, monitoring, and troubleshooting techniques. In addition, we have included guidance to assist you with all aspects of a virtualization project from the early vision and scope setting phase through the project pilot phase. You will also find numerous sidebars contributed by members of the Virtual Server product team, Microsoft Consulting Services, and Microsoft Support Services, that provide feature highlights, best practices and optimization tips, and troubleshooting aids to assist you in getting the most from a Virtual Server 2005 R2 deployment. Finally, the companion media includes tools, additional documentation, feature videos, and sample scripts that you can use and customize to help you automate various aspects of managing Virtual Server 2005 R2 in enterprise environments.

Overview of Book

The four parts of this book cover the following topics:

- **Part I Getting Started with Microsoft Virtual Server 2005 R2 SP1** Provides an in-depth look at the features of Virtual Server 2005 R2, including SP1, and covers the details of the product architecture.

- **Part II Installing and Managing Virtual Server 2005** Provides in-depth information and guidance on installing Virtual Server 2005 R2, using advanced product features, configuring security, tuning performance, developing scripts using the Virtual Server COM API, creating and migrating virtual machines, and troubleshooting common Virtual Server issues.

- **Part III Virtualization Project Methodology**   Provides guidance on how to manage a virtualization project from the initial vision and scope setting phase to the pilot deployment phase.

- **Part IV Virtual Server Infrastructure Management**   Describes how to monitor and maintain the health of a Virtual Server 2005 R2 infrastructure using tools such as the MOM 2005 Virtual Server Management Pack and System Center Virtual Machine Manager 2007. Additional management tools from third-party virtualization software vendors are also covered.

- **Part V Appendices**   Documents additional information that will help you to operate and troubleshoot Virtual Server 2005 R2. Appendix A contains the list of Virtual Server 2005 R2 error codes. Appendix B contains the list of MOM 2005 Virtual Server 2005 R2 Management Pack rules and notifications.

Document Conventions

The following conventions are used in this book to highlight special features or usage:

Reader Aids

The following reader aids are used throughout this book to point out useful details:

Reader Aid	Meaning
Note	Underscores the importance of a specific concept or highlights a special case that might not apply to every situation.
Important	Calls attention to essential information that should not be disregarded.
On the Companion Media	Calls attention to a related script, tool, template, or job aid on the companion media that helps you perform a task described in the text.
Best Practice	Best practices provide advice for best practices that the authors' or the Microsoft Virtualization Team have gained from using and deploying the products.

Sidebars

The following sidebars are used throughout this book to provide added insight, tips, and advice concerning different Virtual Server 2005 R2 features:

Sidebar	Meaning
Direct from the Source	Contributed by experts at Microsoft to provide "from-the-source" insight into how Virtual Server 2005 R2 works, best practices, and troubleshooting tips.
How It Works	Provides unique glimpses of Virtual Server 2005 R2 features and how they work.

Command-line Examples

The following style conventions are used in documenting command-line examples throughout this book:

Style	Meaning
Bold font	Used to indicate user input (characters that you type exactly as shown).
Italic font	Used to indicate variables for which you need to supply a specific value (for example *file_name* can refer to any valid file name).
`Monospace font`	Used for code samples and command-line output.
%SystemRoot%	Used for environment variables.

System Requirements

The following are the minimum system requirements to run the companion media provided with this book:

■ Microsoft Windows XP, with the latest service pack installed and the latest updates installed from Microsoft Update Service. (Note that some of the third-party trial tools require Windows Server 2003 or later to install.)

■ DVD drive

■ Internet Connection

■ Display monitor capable of 1024 × 768 resolution

■ Microsoft Mouse or compatible pointing device

■ Windows Media Player version 9 or newer, or compatible software that will play .wmv files.

■ Adobe Reader for viewing the eBook

Companion Media

The companion media is a valuable addition to this book and includes the following:

Microsoft Virtual Server 2005 R2 SP1

■ A full copy of Virtual Server 2005 R2 that includes SP1. Both x86 and x64 versions are included.

Microsoft Virtual PC 2007

■ A full copy of the latest Microsoft desktop virtualization application, Virtual PC 2007. Both x86 and x64 versions are included.

Scripts, Job Aids, and Resources

- Sample scripts written in Visual Basic Scripting Edition (VBScript) for administering different aspects of Virtual Server 2005 R2 and which can be used either as-is or customized to meet your administrative needs. Scripts provided are electronic versions of scripts from the chapters and bonus scripts that are not referenced in the book. Also included are job aids, troubleshooting tools, and selected whitepapers and guides that supplement the text.

Tools

- Microsoft Active Directory Topology Diagrammer (ADTD) is a tool that documents various aspects of an Active Directory domain.

- Microsoft VMRCPlus is a Windows forms-based application that is an alternative to the Virtual Server Administration Website.

- LeoStream P>V Direct 3.0 is an application that allows you to perform physical-to-virtual machine conversions.

- Xcarab VHDResizer allows you to manipulate a VHD file.

- Invirtus Enterprise VM Converter 2007 and VM Optimizer 3.0 are tools that allow you to perform physical-to-virtual machine conversions, and reduce the size of a VHD, respectively.

- Additional links to third-party tools including PlateSpin PowerConvert and Power-Recon, System Tools Exporter Pro, Xtralogic VHDUtility, and HyperAdmin.

Videos

- Step-by-step process to configure VS host clustering (Quick Migration)
- Guided tour of VMRCPlus
- Step-by-step process to create a Visual Basic script that performs VM file level backups
- Step-by-step procedures to perform a P2V migration using System Center Virtual Machine Manager
- TechEd / IT Forum 2006 presentation by Robert Larson titled "How to Virtualize Infrastructure Workloads"

eBook

- An electronic version of the entire *Microsoft Virtual Server 2005 R2 Resource Kit* is also included on the companion media.

Full documentation of the contents and structure of the companion media can be found in the Readme.txt file on the media.

Web Based Content

In addition to the content that is included with the companion media, additional bonus content is available at *http://vscommunity.com/VSResourceKit/*.

Using the Scripts

Scripts on the Companion DVD must be run using Cscript.exe as the script host. You can do this in several ways:

- Type **cscript** *script_name*.**vbs** **<parameters>** at a command prompt. For a list of available parameters, type **cscript** *script_name*.**vbs** **/?** at a command prompt, or open the script using Notepad and read the comments in the script.

- Configure the default script host on the local computer to Cscript.exe so that you can run scripts by typing **script_name.vbs <parameters>** at a command prompt. To set the default script host to Cscript.exe, type **cscript //h:cscript //nologo //s** at a command prompt.

To function as intended, most scripts on the companion media must also be run using elevated privileges. To open an admin-level command prompt in Windows Vista, click Start and select All Programs. Select Accessories, right-click Command Prompt, and select Run As Administrator. (As an alternative, create a shortcut to an elevated command prompt and save the shortcut on your Quick Launch toolbar.)

Resource Kit Support Policy

Every effort has been made to ensure the accuracy of this book and the companion media content. Microsoft Press provides corrections to this book through the Web at the following location:

http://www.microsoft.com/learning/support/search.asp

If you have comments, questions, or ideas regarding the book or companion media content, or if you have questions that are not answered by querying the Knowledge Base, please send them to Microsoft Press by using either of the following methods:

E-mail:
rkinput@microsoft.com

Postal Mail:
Microsoft Press
Attn: Microsoft Virtual Server 2005 R2 Resource Kit Project Editor
One Microsoft Way
Redmond, WA 98052-6399

Please note that product support is not offered through the preceding mail addresses. For product support information, please visit the Microsoft Product Support Web site at the following address:

http://support.microsoft.com

Part I
Getting Started with Microsoft Virtual Server 2005 R2 SP1

In this part:

Chapter 1: Introducing Virtual Server 2005 R2 SP1. 3

Chapter 2: Virtual Server 2005 R2 SP1 Product Overview 29

Chapter 3: Virtual Server Architecture. 55

Introducing Virtual Server 2005 R2 SP1

In this chapter:

Understanding Virtualization. 4
What Is Software Virtualization?. 4
Making a Business Case for Virtualization 11
Defining Virtualization Scenarios 15
Virtual Server 2005 R2 SP1 Benefits 17
What's New in Virtual Server 2005 R2 SP1? 19
Microsoft Virtual Server 2005 R2 SP1 Support Policies. 24
Microsoft Virtualization Product Roadmap. 25
Summary. 27
Additional Resources. 27

The objective of this book is to provide an in-depth look at Microsoft Virtual Server 2005 Release 2 (R2). Virtual Server 2005 R2 Service Pack 1 (SP1) is the newest release of the product and the basis for the technical information that is presented in this book.

In the last few years, many organizations have turned to virtualization technology, like Virtual Server 2005 R2, to consolidate physical servers and reverse the trend of server sprawl as well as lower data center power, cooling, and space costs to contend with smaller budgets. Increasingly, information technology (IT) departments are also finding that a virtualized infrastructure can be a more flexible environment to operate and can help them more quickly adapt to meet changing business needs.

In this chapter, you will review the major types of virtualization technologies to understand where Virtual Server 2005 R2 SP1 fits in this spectrum. Then, you will learn about the various business and technical scenarios that are addressed with a Virtual Server 2005 R2 SP1 deployment solution. The core of the chapter focuses on an overview of new Virtual Server 2005 R2 SP1 product features and support policies. Finally, the chapter closes with a preview of Microsoft System Center Virtual Machine Manager, an enterprise-class tool to manage a virtualized infrastructure based on Virtual Server 2005 R2 SP1, and Windows Server Virtualization, the next generation, Hypervisor-based virtualization technology for Windows Server 2008.

Understanding Virtualization

Virtualization, in the context of software such as Virtual Server 2005 R2, can be described as the abstraction of physical systems resources such that multiple logical partitions can be created to host a heterogeneous set of operating systems, each running simultaneously on a single server. Each logical partition, also referred to as a *virtual machine*, is the software environment that exposes resources (using hardware emulation or other devices) on top of which an operating system and one or more applications can be loaded and executed. Even though virtualization has only in the last few years become aggressively adopted in x86-based IT environments, the technology was actually first introduced over 40 years ago.

Commercial-grade virtualization technology was conceived by IBM in the mid-1960s to allow the System/360 Model 67 hardware to support multiple, concurrent guest virtual machines, each able to run a single-user operating system. IBM accomplished this by developing two individual operating systems, Virtual Machine (VM) and Conversational Monitor System (CMS), commonly referred to as VM/CMS. VM created and controlled virtual machines, and CMS—a single-user operating system—ran inside the virtual machine, delivering to each user access to underlying system resources. To this day, IBM continues to develop and market VM (rebranded as z/VM), having evolved it to even run itself within a virtual machine in multiple nested levels.

In the last decade, virtualization technology research and product development has resurged with a focus on the x86 (32-bit and 64-bit) platform. In 2006, both Intel and AMD released x86 processor revisions with new instructions and extensions specifically targeted to enable hardware-assisted virtualization. Although differing in implementation details, Intel Virtualization Technology (VT) and AMD Virtualization (AMD-V) provide hardware virtualization features that can be leveraged by software vendors to extend their virtualization solution architectures. Future enhancements of Intel VT and AMD-V are expected as Microsoft and other virtualization software vendors continue to work with Intel and AMD to define areas for improvements.

The shortcomings of the legacy x86 processor platform did not stop virtualization software vendors from developing solutions prior to the release of Intel VT and AMD-V. In fact, several types of virtualization technologies have been created to run on the original x86 processor architecture, using diverse methodologies that differ in the level of abstraction and address specific problem spaces.

What Is Software Virtualization?

Software virtualization includes various techniques to enable multiple secure, isolated partitions to be hosted on a single physical system, simultaneously sharing resources. Accordingly, these different approaches vary in partition density (the number of concurrent partitions), scalability, performance, and breadth of operating system flavors that can be simultaneously supported on a given platform.

Machine-Level Virtualization

At the foundation of a machine-level virtualization solution is a Virtual Machine Monitor (VMM). The VMM is responsible for the creation, isolation, and preservation of the virtual machine state, as well as the orchestration of access to system resources. VMM design is tied to a specific processor architecture; although it allows running various and unmodified operating systems inside a virtual machine, you are usually limited to operating systems that can natively run on the physical system processor.

Figure 1-1 illustrates three different VMM implementations: Type-2 VMM, the "hybrid" model, and Type-1 VMM. The Type-2 VMM runs above a host operating system, such as the Java VM. In the "hybrid" model, the VMM runs as a peer to the host operating system. This is the implementation in Virtual Server 2005 R2. In contrast, the Type-1 VMM, or "Hypervisor," runs directly on the hardware below all virtual machine partitions. Microsoft Windows Server Virtualization is a Hypervisor-based solution.

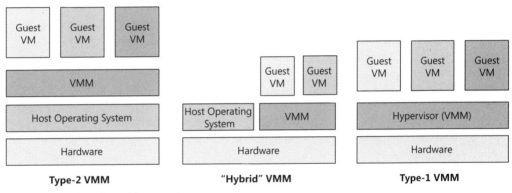

Figure 1-1   Virtual machine monitor types

In terms of performance, the Hypervisor (Type-1 VMM) is generally capable of achieving higher levels of efficiency and, therefore, greater virtual machine density. The other types of VMMs depend on the host operating system for access to resources, which results in more expensive context switches, and greater performance overhead.

Taking a step further into VMM implementations, three major variants are used to create an interface between the virtual machines and the virtualized system resources. These methods are full virtualization, native virtualization, and paravirtualization.

Full Virtualization

In this method, a complete virtual system is created and maintained by the VMM to abstract the real hardware from the virtual machine. This approach allows an operating system to execute in a virtual machine without any modification. Virtual Server 2005 R2 uses this technique along with binary translation, a process that allows the VMM to handle nonvirtualizable x86 instructions to provide system virtualization on the pre–Intel VT and AMD-V x86 processor architectures.

A benefit of full virtualization and the approach of decoupling the physical hardware from the virtual machine is the ability to easily move virtual machines between servers with different physical configurations. This flexibility comes with a performance hit because of the overhead associated with the maintenance of each virtual machine state and latency introduced with binary translation.

Native Virtualization

Native virtualization depends on a virtualizable processor architecture, such as is available with the x86 Intel VT and AMD-V series. These processors implement new execution modes, instructions, and data constructs in hardware that are designed to reduce the complexity of the VMM.

With native virtualization, the VMM is no longer required to maintain virtual machine resource characteristics and state in software; these functions now belong to the processor hardware and logic. Just as in the case of full virtualization, operating systems can run unmodified inside the virtual machines. Windows Server Virtualization uses this method to run legacy operating systems.

This type of implementation has many potential benefits, ranging from the simplification of the VMM architecture to significant performance improvements as a result of the reduction of software-based overhead. By lowering the virtualization overhead, a greater partition density can be achieved on any single system.

How It Works: Virtual Server 2005 R2—A Hosted Virtualization Solution

Within Microsoft, two categorizations are used for virtualization solutions: Hosted and Hypervisor. Virtual Server 2005 R2 is a Hosted virtualization solution because it runs on top of a Windows operating system. In a standard (nonvirtualized) Windows software stack, the operating system runs at the highest x86 privilege level (Ring 0, or "privileged" mode), while applications run in the lowest x86 privilege level (Ring 3, or "user" mode). In Virtual Server 2005 R2, the VMM is installed as a kernel-level driver that runs at the same level as the Windows operating system kernel, Ring 0.

When a virtual machine needs to execute, the operating system kernel yields control and the VMM is switched onto the processor to run the virtual machine guest operating system. Although the guest operating system thinks it is running at Ring 0, it is actually running in an intermediate mode, Ring 1. The applications layered on the guest operating system continue to run in Ring 3. This method is called *ring compression*.

Use of the ring compression method is required because of 17 instructions in the x86 that cannot be fully virtualized but that could result in a fault state, crashing the system. So, to preserve the integrity of the system state, the VMM intercepts and translates the guest operating system instructions to host operating system instructions (binary translation process), handing control back to the Windows operating system kernel when hardware resource access is required or a condition occurs that the VMM cannot handle. Virtual Server 2005 R2 SP1 adds support for hardware-assisted (native) virtualization available with Intel VT and AMD-V, but it remains a Hosted virtualization solution because it still runs on top of a host Windows operating system.

Paravirtualization

Paravirtualization was developed as an alternative to using binary translation to handle x86 nonvirtualizable instructions. In this approach, guest operating systems require modification to enable "hypercalls" from the virtual machine to the Hypervisor. Instead of the Hypervisor (or VMM) having to translate a potentially unsafe instruction from a guest operating system to guarantee system state integrity, a structured hypercall is made from the guest to the Hypervisor to manage the system state changes.

A strict paravirtualization implementation offers greater performance on standard x86 hardware by eliminating the need for costly operations incurred using full virtualization and binary translation. However, it does so at the cost of limiting unmodified guest operating system support and migration of virtual machines back to a physical server. Recognizing these limitations, virtualization products based on paravirtualization implementations also leverage hardware virtualization to host unmodified operating systems. This approach allows a broader range of support, extending to legacy operating systems that are unlikely to be modified, and it allows newer operating systems to be updated, taking advantage of enhancements and performance gains offered through paravirtualization.

Paravirtualization was pioneered and implemented by XenSource, which produces the open-source virtualization solution, Xen. Initial releases of Xen supported only a few, modified operating systems. With the release of Xen 3.0, which leverages the hardware virtualization functionality of Intel VT and AMD-V, an unmodified Windows XP operating system can execute in a guest virtual machine. In July 2006, Microsoft and XenSource entered into an agreement to support a level of interoperability that would allow Xen-modified Linux virtual machines to be migrated seamlessly to Windows Server Virtualization and Windows virtual machines to a Xen solution.

How It Works: Windows Server Virtualization—A Hypervisor Virtualization Solution

As mentioned earlier, Microsoft uses two categories to describe virtualization solutions: Hosted and Hypervisor. In contrast to Virtual Server 2005 R2, Windows Server Virtualization is a Hypervisor solution because it loads and runs directly above the hardware level. This implementation is also commonly referred to as a "bare metal virtualization." Windows Server Virtualization requires a 64-bit Intel VT or AMD-V hardware architecture. Intel VT and AMD-V add two new processor modes: one for execution of the Hypervisor, which now moves to a new ring (sometimes referred to as Ring −1), and another mode for execution of the guest operating system, which is now fully in Ring 0. This implementation eliminates the need for the ring-compression mechanism used in Virtual Server 2005 R2. Windows Server Virtualization does not run on 32-bit x86 or 64-bit Itanium processor architectures.

Windows Server Virtualization leverages native virtualization for legacy Windows operating systems prior to and including Windows Server 2003, but it also implements paravirtualization. A hypercall interface allows guest virtual machines to make action or informational requests to the Hypervisor. Windows Vista and Windows Server 2008 will be the first Windows operating systems to include paravirtualization modifications, which Microsoft refers to as "enlightenments." Initial enlightenments will allow Windows Vista and Windows Server 2008 to determine whether they are running in a virtual machine, as well as provide optimizations in memory management that will increase performance by reducing the levels of abstraction to the real hardware.

Operating System–Level Virtualization

Operating system–level virtualization is based on the abstraction of the operating system layer to support multiple, isolated partitions or to support virtual environments (VEs) on a single-instance host operating system. The virtualization is accomplished by multiplexing access to the kernel while ensuring that no single VE is able to take down the system. Figure 1-2 shows the basic architecture implemented with this approach.

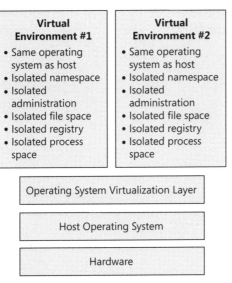

Figure 1-2   Basic operating system–level virtualization architecture

This technique results in very low virtualization overhead and can yield high partition density. However, there are two major drawbacks with this type of solution. The first drawback is the inability to run a heterogeneous operating system mix on a given server because all partitions share a single operating system kernel. The second drawback, also caused by the shared kernel model, is the lack of support for running a mixed 32-bit and 64-bit workload. In addition, any operating system kernel update affects all virtual environments. For these reasons, operating system–level virtualization tends to work best for largely homogeneous workload environments. Virtuozzo, from SWSoft, is an example of a product that uses operating system–level virtualization. Virtuozzo has been extensively adopted and deployed by the Web hosting industry to build high-density infrastructures, offering isolated Web services.

Application-Level Virtualization

All the virtualization techniques discussed to this point have the same objective—increase the number of secure, isolated partitions executing concurrently on physical hardware to maximize use of CPU, storage, network, memory, and other resources. Although they can be applied in a desktop setting, they are mainly geared toward solving resource management problems in server-class environments. They do not address specific client desktop application management issues.

Application-level virtualization is a technology that is geared toward partitioning and isolating client-side applications running on the local operating system. As shown in Figure 1-3, applications are isolated in a virtual environment layered between the operating system and application stack. The virtual environment loads prior to the application, isolates the application from other applications and the operating system, and prevents the application from modifying local resources such as files and registry settings. Applications can read information from the local system registry and files, but writeable versions of these resources are maintained inside the virtual environment. In fact, the application might never be locally installed on the desktop; instead, the code bits can be dynamically streamed and cached in the virtual environment as new portions of the application are needed.

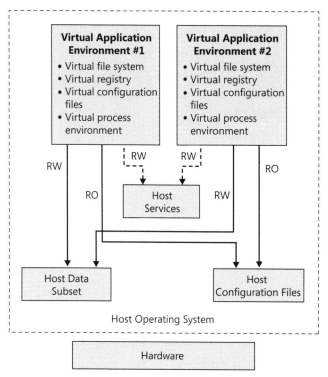

Figure 1-3   Basic application-level virtualization architecture

Application-level virtualization provides several benefits. Of most importance are increased stability of the local desktop; simple application removal without changes to the local environment that could negatively affect other applications; and seamless, conflict-free, side-by-side execution of multiple instances of an application. One or more additional servers might be required to maintain application distributions, application streaming to the desktop, and other enterprise-wide functions.

> **Note**   Microsoft has recently entered the application-level virtualization market with the acquisition of Softricity and the SoftGrid product line. The SoftGrid SystemGuard component runs on the local desktop and maintains the virtual registry, file system, and other data or configuration components needed by the application as it is executing. A SoftGrid Virtual Application Server maintains the application store and streams the application code on demand to the desktop. Other major components included in the SoftGrid solution are: SoftGrid Sequencer to package and virtualize applications; SoftGrid Management Web Service to centralize application policy services; and SoftGrid ZeroTouch to deliver provisioning, access, and reporting for virtualized applications.

Making a Business Case for Virtualization

In today's information technology (IT) shops, the core of any business case made for the adoption of a new technology is minimizing cost while increasing the capacity, security, reliability, availability, and flexibility of the infrastructure to rapidly adapt to changing business needs. Virtualization technology is the foundation that can enable an enterprise to accelerate achievement of the following goals:

- Reduction of IT capital and operational costs

- Implementation of a simplified, dynamic enterprise infrastructure

- Increase in availability of computing resources

- Reduction in time needed to provision or distribute new services

- Reduction in management complexity

Understanding how a virtualized infrastructure can deliver these benefits will clarify the business case to be made for rapid adoption of the technology.

Reducing Capital and Operating Costs

Over the last 15 years, the physical server inventory of mainstream businesses grew extensively as new applications and computing capacity were rolled out to meet organizational growth. To provide application and server management isolation, the majority of deployments resulted in single-server, single-application configurations. The main consequence of this approach was an increasing portion of the IT budget being allocated to operational costs to cover space, power, cooling, administrative personnel, and associated management tools. In tandem, many businesses have experienced one or more data center relocations, outgrowing facilities that could not accommodate an expansion of controlled floor space, additional power requirements, or cooling units to provision the computing environment. Making matters worse, estimates of average server utilization are between 5 percent and 15 percent. So not only are IT shops dealing with server sprawl and a rise in overhead costs, but they are unable, with a traditional architecture, to maximize the return on capital investment from their servers because of the predominant single-server, single-application deployments in their enterprise.

Virtualization of production servers, from the departmental level up to the data center, can help reduce new capital costs by requiring fewer physical servers to be purchased as new workloads need to be rolled out. If one or more deployed servers have spare computing capacity, the new workloads can simply be deployed as new virtual machines. Because virtual machines present a standard, emulated hardware configuration to the operating system and applications running within them, they are also easily moved between servers with different hardware configurations. This flexibility allows for the rebalancing of existing server workloads to dissimilar but available server hardware, creating the required capacity for a new deployment while avoiding new capital budget expenditures. In addition, with physical servers operating at much higher utilization levels when hosting multiple workloads, the return on investment (ROI) per server is improved.

With processor power ratings and server density rising in traditional infrastructures, space, power, and cooling requirements are stated as huge problems by IT organizations. Even with new techniques for power management that balance server power consumption to utilization rates and more efficient power supplies coming onto the market, additional solutions are needed to address the issue. Here again, virtualization of the computing environment can help to reduce operational costs. By consolidating workloads to a smaller number of servers, physical plant footprint, cooling, and power consumption can be significantly reduced. As the computing capabilities of servers grow with multiprocessor, multicore density leaps, workload consolidation ratios will also be trending up in the future, leading to a greater downward impact on the aforementioned operational costs.

Implementing a Simple, Flexible, and Dynamic Infrastructure

Businesses today are only as flexible as their computing infrastructure and processes allow. A traditional infrastructure is complex, somewhat inflexible, and rarely dynamic. IT staff face the challenging task of creating and maintaining hardware standards while hardware and software technology is continually changing. Economic factors are also driving IT managers to maximize the life span of server hardware, extending server refresh cycles to reduce capital expenditures. Unfortunately, this strategy tends to increase facilities management complexity and support issues.

Reducing the complexity of the infrastructure helps to reduce costs. A virtualized environment reduces complexity because a virtual machine is designed to provide a standard hardware solution that is compatible with many operating systems. Because the virtualized hardware is decoupled from the actual physical host devices that it runs on, compatibility across different physical servers is achieved. This flexibility allows you to build a virtual machine on a host using a certain hardware configuration and transfer it to a host using a different hardware configuration, without modification. This eliminates some of the hardships on IT staff, which no longer have to work through the lengthy server certification process that currently takes place to validate that a workload will execute as expected on new hardware.

Furthermore, traditional deployments of applications using a single workload per server to meet service level agreements and eliminate workload compatibility issues can be transformed through virtualization. The core problem is that a traditional deployment method wastes server resources, making the infrastructure too rigid. Virtualization creates a more flexible infrastructure that can be optimized for higher efficiency and server utilization levels and even enables you to host heterogeneous workloads on a single physical machine.

Test and development environments can also benefit from virtualization. In this setting, virtualization can enable virtual machines to be quickly provisioned to create complex application environments across single or multiple host servers. A virtualized environment can also be leveraged to very simply reproduce bugs uncovered during testing without requiring reinstallation of a system, as is often the case when operating a traditional testing infrastructure. Specifically, bug reproduction is accomplished by leveraging the ability of a virtual machine to revert back to its original state, in just a few seconds, by discarding all the tracked state changes made up to the critical point.

Virtualized infrastructures are also much more dynamic than traditional infrastructures when it comes to relocation of workloads. There is no simple, streamlined process in a traditional environment to move a workload on the fly from one server to another. In a virtualized environment, rebalancing of workloads can be easily automated and accomplished with much less risk because the virtual machines abstract away any hardware dependencies.

Increasing the Availability of Computing Resources

One of the great challenges faced by IT organizations, whether they are in a small business or large multinational corporation, is planning for single recovery events such as a server hardware failure, in conjunction with negative impacts to a larger percentage of computing resources. Providing business continuity after a massive natural disaster that causes significant or total loss of capital equipment to local facilities, and instantiating the affected services in alternate locations, is not a simple process when dealing with workloads that are tightly coupled to hardware. Apart from software stack dependencies on hardware configuration, there is complexity and high cost in keeping data synchronized between physical locations separated by large distances. There is also significant complexity in testing and validating recovery procedures to ensure that they are successful and effective.

Virtualization technology can assist with increasing the availability of computing resources through integration with high-availability services, such as clustering, that provide fail-over features. The fine-grained control provided by virtualization solutions gives the ability to cluster single virtual machines across host servers, cluster hosts themselves, or dynamically reallocate workloads to different host servers. This greater degree of control allows traditional single points of failure to be eliminated, making the recovery process simpler and easier.

Dealing with events that can cause a large number of servers and workloads to go offline is also simplified by adopting a virtualized infrastructure. Virtual machine encapsulation into a few portable and easily replicated files can greatly reduce planning, testing, and time to recovery for larger scale outages. Because virtual machine configuration settings are contained in one small file, when they are replicated to a recovery site along with the data files, recovery is a simple matter of registering the virtual machine with the new host and booting the operating system. The abstraction of hardware inherent in virtualization solutions is key to making recovery and business continuity less complex and streamlining processes.

Decreasing Time to Provision or Distribute Services

To gain a business advantage, ways must be found to make business processes and infrastructures able to quickly respond to change. A business advantage could potentially mean a market-share increase, a rise in profit, new market penetration, or other return leading to business growth. If a business can reduce the time to market with a new idea or line of business applications, it can also obtain a faster return on its investment.

The implementation of a new application in a corporate environment is dependent on a complex life cycle, typically involving envisioning, planning, development, test, quality assurance, deployment, and operational phases. Many of these phases require provisioning or deploying new computing resources, or even the purchase of new hardware before the project can effectively begin. Each purchase takes time going through project approval, budgeting, vendor bidding, order placement, delivery, testing, and physical deployment. This timeline can vary widely from one company to the next, ranging anywhere from a few weeks to several months. If multiple hardware resources are required from different vendor sources, additional time impacts can further delay development of the new solution. Minimizing the time from project conception to deployment is crucial to gaining a business edge.

A virtualized computing infrastructure can drive project timeline compression by reducing the need to acquire and deploy new servers for each new project. Instead, using virtualized server pools and pre-created virtual machine libraries, the process of provisioning project computing resources can be reduced to minutes and configuration changes to virtual resources such as storage, network cards, or memory can be done in seconds. Virtualization does not provide this benefit without proper capacity planning efforts. It also does not completely eliminate the need for hardware purchases; instead, new servers are added to increase the capacity to host multiple new workloads and projects instead of single ones. The concrete gain is that once the virtual infrastructure is established, provisioning of new workloads can literally be accomplished in minutes or hours, rather than weeks or months.

Decreasing Management Complexity

Typical IT infrastructures are composed of various vendor hardware components that require regular maintenance and management to ensure that they are up to date with firmware upgrades and patches, and that they are free of hardware faults. When virtualizing a physical infrastructure, the reduction in the number of physical servers is a key benefit that leads to a simplification of the environment and a reduction in the time required for management. Further reducing the number of unique brand servers can also reduce the variety of unique tools required, further driving down management complexity.

Another significant IT management task is the backup process. Backup management typically consists of administering the backup software, backup agents, server backup process, and backup media for each server. Backup management in a virtualized infrastructure is much less complex. Snapshot technologies, available to support backup of complete virtual machine workloads from the physical host level, drive the reduction in management complexity of the backup process. There is no longer a need to install, update, and maintain agents in each guest operating system to perform backups, resulting in faster backups in addition to simplified management.

Defining Virtualization Scenarios

Having examined the business case for virtualization, it is now time to consider the four major scenarios that stand out as prime opportunities for a virtualization solution. These are the areas where, with the current functionality built into Virtual Server 2005 R2 SP1, you can experience the most immediate benefits while addressing areas that have high pain points and a significant impact on business. The four scenarios are as follows:

- Data center consolidation
- Branch office consolidation
- Virtualization of the test and development infrastructure
- Implementation of business continuity and recovery plans

Consolidating the Data Center

This scenario addresses the need of most customers to resolve the power, cooling, and physical space crises currently taking place in data centers. Many workloads running in a data center these days are likely candidates for consolidation, which will enable IT managers and administrators to make fuller use of machine capacity while decreasing the number of physical units to manage. Achieving a consolidated data center can involve a couple of approaches:

- **Homogeneous consolidation**   Combining on a single platform servers with similar applications or workloads
- **Mixed workload**   Combining on a single platform servers with different workloads

Homogeneous and mixed workload consolidations can use virtualization as a method to achieve objectives. In these cases, virtualization provides the following benefits:

- Establishment of a simple physical-to-virtual machine migration process that minimizes the design and testing required to ensure compatibility of workloads on a single platform
- Reduction in the number of physical servers, thereby leading to lower IT costs
- Elimination of duplicate services, thereby decreasing the need for management
- Availability of dynamic tuning to maximize server capacity usage

Consolidating the Branch Office

This scenario addresses the need that a majority of customers have to minimize hardware deployments to a large number of small field offices. Implementation of a virtualized environment in the branch office allows customers to avoid the support and security issues that exist when combining domain controller, file and print, Exchange, and additional workloads directly atop a host operating system. Using virtualization to accomplish the branch office consolidation also has the following benefits:

- Implementation of individual service level agreements (SLAs) for each virtualized workload

- Establishment of a simple physical-to-virtual machine migration process that minimizes the design and testing required to ensure compatibility of workloads on a single platform

- Reduction in the number of physical servers, thereby leading to lower IT costs

- Separation of management for each virtualized workload while securing physical host access

Virtualizing the Test and Development Infrastructure

This scenario addresses the implementation of a virtualized test and development infrastructure. Maintaining and provisioning traditional test and development environments can be a drain on budgets and a huge management challenge. Using virtualization in this scenario provides the following benefits:

- Reduction in the hardware needed to host complex application architectures that include multiple workloads. A single server with appropriate capacity is often sufficient because each workload can run in a separate virtual machine.

- Reduction in time to provision new test and development scenarios, and automation of virtual machine deployment to servers with available capacity.

- Positive impact on test and development life-cycle management. For example, the time needed to accomplish a migration of new applications from the development and test environment to the production environment is greatly reduced by the portability and ease of replication of virtual machine files.

- Simple creation of a virtual machine library to store and retrieve testing scenarios.

- Simple migration of a production environment from physical servers into a test and development virtual machine library.

- Simpler bug reproduction process by using virtual machine state preservation and roll-back features.

Implementing Business Continuity and Recovery

This scenario addresses the implementation of a business recovery process in the event of a single point of failure or major disaster. The challenge for customers when planning for business continuity is defining a simple, low risk, and fast recovery approach that can be validated to meet business continuity requirements. Using virtualization to accomplish business continuity and recovery has the following benefits:

- Support for clustering of individual virtual machines across hosts and clustering of virtualization hosts and workloads to achieve high availability

- Reduced dependencies on expensive, complex hardware

- Ability to establish a physical-to-virtual machine business continuity solution

- Ability to establish a virtual-to-virtual machine business continuity solution

- Ability to use low cost file replication technologies to replicate virtual machine files between hosts and reduce time to recovery

 More Info   You can view and download detailed articles that cover each of the virtualization scenarios in more depth at *http://www.vscommunity.com/scenarios*. In these articles, you will learn how a Virtual Server 2005 R2 solution can be deployed and fine-tuned to address the most common issues that arise in each of the four scenarios.

Virtual Server 2005 R2 SP1 Benefits

Microsoft entered the virtualization arena with the acquisition of the Connectix software virtualization technology in February 2003. Building on the Connectix Virtual PC product, Microsoft released Virtual PC 2004 in November 2003. Virtual PC 2004 is a desktop virtualization solution geared mainly toward enabling client legacy application migration to Windows XP, thereby providing quick access to multiple client images on a single workstation for support organizations and delivering to developers a self-contained software testing platform.

In October 2004, Microsoft followed up with the release of Virtual Server 2005 as an enterprise infrastructure virtualization solution. The initial Virtual Server 2005 solution space was focused on four primary scenarios:

- Consolidation of low-utilization, departmental workloads to reduce the number of deployed servers

- Virtualization of test and development environments to allow rapid provisioning and management of test scenarios

- Migration and consolidation of legacy operating systems and applications from obsolete servers to new servers leveraging Windows Server 2003

- Simplification of disaster recovery plans based on virtual hard disk (VHD) encapsulation of virtual machines to decouple them from hardware dependencies

In conjunction with Virtual Server 2005, Microsoft also released the Virtual Server Migration Toolkit (VSMT), a set of tools based on the Windows Server Automated Deployment Services (ADS), to support physical server migration and encapsulation into the VHD format.

With the release of Virtual Server 2005 R2 in November 2005, Microsoft delivered the following major enhancements:

- Performance improvements through optimization of the VMM memory mapping architecture

- Support for running Virtual Server 2005 R2 on x64 hosts

- High-availability scenarios based on iSCSI to cluster virtual machines across hosts, as well as the ability to cluster Virtual Server 2005 R2 hosts using standard Windows Server 2003 clustering technology

- PXE network boot support in emulated network hardware

- Virtual disk precompactor and compactor to reduce the size of VHD files

Along with these new features, the list of solution scenarios was expanded to include:

- Consolidation of a wider variety and scale of workloads from data center to branch office production environments

- Business continuity management extending beyond single-point disaster recovery to large-scale business contingency and recovery

Virtual Server 2005 R2 SP1 is the latest release of the product. We will take a detailed look at several new features in this release in the next section. A summary of the features is included in Table 1-1, which documents the evolution of the Virtual Server 2005 feature set from initial release to Virtual Server 2005 R2 SP1.

Table 1-1   Virtual Server 2005 Feature Evolution

Microsoft Virtual Server 2005
- Hosted virtualization solution
- Remote Web management
- Scripting Component Object Model (COM) application programming interface (API)
- VHD format
- Multithreaded
- Virtual Server 2005 Migration Toolkit (VSMT)
- Licensed per processor (not core)
- x86 host operating system support
- x86 guest operating system support
- 32-processor support with single CPU virtual machine (VM)
- CPU resource allocation
- Maximum of 64 VMs
- 3.6 GB RAM per VM
- IDE disk and SCSI disk support
- Unlimited number of virtual networks
- Two-node VM-to-VM clustering

Table 1-1   Virtual Server 2005 Feature Evolution

Microsoft Virtual Server 2005 R2

Includes all previous features with the addition of the following:

- x64 host operating system support
- Additional host and guest operating system support
- Virtual hard disk precompactor
- Performance enhancements
- Firewall configuration during installation
- PXE boot support
- Reserved disk space for saved state files
- Virtual floppy disk installation of optimized SCSI driver using F6 option
- Hyperthreading support
- Support for Non-Uniform Memory Access (NUMA) node allocation
- iSCSI support
- Virtual Server host clustering
- Linux guest operating system support and VM additions

Microsoft Virtual Server 2005 R2 SP1

Includes all previous features with the addition of the following:

- Support for 256 GB of host physical memory
- Maximum of 512 VMs when running on Windows x64 editions
- Additional host and guest operating system support
- Intel VT & AMD-V hardware virtualization support
- Hardware virtualization configurable on a per-VM basis
- VHDMount tool
- Volume Shadow Copy Service support
- Active Directory Service Connection Points
- Virtual Server host clustering script and whitepaper
- Default dynamic VHD disk size increased to 127 GB
- Linux guest SCSI emulation fix
- VMRC ActiveX control use of Internet Explorer security zones
- VMRC client option to enable video stretch in full screen mode

What's New in Virtual Server 2005 R2 SP1?

Many new features in Virtual Server 2005 R2 SP1 help to make it the most cost-effective and best software virtualization product for the Windows platform. Following is a list of some of the new features that enable better performance and reliability:

- Intel VT and AMD-V support

- Volume Shadow Copy Service support

- Virtual Server host clustering

- VHDMount command-line tool

- Virtual machine server publication using Active Directory Service connection points

- Host operating system support

- Guest operating system support

This release also includes enhancements that provide more functionality to address areas that IT staff defined as pain points in their existing Virtual Server 2005 R2 implementations. Following is a list of these enhancements:

- Increased capacity for guest virtual machines

- Increased default size for dynamic VHD

- Linux guest virtual machine SCSI emulation fix

Intel VT and AMD-V Support

In 2006, Intel and AMD released extensions to the x86 processor architecture to support native (hardware-assisted) virtualization. With Virtual Server 2005 R2 SP1, hardware assistance is not required to install and use the product, but it will be used if present and enabled. Even though Intel and AMD implemented hardware virtualization differently in their processors, there are no dependencies to prevent moving virtual machines between Intel VT and AMD-V servers after they are cleanly shut down. You can define whether hardware assistance is enabled or disabled by using a configurable setting on an individual virtual machine basis, or a global setting that affects all virtual machines. In some implementations, Intel VT support is also configurable in the host system basic input/output system (BIOS).

In terms of performance, the only real gains for virtual machines running a Windows operating system are during the setup and installation phase, which has shown up to three times faster completion. The reason for this is that Virtual Server 2005 R2 SP1 was already optimized for the best performance of Windows operating systems on the x86 platform prior to hardware-assisted virtualization availability. However, for a non-Windows guest such as Linux, performance gains based on hardware-assisted virtualization should be significant.

Volume Shadow Copy Service Support

The addition of Volume Shadow Copy Service (VSS) support provides stateful, host-side backups, eliminating the need to load an agent in each virtual machine. Any VSS-aware application can leverage this functionality to provide snapshot backup services if it utilizes the VSS writer interface implemented in Virtual Server 2005 R2 SP1. Any virtual machine running a VSS-aware guest Windows operating system (Windows Server 2003 and later) can be backed up in a live state. Any other guest operating system (Windows 2000, Linux, and so on) will need to be in saved state prior to the snapshot. Because snapshots are performed through an extremely fast process (they take seconds), virtual machine downtime is minimized. Additionally, with VSS support, the number of steps involved in archive or restore operations is reduced and the consistency of the data is ensured.

Virtual Server Host Clustering

The Virtual Server host clustering script and whitepaper, originally released shortly after Virtual Server 2005 R2 as Web downloads, are now integrated into SP1. The functionality has not changed, supporting fail-over of an entire Virtual Server host workload across cluster node members as needed to achieve best performance.

VHDMount Command-Line Tool

A widely requested feature, Virtual Server 2005 R2 SP1 now includes a command-line tool to mount a VHD on a host system. VHDMount mounts the VHD and assigns a drive letter to the new virtual disk device. Once mounted, the contents of the VHD can be manipulated through standard file system commands or Windows Explorer.

Using VHDMount does not require the Virtual Server 2005 R2 SP1 Virtual Server service to be installed on the host. It is supported on most Virtual Server 2005 R2 SP1 hosts and can be automated through scripting. VHDMount also supports mounting a VHD that resides on an iSCSI target.

> **Note**   Not all VHDMount options are supported when the host operating system is Windows XP. In particular, the volume mount option that assigns a letter drive uses the Microsoft Virtual Disk Service (VDS) API, which is available only with Windows Server 2003 and later operating systems. Using the VHDMount mount option on a Windows XP host requires that you assign letter drives manually using Disk Manager.

Virtual Machine Server Publication Using Active Directory Service Connection Points

Active Directory defines service connection points (SCPs) that allow servers to publish hosted service data in the directory. This functionality is now supported in Virtual Server 2005 R2 SP1. Through the use of a Lightweight Directory Access Protocol (LDAP) browser, data can be retrieved from Active Directory to identify domain members that are running Virtual Server 2005 R2 SP1.

Host Operating System Support

The following list includes all currently supported host operating systems that can be used with the x86 version of Virtual Server 2005 R2 SP1:

- Microsoft Windows Server 2003, Standard Edition with Service Pack 1 (SP1)
- Microsoft Windows Server 2003, Enterprise Edition with SP1
- Microsoft Windows Server 2003, Datacenter Edition with SP1
- Microsoft Windows Server 2003, Standard Edition with Service Pack 2 (SP2)
- Microsoft Windows Server 2003, Enterprise Edition with SP2
- Microsoft Windows Server 2003, Datacenter Edition with SP2
- Microsoft Windows Server 2003 R2, Standard Edition
- Microsoft Windows Server 2003 R2, Enterprise Edition
- Microsoft Windows Server 2003 R2, Datacenter Edition
- Microsoft Windows Small Business Server 2003 Standard R2
- Microsoft Windows Small Business Server 2003 Premium R2
- Microsoft Windows Server 2008 Beta 3 (non-Production only)
- Microsoft Windows XP Professional with SP2 (non-Production only)
- Microsoft Windows Vista Ultimate (non-Production only)
- Microsoft Windows Vista Business (non-Production only)
- Microsoft Windows Vista Enterprise (non-Production only)

The following list shows all the supported host operating systems that can be used with the x64 version of Virtual Server 2005 R2 SP1:

- Microsoft Windows Server 2003, Standard x64 Edition with SP2
- Microsoft Windows Server 2003, Enterprise x64 Edition with SP2
- Microsoft Windows Server 2003, Datacenter x64 Edition with SP2
- Microsoft Windows Server 2003, Standard x64 Edition
- Microsoft Windows Server 2003, Enterprise x64 Edition
- Microsoft Windows Server 2003, Datacenter x64 Edition
- Microsoft Windows Server 2003 R2, Standard x64 Edition
- Microsoft Windows Server 2003 R2, Enterprise x64 Edition
- Microsoft Windows Server 2003 R2, Datacenter x64 R2 Edition
- Microsoft Windows XP Professional, x64 Edition (non-Production only)
- Microsoft Windows Vista Ultimate, x64 Edition (non-Production only)

■ Microsoft Windows Vista Business, x64 Edition (non-Production only)

■ Microsoft Windows Vista Enterprise, x64 Edition (non-Production only)

 Important   Microsoft Windows XP and Windows Vista are supported only for nonproduction use as the host operating system.

Guest Operating System Support

The following list shows all the supported guest operating systems that can be used with both x86 and x64 versions of Virtual Server 2005 R2 SP1:

■ Microsoft Windows Server 2003 R2, Standard Edition

■ Microsoft Windows Server 2003, Standard Edition with SP1

■ Microsoft Windows Server 2003, Standard Edition with SP2

■ Microsoft Windows Server 2003 R2, Enterprise Edition

■ Microsoft Windows Server 2003, Enterprise Edition with SP1

■ Microsoft Windows Server 2003, Enterprise Edition with SP2

■ Microsoft Windows Server 2003, Wed Edition with SP2

■ Microsoft Windows Server 2008, Beta 3 (non-production only)

■ Microsoft Windows XP Professional with SP2 (non-production only)

■ Microsoft Windows Vista Enterprise (non-production only)

■ Microsoft Windows Vista Business (non-production only)

■ Microsoft Windows Vista Ultimate (non-production only)

■ Red Hat Enterprise Linux 2.1 (Update 7)

■ Red Hat Enterprise Linux 3 (Update 8)

■ Red Hat Enterprise Linux 4 (Update 4)

■ SuSE Linux Enterprise Server 9

■ SuSE Linux Enterprise Server 10

■ Solaris 10

■ Red Hat Linux 7.3

- Red Hat Linux 9.0

- SuSE Linux 9.2

- SuSE Linux 9.3

- SuSE Linux 10.0

- SuSE Linux 10.1

- SuSE Linux 10.2

Guest Virtual Machine Capacity

In Virtual Server 2005 R2, there was a hard limit of 64 virtual machines running concurrently on x86 or x64. The x86 hard limit of 64 virtual machines remains for SP1. However, if you run Virtual Server 2005 R2 SP1 on a Windows x64 edition, the number of concurrent virtual machines has increased to 512.

Default Size for a Dynamic VHD

In Virtual Server 2005 R2 SP1, the default size for dynamically expanding VHDs has been changed from 16 GB to 127 GB.

Linux Guest Virtual Machine SCSI Emulation Fix

Some users encountered an issue when trying to install certain Linux distributions inside a virtual machine using the emulated SCSI bus. The issue occurred most often with the Linux 2.6.x kernel. The fix for this issue has been included in Virtual Server 2005 R2 SP1.

Microsoft Virtual Server 2005 R2 SP1 Support Policies

Microsoft has published a series of Knowledge Base articles that define the support policies for Virtual Server 2005 R2 SP1 and Microsoft Windows Server System (WSS) applications. These articles explain the default support policy for Virtual Server 2005 R2 SP1 and detail WSS products that are not supported. It is useful to revisit these articles periodically as policy changes are made. The three main articles are as follows:

- **KB897613**   "Microsoft Virtual Server Support Policy"

- **KB897614**   "Windows Server System software not supported within a Microsoft Virtual Server environment"

- **KB917437**   "Third-party guest operating systems that are supported for use with Virtual Server 2005 R2"

The support policy information in this section summarizes key points that you should be aware of when designing and deploying Virtual Server 2005 R2 SP1 in your enterprise.

Product Support Policy

Microsoft supports most WSS applications and some Linux and Unix distributions running within a Microsoft Virtual Server 2005 R2 SP1 environment. Virtual Server 2005 R2 SP1 support conforms to the overall Microsoft Support Lifecycle policy and use of the virtual hard disk (.vhd) format. Microsoft has adopted, as part of the Windows Server System Common Engineering Criteria (CEC), that WSS products must be capable of running within a Microsoft Virtual Server 2005 R2 SP1 environment. However, a Windows Server System application that does not meet the criteria will support Virtual Server 2005 R2 SP1 at the next release of the product.

Application Support Policy

Microsoft has published a list of Windows Server System applications that are not supported under Virtual Server 2005 R2 SP1. These applications either require a hardware component that Virtual Server 2005 R2 SP1 does not provide as part of its virtual hardware environment, or they were released prior to Virtual Server 2005 R2 and, therefore, were never tested in a virtual machine.

The current list of applications that are not supported is as follows:

- Microsoft Speech Server (because the telephony hardware required is not emulated in a virtual machine)

- Microsoft ISA Server 2000

- Microsoft ISA Server 2004

- Microsoft SharePoint Portal Server 2003

- Microsoft Identity Integration Server

- Microsoft Identity Integration Feature Pack

Note The fact that these applications are not officially supported in a Virtual Server 2005 R2 SP1 environment does not mean that they will not successfully install and execute in a virtual machine. The key is that you are not guaranteed support from Microsoft Customer Service and Support (CSS) when you place a call regarding a problem.

Microsoft Virtualization Product Roadmap

Figure 1-4 shows the current Microsoft virtualization roadmap, although product features and release dates are always subject to change. In addition to Virtual Server 2005 R2 SP1, two major product releases are expected in 2007. These products are System Center Virtual Machine Manager (VMM) and Windows Server Virtualization. VMM will provide a powerful set of features that will simplify management of a virtualized environment. As previously mentioned, Windows Server Virtualization is the next generation, Hypervisor-based enterprise virtualization solution.

Figure 1-4   Microsoft virtualization roadmap

Microsoft System Center Virtual Machine Manager is an enterprise tool that will allow centralized management of virtualized environments based on Virtual Server 2005 R2 SP1 and Windows Server Virtualization. VMM supports the following tasks:

- Resource optimization to ensure that servers are as fully utilized as possible

- Rapid provisioning of new virtual machines from physical machines, from a virtual machine library store, or built by the user

- Integration with the System Center Operations Manager 2007 database to leverage historical performance data and identify consolidation candidates in ranked order

- Delivery of a physical-to-virtual migration tool based on VSS and block-based transfer technology to create new virtual machines at disk speed

- Intelligent workload allocation based on historical performance data from System Center Operations Manager 2007, performance data from the various potential hosts, and preselected business rules application

Windows Server Virtualization is anticipated to be released as a Server Core role in Windows Server 2008. It will require x64 Intel VT or AMD-V as the underlying hardware architecture and implement paravirtualization to support Windows Vista, Windows Server 2008, and perhaps future Windows operating system releases. Windows Server Virtualization is projected to include the following functionality:

- A micro-kernel-like hypervisor that will run directly on the hardware with a focus on scheduling and isolation as well as management of a minimum set of hardware resources. The hypervisor will also be responsible for the creation of a parent partition that in turn manages one or more child partitions that host guest operating systems

■ A virtualization stack that will run in the parent partition and whose primary function will be the virtualization and emulation of devices for the child partitions

■ Support for 32-bit (x86) and 64-bit (x64) guest operating systems in the child partitions

■ Support for 2 or 4-way symmetric multiprocessing (SMP) virtual machines

■ Support for large memory (greater than 4 GB) virtual machines, including the ability to over-commit memory

■ Support for pass-through disk access for virtual machines, including storage area network (SAN) and direct-attach storage systems

■ Support for multiple virtual machine snapshots (that is, the ability to set a checkpoint for a virtual machine and revert to any saved checkpoint at any time)

■ Support for a simple upgrade path from Virtual Server 2005 R2 SP1 using the same VHD files

In addition to releasing enterprise-class virtualization tools, Microsoft has developed Virtual PC 2007, an update for the Virtual PC 2004 desktop virtualization solution. Virtual PC 2007 was released in February 2007. New features in Virtual PC 2007 provide support for x64 host operating systems, hardware-assisted (native) virtualization, performance improvements, and improved sound support.

Summary

In this chapter, you learned about the different types of software virtualization technologies and how they relate to the development and basic architecture of Virtual Server 2005 R2 SP1. You were exposed to the key drivers to consider when developing a business case for virtualization technology adoption. Core technical virtualization scenarios targeted with a Virtual Server 2005 R2 SP1 solution were reviewed along with associated benefits. An overview of the Virtual Server 2005 R2 SP1 new feature set was provided, along with current support policies. Finally, the chapter concluded with an overview of the Microsoft virtualization product roadmap.

Additional Resources

The following resources contain additional information related to the topics in this chapter:

■ Knowledge Base article 897613, "Microsoft Virtual Server support policy," at *http://support.microsoft.com/kb/897613*

■ Knowledge Base article 897614, "Windows Server System software not supported within a Microsoft Virtual Server environment," at *http://support.microsoft.com/kb/897614*

■ Knowledge Base article 917437, "Third-party guest operating systems that are supported for use with Virtual Server 2005 R2," at *http://support.microsoft.com/kb/917437*

- Whitepaper, "Virtual PC vs. Virtual Server: Comparing Features and Uses," at *http://www.microsoft.com/windowsserversystem/virtualserver/techinfo/vsvsvpc.mspx*

- FAQ, "Virtual Server 2005 Frequently Asked Questions," at *http://www.microsoft.com /windowsserversystem/virtualserver/evaluation/virtualizationfaq.mspx*

- Whitepaper, "Microsoft Virtual Server 2005: Windows Server Virtualization – An Overview," at *http://www.microsoft.com/windowsserversystem/virtualserver/techinfo/virtualization.mspx*

- Whitepaper, "Solution Accelerator for Consolidating and Migrating LOB Applications," at *http://www.microsoft.com/technet/itsolutions/ucs/lob/lobsa/default.mspx*

Chapter 2

Virtual Server 2005 R2 SP1 Product Overview

In this chapter:

Reviewing Virtual Server 2005 R2 29

Managing with the Administration Website 35

Outlining the Virtual Server 2005 R2 COM API 53

Summary 53

Additional Resources 53

This chapter contains an overview of Microsoft Virtual Server 2005 Release 2 (R2) Service Pack 1 (SP1) product features. To provide a robust virtualization platform that abstracts physical hardware dependencies and scales to support numerous concurrent workloads, Virtual Server 2005 R2 presents standard services and resources to create and execute virtual machines. These include a standard virtual hardware environment, virtual hard disks (VHD), and virtual networks. Virtual machine configuration and management functions are performed via the Virtual Server 2005 R2 Administration Website. The Administration Website provides a primary interface to create, inspect, and modify virtual machines, virtual hard disks, virtual networks, and virtual machine processor allocations. Virtual Server 2005 R2 server and Web site properties are also configurable through the Administration Website. Virtual machine remote access is accomplished through the Virtual Machine Remote Control (VMRC), provided as an ActiveX control and standalone Windows application. In addition, Virtual Server 2005 R2 offers a rich Component Object Model (COM) interface that can be leveraged using various scripting and development languages to programmatically control the deployment, administration, and configuration of virtual machines.

Reviewing Virtual Server 2005 R2

Virtual Server 2005 R2 is a hosted virtualization application that runs as a service on both x86 and x64 Microsoft Windows operating systems. As a multithreaded application, Virtual Server 2005 R2 concurrently runs one or more virtual machines (workloads), each in its own thread of execution. Each virtual machine presents a set of virtualized devices to the guest operating system and applications that abstracts the underlying physical hardware, providing workload portability between dissimilar physical servers running Virtual Server 2005 R2.

Virtual Machine Hardware Environment

Table 2-1 lists the standard set of virtualized components that a virtual machine exposes to a guest operating system and application stack. These devices are detected and appear to be the physical hardware resources available to the running workload. When a virtual machine workload requests access to the virtualized resources, Virtual Server 2005 R2 works in conjunction with the host operating system to translate the requested operation from the virtual hardware environment to the physical hardware, and access is achieved via the standard kernel device drivers installed in the host operating system. This approach provides virtual machine workloads the ability to run across a wide variety of server hardware without requiring any modifications to the workload configuration.

Table 2-1   Virtualized Hardware Components

Component	Virtualized Hardware
Basic input/output system (BIOS)	American Megatrends (AMI) BIOS with Intel 440BX chip set and PIIX4, including: ■ Complementary metal oxide semiconductor (CMOS) ■ Real-time clock ■ RAM and video RAM (VRAM) ■ Memory controller ■ Direct memory access (DMA) controller ■ PCI bus ■ ISA bus ■ SM bus ■ Power management ■ 8259 programmable interrupt controller (PIC) ■ Programmable interrupt timer (PIT)
Floppy disk drive	Single 1.44-MB floppy disk drive that maps to real floppy disk drives or floppy drive images.
Serial (COM) port	Dual serial ports that can be mapped to physical serial ports, local named pipes, or files.
Printer (LPT) port	Single printer port that maps to the physical parallel port.
Mouse	Standard PS/2 Microsoft IntelliMouse pointing device mapped to the PS/2 device on the physical computer.
Keyboard	Standard PS/2 101-key Microsoft keyboard, but that can be mapped to a PS/2 keyboard on the physical computer.

Table 2-1   Virtualized Hardware Components

Component	Virtualized Hardware
Network adapter (multifunction)	Up to four Multiport DEC/Intel 21140 Ethernet network adapters.
Processor	Single processor that is the same as the physical computer processor.
Memory	Up to 3.6 GB of RAM per virtual machine.
Video card	S3 Trio64 graphics adapter with 4 MB of VRAM, VGA and SVGA support compliant with VESA 2.0, 2-D graphics accelerator and hardware cursor, and support for DirectX.
IDE/ATAPI storage	Dual IDE channels that support hard drives, CD-ROM or DVD-ROM drives, and ISO images. Each IDE channel supports two disks.
SCSI storage	Up to four Adaptec 7870 SCSI adapters, each supporting seven disks.
Sound card	None.

A few limitations are imposed on virtual machine workloads based on the virtual hardware environment. Operating systems or applications that require direct access to a hardware device that is not listed in Table 2-1 cannot execute in a virtual machine. Because virtual machines expose only a single CPU to a hosted workload, applications that require symmetric multiprocessing (SMP) also cannot execute in a virtual machine.

Virtual Hard Disks

Virtual hard disks (VHDs) are single file representations of a physical hard disk that encapsulate virtual machine data. Virtual hard disks reflect the same internal structure as a physical hard disk, including block allocation tables, data blocks, and sectors. Table 2-2 provides a list of virtual hard disk types available in Virtual Server 2005 R2.

Table 2-2   Virtual Hard Disk Types

Disk Type	Description
Fixed	Virtual hard disk file with all data blocks allocated on the host disk subsystem at creation time. A 10-GB fixed disk consumes 10 GB on the host physical disk where it is created.
Dynamically Expanding	Virtual hard disk file that is preallocated with no data blocks reserved and grows as data is written until it reaches full size. A 10-GB dynamically expanding disk takes less than 2 MB initially and grows to 10 GB in 2-MB data block increments.
	In Virtual Server 2005 R2 SP1, the maximum size for this VHD type is 127 GB.

Table 2-2   Virtual Hard Disk Types

Disk Type	Description
Differencing	Virtual hard disk file that is tied to an existing "parent" virtual hard disk file as an overlay. All writes are made to the differencing disk, the "child," while reads come from the parent and the child. Differencing disks are created as dynamically expanding disks.
Linked	A physical disk volume that you want to convert to a virtual hard disk. Linked disks exist only to perform the migration from physical to virtual hard disk.

Within a virtual machine, a virtual hard disk is represented as a physical disk. On a Virtual Server 2005 R2 server physical disk, a virtual hard disk is stored as a file with a .vhd extension. Virtual machines connect to a virtual hard disk through a virtualized Integrated Drive Electronics (IDE) or Small Computer System Interface (SCSI) adapter. Virtual Server 2005 R2 is responsible for mapping the virtual hard disk to the .vhd file on the physical disk. A VHD can be stored on any IDE, SCSI, storage area network (SAN), or Network-Attached Storage (NAS) storage system supported by the Virtual Server 2005 R2 host operating system.

Virtual hard disks are created using either the Virtual Server Administration Website or scripting through the Virtual Server COM application programming interface (API). A virtual machine can support a maximum of 32 virtual hard disks through a combination of IDE and SCSI-connected VHDs.

Note   Virtual hard disk specifications are independent of the bus type used to connect to the virtual machine. However, the bus type does impose a size limitation on virtual hard disks. Virtual hard disks connected via IDE cannot exceed 127 GB. Virtual hard disks connected via SCSI cannot exceed 2 terabytes.

Virtual IDE Interface

A virtual machine provides built-in primary and secondary virtual IDE interfaces. Each virtual IDE interface can support two devices attached to it, for a total of four IDE devices for every virtual machine. Either virtual hard disks or virtual CD-ROMs can be connected to an IDE interface. By default, the first virtual CD-ROM is attached to the secondary interface as the master device.

Virtual SCSI Interface

Contrary to the built-in virtual IDE interfaces exposed within the virtual machine environment, virtual SCSI interfaces are optional components that must be installed in a virtual machine before they can be used. A virtual machine supports up to four virtual SCSI adapters.

Each virtual SCSI adapter can have up to 7 devices attached, for a total of 28 SCSI devices for every virtual machine.

When you configure a virtual SCSI adapter in a virtual machine, the default SCSI adapter ID is set to 7. Each SCSI adapter is allowed to have the same ID because each virtual SCSI adapter is installed on a separate SCSI bus. Virtual hard disks are the only valid devices that can be connected to a SCSI adapter.

Virtual Networks

A virtual network is a software emulation of a network hub with unlimited ports and a switched uplink that can connect to an external physical network through a physical network adapter or remain disconnected to create an isolated internal network. Each virtual network port simulates a 10/100 Mb Ethernet port. Virtual Server 2005 R2 supports an unlimited number of virtual networks with an unlimited number of virtual machine connections.

By default, Virtual Server 2005 R2 creates a virtual network designated as Internal Network. The Internal Network supports virtual machine to virtual machine connectivity, ensuring that communications between virtual machines are isolated from any physical network. Network packets transmitted through the Internal Network are never processed by a physical network adapter or forwarded to any external physical network.

In addition, Virtual Server 2005 R2 automatically creates a virtual network designated as External Network for each physical network adapter installed in the physical server. If a virtual machine is connected to one of these virtual networks, it appears identical to a networked, standalone physical node and has the ability to communicate with physical or virtual machine nodes across the networks accessible to the physical network adapter.

Virtual Server 2005 R2 also includes a Virtual DHCP server that can be enabled or disabled on each individual virtual network. If enabled on a virtual network, the Virtual DHCP server provides standard network configuration settings to virtual machines connected to the virtual network.

> **Note**   An isolated internal network can also be created to enable network communications between a Virtual Server 2005 R2 host and guest virtual machines. This configuration requires the installation of the Microsoft Loopback Adapter as described in Chapter 4, "Virtual Server 2005 R2 Advanced Features."

Both internal and external virtual networks can be created through the Virtual Server 2005 R2 Administration Website or using the Virtual Server COM API.

Virtual Network Adapters

Virtual machines emulate a virtual Multiport DEC 21140 network adapter to connect to virtual networks. When a virtual network adapter is added to a virtual machine, Virtual Server 2005 R2 allocates a new dynamic media access control (MAC) address from the pool of available addresses. It is also possible to provide a virtual network adapter with a static MAC address that is manually configured.

Virtual machines support a maximum of four virtual network adapters. Virtual network adapters support the Pre-boot Execution Environment protocol (PXE), allowing virtual machines to be provisioned using standard image-deployment tools such as Remote Installation Services, Automated Deployment Services (ADS), or other third-party applications. However, virtual network adapters do not provide support for either Virtual Local Area Networks (VLANs) or network interface card teaming.

Important   Although the DEC 21140 network adapter defines a 10/100 Mb Ethernet interface, there is no network bandwidth limitation imposed on virtual machine workloads. If the underlying physical network adapter is capable of achieving higher network performance (for example, gigabit speed), the virtual machine workload has the ability to exceed the 100 Mb specification.

Virtual Machine Additions

Virtual Machine Additions are a set of performance, integration, and functionality enhancements that are installed in a guest operating system running in a virtual machine. Virtual Machine Additions offer enhancements in the following areas:

- Performance-tuned mouse and keyboard drivers
- Intelligent mouse and cursor focus capture and release
- Virtual machine heartbeat generator
- Time synchronization with the physical host
- Performance-tuned video driver with arbitrary video resizing
- Performance-tuned SCSI controller driver
- Guest kernel patches

Virtual Machine Additions are available for all Virtual Server 2005 R2 SP1 supported versions of Windows and Linux distributions listed in Chapter 1, "Introducing Microsoft Virtual Server 2005 R2 SP1."

Virtual Machine Remote Control

Virtual Machine Remote Control (VMRC) is a client/server remote administration tool provided with Virtual Server 2005 R2. VMRC allows remote access of the guest operating system running in a virtual machine. The VMRC protocol is implemented as a secure version of the Virtual Network Computing (VNC) protocol, and it includes authentication support for NTLM and Kerberos.

The VMRC server is embedded in the Virtual Server 2005 R2 service. In contrast, the VMRC client is implemented in two forms: an ActiveX client for Internet Explorer, and a standalone Windows client. By default, the VMRC server listens on port 5900 for any connections from VMRC clients. When a client connects to the VMRC server, a specific virtual machine can be explicitly chosen. If a virtual machine is not specified, an administrative display is presented. The administrative display contains a thumbnail of each hosted virtual machine. For security purposes, the virtual machines' thumbnails are filtered to include only the virtual machines to which the user running the client has been granted access.

If you click one of the thumbnails, the VMRC client connects to the virtual machine and displays the guest operating system video frame buffer, providing remote control of the guest operating system. Because VMRC provides access to the video frame buffer from the moment a virtual machine is powered on, you have access to the entire boot process, including the BIOS Power-On Self Test (POST). This functionality also allows you to access and change the virtual machine BIOS configuration. This is different than the Remote Desktop Protocol (RDP), which requires the operating system to be up and running before a connection can be achieved and video display is accessible.

Managing with the Administration Website

Virtual Server 2005 R2 provides a Web-based management interface that allows configuration and management of a Virtual Server host and associated virtual machines. Using a Web-based approach allows remote administration from any location or device using a browser that supports ActiveX controls. The administrative Web application (Vswebapp.exe), referred to as the Virtual Server 2005 R2 Administration Website, allows an administrator to manage multiple Virtual Server hosts, albeit serially.

The Virtual Server 2005 R2 Administration Website main page is the Master Status page. The Master Status page is composed of three main panels, as shown in Figure 2-1. The left panel consists of the navigation menu that provides access to the management interfaces for virtual machines, virtual hard disks, virtual networks, and Virtual Server configuration.

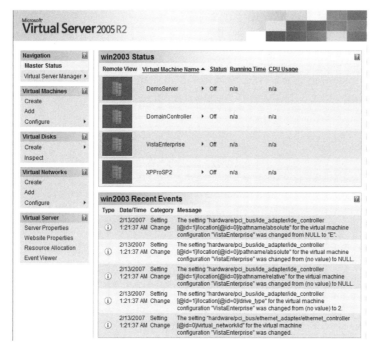

Figure 2-1   Virtual Server 2005 R2 Administration Website—Master Status page

By default, the top right panel provides a 10-entry page-based status view of registered virtual machines. The status information includes a thumbnail graphic of the current video buffer, virtual machine name, current virtual machine state, and virtual machine run time. If a virtual machine is actively running, a processor-usage graph is also displayed.

In the bottom right panel, a recent events log is shown. By default, only the five most recent events are displayed in this view. The number of recent events displayed is configurable in the Website Properties section.

Managing Multiple Virtual Server Hosts

Although the Virtual Server 2005 R2 Administration Website allows only a single Virtual Server host to be managed at a time, it is a simple matter to switch the management focus to a different Virtual Server host. Figure 2-2 shows the Specify Virtual Server form that is displayed when accessed from the Virtual Server Manager navigation menu. This form is where you can specify the name or IP address of a Virtual Server host that you would like to manage.

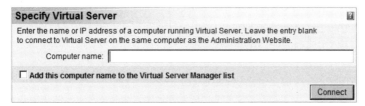

Figure 2-2 Virtual Server 2005 R2 Administration Website—Specify Virtual Server form

On this pane, you also have the option to add entries to the Virtual Server Manager list. To do this, simply select the Add This Computer Name To The Virtual Server Manager List box.

Managing Virtual Machines

The Virtual Server 2005 R2 Administration Website allows you to create, add, or configure virtual machines on the managed Virtual Server host. Virtual machine management is accomplished by selecting the desired management option and then providing or changing information through simple forms.

Creating Virtual Machines

Selecting the Create option in the Virtual Machines menu allows creation of a new virtual machine. If this option is chosen, the Create Virtual Machine form shown in Figure 2-3 is displayed.

Create Virtual Machine

Virtual machine name
Type the name for the virtual machine file to create a virtual machine in its own folder saved in the default configuration folder specified on the Virtual Server Paths page. To create a virtual machine in a different location, provide a fully qualified path.

Virtual machine name:

Memory
The amount of memory can be from 4 MB through 1719 MB (1547 MB maximum recommended).

Virtual machine memory (in MB): 128

Virtual hard disk
Before you can install an operating system on this virtual machine, you must attach a new or existing virtual hard disk to it. A virtual hard disk is a .vhd file that is stored on your physical hard disk and contains the guest operating system, applications and data files.

○ Create a new virtual hard disk

This option creates an unformatted dynamically expanding virtual hard disk in the same directory as the virtual machine configuration file. The maximum size allowed is 127 GB for IDE disks and 2040 GB for SCSI disks.

Size: 127   Units: GB   Bus: IDE

○ Use an existing virtual hard disk

Location: None

File name (.vhd):

Bus: IDE

○ Attach a virtual hard disk later (None)

Virtual network adapter
A virtual machine is preconfigured with one Ethernet network adapter that can be connected to a virtual network.

Connected to: Not connected

Virtual Machine Additions
Important: We highly recommend that you install Virtual Machine Additions. Virtual Machine Additions provides performance and feature enhancements for Windows-based guest operating systems. These features include: time synchronization between guest and host operating systems, mouse integration when using the ActiveX control in Virtual Machine Remote Control (VMRC), and a heartbeat for the guest operating system to monitor the state of the virtual machine.

Create

Figure 2-3 Virtual Server 2005 R2 Administration Website—Create Virtual Machine form

The form gathers basic information about the new virtual machine configuration, including the virtual machine name, memory to assign to the virtual machine, size of the virtual hard disk and bus type (IDE or SCSI) to attach it to, and the virtual network to connect to the virtual machine. Alternatively, you can specify an existing virtual hard drive to attach to the new virtual machine instead of creating a new one.

When the information in the form is submitted to Virtual Server, a new virtual machine configuration file (.vmc) that contains settings information is created. The new virtual machine is registered and visible on the Master Status page; a new virtual hard disk is created, if specified; and a virtual network adapter is connected to the virtual machine. The new virtual machine is then ready to boot and install a new operating system or execute the existing operating system.

Adding Pre-Existing Virtual Machines

Using the Add option in the Virtual Machines menu allows you to add a pre-existing virtual machine to a Virtual Server 2005 R2 host. A simple form that requests only a fully qualified path to an existing virtual machine configuration file is displayed when this option is selected. After the form is submitted, the virtual machine is registered with the Virtual Server host and the configuration page is displayed.

Managing Virtual Machine Configurations

The Configure option in the Virtual Machines menu provides the means to access virtual machine status and configuration panes. The virtual machine status pane, shown in Figure 2-4, displays current performance information and other relevant details, such as the installed guest operating system, the installed version of Virtual Machine Additions, and the path to the virtual machine configuration (.vmc) file.

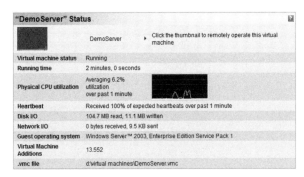

Figure 2-4   Virtual Server 2005 R2 Administration Website—Virtual Machine Status pane

The virtual machine configuration pane, shown in Figure 2-5, displays and summarizes the current virtual machine configuration by major component. In this pane, there are also links to forms that allow modification of the virtual machine configuration.

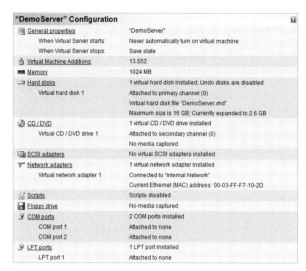

"DemoServer" Configuration

General properties	"DemoServer"
When Virtual Server starts:	Never automatically turn on virtual machine
When Virtual Server stops:	Save state
Virtual Machine Additions	13.552
Memory	1024 MB
Hard disks	1 virtual hard disk installed; Undo disks are disabled
Virtual hard disk 1	Attached to primary channel (0)
	Virtual hard disk file "DemoServer.vhd"
	Maximum size is 16 GB; Currently expanded to 2.6 GB
CD / DVD	1 virtual CD / DVD drive installed
Virtual CD / DVD drive 1	Attached to secondary channel (0)
	No media captured
SCSI adapters	No virtual SCSI adapters installed
Network adapters	1 virtual network adapter installed
Virtual network adapter 1	Connected to "Internal Network"
	Current Ethernet (MAC) address: 00-03-FF-F7-10-2D
Scripts	Scripts disabled
Floppy drive	No media captured
COM ports	2 COM ports installed
COM port 1	Attached to none
COM port 2	Attached to none
LPT ports	1 LPT port installed
LPT port 1	Attached to none

Figure 2-5 Virtual Server 2005 R2 Administration Website—Virtual Machine Configuration pane

Table 2-3 provides a list of virtual machine configuration options and a description of what changes are supported in the associated form.

Table 2-3 Virtual Machine Configuration Options

Configuration Option	Description
General Properties	Allows modifications to the virtual machine name, user account used to run the virtual machine, actions to take during virtual machine start or stop, delay in seconds that will be used if the virtual machine is automatically started, and list of notes for the virtual machine.
Virtual Machine Additions	Allows installation of Virtual Machine Additions and host time synchronization.
Memory	Allows specification of the virtual machine memory allocation.
Hard Disks	Allows the addition, removal, or change in the number of virtual hard disks attached to the virtual machine, as well as the attached bus type (IDE or SCSI). This form also provides the ability to enable or disable undo disks.
CD/DVD	Allows IDE-based CD or DVD drives to be attached to the virtual machine. The CD or DVD can be in the form of an ISO image or physical CD/DVD drive installed on the host.

Table 2-3   Virtual Machine Configuration Options

Configuration Option	Description
SCSI Adapters	Allows the addition, removal, or change in the number of virtual SCSI adapters installed in the virtual machine. There is also an option to specify whether the SCSI bus is configured for shared access to support clustering. The final option allows specification of the SCSI adapter ID (6 or 7) .
Network Adapters	Allows the addition, removal, or change in the number of virtual network cards installed in the virtual machine. For each network adapter, options exist to specify the virtual network connection and whether the network adapter MAC address is assigned dynamically or statically.
Scripts	Allows the specification of scripts that are executed based on virtual machine state changes, such as power on, power off, reset, and so on.
Floppy Drive	Allows the virtual floppy drive to connect to the physical floppy drive on the host or existing floppy disk image.
COM Ports	Allows for the connection of COM ports to or the disconnection of COM ports from the virtual machine. COM ports can be a physical COM port on the host, a text file, or a named pipe.
LPT Ports	Allows for the connection of a printer port to or disconnection of a printer port from the virtual machine. The virtual machine LPT port can only be connected to a physical printer port on the host.

Managing Virtual Hard Disks

The Virtual Server Administration Website allows the creation and inspection of virtual hard disks and virtual floppy disks on the managed Virtual Server host. Just as a virtual hard disk is a single file representation of a physical hard disk, a virtual floppy disk is a single file representation of a physical floppy disk.

Creating Virtual Hard Disks

Virtual hard disk files are a main component of a virtual machine, encapsulating the guest operating system and application data. A virtual hard disk can be created separately from a virtual machine by using the Create option in the Virtual Disks menu. Figure 2-6 shows the menu that is displayed when the Create option is selected. Before a virtual hard disk is created, the virtual hard disk type (fixed, dynamically expanding, differencing, or linked) must be defined. Details for each virtual hard disk type are provided in Chapter 3, "Virtual Server Architecture."

Figure 2-6   Virtual Server 2005 R2 Administration Website—Virtual Disks menu Create option

A virtual machine exposes a single virtual floppy drive to the guest operating system. A virtual machine does not allow the removal of the virtual floppy drive, nor does it support additional floppy drives to be connected. Figure 2-7 illustrates the Virtual Floppy Disk form that enables the creation of a formatted virtual floppy disk (.vfd). Virtual Server 2005 R2 supports only the creation of a 1.44-MB virtual floppy disk, although both 720-KB and 1.44-MB floppy formats can be used.

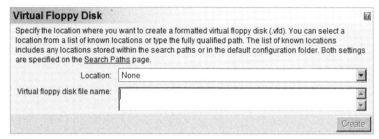

Figure 2-7   Virtual Server 2005 R2 Administration Website—Virtual Floppy Disk form

Inspecting Virtual Hard Disks

If selected, the Inspect option in the Virtual Disks menu will display virtual hard disk properties and potential actions. Once the targeted virtual hard disk is defined, Virtual Server 2005 R2 opens the virtual hard disk, obtains the current and maximum size settings as well as the virtual hard disk type, and displays the information in the Virtual Hard Disk Properties pane. Depending on the type of virtual hard disk, a list of potential actions is displayed in the virtual hard disk Actions pane, as indicated in Table 2-4.

Table 2-4   Virtual Hard Disk Inspect Actions by Drive Type

Disk Type	Action	Description
Fixed	Convert	Convert a fixed disk to a dynamically expanding disk.
Dynamically Expanding	Convert	Convert a dynamically expanding disk to a fixed disk.
	Compact	Compact a dynamically expanding disk to regain unused space.
Differencing	Merge	Merge the changes in a child disk into the parent disk or merge the parent and child disks into a new virtual hard disk.

Managing Virtual Networks

The Virtual Server 2005 R2 Administration Website allows the creation, addition, and configuration of virtual networks on the managed Virtual Server host. Virtual networks allow virtual machines to connect to each other, the host, and other physical or virtual machines on a physical network.

Creating Virtual Networks

The Create option in the Virtual Networks menu allows the creation of new virtual networks using the Network Properties form displayed in Figure 2-8. Creating a new virtual network on a host is an uncommon administrative task because Virtual Server 2005 R2 automatically creates a virtual network for each physical network adapter detected in the host. However, if a new network adapter is added to the Virtual Server host or there is a requirement to construct a complex networking scenario, a new virtual network might also need to be created.

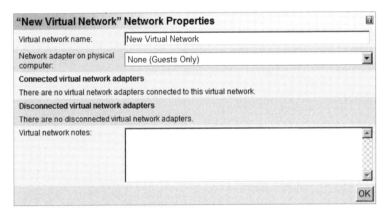

Figure 2-8   Virtual Server 2005 R2 Administration Website—Network Properties form

To create a new virtual network, a virtual network name and physical network adapter to connect to the virtual network must be specified. In the list of network adapters to connect to the virtual network is an entry for each network adapter installed in the host and bound to the Virtual Machine Network Services (VMNS) driver. There is also a None (Guests Only) option in this list. Selecting a physical network adapter from the list allows a virtual network to use the physical adapter to communicate to an attached physical network. Selecting the None (Guest Only) option will create an isolated virtual network. No packets from any attached virtual machine will be transmitted on a physical network, and only virtual machines can attach to this virtual network. Information and settings for a virtual network are stored in a specific configuration file (.vnc) on the Virtual Server 2005 R2 host.

Adding a Virtual Network Configuration File

The Add option in the Virtual Networks menu provides a way to register an existing virtual network configuration file with a Virtual Server 2005 R2 host. Once the fully qualified path to the .vnc file is provided and the Add Virtual Network form is submitted, the virtual network is manageable through the Virtual Network Properties panes.

Configuring Virtual Networks

Similar to the virtual machine configuration file (.vmc), a virtual network configuration file (.vnc) contains virtual network settings and details. Settings include the virtual network name, the connected physical network adapter, and any defined notes. Details include virtual machines connected to the virtual network and virtual machines that have no virtual network connections.

Figure 2-9 shows the Virtual Network Properties panes that are displayed when the Configure menu option is selected for a particular virtual network in the Virtual Networks menu. The lower pane allows the configuration of the virtual network and DHCP server settings.

Figure 2-9   Virtual Server 2005 R2 Administration Website—Virtual Network Properties panes

Figure 2-10 shows the Network Properties form. The Network Properties form allows the modification of the virtual network name, the attached physical network adapter, and any defined notes. There is also an option to enable or disable virtual machine network connections.

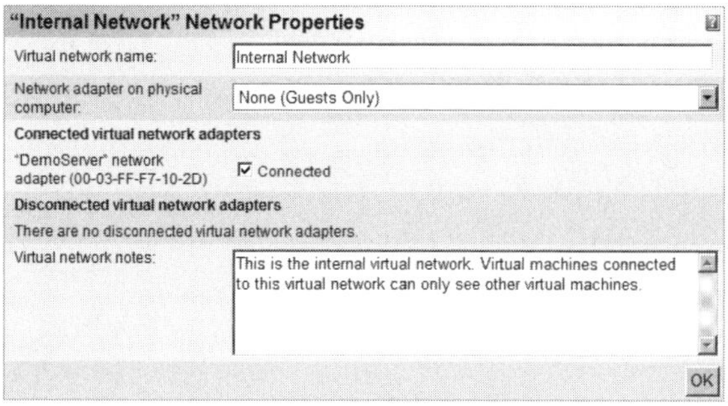

Figure 2-10   Virtual Server 2005 R2 Administration Website—Network Properties form

As shown in Figure 2-11, the DHCP Server Properties form provides the ability to enable or disable the DHCP server and configure the options used to provision virtual machine IP settings.

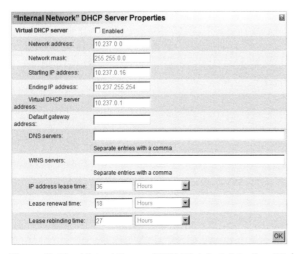

Figure 2-11   Virtual Server 2005 R2 Administration Website—DHCP Server Properties form

Managing Virtual Server Properties

The Virtual Server 2005 R2 Administration Website also provides the ability to configure Virtual Server properties. Figure 2-12 shows the Virtual Server Information and Properties panes displayed when the Server Properties option is selected from the Virtual Server menu.

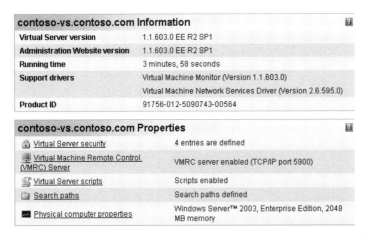

Figure 2-12   Virtual Server 2005 R2 Administration Website—Virtual Server Information and Properties panes

The Virtual Server Information pane contains the Virtual Server and Administration Website version information, as well as the Virtual Server uptime, kernel-level driver versions, and product ID.

The Virtual Server Properties pane contains links that allow the configuration of Virtual Server security settings, VMRC settings, script settings, and search paths settings. There is also a link to a Physical Computer Properties pane that displays the physical computer processor, memory, network, and operating system configuration.

Configuring Virtual Server Security Properties

The Virtual Server Security Properties form, shown in Figure 2-13, provides a means to view and modify security permission entries applied to Virtual Server, virtual machine, and virtual network configuration files that are stored in the default directories. Each permission entry is assigned to a specific user or group. Permission entries can be of either the Allow or Deny type.

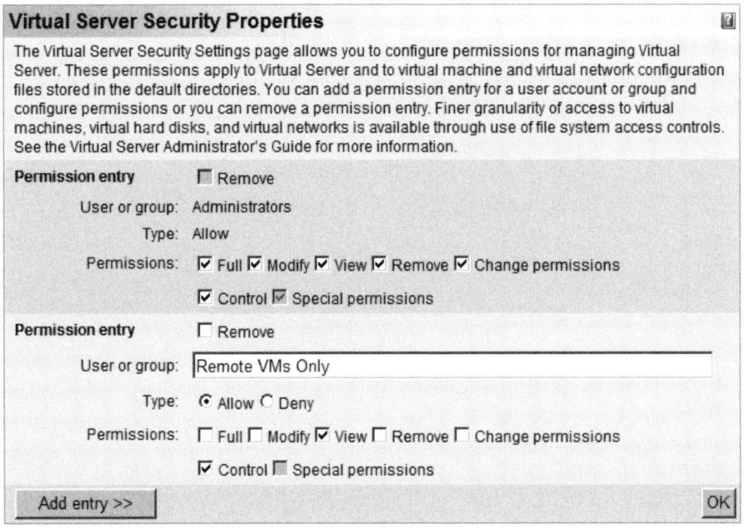

Figure 2-13   Virtual Server 2005 R2 Administration Website—Security Properties form

Table 2-5 lists permissions that can be assigned. By default, only a single permission entry is created for the local administrators group granting Full permissions.

Table 2-5   Permission Entries

Permission	Description
Full	Enables a user or group complete permissions
Modify	Enables a user or group the permissions to do the following: ■ Add virtual machines ■ Add virtual networks ■ Modify VMRC properties ■ Modify Virtual Server search paths ■ Modify Virtual Server script settings
View	Enables a user or group the permissions to do the following: ■ View Virtual Server configuration information ■ View the Virtual Server event log ■ View virtual machine configuration information if READ permissions exist to the .vmc file
Remove	Enables a user or group the permissions to do the following: ■ Remove a virtual machine ■ Remove a virtual network
Change	Enables a user or group to change security permission entries
Control	Enables a user or group permissions to do the following: ■ Access the Component Object Model (COM) interfaces ■ Manage the Virtual Server host using the COM API or the Web interface
Special	Enables the display of special permissions that have been configured

Configuring Virtual Machine Remote Control Server Properties

Figure 2-14 displays the Virtual Machine Remote Control (VMRC) Server Properties form. The VMRC Server accepts client connections that allow remote access and interaction of a virtual machine from the moment the virtual machine is powered on.

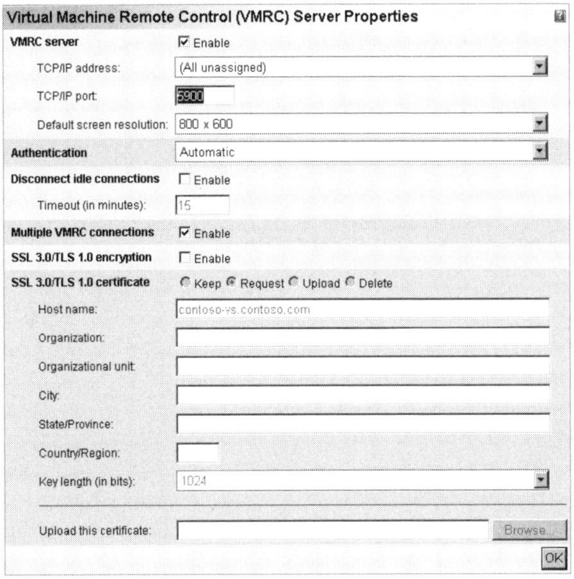

Figure 2-14   Virtual Server 2005 R2 Administration Website—VMRC Server Properties form

The VMRC Server Properties form includes options to enable or disable VMRC, define network communication settings (TCP/IP address and port), configure the default video resolution for remote sessions, select an authentication protocol, configure idle connections settings, enable or disable multiple VMRC connections to a virtual machine, and manage the use of Secure Sockets Layer (SSL) configuration and certificates for the Virtual Server 2005 R2 Administration Website.

Configuring Virtual Server Script Settings

The Virtual Server Script Settings form enables specification of one or more scripts to execute in response to discrete Virtual Server or virtual machine state transitions. A sampling of the Virtual Server Script Settings form is provided in Figure 2-15. The form also contains an option to enable or disable the execution of server or virtual machine scripts.

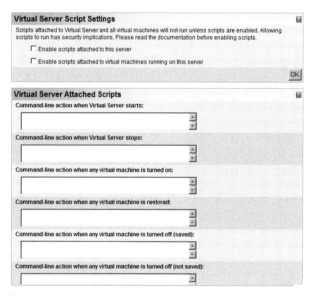

Figure 2-15   Virtual Server 2005 R2 Administration Website—Script Settings form

Virtual machine scripts must be enabled before assignment to a virtual machine. Assigning a virtual machine script will apply that script to all virtual machines running on the Virtual Server host. Each of the following state changes are valid actions that trigger assigned script execution:

- Virtual Server starts

- Virtual Server stops

- Virtual machine is turned on

- Virtual machine is restored

- Virtual machine is turned off (saved)

- Virtual machine is turned off (not saved)

- Virtual machine is turned off within the guest environment

- Virtual machine is reset

- No heartbeat is detected for any virtual machine

- Virtual machine experiences a guest processor error

- Virtual machine receives a warning because of low disk space on the physical computer

- Virtual machine receives an error because of low disk space on the physical computer

Configuring Virtual Server Search Paths

The Virtual Server Search Paths form allows modifications to the default virtual machine configuration folder and search paths. The default folder is used to store the virtual machine configuration file only when a fully qualified path fails to be defined during creation of a new virtual machine.

Search paths require fully qualified paths, as shown in Figure 2-16. In this figure, a default folder and search path configuration have been specified. The search paths are traversed to gather a list of Virtual Server–related files. This list of files is used to populate drop-down selection boxes present in many Virtual Server 2005 R2 Administration Website forms.

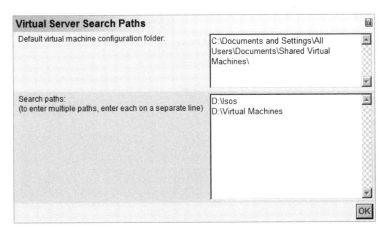

Figure 2-16   Virtual Server 2005 R2 Administration Website—Search Paths form

Managing Website Properties

Selecting the Website Properties option of the Virtual Server menu displays the Administration Website Properties form shown in Figure 2-17. The form allows management of the options that control the layout of the master status page, recent event properties, event viewer properties, VMRC properties, and Virtual Server Manager search paths. The form also allows the configuration of the automatic refresh rate for the Administration Website.

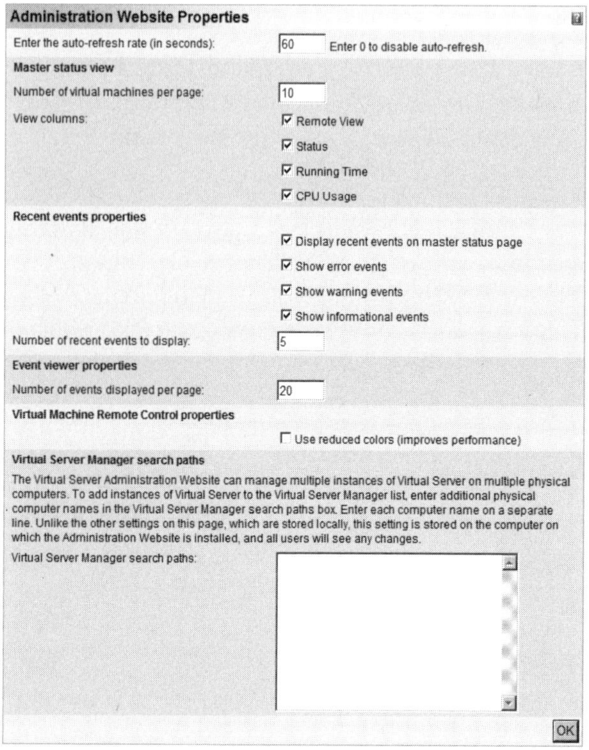

Administration Website Properties   ?

Enter the auto-refresh rate (in seconds):   [60]   Enter 0 to disable auto-refresh.

Master status view

Number of virtual machines per page: [10]

View columns: ☑ Remote View

                                 ☑ Status

                                 ☑ Running Time

                                 ☑ CPU Usage

Recent events properties

                                 ☑ Display recent events on master status page

                                 ☑ Show error events

                                 ☑ Show warning events

                                 ☑ Show informational events

Number of recent events to display: [5]

Event viewer properties

Number of events displayed per page: [20]

Virtual Machine Remote Control properties

                                 ☐ Use reduced colors (improves performance)

Virtual Server Manager search paths

The Virtual Server Administration Website can manage multiple instances of Virtual Server on multiple physical computers. To add instances of Virtual Server to the Virtual Server Manager list, enter additional physical computer names in the Virtual Server Manager search paths box. Enter each computer name on a separate line. Unlike the other settings on this page, which are stored locally, this setting is stored on the computer on which the Administration Website is installed, and all users will see any changes.

Virtual Server Manager search paths:

[   ]

                                                        [OK]

Figure 2-17   Virtual Server 2005 R2 Administration Website—Administration Website Properties form

Configuring the Master Status View

The master status view is the area on the home page of the Virtual Server 2005 R2 Administration Website that displays virtual machine summary performance information and video screen buffer thumbnails. The master status view options allow the configuration of the number of virtual machines displayed before pagination is enabled along with the specific columns of status information included (remote thumbnail view, status, running time, and CPU usage graph).

Configuring Recent Event Properties

By default, the master status view displays the five most recent events. The recent event properties options include the ability to enable or disable the recent events list, in addition to specifying the types of events to display (errors, warnings, or informational events). There is also an option to modify the number of recent events that are reported in the master status view.

Configuring Event Viewer Properties

In addition to the recent events list displayed in the master status view, a complete event history is provided in the Virtual Server Event Viewer. The event viewer properties option allows the configuration of the number of events displayed per page in the event viewer pane.

Configuring VMRC Properties

The VMRC properties section provides the ability to enable the use of a reduced color set for the VMRC server running on the Virtual Server host. Setting this option reduces the size of the video pages that the VMRC server transfers to the VMRC client applications, thereby increasing the refresh performance and reducing the network traffic required during a virtual machine remote control session.

Configuring Virtual Server Manager Search Paths

The Virtual Server manager search paths section allows the specification of a list of Virtual Server hosts that can be managed from the local Administration Website. This list is used to populate a selection of servers in the Virtual Server Manager option of the Navigation menu.

Managing Virtual Machine Resource Allocation

The CPU Resource Allocation form allows the review and configuration of processor resource allocations assigned to registered virtual machines. As shown in Figure 2-18, the following information is available for each active virtual machine:

- Assigned relative weight
- Reserved capacity of a single processor
- Maximum capacity of a single processor
- Reserved system capacity
- Maximum system capacity
- Actual processor usage

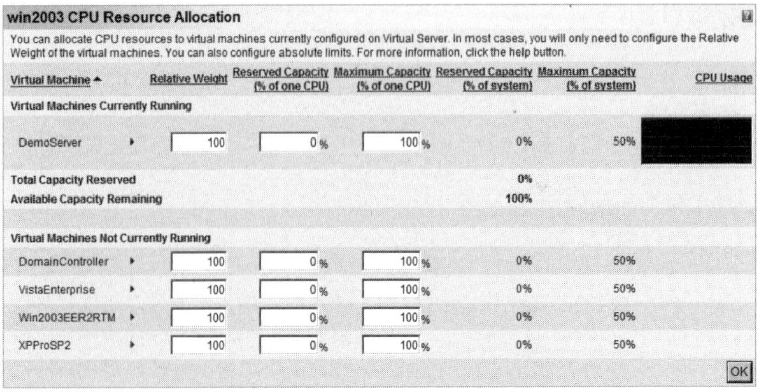

Figure 2-18   Virtual Server 2005 R2 Administration Website—CPU Resource Allocation form

In addition, there are two rollup values that show the total reserved capacity in use and the remaining system capacity available for assignment.

Directly below the rollup values, there is a list of virtual machines that are registered on the host but not currently running. For the virtual machines that are not running, three processor allocation settings can be modified: relative weight, reserved capacity of a single processor, and maximum capacity of a single processor. These settings and their use are described in more detail in Chapter 10, "Virtual Machine Migration Process."

Inspecting the Virtual Server Event Viewer

Accessible from the Virtual Server 2005 R2 Administration Website, the Event Viewer option in the Virtual Server menu displays the complete event history for the managed Virtual Server host. The events listed are the same events displayed in the Windows Event Viewer under the Virtual Server node. The event viewer page, a sample of which is shown in Figure 2-19, allows filtering of events based on event type and source.

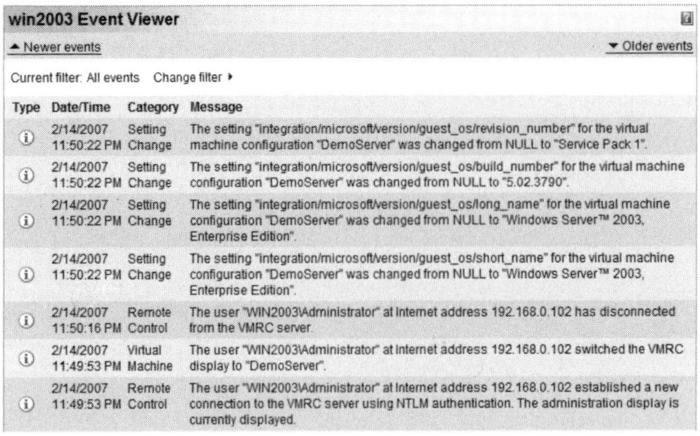

Figure 2-19   Virtual Server 2005 R2 Administration Website—Event Viewer

Outlining the Virtual Server 2005 R2 COM API

Virtual Server 2005 R2 provides a powerful COM API that can be used to programmatically control and monitor Virtual Server, as well as automate deployment and management of virtual machines. All the features offered in the Virtual Server 2005 R2 Administration Website are based on scripts that leverage this development interface.

Scripts and self-developed applications can be created using a variety of languages, including C#, Perl, C++, or Visual Basic to name just a few popular alternatives. Scripts are executed using the Windows Script Host in a new process using the network service account credentials.

> **Note** The Virtual Server 2005 R2 COM API is discussed in detail in Chapter 9, "Developing Scripts with the Virtual Server COM API." This chapter contains many scripts that you can use or modify to use in your environment.

Summary

Virtual Server 2005 R2 SP1 features virtual machines that expose a standard virtual hardware environment to their guest operating system and applications. Becoming familiar with the virtual hardware environment is crucial to making competent decisions concerning physical workloads that can successfully be redeployed as virtual machines.

Creation, inspection, and configuration of virtual machine main components, including virtual hard disks and virtual networks, can be accomplished through the Virtual Server 2005 R2 Administration Website. You can also use the Administration Website to configure Virtual Server 2005 R2 server and Web site properties.

Use the Virtual Machine Remote Control (VMRC) ActiveX or standalone Windows application to remotely access and manipulate virtual machines from the moment they become active. If you anticipate having or already have a significant deployment of Virtual Server hosts and virtual machines, leverage the Virtual Server 2005 R2 COM API to programmatically control the deployment, administration, and configuration of Virtual Server hosts and virtual machines.

Additional Resources

The following resources contain additional information related to the topics in this chapter:

- "Virtual Server 2005 R2 Administrator's Guide" in %systemdrive%\Program Files \Microsoft Virtual Server\Documentation.
- "Virtual Server 2005 R2 Programmer's Guide" in %systemdrive%\Program Files \Microsoft Virtual Server\Documentation.

Chapter 3
Virtual Server Architecture

In this chapter:

Product Architecture. 55
Virtual Machine Monitor Architecture. 57
Virtual Server Service 58
Virtual Machine Helper Service. 58
Virtual Machine Additions 58
Virtual Processors 59
Virtual Server Memory 61
Virtual Networking 61
Virtual Hard Disks 64
Virtual Floppy Disks. 69
Save State File. 69
Summary. 69
Additional Resources. 70

Product Architecture

Microsoft Virtual Server 2005 Release 2 (R2) Service Pack 1 (SP1) uses a Hosted model for virtualization. The Microsoft Windows operating system acts as the host, all resources for virtual machines are allocated from the host's resources, and all I/O with external devices is performed through the host. A virtual machine guest operating system runs in a separate context from the host and has an independent memory address space that does not directly map to the host's address space.

Figure 3-1 provides a high-level view of the relationship between the host hardware and software, and the virtual machine virtual hardware and software. The left side of Figure 3-1 depicts the host hardware application stack, which includes the hardware, the hardware abstraction layer, the host kernel, the host TCP/IP stack, services such as the Virtual Server service, and the applications running on the host. The right-hand side of Figure 3-1 depicts the virtual machine stack. You can see that the virtual machine has the same stack of components as the host down to the hardware abstraction layer. The virtual machine does not see the host's hardware; instead, it sees a set of emulated and virtualized hardware. The Virtual Server service presents the virtual hardware to the virtual machine. The Virtual Server service interfaces to the host hardware through the Virtual Machine Monitor (VMM) kernel implemented as a kernel driver on the host called VMM.SYS. The VMM controls access to the host hardware and manages the processor access.

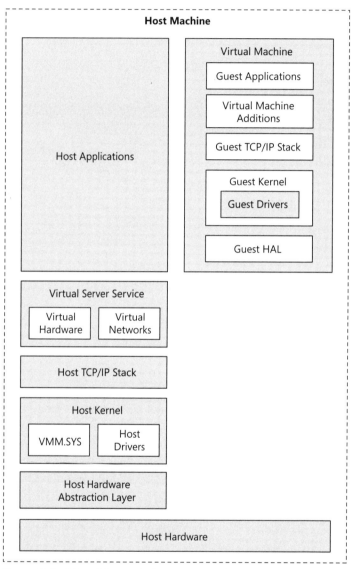

Figure 3-1   Virtual Server 2005 R2 SP1 product architecture

A virtual machine shares the network interface of the host to communicate to other machines on the network. This task is accomplished in two layers. The Virtual Server service implements the virtual networks that the virtual machine network interface can connect. A Network Driver Interface Specification (NDIS) intermediate packet filter driver provides the networking interface between the virtual networks and host network interface card. Using this approach, the Virtual Server service can create unlimited virtual networks and independently bind them to the host network interface cards through the NDIS driver. This arrangement allows virtual machines to send and receive Ethernet packets through the physical host's network interface card.

Virtual Machine Additions are a collection of drivers and services installed in the virtual machine operating system by the end user. Virtual Machine Additions provide optimizations for video, SCSI, networking, mouse, keyboard, and audio. The additions also provide services for tasks such as backup, folder sharing, and CD-ROM management.

The following sections provide a deeper view into each of the major components:

- Virtual Machine Monitor
- Virtual Server service
- Virtual Machine Helper service
- Virtual Machine Additions
- Virtual processors
- Virtual memory
- Virtual networks
- Virtual hard disks
- Virtual floppy disks
- Save state file

Virtual Machine Monitor Architecture

The Virtual Machine Monitor (VMM) is designed to sit between the guest operating system in the virtual machine and the host computer's hardware. The VMM's primary job is to monitor and prevent a guest operating system from accessing resources outside its privilege scope. The VMM accomplishes this by defining a set of application programming interfaces (APIs) that contain the proper access and security limitations, and by trapping privileged instructions and properly handling them. The architecture of VMM is implemented in two parts: the VMM.SYS driver and the VMM kernel. The VMM.SYS driver provides kernel-level services for virtual machines, implements the context-switching mechanism between the host and guest, and handles loading and bootstrapping the VMM kernel. The VMM.SYS driver also implements an interface and a set of APIs to allow user-level code executing on the host operating system to access the services of the VMM.SYS driver.

The VMM kernel is a thin layer of assembly code that executes at processor Ring 0 (zero) and provides exception handling, external interrupt pass-through, and page table maintenance. It also creates and manages the run-time environment that the guest operating system kernel executes. The VMM kernel provides an interface to user- and kernel-level code running in the guest operating system, and it attempts to handle all execution possible before it performs a host context switch and hands the instructions to the host for processing. Each virtual processor has its own instance of a VMM kernel.

Virtual Server Service

The Virtual Server service, VSSRVC.EXE, is the central control point for all virtual machine functionality. It provides the COM+ interfaces to create virtual objects; projects the virtual machine emulated hardware into the virtual machine environment; provides virtual machine device emulation; handles the event logging; manages the CPU resource allocation and monitoring; and provides the Windows Management Instrumentation (WMI) and scripting interfaces, virtual machine configuration creation and editing, virtual machine control, and virtual network configuration and management. The Virtual Server service also includes the Virtual Machine Remote Control (VMRC) server, which allows users to remotely manage and interact with virtual machines. The VMRC server provides remote desktop screen, keyboard, and mouse redirection.

Virtual Machine Helper Service

The Virtual Machine Helper service, VMH.EXE, allows a virtual machine to run in the context of a specified user account to support access to network resources and run scripts. By default, the context of the user that started the virtual machine is used if a specific user account is not configured.

If a virtual machine needs to automatically power on when the Virtual Server process starts, the virtual machine configuration file (.vmc) must specify a user account. The Virtual Machine Helper service then utilizes the user credentials to launch the virtual machine. The Virtual Machine Helper service runs under the Local System account and has limited access to the local computer and anonymous access to network resources.

Virtual Machine Additions

Virtual Machine Additions are a set of drivers and services installed in the virtual machine to provide performance, integration, and functionality enhancements. Microsoft has implemented a common architecture for both Virtual PC 2007 and Virtual Server 2005 R2 SP1. This means that a single set of virtual machine additions has the driver and services for both products included. Figure 3-2 provides a diagram that shows all the drivers and services included in the Virtual Machine Additions package. You can see that there are Virtual PC–specific drivers and services, Virtual Server–specific drivers and services, and then common drivers and services.

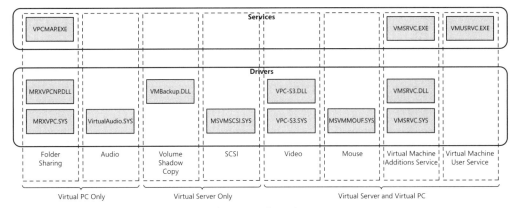

Figure 3-2 Virtual Machine Additions drivers and services

When you install virtual machine additions, all components are installed; however, only the applicable drivers and services are started. If you move a virtual machine between Virtual Server and Virtual PC, the plug-and-play function will enable or disable the correct drivers. Upon startup, the services check which software product they are running under and automatically shut down if not supported on that product.

Virtual Machine Additions driver installation on Virtual Server provides the following enhancements:

- **Video** Enhanced video performance and resizing support for VMRC. This driver replaces the standard S3 Trio driver that Windows installs.

- **Backup** VSS backup writer for Volume Shadow Copy Service (VSS) to allow VSS snapshot-based backups of the virtual machine from the host.

- **SCSI** Enhanced SCSI drive performance and support for shared disk clustering. This driver replaces the standard Adaptec SCSI driver that Windows installs.

- **Mouse** Enhanced mouse detection and focus release support for VMRC. This is implemented as an integration filter driver that enhances the existing Microsoft PS/2 mouse driver.

 Note Hardware-assisted virtualization mode available in the latest processors from Intel and AMD reduces the dependency on Virtual Machine Additions for processor performance tuning, but additions are still required for other purposes such as mouse and keyboard focus detection.

Virtual Processors

The x86-processor architecture is hard to virtualize because it has poor privileged and user state separation, and some instructions that access privilege state are nontrappable. Although emulation is possible, the overhead associated with complete emulation is not acceptable. So a combination of direct execution and emulation is used to obtain the best performance, with direct execution as the preferred execution method. Table 3-1 shows the different processor modes and the execution method implemented for each one.

Table 3-1   Processor and Execution Modes

Processor mode	Execution mode used
Real Mode	Emulation
Virtual 8086 (v86) mode	Direct Execution
Protected Mode Ring 3	Direct Execution with some exceptions
Protected Mode Ring 0	Emulation unless known to be safe

Processor rings define the privilege level of the instructions with Ring 0 having the highest privilege and Ring 3 having the lowest. The kernel of an operating system runs in Ring 0, and any user applications typically run in Ring 3. Figure 3-3 shows the relationship of the rings of execution and the parts of the operating system that execute in each ring.

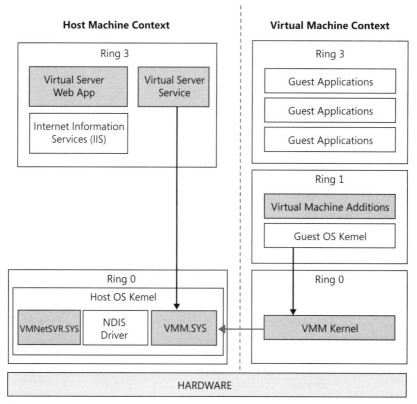

Figure 3-3   Processor execution ring architecture

Virtual Server 2005 R2 SP1 uses a direct execution approach called *ring compression*. Ring compression is the process of executing multiple ring modes for a virtual processor in a single ring mode of the physical processor. Virtual Server 2005 R2 SP1 uses ring compression to run virtual processor Ring modes 0, 1, and 2 in the physical processor Ring 1 mode, while virtual machine Ring 3 executions run in physical processor Ring 3.

During ring compression, direct execution of Ring 0 virtual machine code is allowed only if the execution is considered safe. Known dangerous instructions in the Windows kernel and hardware abstraction layer (HAL) of the virtual machine are patched at run time in memory. The patches are different for each version of a Windows or Linux kernel.

Direct from the Source: How Does Hardware-Assisted Virtualization Affect the Architecture?

Hardware-assisted virtualization available in both Intel's and AMD's latest chips provides a new processor privilege level and instructions that replace the need for ring compression and some emulation. This allows for the simplification of the architecture of Virtual Server 2005 R2 SP1. By using the new processor mode and instructions, the VMM can be more efficient and offload processing to the hardware. Virtual Server 2005 R2 SP1 supports machines with or without hardware virtualization.

Tony Donno
Senior Program Manager, Windows Virtualization

Virtual Server Memory

Virtual Server 2005 R2 SP1 uses only available physical memory to load and run virtual machines. The amount of RAM configured and used by a virtual machine is defined at creation and stored in the virtual machine configuration file. The VMM performs the allocation from physical RAM when the virtual machine is powered on, and the amount of virtual machine system RAM cannot be modified while the virtual machine is running. Because a virtual machine requires the same memory address space as a physical machine, the memory allocated to the virtual machine must be logically mapped to the correct address space the operating system is expecting.

Virtual memory is broken down into memory pages that are 4 KB in length. VMM maintains a set of page tables to support the mapping from virtual machine to physical machine pages. A VMM work area is allocated from the virtual memory to hold the VMM kernel, required data structures, binary translation (emulation) code cache, and device emulation operations and state.

Virtual Networking

The Virtual Server 2005 R2 SP1 network architecture consists of one or more virtual networks on the host and up to four virtual network adapters in a virtual machine. The virtual network is implemented as a hub with unlimited ports for virtual machines to attach to and a single switched uplink port. The uplink port can be connected to a physical network adapter on the host to allow packets to be sent to and received from other computers on the network. The uplink port can be connected only to a single network interface card (adapter) in the host at a time. If the virtual network uplink port is not connected to any network adapter in the host, network traffic is restricted to virtual machines that are connected to the hub ports.

Figure 3-4 shows the Virtual Machine Network Services driver, called VMNetSvr.sys, that handles the interface between the virtual network and the physical host. VMNetSvr.sys is an NDIS intermediate filter driver that can be bound to each Ethernet interface in the host machine. The driver exposes a private Windows Driver Model (WDM) interface to the virtual machine that allows Ethernet packets to be sent and received using the host Ethernet miniport interface. The WDM interface provides some basic Ethernet-level switching on the uplink port so that packets destined for the host are not visible to virtual machines and packets destined for the virtual machines are not visible to the host. All processing of packets is done at the Ethernet Frame level, and therefore, the payload data is never opened. Windows Firewall is a good example of how this works, because Windows Firewall enabled on the host will never see packets destined to any virtual machines and therefore provides no firewall protection. Because the virtual network operates as a hub, it maintains a common broadcast domain between all connected virtual machines.

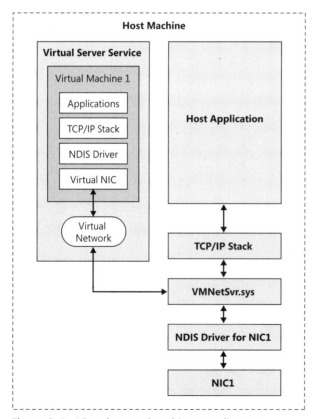

Figure 3-4   Virtual network architecture diagram

Figure 3-5 displays the path that packets take from a virtual machine when being sent to another virtual machine connected to the same virtual network, when being sent to the host, or when being sent to a computer that is connected to the physical network. A virtual machine can send packets to the host, but those packets never pass through the physical network interface in the host.

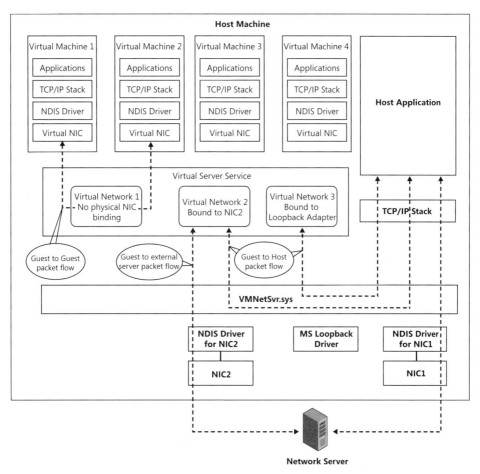

Figure 3-5   Paths that packets take depending on destination

The network adapter in the virtual machine is an emulated 10/100 Mbps DEC/Intel 21140A–based Ethernet card. This network card was selected based on the common availability in both Microsoft Windows and other operating systems. Even though it is presented to the virtual machine as a 10/100 Mbps network adapter, no bandwidth restrictions are implemented in the emulation to restrict the performance to 10/100 Mbps levels. Therefore, if the host network adapter that the virtual network is bound to is faster than 100 Mbps, the virtual machine will achieve speeds faster than 100 Mbps. As a result of the overhead in packet processing, the virtual network adapter will never achieve the speed of the host network adapter.

Every emulated DEC/Intel 21140A network adapter in a virtual machine has its own unique MAC address. Through Virtual Machine Network Services, the virtual network adapter can connect to both 802.3 wired local area network interfaces and 802.11 wireless network interfaces that exist in the host. If connected to a virtual network that is bound to an 802.3 network adapter in the host, each virtual network adapter will maintain a unique presence on the network through its unique MAC address. Virtual Machine Network Services achieves this by placing the host Ethernet adapter into promiscuous mode when bound to the adapter. Each packet routes to the host or the correct virtual machine adapter based on the MAC address. To protect the host, the VMNetSrv.sys driver maintains a packet filter at the Miniport interface to prevent any attempts to exploit the promiscuous mode. Applications with the proper credentials can place the Miniport interface into promiscuous mode. Network Monitor is an example of an application that needs to do this to operate.

Unfortunately, the 802.11 (wireless) specification does not support multiple unique MAC addresses for a single adapter, and an alternate approach is required to achieve the same functionality. Virtual Machine Network Services achieves this by intercepting every packet destined for the external network and replaces the unique MAC address of the virtual machine network adapter with the host's MAC address. When a packet returns, it contains the MAC address of the host, and therefore, Virtual Machine Network Services cannot determine whether the packet belongs to the host or a specific virtual machine. To handle this situation, the Virtual Machine Network Services driver makes a copy of the packet for each virtual machine and replaces the destination MAC address with that of the virtual machine. This action results in a copy of the packet transmitting to every virtual machine running on the host, and the assumption is that the IP stack in each virtual machine will determine whether the packet is destined for itself.

Virtual network management is implemented in the Virtual Server service, and the Virtual Machine Network Services driver provides the interfaces into the hosts networking stack. Binding the Virtual Machine Network service to a network adapter establishes this interface. Because Virtual Machine Network Services is below the TCP/IP stack in the host, the host's TCP/IP stack and any services in the layers above it can be unbound from the network adapter. This arrangement provides the ability to dedicate a network adapter to a single virtual network, and the host is not able to use that network interface for communications. The number of virtual networks is limited only by the available resources.

Virtual Hard Disks

Virtual machines require the same basic hardware that physical machines need to boot and operate: a motherboard, BIOS, memory, network adapter, keyboard, mouse, display, and hard disk. Virtual Server architecture ensures that virtual machines have the highest portability possible. One portability design challenge was how to make a virtual machine hard disk accessible and portable while also providing acceptable performance. Microsoft addressed this issue with the concept of a virtual hard disk (VHD). VHDs are single-file representations of a physical hard disk that are stored on a physical machine's hard disk. Because they are self-contained single files, they are easy to migrate from one host to another.

There are four types of virtual hard disks:

- Fixed hard disk
- Dynamically expanding hard disk
- Differencing hard disk
- Undo hard disk

A fixed virtual hard disk is one for which the disk size on the host's physical disk is pre-allocated based on the size of the drive specified at creation. When creating a 100-GB fixed virtual hard disk, Virtual Server will immediately allocate all 100 GB of data block storage and the additional overhead for the disk headers and footers. A dynamically expanding virtual hard disk is one for which the initial size of the virtual hard disk contains no data blocks and which will grow as data blocks are allocated, up to the maximum size of the specified virtual hard disk. Differencing and undo virtual hard disks are special versions of a dynamically expanding virtual hard disk and differ primarily by disk header content.

How Is a Virtual Hard Disk Structured?

Virtual hard disks share a basic structure, as shown in Figure 3-6. Each virtual hard disk file contains a hard disk footer, a block allocation table (BAT), the actual data blocks, and an optional disk header that varies for each virtual hard disk drive type. Data blocks are 2 MB in size and contain 4096 X 512 byte sectors. A copy of the hard disk footer is maintained in the beginning of the file for redundancy purposes.

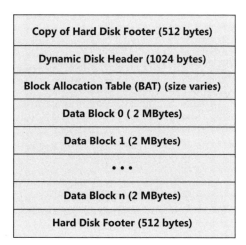

| Copy of Hard Disk Footer (512 bytes) |
| Dynamic Disk Header (1024 bytes) |
| Block Allocation Table (BAT) (size varies) |
| Data Block 0 (2 MBytes) |
| Data Block 1 (2 MBytes) |
| • • • |
| Data Block n (2 MBytes) |
| Hard Disk Footer (512 bytes) |

Figure 3-6   Virtual hard disk structure

> **Note**   The complete Virtual Hard Disk Image Format Specification can be downloaded from Microsoft's Web site at *http://www.microsoft.com/windowsserversystem/virtualserver/techinfo /vhdspec.mspx.*

Hard Disk Footer Definition

The hard disk footer contains the information that defines the size, type, geometry, and features defined in the virtual hard disk. Table 3-2 provides the specification of the field information and size for the 512-byte hard disk footer. The disk footer format is consistent across all the virtual hard disk types.

Table 3-2   Hard Disk Footer Specification

Field name	Size (bytes)	Description
Cookie	8	Used to identify the original creator of the virtual hard disk and is set to "connectix" by default.
Features	4	Used to indicate specific feature support within the virtual hard disk.
File Format Version	4	File specification version of the virtual hard disk file.
Data Offset	8	Contains the absolute byte offset, from the beginning of the file, to the next disk header structure. This field is used for dynamic disks and differencing disks, but not fixed disks. For fixed disks, this field is set to 0xFFFFFFFF.
Time Stamp	4	Stores the original creation time of the virtual hard disk file. It is stored as the number of seconds since January 1, 2000 12:00:00 AM in UTC/GMT.
Creator Application	4	Used to document which application created the virtual hard disk file. It is set to "vs" if the virtual server created the file and "vpc" if Virtual PC created the file.
Creator Version	4	Major/minor version of the application that created the virtual hard disk file.
Creator Host OS	4	Contains a value that indicates the host operating system that created the virtual hard disk file. It is set to "Wi2k" (0x5769326B in hexadecimal) for Windows.
Original Size	8	Size of the virtual hard disk in bytes specified at creation.
Current Size	8	Current size of the virtual hard disk in bytes.
Disk Geometry	4	Value that contains the cylinder, heads, and sectors per track for the hard disk. It is stored as 2 bytes for the cylinder, 1 byte for the heads, and 1 byte for sectors per track.
Disk Type	4	Defines the type of disk this virtual hard disk file contains (fixed, dynamic, or differencing).
Checksum	4	Checksum of the hard disk footer using ones' complement algorithm.

Table 3-2 Hard Disk Footer Specification

Field name	Size (bytes)	Description
Unique Id	16	128-bit universally unique identifier (UUID) used by a differencing virtual hard disk header.
Saved State	1	Flag that indicates whether the virtual machine is in a saved state.
Reserved	427	Reserved are for future fields. It contains zeros.

> **Note**   You can use a HEX file editor to open a VHD file and walk the fields in the disk footer to verify the definition.

Dynamic Disk Header Definition

The Data Offset field in the hard disk footer points to an additional disk header that specifies the information needed to define a dynamic or differencing disk. The header provides the details of the dynamic disk layout and the data it references. For a differencing disk, the header provides the location of the parent virtual hard disk in the form of a locator entry. Table 3-3 provides the definition of the dynamic disk header.

Table 3-3 Dynamic Disk Header Definition

Dynamic Disk Header Fields	Size (bytes)	Description
Cookie	8	Identifies the header, and holds the value "cxsparse" by default.
Data Offset	8	Contains the absolute byte offset to the next structure in the hard disk image. It is currently unused by existing formats and should be set to 0xFFFFFFFF.
Table Offset	8	Stores the absolute byte offset of the BAT in the file.
Header Version	4	Stores the version of the dynamic disk header. Currently, this field must be initialized to 0x00010000.
Max Table Entries	4	The maximum number of entries present in the BAT. This should be equal to the number of blocks in the disk (disk size divided by the block size).
Block Size	4	A block is a unit of expansion for dynamic and differencing hard disks stored in bytes, and it represents only the data section block size. The sectors per block must always be a power of two. The default value of 2 MB is 0x00200000.
Checksum	4	Holds a basic checksum of the dynamic header. The checksum value is a ones' complement of the sum of all the bytes in the header without the checksum field.

Table 3-3 Dynamic Disk Header Definition

Dynamic Disk Header Fields	Size (bytes)	Description
Parent Unique ID	16	Used for differencing hard disks. A differencing hard disk stores a 128-bit UUID of the parent hard disk.
Parent Time Stamp	4	This field stores the modification time stamp of the parent hard disk. This is the number of seconds since January 1, 2000 12:00:00 AM in UTC/GMT.
Reserved	4	Not used, and should be set to zeros.
Parent Unicode Name	512	Contains a Unicode string (UTF-16) of the parent hard disk filename.
Parent Locator Entry 1	24	Each Parent locator entry stores an absolute byte offset in the file where the parent locator for a differencing hard disk is stored. This field is used only for differencing disks and should be set to zero for dynamic disks.
Parent Locator Entry 2	24	
Parent Locator Entry 3	24	
Parent Locator Entry 4	24	
Parent Locator Entry 5	24	
Parent Locator Entry 6	24	
Parent Locator Entry 7	24	
Parent Locator Entry 8	24	
Reserved	256	Currently unused, and must be set to zeros.

Block Allocation Table

The block allocation table (BAT) is a table of absolute sector offsets to the data blocks in the virtual hard disk. The size of the BAT is determined during the creation of the virtual hard disk. Each data block entry is 2 MB in size, and each BAT entry is 4 bytes in size. Each data block consists of a sector bitmap and data. The sector bitmap usage depends on whether the VHD is for a dynamic or differencing disk.

For a dynamic disk, each sector bitmap value indicates which sectors contain valid data. If a sector contains valid data, the corresponding location on the sector bitmap contains a value of "1". If a sector contains no data, the sector bitmap location will contain a "0". For a differencing disk, the sector bitmap value indicates which sectors contain data in the differencing disk (1) versus data in the parent disk (0).

Virtual Floppy Disks

Virtual floppy disks are single-file representations of physical floppy disks. Virtual Server 2005 R2 SP1 reads and writes to 1.44-MB and 720-KB floppy disk images, but it will create only 1.44-MB virtual floppy disk images. A physical 1.44-MB floppy disk has two sides of 80 tracks, with 18 sectors per track and 512 bytes per sector for a total of 1,474,560 bytes per disk. A virtual floppy disk format is the same as a physical floppy, but it maps the two sides of the physical floppy into a single flat file representation.

> **Note**   A virtual machine only has a single floppy drive available in the virtual hardware, and additional drives cannot be added. The virtual floppy drive can be attached to a physical floppy drive or a virtual floppy disk (.vfd) image file.

> **Note**   Virtual Server 2005 R2 does not provide a way to access the contents of a .vfd file unless it is attached to a running virtual machine. There are third-party applications that can mount a .vfd file and allow read and write access without attaching it to a virtual machine.

A Save State File

Each virtual machine has the ability to save the state of current memory and processes to disk in a file with a .vsv extension. You can compare saving the state of a running virtual machine to hibernating a physical machine. When you attempt to power on a virtual machine, it attempts to pre-allocate the disk space required to store the saved state. This behavior ensures that in the event that the Virtual Server service is requested to shut down and there are running virtual machines, those virtual machines' state can be saved to disk. If there is not enough free space on the host drive to create the save state file, Virtual Server will not power on the virtual machine and will place an error in the Virtual Server error log. A save state file is initially allocated the size of the RAM allocated to the virtual machine. This is done to provide space to be able to write the full RAM contents to disk. Only the amount of RAM in use will actually be written to disk.

Summary

This chapter provided details of the Virtual Server 2005 R2 SP1 architecture. It also discussed how the Virtual Machine Monitor (VMM), Virtual Server service, virtual memory, virtual processors, and virtual networks work together to create a virtual machine environment, and how a virtual hard disk is structured.

Additional Resources

The following resources contain additional information and tools related to this chapter:

- Virtual Hard Disk Image Format Specification, at *http://www.microsoft.com /windowsserversystem/virtualserver/techinfo/vhdspec.mspx*

- Channel 9 video on Virtualization Architecture, at *http://channel9.msdn.com /Showpost.aspx?postid=163022*

Part II
Installing and Managing Virtual Server 2005

In this part:

Chapter 4: Installing Virtual Server 2005 R2 SP1 .73

Chapter 5: Virtual Server 2005 R2 Advanced Features 109

Chapter 6: Security in Depth 145

Chapter 7: Best Practices for Configuration and Performance Tuning . .167

Chapter 8: Virtual Machine Creation Process 195

Chapter 9: Developing Scripts with the Virtual Server COM API 227

Chapter 10: Virtual Machine Migration Process .281

Chapter 11: Troubleshooting Common Virtual Server Issues 313

Chapter 4

Installing Virtual Server 2005 R2 SP1

In this chapter:

What Are the Prerequisites?... 73

What Are the Installation Scenarios? 76

Configuring Constrained Delegation 78

Installing Microsoft Internet Information Services 6.0 80

Installing Virtual Server 2005 R2 SP1..................................... 87

Uninstalling Virtual Server 2005 R2 SP1 101

Performing a Command-Line Installation 102

Summary... 107

Additional Resources... 108

This chapter provides the information you need to install Microsoft Virtual Server 2005 Release 2 (R2) Service Pack 1 (SP1). It explains the differences in installing Virtual Server 2005 R2 SP1 on Microsoft Windows XP, Windows Vista, and Windows Server 2003. This chapter also covers a series of installation scenarios and shows how to interactively install Virtual Server for these scenarios, as well as how to use the command-line interface to perform the same tasks.

What Are the Prerequisites?

Before installing Virtual Server 2005 R2 SP1, review the requirements and prerequisites and make sure you have installed the required hardware and software to prevent failed installations. This section describes the minimum and recommended hardware and software requirements for installing Virtual Server 2005 R2 SP1. It separates the requirements into physical computer hardware requirements and operating system requirements. These requirements apply to all installation scenarios. Any scenario-specific requirements are discussed in the section that covers that scenario.

Hardware Requirements

The physical computer hardware requirements for Virtual Server 2005 R2 SP1 can vary widely from the minimum to recommended requirements. Table 4-1 lists the requirements for installing Virtual Server 2005 R2 SP1 to obtain a working system.

> **Important**   The minimum and recommended disk space and memory requirements listed in Table 4-1 are only for the disk space and memory required to install Virtual Server 2005 R2 SP1. These requirements do not include the disk space you will need for creating and storing virtual machines or the memory that you will need for running virtual machines. Planning and designing a Virtual Server host for different numbers and workloads of virtual machines will be covered in Chapter 15, "Virtualization Project: Planning and Design Phase."

Table 4-1   Virtual Server 2005 R2 SP1 Hardware Requirements

Item	Minimum requirement	Recommended requirement
CPU	1 CPU running at 550 MHz or faster	1 dual-core CPU running at 2 GHz or faster Intel VT or AMD-V enabled processor
RAM	256 MB	512 MB
Disk Space	60 MB	100 MB
Video	800 × 600 pixels or higher resolution monitor	1024 × 768 pixels or higher resolution monitor

Operating System Requirements

Virtual Server 2005 R2 SP1 comes in both 32-bit and 64-bit versions. To install the 32-bit version of Virtual Server 2005 R2 SP1, you must have a 32-bit host operating system installed on an x86-class server. To install the 64-bit version of Virtual Server 2005 R2 SP1, you must have a 64-bit operating system installed on an x64-class server. Virtual Server 2005 R2 SP1 does not support the Intel Itanium 64-bit processor line. Refer to Chapter 1, "Introducing Virtual Server 2005 R2 SP1," for a complete discussion of supported and unsupported hosts.

Supported 32-Bit Host Operating Systems

The following list is a summary of the supported host operating systems that can be used with the 32-bit version of Virtual Server 2005 R2 SP1:

- Microsoft Windows Server 2003 R2, Standard, Enterprise, and Datacenter Editions
- Microsoft Windows Server 2003, Standard, Enterprise, and Datacenter Editions with Service Pack 1 (SP1)
- Microsoft Windows Small Business Server 2003 with SP1 and R2 Editions
- Microsoft Windows XP Professional with Service Pack 2 (SP2)
- Windows Vista Enterprise, Business, and Ultimate Editions

Supported 64-Bit Host Operating Systems

The following list shows all the supported host operating systems that can be used with the 64-bit version of Virtual Server 2005 R2 SP1:

- Microsoft Windows Server 2003 R2, Standard, Enterprise, and Datacenter x64 Editions
- Microsoft Windows Server 2003, Standard, Enterprise, and Datacenter x64 Editions
- Microsoft Windows XP Professional, x64 Edition
- Windows Vista Enterprise, Business, and Ultimate, x64 Edition

Important   Microsoft Windows XP and Windows Vista are supported only for nonproduction use as the host operating system.

Active Directory Requirements

Virtual Server 2005 R2 SP1 does not require Active Directory to operate. You can install Virtual Server 2005 R2 SP1 on a server in a workgroup and you will be able to create, modify, run, manage, and operate virtual machines on that host. When the Virtual Server service starts, it verifies whether the host is a member of an Active Directory domain, and if so it attempts to register service principal name (SPN) records with the Active Directory domain it is a member of.

> ### Direct from the Source: Troubleshooting SPNs
>
> To register SPNs, the user or group requires the Validated Write To Service Principal Name permission. By default, a user or computer account has this permission on its own Active Directory object. In addition, the Domain Administrators group has this permission on all objects. If you find that you are receiving errors in the Virtual Server event viewer that indicate failure to register SPNs or you just want to verify registered SPNs, you can use Setspn.exe to list or manually register SPNs for a machine running the Virtual Server service. Refer to Chapter 11, "Troubleshooting a Virtual Server Installation," for details on using Setspn to troubleshoot and register SPNs in Active Directory.
>
> *Allen Stewart*
> *Program Manager, Windows Server Division*

Installing Virtual Server 2005 R2 SP1 on servers that are members of Active Directory domains also allows you to reduce the management and operations of the Virtual Server installation. By joining an Active Directory domain, the security configuration and access control lists (ACLs) can use domain-based groups and users. This functionality allows you to establish a set of groups or specific user accounts that can be centrally managed but used across a pool of Virtual Server hosts in a server farm.

By combining standardized security groups on the Virtual Server hosts with domain global groups, you can establish a standard security configuration across the servers in the farm. If you try to maintain standardized security on each Virtual Server host that is not joined to an Active Directory domain, you will be required to create duplicate local user accounts, track and maintain separate passwords across the hosts, or establish poor practices such as synchronizing the passwords across the hosts.

> **Note** Refer to Chapter 6, "Security in Depth," for a more in-depth discussion on the security features of Virtual Server 2005 R2 SP1 and how to best use them.

To take advantage of some features of Virtual Server 2005 R2 SP1, the host is required to be a member of an Active Directory domain. The Virtual Server service can then publish its binding information in Active Directory as a service connection point (SCP) object. This arrangement allows customers and independent software vendors (ISVs) to write scripts or applications to easily locate all instances of the Virtual Server service within an Active Directory forest.

What Are the Installation Scenarios?

During Virtual Server 2005 R2 SP1 installation, you select components that define how the Virtual Server operates and how it will be managed, choose optional tools to assist in managing the system, and determine how the security of the Virtual Server service is configured. Table 4-2 lists the available components.

Table 4-2   Virtual Server 2005 R2 SP1 Components

Component	Description
Virtual Server service	The Virtual Server service is a required component on any server where you want to define, create, and operate virtual machines.
Virtual Server Administration Website	The Virtual Server administrative interface is browser-based and therefore requires a Web server to host the Administration Website. The Administration Website can reside on the local server or on a separate server. The choice of where the Administration Website resides affects the security configuration of the Virtual Server service.
Virtual Server documentation and developer resources	The Virtual Server documentation and Component Object Model (COM) application programming interface (API) is required on any machine where you want to create, test, and run scripts or applications that will manage one or more Virtual Server hosts. This tool is typically installed with the Virtual Server service and on any development workstations where applications or scripts are being developed for Virtual Server.

Table 4-2   Virtual Server 2005 R2 SP1 Components

Component	Description
VHD Mount tool	The VHD Mount tool is required on any machine where you want to perform offline access to a virtual hard drive. This tool is typically installed with the Virtual Server service and consists of a client tool and a storage bus driver.
Virtual Machine Remote Control (VMRC) Windows client	The VMRC Windows client is required on any machine where you want to remotely manage virtual machines. This tool is typically installed with the Virtual Server service and independently on administrative workstations.

Virtual Server 2005 R2 SP1 comes in a self-extracting executable that contains a Microsoft Installer (MSI) package. As with most MSI packages, you have the option of performing a complete install or performing a custom install. Performing a complete install installs all available components on the local server. Selecting a custom install allows you to select components individually for local installation.

Note   Virtual Machine Network Services (VMNS) and the Volume Shadow Copy Service (VSS) writer are also installed when you install the Virtual Server service. Virtual Machine Network Services provides the virtual network interface and handles all packet receipt and delivery with the virtual machines. The VSS writer provides a VSS-compliant backup interface for backup applications. You can see all installed VSS writers by using the *vssadmin list writers* command.

Table 4-3 provides a breakdown of the typical installation scenarios and a description of what is installed.

Table 4-3   Installation Scenarios

Scenario	Description
Upgrade	Upgrade all components from Virtual Server 2005 R2 to Virtual Server 2005 R2 SP1.
Single Server Installation	Install all components on the same server. Resources can be local or remote.
Central Administration Website Installation	Install all components except for the Administration Web Service on the Virtual Server host machine. The Administration Website is installed on a central server that is providing administrative services for one or more Virtual Server hosts. Resources can be local or remote to the Virtual Server host machines.
Documentation and Developer Resources Only	Install only the documentation and developer resources on the local machine to allow development of applications that make use of the Virtual Server COM API.
VMRC Only	Install only the VMRC client utility on the local machine to allow remote access to Virtual Server host machines.
VHD Mount Only	Install only the VHD Mount utility on the local machine to allow offline read/write modification of a .vhd file.

Configuring Constrained Delegation

When you select a complete install, you are installing all the components of Virtual Server: the Virtual Server service, documentation and development tools, VHD Mount utility, and Virtual Server Administration Website. If you will be accessing all of your resources—such as virtual hard disks, virtual floppy disks, and ISO images—from the local machine, there are no additional setup steps.

If you decide to install the Administration Website on a separate computer or need to access resources that are stored on a separate computer from the Virtual Server service, you have a security delegation requirement and additional configuration, called constrained delegation, is required in most cases.

Constrained delegation is the ability to specify that a computer or service account can perform Kerberos delegation to a limited set of services. This ability allows the user credentials to be passed from the Administration Website to the Virtual Server service or the server hosting the resources files, such as virtual hard disk (.vhd) files and ISO image (.iso) files, so that the user can access the files. In this scenario, you are required to use Integrated Windows authentication. Delegation does not work with Basic authentication.

> **Important**   Constrained delegation is supported only in Windows Server 2003 Active Directory domains in Windows Server 2003 domain functional level. This means that if your domain functional level is Windows 2000 mixed mode or Windows 2000 native, you must raise the domain functional level to Windows Server 2003 native level to configure constrained delegation. In order to raise the domain functional level to Windows Server 2003, you can only have Windows Server 2003 domain controllers; therefore, you must replace, upgrade, or remove any Windows NT 4.0 or Windows 2000 domain controllers that currently exist in the domain.
>
> Constrained delegation is not supported when using Windows XP Professional or Windows Vista as the host operating system. If you install Virtual Server on a Windows XP or Windows Vista system, you will not be able to access resources on remote file servers.

Constrained delegation is configured from the Active Directory Users and Computers Microsoft Management Console (MMC) snap-in. When you configure constrained delegation, you need to know the machine that you want to delegate from and the server and services that you want to delegate to.

> **Important**   In a constrained delegation configuration, when a Kerberos token is passed from a source to a target configured for delegation, it maintains the original user requesting the action intact for complete auditing of user accounts.

In the scenario where you have the Administration Website on a computer separate from the Virtual Server service and the resources are local to the Virtual Server host, you need to delegate from the Web server to the Virtual Server and select the Virtual Server service (VSSRVC) and Common Internet File System (CIFS) services for delegation. Figure 4-1 shows this scenario that uses delegation to one or more Virtual Server hosts.

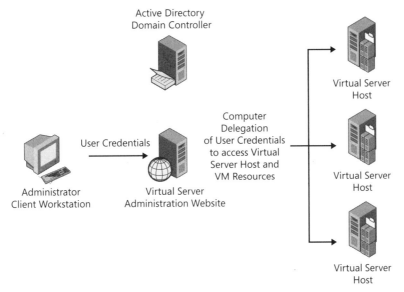

Figure 4-1   Delegation from an Administration Web server to a Virtual Server with local resources

If the virtual machine resource files are stored on a remote file server, you also need to delegate from the Virtual Server to the file server and select the CIFS service for delegation. Figure 4-2 shows this scenario that uses delegation to one or more file servers.

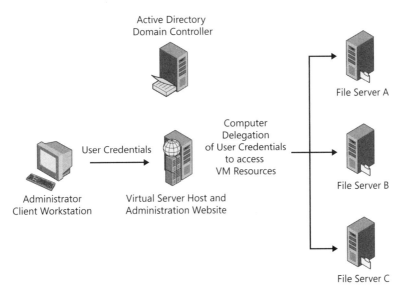

Figure 4-2   Delegation from Virtual Server to file server with remote resources

If the Virtual Server Website is installed centrally and the VM resource files are stored on remote file servers, you need to configure the following two separate delegations, as shown in Figure 4-3:

1. Delegate from the Administration Website to the Virtual Server hosts.

2. Configure a separate delegation from the Virtual Server host to the file servers, and select the CIFS service for delegation.

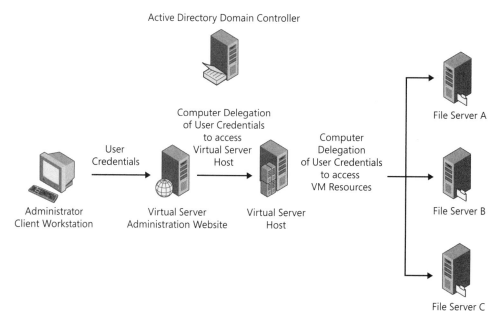

Active Directory Domain Controller

Figure 4-3   Delegation from Web server to Virtual Server and Virtual Server to file server

A constrained delegation configuration can get complicated. Keep detailed documentation on the computer delegations that you have set up and the services that were delegated. You will need this information to troubleshoot access issues and to manage the access in the event that a server is being retired or virtualized.

More Info   For detailed steps for configuring constrained delegation, refer to Chapter 17, "Managing a Virtual Server Infrastructure."

Installing Microsoft Internet Information Services 6.0

Installing Internet Information Services (IIS) 6.0 requires slightly different procedures depending on the operating system. This section provides the procedures for installing IIS 6.0 on Windows XP, Windows Vista, and Windows Server 2003. This section is a reference for the three installation scenarios, and you should select the correct operating system procedure based on the operating system on which you are installing Virtual Server.

Windows XP

Installing IIS 6.0 on Windows XP is a simple process because this version of IIS has no configuration options to select from during install. IIS 6.0 on Windows XP supports only a single Web site and therefore will listen only on a single port. As with most Web servers, the default port is port 80.

 Important   Set the port for the default Web site before you install Virtual Server. Virtual Server will not allow you to change the port during installation. If you want to change the port of the Administration Website to something other than the default port 80 and you did not do so before you installed Virtual Server, you will have to uninstall Virtual Server, change the default port of the Administration Website using the IIS administrative console, and then reinstall Virtual Server.

 Best Practices   Standardize the port you use for Virtual Server Administration Websites. The default port for Windows Server 2003 installations is 1024. You should standardize on this port or select another standard and then use this port across all installations of IIS (Windows XP, Windows Vista, and Windows Server 2003).

To install IIS on Windows XP, follow these steps:

1. From the Start menu, select Control Panel.

2. Click Add Or Remove Programs and then click Add/Remove Windows Components to open the Windows Components Wizard, as shown in Figure 4-4.

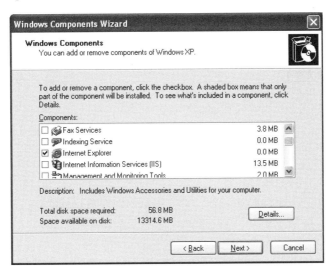

Figure 4-4   Windows Components Wizard

3.   Select the Internet Information Services (IIS) check box to enable IIS for installation.

4.   Click Next and the installation begins.

5.   You might be prompted for the Windows XP or Windows XP service pack CD-ROM. Insert the CD-ROM in the CD-ROM drive and click OK.

6.   When IIS installation is complete, click Finish.

Windows Vista

IIS installation on Windows Vista is an easy process, but selecting all the required components to support Virtual Server 2005 R2 SP1 Administration Website operation is not. Although you could take the simple approach and install all features under IIS, that would open your machine with new attack surfaces and is not a good security practice. The Virtual Server development team received feedback during beta testing that installing Virtual Server on Windows Vista was too error prone. To address this issue, the development team added the ability for the Virtual Server installation process to automatically configure the required IIS options. Although this configuration is done automatically, the steps to verify the IIS configuration are provided below.

> **Note**   If User Access Control is enabled, you will have to approve the launch of the Control Panel application because it requires administrative rights.

To verify that only the required features of IIS to support Virtual Server are installed on a Windows Vista machine, complete the following steps:

1.   Log on to the Windows Vista machine with an account that has administrative rights.

2.   Click the Vista Start button.

3.   Select Control Panel to open the Control Panel page shown in Figure 4-5.

Figure 4-5   Control Panel

4. Click Programs to open the Programs page shown in Figure 4-6.

Figure 4-6   Selecting Programs from Control Panel

5. Under the Programs And Features option, click Turn Windows Features On Or Off to open the Windows Features dialog box shown in Figure 4-7.

Figure 4-7   Windows Features dialog box

6. Expand the Internet Information Services node.

7. Expand the Web Management Tools node.

8. Verify that IIS Management Console is enabled.

9. Expand the IIS 6 Management Compatibility node.

10. Verify that IIS Metabase And IIS 6 Configuration Compatibility options are enabled.

11. Expand the World Wide Web Services node.

12. Expand the Application Development Features node.

13. Verify that CGI is enabled.

14. Expand the Common HTTP Features node.

15. Verify that the following options are enabled:

    ❑ Default Document

    ❑ Directory Browsing

    ❑ HTTP Errors

    ❑ Static Content

16. Expand the Health and Diagnostics node.

17. Verify that the following options are enabled:

    ❑ HTTP Logging

    ❑ Resource Monitor

18. Expand the Performance Features node.

19. Verify that the Static Content Compression algorithm is enabled.

20. Expand the Security node.

21. Verify that the Enable Windows Authentication feature is enabled.

22. Press OK to accept the IIS configuration settings.

> **On the Companion Media**   You will find a batch file on the companion media to auto-
> mate the installation of Internet Information Services (IIS) on Windows Vista using the pkgmgr
> tool. The batch file is called Installiis.bat and is in the \Chapter Materials\Scripts directory.

Windows Server 2003

Installing IIS on Windows Server 2003 can be accomplished in two ways. The first way is similar to the Windows XP installation process and involves the use of the Add/Remove Windows Components option. Windows Server 2003 introduced a new interface for tasks like
this through the Configure Your Server Wizard. This is a wizard approach for selecting server
roles, and it greatly reduces the number of steps that it takes to install a role for a computer.
Since the default options are the correct security options for Windows Server 2003, you can
use the Configure Your Server Wizard approach.

To install IIS 6.0 on Windows Server 2003, complete the following steps:

1. From the Start menu, select Programs, Administrative Tools, and click Configure Your
   Server Wizard.

2. When the wizard starts, click Next.

3. On the Preliminary Steps page, click Next to open the Server Role page, which is shown
   in Figure 4-8. This page enumerates all network devices and connections that will be
   used during server configuration.

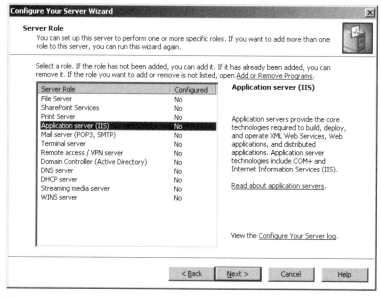

Figure 4-8   Server Role page of the Configure Your Server Wizard

4. Select Application Server and click Next.

    You will be prompted with an option to enable FrontPage Server Extensions and ASP.NET; however, you do not need either for the Virtual Server Administration Website to operate. Click Next.

5. On the Summary Of Selections page, shown in Figure 4-9, review the list of options that will be installed when you proceed, and click Next.

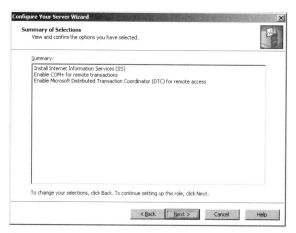

Figure 4-9   Summary Of Selections page of the Configure Your Server Wizard

The wizard scripts the installation based on the selections you made, and it uses that script to install the system in unattended mode. You will be able to see all the steps as the wizard proceeds. When the wizard completes processing, it displays a final page that declares that the machine is now an Application Server.

Installing Virtual Server 2005 R2 SP1

Depending on how Virtual Server will be used, the installation scenario could be an upgrade in place of Virtual Server 2005 R2 or could range from a simple single-server installation to a large multiserver farm of Virtual Server hosts maintained by a central Administration Website. Each installation scenario might require different components of Virtual Server to be installed on different servers, so the installation process supports custom installation and allows you to select any or all components. This section documents the procedures for the most common installation scenarios and important issues to watch out for during installation.

Note   Although Virtual Server 2005 R2 SP1 can be installed on 32-bit or 64-bit versions of the supported operating systems, the procedures are the same for either version.

On the Companion Media   On the companion media, you will find a directory called \Bonus Materials\Applications\Virtual Server 2005 R2 SP1. Inside that directory, you will find two subdirectories: \x86 and \x64. Each directory contains a single file, Setup.exe, for the associated 32-bit or 64-bit version of Virtual Server 2005 R2 SP1. This is the installation file for Virtual Server 2005 R2 SP1. You can install directly off the companion media, or you can copy the correct file version to the local hard disk and install from there.

Important   The Virtual Server 2005 R2 SP1 installation process installs the Virtual Machine Network Services driver. When this driver is installed, it causes the host machine to lose access to the network. Make sure that the installation files are local on the server; otherwise, the installation may fail.

If you are using Remote Desktop to install Virtual Server 2005 R2 SP1 across the network, you will lose your connection while the driver is being installed, but typically it reestablishes the connection quickly. Make sure you use the /console command-line option with Remote Desktop when you establish the connection to the remote server.

Upgrading Virtual Server 2005 R2

Although Virtual Server 2005 R2 SP1 is labeled as a service pack, it is actually a full installation package that can be used to perform a fresh install or upgrade an existing installation of Virtual Server 2005 R2. The uninstall of Virtual Server 2005 R2 and the installation of Virtual Server 2005 R2 SP1 is fully automated in the upgrade process, so you do not have to uninstall Virtual Server 2005 R2 prior to installing Virtual Server 2005 R2 SP1.

Warning   Virtual Server 2005 R2 SP1 required changes to the information stored in the save state (.vsv) file. Therefore, Virtual Server 2005 R2 saved states are not compatible with Virtual Server 2005 R2 SP1 save states. You must resume any virtual machines currently in save state and shut down the guest operating system cleanly before attempting the upgrade to Virtual Server 2005 R2 SP1. If not, you will have to discard the saved state before the virtual machine will power on.

To perform an upgrade of Virtual Server 2005 R2 to Virtual Server 2005 R2 Service Pack 1, complete the following steps:

1. Collect the following information before you start the upgrade:

   ❑ The http port that the Administration Website is currently using

   ❑ The Service account that the Virtual Server service is running under: Local System or Network Service

2. Open the Virtual Server Administration Website, and shut down all running virtual machines. Any virtual machine that is currently in saved state must be resumed from saved state and shut down.

3. Click the Start button, select Administrative Tools, and click Services.

4. Find the Virtual Server and the Virtual Machine Helper services, right-click each one and select Stop. This will stop both services and allow Virtual Server 2005 R2 SP1 to install.

5. On the companion media, obtain the correct version (32- or 64-bit) of Virtual Server 2005 R2 SP1 and launch Setup.exe to start the installation.

6. The dialog box shown in Figure 4-10 prompts you to verify that you want to upgrade the installed version of Virtual Server. Click Upgrade.

Figure 4-10   Verifying the upgrade

7. Click the Install Virtual Server 2005 R2 SP1 button.

8. Read the license terms, select I Accept The Terms Of This License Agreement if you agree, and click Next.

9. In the Customer Information dialog box, enter your User Name and Organization and click Next. The Product ID should be dimmed and already provided.

10. In the Setup Type dialog box, select the default option of a Complete Install and click Next.

11. Select the port that you want to use for the Virtual Server Administration Website, or use the default of 1024. Select the default option of Configure The Administration Website To Always Run As The Authenticated User, and click Next.

12. Accept the default to Enable Virtual Server extensions in Windows Firewall. This auto-matically enables firewall exceptions for the Virtual Server Web site and the VMRC pro-tocol in the Windows Firewall. Click Next.

13. You have now selected all the configuration options for Virtual Server 2005 R2 SP1. Click Install to complete the upgrade.

You should see the upgrade proceed, and then you will see an Internet Explorer window that provides a summary of the installation and the links to the new Virtual Server Administration Website.

Single-Server Configuration

Installing Virtual Server on a single server is a typical scenario for environments where there is no security concern for IIS to be installed locally on the server or if there is a desire for each server to have local administrative capabilities. These procedures assume that no previous version of Virtual Server is installed on the server.

To install all Virtual Server components on a single server, complete the following steps:

1. Ensure that the server meets all the requirements for installation.

2. Install IIS using the procedures detailed in the "Installing Microsoft Internet Information Services 6.0" section of this chapter for the operating system version you are installing.

3. On the companion media, obtain the correct version (32- or 64-bit) of Virtual Server 2005 R2 SP1 and launch Setup.exe to start the installation.

4. Click the Install Microsoft Virtual Server 2005 R2 SP1 button as shown in Figure 4-11.

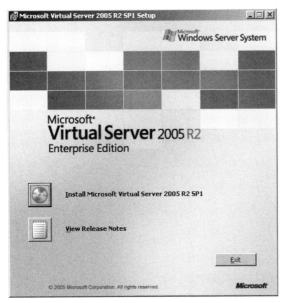

Figure 4-11 Starting the installation

5. Read the license terms, select I Accept The Terms Of This License Agreement if you agree, and click Next.

6. In the Customer Information dialog box, enter your User Name and Organization and click Next. The Product ID should be dimmed and already provided.

7. In the Setup Type dialog box, select the default option of a Complete Install. Click Next.

8. Select the port that you want to use for the Virtual Server Administration Website, or use the default of 1024, as shown in Figure 4-12. Select the default option of Configure The Administration Website To Always Run As The Authenticated User, and click Next.

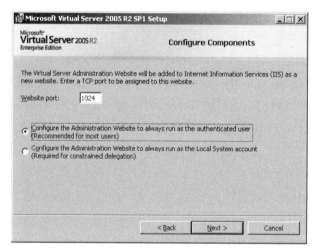

Figure 4-12   Configuring components

9. Verify that the Enable Virtual Server Extensions In Windows Firewall check box is selected as shown in Figure 4-13, and click Next. This automatically enables firewall exceptions for the Virtual Server Web site and the VMRC protocol in the Windows Firewall.

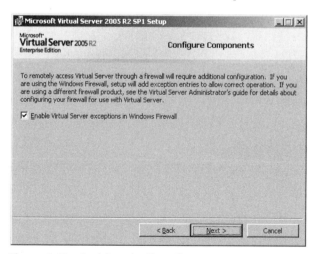

Figure 4-13   Enabling the firewall

10. Click Install to complete the installation.

You should see the installation proceed, and then you will see an Internet Explorer window that provides a summary of the installation and the links to the new Virtual Server Administration Website.

Local Administration Website and Remote Resources

In this scenario, you are installing the Virtual Server host and Website exactly like you would in the Single Server installation scenario. In addition, you must perform the constrained delegation configuration to allow the Virtual Server host to delegate the CIFS service to the file servers where the remote virtual machine resources are stored. The "Configuring Constrained Delegation" section in this chapter covers this scenario. Refer to Figure 4-2 for a diagram that depicts the configuration. The following instructions provide the detailed steps for performing that delegation. Perform these steps after you have installed Virtual Server for a single-server installation.

> **Note** You must perform this step from each Virtual Server host to each file server that will store remote virtual machine files' resources. Therefore, if you have one host and three file servers, you will have to configure the delegation from the Virtual Server host to each file server for the CIFS service.

To allow the Virtual Server service to delegate a user's credentials to a remote file server for the CIFS service, complete the following steps:

1. On the domain controller, open Active Directory Users And Computers.
2. In the console tree, under Domain Name, click Computers, and then click the computer's organizational unit or the organizational unit in which the Virtual Server host is contained.
3. Right-click the Virtual Server host running the Virtual Server service, and then click Properties to open the Virtual Server host's Properties dialog box.
4. On the Delegation tab, select Trust This Computer For Delegation To Specified Services Only.
5. Select Use Any Authentication Protocol, as shown in Figure 4-14.

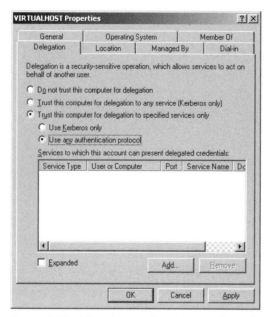

Figure 4-14   Virtual Server host's Properties Delegation tab

6.   Click Add to display the Add Services dialog box, and then click the Users And Computers button.

7.   Type the name of the computer on which the virtual machine resources are stored, and then click OK.

8.   From the list of available services, select CIFS as shown in Figure 4-15, and then click OK. This selects the CIFS service as an approved service to accept delegated user credentials.

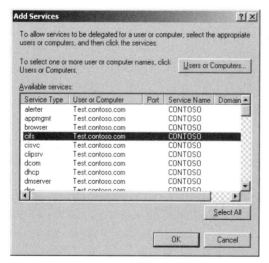

Figure 4-15   Selecting a service for delegation

9. If there is more than one file server that you need to delegate to, repeat steps 6 through 8 for each file server.

10. Click OK, as shown in Figure 4-16, to approve the Virtual Server host's ability to delegate user credentials to the CIFS service on the specified file servers.

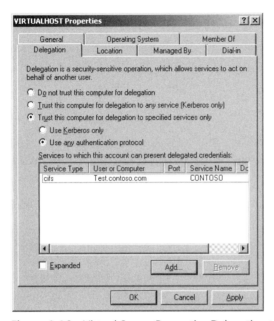

Figure 4-16   Virtual Server Properties Delegation tab

Server Farm with Central Administration Website and Remote Resources

In this scenario, you are installing the Administration Website on a central server to manage all the hosts in a server farm. You'll do this by installing each Virtual Server host with all services but the Administration Website and storing all virtual machine file resources remotely on one or more file servers. This is a typical data center installation scenario that provides a centralized administration point and increases the security of the Virtual Server host machines by reducing the attack surface, because IIS is not required on the host.

In this installation scenario, you must perform two constrained delegation configurations. The first is to allow the central Administration Website to delegate user credentials to the Virtual Server service (VSSRVC) for each host in the server farm. The second is to allow the Virtual Server host to delegate user credentials to the CIFS service running on the file servers on which the remote VM resources are stored. The "Configuring Constrained Delegation" section in this chapter covers this scenario. Refer to Figure 4-3 for a diagram that depicts the configuration. The following instructions provide the detailed steps for performing that delegation.

Installing the Administration Website on a Central Server

To install the Administration Website on a central server, complete the following steps:

1. Ensure that the server meets all the requirements for installation.

2. Install IIS using the procedures detailed in the "Installing Microsoft Internet Information Services 6.0" section of this chapter for the operating system version you are installing.

3. On the companion media, obtain the correct version (32- or 64-bit) of Virtual Server 2005 R2 SP1 and launch Setup.exe to start the installation.

4. Click the Install Microsoft Virtual Server 2005 R2 SP1 button.

5. Read the license terms, select I Accept The Terms Of This License Agreement, and click Next.

6. In the Customer Information dialog box, enter your User Name and Organization and click Next. The Product ID should be dimmed and already provided.

7. In the Setup Type dialog box, shown in Figure 4-17, select the Custom option and click Next.

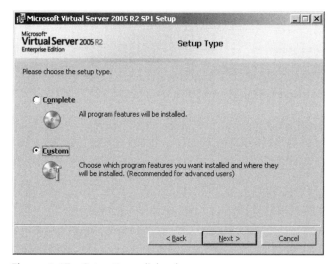

Figure 4-17   Setup Type dialog box

8. In the Custom Setup dialog box, shown in Figure 4-18, click Virtual Server Service, select This Feature Will Not Be Available, and then click Next. You do not want to install the Virtual Server Service.

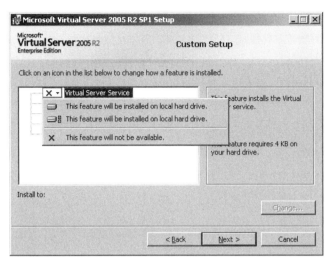

Figure 4-18   Disabling the Virtual Server service in the Custom Setup dialog box

9. In the Configure Components dialog box, shown in Figure 4-19, select the port that you want to use for the Virtual Server Administration Website or use the default of 1024. Select the Configure The Administration Website To Always Run As The Local System Account option, and click Next.

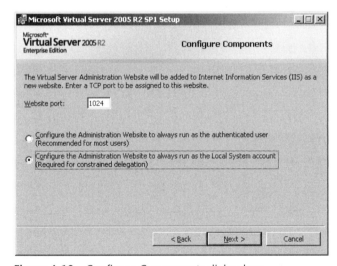

Figure 4-19   Configure Components dialog box

10. Accept the default to Enable Virtual Server Extensions In Windows Firewall, and click Next. This automatically enables firewall exceptions for the Virtual Server Web site and the VMRC protocol in the Windows Firewall.

11. Click Install to complete the installation.

You should see the installation proceed, and then you will see an Internet Explorer window display that provides a summary of the installation and the links to the new Virtual Server Administration Website.

Installing the Virtual Server Host Server with No Local Administration Website

To install the host server without a local Administration Website, complete the following steps:

1. Ensure that the server meets all the requirements for installation.

> **Important**   Do not install IIS on this machine; you will not be installing the Virtual Server Administration Website and you do not require IIS.

2. On the companion media, obtain the correct version (32- or 64-bit) of Virtual Server 2005 R2 SP1 and launch Setup.exe to start the installation.

3. Click the Install Microsoft Virtual Server 2005 R2 SP1 button.

4. Read the license terms, select I Accept The Terms Of This License Agreement if you agree, and click Next.

5. In the Customer Information dialog box, enter your User Name and Organization and click Next. The Product ID should be dimmed and already provided.

6. In the Setup Type dialog box, select the Custom Install option and click Next.

7. In the Custom Setup dialog box, shown in Figure 4-20, click Virtual Server Web Application, select This Feature Will Not Be Available, and then click Next.

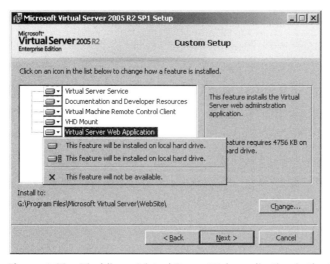

Figure 4-20   Disabling a Virtual Server Web application in the Custom Setup dialog box

> **Note**   Because you are not installing the Virtual Server Web Application on this server, you are not prompted to configure the port for the Web server.

8. Accept the default to Enable Virtual Server Extensions In Windows Firewall, and click Next. This automatically enables firewall exceptions for the VMRC protocol in the Windows Firewall.

9. Click Install to complete the installation.

You should see the installation proceed, and then you will see an Internet Explorer window that provides a summary of the installation.

Documentation and Developer Resources Only

In scenarios where you need to perform development for Virtual Server, you might need to install only the development tools and documentation on a development workstation and none of the other services, such as the Virtual Server service or the Administration Website. You must have Virtual Studio or one of the Express development products installed on the development workstation before you install the development tools. Use the following instructions to install only the development tools and documentation.

To install the Virtual Server documentation and developer resources, complete the following steps:

1. On the companion media, obtain the correct version (32- or 64-bit) of Virtual Server 2005 R2 SP1 and launch Setup.exe to start the installation.

2. Click the Install Microsoft Virtual Server 2005 R2 SP1 button.

3. Read the license terms, select I Accept The Terms Of This License Agreement if you agree, and click Next.

4. In the Customer Information dialog box, enter your User Name and Organization, and click Next. The Product ID should be dimmed and already provided.

5. In the Setup Type dialog box, select the Custom Install option and click Next.

6. In the Custom Setup dialog box, shown in Figure 4-21, select each of the listed options except the Documentation And Developer Resources option, and select This Feature Will Not Be Available from the drop-down menu. Once you have disabled all components except Documentation And Developer Resources, click Next.

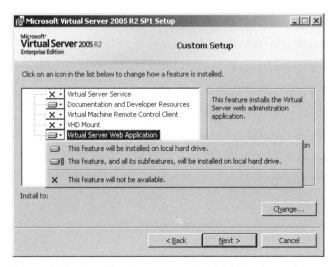

Figure 4-21   Installing Documentation And Developer Resources Only

7. Click Install to complete the installation.

You should see the installation proceed, and then you will see an Internet Explorer window that provides a summary of the installation.

Virtual Machine Remote Control Client Tool Only

In scenarios where you need to perform remote management of virtual machines, you might need to install the Virtual Machine Remote Control (VMRC) Client tool on an administrative workstation and none of the other services, such as the Virtual Server service or the Administration Website.

To install the Virtual Server VMRC tool only, complete the following steps:

1. On the companion media, obtain the correct version (32- or 64-bit) of Virtual Server 2005 R2 SP1 and launch Setup.exe to start the installation.

2. Click the Install Microsoft Virtual Server 2005 R2 SP1 button.

3. Read the license terms, select I Accept The Terms Of This License Agreement if you agree, and click Next.

4. In the Customer Information dialog box, enter your User Name and Organization and click Next. The Product ID should be dimmed and already provided.

5. In the Setup Type dialog box, select the Custom Install option and click Next.

6. In the Custom Setup dialog box, shown in Figure 4-22, select each of the listed options except the Virtual Machine Remote Control Client, and select This Feature Will Not Be Available from the drop-down menu. After you have disabled all components except the VMRC Client, click Next.

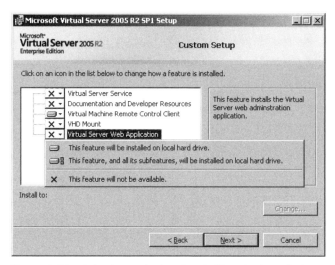

Figure 4-22 Selecting only the VMRC Client for installation

7. Click Install to complete the installation.

You should see the installation proceed, and then you will see an Internet Explorer window that provides a summary of the installation.

At this point, the VMRC client is installed into the C:\Program Files\Microsoft Virtual Server\VMRC Client\ directory. A Start menu program group is also created, and a shortcut to the VMRC client will be created. You should be able to launch the VMRC client utility from the shortcut in the menu.

> **Note** The VMRC Client is a Windows application instead of a Web browser interface. The Windows VMRC Client actually uses the same ActiveX control as the Web browser version; it just has more features because it is a Windows application. For example, the VMRC client will allow you to expand the display to full screen and allow you to switch to other running virtual machines using the host key plus the left or right arrow keys.

VHD Mount Tool Only

In scenarios where you need to perform maintenance of virtual hard drive (.vhd) files or maybe offline modification of sysprep files in a virtual hard drive used as a template for provisioning new virtual machines, you might need to install the VHD Mount tool on an administrative workstation and none of the other services, such as the Virtual Server service or the Administration Website.

To install the Virtual Server VHD Mount tool, complete the following steps:

1. On the companion media, obtain the correct version (32- or 64-bit) of Virtual Server 2005 R2 SP1 and launch Setup.exe to start the installation.

2. Click the Install Microsoft Virtual Server 2005 R2 SP1 button.

3. Read the license terms, select I Accept The Terms Of This License Agreement if you agree, and click Next.

4. In the Customer Information dialog box, enter your User Name and Organization, and click Next. The Product ID should be dimmed and already provided.

5. In the Setup Type dialog box, select the Custom Install option and click Next.

6. In the Custom Setup dialog box, shown in Figure 4-23, select each of the listed options except VHD Mount, and select This Feature Will Not Be Available from the drop-down menu. After you have disabled all components except the VHD Mount tool, click Next.

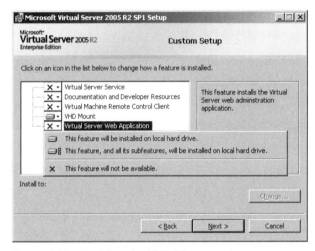

Figure 4-23   Enabling the VHD Mount tool

7. Click Install to complete the installation.

You should see the installation proceed, and then you will see an Internet Explorer window that provides a summary of the installation.

At this point, VHD Mount is installed into the C:\Program Files\Microsoft Virtual Server \VHDMount directory. A Start menu program group is not installed when you install VHD Mount because it is a command-line tool. To use VHD Mount, you must open a command prompt window and run the vhdmount.exe command with the correct command-line options to mount or unmount a .vhd file.

More Info   For more information on VHDMount and the command-line options, refer to Chapter 5, "Advanced Features."

Uninstalling Virtual Server 2005 R2 SP1

Uninstalling Virtual Server 2005 R2 SP1 is a straightforward process. When you launch the uninstall process, the Virtual Server 2005 SP1 MSI file executes the predefined uninstall routine. This routine performs the following actions:

- Uninstalls the Virtual Server service
- Uninstalls the Virtual Machine Helper service
- Removes the Virtual Machine Monitor (VMM)
- Removes the Virtual Machine Network Services from all network interface cards that it is bound to
- Removes the Start menu Programs menu group and all shortcuts

If the Virtual Server Administration Website is installed on the local machine, the uninstall process also removes the IIS virtual directory, deletes the Administration Website files, removes any application pool configuration changes, and removes any files related to the Administration Website from the machine. The uninstall process does not remove IIS from the machine—that requires a separate uninstall step. Refer to Help and Support for your operating system version for instructions on how to uninstall IIS.

Any resource files that are stored locally on the machine or on a remote server will not be touched during the uninstall process. This means that you can uninstall Virtual Server 2005 R2 SP1 with no concern for loss of your virtual machines, virtual hard disks, or their configuration files. In addition, the Virtual Server configuration information file Options.xml is not removed from the system, so you can uninstall and reinstall Virtual Server without fear of losing your configuration settings.

The following procedures describe uninstalling Virtual Server 2005 R2 SP1. Instead of presenting one procedure for Windows XP and another procedure for Windows Server 2003 and Windows Vista, the various options are included in the appropriate steps. The Windows XP and Windows Server 2003 selections are presented first, followed by the Windows Vista selections.

To uninstall Virtual Server 2005 R2 SP1, complete the following steps:

1. Click the Start button, select Administrative Tools, and click Services.
2. Find the Virtual Server and the Virtual Machine Helper, right-click each one, and select Stop. This will stop both services and allow Virtual Server 2005 R2 SP1 to install. You cannot uninstall Virtual Server while the services are running.
3. Click the Start button, select Control Panel, click Add/Remove Programs or Uninstall A Program, depending on your operating system.

4. Find the entry for Virtual Server 2005 R2 SP1 in the list, and click either Remove or Uninstall, depending on your operating system. Figure 4-24 shows the dialog box for Windows XP and Windows Server 2003.

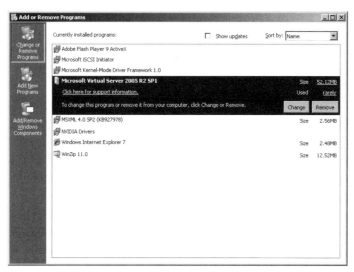

Figure 4-24   Uninstalling a program in Windows Server 2003 or Windows XP

5. Click Yes to confirm that you want to uninstall the Virtual Server 2005 R2 SP1 application and then click OK.

The uninstall process will launch, uninstall all components, and then finish.

Performing a Command-Line Installation

Microsoft Virtual Server 2005 R2 SP1 has a command-line installation interface that you can use to install or uninstall any combination of the installable Virtual Server components. The command-line interface is provided as part of the MSI file that is extracted from the Setup.exe provided by Microsoft. The command-line syntax contains a list of options that allow you to control the level of interface that is presented, from a full user interface to a quiet install with no visible interface. In addition, the command-line options allow you to control parameters such as the port used for the Administration Website and the state of the Virtual Server services.

This section presents the command-line options and explains how to use them to achieve the installation scenarios that were described in this chapter: single-server installation, central Administration Website, Virtual Server service, VMRC Client installation, Documentation and Developer Resources, and VHD Mount.

Command-Line Options

Performing a command-line installation of Virtual Server requires you to execute the command line from the local machine. To execute the command line with all available options, you must extract the Virtual Server 2005 Install.msi file from the Setup.exe file. Extracting the files requires the following syntax:

```
Setup.exe /c /t [drive letter:\path]
```

The meaning of each element in the syntax is as follows:

/c   Extracts the contents of the Setup.exe file

/t   Indicates the drive letter and path to use to extract the file will follow

drive letter:\path   Specifies the drive letter and path in which to store the extracted files

For example, if you want to extract the Virtual Server 2005 Install.msi file to C:\VirtualServerSetupFiles, you would type the following on the command line and execute it.

```
Setup.exe /c /t c:\VirtualServerSetupFiles
```

Once you have extracted the Virtual Server 2005 Install.msi file, you need to understand the command-line options, the supporting parameters that are available to you, and how to use the .MSI file and Msiexec.exe file to achieve an installation from the command line. Table 4-4 lists the specific Msiexec.exe command-line options for Virtual Server 2005 Install.msi.

Table 4-4   Msiexec.exe Command-Line Options for Virtual Server 2005 Install.msi

Command-line option	Description
/i	Performs an installation of Virtual Server.
/a	Performs an administrative install of Virtual Server to a network location.
/x	Uninstalls an existing installation of Virtual Server.
/q[n,b,r,f]	Sets the user interface level based on the optional parameters specified.
	/q or /qn – No interface is provided (and no summary screen either)
	/qb – Basic user interface provided
	/qr – Reduced user interface provided
	/qf – Full user interface provided
/l {logfile}	Specifies where the setup log file is stored and the name of the log file. The *logfile* parameter must be specified as a full path, and environment variables can be used in the path.
	Examples:
	/l C:\logfiles\VirtualServerInstall.log
	/l %TEMP%\VirtualServerInstall.log

Table 4-4   Msiexec.exe Command-Line Options for Virtual Server 2005 Install.msi

Command-line option	Description
MSIFILE	Specifies the name of the MSI file that the Msiexec.exe file will launch. This must provide the full path to the MSI file or must be in the current directory.
ALLUSERS	Determines what users see in the Start menu and in Add Or Remove Programs. If ALLUSERS is not specified, a per-machine installation is performed (default). If ALLUSERS="", the installer performs a per-user installation for the user that started the installation.
PIDKEY	Obsolete. This option is no longer needed. The PIDKEY is embedded in the installation MSI file and does not need to be specified.
SERVICESTARTUPMANUAL	Specifies whether the Virtual Server services (VSSRVC.EXE and VMH.EXE) are configured to start manually or automatically. 1 = Manual 0 = Automatic For example, to start the services manually: SERVICESTARTUPMANUAL=1
WEBSITEDEFAULTPORT	Specifies the default port that will be used for access to the Administration Website. If you do not specify a value, the default port number 1024 is used. Value = Port number For example: WEBSITEDEFAULTPORT=80
INSTALLDIR	Used in conjunction with the /i parameter to specify the custom directory path where you want Virtual Server to be installed. Not specifying this option will install Virtual Server to the default location C:\Program Files\Microsoft Virtual Server\. Value = the full path to the directory For example: INSTALLDIR=C:\VirtualServer
TARGETDIR	Used in conjunction with the /a parameter to specify the target directory in which you want Virtual Server administration installation to be placed. This option can be specified as a UNC path or a mapped driver letter and path. For example: TARGETDIR=\\SERVERA\Software\VirtualServer TARGETDIR=S:\VirtualServer

Table 4-4   Msiexec.exe Command-Line Options for Virtual Server 2005 Install.msi

Command-line option	Description
ADDLOCAL	Specifies the Virtual Server components that will be installed. One or more components can be specified, separated by commas. ADDLOCAL must be specified with all uppercase letters.
	VirtualServer – Virtual Server services
	VMRCClient – VMRC Client
	DevAndDoc –Documentation and Developer Resources
	VSWebApp – Administration Website
	VHDMount – VHD Mount tool
	For example, to install only the Administration Website, use the following:
	ADDLOCAL=VSWebApp
	To install the Virtual Server services, documentation and developer resources, and VHD Mount tool, use the following:
	ADDLOCAL=VirtualServer, DevAndDoc, VHDMount
NOSUMMARY	Specifies whether you want to display the summary screen at the end of the installation. Use a value of 1 to indicate the summary should not be displayed. The default is to display the summary.
	For example:
	NOSUMMARY=1

Command-Line Syntax

The MSIEXEC full command-line syntax is as follows:

```
msiexec.exe {/i|/a|/x} "msifile" [allusers=value] [servicestartupmanual=value]
[websitedefaultport=value] [{installdir=value|targetdir=value}] [ADDLOCAL=value,value]
[nosummary=value] [/qb | /qn | /qr | /qf] [/l logfile]
```

The following syntax line examples are for different scenarios (install on a local computer, administration installation, and uninstall) in which not all options are required.

Installing on a Local Computer

The following code block is a list of all the options and parameters that are available when performing an installation of Virtual Server 2005 R2 SP1 from the command line on a single server:

```
msiexec.exe /i "msifile" [allusers=value]
[servicestartupmanual=value] [websitedefaultport=value] [{installdir=value}]
[ADDLOCAL=value,value]
[nosummary=value] [/qb | /qn | /qr | /qf] [/l logfile]
```

Performing an Administrative Installation

The following code block is a list of all the options and parameters that are available when performing an administration installation of Virtual Server 2005 R2 SP1 on a remote server:

```
msiexec.exe /a "msifile" targetdir=value [/qb | /qn | /qr | /qf] [/l logfile]
```

Uninstalling an Existing Virtual Server Installation

The code block that follows is a list of all the options and parameters that are available when performing an uninstall of an existing installation of Virtual Server 2005 R2 SP1 on a local server:

```
msiexec.exe /x "msifile" [ADDLOCAL=value,value] [/qb | /qn | /qr | /qf] [/l logfile]
```

 Important   When you specify any path values in the command line and those paths contain spaces, you must enclose the entire path in quotes (" ").

Command-Line Examples

To perform a full installation of Virtual Server 2005 R2 SP1 on the local machine with no user interface and no logfile, use the following command line. This command line will use the default installation path, select the default Web administration port of 1024, and not provide a summary screen at the end of the installation.

```
msiexec.exe /I "virtual server 2005 install.msi" /qn
```

To change the default port that the Administration Website listens on from 1024 to port 80, you add the WEBSITEDEFAULTPORT=80 parameter to the command line:

```
msiexec.exe /I "virtual server 2005 install.msi" websitedefaultport=80 /qn
```

To perform an Administration install of Virtual Server 2005 R2 SP1 on a server named SERVER1, share named SOFTWARE, in a directory called VS2005R2SP1, with basic user interface (all on one line), use the following command line:

```
msiexec.exe /a "virtual server 2005 install.msi" targetdir=\\Server1\Software\VS2005R2SP1 /qb
```

To uninstall an existing Virtual Server installation with no user interface and a log file created and stored at C:\temp and called VS-UNINSTALL.LOG, use the following command line:

```
Msiexec.exe /X "Virtual Server 2005 Install.msi" /L C:\TEMP\VS-UNINSTALL.LOG /qn
```

> ### Direct from the Source: Why Won't My Uninstall Command Line Work?
>
> The Virtual Server uninstall process does not stop the Virtual Server and Virtual Machine Helper services prior to attempting to uninstall. You can use the NET STOP *<service name>* command for each service before launching an uninstall of the software. If you create a simple batch file with the following lines, uninstall will be successful:
>
> ```
> Net Stop "Virtual Server"
> Net Stop VMH
> Msiexec /x "Virtual Server  2005 Install.msi" /qn
> ```
>
> *Mike Williams*
> *Microsoft Services, Senior Consultant*

Performing the Installation Scenarios Using the Command Line

This section describes how to use the command-line process to perform the same installation scenarios of Virtual Server 2005 R2 SP1: single-server installation, local Administration Website only, Virtual Server services only, Documentation and Developer Resources only, and VHD Mount tool only. You will specify that all of these command-line scenarios specify no user interface.

Single-Server Installation
```
Msiexec.exe /I "Virtual Server 2005 Install.msi" /qn
```

Local Administration Website Only
```
Msiexec.exe /I "Virtual Server 2005 Install.msi" ADDLOCAL=vswebapp /qn
```

Virtual Server Services Only
```
Msiexec.exe /I "Virtual Server 2005 Install.msi" ADDLOCAL=virtualserver /qn
```

Documentation and Developer Resources Only
```
Msiexec.exe /I "Virtual Server 2005 Install.msi" ADDLOCAL=devanddoc /qn
```

VMRC Client Tool Only
```
Msiexec.exe /I "Virtual Server 2005 Install.msi" ADDLOCAL=vmrcclient /qn
```

VHD Mount Tool Only
```
Msiexec.exe /I "Virtual Server 2005 Install.msi" ADDLOCAL=vhdmount /qn
```

Summary

In this chapter, we covered the installation and removal of Virtual Server 2005 R2 SP1, as well as how to upgrade an existing Virtual Server 2005 R2 installation. There are multiple possible installation scenarios based on operating system, desired Virtual Server components, and component placement on servers. Determining which installation scenario applies to your environment and proactively collecting the required information will reduce installation issues. Distributing the Virtual Server 2005 R2 SP1 components across multiple servers will reduce the security risk of your environment, but that approach requires constrained delegation to be configured. The command-line installation process is the most flexible and easiest to use, and it should be your preferred method of installing or removing Virtual Server 2005 R2 SP1 in your environment.

Additional Resources

The following resources contain additional information and tools related to this chapter:

- Knowledge Base Article 890893, "The SPNs that Virtual Server requires are not registered in Active Directory when you try to install Virtual Server 2005 on a Windows-based domain controller," at *http://support.microsoft.com/kb/890893*

- Knowledge Base Article 322692, "How to raise domain and forest functional levels in Windows Server 2003," at *http://support.microsoft.com/kb/322692*

- Virtual Server 2005 R2 SP1 Administrator's Guide and Release notes available in the Microsoft Virtual Server menu option under the Start Menu

- Knowledge Base Article 314881, "The Command-Line Options for the Microsoft Windows Installer Tool Msiexec.exe," at *http://support.microsoft.com/kb/314881*

- IIS 6.0 Technical Reference in the Windows Server 2003 TechCenter, at *http://www.microsoft.com/technet/prodtechnol/WindowsServer2003/Library/IIS /69a58513-141a-4adb-b6bc-2aaad4ea77b8.mspx*

Chapter 5

Virtual Server 2005 R2 Advanced Features

In this chapter:

Using Virtual Hard Disk Advanced Features 109

Using Virtual Network Advanced Features 126

Using Clustering Advanced Features 130

Summary. 142

Additional Resources. 143

This chapter describes advanced features in Microsoft Virtual Server 2005 Release 2 (R2). You will learn about virtual hard disk, network, and clustering options that you can use to deploy broad virtualization infrastructure solutions. Technical descriptions and configurations are discussed along with common usage scenarios.

Using Virtual Hard Disk Advanced Features

Virtual Server 2005 R2 uses the virtual hard disk (VHD) format to encapsulate virtual machine data into one or more files that are equivalent to physical drives associated with a traditional server. Using the VHD format as a basic building block, Virtual Server 2005 R2 provides advanced virtual hard disk features that enable the creation of virtualized environments that are more functional and flexible than physical equivalents, particularly for disciplines such as development, testing, training, and support. Table 5-1 lists the advanced virtual hard disk features covered in this section.

Table 5-1 Virtual Hard Disk Advanced Features

Feature	Description
Differencing disks	A special type of dynamically expanding virtual hard disk that stores virtual machine data changes while isolating them from the base virtual hard disk.
Undo disks	A special type of dynamically expanding virtual hard disk that stores virtual machine data changes while isolating them from the base virtual hard disk. There are similarities with differencing disks, but differences in options and applicable scenarios.

Table 5-1   Virtual Hard Disk Advanced Features

Feature	Description
Linked disks	A special type of virtual hard disk designed specifically to convert a physical hard disk into a virtual hard disk file. The process associated with the use of linked disks is potentially time consuming depending on the size of the physical disk.
VHDMount command-line tool	This is a new feature provided with Virtual Server 2005 R2 SP1. VHDMount is an essential tool to manipulate virtual hard disk files without booting into a virtual machine.
VHD compaction	This tool is used to regain unused space within a virtual hard disk. The compaction process works only for dynamically expanding virtual hard disks. No other type of virtual hard disk can be compacted.

Differencing Disks

A virtual machine running within Virtual Server 2005 R2 has its data encapsulated in one or more base virtual hard disks. When data changes occur to the guest operating system or the applications running in it, modifications are committed to the virtual hard disks. The changes made to the virtual hard disks are permanent, paralleling the process that would occur with a standard physical system. However, a variety of compelling scenarios are enabled by preserving a base virtual hard disk in an unchanged state, while still capturing and storing ongoing virtual machine changes.

A differencing disk is a special type of dynamic disk that stores changes to virtual machine data in a separate file from a base virtual hard disk. The association of the base virtual hard disk to the differencing disk is defined as a parent-child relationship. In this parent-child relationship, each child differencing disk can derive from only one parent disk, but parent disks can be used as the basis to create multiple, distinct child differencing disks.

Figure 5-1 shows that differencing disks can be created in very simple or very complex parent-child hierarchies. A multilevel differencing disk hierarchy is commonly referred to as a *chain* of differencing disks, reflecting that a child differencing disk can have a parent disk that is also a differencing disk. The chain can consist of several levels, but it always stems from either a standard dynamically expanding or fixed-size virtual hard disk at the top of the hierarchy. This concept is important because data changes in a differencing disk are simply represented as modified blocks in relation to the parent disk. Therefore, a differencing disk is never used independently, but in conjunction with all parent disks in its hierarchy. (See Figure 5-1.)

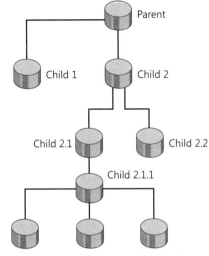

Figure 5-1   Multilevel differencing disk hierarchy

If you examine a Virtual Server 2005 R2 host file system, you will see each differencing disk stored as an individual file. Within the virtual machine file system, you see only a single disk, independent of how many levels of differencing disks are actually associated with a specific virtual hard disk.

Best Practices   To quickly and easily identify parent-child differencing disk relationships in a complex chain, adopt a standardized virtual hard disk naming convention. The Virtual Server Administration Website allows you to inspect a differencing disk and discover its parent disk, but it does not report any child differencing disks related to it.

Creating a Differencing Disk

When you create a new differencing disk, the location of the base virtual hard disk that will be the parent for the new differencing disk must be specified. The parent disk can be either a fixed-size or dynamically expanding virtual hard disk. A differencing disk grows as needed, up to the size specified for the parent virtual hard disk.

To create a differencing disk, follow these steps:

1. Open the Virtual Server 2005 R2 Administration Website.

2. In the navigation pane, under Virtual Disks, point to Create and then click Differencing Virtual Hard Disk.

3. In Location, select the folder to store the new virtual hard disk file. If the folder does not appear in the list, type the fully qualified path to the folder as described in the next step.

4. In the Virtual Hard Disk File Name text box, type the fully qualified path to the folder followed by a name for the differencing virtual hard disk. You do not need to include a filename extension.

5. In Known Virtual Hard Disks, select the virtual hard disk file to use as the parent disk.

6. If the virtual hard disk file does not appear in the Known Virtual Hard Disks list, in the Fully Qualified Path To Parent Virtual Hard Disk text box, type the fully qualified path to the parent virtual hard disk file.

7. Click Create.

> **Note**   By default, differencing disks use the .vhd file extension, which makes them difficult to distinguish from standard virtual hard disks.

Examining Parent-Child Differencing Disk Relationships

Every dynamic disk contains a standard virtual hard disk header that embeds a specific dynamic disk header. The dynamic disk header format is identical for both standard dynamically expanding and differencing disks. However, several fields in this header are only relevant to differencing disks, as they identify parent disk attributes. A list of the dynamic disk header fields is provided in Table 5-2, with those relating only to differencing disks appearing in bold-face type.

Table 5-2   Dynamic Disk Header

Dynamic disk header fields	Description
Cookie	A set field that identifies the header.
Data Offset	Absolute byte offset to next hard disk image structure (*currently unused*).
Table Offset	Absolute byte offset of the block allocation table (BAT) in the file.
Header Version	Dynamic disk header version.
Max Table Entries	Maximum number of entries in the BAT.
Block Size	Size of unit that is used to incrementally expand the dynamic disk.
Checksum	Checksum of the dynamic disk header.
Parent UUID	**128-bit universally unique identifier (UUID) of the parent disk (used only for differencing disks).**
Parent Time Stamp	**Modification time stamp of the parent disk (used only for differencing disks).**
Reserved	Field is set to zero.
Parent Unicode Name	**Unicode string for filename of the parent disk (used only for differencing disks).**

Table 5-2   Dynamic Disk Header

Dynamic disk header fields	Description
Parent Locator Entry 1	**Platform-specific format containing the absolute byte offset in the file where the parent locator is stored (used only for differencing disks).**
Parent Locator Entry 2	**Platform-specific format containing the absolute byte offset in the file where the parent locator is stored (used only for differencing disks).**
Parent Locator Entry 3	**Platform-specific format containing the absolute byte offset in the file where the parent locator is stored (used only for differencing disks).**
Parent Locator Entry 4	**Platform-specific format containing the absolute byte offset in the file where the parent locator is stored (used only for differencing disks).**
Parent Locator Entry 5	**Platform-specific format containing the absolute byte offset in the file where the parent locator is stored (used only for differencing disks).**
Parent Locator Entry 6	**Platform-specific format containing the absolute byte offset in the file where the parent locator is stored (used only for differencing disks).**
Parent Locator Entry 7	**Platform-specific format containing the absolute byte offset in the file where the parent locator is stored (used only for differencing disks).**
Parent Locator Entry 8	**Platform-specific format containing the absolute byte offset in the file where the parent locator is stored (used only for differencing disks).**
Reserved	Field is set to zero.

A differencing disk uses the parent UUID and Unicode file name information stored in its dynamic disk header to locate and open the parent disk. Because a parent disk can also be a differencing disk, it is possible that the entire hierarchy of parent disks will be opened, up to the base virtual hard disk.

Portability of parent and child differencing disks across server platforms is provided by the Parent Locator entries listed in Table 5-2. Parent locator entries store platform-specific information to locate the parent differencing disk on the physical drive.

Important   For the Microsoft Windows platform, both the absolute (for example, c:\parent\parent.vhd) and relative (for example, .\parent\parent.vhd) paths of the parent disk are stored in the Parent Locator entry of a differencing disk. As long as you copy the virtual hard disks to the same relative directory hierarchy on a new host, you will be able to add the virtual machine to Virtual Server and turn it on without having to make any additional changes.

When a virtual machine using differencing disks issues a write operation, the data is written only to the child differencing disk. As part of the process, an internal virtual hard disk data structure is updated to reflect changes that supersede data in the parent disk. During read operations, the same internal virtual hard disk data structure is checked to determine which data to read from the child differencing disk. Unchanged data is read from the parent disk.

Direct from the Source: Configure Parent Disks as "Read-Only"

A child differencing disk stores the parent disk modification time stamp when it is created. Any modifications made to the parent disk after creation of the child differencing disk will be detected and will invalidate the child differencing disk. To ensure that nothing can be written to the parent disk that will corrupt the parent-child disk relationship, configure the parent disk as "read-only."

Bryon Surace
Program Manager, Windows Virtualization

Merging Differencing Disks

Although a differencing disk can be used to permanently store virtual machine data changes, you might need to combine the child differencing disk with the parent disk. Virtual Server 2005 R2 provides two ways to accomplish this. You can either merge the differencing disk into the parent disk or merge the differencing disk and the parent disk into a new virtual hard disk. If you merge a differencing disk into the parent disk, the differencing disk is deleted upon completion of the process and any other differencing disk that pointed to the original parent disk is invalidated. If you need to retain the differencing disk, you should choose to merge the differencing disk and parent disk into a new virtual hard disk. This approach is recommended to lower the risk of data loss. You can verify that the merge operation is successful prior to deleting the original files.

To merge differencing disks, follow these steps:

1. Open the Virtual Server R2 Administration Website.

2. In the navigation pane, under Virtual Disks, click Inspect.

3. In the Inspect Virtual Hard Disk pane, do one of the following, and then click Inspect:

    ❑ In Known Virtual Hard Disks, select the virtual hard disk that you want to merge.

    ❑ In the Fully Qualified Path To File text box, type the fully qualified path to the virtual hard disk file that you want to merge.

4. In the Actions pane, click Merge Virtual Hard Disk.

5. Proceed with one of the following two choices:

    ❑ Select the Merge With Parent Virtual Hard Disk option.

❏ Select the Merge To New Virtual Hard Disk option, and then select a folder in which to store the new virtual hard disk. If the folder is not listed, type a fully qualified path and filename for the new virtual hard disk. You do not need to include a filename extension.

6. In Merged Virtual Hard Disk Type, select a type for the new virtual hard disk.

7. Click Merge.

Important   Prior to merging a differencing disk and parent disk into a new virtual hard disk, make sure there is enough space on the physical disk to perform the operation.

Using Differencing Disks

Functionality gains from using differencing disks become evident when considering a typical support scenario. A support engineer often needs to troubleshoot server configurations for different operating system update levels or with different applications. Using one or more physical test servers, even with preconfigured build images, the setup and testing of multiple server configurations is a lengthy, complex process that results in protracted problem response time. Using Virtual Server 2005 R2 with differencing disks, a support engineer can quickly create a virtual machine for each unique server configuration. Starting with a common parent virtual hard disk that contains the base operating system, each individual server configuration is created as a new virtual machine with one or more differencing disks to capture incremental operating system patches and application stacks.

Important   Differencing disks should not be used with cluster configurations.

As shown in Figure 5-2, implementing a virtualized support environment using differencing disks can help significantly reduce the setup and test cycle associated with problem resolution response time. Even with a single physical server constraint, a Virtual Server 2005 R2 host can run multiple virtual machines (VMs) concurrently, allowing parallel testing of distinctive server configurations. In addition to creating an environment that can lead to faster support response time, this solution also has the additional benefit of saving significant amounts of physical disk space for any scenario that requires multiple complex configurations sharing a large common software base.

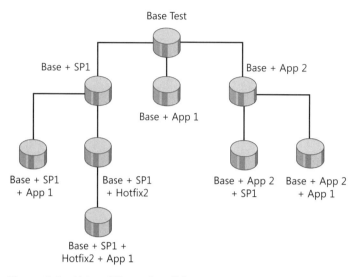

Figure 5-2   Using differencing disks to create guest VMs for concurrent testing

Undo Disks

Undo disks are quite similar to differencing disks. Like a differencing disk, an undo disk is used to isolate virtual machine data changes from a base virtual hard disk. Undo disks also share the special dynamic disk characteristics previously defined for differencing disks. However, in an environment where virtual machine data changes need to be quickly discarded or a rapid rollback to the base virtual machine state is required, undo disks are a better solution than differencing disks. There are other environments that require the use of a shared common software base and rapid rollbacks to a baseline state. In these cases, differencing disks can be used in combination with undo disks to implement the virtualization solution.

> **Note**   Unlike a differencing disk, which has a .vhd filename extension, an undo disk uses a .vud filename extension. Also, undo disks are stored in the same directory as the virtual machine configuration file (which uses a .vmc filename extension).

Configuring Undo Disks

One major distinction between differencing disks and undo disks is in the configuration process. A differencing disk is created at an individual virtual hard disk level and usually associated with the creation of a new virtual machine. In contrast, undo disks are either enabled or disabled for an existing virtual machine and created for every virtual hard disk associated with the virtual machine. In other words, you do not have the ability to individually choose the virtual hard disks for which undo disks are generated.

Important   If you need to move a virtual machine from one Virtual Server 2005 R2 host to another, don't forget to move parent disks and virtual machine configuration files (.vmc) along with child differencing disks and undo disks.

To configure undo disks for a virtual machine, follow these steps:

1. Open the Virtual Server 2005 R2 Administration Website.

2. In the navigation pane, under Virtual Machines, point to Configure and then click the desired virtual machine.

3. In the Configuration section, select Hard Disks.

4. In the Virtual Hard Disk Properties section, select the Enable Undo Disks check box and then click OK.

Important   Undo disks can be enabled or disabled only when a virtual machine is in a powered-off state. The option to enable undo disks is not available if the virtual machine is in a saved state.

Managing Undo Disks

Another major distinction between differencing disks and undo disks is that you are required to decide what to do with the changes saved in undo disks every time a virtual machine is shut down or placed in a saved state. Virtual Server 2005 R2 provides three options to manage undo disks:

- **Keep Undo Disks**   This option saves the changes stored in the undo disk and preserves the state of the base virtual hard disk.

- **Commit Undo Disks**   This option saves the changes stored in the undo disk to the base virtual hard disk.

- **Discard Undo Disks**   This option deletes the undo disk without saving any changes to the base virtual hard disk.

If you shut down the guest operating system from within the virtual machine, undo disks are saved. If you choose to discard undo disk changes, new undo disks are created when the virtual machine is turned back on.

Caution   If you disable undo disks while a virtual machine is turned off, the undo disks are immediately deleted.

Using Undo Disks

Undo disks are most useful in scenarios where frequent rollbacks to a base configuration are required. Two mainstream examples are software testing and end-user training. Working in these scenarios with only physical components, one of the most time consuming and tedious tasks is rebuilding the baseline environment—whether it is to re-create the steps to isolate a software bug or to prepare the system for the next user of a training lab. This is even more of a burden if the environment consists of several, incrementally different workloads, although the process can again be somewhat simplified by using imaging tools to more quickly reset each system. A better solution for working in these scenarios is to use Virtual Server 2005 R2 virtual machines that enable undo disks. As illustrated in Figure 5-3, the more complex software testing scenario—which requires multiple, incrementally different virtual machine configurations—is optimized by using undo disks in conjunction with differencing disks. The simple end-user training configuration only requires the implementation of undo disks. At the end of each training session, the system only needs to be reset to the base configuration.

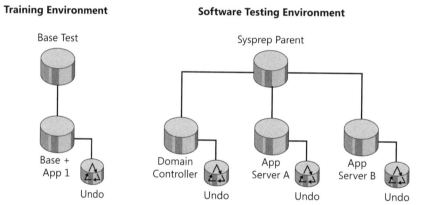

Figure 5-3   Using undo disks with and without differencing disks to achieve a quick rollback

In either case, a rollback to a baseline configuration is accomplished by simply choosing to discard the changes in the undo disks. This process takes just a few moments to complete before the system software is reset to the original configuration.

Best Practices   To restrict the ability to commit undo disk changes and ensure the integrity of the virtual machine baseline configuration, you should set the base virtual hard disk files to read-only.

Linked Disks

A linked disk is a virtual hard disk that points to a physical drive with the single purpose of duplicating the contents into a new virtual hard disk. There are several requirements to consider when using this method to migrate the contents of the physical disk into a virtual hard disk. The limitations are as follows:

- A linked disk can be associated only with a physical disk, not a volume.

- A linked disk must be used only to migrate a data disk; startup disks are not supported.

- A linked disk must be stored on a physical disk that is separate from the drive being converted.

- The physical disk must not be accessed by the host operating system or applications during the conversion process.

- If the physical disk that is being converted is larger than 127 GB, you must attach the virtual hard disk into which the disk contents will be copied to a virtual SCSI adapter.

> **Best Practices**   Prior to creating the linked disk, you should use the Disk Management Microsoft Management Console (MMC) or other similar tool to remove the drive letter for the target drive. This will make the drive inaccessible to the host operating system, preventing disk corruption during the conversion process.

Creating a Linked Disk

The creation of a linked disk is simple, but it is only the first step in converting a physical disk into a new virtual hard disk. Follow these steps to create a linked disk:

1. Open the Virtual Server 2005 R2 Administration Website.

2. In the navigation pane, under Virtual Disks, point to Create, and then click Linked Virtual Hard Disk.

3. In Location, select the folder in which to store the virtual hard disk file. If the folder you want does not appear in the list, you must type the fully qualified path to the folder in the following step.

4. In the Virtual Hard Disk File Name text box, after the path to the folder, type a name for the virtual hard disk. You do not need to include a filename extension.

5. In the Physical Computer Drive section, select the physical hard disk to which you want to link the virtual hard disk and then click Create.

At this point, you have only created a virtual hard disk that is essentially a pointer to the physical drive.

Using the Linked Disk to Convert the Physical Disk

To complete the process and copy the physical drive content to a new virtual hard disk, follow these additional steps:

1. Open the Virtual Server 2005 R2 Administration Website.

2. In the navigation pane, under Virtual Disks, click Inspect.

3. In the Inspect Virtual Hard Disk pane, select the virtual hard disk to convert in Known Virtual Hard Disks. If the file does not appear in the list, in the Fully Qualified Path To File text box, type the fully qualified path to the virtual hard disk file to convert.

4. Click Inspect.

5. Under Actions, click Convert Virtual Hard Disk.

6. In Location, select the folder in which to store the converted virtual hard disk file. If the folder you want does not appear in the list, in the Converted Virtual Hard Disk Name text box, type the fully qualified path including the filename.

7. In Converted Virtual Hard Disk Type, select the type of virtual hard disk that you want to create.

8. Click Convert.

Once the conversion process completes, you can attach the new virtual hard disk to a virtual machine. You should delete the linked disk that you created prior to the physical disk conversion.

Note   Virtual Server 2005 R2 will prevent you from attaching a linked disk to a virtual machine.

VHDMount Command-Line Tool

The VHDMount command-line tool is a new feature delivered with Virtual Server 2005 R2 Service Pack 1 (SP1). This tool allows you to mount a virtual hard disk file as a virtual disk device on a host machine. Using this method, you can inspect, inject, or delete files in the virtual hard disk without having to boot into a virtual machine.

Note   By default, the VHDMount command-line tool is located in %systemdrive%\Program Files\Microsoft Virtual Server\Vhdmount.

VHDMount leverages the Virtual Disk Service (VDS), which is a set of application programming interfaces (APIs) that permit management of disks and volumes at the operating system level. Although VDS is available only with Windows Server 2003 and later operating systems, you can still run VHDMount in Windows XP.

When VHDMount is used to mount a virtual hard disk file, VDS interacts with the Plug and Play Manager to discover the virtual hard disk as a new disk and mount it (assigning a drive letter) in the host operating system. Once the virtual hard disk is successfully mounted, a new entry is listed in Device Manager | Disk Drives and is registered as *MS Virtual Server SCSI Disk*

Device. There is also a new entry listed in Device Manager | Microsoft Server Virtual Storage Devices that is registered as *Microsoft Server Virtual Storage DeviceXX*, where *XX* is a unique number that increases sequentially with each mounted device. At this stage, the virtual hard disk file contents can be accessed using standard file system browsing tools such as Windows Explorer.

> **Important**   By default, all changes made by VHDMount to a mounted disk are written to an undo disk that is created in the temporary folder for the current user. You can use the /f option to mount a VHD without an undo disk. You can also use the /c option to commit or /d option to discard changes when unplugging a mounted disk.

Defining VHDMount Command-Line Options

VHDMount is a simple utility to use, with only a few options needed to mount and dismount virtual hard disks. Table 5-3 lists the VHDMount command-line options.

Table 5-3   VHDMount Command-Line Options

Command-line option	Description
/p	Plugs in a virtual hard disk file as a virtual disk device without mounting the volume.
/m	Plugs in a virtual hard disk file as a virtual disk device and mounts the volume.
/u	Unplugs a virtual disk device.
/q	Returns the disk name of a mounted virtual disk device.

> **Important**   Even though VDS is not available in Windows XP, the virtual disk device should be automatically detected and mounted. However, because you cannot use the /m option with VHDMount, you are unable to specify a starting drive letter to mount a virtual hard disk in Windows XP.

Using VHDMount to Plug In a Virtual Hard Disk File

The following command-line shows the VHDMount option and parameter needed to plug in a virtual hard disk file without mounting the volume:

```
VHDMOUNT.EXE /p [/f] VHDFileName
```

VHDFileName VHDFileName indicates the fully qualified path to the virtual hard disk file. If you use the /f option, an undo disk will not be created. For example, to plug in a virtual hard disk file named test.vhd (with an undo disk) located in folder c:\virtual machines, you type the following:

```
VHDMOUNT.EXE /p "c:\virtual machines\test.vhd"
```

> **Important**   When you specify any path values in the command line and those paths contain spaces, you must enclose the entire path in quotes.

Using VHDMount to Plug In and Mount a Virtual Hard Disk File

The next command line shows the VHDMount option and parameter needed to plug in and mount a virtual hard disk file:

```
VHDMOUNT.EXE /m [/f] VHDFileName [DriveLetter]
```

DriveLetter is an optional parameter that defines the starting drive letter used to mount virtual hard disk files.

For example, to plug in and mount the virtual hard disk file used in the previous example as drive E, you type the following:

```
VHDMOUNT.EXE /m "c:\virtual machines\test.vhd" E
```

> **Important**   When you specify a drive letter in your VHDMount command, do not type a colon after the drive letter. If you do, the VHDMount help screen will display and your command will be ignored.

Using VHDMount to Unmount a Virtual Hard Disk File

The following command line represents the VHDMount option and parameters needed to unmount a virtual hard disk file:

```
VHDMOUNT.EXE /u [/c | /d] VHDFileName | All
```

All is an optional parameter that applies the operation to all mounted virtual disk devices. The /c option updates the original VHD with all the changes stored in the undo disk (if one was created) and deletes the undo disk after unplugging the disk. The /d option discards all changes to the mounted disk and deletes the undo disk after unplugging the disk. The /c and /d options are only applicable if the VHDMount /p and /m commands were used without the /f option.

For example, to dismount a virtual hard disk file, update the original VHD, and delete the undo disk, you type the following:

```
VHDMOUNT.EXE /u /c "c:\virtual machines\test.vhd"
```

Using VHDMount to Determine a Virtual Hard Disk Name

The next command line shows the VHDMount option and parameter needed to determine the disk name associated with the mounted virtual hard disk file:

```
VHDMOUNT.EXE /q VHDFileName | All
```

All is an optional parameter that applies the operation to all mounted virtual disk devices.

For example, to get a listing of disk names associated with all mounted virtual hard disk files, you type the following:

```
VHDMOUNT.EXE /q All
```

On the Companion Media   On the companion media, you will find a directory called \Chapter Materials\Files\VHDMount. Inside the directory there is a registry file named Vhdmenu.reg. This file will make registry modifications that add mount and dismount selections to the context menu that appears when you right-click a virtual hard disk file.

VHD Compaction

VHD compaction is a process that reduces the size of a virtual hard disk file on the physical disk. Virtual Server 2005 R2 provides a compaction tool that achieves minor reductions in a virtual hard disk file size if used solely on its own. A better approach is to use a three-step process that includes defragmentation, precompaction, and compaction. Defragmentation and precompaction prepare the virtual hard disk file for the compaction process, resulting in greater reductions in virtual hard disk file size.

Note   Prior to virtual hard disk file defragmentation, remove temporary files and folders, delete any other unwanted data, and empty the recycle bin.

VHD compaction can be performed only on dynamically expanding disks. Fixed-size virtual hard disks have to be converted to a dynamically expanding disk prior to being compacted. Special dynamically expanding virtual hard disks, such as differencing or undo disks, cannot be directly compacted. Differencing disks and undo disk changes must be merged into their parent disk, and the parent disk can be compacted if it is a dynamically expanding disk.

Best Practices   Because of processor and disk resource requirements, you should use a non-production server, when possible, to perform the virtual hard disk compaction process. In Virtual Server 2005 R2, you can perform the defragmentation step within the virtual machine or while the virtual hard disk is offline. However, it is best to perform defragmentation, pre-compaction, and compaction with the virtual hard disk file offline.

Defragmenting the Virtual Hard Disk File

The first step in the process to reduce the size of a virtual hard disk file is defragmentation. As new information is written to disk, data might not be saved in contiguous disk blocks. In time, as you delete data on the disk, empty blocks will be randomly filled with file fragments. Performance is adversely affected when the disk fragmentation is excessive because it takes longer to retrieve related data spread across a disk than if it were located in a contiguous set of blocks. Defragmentation reduces or eliminates the number of fragmented files on a disk, resulting in larger areas of empty contiguous blocks.

To defragment a virtual hard disk offline, you first have to use the VHDMount command-line tool to mount the virtual hard disk file. You can find the VHDMount command syntax in the

"Using VHDMount to Plug In and Mount a Virtual Hard Disk File" section earlier in this chapter. Once the virtual hard disk file is mounted, use the Windows Defrag utility on the host system to defragment the virtual hard disk file. Table 5-4 lists the defrag command lines for Windows XP, Windows Server 2003, and Windows Vista. The time required to defragment the virtual hard disk file depends on several factors, including the degree of fragmentation, file size, and disk characteristics.

Table 5-4   Platform-Specific Defragmentation Command Lines

Command line	Operating system
Defrag *DriveLetter* ■ *DriveLetter* is the drive letter associated with the mounted virtual hard disk.	Windows XP Windows Server 2003
Defrag *DriveLetter* –w ■ *DriveLetter* is the drive letter associated with the mounted virtual hard disk. ■ –w specifies that all file fragments should be consolidated, regardless of size.	Windows Vista

Precompacting the Virtual Hard Disk File

The second step in the process is precompaction. Virtual Server 2005 R2 includes the Virtual Disk Precompactor tool, which is designed to overwrite any unallocated disk blocks in a virtual hard disk file with zeros. This step is crucial to ensure that the compaction tool can make the virtual hard disk file as small as possible.

The Virtual Disk Precompactor tool is contained in the Precompact.iso disk image located in the %systemdrive%\Program Files\Microsoft Virtual Server\Virtual Machine Additions folder. Use your favorite virtual CD tool to mount the Precompact.iso image on your Virtual Server 2005 R2 host and retrieve the Precompact.exe tool. Table 5-5 lists the options that are available when you invoke the Virtual Disk Precompactor tool from the command line.

Table 5-5   Virtual Disk Precompactor Command-Line Options

Command-line option	Description
-Help	Displays the help dialog box that lists the command-line options, product version, and syntax examples.
-Version	Displays the help dialog box that lists the command-line options, product version, and syntax examples.
-Silent	Executes the precompactor in unattended mode, and suppresses all dialog boxes.

Table 5-5   Virtual Disk Precompactor Command-Line Options

Command-line option	Description
-SetDisks:<list> *<list>* is an optional parameter that represents one or more drive letters.	Defines the list of virtual hard disks to precompact. If this option is not specified, all virtual hard disks attached to a virtual machine are compacted.

For example, the following command precompacts virtual hard disks mounted to drive letters F and G, in unattended mode:

```
Precompact -Silent -SetDisks:FG
```

> **More Info**   Virtual Server 2005 R2 allows precompacting virtual hard disk files from within a virtual machine. Once you capture the Precompact.iso image on the virtual machine CD or DVD drive, you can double-click the drive to launch Virtual Disk Precompactor. Using this process, you cannot specify which virtual hard disk to precompact. Instead, Virtual Disk Precompactor precompacts all virtual hard disks attached to the virtual machine.

Compacting the Virtual Hard Disk File

The third and final step in the process to reduce the virtual hard disk size is disk compaction. After running the Virtual Disk Precompactor tool, empty disk blocks in the virtual hard disk file contain zeros. The Virtual Server compaction tool finds the disk blocks that contain zeros and removes them, reducing the virtual hard disk file size.

> **Caution**   The Virtual Server compaction tool requires that you have enough disk space to concurrently store the original virtual hard disk file and an additional temporary file that contains the compacted virtual hard disk. The original virtual hard disk file will be deleted at the end of the compaction process and replaced with the compacted virtual hard disk file. If the disk runs out of space before completing the compaction process, an event will be recorded in the Virtual Server event log and no changes will be made to the disk.

To use the Virtual Server compaction tool, follow these steps:

1. Open the Virtual Server 2005 R2 Administration Website.

2. Turn off the virtual machine associated with the dynamically expanding virtual hard disk that you want to compact.

3. In the navigation pane, under Virtual Disks, click Inspect.

4. In the Inspect Virtual Hard Disk pane, select the virtual hard disk to compact in Known Virtual Hard Disks. If the virtual hard disk file does not appear in the list, type the fully qualified path to the virtual hard disk in the Fully Qualified Path To File text box.

5. Click Inspect.

6. Under Actions, click Compact Virtual Hard Disk.

7. In the Compact Virtual Hard Disk pane, click Compact.

The VHD compaction process can also be scripted using the Virtual Server 2005 R2 COM API. This API allows you to create scripts and compact the virtual hard disk files outside of the Virtual Server Administration Website.

> **On the Companion Media**   On the companion media, you will find a directory called \Chapter Materials\Scripts\Compact. Inside the directory there are two files, Vhdprep.bat and Compaction.vbs. The Vhdprep.bat file mounts the virtual hard disk file and runs the defragmenter and Virtual Disk Precompactor before calling the Compaction.vbs script. The Compaction.vbs script invokes the Virtual Server compaction tool to compact the virtual hard disk offline.

Using Virtual Network Advanced Features

The Virtual Server 2005 R2 network architecture allows virtual machine network traffic to be isolated from other virtual machines, the Virtual Server 2005 R2 host, and external networks. It also allows virtual machines to be connected to each other, the Virtual Server 2005 R2 host, corporate networks, and the Internet. Many configuration options are available and some depend on the implementation of advanced network settings. Table 5-6 lists Virtual Server 2005 R2 advanced network features covered in this section.

Table 5-6   Virtual Network Advanced Features

Configuration	Description
Microsoft Loopback Adapter	A software-based network adapter that is used to connect virtual machines to internal networks.
Host-to-Guest Networking	Uses the Microsoft Loopback Adapter to enable network connectivity between a Virtual Server 2005 R2 host and virtual machines.
Internet Connection Sharing with Network Address Translation	Uses the Microsoft Loopback Adapter to enable virtual machines to share the Virtual Server 2005 R2 server network access to the Internet.

Using the Microsoft Loopback Adapter

The Microsoft Loopback Adapter is a built-in, software-based network interface that can be attached to virtual networks to provide connectivity between virtual machines. The Microsoft Loopback Adapter can also be used to attach to internal virtual networks linking virtual machines to the Virtual Server 2005 R2 host. Network traffic between virtual machines and the Virtual Server 2005 R2 host is constrained to the internal virtual networks and isolated from external, physical networks.

Installing the Microsoft Loopback Adaptor

The Microsoft Loopback Adaptor is installed on the Virtual Server 2005 R2 host just like a physical network adapter. Here are the steps to install the Microsoft Loopback Adaptor on Windows Server 2003 R2:

1. On the Virtual Server 2005 R2 host, click Start and then click Control Panel.

2. In Control Panel, click Add Hardware and then click Next.

3. In the Is The Hardware Connected dialog box, choose Yes (I Have Already Connected The Hardware) and then click Next.

4. In the Installed Hardware list, choose Add A New Hardware Device and then click Next.

5. In the What Do You Want The Wizard To Do check list, choose Install The Hardware That I Manually Select From A List (Advanced) and then click Next.

6. In the Common Hardware Types list, choose Network Adapters and then click Next.

7. In the Manufacturer list, click Microsoft.

8. In the Network Adapter list, choose Microsoft Loopback Adapter and then click Next.

9. In the Hardware To Install dialog box, click Next.

10. In the Completing The Add Hardware Wizard dialog box, click Finish.

> **Important** You must be a member of the administrators group to install a new network adapter in the Virtual Server host operating system.

Configuring the Microsoft Loopback Adaptor

Before you can use the Microsoft Loopback Adaptor, you must ensure that it is properly configured on your Virtual Server 2005 R2 host. The Microsoft Loopback Adaptor must be bound to Virtual Machine Network Services to allow communications through a virtual network. Once the configuration is complete, you can create virtual networks in the Virtual Server 2005 R2 Administration Website to enable virtual machine network connectivity. Follow these steps to configure the Microsoft Loopback Adaptor bindings on the Virtual Server 2005 R2 host:

1. On the Virtual Server 2005 R2 host, click Start and select Control Panel.

2. Select Network Connections, right-click the local area connection associated with the Microsoft Loopback Adapter and then click Properties.

3. In This Connection Uses The Following Items, ensure that the Virtual Machine Network Services check box is selected.

4. Click Internet Protocol (TCP/IP), and then click Properties.

5. On the General tab, select Use The Following IP Address and then type the IP address and subnet mask, but do not enter a gateway address.

6. Click OK, and then click Close.

> **Note**   Use one of the reserved ranges of nonroutable TCP/IP addresses when you configure the Microsoft Loopback Adaptor network address properties. The network address and network mask must be the same on the Virtual Server 2005 R2 host as on the virtual machines that you want to connect to the virtual network.

Implementing Host-to-Guest Networking

Virtual PC 2007 has a Shared Folders feature that allows file sharing between the Virtual PC host and virtual machines. Although no similar feature exists in Virtual Server 2005 R2, you can use the Microsoft Loopback Adapter and virtual networks to enable network connectivity between a Virtual Server 2005 R2 host and virtual machines. Once you have configured this arrangement, you can use standard Windows file sharing features between the physical server and virtual machines.

Creating a Virtual Network for Host-to-Guest Networking

After the Microsoft Loopback Adapter has been installed and configured on the Virtual Server 2005 R2 host, you can create a new virtual network to which you connect the virtual machines. To accomplish this, perform the following steps:

1. Open the Virtual Server 2005 R2 Administration Website.

2. In the navigation pane, under Virtual Networks, click Create.

3. In the Virtual Network Name text box, type a name for the virtual network.

4. In Network Adapter On Physical Computer, select the Microsoft Loopback Adapter.

5. In Disconnected Virtual Network Adapters, select the Connected check box for any virtual machine network adapter that you want to attach to the new virtual network.

6. In the Virtual Network Notes text box, type in a description for the new virtual network and then click OK.

You can now boot the virtual machines, configure the network address for the new local connection, and configure firewall settings to enable resource sharing, as required.

Enabling a Virtual DHCP Server on a Virtual Network

If you intend to connect several virtual machines to the host-to-guest virtual network, you should configure the Virtual DHCP Server option on the virtual network. The Virtual DHCP server will manage and provide network configuration options to connecting virtual machines. These are the steps to enable the Virtual DHCP Server option:

1. Open the Virtual Server 2005 R2 Administration Website.

2. In the navigation pane, under Virtual Networks, select Configure and then click the appropriate virtual network.

3. In the Virtual Network Properties pane, click DHCP server.

4. Choose the Enabled check box, and configure the DHCP server options as needed.

5. Click OK.

> **Note** In the DHCP Server options, you can see that the first 16 IP addresses from the start of the specified range are reserved. These 16 IP addresses are never assigned; use one in that range to configure the Virtual Server host adapter.

Configuring Internet Connection Sharing and Network Address Translation

Using the Microsoft Loopback Adapter, you can also configure Internet Connection Sharing (ICS) on the Virtual Server 2005 R2 host to provide virtual machine connectivity to external networks using Network Address Translation (NAT). This configuration provides external network access without the provisioning of official network addresses or direct virtual machine connection to the physical network. The major steps to implement this scenario are as follows:

1. Install the Microsoft Loopback Adapter on the Virtual Server 2005 R2 host.

2. Configure Internet Connection Sharing on the Microsoft Loopback Adapter.

3. Create a virtual network using the Microsoft Loopback Adapter.

4. Connect virtual machines to the virtual network.

All steps are covered in previous examples, with the exception of the Internet Connection Sharing configuration on the Virtual Server 2005 R2 host. Here are the steps to complete the Internet Connection Sharing configuration on Windows Server 2003 R2:

1. On the Virtual Server 2005 R2 host, click Start and select Control Panel.

2. Select Network Connections, and click on the connection that provides Internet connectivity.

3. In the Local Area Connection Status dialog box, on the General tab, click Properties.

4. Click the Advanced tab.

5. In Internet Connection Sharing, select the Allow Other Network Users To Connect Through This Computer's Internet Connection check box.

6. Click OK.

You can use the network connection Repair option in the virtual machines to force connections to refresh the IP address configuration from the Internet Connection Sharing host.

> **Caution**   If IPSec is configured on the Virtual Server 2005 R2 host, you cannot use Internet Connection Sharing to provide external network access to virtual machines.

Using Clustering Advanced Features

A common issue that arises when considering the deployment of a virtualized infrastructure is that a single physical server running multiple workloads becomes a more critical point of failure, with an impact on a larger user and business base than a single physical server running a single workload. Clustering addresses this risk by providing high-availability solutions that are as applicable in the virtualization space as in the physical server space. In this section, you will learn how to configure virtual machines and Virtual Server 2005 R2 hosts to implement the clustering scenarios listed in Table 5-7.

Table 5-7   Virtual Server 2005 R2 Advanced Cluster Configurations

Feature	Description
Virtual Machine Cluster Using iSCSI	A cluster based on Microsoft Cluster Server (MSCS) that consists of two or more virtual machine cluster nodes supporting a cluster-aware application. Virtual machine cluster nodes can be located across Virtual Server 2005 R2 hosts, but they require iSCSI-based disks.
Virtual Server Host Cluster	A cluster based on Microsoft Cluster Server that consists of two or more Virtual Server 2005 R2 host cluster nodes.

In Virtual Server 2005, you could create only a two-node virtual machine cluster based on virtual SCSI adapters. This required the cluster nodes to be located on the same Virtual Server 2005 host. A two-node virtual machine cluster could be useful in test environments using cluster-aware applications, but it was not a solution that could be deployed and supported in a production environment. In effect, the Virtual Server 2005 host represented a single point of failure, so the solution could not meet high-availability production requirements.

Virtual Server 2005 R2 removed the two-node and single-host virtual machine cluster limitations by adding support for the iSCSI protocol. Using iSCSI shared disks, multinode clusters can be created using virtual machines hosted on separate Virtual Server 2005 R2 hosts. This type of cluster is still recommended for virtual machines running cluster-aware applications.

Virtual Server 2005 R2 also introduced support for Virtual Server host clusters. Virtual Server 2005 R2 host clusters allow failing over individual or all virtual machine workloads to other Virtual Server 2005 R2 host cluster member nodes. For virtual machines running non–cluster aware applications, Virtual Server 2005 R2 host clusters are a basic building block for the implementation of high-availability solutions.

Virtual Server 2005 R2 SP1 includes all the clustering features found in Virtual Server 2005 R2. Once you have installed Virtual Server 2005 R2 SP1 on a host, you will have access to a whitepaper with detailed information concerning Virtual Server 2005 R2 host clusters. Previously provided as a download from the Microsoft Web site, the whitepaper is now packaged in the Virtual Server 2005 R2 SP1 distribution media. You can find the whitepaper in the %systemdrive%\Program Files\Microsoft Virtual Server\Host Clustering directory on your Virtual Server 2005 R2 SP1 host.

Implementing a Virtual Machine Cluster Using iSCSI

With Virtual Server 2005 R2 SP1, virtual machine clusters are now supported for production workloads when used in conjunction with iSCSI-based shared disk systems. Using iSCSI to deploy a cluster eliminates the need for the specialized hardware that was previously required to configure clustering. The requirements for an iSCSI-based solution are network adapters to connect the storage to the cluster nodes, and a storage unit that uses iSCSI. The iSCSI protocol defines the rules and processes for transmitting and receiving block storage data over TCP/IP networks. iSCSI-based implementations consist of an iSCSI initiator and an iSCSI target with an interconnecting network.

Virtual machine clusters implemented with iSCSI require each cluster node to be located on separate Virtual Server 2005 R2 hosts. Virtual machine clusters can range from two-node to eight-node active clusters. Physical distance between cluster nodes is restricted by the iSCSI protocol and the maximum latency that a cluster heartbeat signal can support.

Table 5-8 lists implementation requirements prior to creating a two-node virtual machine cluster based on an iSCSI storage device.

Table 5-8   Requirements for an ISCSI-Based Virtual Machine Cluster

Requirement	Description
Operating System	Windows Server 2003 R2 Enterprise Edition must be installed on each virtual machine cluster node.
Virtual Machine Additions	Virtual Machine Additions must be installed on each virtual machine node.
iSCSI Quorum and Shared Disks	iSCSI Quorum and Shared Disks targets must be created prior to configuring the cluster nodes. The Quorum disk must be at least 50 MB in size to satisfy Microsoft Cluster Server requirements.

Table 5-8   Requirements for an ISCSI-Based Virtual Machine Cluster

Requirement	Description
Network Adapters	Three network adapters must be added and configured for the Public, Private, and iSCSI networks on each virtual machine cluster node.
Virtual Networks	Virtual networks must be created for non-cluster traffic and iSCSI traffic (Public, Private, and iSCSI).
Active Directory	Virtual machine cluster nodes must be members of an Active Directory domain.
Cluster Service Account	A cluster service account must be created in Active Directory.

To deploy a two-node virtual machine cluster using iSCSI, you must perform the following major steps:

1.   Create a shared drive for quorum and data storage using the iSCSI Initiator.

2.   Configure virtual networks on each of the Virtual Server 2005 R2 hosts.

3.   Configure shared drives on each virtual machine cluster node.

4.   Install Microsoft Cluster Server on the first virtual machine cluster node and assign the shared drive.

5.   Install Microsoft Cluster Server on the second virtual machine cluster node, join it to the cluster, and assign the shared drive.

Note   The Microsoft iSCSI Initiator service is included in the Microsoft iSCSI Software Initiator package, which you can download from the Microsoft Web site at *http://go.microsoft.com /fwlink/?linkid=44352*.

Configuring the iSCSI Shared Disks

After you build your base virtual machines, you can configure the cluster shared disks. Follow these steps to configure virtual machine cluster node access to iSCSI shared disks:

1.   Install the Microsoft iSCSI Initiator software in the first virtual machine.

2.   Click Start, click All Programs, click Microsoft iSCSI Initiator, and then click Microsoft iSCSI Initiator again.

3.   Click the Discovery tab, and in Target Portals, click Add.

4.   Enter the name or IP address of the server where the target iSCSI drive is defined.

5.   Click the Targets tab to display a list of disk targets.

6.   Select Quorum and click Log On.

7. Select Automatically Restore This Connection When The System Boots And Enable Multipath, if you have multipath software installed.

8. Repeat steps 6 and 7 for the Shared target, and then click OK.

9. In the Disk Management MMC, format each disk with a single partition, using drive letter Q for the Quorum disk and drive letter S for the Shared disk.

10. Shut down the virtual machine.

11. Repeat steps 1 to 8 for the second virtual machine.

12. In the Disk Management MMC, set the Quorum drive letter to Q and the Shared drive letter to S.

Configuring Microsoft Cluster Server on the First Virtual Machine

When you create the first node in a cluster, you specify all parameters that define the cluster configuration. The Cluster Configuration Wizard guides you through the installation and completes the cluster setup when you have entered all the required information.

> **Caution** During the configuration of Microsoft Cluster Server on the first cluster node, you must power-off all other nodes. This is to avoid data corruption on the shared disks. Ensure that the first cluster node can successfully access all volumes before attempting to join additional cluster nodes.

Follow these steps to configure Microsoft Cluster Server on the first virtual machine cluster node:

1. Log in to the virtual machine with Domain Administrator credentials.

2. Click Start, click All Programs, click Administrative Tools, and then click Cluster Administrator.

3. When prompted with the Open Connection To Cluster dialog box, select Create New Cluster in the Action drop-down list.

4. Review the information list in the New Server Cluster Wizard, and then click Next.

5. In the Cluster Name text box, type a name for the cluster and then click Next.

6. In the Computer Name text box, type the computer name of the virtual machine that is the first node in the cluster.

7. Click Next.

8. Remedy any errors found in the Analyzing Configuration step, and then re-analyze. If there are no further errors, click Next.

9. In the IP Address text box, type an IP address on the public network that will be used to manage the cluster and click Next.

10. In the User Name text box, type the name of the cluster service account that you created in Active Directory.

11. In the Password text box, type the password for the cluster service account.

12. In Domain, select your domain name from the drop-down list and then click Next.

13. Review the Summary page to verify that all information used to create the cluster is correct.

14. Click Quorum, select Disk Q: from the drop-down list, and then click OK.

15. Click Next.

16. Once the cluster creation is complete, click Next.

17. Click Finish to complete the installation.

Configuring Microsoft Cluster Server on the Second Virtual Machine

Installing Microsoft Cluster Server on the second virtual machine is much quicker because the cluster configuration already exists. Additional cluster nodes are simply joined to the defined cluster.

When adding subsequent nodes, leave the first cluster node and all shared disks turned on, and power-up additional nodes. The cluster service will control access to the shared disks to eliminate any chance of corruption. Follow these steps to configure the second node (and any subsequent node) in the cluster:

1. Open Cluster Administrator on the first cluster node.

2. Click File, click New, and then click Node.

3. On the Add Cluster Computers Wizard Welcome page, click Next.

4. In the Computer Name text box, type the computer name for the second cluster node and then click Add.

5. Click Next.

6. Remedy any errors found in the Analyzing Configuration step, and then re-analyze. If there are no further errors, click Next.

7. Type the password for the cluster service account, and then click Next.

8. Review the summary information that is displayed for accuracy, and then click Next.

9. Review any warnings or errors encountered during cluster creation, and then click Next.

10. Click Finish to complete the installation.

To quickly verify that cluster failover is successful, you can shut down the first cluster node. When you open Cluster Administrator on the second cluster node, you will see that it now owns all cluster resources. Once you have tested that cluster failover is successful, you can proceed with the installation of the cluster-aware application.

Implementing a Virtual Server Host Cluster Using iSCSI

To achieve high availability for non–cluster aware applications running in virtual machines, you must implement a Virtual Server 2005 R2 host cluster. Virtual Server 2005 R2 host clusters can be deployed using SCSI, SAN, or iSCSI-based shared storage. Like virtual machine clusters, Virtual Server 2005 R2 host clusters can range from two-node to eight-node active clusters. It is important to understand that in this configuration, you are clustering the Virtual Server 2005 R2 hosts, not the applications running in the virtual machines. If one of the Virtual Server 2005 R2 host cluster nodes fails, virtual machines defined as resource groups in the cluster configuration are restarted on other Virtual Server 2005 R2 host cluster member nodes. In contrast, failure of an application running within a virtual machine will not result in a failover event.

> **Important** The complete set of hardware used to implement a Virtual Server Host cluster must be listed in the Windows Server Catalog as a qualified cluster solution for Windows Server 2003.

There are many scenarios to which you can apply a Virtual Server 2005 R2 host cluster solution. Table 5-9 lists the most common scenarios that benefit from a Virtual Server 2005 R2 host cluster implementation.

Table 5-9   Virtual Server Host Cluster Scenarios

Scenario	Virtual Server host cluster benefits
Host hardware scheduled maintenance	Prior to performing hardware maintenance on a Virtual Server cluster node, hosted virtual machines can move groups over to other nodes in the cluster with minimal impact on application availability.
Host software updates	Before applying potentially disruptive software updates to the host, hosted virtual machines can fail over to other nodes in the cluster with minimal impact on application availability.
Non–cluster aware applications	Non–cluster aware applications running in virtual machines on a Virtual Server 2005 R2 host cluster node are protected from unexpected downtime caused by a host failure. If the Virtual Server 2005 R2 host cluster node fails, the virtual machine can fail over to other nodes in the cluster with minimal impact on application availability.

Table 5-9   Virtual Server Host Cluster Scenarios

Scenario	Virtual Server host cluster benefits
Workload rebalancing	Virtual machine performance might dictate a need to rebalance the workload on a Virtual Server 2005 R2 host cluster node. If there is another cluster node with the required resources available, the virtual machine can be quickly failed over with minimal impact on application availability.

During an unplanned cluster failover event, there is always some short period of time during which the cluster-defined resources are unavailable as they are restarted on a different cluster node. Microsoft Cluster Server ensures that the applications experience minimal service disruptions. If an administrator performs a normal shutdown on a cluster node or moves a guest from one host to another for planned maintenance, Virtual Server 2005 R2 can save the virtual machine state before it is moved.

Because virtual machines running in Virtual Server 2005 R2 are not cluster-aware, Microsoft created a script that ensures that virtual machines function correctly during cluster failover events. Each virtual machine is configured as a cluster resource group. Inside each cluster resource group, the script is configured as a Generic Script resource that has the effect of turning a virtual machine into a cluster-aware-like application. The script can also restart a virtual machine when it stops running. Underlying this whole process is the Microsoft Cluster Server, which provides the health monitoring and automatic recovery for the virtual machine.

> **On the Companion Media**   On the companion media, you will find a directory called \Chapter Materials\Scripts\Cluster. Inside the directory there are two files: Stop_clussvc_script.cmd and Havm.vbs. These files are needed during the configuration of Virtual Server 2005 R2 host cluster nodes. A listing of the script is also included in the Virtual Server Host Clustering Step-by-Step Guide for Virtual Server 2005 R2," located at %systemdrive%\Program Files\Microsoft Virtual Server\Host Clustering.

Table 5-10 lists implementation requirements prior to creating a Virtual Server 2005 R2 host cluster based on iSCSI shared storage that is supported in a production environment.

Table 5-10   Requirements for iSCSI-Based Virtual Server Host Cluster

Requirement	Description
Physical Hardware	Creation of a Virtual Server 2005 R2 host cluster supported in production requires two or more identical physical servers that are listed in the Windows Server Catalog.

Table 5-10   Requirements for iSCSI-Based Virtual Server Host Cluster

Requirement	Description
Operating System	Windows Server 2003 Enterprise Edition (SP1 or R2).
	Windows Server 2003 Datacenter Edition (SP1 or R2).
iSCSI	Microsoft iSCSI Software Initiator 2.0 or later version.
iSCSI Quorum and Shared Disks	iSCSI Quorum and Shared Disks targets must be created prior to configuring the cluster nodes. The Quorum disk must be at least 50 MB to satisfy Microsoft Cluster Server requirements. The Shared disk must be sized to contain virtual machine VHD files.
Network Adapters	Three network adapters must be added and configured for the Public, Private, and iSCSI networks on each Virtual Server 2005 R2 host cluster node.
Active Directory	Virtual Server 2005 R2 host cluster nodes must be members of an Active Directory domain.
Cluster Service Account	A cluster service account must be created in Active Directory.
Virtual Machine Additions	Virtual Machine Additions must be installed on each virtual machine.
Support Files	Havm.vbs and Stop_clussvc_script.cmd, located on the companion media.

To deploy a two-node Virtual Server 2005 R2 host using iSCSI, you must perform the following major steps:

1. Create a shared drive for quorum and data storage using the iSCSI Initiator.

2. Configure Microsoft Cluster Server on each Virtual Server 2005 R2 host.

3. Configure both Havm.vbs and Stop_clussvc_script.cmd on each Virtual Server 2005 R2 host.

4. Configure a cluster disk resource, resource group, and resource script.

5. Configure a virtual machine on one of the Virtual Server 2005 R2 hosts.

Important   For a more detailed list of limitations and requirements, refer to the Virtual Server Host Clustering Step-by-Step Guide for Virtual Server 2005 R2 SP1.

Configuring the iSCSI Shared Disks

Follow these steps to configure virtual machine cluster node access to iSCSI shared disks:

1. Install the Microsoft iSCSI Initiator software on the first Virtual Server 2005 R2 host.

2. Click Start, click All Programs, click Microsoft iSCSI Initiator, and then click Microsoft iSCSI Initiator again.

3. Click the Discovery tab, and in Target Portals, click Add.

4. Enter the name or IP address of the server where the target iSCSI drive is defined.

5. Click the Targets tab to display a list of disk targets.

6. Select Quorum and click Log On.

7. Select Automatically Restore This Connection When The System Boots And Enable Multipath if you have multipath software installed.

8. Repeat steps 6 and 7 for the Shared target, and then click OK.

9. In the Disk Management MMC, format each disk with a single partition, using drive letter Q for the quorum disk and drive letter S for the Shared disk.

10. Shut down the Virtual Server 2005 R2 host.

11. Repeat steps 1 through 8 for the second Virtual Server 2005 R2 host.

12. In the Disk Management MMC, set the Quorum drive letter to Q and the Shared drive letter to S.

Configuring Microsoft Cluster Server on the First Virtual Server Host

Follow these steps to configure Microsoft Cluster Server on the first virtual server host:

1. Log in to the first Virtual Server 2005 R2 host with Domain Administrator credentials.

2. Click Start, click All Programs, click Administrative Tools, and then click Cluster Administrator.

3. When prompted with the Open Connection To Cluster dialog box, select Create New Cluster in the Action drop-down list.

4. Review the information list on the New Server Cluster Wizard Welcome page, and then click Next.

5. In the Cluster Name text box, type a name for the cluster and then click Next.

6. In the Computer Name text box, type the computer name of the virtual machine that is the first node in the cluster.

7. Click Next.

8. Remedy any errors found in the Analyzing Configuration step and then re-analyze. If there are no further errors, click Next.

9. In the IP Address text box, type an IP address on the public network that will be used to manage the cluster and click Next.

10. In the User Name text box, type the name of the cluster service account that you created in Active Directory.

11. In the Password text box, type the password for the cluster service account.

12. In Domain, select your domain name from the drop-down list and then click Next.

13. Review the Summary page to verify that all information used to create the cluster is correct.

14. Click Quorum, select Disk Q: from the drop-down list, and then click OK.

15. Click Next.

16. Once the cluster creation is complete, click Next.

17. Click Finish to complete the installation.

Configuring Microsoft Cluster Server on the Second Virtual Server Host

Installing Microsoft Cluster on the second Virtual Server 2005 R2 host is again a quick process because the cluster configuration already exists. Additional cluster nodes just have to be added to the existing cluster.

When adding subsequent nodes, leave the first cluster node and all shared disks turned on, and power-up additional nodes. The cluster service will control access to the shared disks to eliminate any chance of corruption. Follow these steps to configure the second node (and any subsequent node) in the cluster:

1. Open Cluster Administrator on the first cluster node.

2. Click File, click New, and then click Node.

3. On the Add Cluster Computers Wizard Welcome page, click Next.

4. In the Computer Name text box, type the computer name for the second cluster node and then click Add.

5. Click Next.

6. Remedy any errors found in the Analyzing Configuration step and then re-analyze. If there are no further errors, click Next.

7. Type the password for the cluster service account, and then click Next.

8. Review the summary information that is displayed for accuracy, and then click Next.

9. Review any warnings or errors encountered during cluster creation, and then click Next.

10. Click Finish to complete the installation.

Configuring the Shutdown Script for Virtual Server Host Cluster Nodes

Because Virtual Server 2005 R2 is not a cluster-aware application, you have to ensure that the cluster service shuts down and all virtual machines are failed over prior to a Virtual Server Host shutdown. Follow these steps to configure the shutdown script for the Virtual Server 2005 R2 host cluster nodes:

1. In the root directory of the local hard disk on each Virtual Server 2005 R2 host, copy the Stop_clussvc_script.cmd file from the companion media.

2. Click Start, click Run, and then type **gpedit.msc**.

3. Click Enter.

4. Navigate to Local Computer Policy, click Computer Configuration, click Windows Settings, and then click Scripts.

5. In the right-hand pane, double-click Shutdown, and click Add.

6. In the Script Name text box, type the fully qualified path name of the batch file, and then click OK twice.

Configuring the Disk Resource, Resource Group, and Havm.vbs Script

Follow these steps to configure the cluster disk resource, resource group, and cluster control script:

1. On the first Virtual Server 2005 R2 host, click Start, click Control Panel, click Administrative Tools, and then click Cluster Administrator.

2. In Cluster Administrator, create a new resource group and name it **Group0**. If you want to specify a Preferred Owner for the group, specify the node on which you want the guest to run most of the time.

3. In Cluster Administrator, create a new disk resource, or use the appropriate disk resource if it has already been created. Verify that it is the Shared disk configured as a Physical Disk Resource with no dependencies, assigned to resource group Group0, and both cluster nodes are listed as Possible Owners.

4. With Group0 online, create a folder on the Shared disk called **GuestVM1**.

5. On each Virtual Server 2005 R2 host cluster node, create a folder on the local disk in %systemroot%\Cluster and copy the Havm.vbs script into it from the companion media.

> **Important**   If you want to create and fail over multiple virtual machines independently, you have to configure each guest in its own resource group. If you want to fail over certain virtual machines together, you need to configure them in the same resource group.

Creating a Virtual Machine on the First Virtual Server Host

Follow these steps to configure the virtual network and virtual machine on the first Virtual Server 2005 R2 host cluster node:

1. Click Start, click All Programs, click Microsoft Virtual Server, and then click Virtual Server 2005 R2 Administration Website.

2. In the navigation pane, under Virtual Networks, click Create.

3. In the Virtual Network Name text box, type in a name for the cluster network.

4. In Network Adapter On Physical Computer, select the network adapter associated with the public network, and then click OK.

5. In the navigation pane, under Virtual Networks, click Configure, and then click View All.

6. In Virtual Networks, click on the virtual network you created, and then click Edit Configuration.

7. Copy the fully qualified path of the .vnc file.

8. Open Explorer, and paste the fully qualified path of the .vnc file (without the filename) into the address bar.

9. Right-click the cluster network name you just created, and then click Cut.

10. In Explorer, navigate to the GuestVM1 folder on the Shared disk and paste the .vnc file.

11. Open the Virtual Server 2005 R2 Administration Website.

12. In the navigation pane, under Virtual Networks, click Add.

13. In the Existing Configuration (.vnc) File text box, type the fully qualified path to the new .vnc file that you created in the Shared disk GuestVM1 folder and then click Add.

14. Copy an existing virtual machine into the Shared disk GuestVM1 folder.

15. In the navigation pane, under Virtual Machines, click Add.

16. In the Fully Qualified Path To File text box, type the fully qualified path to the virtual machine .vmc file and then click Add.

17. In the virtual machine Configuration pane, click Network Adapters.

18. In the Virtual Machine Network Adapter Properties pane, in the Connected To drop-down box, select the cluster network that you created and then click OK.

Completing the Virtual Machine Configuration on the Second Virtual Server Host

Follow these steps to complete the configuration of the virtual machine on the second Virtual Server 2005 R2 host:

1. On the second Virtual Server 2005 R2 host, click Start, click All Programs, click Administrative Tools, and then click Cluster Administrator.

2. Move Group0 to the second Virtual Server 2005 R2 host cluster node.

3. Open the Virtual Server 2005 R2 Administration Website.

4. In the navigation pane, under Virtual Networks, click Add.

5. In the Existing Configuration (.vnc) File text box, type the fully qualified path to the .vnc file located on the Shared disk in the GuestVM1 folder and then click Add.

6. In the navigation pane, under Virtual Machines, click Add.

7. In the Fully Qualified Path To File text box, type the fully qualified path to the virtual machine .vmc file and then click Add.

8. Open Cluster Administrator, and create a new script resource called **GuestVM1Script**.

9. Configure the resource as a Generic Script resource, assign it to Group0 with Possible Owners listing both cluster nodes, and add a Shared disk as a resource dependency.

10. In the Script Filepath text box, type **%windir%\Cluster\Havm.vbs**.

11. Click Start, and then click Run.

12. Type '**cluster res "Guest1Script" /priv VirtualMachineName=***GuestVM1*', replacing *GuestVM1* with the name of the virtual machine that you added, and then press Enter.

13. Open Cluster Administrator and bring Group0 online.

14. Open the Virtual Server 2005 R2 Administration Website.

15. Verify that the virtual machine is in the Running state.

You can now verify that the virtual machine fails over to the first Virtual Server 2005 R2 host cluster node. To do this, open the Cluster Administrator and choose the Move Group option for the Group0 resource group. You should see the Owner field change when the virtual machine has failed over.

Summary

There are many advanced features in Virtual Server 2005 R2 that you can leverage to optimize virtualization infrastructure deployments. If you are going to create complex testing, support desk, or user-training scenarios, use differencing disks and undo disks to enable quick provisioning of new virtual machine configurations with the ability to roll back to the baseline state. When you need to reduce the size of dynamically expanding disks, use defragmentation and precompaction prior to the VHD compaction tool to minimize the size of compacted virtual hard disks. Configure the Microsoft Loopback Adapter to create isolated network connections between a Virtual Server 2005 R2 host and its hosted virtual machines. For cluster-aware applications running within virtual machines, use a virtual machine cluster to minimize downtime from virtual machine failures. In the case of non–cluster aware applications, deploy high-availability Virtual Server 2005 R2 host clusters to reduce planned and unplanned downtime.

Additional Resources

The following resources contain additional information related to the topics in this chapter:

- Knowledge Base article 311272, "The DevCon command-line utility functions as an alternative to Device Manager," at *http://support.microsoft.com/kb/311272*

- White paper, "Virtual Hard Disk Image Format Specification," at *http://www.microsoft.com/windowsserversystem/virtualserver/techinfo/vhdspec.mspx*

- White paper, "Using iSCSI with Virtual Server 2005 R2," at *http://go.microsoft.com/fwlink/?LinkId=55646*

- White paper, "Virtual Server Host Clustering Step-by-Step Guide for Virtual Server 2005 R2," in %systemdrive%\Program Files\Microsoft Virtual Server\Host Clustering

Chapter 6
Security in Depth

In this chapter:

Securing Virtual Server 2005 R2 145

Securing Virtual Machine Access. 159

Securing Remote Administration Sessions. 164

Virtual Server Services Security 164

Virtual Server Network Ports 165

Summary 165

Additional Resources 166

This chapter describes the security features in Microsoft Virtual Server 2005 R2. You will learn how to secure Virtual Server 2005 R2 access; how to configure security settings and NTFS permissions to control virtual machine, virtual disk, and virtual network access; and how to enable the Secure Sockets Layer (SSL) protocol to protect Virtual Server 2005 R2 Administration Website and Virtual Machine Remote Client (VMRC) sessions.

Securing Virtual Server 2005 R2

In a default installation of Virtual Server 2005 R2, only members of the administrators group are granted rights to manage the Virtual Server configuration as well as create new virtual machines, virtual hard disks, and virtual networks. Additional permission entries must be specifically added to grant other users or groups permissions to access and manage Virtual Server resources. Until new permission entries are created, VMRC use is also restricted to members of the administrators group. New standard permission entries are configured through the Virtual Server Administration Website. To properly configure new Virtual Server 2005 R2 permission entries, it is crucial to understand the Virtual Server 2005 R2 components that must be protected to achieve a secure configuration. During the installation of Virtual Server 2005 R2, several folders are created on the file system, each of which contains critical application files. Table 6-1 contains a list of the folders, the location in which they are created during a default installation, and their contents. In point of fact, Virtual Server 2005 R2 access control is achieved by translating the permission entries created through the Virtual Server Administration Website into specific NTFS permissions applied on an appropriate subset of these files and folders. Therefore, you must thoroughly comprehend the folder and file permission settings that are modified for each permission entry setting, so that you can develop, implement, and manage a successful, robust security model for your Virtual Server infrastructure.

Table 6-1   Virtual Server 2005 R2 Application Folders

Folder	Description
Windows Server 2003, Windows XP %Systemdrive%\Program Files\Microsoft Virtual Server **Windows Vista** %Systemdrive%\Program Files\Microsoft Virtual Server	This is the primary Virtual Server 2005 R2 application folder that contains the following files: ■ Virtual Server service (Vssrvc.exe) and virtual machine helper executables (vhm.exe). ■ Virtual Server VSS writer (vswriter.dll). ■ Summary HTML file (summary.html) that is displayed at the end of installation. ■ Licensing file (License.rtf) that describes the Virtual Server 2005 R2 license agreement. It also contains the following folders: ■ Documentation Virtual Server help files, release notes, COM application programming interface (API) dynamic-link libraries (DLLs), and the header file. ■ Drivers Virtual network driver files. ■ Event Log Virtual Server event log DLL. ■ Host Clustering Host clustering whitepaper. ■ Vhdmount VHDMount executable, storage drivers, and COM API header file. ■ Virtual Machine Additions Virtual Machine Additions ISO image and virtual floppy images. ■ VMRC Client VMRC Windows client. ■ Website Administration Website application, VMRC ActiveX client, and associated files.

Table 6-1 Virtual Server 2005 R2 Application Folders

Folder	Description
Windows Server 2003, Windows XP %Systemdrive%\Documents and Settings\All Users\Application Data\Microsoft\Virtual Machine Helper **Windows Vista** %Systemdrive%\ProgramData\Microsoft\Virtual Machine Helper	This folder contains a single encrypted file named NETWORK SERVICE that stores information about user accounts and passwords associated with virtual machines.
Windows Server 2003, Windows XP %Systemdrive%\Documents and Settings\All Users\Application Data\Microsoft\Virtual Server **Windows Vista** %Systemdrive%\ProgramData\Microsoft\Virtual Server	This folder contains the following files: ■ Options.xml This XML file stores Virtual Server configuration settings. ■ VSLicense.xml This XML file contains the Virtual Server license parameters. It also contains the following folders: ■ Virtual Machines Includes a shortcut to every registered virtual machine configuration file. ■ Virtual Networks Includes a shortcut to every virtual network configuration file. ■ CrashLogs Log files named VSCrashLog*number*.txt that capture Virtual Server problem information.
Windows Server 2003, Windows XP %Systemdrive%\Documents and Settings\All Users\Application Data\Microsoft\Virtual Server Webapp **Windows Vista** %Systemdrive%\ProgramData\Microsoft\Virtual Server Webapp	This folder contains a single file named ServerPaths.xml that stores information about the Virtual Server Manager search paths.
Windows Server 2003, Windows XP %Systemdrive%\Documents and Settings\All Users\Documents\Shared Virtual Machines **Windows Vista** %Systemdrive%\Users\Public\Documents\Shared Virtual Machines	By default, this folder contains a subfolder created for each new virtual machine. Each subfolder contains the new virtual machine configuration file (.vmc), associated saved-state file (.vsv), virtual hard disk file (.vhd), and virtual floppy disk file (.vfd).

Table 6-1   Virtual Server 2005 R2 Application Folders

Folder	Description
Windows Server 2003, Windows XP %Systemdrive%\Documents and Settings \All Users\Documents\Shared Virtual Networks	By default, this folder contains the virtual network configuration files (.vnc) for each new virtual network.
Windows Vista %Systemdrive%\Users\Public\Public Documents\ Shared Virtual Networks	

As shown in Figure 6-1, the permission entry for the administrators group is listed in the Virtual Server Security Properties section of the Administration Website.

Figure 6-1   Administrators Permission Entry in Virtual Server Security Properties

> **Best Practices**   Although the Virtual Server Administration Website user interface (UI) does not allow you to remove the Administrators permission entry, you should not use the default local administrators group to assign Virtual Server resource permissions to new users. Instead, create new groups and use the well-documented group nesting model before creating new Virtual Server permission entries. For example, within a single domain, create a new global group (such as Virtual Server Admins – GG to designate a global group) and add the target users to the group. Then, create a domain local group (such as Virtual Server Local Admins – DLG to designate a domain local group) and nest the global group into it. Finally, use the domain local group when creating new Virtual Server permission entries.

The default permission entry displayed in Figure 6-1 shows that all available permission settings are assigned to the administrators group. Essentially, creating or changing a permission entry in Virtual Server Security Properties results in a modification of the discretionary access control list (DACL) for three primary Virtual Server folders:

- %systemdrive%\Documents and Settings\All Users\Application Data\Microsoft \Virtual Server

- %systemdrive%\Documents and Settings\All Users\Documents\Shared Virtual Machines

- %systemdrive%\Documents and Settings\All Users\Documents\Shared Virtual Networks

These are the folder paths for Microsoft Windows Server 2003 and Windows XP. Refer to Table 6-1 for the exact location of the folders in Windows Vista. Table 6-2 lists the NTFS permissions that are applied to the DACLs of the Virtual Server folders when each permission setting is enabled.

Caution   The %systemdrive%\Documents and Settings\All Users\Documents\Shared Virtual Machines represents the default virtual machine configuration folder that was set during Virtual Server 2005 R2 installation. You should modify the location of this folder to avoid storing virtual machine files on your system drive. This will prevent the host operating system from possibly crashing because of growing virtual machine files filling up the system drive. The folder location can be changed by specifying a new path for the default virtual machine configuration folder entry in Virtual Server search paths.

Table 6-2   **Virtual Server Security Permissions**

Permission	Corresponding NTFS permissions
Full	Selecting this permission automatically selects all other permissions and assigns the following NTFS settings to the targeted user or group: ■ Traverse Folder/Execute File ■ List Folder/Read Data ■ Read Attributes ■ Read Extended Attributes ■ Create Files/Write Data ■ Create Folders/Append Data ■ Write Attributes ■ Write Extended Attributes ■ Delete ■ Read Permissions ■ Change Permissions ■ Take Ownership

Table 6-2   Virtual Server Security Permissions

Permission	Corresponding NTFS permissions
Modify	Selecting this permission assigns the following NTFS settings to the targeted user or group: ■ Create Files/Write Data ■ Create Folders/Append Data ■ Write Attributes ■ Write Extended Attributes ■ Read Permissions
View	Selecting this permission assigns the following NTFS settings to the targeted user or group: ■ List Folder/Read Data ■ Read Attributes ■ Read Extended Attributes ■ Read Permissions
Remove	Selecting this permission assigns the following NTFS settings to the targeted user or group: ■ Delete ■ Read Permissions
Change	Selecting this permission assigns the following NTFS settings to the targeted user or group: ■ Read Permissions ■ Change Permissions ■ Take Ownership
Control	Selecting this permission assigns the following NTFS settings to the targeted user or group: ■ Traverse Folder/Execute File ■ Read Permissions
Special Permissions	This is only an indicator that special permissions have been granted to the user or group defined in the permission entry. It cannot be selected or deselected.

Note   You can find more information on permission settings for files and folders at *http://www.microsoft.com/resources/documentation/windows/xp/all/proddocs/en-us /acl_special_permissions.mspx*.

Although you can directly modify the DACL of the Virtual Server folder to assign permissions, you should not pursue this strategy because subsequent changes made through the Virtual Server Administration Website will result in the replacement of DACL settings.

Warning   Do not attempt to directly modify a DACL unless you thoroughly understand the security model and need to configure a very specific permissions set. Instead, modify permissions through the Virtual Server Security Properties to avoid misconfiguring Virtual Server resources. Incorrectly setting permissions on Virtual Server or virtual machine folders and files can result in allowing users access to reconfigure Virtual Server settings, compromise virtual machines, virtual hard disks, and virtual network resources, and change virtual machine state resulting in applications going offline.

In addition, when the Virtual Server folder DACL is directly modified, the Virtual Server service (Vssrvc.exe) must be restarted before the new settings take effect. This step is not required if you make the modifications using the Administration Website Virtual Server Security Properties.

Note   You can use net stop "virtual server" and net start "virtual server" (with the quotes) at a command line to start and stop the Virtual Server Service.

You should also be aware that direct DACL modifications might not be reflected in the Virtual Server Security Properties permission entry. In other words, the Special Permissions setting is not necessarily enabled to indicate that the current Virtual Server folder DACL represents customized NTFS security settings.

Best Practices   As stated earlier, create and assign permissions to groups rather than individual users. More specifically, create groups that correspond to basic roles that exist in your organization, and define the permissions that will be required to perform the role. Place the individuals that will perform the role in a global group and nest the global group in a Domain Local Group. When you add a new permission entry through the Virtual Server Security Properties in the Virtual Server Administration Website, assign the role permissions to the Domain Local Group.

The next several sections describe common Virtual Server management roles in conjunction with the Virtual Server permissions and NTFS settings required to enable specific resource access rights. To implement one or more of these roles in your environment, define a group that corresponds to the role, add the appropriate individuals as members of the group, and assign the recommended permissions and security settings to the group. In organizations where there is a very strict separation of duties, the roles represented by the individual groups are populated with various teams and individuals. In organizations with multifunction teams, teams or individuals can be easily granted multiple roles by being assigned to more than one of the defined groups.

Direct from the Source: Administration Website Properties

The Administration Website Properties allow you to configure settings that control the Web page refresh rate, the number of virtual machines displayed in the Master Status view and the information columns that are visible, the number and types of recent events displayed in the Master Status view, the number of events displayed on an event viewer page, and the VMRC color depth.

The configuration changes made to these properties are stored in a cookie that is associated with the user browser session. The cookie is stored on the local computer hosting the browser session. A separate cookie is also created for each individual Virtual Server Administration Website.

The Virtual Server manager search paths, which define the instances of Virtual Server managed from the Administration Website, are also configurable through the Administration Website Properties. However, these settings are stored on the computer where the Administration Website is running, and all authorized users are affected by changes made to it.

Ben Armstrong
Program Manager, Windows Virtualization

Configuring a Virtual Server View Only Role

One of the common roles that you might want to implement in your Virtual Server environment is one that provides basic access to examine Virtual Server configuration settings without allowing any modification rights. For example, you might have a team responsible for monitoring Virtual Server or virtual machine performance and settings. Table 6-3 lists the permission settings that must be enabled and the access rights granted for this role.

Table 6-3   Virtual Server View Only Role

Permission settings	Access rights
View, Control	Selecting these permissions enables the following access rights for the targeted user or group: ■ View Administration Website ■ View virtual machine status ■ View recent events ■ View registered virtual machine configurations* ■ View virtual network configurations ■ View Virtual Server properties ■ View and set most Administration Website properties ■ View resource allocations ■ View event viewer entries ■ Use the VMRC client or ActiveX control to remotely connect to a running virtual machine. ■ Access the Component Object Model (COM) API

* If virtual machine files are stored in locations other than the default configuration folder, you have to manually add NTFS permissions that allow access to the folder hierarchy and virtual machine configuration file (.vmc). Refer to Table 6-2 to determine the NTFS permissions that are applied to the default folder when selecting the View and Control permissions, apply them to the required virtual machine folders, and ensure that the permissions are inherited by subfolders and files.

You can further restrict the role and remove access rights to view virtual machines in the Master Status view, virtual machine configuration details, and virtual network configuration details. This is achieved by removing the group entry from the NTFS security settings for the default virtual machine configuration folder and Shared Virtual Network folder, as well as for any other virtual machine folders defined in the Virtual Server search paths.

> **Note**   At first glance, you might question why removing the Traverse Folder/Execute File permission from the virtual machine folders listed in the Virtual Server search paths does not achieve the desired goal of disallowing viewing virtual machine and virtual network details in the Virtual Server Administration Website. Basically, a default group policy exists that applies the Bypass Traverse Checking user right to the Everyone group, allowing traversal of folders even if the Traverse Folder/Execute File permission is not directly granted. The reasons for giving this right to all users and the consequences if it is removed are documented in Knowledge Base article 823659, which is found at *http://support.microsoft.com/kb/823659*.

Configuring a Virtual Server Security Manager Role

Another role that you might be required to provide is the ability to only view and modify Virtual Server security settings. Table 6-4 lists the permission settings that must be enabled and the access rights granted for this role. For example, you might have a team responsible for auditing application security and enforcing compliance based on the organization's security policy.

Table 6-4   Virtual Server Security Manager Role

Permission settings	Access rights
Change Permissions, Control	Selecting these permissions enables the following access rights for the targeted user or group:
	■ View Administration Website
	■ View and modify Virtual Server Security Properties
	■ View and set most Administration Website properties
	■ View Physical Computer Properties
	■ Access the COM API

A user that is assigned the Virtual Server Security Manager role could elevate her rights by creating a new permission entry for her account and selecting the Full permission setting. Therefore, it is critical to implement strict audit policies and perform regular audit log reviews of Virtual Server events listed in Table A-5 of Appendix A, to assist in the detection of any abuse of privilege.

Planning   Prior to deployment of your Virtual Server infrastructure, you should extend your current audit strategy to include the collection, analysis, and reporting of Virtual Server security-related events. If you are in the planning stage and developing an audit strategy, you can use any third-party auditing tool or Microsoft System Center Operations Manager 2007 Audit Collection Services (ACS). ACS collects, consolidates, and generates reports on Windows security log data in real-time. You can learn more about this tool at *http://download.microsoft.com /download/E/E/7/EE797D69-02B2-420D-B0F2-196906CCE063 /Whitepaper-Audit_Collection_with_System_Center_Operations_Manager_2007_final.pdf.*

Configuring a Virtual Machine Manager Role

The Virtual Machine Manager role provides the ability to create, add, and modify virtual machines and virtual hard disks. Virtual machines can also be removed from the Virtual Server. In addition, this role provides the ability to view, but not manage, virtual networks. Table 6-5 lists the permission settings that must be enabled and the access rights granted for this role. For example, this role might be implemented in a test lab or production staging environment, where a specific team needs to maintain, create, and provision virtual machines prior to release for an integrated test scenario or production deployment.

Table 6-5   Virtual Machine Manager Role

Permission settings	Access rights
Modify, View, Remove, Control	Selecting these permissions enables the following access rights for the targeted user or group: ■ View Administration Website ■ View and modify virtual machine status ■ Create, add, and configure virtual machines ■ Remove virtual machines ■ Create and inspect virtual hard disks ■ View and add virtual networks ■ View and set most Administration Website properties ■ View and modify resource allocations ■ View event viewer entries ■ Use the VMRC client or ActiveX control to remotely connect to a running virtual machine. ■ Access the COM API

The NTFS settings of the default virtual network folders, Options.xml, and virtual machine folders not located in the default folder must be manually modified to restrict the access rights for this role. Table 6-6 contains the list of specific NTFS settings to change. Because DACLs in the Virtual Server folder hierarchy require modification, remember to restart the Virtual Server service after making the changes.

Table 6-6   Virtual Machine Manager Role NTFS Settings Changes

File/Folder	NTFS settings
Options.xml (in Virtual Server folder) Virtual Networks (in Virtual Server folder) Shared Virtual Networks	Deny the following permission settings for the targeted user or group: ■ Create Files/Write Data ■ Create Folders/Append Data ■ Write Attributes ■ Write Extended Attributes ■ Delete *Use of Deny entries preserves permission inheritance.*

Table 6-6   Virtual Machine Manager Role NTFS Settings Changes

File/Folder	NTFS settings
Virtual Machine folders (outside the default virtual machine configuration folder hierarchy)	Allow the following permission settings for the targeted user or group: ■ Traverse Folder/Execute File ■ List Folder/Read Data ■ Read Attributes ■ Read Extended Attributes ■ Create Files/Write Data ■ Create Folders/Append Data ■ Write Attributes ■ Write Extended Attributes ■ Read Permissions ■ Delete

> **Warning**   If you plan to assign multiple roles to a group of users, you should thoroughly review the permission settings for each role to determine whether any Deny permission setting will override an Allow permission in another role. If this is the case, you might need to define a custom role.

Configuring a Virtual Network Manager Role

The Virtual Network Manager role provides the ability to create, add, and modify virtual networks. Virtual networks can also be removed from the Virtual Server. This role does not provide the ability to view or manage virtual machines. Table 6-7 lists the permission settings that must be enabled and the access rights granted for this role. For example, this role might be implemented when a team wants to maintain a strict virtual network structure.

Table 6-7   Virtual Network Manager Role

Permission settings	Access rights
Modify, View, Remove, Control	Selecting these permissions enables the following access rights for the targeted user or group: ■ View Administration Website ■ Create, add, and configure virtual networks ■ View and set most Administration Website properties ■ View event viewer entries ■ Use the VMRC client or ActiveX control to remotely connect to a running virtual machine. ■ Access the COM API

The NTFS settings of the default virtual machines folders, Options.xml, and virtual machine folders not located in the default folder must be manually modified to restrict the access rights for this role. Table 6-8 contains the list of specific NTFS settings to change.

Table 6-8   Virtual Network Manager Role NTFS Settings Changes

File/Folder	NTFS settings
Options.xml (in Virtual Server folder)	Deny the following permission settings for the targeted user or group: ■ Create Files/Write Data ■ Create Folders/Append Data ■ Write Attributes ■ Write Extended Attributes ■ Delete *Use of Deny entries preserves permission inheritance.*
Virtual Machines (in Virtual Server folder) Shared Virtual Machines (or the current default virtual machine configuration folder specified in the Virtual Server search paths)	Deny the following permission settings for the targeted user or group: ■ List Folder/Read Data ■ Create Files/Write Data ■ Create Folders/Append Data ■ Write Attributes ■ Write Extended Attributes ■ Delete *Use of Deny entries preserves permission inheritance.*
Virtual Machine folders (outside the default virtual machine configuration folder hierarchy)	No changes are needed.

Configuring a Virtual Server Manager Role

The Virtual Server Manager role provides the ability to manage all aspects of the Virtual Server configuration with the exception of security settings. Creation and management of virtual machines, virtual networks, and virtual hard disks are also included in this role. Table 6-9 lists the permission settings that must be enabled and the access rights granted for this role. For example, this role might be implemented within a team that has one or more users with wide responsibilities for management of a Virtual Server infrastructure.

Table 6-9   Virtual Server Manager Role

Permission settings	Access rights
Modify, View, Remove, Control	Selecting these permissions enables the following access rights for the targeted user or group: ■ View Administration Website ■ View and modify virtual machine status ■ View recent events ■ Create, add, and configure registered virtual machines ■ Remove virtual machines ■ Create and inspect virtual disks ■ Create, add, and configure virtual networks ■ Remove virtual networks ■ View and modify Virtual Server properties (except security settings) ■ View and modify Administration Website properties ■ View and modify resource allocations ■ View event viewer entries ■ Use the VMRC client or ActiveX control to remotely connect to a running virtual machine ■ Access the COM API

The Virtual Server Manager role differs from a role given Full control by not including the ability to modify Virtual Server security properties. As described in the "Configuring a Virtual Server Security Manager Role" section, that privilege is granted as a result of enabling the change permissions entry for the targeted group.

Configuring a VMRC Client Role

The VMRC client allows you to remotely connect to a virtual machine to which you have appropriate rights. Unlike the Administration Website, the VMRC client does not display or provide the ability to perform Virtual Server administrative tasks, such as changing Virtual Server properties or creating and modifying virtual machine configurations.

The VMRC client is a single executable that is installed during the Virtual Server 2005 R2 setup process. Because it is a standalone tool, it can be installed on any client workstation with a user that requires the ability and privileges to remotely view, connect, log in, and administer a running virtual machine. Table 6-10 lists the permission settings that must be enabled and the access rights granted for this role.

Table 6-10 VMRC Client Role

Permission settings	Access rights
View	Selecting these permissions enables the targeted user or group to connect remotely to running virtual machines using the VMRC client.

This configuration will allow remote connection only to a running virtual machine. To provide the ability to turn on an inactive virtual machine using VMRC, NTFS write permissions (Create Files/Write Data, Create Folders/Append Data, Write Attributes, and Write Extended Attributes) must be added to the DACL of the default virtual machine configuration folder and other virtual machine folders for the targeted user or group. Virtual machines cannot be started unless read, execute, and write access is provided to the configuration file (.vmc) and virtual hard disk (.vhd) files. This role can be assigned to any user or group that needs to manage the guest operating system or applications running in a virtual machine.

Securing Virtual Machine Access

As described in Table 6-1, Virtual Server 2005 R2 creates a Shared Virtual Machines folder as the default location where virtual machine files (.vmc, .vhd, .vsv, and .vud) are stored. When a new virtual machine is created, a corresponding folder is generated in the Shared Virtual Machines folder hierarchy and the virtual machine files are placed in it. However, virtual machine files do not have to be stored in the default location. In most enterprise environments, architecture and performance requirements commonly drive virtual machine folders to be located on one or more centrally managed storage systems or file servers.

Virtual machine files that are not located in the Shared Virtual Machines folder hierarchy cannot be secured directly through Virtual Server security properties. Instead, each virtual machine folder hierarchy must be secured by direct application of NTFS permissions based on organizational needs. For instance, in a typical production environment, there is likely a requirement to accommodate multiple scenarios, including administration of core business workloads by a central administrator group, line of business workloads by departmental or business groups, and test and development workloads by project teams or individual team members.

Configuring Centrally Managed Virtual Machine Security

Several critical business workloads are commonly managed by a central administration team. Workloads that usually fall in this category are core infrastructure services such as Active Directory, Domain Name Service (DNS), and Dynamic Host Configuration Protocol (DHCP).

Enterprise-wide applications, such as Microsoft Exchange Server, are another category of workloads that are often centrally managed. Figure 6-2 depicts how to organize and manage permissions on a virtual machine folder hierarchy in a scenario where there is a centralized administration team (which can be composed of subteams) with responsibilities to manage core workloads.

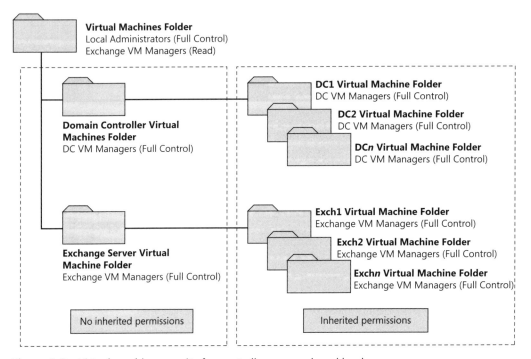

Figure 6-2 Virtual machine security for centrally managed workloads

In this model, workload folders are created to contain individual virtual machine folders. NTFS permissions applied to the workload and virtual machine folders are strictly configured to restrict access to the virtual machine manager group responsible for it. Furthermore, permission inheritance is implemented only at the virtual machine folder level.

Important In highly secure or regulated environments, virtual machine files for distinct core workloads might need to be isolated on servers and storage with very tightly controlled access rights.

Configuring Organizationally Managed Virtual Machine Security

In most environments, many line of business workloads are managed using a decentralized administration model. These workloads are typically administered at a departmental, business unit, or other organizationally based level. In this scenario, it is crucial to apply the appropriate permissions to the virtual machine folders on shared storage and ensure that only the appropriate administrative team is assigned access rights. Figure 6-3 depicts how you can organize and manage permissions for a folder hierarchy in an environment where one or more virtual machines are departmentally managed.

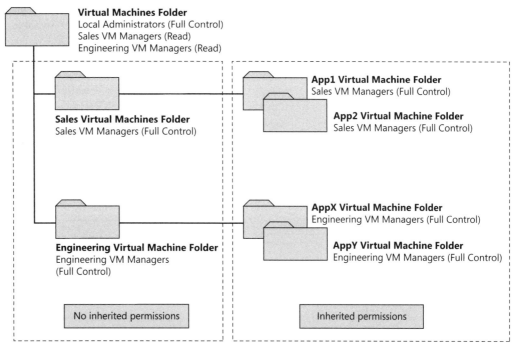

Figure 6-3   Virtual machine security for departmentally managed workloads

In this model, departmental folders are created to contain individual virtual machine folders. NTFS permissions applied to the departmental and virtual machine folders are strictly config-ured to restrict access to the departmental virtual machine manager group. Again, permission inheritance is implemented only at the virtual machine folder level.

Configuring Project-Managed Virtual Machine Security

In test and development environments, usually multiple, concurrent projects are in progress. Each project has a defined team, and individual responsibilities are assigned to team members. In this scenario, both project-level and individual-level virtual machines are needed throughout the project life cycle. Here again, it is crucial to apply the appropriate permissions to virtual machine folders on shared storage and ensure that only the appropriate team or individual is assigned access rights to specific virtual machines. Figure 6-4 depicts how you can organize and manage permissions for a folder hierarchy in a test and development environment.

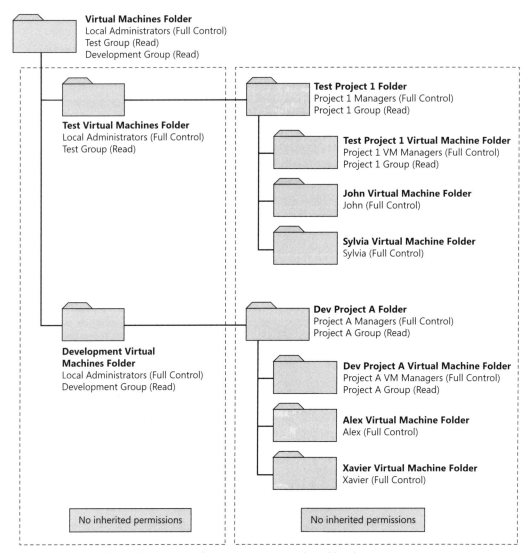

Figure 6-4   Virtual machine security for project-managed workloads

In this model, high-level test and development group folders are defined that contain individual project subfolders. Within each of the project subfolders, discrete virtual machine folders are created and access is restricted to each team member. There is also a project-level virtual machine folder that can be accessed by individual team members to refresh their environment, but it can be modified only by the project virtual machine managers groups. Inherited permissions are not enabled in this folder hierarchy.

Enabling Constrained Delegation

If you deploy one or more Virtual Server 2005 R2 servers in an Active Directory environment with access to virtual machine files on a remote file server, or implement a central Virtual Server Administration Website, you must configure constrained delegation. Constrained delegation allows the Administration Website to pass authentication credentials through the Virtual Server to the remote file server to access hosted virtual machine files. Constrained delegation is compatible only with integrated Windows authentication. It will not work if basic authentication is configured for the Administration Website. Chapter 4, "Installing Virtual Server 2005 R2 SP1," contains step-by-step instructions to implement constrained delegation in an Active Directory environment.

Configuring a Virtual Machine User Account

To automatically start a virtual machine after the Virtual Server service restarts, you must configure the virtual machine to run under the context of a specific user account. This option is configured in the virtual machine configuration General Properties section as shown in Figure 6-5.

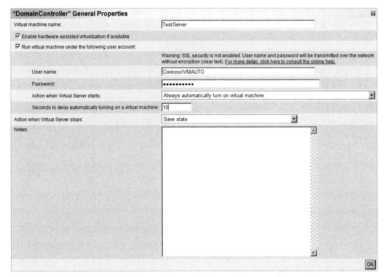

Figure 6-5   Virtual machine General Properties configuration

When configuring this option, assign a domain user account. Once defined, you can configure one or more virtual machines to run in the context of that user account. This user account is also used to execute scripts assigned to the virtual machine. Table 6-11 lists the NTFS permissions to assign to the virtual machine and virtual network folders to allow the user account to execute the virtual machine.

Table 6-11   Virtual Machine Account Minimum Permissions

File	Required permissions
Virtual machine folder	Read and Execute
	List Folder Contents
	Read
	Write
Virtual network configuration folder	Read and Execute
	List Folder Contents
	Read

Important   You should manage the user account similarly to service accounts defined in your environment, taking special notice that when the user account password changes, you will have to update the user account settings for each virtual machine that runs in the context of that account. For information on managing service accounts, download the "Services and Service Accounts Security Planning Guide" at *http://go.microsoft.com/fwlink/?LinkId=41312*.

Securing Remote Administration Sessions

By default, communications to the Administration Website and virtual machines sessions using the VMRC client are non-encrypted Hypertext Transfer Protocol (HTTP) traffic. To encrypt these data streams, you can configure the Administration Website and VMRC client to use the Secure Sockets Layer (SSL) protocol. To configure SSL for the Administration Website, use the standard Internet Information Services (IIS) management tool and configuration process. The VMRC client SSL configuration is accomplished through the VMRC Server Properties on the Administration Website.

Virtual Server Services Security

Virtual Server 2005 R2 services run under the context of system accounts with the lowest possible privilege level. The main Virtual Server service (Vssrvc.exe) runs under the Network Service account (NT AUTHORITY\Network Service). The Network Service account has limited access to local computer resources and uses the computer account for authenticated access to network resources. The Virtual Machine Helper service (Vmh.exe) runs under the Local Service account (NT AUTHORITY\Local Service).

> **Warning** You should not change the system account settings for the Virtual Server service and Virtual Machine Helper service.

Virtual Server Network Ports

During the installation of Virtual Server, the installer attempts to configure firewall exceptions if the host machine uses Windows Firewall. If a different firewall product is used, these firewall exceptions must be configured manually:

- TCP Port 135, which is used for Remote Procedure Call (RPC)

- TCP Port 1024, which is the default port for the Virtual Server Administration Website application (VSWebapp.exe) in Windows Server 2003

- Virtual Server service (Vssrvc.exe)

The default port for the VMRC server, TCP 5900, is opened as a result of the exception configured for the Virtual Server service. In addition, the VMRC client uses TCP ports 137 and 138 when Kerberos authentication is enabled for VMRC.

If you change the default ports for the Virtual Server Administration Website application and VMRC server, use these ports to configure firewall exceptions. For Windows Vista, TCP Port 80 is used for the Virtual Server Administration Website application. If you plan to install Virtual Server 2005 R2 on Windows XP SP2, you may need to manually add the TCP Port 80 exception for the Virtual Server Administration Website application.

> **More Info** If you plan to run remote scripts using the Virtual Server COM API, you also have to open ports for Distributed COM (DCOM). In a default configuration, DCOM uses a random port above 1024. However, DCOM can be restricted to use a defined range of ports, as documented in *http://msdn2.microsoft.com/en-us/library/ms809327.aspx*.

Summary

To properly secure access to Virtual Server 2005 R2 resources, it is critical to understand the application components that need protection. You should set and modify permissions to Virtual Server resources through the Virtual Server Security Properties, if possible. In all cases, identify the management roles needed in your environment, create corresponding security groups, and place the appropriate members in the groups. Virtual Machine folder hierarchies should be clearly defined and secured based on the virtual machine management requirements in your environment. Enable SSL to encrypt the Administration Website and VMRC data streams, and restrict sensitive data from being transmitted in the clear. The Virtual Server service (Vssrvc.exe) and Virtual Machine Helper service (Vmh.exe) run under the context of the system account with very limited rights.

Additional Resources

The following resources contain additional information related to the topics in this chapter:

- Virtual Server help file, vs.chm, in %systemdrive%\Program Files\Microsoft Virtual Server \Documentation

- Microsoft Technet, "Configuring SSL on a Web Server or Web Site (IIS 6.0)," at *http://www.microsoft.com/technet/prodtechnol/WindowsServer2003/Library/IIS /56bdf977-14f8-4867-9c51-34c346d48b04.mspx?mfr=true*

Chapter 7

Best Practices for Configuration and Performance Tuning

In this chapter:

Configuring the Administration Website. 167

How to Obtain the Best Host Performance 173

Optimizing Hard Disk Performance 179

Optimizing Network Performance 183

Optimizing Virtual Machine Performance. 184

Operational Considerations 189

Summary. 193

Additional Resources. 194

This chapter provides recommendations and best practices to configure a Microsoft Virtual Server 2005 Release 2 (R2) Service Pack 1 (SP1) host and virtual machines to optimize performance. The chapter covers Virtual Server 2005 R2 SP1 Administration Website configuration, host and virtual machine performance tuning, and operational considerations. Performance tuning modifications are included for processor, memory, display graphics, hard disk, and networking components.

Configuring the Administration Website

The Virtual Server 2005 R2 SP1 default Administration Website configuration is designed for generic deployments. Additional tuning is required to provide an optimized experience for managing hosts and virtual machines. This section reviews configuration options for Virtual Server 2005 R2 SP1 search paths, default configuration folder location, and remote control.

Configuring Search Paths

The Virtual Server Administration Website is the primary interface to manage the configuration of virtual machines, virtual hard disks, and virtual networks on any Virtual Server host in your network. As a browser-based tool, it offers flexibility and a few limitations. When creating a new virtual machine, for example, you can enter a fully qualified path to an existing virtual hard disk or create a new virtual hard disk and provide the fully qualified path to the location to store the .vhd file. Unfortunately, the Virtual Server Administration Website does not provide the ability to browse the file system to select the fully qualified path. Therefore, before you enter a path to a file, you will probably identify and copy the fully qualified path in Explorer, paste it into the input box, and add the name of the file that you want to read or write to.

To simplify this process, the Virtual Server 2005 R2 Administration Website provides a way to specify search paths that will be parsed and cached for display. The Administration Website applies filters based on the action that you are performing, and it displays only the relevant files in the appropriate drop-down boxes. Figure 7-1 shows the Search Paths configuration screen.

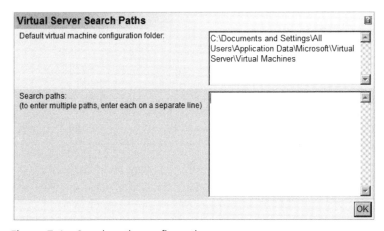

Figure 7-1   Search paths configuration screen

For example, if you are attempting to select a CD-ROM ISO image file to attach to a running virtual machine, the only ISO files that are presented are the ones copied during Virtual Server installation. By default, these are displayed because the directory is automatically added to the search paths list at installation time.

 Best Practices   Create a directory on the Virtual Server host to store all the files that are commonly used by virtual machines (ISO, VFD, and so on). You should use subdirectories to organize the different types of files and simplify selection.

 Best Practices   Add all directories in which you store virtual machine files to the Virtual Server Search Paths. Once this is configured, files in the specified directories will automatically be parsed and displayed in any drop-down list on the Web site. This allows you to select a file rather than typing the fully qualified path.

Modifying the Search Paths Configuration

To configure the search paths options on your server, follow these steps:

1. Determine the paths that you would like to add to the Administration Website.

2. Open the Virtual Server 2005 R2 Administration Website.

3. In Virtual Server, click Server Properties.

4. Click Search Paths to open the Search Paths configuration page, as shown in Figure 7-1.

5. Type the search paths (one per line) as full path statements, as shown in the following example:

```
C:\ISOs
D:\Virtual Machines
```

6. Click OK to save the search paths entered.

Configuring the Default Virtual Machine Configuration Folder

The virtual machine configuration folder defines the default storage location for any new virtual machine. Table 7-1 lists the default location for the virtual machine configuration folder for various operating systems.

Table 7-1 Virtual Machine Configuration Folder Defaults

Operating system	Default location
Microsoft Windows XP and Windows Server 2003	C:\Document and Settings\All Users\Application Data\Microsoft \Virtual Server\Virtual Machines
Windows Vista	C:\Users\Public\Documents\Shared Virtual Machines

If you create new virtual machines and specify only the name of the virtual machine instead of a full path to the configuration file (.vmc), Virtual Server 2005 R2 creates a subdirectory using the name of the virtual machine and stores the .vmc file at that location. Virtual Server 2005 R2 stores the save state file (.vsv) and any undo disk files (.vud) in the same directory as the .vmc file. Because the default folder location is on the system volume, it has the potential to cause disk space issues that can significantly affect Virtual Server 2005 R2 performance.

Best Practices   Modify the default virtual machine configuration folder location to store virtual machines on a volume other than the system volume. When you change this path, the folder access control is reset to the security configuration specified in the Virtual Server 2005 R2 Administration Website.

Modifying the Default Virtual Machine Configuration Folder

To modify the default folder for virtual machines, follow these steps:

1. Determine the path that you would like to use as the new virtual machine default folder.

2. Open the Virtual Server 2005 R2 Administration Website.

3. On the left navigation menu, click Server Properties.

4. Click Search Paths. You will see the Search Paths configuration screen shown in Figure 7-1.

5. In the Default Virtual Machine Configuration Folder text box, type the new default folder location as full path statements, as shown in the following example:

   ```
   D:\Shared Virtual Machines\
   ```

6. Click OK to save the settings.

Direct from the Source: Beware of Automatic ACL Changes

When you change the default virtual machine configuration folder to a new location, or when you add or remove an entry in the Virtual Server 2005 R2 Security Settings, the default virtual machine configuration folder specified and all subdirectories will have the access control lists (ACLs) reset to the current security configuration of the Virtual Server site. You will not receive a warning that this is going to occur.

The ACLs of the default virtual machine configuration folder root are completely replaced, and the subdirectories are reset in an overlay mode. If there is a group with ACLs defined on a subdirectory of the default virtual machine configuration folder and that group is being used in a security setting in Virtual Server, that ACL entry will be overwritten with the ACL settings defined in the Virtual Server 2005 R2 security setting.

Joseph Conway
Support Escalation Engineer, Virtualization

Enabling Virtual Machine Remote Control

Microsoft Virtual Machine Remote Control (VMRC) is disabled by default when you install Virtual Server 2005 R2. This ensures that the default installation of Virtual Server has a reduced remote attack surface. To remotely manage a virtual machine from a power-on state, you need to enable VMRC. VMRC allows access to all virtual machines on the Virtual Server 2005 R2 host based on access permissions. Unless you provide the name of a specific virtual machine, an administrative screen will be displayed containing thumbnail snapshots of all the virtual machines' current video buffers.

When you enable VMRC, there are a series of options that you can configure, as shown in Table 7-2.

Table 7-2   VMRC Configuration Options

Option	Description
TCP/IP address	TCP/IP address that VMRC uses for communications.
TCP/IP Port	TCP port number that VMRC uses for communications. The default port number is 5900.
Default Screen Resolution	Screen resolution that the VMRC client uses when establishing a remote session with a virtual machine.
Authentication	Authentication Protocol that is used for authenticating access to the VMRC client: Automatic, NTLM, or Kerberos.
Disconnect idle connections	Amount of time in minutes that the VMRC server waits with no activity before disconnecting the VMRC client session.
Multiple VMRC Connections	Enables the ability for a VMRC client session to allow more than one user to connect to a virtual machine.
SSL 3.0/TLS 1.0 encryption	Enables or disables the use of Secure Sockets Layer (SSL) or Transport Layer Security (TLS) encryption for the VMRC sessions.
SSL 3.0/TLS 1.0 certificate	Required information to configure the certificate used for establishing the encrypted VMRC session.

There are two interfaces to the VMRC protocol: an ActiveX control and a Windows client. The ActiveX control is the interface presented by the Virtual Server 2005 R2 Administration Website. The Windows VMRC Client is accessible from the Virtual Server program menu option. The configuration options in Table 7-2 affect both VMRC interfaces. You should consider each of the best practices in the following sections to modify the configuration of your Virtual Server 2005 R2 installations.

Enabling VMRC

To enable VMRC after installing Virtual Server 2005 R2 to allow remote management of virtual machines, follow these steps:

1. Open Virtual Server 2005 R2 SP1 Administration Website in an Internet Explorer browser window.

2. On the Virtual Server menu, click Server Properties.

3. In the Properties window, click Virtual Machine Remote Control (VMRC) Server.

4. To enable VMRC on this server, select the Enable check box as shown in Figure 7-2.

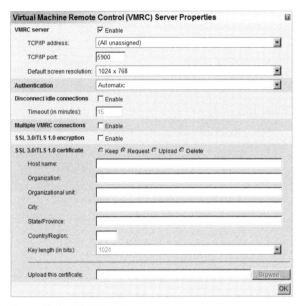

Figure 7-2   VMRC options screen

5. Optionally, disable idle connections by selecting the Enable check box in the Disconnect Idle Connections section.

6. Optionally, enable multiple VMRC connections by selecting the Enable check box in the Multiple VMRC Connections section.

7. Click OK.

Best Practices   Configure VMRC to listen only on a specific TCP/IP address if the host has multiple network adapters. This ensures that all VMRC traffic goes only across a single network card and a single TCP/IP address. This configuration makes it easier to troubleshoot any issues with VMRC.

Best Practices   Change the default port for VMRC. Changing the default port provides additional protection to the VMRC service against denial of service attacks or other security threats. Changing the default port forces you to specify the port number as part of the query string in the VMRC client.

Best Practices   Configure the authentication setting of VMRC to Kerberos to ensure that only Active Directory domain member servers can remotely manage the Virtual Server 2005 R2 host. This configuration provides an additional layer of security from remote systems that are not members of the Active Directory domain. Enabling this feature requires contacting a domain using Kerberos to authenticate the remote user session.

Best Practices Only enable multiple VMRC connections when you need the ability for multiple people to connect to a virtual machine concurrently. Scenarios might include debugging, training, or installation support purposes.

Best Practices Enable and configure SSL/TLS to protect the Internet Information Services (IIS) and VMRC network traffic when you enable basic authentication. By default, the Administration Website pages are not encrypted during transfer. When Windows authentication is used, user IDs and passwords are encrypted. Refer to Chapter 6, "Security in Depth," for more information on securing Virtual Server and configuring SSL/TLS.

How to Obtain the Best Host Performance

Configuring your Virtual Server host to obtain the best performance requires focusing on five key configuration areas: processor, memory, display graphics, disk subsystem, and network adapters. Using the fastest hardware components available is a good beginning, but how you combine them to obtain the optimum configuration is not always obvious. In this section, you will learn more about the five key configuration areas and best practices to obtain the optimum performance for your Virtual Server 2005 R2 host.

Maximizing Processor Performance

Virtual Server 2005 R2 is a multithreaded application that performs best on servers containing multiple processors. Processors today are single core or multiple core and come with or without virtualization hardware assistance—such as Intel Virtualization Technology (Intel VT) and AMD Virtualization (AMD-V). They can also have hyperthreaded logical processors.

Because the number of simultaneous threads is directly related to the number of processor cores that are available to execute them, the best host configuration is one that has multiple cores. To maximize the number of processors available and minimize the footprint of the server that you are using, purchasing servers with the latest quad-core processors will provide you with the best price-to-performance solution.

Virtual Server 2005 R2 SP1 now supports the processors from Intel and AMD with hardware virtualization support: Intel VT and AMD-V. Hardware virtualization-assisted processors relieve Virtual Server 2005 R2 SP1 from performing some virtualization operations in software, thereby providing performance gains. Virtual Server 2005 R2 SP1 uses virtual machine additions to tune the performance of supported Windows and Linux operating systems. Most performance gains from the current series of hardware virtualization-assisted processors are obtained when the virtual machine additions have not yet been loaded, mainly during virtual machine boot and operating system installation.

Buying servers that have hyperthreaded processor cores will provide you nominal performance improvement. Hyperthreaded processors are logical and operate well in low workload conditions, using available physical cycles to process more instructions. As the load on the physical processor cores increase, the hyperthreaded processors become starved for processor cycles, and performance of threads and processes depending on a hyperthreaded processor can be significantly affected. To ensure that a thread of execution for a virtual machine does not experience this degradation, Virtual Server does not schedule any Virtual Server threads of execution on hyperthreaded processors.

Best Practices   Purchase servers with multicore Intel VT or AMD-V processors as Virtual Server 2005 R2 SP1 hosts. Quad-core systems should be the minimal multicore processor configuration. Although it's not required, you should consider disabling hyperthreading on the cores in a Virtual Server host to remove them from operating system management and monitoring cycles. If you do not do this, any workload analysis tool that determines the maximum available and utilized processing power will incorrectly include hyperthreaded processors and invalidate the calculations.

Maximizing Memory Performance

Available memory is a critical requirement in a Virtual Server 2005 R2 environment because Virtual Server uses only physical RAM to load and run virtual machines. Properly planning the memory requirements and configuration of a Virtual Server can have positive performance results for a virtual machine.

Understanding Memory Types

Most motherboards can use different types of memory, depending on the processor and chipset in use. Memory choices typically involve a tradeoff between speed and capacity. By choosing the faster memory chips, you typically reduce the maximum capacity of memory available in the system. This difference can be significant and as large as a 75-percent reduction in memory capacity. For example, the same motherboard might be able to install 128 GB of 266-MHz PC2700 memory, 64 GB of 333-MHz PC2700 memory, or only 32 GB of 400-MHz PC3200 RAM. Using the fastest RAM will dramatically reduce the amount of total RAM available and the number of virtual machines that your host can support. You should always verify the configuration with your hardware vendor to be assured that you are using the correct configuration settings.

Best Practices   Determining the best practice configuration for memory in a Virtual Server 2005 R2 host is really driven by the goals of the system. If the goal is to obtain the fastest memory performance possible on the Virtual Server host, use the fastest memory available. If the goal is to obtain the best performance possible but run the maximum number of virtual machines on the host as possible, use the memory that gives you the highest capacity and attempts to compensate with other components, such as faster processors or a faster speed disk subsystem.

Understanding Memory Configuration

Memory chip performance is not the only consideration when evaluating the performance of virtual machines. Virtual machines that have too little memory allocated to them suffer from excessive amounts of memory paging to disk. Disk access is typically measured in milliseconds (10^{-3} seconds), while memory access is measured in nanoseconds (10^{-9} seconds). That makes memory access 1 million times faster than disk systems in retrieving data. Because disk access in a virtual environment has additional overhead, the actual impact on performance is even higher. Reducing the amount of memory paging to disk will increase the performance of the virtual machines.

Operating systems inside virtual machines require no less memory than on their physical counterparts. Virtual machines incur memory overhead for interfaces to the Virtual Machine Monitor (VMM), video buffer, keyboard buffer, and mouse buffer, whereas purely physical environments do not. Memory overhead varies but typical values are 32 MB of additional space over the standard memory assigned.

Physical servers are typically purchased based on a standard configuration. In the case of memory, many physical servers were purchased with more memory than the workloads required. When virtualizing the servers, it is a good time to reevaluate the actual physical server memory requirements.

Best Practices   Once you have determined the actual memory required for the physical server, you should use a scaling factor when planning the amount of memory that you allocate to a virtual machine. A good value is 1.25 times the memory that you would have allocated to a purely physical machine with the additional 32 MB for overhead. This increased allocation will provide more memory for the virtual machine, increase the number of applications that can be loaded in the virtual machine's RAM, and reduce the amount of paging to disk. The formula is as follows: Virtual Machine required memory = 32 MB + (1.25 × original physical server RAM in MB).

Understanding Non-Uniform Memory Access

Another memory consideration involves the architecture of the processor and motherboard. Non-Uniform Memory Access (NUMA) is an architectural feature of modern multiprocessor platforms. NUMA architecture combines the processor, I/O bus, and memory into a "node" that is tuned for performance. These nodes are interconnected by a high-speed bus system. The processor has faster access, with lower latency and greater bandwidth to the memory contained within the node. When the server needs to access memory on another node using the system interconnect, the performance will be affected by increased latency and reduced bandwidth. Proper configuration of a NUMA-based machine allows for maximizing local memory access while minimizing memory access using the system interconnect. An improperly configured NUMA-based server can suffer from significant performance issues.

Configuration of a NUMA architecture server requires understanding the memory requests of the virtual machines that will be running in the system. To properly configure the memory on a NUMA system, you need to evenly distribute the memory assigned to each processor. This gives each processor the same size of local cache and minimizes the memory requests between nodes. Figuring out how much memory to put in the system depends on a combination of factors, including the largest memory block a virtual machine requires, the number of processors in the system, and the size of the memory sticks that the system will accept.

If you have a virtual machine that is assigned 3.6 GB of memory, you need to ensure that you have at least 4 GB of memory installed on each processor node in the NUMA system so that the virtual machine thread running on a processor will be able to have all of its memory loaded in the local node. If you have 4 processor nodes, the minimum amount of memory you should be placing in the server is 16 GB, or 4 GB per node.

Direct from the Source: NUMA Ratio

NUMA vendors have established a NUMA ratio value that describes the amount of time it takes for a node to access "remote" memory, or memory that is assigned to another node, versus its own "local" memory. Generally, performance is not affected if the NUMA ratio is between 1.0 and 1.5. Once the ratio is 3.0 or greater, performance will degrade.

On NUMA systems that have one or more nodes without memory assigned, you will find Event IDs 1100 and 1101 in the application event log when the Virtual Server service starts. These events will be logged when a NUMA configuration is not set up properly. You will also see these errors on multicore systems where memory allocation to additional cores is not defined in the Static Resource Affinity Table (SRAT) but is handled instead at the BIOS level. Please check with your hardware vendors regarding their specific NUMA configurations to understand how to properly configure the memory.

Rob Hefner
Microsoft Services Support Engineer, Virtualization

Best Practices   Determine the largest block of memory that will be requested on the NUMA system, and then purchase at least that much memory per processor. Because a virtual machine can be configured with a maximum of 3.6 GB of RAM, the minimum amount of memory per processor should be 4 GB of RAM. You should evenly distribute the memory to each processor to maximize local node use of memory and reduce the number of memory calls to another node.

Increasing Display Graphics Performance

Display graphics performance has two primary areas: the performance on the host, and the performance of the virtual machines. Increasing graphics performance on the host provides a better user experience when interacting at the console of the Virtual Server 2005 R2 host. Increasing graphics performance of virtual machines provides a better user experience when interacting with the Virtual Machine Remote Control (VMRC) console application.

Increasing the display graphics performance involves adjusting the display configuration and the visual effects configuration of the hosts and virtual machines. Windows display adapter drivers have an advanced setting that controls the level of hardware acceleration that is being used. The value ranges from No hardware acceleration to Full hardware acceleration. Most Windows Server installations do not automatically set the acceleration level to Full, preventing the maximum performance for the display subsystem.

Best Practices   Enable Full hardware acceleration on the Virtual Server host and every virtual machine to obtain the best display adapter performance. In rare instances, increasing the hardware acceleration level will decrease performance. In these instances, an older display graphics driver that requires an update to the latest version is usually the source of the problem.

Adjusting the Display Hardware Acceleration

To adjust the display hardware acceleration, follow these steps:

1. On Windows XP and Windows Server 2003, right-click the desktop and select Properties.

   On Windows Vista, right-click the desktop, select Personalize, and then select Display Settings.

2. Click the Settings tab, and then click the Advanced button.

3. Click the Troubleshoot tab and you will see a Hardware Acceleration slider bar dialog box as shown in Figure 7-3.

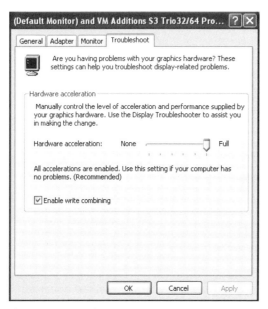

Figure 7-3   Hardware acceleration slider bar

4. Move the slider to the right side where it says Full, and click OK.

Increasing VMRC Performance

VMRC allows you to remotely connect to the Virtual Server host and view the screens of virtual machines to which you have access. The Virtual Server service (Vssrvc.exe) contains the VMRC server-side interface that communicates with the VMRC client-side component. The default port that the VMRC service listens on is TCP port 5900.

The VMRC interface does not use the on-board display graphics adapter to generate virtual machine screens. All VMRC operations are performed purely in software. Therefore, one way to increase the graphics performance of VMRC sessions is to use faster processors and network adapters in the host.

You can also improve the performance across the network by enabling the option to use reduced colors. Enabling reduced colors can be accomplished two ways: enabling the option from the Virtual Server Administration Website, or enabling the option from the VMRC Windows client. When enabled from the Administration Website, all VMRC sessions to the Virtual Server configured to use reduced colors are affected. When enabled from the VMRC client, only the active server connection is affected.

Enabling Reduced Colors from the Administration Website

To enable reduced colors for all VMRC sessions to a Virtual Server host, follow these steps:

1. Open the Administration Website on the desired Virtual Server host.

2. Select Website Properties from the left menu.

3. In the Virtual Machine Remote Control Properties section, select the Use Reduce Colors check box and then click OK.

Enabling Reduced Colors from the VMRC Windows Client

To enable reduced colors for a specific VMRC session to a Virtual Server host, follow these steps:

1. Click the Start button, select Programs, select Microsoft Virtual Server, and click Virtual Machine Remote Control Client.

2. Select the Reduce Colors check box as shown in Figure 7-4.

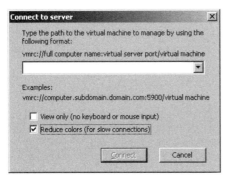

Figure 7-4   VMRC dialog box

3. Type the name of the Virtual Server to manage in the Path box, and click Connect.

Best Practices   Enable reduced colors in the VMRC client interface when connecting to a Virtual Server host across a slow wide area network (WAN) connection. Enable reduced colors on the Web properties of a Virtual Server host if all administration will be performed over a slow WAN connection.

Optimizing Hard Disk Performance

Virtual Server host scalability is heavily dependent on the disk subsystem. As you add more virtual machines to a host, the disk I/O workload increases. A single virtual machine performing heavy disk I/O can adversely affect the performance of other running virtual machines. In addition, applications that are running on the Virtual Server 2005 R2 host can affect disk performance.

Evaluating Virtual Server Host Applications that Are Affecting Disk Performance

Applications that can affect a Virtual Server host disk performance should be eliminated or reconfigured to minimize the effects on disk performance. Antivirus software is an example of a common application that is installed on Virtual Server hosts. Antivirus software is typically implemented as a disk filter driver that intercepts all calls for read access and writes to the hard disk and that scans the information for viruses before allowing the operation to complete. Antivirus software typically targets executables and other file types that can present a threat to the host operating system.

Virtual Server services and associated file extensions are not excluded by default from most antivirus applications. Most antivirus applications allow you to exclude file extensions or processes from virus scans. If you exclude the file extension, it excludes any application that might be reading and writing to those files, which might include a virus or Trojan horse. However, if you exclude processes, any other application that attempts to open the files would be scanned and the potential for catching a virus or Trojan horse is much higher.

> **Best Practices**   You should configure the antivirus application to exclude file extensions or processes. Using the process exclusion method rather than the file exclusion method is recommended because it provides better protection. When configuring the antivirus software to exclude the Virtual Server processes, you should exclude the Virtual Server service (Vssrvc.exe) and the Virtual Machine Helper service (Vmh.exe).
>
> If your antivirus application does not support excluding processes, you should add .vhd, .vmc, .vud, .vfd, .vsv, and .vnc file extensions to your antivirus file exclusion list so that they are not scanned.

Understanding Disk Hardware Performance

Obtaining the best disk performance for your virtual machines requires the use of high-speed disks and spreading the disk I/O load over as many spindles as possible. The speed of the disk is directly related to how fast data can be read from and written to the disk. Hard drives typically come in speeds of 4200, 5400, 7200, 10,000, and 15,000 revolutions per minute (RPM). The most common drive speed today is the 7200-RPM drive.

Hard disk platters are arranged in concentric circles called *tracks*. Each track is divided into sectors that look like smaller arcs. As the platter spins, the read/write head is positioned over the track where sectors are located. The faster the platter spins, the faster the read/write head can access the sector, increasing throughput.

> **Best Practices**   You should use 10,000-RPM or faster drives in the Virtual Server host to minimize the data read/write times for virtual machines. Using a 10,000-RPM drive rather than a 7200-RPM drive significantly increases the number of read and write operations performed per minute.

Understanding How Disk Types Affect Performance

Disk speed is only one part of the equation. The type of drive is also very important. Drive types available today include Parallel-ATA, Serial-ATA, Serial Attached SCSI (SAS), and SCSI. All drive types have different performance specifications, and most even have different grades of drives, with higher throughput capabilities as the grades and prices increase. Table 7-3 shows a comparison of the performance ratings of standard SATA, SAS, and SCSI drives currently available.

Table 7-3 **Drive Performance Comparison**

Drive type	Throughput	Queuing
SATA	2.4 gigabits/second per drive	NCQ
SAS	6 gigabits/second per drive	TCQ
SCSI	2.5 gigabits/second per shared bus	none

Drives also operate using different protocols. Parallel Advanced Technology Attachment (PATA) drives must complete a read or write request before they will perform the next read or write in the queue. Serial Advanced Technology Attachment (SATA), Small Computer System Interface (SCSI), and Serial Attached SCSI (SAS) drives can queue multiple requests and make intelligent decisions about which sequence the operations should be performed in. The latest SATA drives use a method called Native Command Queuing (NCQ), while SCSI and SAS drives use a similar method called Tagged Command Queuing (TCQ). Both methods are designed to increase performance by allowing an individual hard disk to queue more than one I/O request at a time and dynamically modify the order in which the operations are performed.

Figure 7-5 shows the comparison of two disk operations accessing different tracks with and without command queuing. Without command queuing, the read/write head has to perform the operations in the order they were submitted into the queue. It might have to bypass the track that the second operation needs in order to access the track for the first operation. Then it would have to complete additional revolutions and head movement to perform the second operation, decreasing efficiency. With command queuing, operations can be optimized to perform the second operation and then the first operation. This flexibility reduces disk latency.

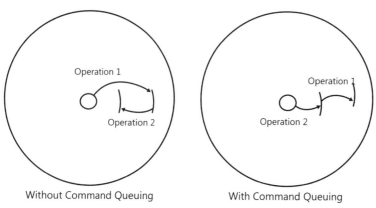

Without Command Queuing   With Command Queuing

Figure 7-5   Command queuing comparison

> **Best Practices**   You should use the SATA or SAS drive type in the Virtual Server 2005 R2
> host to obtain the benefits of command queuing. Although 10,000-RPM or faster drives are
> recommended, the exact drive type and speed will be driven by your available budget and,
> potentially, the original equipment manufacturer (OEM) contracts or standards that are in
> place.

Understanding Disk Drive Configuration

Designing a disk drive configuration that provides the best performance is dependent on the workload and the number of virtual machines that will be running on the Virtual Server 2005 R2 host. Running one virtual machine on a single dedicated spindle will provide good performance. As the number of virtual machines increases, so will the disk activity, and a single drive will no longer be able to provide acceptable read/write performance. Creating a disk array is the best way to spread the disk I/O load across multiple spindles. Redundant Array of Inexpensive Disks (RAID) level 10 is the fastest redundant disk subsystem in regular use today. RAID 10 is achieved by creating a mirrored set (RAID 1) of striped disks (RAID 0).

Storage area networks (SANs) are disk systems that have high-speed connections to drive arrays. SANs have software interfaces that allow the disk space to be combined into logical unit numbers (LUNs) and quickly reconfigured. Host bus adapters (HBAs) provide the high-speed connection between the host and the disk array. Most HBAs use fiber-optic cable connections called fiber channel.

Internet SCSI (iSCSI) is a network protocol that allows data transfer using the SCSI protocol over TCP/IP networks. iSCSI requires only an Ethernet network adapter to operate. iSCSI does not require expensive HBAs or storage protocols such as Fibre Channel, and it does not require SCSI disks to be used on the target system. This allows iSCSI to provide inexpensive access to centralize storage.

iSCSI uses a client/server metaphor for communication The iSCSI client is called an *initiator*, and the iSCSI server is called a *target*. An iSCSI initiator is a client device that connects to an iSCSI target, providing block-level access to its disk storage. One limitation of an iSCSI initiator/target system is that only one iSCSI initiator can talk to a specific iSCSI target at a time.

> **Best Practices**   You should consider a SAN that provides the redundancy of RAID 10 configurations, iSCSI target capability, and the ability to use high RPM queued I/O hard drives. Selecting one that supports SATA and SAS hard drives in the same enclosure will provide you with the most flexibility. When creating the RAID 10 disk array, you should use as many spindles as feasible to distribute the I/O load.

Optimizing Network Performance

Virtual Server shares the host's physical network adapters with virtual machines. Networking performance of the host and the virtual machines is affected by the number of virtual machines sharing an adapter, the speed of the adapter, and the adapter configuration settings. This section describes common issues involved with configuring networking on the physical and virtual machines and best practice–based solutions.

Understanding Virtual Networks and Adapters

The Virtual Machine Network Services (VMNS) driver provides the interface between the virtual networks and the physical network adapters in the host. VMNS redirects packets to the correct virtual network and attached virtual machine network adapter. Virtual networks can be bound only to a single physical network adapter at a time. One or more virtual machines are assigned to a virtual network, and the combined network traffic of the assigned virtual machines is transmitted over the single physical network adapter. Sharing a physical network adapter with multiple virtual machines can affect network performance. Installing multiple network adapters in the Virtual Server host allows you to distribute the virtual networks load and performance effects across physical interfaces.

The virtual machine emulated network adapter was selected for universal driver availability in multiple operating system releases from multiple vendors. However, this choice of network adapter reduced the available advanced features found in more recent adapters such as the following features:

- TCP/IP offloading features (checksum, segmentation, and so on)
- Jumbo frame support
- Flow Control
- Teaming
- Quality of Service (QoS) offloading

Leaving these features enabled on the physical network adapter that will be used for virtual machine traffic can potentially cause data corruption, traffic loss, and reduced throughput.

> **Best Practices**   You should dedicate a network adapter for host traffic on every Virtual Server host. This arrangement prevents the virtual machine traffic from affecting Virtual Server management tasks. This is accomplished by unbinding the VMNS driver from the physical network adapters that will be the dedicated host network adapter.

> **Best Practices**   You should dedicate network adapters for virtual machine traffic on every Virtual Server host. This arrangement prevents the Virtual Server management traffic from affecting the virtual machine traffic. This is accomplished by unbinding all services, protocols (including TCP/IP), and drivers listed in the network properties dialog box except for the VMNS driver.

> **Best Practices**   You should disable hardware acceleration features of the host physical network adapter for all virtual machine dedicated network adapters. The virtual machine emulated network adapter does not provide support for these advanced features, and leaving them on will decrease performance and potentially cause data corruption.

Optimizing Virtual Machine Performance

Virtual machine performance can be affected by different variables, including the performance of the host, the configuration options for the operating system, the type and configuration of the selected virtual hardware in the virtual machine, and how resources are allocated to the virtual machine. This section reviews these component issues and the best-practice solutions for minimizing their effects.

Virtual Machine Additions

Virtual machine additions are features that improve the performance and integration of virtual machines by installing a series of drivers in the virtual machine. Driver updates are included for the mouse, keyboard, video, and SCSI systems. However, virtual machine additions are available only for a certain subset of Windows and Linux operating systems. They are installed in the virtual machine after the Windows or Linux operating system is installed. After additions have been installed, new integration features are enabled.

> **Best Practices**   You should install the virtual machine additions as soon as possible after the operating system has been installed. This approach allows you to take advantage of the performance improvements and integration features while you are finishing the configuration of the virtual machine.

Best Practices   You should update the virtual machine additions on any pre-existing virtual machines or when you migrate virtual machines from Virtual PC to Virtual Server. By updating the additions to the latest version, you ensure the best performance and the latest additions features. You should use the latest additions version available for Virtual PC or Virtual Server.

Understanding Processor Resource Allocation

Virtual Server manages processor allocation to virtual machines through the CPU resource allocation settings accessible from the Virtual Server 2005 R2 Administration Website. CPU resource allocation configuration provides three settings options: relative weight, reserved capacity, and maximum capacity. Table 7-4 defines the three resource allocation settings and the allowed ranges of the values.

Table 7-4   Resource Allocation Settings

Allocation setting	Description	Range
Relative weight	Relative values assigned to virtual machines that define the amount of processing power a virtual machines receives. A virtual machine with a high relative weight obtains more processing power than a virtual machine with a low relative weight.	1-10,000
Reserved Capacity	Reserved capacity is the percentage of a logical processor that Virtual Server will guarantee is available for a virtual machine. The maximum percentage is 100.	0-100
Maximum Capacity	Maximum capacity is the percentage of a logical processor that Virtual Server will not allow a virtual machine to exceed.	0-100

By default, all virtual machines have a relative weight of 100 and a maximum logical processor capacity set to 100 percent so that the resource requirements of each virtual machine are equal and none is given preference over another.

Understanding the Resource Allocation Management Page

The resource allocation page of a Virtual Server 2005 R2 host with two processor cores is shown in Figure 7-6. For each virtual machine, the page displays the processor resource allocation settings, the system-level processor resource allocation, and a processor utilization history graph.

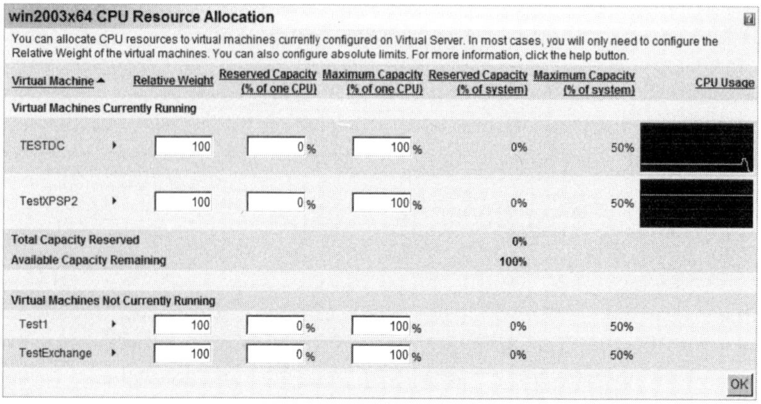

Figure 7-6 Processor Resource Allocation management page

Resource allocation has two aspects: the values that you can set on the virtual machines for relative weight, maximum capacity, and reserved capacity; and the available capacity of the host when you attempt to turn on a virtual machine. It is possible to set the reserved capacity for every virtual machine to 100 percent. Although it seems that you can oversubscribe the capacity of the processing power of the host, processor resource allocation manages the available capacity automatically for you. As you start a virtual machine that has reserved capacity set, the amount of available capacity on the system is reduced. When you attempt to start a virtual machine that has a reserved capacity allocation that is larger than the available capacity left on the system, Virtual Server will return an error and not power on the virtual machine.

The reserved and maximum capacity is calculated based on the number of processors in the host. In Figure 7-6, the host has two processors, so the maximum capacity of the system that can be allocated to a single virtual machine is 50 percent. This value is calculated by taking 100 percent and dividing it by the number of processors. But when you actually set the value for reserved capacity of the virtual machine, you are setting a percentage of the logical processor that you want to reserve. So if you want to reserve an entire logical processor for a virtual machine, you enter 100 percent for the setting, and the system will calculate the amount of system capacity that will be allocated from the available pool of capacity when you turn on the virtual machine—in this case, that would be 50 percent of the system capacity. If you set the reserved capacity of a virtual machine to 50 percent, the reserved capacity of the system would display as 25 percent, or 50 percent of the maximum value for a processor.

Resource allocation should always be part of the planning process for the placement of virtual machine workloads on a Virtual Server host. You should also revisit the current allocation on a host on a regular basis to ensure that the addition or removal of virtual machines on the host has not upset the balance of the system. Once you modify the default resource allocation approach for a host, you risk starving virtual machines for processing power. You should consider the best practices listed in this section to configure the processor resource allocation of your Virtual Server 2005 R2 host.

> **Best Practices**   You should use a tiered approach to configure processor resource alloca-
> tion settings. Unless you are going to manage the resource allocation settings and modify
> them regularly, you should maintain the default configuration. If you have a host with virtual
> machines for which you want to guarantee a certain amount of processing power, you should
> use the reserved capacity allocation approach for those machines. Typically, you do this for a
> machine that has dependencies to provide services to other physical or virtual machines, such
> as a domain controller, or for machines that you know will have high performance require-
> ments, such as an SQL server. If you have a host for which you want to maintain equal process-
> ing power but you know the virtual machines do not provide critical services, you should use
> the maximum capacity allocation to limit the effect they will have on the other virtual
> machines in the system.

Understanding Virtual Machine Graphics Performance

Graphics performance inside a virtual machine is dependent on the emulated graphics card.
Some advanced features that are easily handled by a hardware graphics adapter can cause
screen repainting issues in a virtual machine and cause the virtual machine screen refreshes
to be slow. This effect is most noticeable on a Windows client operating system such as
Windows XP or Windows Vista, where the visual experience uses advanced graphics features
such as shadowing.

To obtain the best repaint and refresh user experience in virtual machines, you have to tune
the virtual machine user interface to provide best performance instead of best user experience. By default, the user interface experience is managed by the Windows operating system.
You can modify the default and adjust for best performance.

> **Best Practices**   You should adjust the Windows visual interface settings to use a "best per-
> formance" setting instead of letting Windows adjust the settings to achieve the best user expe-
> rience. This is required on the Virtual Server 2005 R2 host as well as every virtual machine.

Configuring the Windows User Interface for Best Performance

To adjust the default Windows user interface to obtain the best performance, follow these
steps:

1. Click the Start button, select Control Panel, and choose System.

2. Click the Advanced tab and then the Performance button. The Performance Options
    dialog box will be displayed as shown in Figure 7-7.

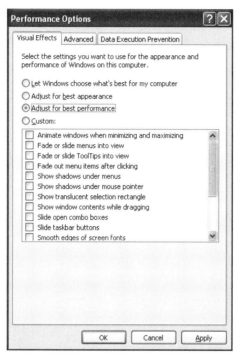

Figure 7-7   Visual effects Performance Options dialog box

3. Select the Adjust For Best Performance option.

4. Click OK.

Virtual Hard Disk Performance

Virtual hard disks are stored on the physical disk as single files with a .vhd extension. The initial size of the VHD file is dependent on the type of virtual hard disk selected. You can use a fixed-size virtual hard disk or a dynamically expanding virtual hard disk. When you create a fixed-size virtual hard disk, the entire size of the drive is allocated on the physical disk as a single file. For example, if you elect to create a 10-GB hard disk, Virtual Server 2005 R2 will create a 10-GB file on the host's drive and internally structure it like a physical hard disk. It creates a master boot record and a file table, and it stores data in virtual tracks and sectors. Initial creation of a fixed-size virtual hard disk takes longer, but once the disk space allocation is complete, the file size is not modified again. A dynamically expanding virtual hard disk has the same internal structure as a fixed-size virtual hard disk, but when it is created it does not preallocate all the disk space in the file. As you write to a dynamically expanding disk and more space is needed, it allocates 2-MB chunks of space to extend the VHD file size to the maximum size of the VHD.

Fixed-size VHD files are less prone to be fragmented when created and do not have the overhead of allocation of space on the fly. Dynamically expanding disks allow you to use physical disk space as you go instead of pre-allocating space that is not being used. Proper disk space management is required if you elect to use dynamically expanding disks. Virtual Server does not prevent you from oversubscribing the disk space on the physical server when creating a dynamically expanding VHD. Proper planning is also required when provisioning fixed-sized virtual hard disks across the network because of the amount of data that needs to be transferred.

Virtual hard disks can also be connected to two different types of adapters in a virtual machine. The type of adapter you connect defines the size limits and virtual hard disk performance. Virtual machines provide both Integrated Drive Electronics (IDE) and SCSI adapters. Virtual hard disks attached to an IDE adapter can be a maximum of 127 GB, and virtual hard disks attached to a SCSI adapter can be up to 2 TB in size.

Virtual Server 2005 R2 IDE and SCSI virtual adapters have the same characteristics as physical adapters. A virtual SCSI adapter performs faster than a virtual IDE adapter because of architecture limitations on data transfer and SCSI adapter ability to perform multiple transactions simultaneously. Overall, virtual SCSI adapters provide approximately 20 percent performance gains over an IDE adapter on a virtual machine with virtual machine additions installed. The virtual machine additions install an optimized virtual SCSI adapter driver that provide performance enhancements over the out-of-the-box Adaptec SCSI adapter driver.

Best Practices To obtain best performance, you should create virtual hard disks as fixed disks and connect them to a SCSI bus adapter. A fixed disk eliminates the dynamic allocation overhead and oversubscription concerns on the host. Attaching the fixed disk to a SCSI adapter allows you to create larger virtual hard disks and obtain approximately a 20 percent improvement in performance.

Best Practices You should use compression software to reduce the size of the fixed virtual hard disks before you attempt to transfer them over the network. Compression technologies such as ZIP and RAR (Roshal ARchive) can achieve significant size reductions on VHD files that are mostly empty space.

Operational Considerations

Using Virtual Server 2005 R2 in test, development, or production environments requires that operational standards be established to maintain efficiency. This section addresses establishing naming standards and creating and operating a library of virtual machines.

Establishing Standards

Establishing a set of configuration standards before you roll out virtualization on an enterprise basis will save you many hours of configuration changes. Standards are critical to minimizing virtual machine migration efforts between hosts, provisioning virtual machines, and making virtual machines and virtual networks easily identifiable.

Virtual machines are listed in the Administration Website according to the virtual machine configuration (.vmc) filename, and they are sorted in ascending alphabetical order. The .vmc filename is not required to match the actual computer name of the virtual machine. This approach provides both flexibility and confusion. You are allowed to specify a different name for the .vmc file than the virtual machine, giving you flexibility for sorting and grouping in the user interface. However, you must maintain a mapping of the .vmc name to the machine name. The virtual machine configuration filename is required to be unique on a single host, but duplicate names can exist on other Virtual Server 2005 R2 hosts.

Virtual hard disks are stored in the virtual machine configuration file by absolute and relative paths to the vmc file. This arrangement provides Virtual Server 2005 R2 file portability, allowing it to find VHD files moved to other hosts with a different drive or path location. The relative path is used to prevent collisions if you made a copy on the same server.

Virtual network configuration files (.vnc) consist of a virtual network name, a bound physical adapter, and the configuration of the virtual Dynamic Host Protocol (DHCP) server. Virtual network names must be unique on a single host. Each virtual machine can have up to four virtual network adapters and be attached to four different virtual networks. The partnerships between virtual network adapters and virtual networks are stored in the virtual machine configuration file.

How It Works: Mapping a Virtual Network Adapter to a Physical Adapter

Mapping a virtual network adapter to a virtual network and then to a physical network adapter involves three files: the virtual machines .vmc, the virtual networks .vnc, and the options.xml host configuration file.

The .vmc file has an entry for each network adapter that specifies the *ID* of the *virtual_network* entry that is the virtual network it is attached to.

```
<ethernet_controller id="0">
        <ethernet_card_address type="bytes">0003FF1B6AD5</ethernet_card_address>
        <id type="integer">5</id>
        <virtual_network>
              <id type="bytes">00D67AACDFC2499DBD9222F7A0A29D54</id>
            <name type="string">Wireless</name>
        </virtual_network>
```

This maps to the .vnc file for the virtual network and the value for id. When these two values match, this is the virtual network that the virtual machine is attached to.

```
<settings>
        <gateway type="integer">22</gateway>
        <id type="bytes">00D67AACDFC2499DBD9222F7A0A29D54</id>
```

The options.xml file contains the binding to the physical network adapter using the gateway value of the .vnc file which maps to the id property value of the virtual_gateway entry.

```
<virtual_gateway id="7">
        <adapter type="string">\DosDevices\VPCNetS2_{CA746289-F2E6-405A-B7C2-
E2595ACA750A}</adapter>
        <id type="integer">22</id>
        <name type="string">Intel(R) PRO/Wireless 3945ABG Network Connection #2</name>
        <type type="integer">2</type>
    </virtual_gateway>
```

When you move the VNC from one machine to the other, only when the Virtual_gateway id matches between servers will it map properly to the physical adapter. It might be possible to have identical IDs between servers, but connected to different physical networks, so it is always better to reattach the VNC to the desired physical network adapter to be sure it is connected to the adapter you intended.

Best Practices   You should establish naming standards for virtual machine configuration files as well as the computer name of the virtual machine. Virtual machine computer names should use the company naming standard for servers. Virtual machine configuration filenames should either match the virtual machine computer name or provide a way to group the machines in the user interface while including the virtual machine computer name.

For example, the company naming standard might be a three-letter location name followed by a server role designator, followed by a unique numeric value such as the following name:

HOUFS01

Using the standard three letter airport code designators will provide a preexisting recognized standard. The corresponding virtual machine name could be one of the following:

HOUFS01
F&P – HOUFS01

Using F&P in the beginning groups all file and print servers together in the Virtual Server 2005 R2 Administration Website user interface.

Best Practices   You should establish virtual network naming standard to indicate the type of network attached: INTRANET, INTERNET, or TEST1. You should use a generic name that applies across multiple Virtual Server 2005 R2 hosts in a server farm. Refrain from using the network's address, such as 10.10.10.0, for virtual network names. Using common virtual network names throughout the server farm allows you to migrate a virtual machine between hosts without having to reset the virtual network connection.

Best Practices   You should establish a virtual hard drive naming standard that allows you to quickly determine the computer name, drive type, and the drive number. The standard you choose should be well documented and followed to allow proper asset tracking.

Sample VHD Naming Standard

A sample VHD naming standard includes computer name, drive type, and drive number combined together to form a name like the following one:

```
ComputerName-Drivetype-drivenumber.vhd
```

The following table summarizes VHD naming standard components.

Naming standard component	Description
Computer Name	Virtual machine computer name
Driver type	I = IDE disk
	S = SCSI disk
	ID = IDE Differencing disk
	SD = SCSI Differencing disk
Drive number	VHD drive number for multiple VHD drives attached to a single machine

Using this standard, a virtual machine called HOUFS01 with two SCSI disks would produce the following:

```
HOUFS01-S-01.vhd - Disk 1
HOUFS01-S-02.vhd - Disk 2
```

Library of Virtual Machines

Provisioning a virtual machine in Virtual Server 2005 R2 is as simple as copying a set of files that combine to give virtual machines an identity. A library of virtual machines could include base machines with only the operating system installed, specific types of pre-installed application servers, and special-purpose virtual machines that have unattended installations of applications scripted to launch on boot and complete the installation.

Challenges to creating and maintaining a library of virtual machines include issues such as sysprepping images, minimizing provisioning time, managing updatess, and maintaining an authoritative source and replication system for distributing virtual machines.

Best Practices   You should install and run sysprep on any virtual machine that will be added to the virtual machine library. While you are not limited to the number of times you can run sysprep on a machine, you are limited to the number of times that you can execute sysprep and reset product activation. That limit is three times. If you are going to sysprep a machine on a regular basis, you should not reset activation. Refer to the "Additional Resources" section of this chapter for more information about sysprep limitations.

Best Practices   You should use dynamically expanding disks rather than fixed virtual hard disks to minimize the size of the virtual machines in the library. Doing so will dramatically reduce the amount of traffic transferred and reduce the load on your network.

You should automate the process of updating machines in the virtual machine library. Currently, there is no way to offline update a Windows operating system. Managing updates requires a script that automates the process or a procedure that describes the manual processes. An automated script requires the following steps:

1. Provision the virtual machines to a host machine.
2. Register the new virtual machine.
3. Power on the virtual machine.
4. Silently install all updates.
5. Power down the virtual machine.
6. Unregister the virtual machine.
7. Copy back the patched image to the library.

System Backup

Virtual Server 2005 R2 SP1 provides a new Volume Shadow Copy Service (VSS) writer. VSS writers are software interfaces included in applications and services that help provide consistent backups through the Volume Shadow Copy Service. The Virtual Server 2005 R2 SP1 writer responds to signals provided by the Volume Shadow Copy Service interface to allow the host and virtual machines to prepare their data stores for shadow copy creation by flushing all pending writes and to ensure that no writes occur on the volume while the shadow copy is being created. The VSS writer allows host and virtual machine backups to be performed from the host while the virtual machine is running. Without a VSS writer available, you would have to load a backup agent in every virtual machine, save the state, or shut down every virtual machine to ensure that memory and disk buffers are flushed to disk so that no data is lost.

The Virtual Server 2005 R2 SP1 VSS writer fulfills only half of the requirement. The backup application must implement support for the writer and have the ability to query the writer interfaces before it starts to back up the system. Refer to Chapter 17, "Managing a Virtual Server Infrastructure," for a detailed discussion of Virtual Server backup and the VSS writer.

Important   Because Windows Server 2003 SP1 and R2 versions were released before Virtual Server 2005 R2 SP1, Windows Server 2003 SP1 and R2 versions of NTBackup are not aware of the Virtual Server 2005 R2 SP1 VSS writer interface. Therefore, NTBackup will not properly signal Virtual Server or virtual machines to quiesce all disk and memory buffers before trying to back up the files.

Best Practices   You should purchase a backup application that is aware of the Virtual Server 2005 R2 SP1 VSS writer to perform backups on Virtual Server 2005 R2 SP1 hosts. This will allow you to minimize the effort and load associated with performing backups of virtual machines.

Summary

This chapter covered best practices to address common configuration, performance, and operational issues associated with deployments of Virtual Server 2005 R2. You can avoid configuration issues by modifying the default virtual machine configuration folder, adding custom search paths for easy selection of files in the Administration Website user interface, enabling VMRC, and selecting configuration options to provide a secure remote virtual machine management solution.

Host performance issues can be avoided by selecting appropriate memory configurations, enabling full acceleration for your graphics display adapter, selecting and correctly configuring the right network adapters, and purchasing a SAN with high-RPM SATA or SAS hard disks and iSCSI support. You can avoid virtual machine performance issues by following best practices for your host hardware configuration, using proper resource allocation settings, improving your display graphics performance by configuring for performance and not visual effects, installing virtual machine additions, and using fixed-size SCSI virtual hard drives.

Finally, you can keep operational headaches to a minimum by establishing naming standards, establishing a library of sysprep virtual machines, and using the new Virtual Server 2005 R2 SP1 VSS writer to obtain the most flexible and best-performing backups of host and virtual machines.

Additional Resources

The following resources contain additional information related to this chapter:

- Knowledge Base Article 830958, "Summary of the limitations of the System Preparation tool," at *http://support.microsoft.com/kb/830958/*

- White paper, "How Sysprep Works," at *http://technet2.microsoft.com/WindowsVista/en /library/fd2f79c9-3049-4b8c-bcfd-4e6dc5771ace1033.mspx?mfr=true*

- Knowledge Base Article 903748, "Virtual Server 2005 performance tips," at *http://support.microsoft.com/kb/903748/*

- Knowledge Base Article 925477, "Event IDs 1100, 1101, and 1102 are logged every time that the Virtual Server service starts in Virtual Server 2005 R2," at *http://support.microsoft.com/kb/925477/*

- White paper, "How Volume Shadow Copy Service Works," at *http://technet2.microsoft.com/WindowsServer/en/Library /2b0d2457-b7d8-42c3-b6c9-59c145b7765f1033.mspx?mfr=true*

- White paper, "Virtual Hard Disk Image Format Specification," at *http://www.microsoft.com/windowsserversystem/virtualserver/techinfo/vhdspec.mspx*

- White paper, "Using iSCSI with Virtual Server 2005," at *http://www.microsoft.com /downloads/details.aspx?FamilyID=d112aa63-a51e-4722-a41b-98b3ab3700a3&displaylang=en*

- White paper, "Application Software Considerations for NUMA-Based Systems," at *http://www.microsoft.com/whdc/system/platform/server/datacenter/numa_isv.mspx*

Chapter 8
Virtual Machine Creation Process

In this chapter:

Defining Basic Virtual Machine Configuration Parameters. 196

Creating a New Virtual Machine 197

Tuning Virtual Machine Key Configuration Settings 198

Adding a Virtual Machine. 209

Removing a Virtual Machine 211

Configuring Virtual Machine BIOS Settings 211

Installing a Guest Operating System. 213

Installing Virtual Machine Additions 215

Controlling Virtual Machine State. 217

Understanding the Benefits of a Virtual Machine Library. 218

Creating a Virtual Machine Library. 219

Managing a Virtual Machine Library 223

Summary. 225

Additional Resources. 226

In this chapter, you will learn the process to create new virtual machines using Microsoft Virtual Server 2005 R2. You will review the virtual machine configuration options that must be defined prior to virtual machine creation and learn the step-by-step procedure to create a new virtual machine by using the Virtual Server 2005 R2 Administration Website. The procedure includes the following tasks:

- Defining a virtual machine configuration file
- Creating a virtual hard disk (VHD)
- Connecting to a virtual network
- Tuning the virtual machine configuration
- Installing a guest operating system
- Installing Virtual Machine Additions to enhance performance and functionality

Additionally, you will learn about the benefits of setting up, configuring, and managing a virtual machine library to enable rapid provisioning in your Virtual Server 2005 R2 environment.

Defining Basic Virtual Machine Configuration Parameters

Creating a new virtual machine using the Virtual Server 2005 R2 Administration Website is a straightforward process. However, before bringing up the Administration Website in a browser and proceeding with the task, you should define the configuration items listed in Table 8-1. These are the basic parameters required to create a new virtual machine.

Table 8-1   Basic Parameters for New Virtual Machine Creation

Parameter	Description
Virtual machine name	The name that will be associated with the new virtual machine folder, virtual machine configuration file, and virtual hard disk. This is also the virtual machine name that will be displayed in the Administration Website Master Status view.
Memory	The amount of memory to allocate to the new virtual machine, not to exceed 3.6 GB. The memory allocation should take into consideration the amount of RAM in the physical server in conjunction with the memory requirements of the host operating system and other running virtual machines.
Virtual hard disk	The size and bus type (IDE or SCSI) for a new dynamically expanding virtual hard disk. By default, a new virtual hard disk is created in the same directory as the virtual machine configuration file. If the virtual hard disk size must be greater than 127 GB, the SCSI bus option must be specified. Specifying this option will allow creating a virtual hard disk up to 2040 GB.
	If an existing virtual hard disk should be connected to the new virtual machine, the virtual hard disk location, name, and bus type desired are specified.
	Alternatively, virtual hard disk association to the new virtual machine can be deferred.
Virtual network adapter	The virtual network to connect the virtual machine is specified. Otherwise, no connection can also be selected.

Once you have defined these basic parameters, you are ready to load the Virtual Server Administration Website, and begin the process to create a new virtual machine.

Creating a New Virtual Machine

Figure 8-1 shows the Virtual Server 2005 R2 Administration Website page from which you can create a new virtual machine. To create a new virtual machine, follow these steps:

1. Open the Virtual Server 2005 R2 Administration Website.

2. In the navigation pane, under Virtual Machines, click Create.

3. If you want the new virtual machine folder and files to be saved in the default configuration folder specified in Virtual Server Search Paths, type only the name of the new virtual machine in the Virtual Machine Name text box. If you want to create the folder and files in a different location, type in a fully qualified path for the new virtual machine configuration file (for example, d:\VMs\NewVM\NewVM.vmc). If the folder does not exist, it will be created.

4. In the Virtual Machine Memory text box (which specifies the memory in MBs), type the memory allocation for the new virtual machine. The default value reflects a minimum allocation that you should replace based on the factors listed in Table 8-1.

5. If you want to create a new dynamically expanding virtual hard disk, select Create A New Virtual Hard Disk. Then, in Size, enter the desired size of the virtual hard disk. The Units pull-down menu allows you to switch between MB and GB. The Bus pull-down menu allows you to connect the virtual hard disk to either an IDE (integrated development environment) or SCSI (Small Computer System Interface) virtual bus adapter.

6. If you pre-created a virtual hard disk, select Use An Existing Virtual Hard Disk. The Location pull-down menu allows you to choose a virtual hard disk located in the defined Virtual Server Search Paths and will populate the File Name (.vhd) text box. If you want to use a virtual hard disk located in another path, type in the fully qualified path and file name. The Bus pull-down menu allows you to connect the virtual hard disk to either an IDE or SCSI virtual bus adapter.

7. If you want to defer attaching a virtual hard disk, select Attach A Virtual Hard Disk Later (None).

8. The Connected To pull-down menu allows you to choose a preconfigured virtual network to connect the new virtual machine to. If you plan to install an operating system that requires updates, you might want to choose Not Connected to ensure that the new virtual machine remains isolated until it is fully updated.

9. Click Create to create the new virtual machine.

Create Virtual Machine

🖳 **Virtual machine name**

Type the name for the virtual machine file to create a virtual machine in its own folder saved in the default configuration folder specified on the <u>Virtual Server Paths</u> page. To create a virtual machine in a different location, provide a fully qualified path.

Virtual machine name:

━━ **Memory**

The amount of memory can be from 4 MB through 1847 MB (1662 MB maximum recommended).

Virtual machine memory (in MB): 128

💾 **Virtual hard disk**

Before you can install an operating system on this virtual machine, you must attach a new or existing virtual hard disk to it. A virtual hard disk is a .vhd file that is stored on your physical hard disk and contains the guest operating system, applications and data files.

◉ Create a new virtual hard disk

This option creates an unformatted dynamically expanding virtual hard disk in the same directory as the virtual machine configuration file. The maximum size allowed is 127 GB for IDE disks and 2040 GB for SCSI disks.

Size: 127   Units: GB   Bus: IDE

○ Use an existing virtual hard disk

Location: None

File name (.vhd):

Bus: IDE

○ Attach a virtual hard disk later (None)

⚟ **Virtual network adapter**

A virtual machine is preconfigured with one Ethernet network adapter that can be connected to a virtual network.

Connected to: Not connected

👤 **Virtual Machine Additions**

Important: We highly recommend that you install Virtual Machine Additions. Virtual Machine Additions provides performance and feature enhancements for Windows-based guest operating systems. These features include: time synchronization between guest and host operating systems, mouse integration when using the ActiveX control in Virtual Machine Remote Control (VMRC), and a heartbeat for the guest operating system to monitor the state of the virtual machine.

Create

Figure 8-1   Create Virtual Machine page

The new virtual machine folder is created, as well as the virtual machine configuration file and virtual hard disk. When the new virtual hard disk is created, you will find that it is only a few kilobytes in size. Because the default new virtual hard disk type is dynamically expanding, the file contains only basic header information until an operating system is installed. File space will be allocated to the virtual hard disk as required, up to the defined maximum size. Once the configuration file and virtual hard disk are created, the virtual machine is registered and the Administration Website virtual machine status and configuration page is displayed.

> **Note**   To attach a fixed-size or differencing virtual hard disk, use the Create option in the Virtual Disks menu of the Administration Website prior to generating the new virtual machine. From this menu, you can create any of the supported virtual hard disk types or a virtual floppy disk, if needed. When you create the new virtual machine, select the Use An Existing Virtual Hard Disk option, choose the pre-created virtual hard disk, and specify the bus connection as either IDE or SCSI.

Tuning Virtual Machine Key Configuration Settings

When you use the Virtual Server 2005 R2 Administration Website to create a new virtual machine, several virtual components—such as the CD/DVD drive, floppy drive, COM ports, and LPT ports—are configured with default settings. However, you might want to tune one or more of these key components before proceeding with loading the operating system and applications in the virtual machine. In most cases, when you are adding or removing components, the virtual machine is required to be powered off. Other configuration settings, such as changing a virtual CD/DVD drive mapping or connecting a virtual network adapter to a different virtual network, can be modified even if the virtual machine is running. All the configuration settings are accessible from the Administration Website virtual machine configuration page.

Follow these steps to select and load a virtual machine configuration page in your browser:

1. Open the Virtual Server 2005 R2 Administration Website.

2. In the navigation pane, under Virtual Machines, click Configure.

3. Click the appropriate entry in the list of registered virtual machines.

Note   You can also script modifications to virtual machine configuration settings. In Chapter 9, "Developing Scripts with the Virtual Server COM API," you will learn how to develop scripts using the Virtual Server 2005 R2 COM API.

Changing the Virtual Machine Name

If you mistype a virtual machine name or need it to conform to a new naming standard, follow these steps to rename the virtual machine:

1. In the virtual machine Status pane, verify that the virtual machine status is Off.

2. In the virtual machine Configuration pane, click General Properties.

3. In the Virtual Machine Name text box, type the new virtual machine name, and then click OK.

Performing these actions will change the name of the virtual machine and the name of the virtual machine configuration file (.vmc). However, the virtual machine folder and virtual hard disk name will be unaffected by the change.

Best Practices   It is recommended that you also change the virtual machine folder name if you change the virtual machine name. To do this, you must first remove the virtual machine from Virtual Server. This step is necessary to delete the shortcut entry (refer to Chapter 6, "Security in Depth," for folder locations) that Virtual Server creates when a new virtual machine is registered. Virtual Server uses the shortcut entries to determine the folder location of registered virtual machines. Once the virtual machine is removed from Virtual Server, you can change the folder name and re-register it. If you do not follow this procedure, the shortcut entry will be obsolete, but Virtual Server will still retain it.

Automating Virtual Machine Startup and Shutdown

By default, a new virtual machine runs under the context of the user that starts the virtual machine. If you intend to assign one or more scripts to a virtual machine, you must assign a specific user account to run the virtual machine. Furthermore, you must assign a specific user account if you want the virtual machine to automatically turn on when Virtual Server starts. Use the guidelines in Chapter 6 (in the "Configuring a Virtual Machine User Account" section) to configure the user account. Then follow these steps to change the virtual machine startup and shutdown settings:

1. In the virtual machine Status pane, verify that the virtual machine status is Off.

2. In the virtual machine Configuration pane, click General Properties.

3. Click Run Virtual Machine Under The Following User Account.

4. In the User Name text box, type the user account name.

5. In the Password text box, type the password associated with the user account name.

6. In Action When Virtual Server Starts, select Automatically Turn On Virtual Machine If It Was Running When Virtual Server Stopped to enable automatic startup.

7. In Seconds To Delay Automatically Turning On A Virtual Machine, type in the number of seconds that you need to stagger the startup of the virtual machine (typically, 60 to 90 seconds). The value cannot exceed 86,400 seconds (24 hours).

8. In Action When Virtual Server Stops, choose Save State to enable a fast restart of the virtual machine in the same state.

9. Enter a note that describes the modifications made to the startup and shutdown settings, and then click OK.

Once the startup modifications are completed, the Virtual Machine Helper service (discussed in Chapter 3, "Virtual Server Architecture") will use the specified user account context to run the virtual machine.

Use the Save State option when Virtual Server stops to allow restarting the virtual machine from the current state in the shortest delay. This option directs Virtual Server to capture the current contents of virtual machine memory to a file (.vsv), which it uses to reload into memory during a quick and stateful restart of the virtual machine. Avoid using the virtual machine Turn Off option, as this is equivalent to pulling the power plug on a physical computer and can result in data corruption.

Important It is not possible to move a virtual machine in a saved stated from Virtual Server 2005 R2 to Virtual PC 2004 or Virtual PC 2007. Although virtual machine configuration files (.vmc) and virtual hard disks (.vhd) are compatible between Virtual Server and Virtual PC, Save State (.vsv) files are incompatible.

Changing the Memory Setting

Based on changing performance needs driven by requirements such as servicing a larger user population or significant increase in workload transactions, you might need to adjust a virtual machine memory setting. When revising virtual machine memory allocation, it is important to consider that the value allocated to the virtual machine by the host is increased by 32 MB to account for the emulated video RAM (VRAM) and code cache that is maintained to enhance performance. For example, a virtual machine with a 512-MB memory setting receives an adjusted allocation of 544 MB from Virtual Server. If the Virtual Server host cannot allocate the additional memory, the virtual machine performance might be impacted. Use the following steps to adjust the virtual machine memory setting:

1. In the virtual machine Status pane, verify that the virtual machine status is Off.

2. In the virtual machine Configuration pane, click Memory to display the Memory Properties page.

3. In the Virtual Machine Memory text box, type in the new value.

4. Click OK.

Depending on the amount of memory installed in the physical server, Virtual Server will display the maximum memory available to allocate to the virtual machine. If you attempt to enter an allocation greater than the maximum available memory, Virtual Server will refresh the virtual machine Memory Properties page with an error, as shown in Figure 8-2.

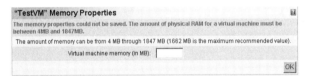

Figure 8-2 Virtual machine Memory Properties page—Maximum memory allocation error

Important Virtual Server 2005 R2 does not support memory over-commit or memory sharing. The sum of memory allocated to virtual machines must be less than the total memory installed in the physical server.

Changing the Virtual Hard Disk Settings

The Virtual Server 2005 R2 Administration Website allows only the definition of a single virtual hard disk during the creation of a new virtual machine. However, for most workloads, two or more virtual hard disks will be required to separate the guest operating system files and application data files to achieve greater recoverability, security, and performance levels. A maximum of 32 VHDs (4 IDE and 28 SCSI) can be attached to a single virtual machine. Maximum disk performance is achieved by attaching VHDs to a virtual SCSI adapter. The IDE protocol does not allow concurrent transactions on the bus; rather, transactions occur serially. The SCSI protocol, on the other hand, allows multiple transactions simultaneously, leading to greater overall disk performance.

Use the following steps to create and attach an additional VHD connected to the virtual machine by a virtual SCSI bus:

1.   In the virtual machine Status pane, verify that the virtual machine status is Off.

2.   If a virtual SCSI adapter is already installed in the virtual machine, you can use it to attach the new VHD and skip to step 6.

3.   To install a new virtual SCSI adapter in the virtual machine, click SCSI Adapters in the virtual machine Configuration pane to display the SCSI Adapter Properties page.

4.   Click Add SCSI Adapter.

5.   Click OK.

6.   Back in the navigation pane, under Virtual Disks, click Create and then click on either Dynamically Expanding Virtual Hard Disk or Fixed Size Virtual Hard Disk.

7.   On the virtual hard disk page, select the folder in which to store the virtual hard disk from the Location drop-down menu. If the folder does not appear in the list, you must type the fully qualified path to the folder in the following step.

8.   In the Virtual Hard Disk File Name text box, type a name for the new virtual hard disk after the folder path or type the fully qualified path as mentioned in the previous step. It is not necessary to include a filename extension.

9.   In Size, type the maximum size for the new virtual hard disk.

10.   In Units, select MB or GB as required.

11.   Click Create.

12.   Back in the navigation pane, under Virtual Machines, click Configure and then click the appropriate virtual machine.

13.   In the virtual machine Configuration pane, click on Hard Disks to display the Virtual Hard Disk Properties.

14.   Click Add Disk.

15.   In Attachment, select the first unused SCSI channel and ID.

16.   In Known Virtual Hard Disks, select the VHD to attach to the virtual machine. If the VHD does not appear in the list, you must type the fully qualified path to the VHD in the Fully Qualified Path To File text box.

17.   Click OK.

Important To get maximum performance within a virtual machine, install the accelerated SCSI controller driver. Perform this procedure on the guest operating system when you add a virtual SCSI adapter to a virtual machine after installing Virtual Machine Additions. When the accelerated driver is installed, Device Manager lists it as "Microsoft Virtual Machine PCI SCSI Controller."

In the virtual machine Configuration pane, under the Hard Disks section, you can view the new virtual hard drive configuration details, including the SCSI bus channel and ID, maximum VHD file size, and current VHD file size.

Important For a general review of VHD types, refer to Chapter 2, "Virtual Server 2005 R2 SP1 Product Overview." If you need in-depth information concerning the use of differencing, undo, and linked disks, or the new VHD Mount tool included in Virtual Server 2005 R2 SP1, refer to Chapter 5, "Virtual Server R2 Advanced Features."

Changing the Virtual CD/DVD Settings

When a new virtual machine is created, it is configured with a virtual CD/DVD drive attached to the secondary virtual IDE channel. By default, the virtual CD/DVD drive is mapped to the physical server CD or DVD drive. Virtual Server 2005 R2 allows up to four virtual CD or DVD drives to be configured in a virtual machine (using all virtual IDE channels). Keep in mind that virtual machines must be powered off to add or remove virtual CD/DVD drives.

In addition to capturing physical drives, virtual CD/DVD drives can be mapped to standard ISO 9660 images or configured without any mapping. Virtual Server 2005 R2 SP1 removes the 2.2-GB ISO image size limitation of previous releases. Two basic ISO images are included with Virtual Server, precompact.iso and VMAdditions.iso, to support installation of the virtual hard disk precompactor tool and Virtual Machine Additions. If a virtual CD/DVD drive is mapped to an operating system ISO image, the virtual machine can boot and install from the drive, resulting in a shortened installation time when compared with a physical CD installation because of the faster ISO image data access.

Note Virtual Server 2005 R2 SP1 does not have a limit in code to restrict the ISO image size that can be mapped to a virtual CD/DVD drive. ISO images greater than 4.2 GB were successfully tested in the SP1 release.

Use the following steps to create and attach an additional virtual CD/DVD to the virtual machine:

1. In the virtual machine Status pane, verify that the virtual machine status is Off.

2. In the virtual machine Configuration pane, click CD/DVD to display the CD/DVD Drive Properties page.

3. Click Add CD/DVD Drive.

4. In Attachment, select the virtual IDE channel to attach the CD/DVD drive. Unavailable virtual IDE channels will display as "in use."

5. In Capture, select one of the following mapping options for the new virtual CD/DVD drive:

    ❑ If you do not want to immediately map to a physical drive or ISO image, click No Media.

    ❑ If you want to map to a physical drive, click Physical CD/DVD Drive. Then select the appropriate physical drive from the list.

    ❑ If you want to map to an ISO image, click Known Image Files. Then select an available ISO image file from the list. If the ISO image file is not displayed (that is, it's not located in the specified search paths), type the fully qualified path and ISO image file name in the Fully Qualified Path To File text box.

6. Click OK.

Changing the Virtual Network Adapter Settings

A virtual machine is created with a single virtual network adapter. However, up to three additional virtual network adapters can be added to the virtual machine configuration. Virtual Server 2005 R2 dynamically assigns a unique MAC address (within the 00-03-FF-xx-xx-xx range) to each virtual network adapter, enabling each adapter to connect independently to one of the available virtual networks.

By default, Virtual Server 2005 R2 creates a virtual network for each physical Ethernet network adapter to allow rapid configuration of virtual machines to external networks. An internal virtual network is also created to allow connectivity between virtual machines hosted on the same Virtual Server. Internal virtual network transmissions are confined within a software-emulated network hub and are never transmitted through any of the physical network adapters. For example, if you want to import multiple production servers into interconnected virtual machines hosted on a single Virtual Server without risking data transmission to the production network, use the default internal network or create a new internal virtual network (one not attached to any network adapter), and connect all the virtual machines to it via a virtual network adapter. If you must spread the virtual machines across multiple Virtual Server hosts, create an external virtual network connected to a physical network adapter on each of the Virtual Server hosts. The physical network adapter should itself be connected to an isolated physical network to ensure that no data is transmitted across the production network. Then connect each virtual machine to the external virtual network to allow network interconnectivity. Virtual Server 2005 R2 supports an unlimited number of virtual networks to allow flexibility in the network connection configuration of virtual machines.

 Important   If you need to configure internal virtual network connectivity between the Virtual Server host and one or more virtual machines, setup and configuration of the Microsoft Loopback Adapter is explained in Chapter 5.

Use the following steps to create and attach additional virtual network adapters to the virtual machine:

1. In the virtual machine Status pane, verify that the virtual machine status is Off.

2. In the virtual machine Configuration pane, click Network Adapters to display the Network Adapter Properties page.

3. Click Add Network Adapter.

4. In Connected To, select the appropriate virtual network from the list, and then click OK.

Changing the Virtual Machine Script Settings

Before any script can be associated with a virtual machine, Virtual Server script settings must be modified to enable the feature, and the virtual machine must be configured to run in the context of a specific user account as described in the "Automating Virtual Machine Startup and Shutdown" section of this chapter.

Once these configuration modifications are performed, Virtual Server 2005 R2 allows assignment of scripts that execute based on the occurrence of these specific virtual machine events:

- Virtual machine is turned on

- Virtual machine is restored

- Virtual machine is saved and turned off

- Virtual machine is turned off and not saved

- Virtual machine is turned off within the guest environment

- Virtual machine is reset

- Virtual machine heartbeat is not detected for three minutes

- Virtual machine guest processor error has occurred

- Virtual machine receives a low disk space warning for a virtual hard disk

- Virtual machine receives a low disk space error for a virtual hard disk

If an assigned script does not successfully execute, an entry is recorded in the Virtual Server event log. However, if a script executes but fails with an error, no indication will be recorded in the Virtual Server event log. Virtual Server 2005 R2 does not directly monitor the status of each script command.

Use the following steps to associate a script with one or more of the specified virtual machine events:

1. In the virtual machine Configuration pane, click on Scripts to display the Scripts Properties page.

2. In the Command text box of the event that you want to trigger the execution of the script, type in the fully qualified path to the script.

3. Repeat step 2 for any additional events.

4. Click OK.

Changing the Virtual Floppy Drive Settings

When a virtual machine is created, a single virtual floppy drive is configured without any direct mapping to media. Unlike most other virtual components, the virtual floppy drive cannot be removed and no additional floppy drives can be added to a virtual machine. A virtual floppy drive can be mapped to a physical floppy drive on the Virtual Server host or to a floppy disk image. Only a single virtual machine can be mapped to a physical floppy drive or a writable virtual floppy disk image. However, multiple virtual machines can concurrently access a read-only virtual floppy disk. Virtual Server 2005 R2 supports floppy disk images of 720 KB or 1.44 MB in size, but it will create images only in the latter format. As described in Table 8-2, three basic floppy disk images are included with Virtual Server 2005 R2.

Table 8-2   Floppy Disk Images Included with Virtual Server 2005 R2

Floppy disk image	Description
DOS Virtual Machine Additions.vfd	This floppy disk image contains Virtual Machine Additions to install in a DOS guest operating system.
NT4 Network Driver.vfd	This floppy disk image contains an updated driver for the DEC 21140A Network Adapter. The updated driver is required to enable multifunction support and enable a Microsoft Windows NT Server 4.0 guest operating system to access more than one network adapter.
SCSI Shunt Driver.vfd	This floppy disk image contains emulated SCSI drivers that you can load when prompted to hit F6 during installation of a Windows Server 2003, Windows Server 2000, or Windows XP Professional guest operating system. Use of these drivers can greatly reduce installation time.

Use the following steps to change the virtual floppy drive mapping for the virtual machine:

1. In the virtual machine Configuration pane, click Floppy Drive to display the Floppy Drive Properties page.

2. In Capture, select one of the following mapping options for the virtual floppy drive:

   ❑ If you do not want to immediately map to a physical drive or floppy disk image, click No Media.

   ❑ If you want to map to a physical drive, click Physical Floppy Drive. Then select the appropriate physical drive from the list.

   ❑ If you want to map to a floppy disk image, click Known Floppy Disks. Then select an available floppy image file from the list. If the floppy disk image file is not displayed (that is, it's not located in the specified search paths), type the fully qualified path and floppy disk image file name in the Fully Qualified Path To File text box.

3. Click OK.

 Note The floppy disk images can be found in %SystemDrive%\Program Files\Microsoft Virtual Server\Virtual Machine Additions. This is also the location of the ISO images included with Virtual Server 2005 R2.

Changing the Virtual COM Port Settings

There are two virtual COM ports available to enable a virtual machine to communicate through a host serial device, file, or named pipe. By default, the virtual COM ports are configured without any device connection. The virtual COM ports cannot be removed from the virtual machine configuration. Concurrent access by multiple virtual machines to a device attached to a virtual COM port is not permitted. The device becomes available for use by another virtual machine when it is released or the controlling virtual machine is powered off.

Table 8-3 describes the four virtual COM port connection settings that are available in Virtual Server 2005 R2.

Table 8-3   Table Virtual COM Port Connection Settings

Setting	Description
None	This is the default setting for a new virtual machine, ensuring that no device is connected to a virtual COM port.
Physical Computer Serial Port	This setting maps a serial port on the physical host to a virtual COM port in the virtual machine. Virtual Server 2005 R2 only supports mapping a virtual COM port to physical host ports COM1 through COM4. The physical host COM port is mapped when the virtual machine starts and is released when the virtual machine COM port configuration is changed or the virtual machine is shut down. Alternatively, there is an option to capture the physical host COM port only when the virtual machine accesses the virtual COM port. Virtual Server will wait for an AT modem command before mapping the physical host COM port to the virtual machine.
Text File	This setting allows sending output from a virtual COM port to a text file located on the hard drive of the physical host.
Named Pipe	This setting allows mapping a virtual COM port to a named pipe on the physical host or virtual machine connected on the same virtual network.

Use the following steps to configure the virtual COM port settings:

1. In the virtual machine Configuration pane, click COM Ports to display the COM Port Properties page.

2. In the appropriate virtual COM port section, click to select the required Attachment setting based on the descriptions in Table 8-3, and then click OK.

> **Note**   You can set up a virtual COM port with a named pipe mapping to simulate a null modem connection. This is useful to run a debugging session involving a virtual machine. You can find the steps to set up a kernel debugging session for Windows XP inside a virtual machine at *http://blogs.msdn.com/virtual_pc_guy/archive/2005/10/20/482413.aspx*.

Changing the Virtual LPT Port Settings

Only a single virtual LPT port is available in a virtual machine. By default, the virtual LPT port is not mapped to any device, and it cannot be removed from the virtual machine configuration. There is only one additional configuration setting for the virtual LPT port, which is a mapping to the physical host LPT1 port. Concurrent access by multiple virtual machines to a device attached to a virtual LPT port is not permitted. The device becomes available for use by another virtual machine when it is released or the controlling virtual machine is powered off.

Use the following steps to configure the virtual LPT port settings:

1. In the virtual machine Configuration pane, click LPT Ports to display the LPT Port Properties page.

2. Select LPT1 (378h-37Fh) to connect the virtual LPT port to the physical LPT1 port. If you want to disassociate the virtual LPT port from the physical LPT1 port, select None. Click OK.

Adding a Virtual Machine

Virtual machines created on another Virtual Server host or Virtual PC can be easily moved to a new Virtual Server host. The first step in moving a powered-off virtual machine is the relocation of the virtual machine configuration file (.vmc), virtual hard disk files (.vhd), and virtual network configuration files (.vnc) to a disk storage device that is accessible to the new Virtual Server host.

Direct from the Source: Saved State File Compatibility

Special consideration must be given to moving virtual machines between Virtual PC and Virtual Server hosts if the VMs are in a saved state as opposed to cleanly powered off. Generally, to move VMs in a saved state, you must do so between Virtual Server hosts with identical processors and product versions.

Virtual machine saved state files (.vsv) are incompatible between the Virtual PC and Virtual Server products shown in the following list:

- Virtual Server 2005 R2 not compatible with Virtual Server 2005 R2 SP1
- Virtual Server 2005 not compatible with Virtual Server 2005 R2
- Virtual Server 2005 (any version) not compatible with Virtual PC 2007
- Virtual Server 2005 (any version) not compatible with Virtual PC 2004
- Virtual PC 2004 not compatible with Virtual PC 2007
- Virtual PC 2004 not compatible with Virtual PC 2004 SP1

> Virtual machine saved state files are also incompatible between hosts with different
> physical processor configurations, such as Intel and AMD, as well as across processor
> steppings, such as Intel Pentium 4 Northwood and Prescott.
>
> *John Howard*
> *Program Manager, Windows Virtualization*

If you are moving a virtual machine from Virtual PC to Virtual Server 2005 R2, there are a few
key points to consider:

- Virtual Server does not provide a sound card emulation, so sound functionality available
  in Virtual PC will be lost.

- Virtual PC supports only virtual IDE adapters, whereas Virtual Server also supports virtual SCSI adapters. To take advantage of the increased disk performance available with
  a virtual SCSI adapter, you have to update virtual hard disk adapter configurations.

- Virtual Server does not provide the Shared Folders feature available in Virtual PC. You
  should configure a Microsoft Loopback Adapter to enable network connectivity
  between the Virtual Server host and virtual machines.

Use the following steps to add an existing virtual machine to a new Virtual Server host:

1. Open the Virtual Server 2005 R2 Administration Website.

2. In the navigation pane, under Virtual Machines, click Add.

3. In Known Configuration Files, select the virtual machine from the list of VMs found in
   the defined Virtual Server Search Paths and it will automatically populate the Fully
   Qualified Path To File text box.

4. If the virtual machine configuration file is not located in one of the directories defined in
   the Virtual Server Search Paths list, type the fully qualified path to the file in the Fully
   Qualified Path To File text box.

5. Click Add.

Once the virtual machine is registered, the virtual machine status and configuration page is
displayed. If necessary, you should update the virtual machine with the latest virtual machine
additions before putting it back into production.

> **Note**   Virtual Server creates a shortcut entry (refer to Chapter 6 for folder locations) when a
> virtual machine is registered. The shortcut entry is used to determine the folder location of
> registered virtual machines. If a new virtual machine reuses a previously registered virtual
> machine name and the shortcut entry for the previous virtual machine was not deleted, then
> registration of the new virtual machine fails.

Removing a Virtual Machine

Completely removing a virtual machine and associated files from a Virtual Server host requires two steps. First, you unregister the virtual machine through the Administration Web-site. This step does not delete any of the virtual machine files, except for the shortcut entry that points to the location of the virtual machine configuration file. This prevents mistakenly deleting virtual machine files from the Virtual Server host. If you are certain that you will no longer execute the virtual machine on the specific Virtual Server host, the next step you take is to manually delete all the associated files after unregistering the virtual machine.

To unregister a virtual machine from a Virtual Server host, follow these steps:

1. Open the Virtual Server 2005 R2 Administration Website.

2. In the Master Status pane, ensure that the virtual machine status is Off. Otherwise, power down the virtual machine.

3. Point to the virtual machine name to display the action list.

4. Click Remove.

On the Companion Media   The companion media contains a Visual Basic script named DeleteVM.vbs in the \Chapter Materials\Scripts directory that you can run (and customize) for your environment to unregister a virtual machine and delete the associated virtual hard disk files (.vhd), saved state file (.vsv), and virtual machine configuration file (.vmc).

Configuring Virtual Machine BIOS Settings

After tuning the configuration of a new virtual machine, you need to install the guest operating system and applications. As you would do with a physical computer, you should review and modify any configuration settings in the virtual machine basic input/output system (BIOS) before proceeding with the operating system installation. More than likely, the only configuration option that you would change is the boot order. Figure 8-3 shows the Main screen of the virtual machine BIOS setup utility, accessed by pressing the Delete key during the initial boot sequence.

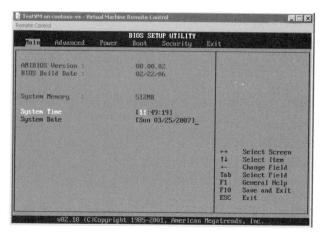

Figure 8-3   Virtual machine BIOS Setup Utility Main screen

From this screen, you can navigate to the Advanced, Power, Boot, Security, and Exit menu options using the arrow keys. Table 8-4 lists the configuration settings that are available in each section.

Table 8-4   Virtual Machine BIOS Configuration Settings

Setting	Description
Main	AMIBIOS Version (View Only)
	BIOS Build Date (View Only)
	System Memory (View Only)
	System Time (Configurable)
	System Date (Configurable)
Advanced	IDE Configuration (Configurable)
	Floppy Configuration (Configurable)
	Boot Settings Configuration (Configurable)
Power	Power Management/APM (Configurable)
	ACPI Aware OS (Configurable)
Boot	Boot Device Priority (Configurable)
	Hard Disk Drives (Configurable)
	Floppy Drives (View Only)
	CDROM Drives (View Only)
Security	Change Supervisor Password (Configurable)
	Change User Password (Configurable)
	Clear User Password (Configurable)

Table 8-4   Virtual Machine BIOS Configuration Settings

Setting	Description
Exit	Exit Saving Changes
	Exit Discarding Changes
	Load Optimal Defaults
	Load Failsafe Defaults
	Discard Changes

The default order in which boot devices are checked for a valid operating system or boot loader is as follows:

1. Floppy Drive
2. CDROM
3. Hard Drive
4. PXE

If startup media is not found on either the floppy drive or CDROM, the virtual machine first scans the virtual IDE bus channels and then scans the virtual SCSI bus channel for a bootable drive (if both types of adapters are present). Only the first SCSI adapter (SCSI 0) is scanned for a bootable drive. To directly boot using the first SCSI adapter, bypassing the IDE channel scan, you can specify the bootable virtual hard drive in the BIOS Boot Menu under the Hard Disk Drives options.

Installing a Guest Operating System

A virtual machine does not usually provide any useful service until it is configured with a workload that consists of an operating system and one or more applications. Installing an operating system in a virtual machine is a process that very much parallels that of a physical computer. A virtual machine operating system can be installed using original media, an imaging tool, ISO images, or PXE-based installation. Table 8-5 lists the virtual machine requirements for each of these installation methods.

Table 8-5   Virtual Machine Operating System Installation Options

Setting	Description
Original Media	The virtual CD/DVD must be mapped to the physical host drive containing the original media.
Imaging Tool	The virtual floppy or CD/DVD must be mapped to the physical host drive containing a CD-based image.
	—Or—
	The virtual machine is created using a VHD that was prepared with the System Preparation tool (Sysprep) or other supported tool.

Table 8-5 Virtual Machine Operating System Installation Options

Setting	Description
ISO Image	The virtual CD/DVD must be mapped to the ISO image file.
PXE-Based Installation	The virtual machine must PXE boot to connect to Remote Installation Services (RIS) or to a physical-to-virtual (P2V) migration tool such as the Virtual Server 2005 Migration Toolkit (VSMT).

If an operating system must be installed from scratch, use an ISO image stored on a physical host drive when possible, instead of using original media. Installing an operating system from an ISO image mapped to the virtual machine CD/DVD is faster than installing from original media. In addition, if you intend to deploy the same operating system configuration repetitively, use the Sysprep tool to create a baseline VHD that can be copied and reused to quickly provision new virtual machines. The Sysprep utility prepares an operating system for distribution by resetting it to run the setup at the next boot, eliminating security identifier (SID) and machine name duplication issues that would otherwise take place. Sysprep should be used only after the operating system has been updated, Virtual Machine Additions have been installed, and any baseline applications have been included in the configuration.

Note The Windows Server 2003–compatible Sysprep tools and documentation are packaged in \Support\Tools\Deploy on the Windows Server 2003 media.

The basic steps to install an operating system in a virtual machine using an ISO image file, assuming a single virtual CD/DVD configuration, are as follows:

1. Open the Virtual Server 2005 R2 Administration Website.

2. In the navigation pane, under Virtual Machines, click Configure and select the target virtual machine.

3. In the virtual machine Configuration pane, click CD/DVD to display the CD/DVD Drive Properties page.

4. In Capture, click Known Image Files and select the target ISO image file or enter the fully qualified path and filename in the Fully Qualified Path To File text box.

5. Click OK.

6. Navigate back to the Master Status page, and click the thumbnail to turn on the virtual machine.

7. Click the virtual machine thumbnail again to launch the VMRC ActiveX control and connect to the virtual machine console.

8. Once the virtual machine boots and begins the setup process, follow normal procedures to install the operating system.

> **Note**   You can also use the VMRC client application to remotely connect to the virtual machine console. In Windows Server 2003, click Start, click All Programs, click Microsoft Virtual Server, and then click Virtual Machine Remote Control Client to launch the application. The VMRC Server must be enabled prior to attempting a connection using either the VMRC ActiveX or client application.

Installing Virtual Machine Additions

Once the virtual machine guest operating system configuration is complete, Virtual Machine Additions should be installed. Virtual Machine Additions are a set of performance, integration, and functionality enhancements that are installed in a guest operating system running in a virtual machine. Virtual Machine Additions offer enhancements in the following areas:

- Performance-tuned mouse and keyboard drivers
- Intelligent mouse and cursor focus capture and release
- Virtual machine heartbeat generator
- Time synchronization with the physical host
- Performance-tuned video driver with arbitrary video resizing
- Performance-tuned SCSI controller driver
- Guest kernel updates

Virtual machine performance is significantly increased once virtual machine–specific driver updates replace standard guest operating system driver files. Virtual Machine Additions are updated from time to time, so it is also important to incorporate these updates into your maintenance procedures and schedule as new versions are released.

When you install Virtual Machine Additions, the registry keys (which are all REG_SZ) listed in Table 8-6 are added in the guest operating system under \HKEY_LOCAL_MACHINE\SOFTWARE \Microsoft\Virtual Machine\Guest\Parameters. These registry entries contain Domain Name System (DNS) naming information about the Virtual Server host and virtual machine.

Table 8-6   Virtual Machine Additions Registry Keys

Registry key	Description
HostName	The DNS name assigned to the Virtual Server host. If the Virtual Server host is a node in a cluster, this is the domain name of the cluster virtual server.
PhysicalHostName	The DNS name of the Virtual Server host. If the Virtual Server host is a node in a cluster, this is the domain name of the individual node, not the cluster virtual server.

Table 8-6   Virtual Machine Additions Registry Keys

Registry key	Description
PhysicalHostNameFullyQualified	The fully qualified DNS name of the Virtual Server host. The fully qualified DNS name is a concatenation of the DNS host name and the DNS domain name.
VirtualMachineName	The virtual machine name under which the guest operating system is running.

Virtual Machine Additions can be automatically installed using the link provided at the bottom of the VMRC page when connected to the virtual machine. You can do this either by manually capturing the ISO image that contains the Virtual Machine Additions and mapping it to the virtual CD/DVD or by scripting the installation.

Follow these steps to easily install the Virtual Machine Additions from the virtual machine Status page:

1. Open the Virtual Server 2005 R2 Administration Website.

2. In the navigation pane, under Virtual Machines, click Configure and select the target virtual machine.

3. In the virtual machine Configuration pane, click CD/DVD to display the CD/DVD Drive Properties page.

4. In Capture, click Known Image Files and select the VMAdditions.iso image file.

5. Click OK.

6. Navigate back to the Master Status page and click the thumbnail to connect to the virtual machine console.

7. If Autoplay is enabled, the Virtual Machine Additions installation starts automatically.

8. If Autoplay is not enabled, double-click the virtual CD/DVD drive to start the installation.

9. In the Welcome To Setup For Virtual Machine Additions dialog box, click Next.

10. In the Setup Completed dialog box, click Finish.

11. When prompted, click Yes to restart the virtual machine.

Note   More details on the architecture of Virtual Machine Additions can be found in Chapter 3, "Virtual Server Architecture."

Controlling Virtual Machine State

Table 8-7 includes a list of options that Virtual Server 2005 R2 provides to control and change the state of a virtual machine. In all cases, available options depend on the existing virtual machine state. It is critical to understand virtual machine state and transition paths to prevent corruption, data loss, or service interruptions caused by incompatibilities with applications or services running in the virtual machine.

Table 8-7   Virtual Machine State Control Options

Registry key	Description
Turn On	Powers on the virtual machine to boot into a guest operating system, if one is installed.
Turn Off	Turns off the virtual machine without saving any state information. This has the same effect as pulling a power plug on a physical machine.
Pause	Stops the execution of the virtual machine, maintaining the current state of the memory.
Resume	Resumes execution of the virtual machine from the exact state that it was in when paused.
Save State	Saves the memory contents of the virtual machine into a file (.vsv), and stops execution. This allows restoring a virtual machine to the condition that it was in when its state was saved.
Save State and Commit Undo Disks	Saves the current memory contents of the virtual machine into a file (.vsv), merges undo disks with their parent disks, and stops execution. This allows restoring a virtual machine to the condition that it was in when its state was saved.
Save State and Keep Undo Disks	Saves the current state of the virtual machine into a file (.vsv), keeps undo disks, and stops execution. This allows restoring a virtual machine to the condition that it was in when its state was saved.
Shut Down Guest OS	Shuts down the guest operating system, simulating a clean shutdown of a physical machine.
Shut Down Guest OS and Keep Undo Disks	Shuts down the guest operating system, and keeps undo disks. This provides the option to roll back the virtual machine to the state that it was in when undo disks were enabled.
Shut Down Guest OS and Commit Undo Disks	Shuts down the guest operating system, and merges undo disks with the parent disks. There is no longer an option to roll back the virtual machine to the state that it was in when undo disks were enabled.

Table 8-7   Virtual Machine State Control Options

Registry key	Description
Turn Off Virtual Machine and Keep Undo Disks	Turns off the virtual machine without saving any state information, and keeps undo disks. This has the same effect as pulling the plug on a physical machine. It also preserves the option to roll back the virtual machine to the state that it was in when undo disks were enabled.
Turn Off Virtual Machine and Commit Undo Disks	Turns off the virtual machine without saving any state information, and merges the undo disk with the parent disk. This has the same effect as pulling the plug on a physical machine.
Turn Off Virtual Machine and Discard Undo Disks	Turns off the virtual machine, discards undo disks, and does not save any state information. This has the same effect as pulling the plug on a physical machine. When the virtual machine is turned on, new undo disks are created.
Reset	Resets the virtual machine. This has the same effect as pressing the reset button on a physical machine.
Restore From Saved State	Turns on the virtual machine, and restores it to the state that it was in when the state was saved.
Discard Saved State	Discards the .vsv file that contains state information for the virtual machine, and keeps the virtual machine turned off.

For example, a virtual machine configured as a domain controller should never be placed in a saved state and later restored. Bringing an Active Directory database back online after being in saved state can cause database corruption and replication failures that have a severe impact on the integrity of the Active Directory domain and forest. Typically, any application with transactional dependencies should be very carefully managed to avoid critical data-integrity issues caused by improperly suspending or turning off a virtual machine, and then eventually bringing it back online.

Important   For more information on special considerations when hosting domain controllers in a virtualized environment, refer to Knowledge Base article 888794 at http://support.microsoft.com/kb/888794.

Understanding the Benefits of a Virtual Machine Library

A virtual machine library is a managed collection of baseline virtual machines, typically controlled by a centralized virtual machine library management team, and used to rapidly provision new production, test, development, and training environments. Instead of having to install each virtual machine from scratch or use a complicated tool to restore an image, virtual machines can be ready to boot and execute almost immediately. The virtual machine library management team is responsible for keeping virtual machines current with updates and service packs, removing unnecessary files, compacting virtual machines to conserve space, and managing virtual machine configuration file settings.

The features and benefits of having a virtual machine library in your organization are summarized in Table 8-8.

Table 8-8   Virtual Machine Library Features and Benefits

Features	Benefits
Centralized virtual machine management team	Establishes single source of virtual machines
	Establishes compulsory standards
	Reduces duplication of effort
Centralized testing and installation of updates and service packs for baseline virtual machines	Reduces duplication of effort
	Provides for more standard update levels across environments
Sysprepped virtual machines	Ensures unique virtual machine identity
	Enables custom configuration of guest operating system and faster deployment
Prebuilt scenarios involving multiple virtual machines	Reduces post provisioning steps
	Eliminates rework
Automation	Allows for automation of post-configuration steps to decrease human error and repetitive effort
License tracking	Provides the ability to track the number of new virtual machines, as well as the operating system version and license requirements
	Provides the ability to track the number of application licenses required based on provisioned virtual machines
Standards	Helps in developing and enforcing standards for configuration, installed applications, and naming conventions, to cite just a few critical areas

As you can see, there are many benefits related to the deployment of a virtual machine library to provision a virtualized infrastructure. In the following sections, we will cover in more depth items to consider when creating and managing a virtual machine library.

Creating a Virtual Machine Library

Creating a virtual machine library can be approached from two main angles: the development of processes to manually manage storage, access, and security of the library; or the purchase of a software application that enables the desired functionality. Here we will review the overall requirements when manually managing a virtual machine library. Chapter 19, "System Center Virtual Machine Manager 2007," is dedicated to the review of a new application in the System Center family called System Center Virtual Machine Manager (VMM). A core function of VMM is to enable and control a virtual machine library for a farm of Virtual Server hosts.

Components of a Virtual Machine Library

Although a virtual machine library can be as simple as a directory on a central file server that stores prepped virtual hard disks, the benefits of this type of approach are minimal. The following set of key components represents the minimum baseline required to achieve significant and tangible benefits:

- Centralized storage
- Structured roles
- Effective security

Centralized Storage

Centralized storage is a key building block for a virtual machine library. A centralized storage solution must have the following capabilities:

- High-speed network interfaces to minimize virtual machine deployment times
- Scalable, high-performance disk subsystem for compartmental storage areas
- Area for virtual machines in development
- Area for virtual machines managed storage
- Area for user storage of customized virtual machines
- Area for components such as operating system and application ISO images
- Area for tested and certified updates and service packs

High-Speed Network Interfaces

Virtual machines provisioned from a centralized storage solution are transferred over the network to Virtual Server hosts. The viability of a centralized solution is affected by the speed and number of virtual machines provisioned concurrently. Therefore, a centralized storage solution would likely require multiple high-speed network connections to achieve scalability and performance goals. Network interfaces should be no less than 1-gigabit Ethernet or 10-gigabit Ethernet, depending on the capacity of the existing network. At a minimum, there should be three high-speed interfaces to the central storage system. One should be dedicated to managing the central storage system, and two should be used for provisioning virtual machines.

Scalable and High-Performance Disk Subsystem

The scalability of a central storage solution is affected by the configuration of the disk subsystem. High disk I/O performance is also crucial to minimize provisioning time. Different data sets will be stored in the central storage solution, requiring different levels of read/write performance. Table 8-9 lists different solution storage areas and the required disk I/O performance.

Table 8-9 Storage Areas and Disk I/O Requirements

Area	Read/write performance configuration
Virtual machines in development storage	Read/write disk performance
Managed virtual machine storage	Read disk performance
User-customized virtual machine storage	Write disk performance
Supplemental tools storage	Read disk performance
Updates and service packs storage	Read disk performance

Structured Roles

Structured roles define the characteristic actions that users or groups of users will perform in relation to a virtual machine library. Roles differ from security groups in that they do not directly define the access control that must be implemented to secure the virtual machine library. For example, departmental managers who manage only a certain type of virtual machine or departmental virtual machines each need access rights to a different subset of virtual machines stored in the virtual machine library, while still performing identical functions for their department in relation to the virtual machine library. To enforce control access to the compartmental storage areas, you still need to define and manage security groups. In some cases, roles and security group might map one to one. However, this can be determined only after clearly defining the roles needed in an organization.

A role should reflect the system that will be managed, actions that will be performed, and resources that will be needed to perform the actions. Table 8-10 lists the bare minimum roles for a rudimentary virtual machine library. The builder role encompasses individuals who create virtual machines and place them in the managed storage area. The manager role is responsible for modifying and managing virtual machines once they are placed in the managed storage compartments. The user role provisions virtual machines to create new production or test environments.

Table 8-10 Virtual Machine Library Roles and Responsibilities

Role	Responsibilities
Builder	Create base virtual machines
	Install operating system and centrally managed applications
	Sysprep virtual machines
	Upload virtual machines to the library
Manager	Manage security
	Manage configuration settings of pre-built virtual machines
	Manage supplemental tools
	Retire outdated virtual machines from the library
	Retire outdated supplemental tools from the library
User	Provision virtual machines from the library

Note There are other roles that would bring value to manage virtual machines once provisioned to a Virtual Server host. You should define all of the roles that you will need based on the requirements for your specific environment.

Effective Security

Security groups are required to control access to storage compartment areas in the virtual machine library. The number of required security groups is driven by the granularity of the access controls that your organizational structure imposes. Table 8-11 describes three basic security groups required to control access of resources stored in the virtual machine library: Virtual Machine Builders, which is the team that creates the virtual machines; Virtual Machine Managers, which is the team that manages the configuration of stored virtual machines; and Virtual Machine Users, which is the group of users that use the library to provision new machines.

Table 8-11 Security Group Definitions

Security group	Access rights	Storage area or function
Virtual Machine Builders	Read, Write—All Files	In-development virtual machines
		Managed virtual machines
Virtual Machine Managers	Read, Write—All Files	Managed virtual machines
Virtual Machine Users	Read—All Files	Managed virtual machines

There are many reasons why you might require more granular security groups. You might want to further subdivide the virtual machine storage area and provide restricted access to only the subsections needed by each group. You might do this to divide management responsibilities or access to ready-to-be-deployed virtual machines. For example, you might want to limit who can manage or provision an Active Directory domain controller or a Microsoft Exchange mailbox server. To accomplish this, you need to create new storage compartments under the Managed Virtual Machines storage location for domain controllers and Exchange servers, and then place the appropriate domain controller and Exchange server managed virtual machines in those directories. You then need to create the new security groups shown in Table 8-12.

Table 8-12   Additional Security Group Definitions

Security group	Access rights	Storage area or function
Domain Controller Managers	Read, Write—All Files	Managed virtual machines\Domain controllers
Exchange Server Managers	Read, Write—All Files	Managed virtual machines\Exchange servers
Domain Controller Users	Read—All Files	Managed virtual machines\Domain controllers
Exchange Server Users	Read—All Files	Managed virtual machines\Exchange servers

You do not want to permit access to anyone else to the Managed Virtual Machines\Domain Controllers and Managed Virtual Machines\Exchange Servers directories.

Managing a Virtual Machine Library

Managing a virtual machine library presents some unique challenges. The following set of management tasks are common to all types of virtual machine libraries and must be performed on a regular basis:

- Capacity planning
- Patch management
- Security
- Content refresh

Capacity Planning

Capacity planning is a key management task to ensure that the central storage system does not run out of disk space or suffer from reduced performance because of low disk space. This task requires a tool such as Microsoft Operations Manager to track the disk space usage on the central storage system and define a set of thresholds to notify you when the disk space is getting low so that you can proactively add capacity. You should have a minimum of two levels of notifications: Warning and Danger. A warning notification is defined to provide early notification of a low disk space issue, allowing enough time to purchase the hard disks and schedule a maintenance window. A danger notification is typically sent when you are close to a defined threshold that, if triggered, would possibly have an impact on performance or result in the loss of data.

Patch Management

Patch management is the next key management task that is required to ensure that the virtual machines in the library have the latest set of security and nonsecurity updates. Patch management can be handled with different methods: CD-based updates distribution with scripted install, dedicated updates management tools such as Microsoft Software Update Service (MSUS), general-purpose tools such as Systems Management Server, or other methods. Table 8-13 describes the pros and cons of each approach for a virtual machine library.

Table 8-13   Patch Management Methods

Patch management method	Pros	Cons
CD-based distribution with automated script	Self contained No update management tool required No network access required Reporting on update success or failure is easy	Must maintain multiple versions of updates on CD Space limitation Installation method requires all updates to be installed every time No ability to restrict application of an update to a machine
Dedicated Patch Management Solution	Designed for optimal update management process Installs only required updates Allows targeting of updates to certain machines	Network access required Solution typically requires the updates to come from Windows Update Some solutions might require building custom deployment packages
General-Purpose Tool	Minimizes the number of tools required for updates Allows targeting of updates to certain machines	More labor intensive

Security

Properly managing security is a crucial task for a virtual machine library. A properly managed security environment helps the library run smoothly, restricts data access to the appropriate subset of needed resources, and maintains data integrity of the managed virtual machines. Managing virtual machine library security mainly revolves around keeping up-to-date security groups that control access rights, designing and tuning the required secure directory structure to properly compartmentalize stored virtual machines, and assigning security groups to the directory structure to ensure that proper security is enforced.

Content Refresh

A virtual machine library that contains versions of virtual machines that are no longer required or used reduces the value of the library and wastes valuable disk space. The tasks in the following list should be performed on a regular basis to keep the virtual machine library current:

- Creating new virtual machines
- Updating existing virtual machines
- Updating tool set
- Retiring unused virtual machines
- Retiring supplemental tools

Virtual machines usage will subside. When new versions of operating systems or applications are shipped and organizations migrate to the latest versions, there is a need to review and retire virtual machines and supplemental tools that are no longer required. This is a crucial task for which a process and solution must be developed and implemented in the absence of any sophisticated tool set to maintain a viable virtual machine library.

Summary

Remember to define the basic configuration settings prior to creating a new virtual machine. Prior to installing an operating system, tune the configuration of virtual machine components not specified during virtual machine creation time. If you have created virtual machines on other instances of Virtual Server, you can easily add them to the new Virtual Server host. If you want to permanently remove a virtual machine, you must manually delete the associated files, as these are not deleted automatically by Virtual Server.

Although many virtual machine BIOS settings are configurable, more than likely, you will only very occasionally adjust boot devices and boot order settings. There are several methods to install an operating system in a virtual machine, but use ISO image files for higher performance when doing a complete installation, rather than using a physical CD or DVD. Also, if repeated deployments are planned, use the Sysprep utility to prepare a VHD for duplication and fast provisioning of new virtual machines.

Install the Virtual Machine Additions after the operating system configuration to enhance the virtual machine performance and functionality. Finally, consider the benefits of creating a virtual machine library to store sysprepped VHDs and supplemental tools that can be used to very quickly provision new production or test-and-development virtual machine environments.

Additional Resources

The following resources contain additional information related to the topics in this chapter:

- Knowledge Base article 162001, "Do not disk duplicate installed versions of Windows," at *http://support.microsoft.com/kb/162001*

- Knowledge Base article 928386, "Sysprep functions and known issues," at *http://support.microsoft.com/kb/928386*

Chapter 9

Developing Scripts with the Virtual Server COM API

In this chapter:

Scripting with the COM API 227

What's New in SP1 235

Advanced Scripting Concepts 236

Managing Virtual Hard Disks 245

Managing Virtual Machines 253

Managing Virtual Networks 262

Managing a Virtual Server Configuration 267

Advanced Example 274

Summary 279

Additional Resources 280

Microsoft Virtual Server 2005 R2 provides a rich Component Object Model (COM) application programming interface (API) that can be accessed from any COM-compatible language, including Microsoft Visual Basic Script, Microsoft Visual Basic, JavaScript, J#, C++, and C#. The COM API provides over 300 interfaces and allows you to manage Virtual Servers and virtual machines locally or remotely. A complete programmer's reference guide to the API, *Virtual Server Programmer's Guide*, is installed with Virtual Server and can be found in \Program Files\Microsoft Virtual Server\Documentation folder. This chapter assumes that the reader has access to the programmer's guide and will use it as the primary reference for syntax requirements.

Scripting with the COM API

Unless you are a programmer using languages such as Visual Basic, C++, or C#, the scripting interface will be your primary method of using the Virtual Server COM API. Microsoft provides a programmer's guide with Virtual Server 2005 R2 that provides a reference to the syntax of all the available methods, functions, subroutines, properties, and constants. There are very few examples in the programmer's guide that actually show how to use the COM API. The remaining sections in this chapter detail how to use the COM API with Visual Basic Script.

The approach of the chapter is to provide you with building blocks and sample scripts that will minimize the time it takes you to learn the Virtual Server COM API. There are sections on connecting to the Virtual Server object locally and remotely; retrieving and displaying information; error handling; and advanced topics such as file and folder management, logging and retrieving events from the event log, understanding tasks, and using the Virtual Server WMI interfaces.

Once that basic knowledge has been provided, it is put to use while building scripts for managing virtual hard disks, virtual machines, virtual networks, and Virtual Server configuration information. The last script rolls everything covered into a single script example of how to back up and archive virtual machines files.

All the sample scripts provided incorporate error handling throughout the script to demonstrate how to properly handle and process errors in Visual Basic Script.

> **On the Companion Media**   All the scripts in this chapter are written in Visual Basic Script and provided on the companion media in the \Chapter Materials\Scripts directory.

> **On the Companion Media**   In addition to the scripts provided in the chapter as examples, you will find additional scripts in the \Bonus Materials\Scripts directory.

> **Note**   You can find additional sample scripts at the Microsoft TechNet Script Center for Virtual Server at *http://www.microsoft.com/technet/scriptcenter/scripts/vs/default.mspx*.

Connecting to the Virtual Server Object

Before you can interact with the Virtual Server COM API, you must establish a connection to the Virtual Server service using the *VMVirtualServer* interface. With Visual Basic Script, this is accomplished using the *CreateObject()* method and the "VirtualServer.Application" parameter. The following code declares a variable to hold the Virtual Server object reference and then assigns the object to the variable when the connection is established:

```
Option Explicit
Dim objVS
Set objVS = CreateObject("VirtualServer.Application")
```

In the first line of the script, *Option Explicit* is specified to ensure that you declare all variables. Without *Option Explicit*, typing errors or undeclared variables can cause unexpected results that are hard to troubleshoot. The next line, *Dim objVS*, declares a variable to be used as an object reference to the Virtual Server object. The third line, *Set objVS = CreateObject("VirtualServer.Application")*, calls the VBScript function *CreateObject*, passing the *servicename.typename* for an automation object. In this case, *servicename* is *VirtualServer* and the type is *Application*. The *CreateObject* function returns an object reference, which is assigned to the variable you created using the *Set* command.

Once you have a reference to the *VMVirtualServer* interface, you can access the properties and use its methods. Properties of the *VMVirtualServer* interface allow you to obtain information about the current Virtual Server configuration, such as information about the host running Virtual Server or what version of Virtual Server this host is running. Some properties can be accessed directly; others are stored in collections. Collections are arrays of objects that you can enumerate to find out more information.

Retrieving and Displaying Information

Once you have the Virtual Server object, you can access any property by referencing the property as a child object of the Virtual Server object. For example, to find out the version of Virtual Server running on this machine, you retrieve the *Version* property. Property variables must be declared like object references, but unlike object references property variables do not require you to assign the retrieved property to the declared variable using the *Set* command. For example, to retrieve the version of the Virtual Server software running on the machine, you declare a variable to hold the version property and then store the retrieved value in the variable:

```
Dim strVersion
strVersion = objVS.Version
```

Now that you have the property value in a variable, you can display the value on the screen. The easiest way to do this is with the *WScript.Echo* command. The *Echo* command allows you to combine text and the variable value in a string for display on the screen. The & symbol is a concatenation symbol for combining text strings and variables in an *Echo* statement:

```
WScript.Echo "Text before the variable" & strVersion & "text after the variable"
```

Direct from the Source: Configuring the Default Scripting Host

The *WScript.Echo* behavior you get depends on whether *CScript* or *WScript* is the script host. While both versions will execute a Visual Basic script, *CScript* is the command-line version and *WScript* is the Windows version. By default, if you execute a Visual Basic Script without specifying the scripting host, *WScript* executes the script. Any *WScript.Echo* commands result in a popup dialog box that must be dismissed by pressing the OK button. Until the dialog box is dismissed, the script execution is paused. Although this can be helpful when troubleshooting a script, this is not desirable for production scripts. Executing the scripts using *CScript* allows all output to be written to the console and not require any confirmation. You can change the default behavior in one of two ways. The first way is to run the script from the command line using CSCRIPT <*vbscript filename*>. This forces the script to use the *CScript* scripting host. The second way is to make *CScript* the default script host. To accomplish this, open a command prompt window and run CSCRIPT //H:CSCRIPT This sets the host to *CScript* and saves the settings for the active user.

John Howard
Program Manager, Windows Virtualization Product Group

For properties that are stored in collections, the retrieval process is slightly different. For example, to retrieve the virtual machines that are registered on the Virtual Server you must obtain a reference to the collection in which they are stored, assign it to the variable using the *Set* command, and then enumerate the collection to obtain the properties of the virtual machine. The *VirtualMachines* property of the Virtual Server object returns an object reference to the collection of virtual machines:

```
Dim objVMCollection
Set objVMCollection = objVS.VirtualMachines
```

Once you have the object reference to the virtual machine collection, you can enumerate through the virtual machine collection using a *For Next* loop and retrieve the properties of each virtual machine. Looping through the virtual machine objects requires a reference to access the items in the list. In the following example, the object reference *objVM* is used:

```
Dim objVM
For Each objVM in objVMCollection
   WScript.Echo " VM Name: " & objVM.Name
Next
```

The collection object also has properties. A useful property is *Count*. *Collection.Count* provides the number of items in the collection. You can use the *Count* property and a conditional statement to determine whether you should enumerate the collection.

You can combine all the code into a single script that connects to Virtual Server, gets a reference to a collection of virtual machines, and then lists the name of all the virtual machines to the screen.

```
GetVMList.vbs
Option Explicit
Dim objVS, objVMCollection, objVM

Set objVS = CreateObject("VirtualServer.Application")
Set objVMCollection = objVS.VirtualMachines

If objVMCollection.Count > 0 Then
   WScript.Echo "Number Virtual machines: " & objVMCollection.Count
   For Each objVM in objVMCollection
      WScript.Echo " VM Name: " & objVM.Name
   Next
Else
   WScript.Echo "Number Virtual machines: [none]"
End If
```

Error Handling

Visual Basic script has error-handling support. The two primary interfaces available to detect and deal with errors are the *Err* object and the *ON ERROR* statement. The *Err* object is available by default and does not have to be declared. The properties of the *Err* object are automatically set in the event of a run-time error. The five properties of the *Err* object are described in Table 9-1.

Table 9-1   *Err* Object Properties

Property	Description
Description	Short description of the error
Number	Run-time error number in the range of 0 through 65535
Source	Name of the object that generated the error
HelpFile	Help file name to use for error responses
HelpContext	Context ID for the help topic to be displayed

The properties of *Err* object allow you to determine the error number that was raised, the description (if one is defined), and the help information based on the context identifier. In addition to allowing you to determine the *Err* properties, the *Err* object has two methods that can be of assistance in error handling. Table 9-2 provides a description of the two methods.

Table 9-2   *Err* Object Methods

Method	Description
Clear	Resets the *Err.Number* value to zero.
Raise	Raises an error. The error can be a system-defined or user-defined error number. You can optionally specify *Source*, *Description*, *HelpFile*, and *HelpContext* values.

Use the *Clear* method when you want to reset the error description, and use the *Raise* method when you want to force a system error to occur or when you want to create custom errors for your application. If you decide to create custom errors for a script or application, be sure to specify the optional parameter *Description* at a minimum.

> **Note**   You will find the reference for Visual Basic Script run-time and syntax errors on the Microsoft Developer Network (MSDN) site at *http://msdn2.microsoft.com/en-us/library /5ta518cw.aspx*.

The *On Error* statement enables or disables error-handling inline in the script. When you want to detect an error and provide error handling, you place *On Error Resume Next* in your script and then provide code to detect an error and perform the appropriate action. *On Error Resume Next* handles the error by allowing the script to continue and assumes that the script will process the error and do the correct action. Placing *On Error Resume Next* in your script and no error handling code is a bad scripting practice. To disable the error handler, place *On Error GoTo 0* after the error-handling code.

The ConnectToVS.vbs script combines the *Err* object and the *On Error* statement to detect whether an error has occurred when connecting to the *VMVirtualServer* interface.

```
ConnectToVS.vbs
Option Explicit
Dim objVS, strVersion
On Error Resume Next
Set objVS = CreateObject("VirtualServer.Application")

If Err.number <> 0 Then
    WScript.Echo "Failed to connect to Virtual Server"
    WScript.Echo "Error Number=" & Err.Number & " Description=" & _
       Err.Description
    WScript.Quit
Else
    WScript.Echo "Successfully connected to Virtual Server"
    On Error GoTo 0
End if

strVersion = objVS.Version
WScript.Echo "Connected to Virtual Server version:" & strVersion
```

To enable error handling, place *On Error Resume Next* before the call to *CreateObject* and then place the code to handle the error directly after the call to *CreateObject*. This ensures that the error is detected and properly handled.

The error-handling code in the *If* block checks for an error first using *Err.number <> 0*. If *Err.number* is not zero, an error has occurred. Using the *WScript.Echo* command, a message is provided to the user that explains that an error has occurred and that provides the specific error number and error description. Then the script quits by executing the script using the *WScript.Quit* command. If there is no error, the script outputs a successful connection message, clears any error messages, and disables error handling by calling *On Error GoTo 0*. To verify the connection, the version of Virtual Server is retrieved using the *objVS.Version* property and displayed using the *WScript.Echo* command.

Note   There are lines of sample scripts in this chapter that are too long to fit on a single line because of the width of the page. These lines will use the line continuation character "_" to indicate that the line is continued on the next line.

Direct from the Source: Debugging Scripts

Visual Basic scripts are programs. Do not underestimate the complexity or size of code possible just because you are writing scripts. There are several tools that can be used to make your job much easier when debugging complex scripts. A free interactive debugger is available from Microsoft at the following location: *http://www.microsoft.com/downloads/details.aspx?familyid=2f465be0-94fd-4569-b3c4-dffdf19ccd99&displaylang=en.*

> To use the script debugger, you specify the //x and //d command-line options to cscript.exe as follows: cscript //x //d yourscript.vbs. When the script starts, the debugger will automatically start and wait at the first executable line in the script. You can press F8 to step through the code line by line, press F9 to set breakpoints, or press F5 to start execution until either the script terminates or until a breakpoint or error is encountered. You can also place STOP statements anywhere in your script to force the debugger to stop at that location. Using the debugger command window allows you to display or change the value of variables at any point during the execution of the script. You can also enter VBScript commands directly to see values returned by VBScript statements. Other commercially available debuggers that offer additional capabilities are available for purchase from Microsoft and third parties. A script debugger should be part of every scripter's toolbox to help create high quality, fully debugged scripts.
>
> *Ken Durigan*
> *Architect, Microsoft Consulting Services*

Connecting to Remote Virtual Server

Connecting to a remote Virtual Server requires a simple change to the *CreateObject* command that consists of adding the remote server name as a second parameter:

```
Set objVS = CreateObject("VirtualServer.Application", <remote server name>)
```

The remote server name can be specified as just the name of the server (server1), the fully qualified name of the server (server1.contoso.com), or an IP address (192.168.0.1). Typically, you do not want to hard code the remote server parameter when you use this option. To pass the parameter to the script, use the *WScript.Arguments* interface. *WScript.Arguments* returns an object reference to a collection that stores the parameters specified on the command line. Once you have a reference to the collection, you can access any command-line parameters and use them in the script.

Modifying the sample script to connect to a remote Virtual Server specified as a single command-line parameter requires the addition of a line that retrieves the command-line parameters and assigns them to an object reference:

```
Set objArgs = WScript.Arguments
```

Once that object reference has been set, the first command-line parameter *objArgs(0)* can be retrieved and used as the remote server name. Using command-line parameters requires that you add more error checking to ensure that the expected command-line parameter was provided:

```
If objArgs.Count = 0 then
   WScript.Echo "ERROR: Remote server not specified"
   WScript.Quit
End if
```

This code checks the first command-line object to see whether there are any arguments by using *If objArgs.Count = 0*. If no arguments exist, it provides an error message and quits the script. If arguments exist, it continues assuming the argument is properly specified. Connect-ToRemoteVS.vbs incorporates the changes to connect to a remote Virtual Server and obtain the version of Virtual Server software that is running.

```
ConnectToRemoteVS.vbs
Option Explicit
Dim objVS, strVersion, objArgs

Set objArgs = WScript.Arguments

If objArgs.count = 0 then
   WScript.Echo " ERROR: Remote server not specified"
   WScript.Quit
End if


On Error Resume Next
Set objVS = CreateObject("VirtualServer.Application", objArgs(0))

If Err.number <> 0 Then
   WScript.Echo "Failed to connect to Virtual Server"
   WScript.Echo "Error Number=" & Err.Number & " Description=" & _
     Err.Description
   WScript.Quit
Else
   WScript.Echo "Successfully connected to Virtual Server" & objArgs(0)
   Err.Clear
   On Error GoTo 0
End if

strVersion = objVS.Version
WScript.Echo "Virtual Server version:"& strVersion
```

To run the script from the command line, you use the following syntax: *Cscript ConnectToRemoteVS.vbs <remoteservername>*. If you want to connect to the local computer, you can specify the computer name or *localhost*. You could also modify the script to use the local host automatically if no remote server name is specified.

Important   Connecting to a remote server requires that the account that executes the ConnectToRemoteVS.vbs script has permissions to the remote server. If the account does not have correct permissions, you will receive an *Error=70* message and a description of *Permission Denied*.

What's New in SP1

Virtual Server 2005 R2 SP1 brings the first changes to the COM API since its release. The changes are minor, and they are additive to the overall API.

VHDMount Functions

Three new functions have been added to the COM API to provide support for VHDMount released with Virtual Server 2005 R2 SP1. Table 9-3 provides the function name and description of the new functions.

Table 9-3   VHDMount Functions

Function	Description
GetSCSIAddress	Returns the SCSI address of the virtual hard disk (VHD) mounted using the *MountVHD* function
MountVHD	Mounts the specified virtual hard disk file (.vhd file) as a virtual disk device
UnMountVHD	Unmounts a virtual hard disk file (.vhd file) that had been mounted with the *MountVHD* function

These functions allow you to programmatically mount and interact with VHD files. The new interfaces are available only from nonscripting languages.

VMTask Properties

The *VMTask* interface has been extended with two new properties: *VMTask.Error* and *VMTask.ErrorDescription*. The *Error* property contains the error recorded for the task, and the *ErrorDescription* property has the description of the error. When using a method that returns a task such as *CreateDifferencingVirtualHardDisk*, the task object reference allows you to retrieve the two new parameters. The following Visual Basic Script code provides an example:

```
Set CreateDiffTask = objVS.CreateDifferencingVirtualHardDisk _
                    ("c:\diff1.vhd", "C:\test1.vhd")
WScript.Echo CreateDiffTask.Error
WScript.Echo CreateDiffTask.ErrorDescription
```

The usage of these properties might not be intuitive. If the *CreateDifferencingVirtualHardDisk* method experiences an error when trying to start the operation, it will not return an object reference, and therefore, you will not be able to access the *Error* and *ErrorDescription* properties of the task. The new properties apply only to the running task itself, and they provide information if a failure occurs during the task operation.

VMGuestOS Properties and Methods

The *VMGuestOS* class has been extended with a new method and a new property. The new method, *VMGuestOS.GetParameter*, retrieves a predefined or user-defined configuration parameters from inside the guest operation system. The virtual machine must be running, and the latest virtual machine additions must be installed for this method to work. This method is supported only for Microsoft Windows–based guest operating systems. When virtual machine additions are installed, the following key is automatically added to the guest operating system's registry:

```
HKEY_LOCAL_MACHINE\SOFTWARE\Microsoft\Virtual Machine\Guest\Parameters
```

When the guest operating system starts, the following registry string values are populated in the *Parameters* key:

- *HostName*
- *PhysicalHostName*
- *PhysicalHostNameFullyQualified*
- *VirtualMachineName*

The following sample Visual Basic Script code shows how to retrieve the *HostName* parameter from a running virtual machine with Virtual Machine Additions installed:

```
Dim hostname
hostname = objVM.GuestOS.GetParameter("HostName")
WScript.Echo hostname
```

The new property, *GuestOS.ComputerName*, retrieves the computer name of the virtual machine. This property also requires that the virtual machine is running and the latest virtual machine additions are installed. The following sample Visual Basic Script code shows how to retrieve the computer name from a running virtual machine and display it on the screen:

```
WScript.Echo objVM.GuestOS.ComputerName
```

VMRCClientControl Property

A new property was added to *VMRCClientControl* called *ShrinkEnabled*. The *VMRCClientControl.ShrinkEnabled* property contains a Boolean value of *True* if the client window that contains the VMRC control can stretch its contents to fit the current window size.

Advanced Scripting Concepts

Writing scripts using the Virtual Server COM API eventually requires access to some advanced scripting functionality such as modifying files and folders, logging events to the Windows event log, monitoring task completion, or using the Windows Management Interface (WMI).

File and Folder Management

Visual Basic Script has a class called *Scripting* with an interface called *FileSystemObject*. This interface has a long list of methods, but the key methods for file and folder management are listed in Table 9-4.

Table 9-4   *Scripting.FileSystemObject* **File and Folder Methods**

Method	Description
CopyFile	Copies one or more files from a source to a destination with the option to overwrite the file if it already exists.
CopyFolder	Copies one or more folders and their contents from a source to a destination with the option to overwrite the folder if it already exists.
CreateFolder	Creates a folder using the specified path.
DeleteFile	Deletes one or more files with the option to force the deletion of a file if it is read-only.
DeleteFolder	Deletes one or more folders with the option to force the deletion of a folder if it is read-only.
FileExists	Checks for a file using the path and filename specified, and returns *True* if it exists or *False* if it does not.
FolderExists	Checks for a folder using the path specified, and returns *True* if it exists or *False* if it does not.
MoveFile	Moves one or more files from a source to a destination.
MoveFolder	Moves one or more folders from a source to a destination.

Before you can use any of the *FileSystemObject* methods, you must obtain an object reference to the *Scripting.FileSystemObject* interface as shown here:

```
Dim objFSO
Set objFSO = CreateObject("Scripting.FileSystemObject")
```

Once you have the object reference assigned to the *objFSO* variable, you can use that variable to access all the methods. For example, if you want to move and copy some files from a source directory to a backup directory, you need to use the following methods:

- *FolderExists*, to make sure the source and backup directories exist
- *CreateFolder*, to create the backup folder
- *DeleteFile*, to delete any old copies of the files
- *MoveFile*, to move files from the source directory to the backup directory
- *CopyFile*, to copy files from the source directory to the backup directory

As an alternative to copying or moving files, you can copy or move the entire folder.

BackupFiles.vbs is an example of how to use the *FileSystemObject* methods to back up files from a source directory to a backup directory.

```
BackupFiles.vbs
Option Explicit

Dim objFSO
Dim strBackupPath, strSourcePath
'=========================================================================
' Create a reference to the FileSystemObject
'=========================================================================
Set objFSO = CreateObject("Scripting.FileSystemObject")

strSourcePath = "E:\FILES"
strBackupPath = strSourcePath & "\" & "BACKUP"


'=========================================================================
' Check if the source path exists
'=========================================================================
If (NOT objFSO.FolderExists(strSourcePath)) then
    WScript.Echo "ERROR: Source path does not exist"
    WScript.Quit
End If


'=========================================================================
' Create the Backup folder if it does not exist
' or delete all the files in the backup folder if it does exist
'=========================================================================
If (NOT objFSO.FolderExists(strBackupPath)) then
    objFSO.CreateFolder(strBackupPath)
else
    objFSO.DeleteFile strBackupPath & "\*"
End if

objFSO.MoveFile strSourcePath & "\*.txt", strBackupPath
objFSO.CopyFile strSourcePath & "\*.doc", strBackupPath

WScript.Echo "Copy and Move Complete"
```

Logging Events

When you create small simple scripts or large complicated scripts, you might want to log the script progress. You can do this by creating your own custom log file and a tool to parse it, or you can use the Windows event logs. If you want to log errors to the Application event log on the local computer, you can use the Windows Scripting Host *LogEvent* method. *LogEvent* allows you to specify the event types shown in Table 9-5 and provide a message to log with the event. If the event was written to the log successfully, *LogEvent* returns *True*; otherwise, it is *False*.

Table 9-5 Event Log Types

Event type	Description
0	Success
1	Error
2	Warning
4	Information
8	Audit_Success
16	Audit Failure

Before you can log any errors, you must create a connection to the shell interface *WScript.Shell*. Once you have the object reference, you can then call the *LogEvent* method. The syntax for *LogEvent* is

```
object.LogEvent(Type, Message)
```

where *Type* is one of the event types listed in Table 9-5 and *Message* is the text string that will be recorded in the event. LogEvent.vbs provides a simple example of creating an object reference to the *Shell* and then calling the *LogEvent* method for an event type of success and failure.

```
LogEvent.vbs
Option Explicit
Dim objShell

'===========================================================================
' Get a connection to the Windows Shell
'===========================================================================
Set objShell = WScript.CreateObject("WScript.Shell")

objShell.LogEvent 0, "Successful operation"
objShell.LogEvent 1, "ERROR: Failed operation"
```

If you run this on a machine, you can open the Event Viewer administration tool and see two new events in the application log showing the source application as Windows Scripting Host (WSH), the event id as 0 or 1, and the text messages in the description text box.

The *Shell* object does not have a method to retrieve events from the event log. To do this, you must use WMI. To retrieve the errors that you logged, you can use *GetObject* function with a WMI object path as the input parameter. If you use an object path that contains the winmgmts prefix and the default namespace of \root\cimv2, you get an object reference to the WMI service. Once the object is obtained, you can use the *ExecQuery* method and a Transact SQL statement to retrieve a collection of Event log entries. Depending on how you format the Transact SQL query string, you can filter the returned events. For example, if you want to query the Application event log and retrieve only the events that have a source name of WSH, the query string looks like this:

```
Select * from Win32_NTLogEvent Where Logfile = 'Application'_
    AND SourceName = 'WSH'
```

ReadEvents.vbs is a sample script that uses this query string to retrieve all the WSH Source-Name event log entries from the application event log. Once you have the filtered collection of Event log entries, the script prints out the information contained in the Event log entry.

```
ReadEvents.vbs
Option Explicit

Dim strComputer, objWMIService, colLoggedEvents, objEvent
strComputer = "."

Set objWMIService = GetObject("winmgmts:\\" & strComputer & "\root\cimv2")

Set colLoggedEvents = objWMIService.ExecQuery _
  ("Select * from Win32_NTLogEvent " _
    & "Where Logfile = 'Application' AND SourceName = 'WSH'")

If colLoggedEvents.Count = 0 Then
  WScript.Echo "ERROR: No Events match the query"
  WScript.Quit
End If

For Each objEvent in colLoggedEvents
  WScript.Echo "Category: " & objEvent.Category & VBNewLine _
  & "Computer Name: " & objEvent.ComputerName & VBNewLine _
  & "Event Code: " & objEvent.EventCode & VBNewLine _
  & "Message: " & objEvent.Message & VBNewLine _
  & "Record Number: " & objEvent.RecordNumber & VBNewLine _
  & "Source Name: " & objEvent.SourceName & VBNewLine _
  & "Time Written: " & objEvent.TimeWritten & VBNewLine _
  & "Event Type: " & objEvent.Type & VBNewLine _
  & "User: " & objEvent.User
Next
```

Using Tasks

Tasks are used to track and obtain the status of asynchronous actions of COM methods. There are many Virtual Server COM API methods that return a *VMTask* interface so that the progress of the task can be tracked. Table 9-6 shows the *VMTask* methods that you can use to manage the task that is running.

Table 9-6   *VMTask* Methods

Method	Description
WaitForCompletion	Waits for the task to complete or until the specified timeout expires
Cancel	Cancels the task
PercentCompleted	Returns the completion percentage of the task
Description	Returns the description of the task
Result	Returns the result of the task
IsCancelable	Returns TRUE if the task can be canceled before completion

Table 9-6   *VMTask* Methods

Method	Description
ID	Returns the unique ID for the task
IsComplete	Returns TRUE if the task has completed

Virtual Server 2005 R2 SP1 introduces two new extensions to the *VMTask* interface. *VMTask2* is an extended version of the *VMTask* class that adds the two new properties shown in Table 9-7.

Table 9-7   *VMTask2* Methods

Property	Description
Error	Contains the value (HRESULT) of the error
ErrorDescription	Contains the description of the error

The simplest usage of the *VMTask* interface is to define a variable to hold a *VMTask* object reference and assign the *VMTask* return value from a method. Once you have that reference, you can then call a *VMTask* method such as *WaitForCompletion* to wait for the asynchronous task to complete:

```
Dim objTask

Set objTask = interface.method()
objTask.WaitForCompletion(10000)

If objTask.IsComplete Then
   wScript.Echo "Task Successful"
Else
   wScript.Echo "Task still not Complete"
End If
```

The sample code demonstrates the declaration and assignment of the *objTask* variable, which is the task from the method. The *WaitForCompletion* method is then called with a value of 10000 milliseconds. The script waits for one of two actions to happen: the task completes within 10 seconds and the method returns early, or the task does not complete within 10 seconds and the method exits. In the first case, the *IsComplete* method returns *True*; in the second case, the *IsComplete* method returns *False*.

Caution   Be careful when using *WaitForCompletion* within loops such as *Do..While* and *While..Wend*. There is no built-in safety mechanism in the *WaitForCompletion* method that will prevent an infinite loop. There is also no guarantee that the task will ever complete, so checking for *IsComplete* without a limit on the number of times you check is not a good idea.

Using the Virtual Server WMI Namespace

Virtual Server has a WMI namespace that is not very well documented. The root of the namespace is \root\vm\virtualserver, and it contains only two classes: *VirtualMachine* and *VirtualNetwork*. Each class has a series of properties that can be accessed. Table 9-8 lists the *VirtualMachine* class properties. The WMI properties of the *VirtualMachine* object allow you to obtain information about uptime, processor, disk, memory, and network usage by each virtual machine, in addition to heartbeat information.

Table 9-8   *VirtualMachine* WMI Class Properties

Counter	Information
Name	Name of the virtual machine
CpuUtilization	Percentage of CPU resources allocated to this virtual machine that are currently in use
DiskBytesRead	Number of bytes read by all the virtual hard disks assigned to this virtual machine since the virtual machine was last turned on
DiskBytesWritten	Number of bytes written by all virtual hard disks assigned to this virtual machine
DiskSpaceUsed	Total disk space used by this virtual machine on all the disks that are assigned to it
HeartbeatCount	Number of heartbeats received since the virtual machine was last turned on
HeartbeatInterval	Duration of the heartbeat interval in seconds
HeartbeatPercentage	Percentage of total expected heartbeats that have been received in the last heartbeat interval
HeartbeatRate	The number of heartbeats expected per heartbeat interval
NetworkBytesReceived	Total bytes received by all virtual networks assigned to this virtual machine
NetworkBytesSent	Total bytes sent by all virtual networks assigned to this virtual machine
PhysicalMemoryAllocated	The system memory allocated to this virtual machine
Uptime	Number of seconds that the virtual machine has been running since it was last turned on

The VM_WMI_Properties.vbs script displays all properties of every running virtual machine on the specified Virtual Server host. If there are no running virtual machines, verified by *colItems.Count = 0*, an error message is provided. The property information retrieved is for each virtual machine, not a cumulative total.

VM_WMI_Properties.vbs

```
Option Explicit

dim strComputer, objWMIService, colItems, objItem

strComputer = "localhost"

Set objWMIService = GetObject("winmgmts:\\" & strComputer & _
    "\root\vm\virtualserver")

Set colItems = objWMIService.ExecQuery("SELECT * FROM VirtualMachine")

If colItems.Count = 0 Then
    WScript.Echo "ERROR: No virtual machines running"
    WScript.Quit
End If

For Each objItem in colItems
    WScript.Echo "---------------------------------"
    WScript.Echo "VirtualMachine instance"
    WScript.Echo "---------------------------------"
    WScript.Echo "Name: " & objItem.Name
    WScript.Echo "CpuUtilization: " & objItem.CpuUtilization
    WScript.Echo "DiskBytesRead: " & objItem.DiskBytesRead
    WScript.Echo "DiskBytesWritten: " & objItem.DiskBytesWritten
    WScript.Echo "DiskSpaceUsed: " & objItem.DiskSpaceUsed
    WScript.Echo "HeartbeatCount: " & objItem.HeartbeatCount
    WScript.Echo "HeartbeatInterval: " & objItem.HeartbeatInterval
    WScript.Echo "HeartbeatPercentage: " & objItem.HeartbeatPercentage
    WScript.Echo "HeartbeatRate: " & objItem.HeartbeatRate
    WScript.Echo "NetworkBytesReceived: " & objItem.NetworkBytesReceived
    WScript.Echo "NetworkBytesSent: " & objItem.NetworkBytesSent
    WScript.Echo "PhysicalMemoryAllocated: " & objItem.PhysicalMemoryAllocated
    WScript.Echo "Uptime: " & objItem.Uptime
Next
```

Table 9-9 has the listing of *VirtualNetwork* class properties. The WMI properties of the *VirtualNetwork* class allow you to obtain dropped, received, and sent information for packets on the virtual network. You can obtain the information in either bytes or packet numbers. Only virtual networks that are attached to physical network adapters and have running virtual machines attached will show information.

Table 9-9 *VirtualNetwork* WMI Class Properties

Counter	Information
Name	Name of the physical network adapter to which this virtual network is attached.
BytesDropped	Number of bytes dropped by this virtual network. Any number above zero indicates a virtual network failure.

Table 9-9   *VirtualNetwork* WMI Class Properties

Counter	Information
BytesReceived	Total bytes received by this virtual network since the first virtual machine attached to it was turned on.
BytesSent	Total bytes sent by this virtual network since the first virtual machine attached to it was turned on.
PacketsDropped	Number of packets of data dropped by this virtual network. Any number above zero indicates a virtual network failure.
PacketsReceived	Total packets of data received by this virtual network since the first virtual machine attached to it was turned on.
PacketsSent	Total packets of data sent by this virtual network since the first virtual machine attached to it was turned on.

The VNET_WMI_Properties.vbs script displays all properties of every virtual network on the specified Virtual Server host. If there are no virtual networks with running virtual machines, verified by *colItems.Count = 0*, an error message is provided.

```
VNET_WMI_Properties.vbs
Option Explicit

dim strComputer, objWMIService, colItems, objItem

strComputer = "localhost"

Set objWMIService = GetObject("winmgmts:\\" & strComputer & "\root\vm\virtualserver")

Set colItems = objWMIService.ExecQuery("SELECT * FROM VirtualNetwork")

If colItems.Count = 0 Then
    WScript.Echo "ERROR: No virtual machines running on any virtual network"
    WScript.Quit
End If

For Each objItem in colItems
    WScript.Echo "----------------------------------"
    WScript.Echo "VirtualNetwork instance"
    WScript.Echo "----------------------------------"
    WScript.Echo "Name: " & objItem.Name
    WScript.Echo "BytesDropped: " & objItem.BytesDropped
    WScript.Echo "BytesReceived: " & objItem.BytesReceived
    WScript.Echo "BytesSent: " & objItem.BytesSent
    WScript.Echo "PacketsDropped: " & objItem.PacketsDropped
    WScript.Echo "PacketsReceived: " & objItem.PacketsReceived
    WScript.Echo "PacketsSent: " & objItem.PacketsSent
Next
```

> ## Direct from the Source: WMI Made Simple
>
> The Windows Management Interface (WMI) is a very powerful API that allows scripters to get at a variety of system information. It can be difficult to learn such a large API for anyone starting out with scripting. Fortunately, there is a free tool called Scriptomatic 2.0 available from Microsoft at the following location: *http://www.microsoft.com/downloads/details.aspx?FamilyID=09dfc342-648b-4119-b7eb-783b0f7d1178&DisplayLang=en*.
>
> Scriptomatic 2.0 writes WMI code for you and allows you to copy and paste the resulting source code into your scripts. Scriptomatic also allows you to explore the WMI classes to help you to find exactly what you are looking for.
>
> *Ken Durigan*
> *Architect, Microsoft Consulting Services*

Managing Virtual Hard Disks

Managing virtual hard disks (VHDs) by using scripts allows you to quickly obtain information about existing virtual hard disks, create new virtual hard disks, and add created virtual hard disks to virtual machines. Operations that affect an existing virtual hard disk require obtaining an object reference to the virtual hard disk first. This can be accomplished in two ways: by using the *VMVirtualServer.GetHardDisk* method if you know the full path to the VHD file, or by enumerating all the virtual hard disks connected to a virtual machine to identify the disk and obtain an object reference.

Virtual Server supports four types of virtual hard disks: dynamic, fixed, differencing, and linked. Table 9-10 shows the *VMVirtualServer* methods to manage virtual hard disks.

Table 9-10   *VMVirtualServer* Methods to Create VHDs

Method name	Description
CreateDynamicVirtualHardDisk	Creates a dynamically expanding virtual hard disk
CreateFixedVirtualHardDisk	Creates a fixed-size virtual hard disk
CreateDifferencingVirtualHardDisk	Creates a differencing virtual hard disk from a parent
CreateHostDriveVirtualHardDisk	Creates a linked disk to a host volume

> **Note**   There is no method to delete virtual hard disks, and you will find no operation in the Virtual Server COM API that will delete virtual hard disks. This was a deliberate decision by the Virtual Server team to ensure that no Virtual Server COM API method could accidently delete critical VHD files. If you want to delete VHD files, you can use the *FileSystemObject's DeleteFile* method.

Once you have created virtual hard disks, you need to add the virtual hard disk to a virtual machine or remove it from a virtual machine. You can perform these operations only if the virtual machine is in a turned-off state and no saved state exists. Table 9-11 shows the VMVirtualMachine methods to manage adding virtual hard disks to a virtual machine or removing them from a virtual machine.

Table 9-11   VMVirtualMachine Methods to Add or Remove VHDs

Method name	Description
AddHardDiskConnection	Adds a new virtual hard disk to the virtual machine
RemoveHardDiskConnection	Removes an existing virtual hard disk from the virtual machine, but does not delete the VHD file

Obtaining Virtual Hard Disk Information

As part of a virtual machine management regiment, you might want to routinely obtain information about virtual hard disks attached to registered virtual machines. GetHardDiskInfo.vbs provides an example of how to enumerate all the connected virtual hard disks of a virtual machine and obtain the following information:

- How the hard disk is connected (Bus, device number, and bus type)

- The path to the virtual hard disk file

- The amount of free host disk space available for VHD expansion

- The maximum size of the VHD as reported in the guest

- The current size of the VHD as reported on the host

- The type of virtual hard disk (dynamic, fixed, differencing, linked)

- For linked disks, which host drive is linked

GetHardDiskInfo.vbs accomplishes this by obtaining an object reference to the virtual machine, using that reference to get the property *HardDiskConnections* (which points to a collection), using the hard disk collection to enumerate each drive, and using the drive's *HardDisk* property to obtain information about the virtual hard disk.

GetHardDiskInfo.vbs

```
'=============================================================================
' GetHardDiskInfo.vbs - Retrieves hard disk info from every hard disk
' connection of a virtual machine
'=============================================================================
Option Explicit

Dim objVM1, objVS, objArgs, objHD, objDrive, objHardDisk, objUndoDrive
Dim colHDs
Dim strVMName
Dim VMDiskType(5)
```

```
VMDiskType(0) = "Dynamic"
VMDiskType(1) = "Fixed"
VMDiskType(2) = "Differencing"
VMDiskType(3) = "Undefined"
VMDiskType(4) = "Linked"


'===================================================================
' Retrieve Command-Line Arguments
'===================================================================
set objArgs = WScript.Arguments

If objArgs.Count<> 1 Then
  WScript.Echo "Missing command line argument"
  WScript.Echo "VMName"
  WScript.Quit
End If


strVMName = objArgs(0)
'===================================================================
' Get a connection to Virtual Server on local machine
'===================================================================
On Error Resume Next
Set objVS = CreateObject("VirtualServer.Application")

If Err.number <> 0 Then
   WScript.Echo "Failed to connect to Virtual Server"
   WScript.Echo "Error Number=" & Err.Number & " Description=" & _
      Err.Description
   WScript.Quit
Else
   WScript.Echo "Successfully connected to Virtual Server"
   On Error GoTo 0
End if


'===================================================================
' Get an Object link to the strVMName virtual machine
'===================================================================
Set objVM1 = objVS.FindVirtualMachine(strVMName)

If objVM1 is nothing then
   WScript.Echo "Unable to Find " & strVMName
   WScript.Quit
End If

On Error Resume Next
Set colHDs = objVM1.HardDiskConnections

If colHDs.Count > 0 Then
   WScript.Echo "Hard disk connections: " & colHDs.Count

   For Each objDrive in colHDs
      WScript.Echo "Virtual machine: " & objVM1.Name
      WScript.Echo "Bus number: " & objDrive.BusNumber
      WScript.Echo "Bus type: " & objDrive.BusType
```

```
        WScript.Echo "Device number: " & objDrive.DeviceNumber

        Set objHardDisk = objDrive.HardDisk
        WScript.Echo "Hard disk file: " & objHardDisk.File
        WScript.Echo "Host drive identifier: " & _
            objHardDisk.HostDriveIdentifier
        WScript.Echo "Host free disk space: " & _
            objHardDisk.HostFreeDiskSpace
        WScript.Echo "Size in guest: " & objHardDisk.SizeInGuest
        WScript.Echo "Size on host: " & objHardDisk.SizeOnHost
        WScript.Echo "Type: " & VMDiskType(objHardDisk.Type)

        If objVM1.Undoable Then
         Set objUndoDrive = objDrive.UndoHardDisk
         WScript.Echo "Undo disk file: " & objUndoDrive.File
        End If
    Next
Else
    WScript.Echo "Error: No Hard disk connections"
End If
```

Creating Virtual Hard Disks

Creating virtual hard disks is an easy process when you use the Administrative Console, but it takes a few minutes to accomplish. CreateVHD.vbs is a sample script for creating dynamically expanding, differencing, or fixed virtual hard disks from a single script. The objective of the script is to simplify the process and dramatically reduce the amount of time it takes to create virtual hard disks.

CreateVHD.vbs requires three command-line arguments:

1. The type of virtual hard disk to create, expressed as a three-letter code:
   - ❑ DYN = Dynamically expanding
   - ❑ DIF = Differencing
   - ❑ FIX = Fixed

2. The path where the VHD should be created

3. For DYN or FIX type disks, the size of the VHD to create in megabytes. For DIF type disks, the path to the parent VHD file.

CreateVHD.vbs operates in the following manner. CreateVHD.vbs uses a *select case* to conditionally assign the correct command-line parameter to the correct variable based on the type of virtual hard disk specified. The script then performs error checking on the command-line parameters to be sure that the VHD size specified was a numeric value and that it is not larger than the maximum virtual hard disk size of 2 TB. The numeric value check is to validate that the user did not incorrectly provide a text string instead of an number for the VHD size.

CreateVHD.vbs then makes a connection to the Virtual Server interface and runs the appropriate method to create a dynamic, differencing, or fixed virtual hard disk. Both the *CreateDynamicVirtualHardDisk* and *CreateFixedVirtualHardDisk* methods use the same parameters: path and size. *CreateDifferencingVirtualHardDisk* creates a new hard disk child based on an existing parent virtual hard disk; therefore, the path to the parent virtual hard disk is required instead of the virtual hard disk size.

CreateVHD.vbs

```
'=========================================================================
' CreateVHD.vbs
'=========================================================================
Option Explicit
Dim objVS, objArgs
Dim strHardDiskPath, strVHDType, strVHDParent
Dim intVHDSize
Dim diskTask

' Verify correct number of arguments
set objArgs = WScript.Arguments
If objArgs.Count<> 3 Then
  WScript.Echo "Missing command line arguments"
  WScript.Echo "VHDType VHDPath VHDSize(MB) for dynamic or fixed disks"
  WScript.Echo "VHDType VHDPath VHDParentPath for differencing disks"
  WScript.Echo "VHDType= DYN, DIF, or FIX"
  WScript.Quit
End If

strVHDType = ucase(objArgs(0))
strHardDiskPath = objArgs(1)

' Verify correct VHD type specified
Select Case strVHDType
  Case "DYN"
    intVHDSize = objArgs(2)
  Case "FIX"
    intVHDSize = objArgs(2)
  Case "DIF"
    strVHDParent = objArgs(2)
  Case Else
    WScript.Echo "Error: VHDType not specified as DYN, DIF, or FIX"
    WScript.Quit
End select

' Verify disk size specified is not over 2 TB
On Error Resume Next
If strVHDType <> "DIF" Then
  If IsNumeric(intVHDSize)=False Then
    WScript.Echo "Error: VHD Size specified is not a number"
    WScript.Quit
  ElseIf intVHDSize > 2088960 Then
    WScript.Echo "Error: VHD Size specified is larger than 2-TB maximum"
    WScript.Quit
  End If
End If
```

```
' Connect to Virtual Server
Set objVS = CreateObject("VirtualServer.Application")

If Err.number <> 0 Then
  WScript.Echo "Failed to connect to Virtual Server"
  WScript.Echo "Error Number=" & Err.Number & " Description=" & _
    Err.Description
  WScript.Quit
Else
  WScript.Echo "Successfully connected to Virtual Server"
  Err.Clear
  On Error GoTo 0
End if


' Create a Dynamic, Differencing, or Fixed Virtual Hard Disk

On Error Resume Next
Select Case strVHDType
  Case "DYN"
    Set diskTask = objVS.CreateDynamicVirtualHardDisk(strHardDiskPath, _
                intVHDSize)
  Case "FIX"
    Set diskTask = objVS.CreateFixedVirtualHardDisk(strHardDiskPath, _
                intVHDSize)
  Case "DIF"
    Set diskTask=objVS.CreateDifferencingVirtualHardDisk(strHardDiskPath,_
              strVHDParent)
End Select

'Catch errors
If Err.Number <> 0 Then
  WScript.Echo "Error:" & Err.Description
  Err.Clear
Else
  diskTask.waitforCompletion(10000)

  If Err.Number = 0 Then
    WScript.Echo "Created hard disk: " & strHardDiskPath
  Else
    WScript.Echo "Error:" & Err.Number & "- " & Err.Description
  End If
End If
```

Adding VHDs to a Virtual Machine

Creating a virtual machine using the Administrative Console allows you to create or add only
a single virtual hard disk to the machine. You can use the Administrative Console to create and
add more virtual hard disks to virtual machines. If you need to add virtual hard disks to a
series of virtual machines, you want a more efficient way to accomplish this. AddVHD.vbs
allows you to do this easily and powerfully. AddVHD.vbs supports not only defining the vir-

tual machine and path to the virtual hard disk to add, it also requires you to specify the bus type, SCSI or IDE, bus number, and device connection on the bus.

The script provides error checking to ensure the command-line arguments are specified correctly and that values provided are in the correct ranges for the bus and device numbers. AddVHD.vbs verifies that the virtual machine specified on the command line exists before it attempts to add the virtual hard disk. The script then verifies that if a SCSI controller is specified on the command line, the virtual machine has a SCSI controller. It does this by determining the number of SCSI controllers in the collection returned from *VMVirtualMachine.SCSIControllers*. If no SCSI controllers are in the collection, one is automatically added using the *AddSCSIController* method:

```
If strBusType = "SCSI" Then
    ' Check for SCSI controllers, and add one if one does not exist
    Set colSCSIControllers = objVM.SCSIControllers
    If colSCSIControllers.Count = 0 Then
        Set objController = objVM.AddSCSIController
    End If
End If
```

Then the very last step is adding the virtual hard disk by using the *VMVirtualMachine.AddHardDiskConnection* method, specifying the path, bus type, bus number, and device number.

AddVHD.vbs

```
'=========================================================================
' AddVHD.vbs
'=========================================================================
Option Explicit
Dim objVS, objArgs, objVM, objDisk, objController
Dim strVMName, strHardDiskPath, strBusType
Dim intBusType, intBusNumber, intDeviceNumber, colSCSIControllers


' Verify correct number of arguments
set objArgs = WScript.Arguments
If objArgs.Count<> 5 Then
   WScript.Echo "Missing command line arguments"
   WScript.Echo "VMName VHDPath BusType BusNumber DeviceNumber"
   WScript.Echo "BusType= SCSI or IDE"
   WScript.Quit
End If

strVMName = objArgs(0)
strHardDiskPath = objArgs(1)
strBusType = ucase(objArgs(2))
intBusNumber = objArgs(3)
intDeviceNumber = objArgs(4)


' Verify correct VHD type specified
Select Case strBusType
```

```
    Case "SCSI"
      intBusType = 1
      If intDeviceNumber > 6 Then
        WScript.Echo "Error: SCSI Device Number not between 0-6"
        WScript.Quit
      End If
    Case "IDE"
      intBusType = 0
      If intDeviceNumber > 1 Then
        WScript.Echo "Error: IDE device number not 0 or 1"
        WScript.Quit
      End If
    Case Else
      WScript.Echo "Error: BusType not specified as SCSI or IDE"
      WScript.Quit
End select

'Connect to Virtual Server
On Error Resume Next
Set objVS = CreateObject("VirtualServer.Application")

If Err.number <> 0 Then
  WScript.Echo "Failed to connect to Virtual Server"
  WScript.Echo "Error Number=" & Err.Number & " Description=" & _
    Err.Description
  WScript.Quit
Else
  WScript.Echo "Successfully connected to Virtual Server"
  Err.Clear
  On Error GoTo 0
End if

' Get an Object link to the strVMName virtual machine
On Error Resume Next
Set objVM = objVS.FindVirtualMachine(strVMName)

If objVM is nothing then
  WScript.Echo "Unable to find " & strVMName
  WScript.Quit
End If

If strBusType = "SCSI" Then
  ' Check for SCSI controllers, and add one if one does not exist
  Set colSCSIControllers = objVM.SCSIControllers
  If colSCSIControllers.Count = 0 Then
    Set objController = objVM.AddSCSIController
  End If
End If

' Add VHD to VM
Set objDisk = objVM.AddHardDiskConnection(strHardDiskPath, _
              intBusType, intBusNumber, intDeviceNumber)

' Catch errors
```

```
If objDisk Is Nothing Then
  WScript.Echo "Error:" & Err.Description
  Err.Clear
Else
  WScript.Echo "Attached hard disk: " & strHardDiskPath & "to " & strVMName
End If
```

Managing Virtual Machines

Managing virtual machines using the Virtual Server Administration Website is reasonable for small tasks, but when you need to manage large numbers of virtual machines or you need to do a repetitive task to a virtual machine, using the Virtual Server COM API is the best approach. Table 9-12 shows the *VMVirtualServer* methods to find and manage the creation, deletion, and registration of virtual machines.

Table 9-12   *VMVirtualServer* Methods to Create, Delete, and Register Virtual Machines

Method name	Description
CreateVirtualMachine	Creates a new virtual machine, and returns an object reference. It requires the name of a virtual machine configuration (.vmc) file and the path to where the .vmc file should be created.
DeleteVirtualMachine	Removes the virtual machine configuration registration from the Virtual Server Administrative Console, and deletes the VMC file, any save state files, and any undo disks. The VHD file is not deleted.
FindVirtualMachine	Searches for an existing virtual machine, and returns an object reference to it if a virtual machine is found.
GetVirtualMachineFiles	Retrieves an array of known virtual machine configuration (.vmc) files. Additional search paths can be specified, and registered virtual machines can be excluded from the array.
RegisterVirtualMachine	Registers a virtual machine configuration file in the Virtual Server Administrative Console.

Creating a Virtual Machine

Creating a virtual machine is a multistep process. The *CreateVirtualMachine* method creates only the virtual machine configuration file in the specified path. You must also configure the virtual machine hardware to obtain a usable virtual machine. This typically involves setting the amount of memory, adding a virtual SCSI adapter, creating a virtual hard disk and attaching it to the SCSI adapter, and attaching the virtual network card to a virtual network:

```
Set objVM = objVS.CreateVirtualMachine(strVmName, strVmPath)
```

When you make the call to *CreateVirtualMachine*, the return value is an object reference to a *VMVirtualMachine* object. Using this object reference allows you to assign properties and call methods to manage the configuration of the virtual machine. To configure the memory of the virtual machine, you could use the *Memory* property of the virtual machine object:

```
objVM.Memory = intMemory
```

There are problems with just attempting to assign the memory amount requested. The minimum amount of memory for a virtual machine is 4 MB, and the maximum is based on the amount of physical RAM in the host. Therefore, setting the requested amount of memory requires verification that it is a valid request. Checking the minimum amount is easy because it is a known value. The maximum value varies by host, so accessing the *VMVirtualServer.MaximumMemoryPerVM* property allows you to determine the maximum memory that can be assigned to a virtual machine. If the requested amount of memory is above the maximum, the maximum value is used instead:

```
If (intMemory > 4) And (intMemory < objVS.MaximumMemoryPerVM) Then
   objVM.Memory = intMemory
Else
   If intMemory < 4 Then
      WScript.Echo "Memory specified was smaller than VM minimum"
      WScript.Echo "Setting memory to minimum value: 4MB"
      objVM.Memory = 4
   Else
      WScript.Echo "Memory specified was larger than VM maximum"
      WScript.Echo "Setting memory to maximum value: " & _
         objVS.MaximumMemoryPerVM
      objVM.Memory = objVS.MaximumMemoryPerVM
   End If
End If
```

To add an existing virtual hard disk to a virtual machine, use the *AddHardDiskConnection* method of the *VMVirtualMachine* object. This requires that you specify the path to the virtual hard disk (.vhd) file, the bus type (IDE or SCSI), the bus number (0–1 for IDE, and for SCSI it is based on the number of SCSI controllers), and the device number (0–1 for IDE, 0–6 for SCSI). So to attach a virtual hard disk on an IDE interface, the primary bus, and the primary device, you specify the following:

```
Set objDrive = objVM.AddHardDiskConnection(strHardDiskPath,0,0,0)
```

The *AddHardDiskConnection* method returns an object reference to the virtual hard disk that was just added to the virtual machine. Using this object, you can view and modify the parameters of the hard disk.

To assign a virtual network to a specific network adapter is a little more complicated. First you must obtain an object reference to the virtual network by using the *FindVirtualNetwork* method of the *VMVirtualServer* interface. Then obtain an object reference to the virtual machines network adapter and use the *AttachToVirtualNetwork* method to assign the virtual network. Assuming you want to attach the Internal Network virtual network to the first network adapter in the virtual machine, the code is as follows:

```
Set objNetwork = objVS.FindVirtualNetwork("Internal Network")

Set colNetworkAdapters = objVM.NetworkAdapters
errReturn = colNetworkAdapters.item(1).AttachToVirtualNetwork(objNetwork)
```

CreateVM.vbs is a sample script for creating a virtual machine. The script requires three command-line arguments: the virtual machine name, the memory in megabytes, and the size of the virtual hard disk in megabytes.

CreateVM.vbs

```
'=======================================================================
' CreateVM.vbs - Creates a virtual machine
'
' Script takes three command-line arguments
' Arg(0) = VMName
' Arg(1) = Memory in MB
' Arg(2) = VHD size in MBs
'
' VHDs will be stored in C:\NewVMs\ using the VMNAME as the directory name
'=======================================================================
Option Explicit

Dim objArgs, objVS, objVM, objDrive, objNetwork
Dim colNetworkAdapters
Dim strVmName, strVmPath, strHardDiskPath
Dim intMemory, intVHDSize, intBusType, intBusNumber, intDeviceNumber
Dim diskTask, errReturn

set objArgs = WScript.Arguments
If objArgs.Count<> 3 Then
  WScript.Echo "Missing command line arguments"
  WScript.Echo "VMName Memory(MB) VHDSize(MB)"
  WScript.Quit
End If

strVmName = objArgs(0)
strVmPath = "C:\NewVMs\" & strVmName & "\"

intMemory = objArgs(1)
intVHDSize = objArgs(2)

strHardDiskPath = "C:\NewVMs\" & strVmName & "\" & strVmName & ".VHD"

intBusType = 0
intBusNumber = 0
intDeviceNumber = 0


'=======================================================================
' Get a connection to the base object for Virtual Server
'=======================================================================
```

```
On Error Resume Next
Set objVS = CreateObject("VirtualServer.Application")

'======================================================================
' Create the virtual machine, obtain objVM
'======================================================================
Set objVM = objVS.CreateVirtualMachine(strVmName, strVmPath)

If Err.Number = 0 Then
  WScript.Echo "Created virtual machine named " & strVmName
Else
  WScript.Echo "Unable to create virtual machine named " & strVmName
  WScript.Quit
End If


'======================================================================
' Set the amount of memory
'======================================================================
If (intMemory > 4) And (intMemory < objVS.MaximumMemoryPerVM) Then
  objVM.Memory = intMemory
Else
  If intMemory < 4 Then
    WScript.Echo "Memory specified was smaller than VM minimum"
    WScript.Echo "Setting memory to minimum value: 4MB"
    objVM.Memory = 4
  Else
    WScript.Echo "Memory specified was larger than VM maximum"
    WScript.Echo "Setting memory to maximum value: " & _
        objVS.MaximumMemoryPerVM
    objVM.Memory = objVS.MaximumMemoryPerVM
  End If
End If
'======================================================================
' Create a dynamic expanding Virtual Hard Disk
'======================================================================
Set diskTask = objVS.CreateDynamicVirtualHardDisk(strHardDiskPath, _
  intVHDSize)

diskTask.WaitforCompletion(5000)

If Err.Number = 0 Then
  WScript.Echo "Created hard disk."
else
  WScript.Echo "Unable to create hard disk."
  WScript.Quit
End If


'======================================================================
' Add the hard disk to the VM
'======================================================================
Set objDrive = objVM.AddHardDiskConnection(strHardDiskPath,0,0,0)

If Err.Number = 0 Then
  WScript.Echo "Added Hard disk"
Else
```

```
    WScript.Echo "Unable to add hard disk."
    Err.Clear
    WScript.Quit
End If



'=======================================================================
' Attach to the virtual network
'=======================================================================
Set objNetwork = objVS.FindVirtualNetwork("Internal Network")

Set colNetworkAdapters = objVM.NetworkAdapters
errReturn = colNetworkAdapters.item(1).AttachToVirtualNetwork(objNetwork)

If Err.Number = 0 Then
  WScript.Echo "Added Virtual Network Connection"
Else
  WScript.Echo "Unable to add Virtual Network Connection"
  Err.Clear
End If
WScript.Echo "Virtual Machine Created Successfully"
```

Deleting a Virtual Machine

Deleting a virtual machine from the Virtual Server Administrative Console via script using the *DeleteVirtualMachine* method should be used only when you are going to stop using the virtual machine. This method unregisters the virtual machine, deletes the virtual machine configuration file, deletes the saved state file, and deletes all undo disk files. It does not delete the virtual hard disk file. If you only want to remove the virtual machine from the console and not affect any of the virtual machine files, you should use the *UnregisterVirtualMachine* method.

DeleteVM.vbs is a sample script for deleting a virtual machine. The virtual machine name is provided as a command-line argument. The script verifies the command-line argument, connects to the *VMVirtualServer* interface, and searches for the virtual machine using the *FindVirtualMachine* method.

Determining whether the virtual machine was found is tricky. The *FindVirtualMachine* method returns a *VMVirtualMachine* object reference only if the virtual machine was found. The *objVM* variable starts out as empty, but if the virtual machine is not found it has no assignment and points to nothing. Using a conditional operation, *objVM Is Nothing*, in the *If* statement allows you to determine whether the *FindVirtualMachine* method found a matching virtual machine and returned an object reference to it. If the virtual machine was not found, an error message is output and the script quits.

The *DeleteVirtualMachine* method will not delete the virtual machine if it is not turned off, so the script verifies that the *objVM.State* value is 1 (Turned Off) or 2 (Saved State) before attempting to call the *DeleteVirtualMachine* method.

DeleteVM.vbs

```vbscript
'========================================================================
' DeleteVM.vbs - Delete a Virtual Machine
'========================================================================
Option Explicit

Dim objVS, objVM, objArgs
Dim strVMName

set objArgs = WScript.Arguments

If objArgs.Count<> 1 Then
  WScript.Echo "Missing command line argument"
  WScript.Echo "VMName"
  WScript.Quit
End If


strVMName = objArgs(0)

On Error Resume Next
'========================================================================
' Connect to Virtual Server
'========================================================================

Set objVS = CreateObject("VirtualServer.Application")

If Err.number <> 0 Then
  WScript.Echo "Failed to connect to Virtual Server"
  WScript.Echo "Error Number=" & Err.Number & " Description=" & _
       Err.Description
  WScript.Quit
Else
  WScript.Echo "Successfully connected to Virtual Server"
  Err.Clear
  On Error GoTo 0
End If


'========================================================================
' Find the Virtual Machine
'========================================================================


Set objVM = objVS.FindVirtualMachine(strVMName)

On Error Resume Next

If objVM is Nothing Then
  WScript.Echo "Specified Virtual Machine does not exist"
  Err.Clear
  On Error Goto 0
  WScript.Quit
Else
  WScript.Echo "Successfully found Virtual Machine"

'========================================================================
```

```
' Verify the Virtual Machine is turned off before deleting it
' State=1 means turned off
' State=2 means turned off with a saved state
'=====================================================================
  If (objVM.State = 1) Or (objVM.State = 2) Then
     objVS.DeleteVirtualMachine(objVM)
     WScript.Echo "VM deleted"
     WScript.Quit
  End If
  WScript.Echo "Virtual Machine is running and cannot be deleted"
  Err.Clear
  On Error Goto 0

End if
```

Registering a Virtual Machine

Registering a virtual machine typically happens only when you are moving virtual machines from one server to another or when you are using prebuilt virtual machines from a central authority. The virtual machine must be in a powered-off state or in a saved state that is compatible with the version of Virtual Server and the hardware. You cannot register a virtual machine in a saved state that was running on any version of Virtual PC because the saved state files are not compatible. You must either discard the saved state file before registering the virtual machine in Virtual Server or resume the saved state under Virtual PC and perform a shutdown before attempting to register the machine in the Virtual Server host. Registering a virtual machine uses the *RegisterVirtualMachine* method of the *VMVirtualServer* interface. *RegisterVirtualMachine* requires two parameters: the virtual machine name, and the full path to the virtual machine configuration file.

RegisterVM.vbs demonstrates how to use the *RegisterVirtualMachine* method. RegisterVM.vbs establishes a connection to the local Virtual Server, processes the two command-line arguments, verifies that a virtual machine with the same name does not already exist on this server, and then registers the virtual machine.

RegisterVM.vbs

```
'=====================================================================
' RegisterVM.vbs - Register an existing VMC file
'=====================================================================

Option Explicit

Dim objVS, objVM, objArgs
Dim strVMName, strVMPath

set objArgs = WScript.Arguments

If objArgs.Count<> 2 Then
  WScript.Echo "Missing command line arguments"
```

```
    WScript.Echo "VMName PathtoVMC"
    WScript.Quit
End If

strVMName = objArgs(0)
strVMPath = objArgs(1)

On Error Resume Next
'================================================================================
' Connect to Virtual Server
'================================================================================

Set objVS = CreateObject("VirtualServer.Application")

If Err.number <> 0 Then
  WScript.Echo "Failed to connect to Virtual Server"
  WScript.Echo "Error Number=" & Err.Number & " Description=" & _
    Err.Description
  WScript.Quit
Else
  WScript.Echo "Successfully connected to Virtual Server"
  Err.Clear
  On Error GoTo 0
End If


'================================================================================
' Look for a Virtual Machine with the same name
'================================================================================

Set objVM = objVS.FindVirtualMachine(strVMName)
'================================================================================
' Verify that you did not find the Virtual Machine
'================================================================================
On Error Resume Next
If objVM Is Nothing Then

  Set objVM = objVS.RegisterVirtualMachine(strVMName, strVMPath)

  If objVM Is Nothing Then
    WScript.Echo "ERROR: Failure registering VM named " & strVMName
  Else
    WScript.Echo "VM named " & strReturn & " registered successfully"
  End If
  Err.Clear
  On Error Goto 0
Else
  WScript.Echo "VM named " & strVMName & " already exists"
  WScript.Quit
End if
```

Unregistering a Virtual Machine

Unregistering a virtual machine from a host removes all references of the virtual machine from the Administrative Console. If you need to modify the directory structure where the virtual machine files are stored, you must unregister the virtual machine, modify the directory structure, and then register the virtual machine to ensure proper operation. Unregistering a virtual machine requires that the virtual machine cannot be running. It can be in a saved state or a fully shut down state.

UnRegisterVM.vbs uses the *VMVirtualServer* method *UnregisterVirtualMachine* to unregister virtual machines. UnRegisterVM.vbs requires a single command-line argument: the name of the virtual machine to unregister. The virtual machine name is verified to exist on the server using the *FindVirtualMachine* method. Once the name is verified to exist, the virtual machine state is checked to ensure that the current state is turned off or saved:

```
If objVM.State = TurnedOff Or objVM.State = Saved Then
```

Once the virtual machine has been verified to be in the correct state, the name of the virtual machine is then passed to the *UnregisterVirtualMachine* method to unregister the virtual machine. No virtual machine files are deleted during the operation.

```
UnRegisterVM.vbs
'================================================================
' UnRegisterVM.vbs - Remove a VM configuration registration
'================================================================
Option Explicit

Dim objVS, objVM, objArgs
Dim strVMName

Const TurnedOff = 1
Const Saved = 2

set objArgs = WScript.Arguments

If objArgs.Count<> 1 Then
  WScript.Echo "Missing command line argument"
  WScript.Echo "VMName"
  WScript.Quit
End If

strVMName = objArgs(0)

On Error Resume Next
'================================================================
' Connect to Virtual Server
'================================================================

Set objVS = CreateObject("VirtualServer.Application")
```

```
If Err.number <> 0 Then
  WScript.Echo "Failed to connect to Virtual Server"
  WScript.Echo "Error Number=" & Err.Number & " Description=" & _
    Err.Description
  WScript.Quit
Else
  WScript.Echo "Successfully connected to Virtual Server"
  Err.Clear
  On Error GoTo 0
End If


'========================================================================
' Find the Virtual Machine
'========================================================================


Set objVM = objVS.FindVirtualMachine(strVMName)


'========================================================================
' Verify that you found the Virtual Machine
'========================================================================
On Error Resume Next
If objVM Is Nothing Then
  WScript.Echo "Specified Virtual Machine does not exist"
  WScript.Quit

Else
  WScript.Echo "Virtual Machine is currently registered"
'========================================================================
' Verify the Virtual Machine is turned off before unregistering it
'========================================================================
  If (objVM.State = TurnedOff) Or (objVM.State = Saved) Then
    objVS.UnregisterVirtualMachine(objVM)
    WScript.Echo "Virtual Machine successfully unregistered"
    WScript.Quit
  Else
    WScript.Echo "Virtual Machine is running and cannot be unregistered"
    Err.Clear
    On Error Goto 0
  End If
End if
```

Managing Virtual Networks

Virtual networks are the path from the virtual world to the physical world. A virtual network can be bound to a physical adapter to allow traffic from the virtual machine, through the virtual network, and then onto the physical network. Virtual networks can also be connected to Microsoft loopback adapters or not connected to adapters at all.

Managing virtual networks involves managing the creation, registration, and configuration of the virtual network. There is a virtual machine side to managing virtual network adapter connections to virtual networks. That scenario is covered in the section on managing virtual machines. Table 9-13 shows the *VMVirtualServer* methods that exist for managing creation and registration of virtual networks.

Table 9-13 *VMVirtualServer* **Methods to Create, Register, and Remove Virtual Networks**

Method name	Description
CreateVirtualNetwork	Creates a new virtual network, and returns an object reference. It requires the name of a virtual network configuration (.vnc) file and the path to where the .vnc file should be created.
DeleteVirtualNetwork	Removes the virtual network configuration registration from the Virtual Server Administrative Console, and deletes the VNC file.
FindVirtualNetwork	Searches for an existing virtual network by name, and returns an object reference to it if found.
GetVirtualNetworkFiles	Retrieves and returns an array of known virtual network configuration files. You can specify alternate search paths and whether registered virtual networks should be excluded from the array.
RegisterVirtualNetwork	Registers a virtual network configuration file in the Virtual Server Administrative Console.

In addition to the methods for managing virtual networks, *VMVirtualServer* has a property called *VirtualNetworks* that contains a *VMVirtualNetworkCollection*. Using this collection, you can enumerate all the registered virtual networks on a Virtual Server host:

```
Set objVNColl = objVS.VirtualNetworks
If objVNColl.Count = 0 Then
  WScript.Echo "Virtual networks: [none]"
Else
  WScript.Echo "Virtual networks: " & objVNColl.Count
  For Each objVN in objVNColl
    WScript.Echo "    Name: " & objVN.Name
  Next
End If
```

The default location for virtual network configuration files is stored in the *VMVirtualServer.DefaultVNConfigurationPath* property. By default, this property value is set to the "%ALLUSERSPROFILE%\Documents\Shared Virtual Networks\" directory. This property is ready only.

```
WScript.Echo "Default VNC path: " & objVS.DefaultVNConfigurationPath
```

Creating Virtual Networks

Creating virtual networks is typically required in every deployment of Virtual Server. As you install your hosts, it is a best practice to set up consistently named virtual networks across the hosts to minimize issues with moving virtual machines between hosts. Without common virtual network names, manual intervention is typically needed to verify the correct network or networks the virtual machine must be attached to.

The CreateVNET.vbs script is designed to safely create virtual networks rapidly by using the *CreateVirtualNetwork* method. CreateVNET.vbs requires a single command-line argument for the virtual network name at a minimum. You can optionally specify a different path to store the virtual network configuration file. This should be used only if you have decided to store virtual network configuration files in a different path than the default.

CreateVNET.vbs performs the following steps:

1. Verifies the command-line parameters

2. Connects to Virtual Server

3. Determines whether an optional path has been specified or whether the defined default configuration path property *DefaultVNConfigurationPath* should be retrieved and used

4. Verifies, by using *FindVirtualNetwork*, that a virtual network with the name specified does not already exist

5. Creates the virtual network by using the *CreateVirtualNetwork* method

6. Obtains an array of the host network adapters by using *HostInfo.NetworkAdapters*, and then assigns the first physical adapter to the newly created virtual network

You can modify the script slightly to allow the user to select the physical adapter to attach to the new virtual network. To do that, you have to retrieve the array of physical network adapters, display them on the screen in a numeric list format, prompt the user to select a physical adapter in the list, and then use that selection to assign the physical network adapter to the created virtual network. The problem with that modification is the script requires user input to complete and eliminates the ability to fully automate the script.

CreateVNET.vbs

```
'===============================================================================
' CreateVNET.vbs
'===============================================================================
Option Explicit
Dim objVS, objArgs, objVNET, objNICs
Dim strVNETName, strVNETPath

' Verify correct number of arguments
set objArgs = WScript.Arguments
If Not ((objArgs.Count = 2) Or (objArgs.Count = 1)) Then
  WScript.Echo "Missing command line arguments"
  WScript.Echo "VNETName <VNETPath>"
  WScript.Quit
End If

strVNETName = objArgs(0)
```

```
' Connect to Virtual Server
On Error Resume Next
Set objVS = CreateObject("VirtualServer.Application")

If Err.number <> 0 Then
  WScript.Echo "Failed to connect to Virtual Server"
  WScript.Echo "Error Number=" & Err.Number & " Description=" & _
    Err.Description
  WScript.Quit
Else
  WScript.Echo "Successfully connected to Virtual Server"
  Err.Clear
  On Error GoTo 0
End if

'Set the path to the passed value or the default location
If objArgs.Count=2 Then
  strVNETPath = objArgs(1)
Else
  strVNETPath = objVS.DefaultVNConfigurationPath
End If

' Check if VNET already exists
On Error Resume Next
Set objVNET = objVS.FindVirtualNetwork(strVNETName)

If Not objVNET is nothing then
  WScript.Echo "Error: Virtual Network " & strVNETName & " already exists"
  WScript.Quit
End If

' Add VNET
Set objVNET = objVS.CreateVirtualNetwork(strVNETName, strVNETPath)

' Catch errors
If objVNET Is Nothing Then
  WScript.Echo "Error:" & Err.Description
  Err.Clear
Else
  ' Assign the network to the first physical network adapter
  Set objNICs = objVS.HostInfo.NetworkAdapters
  objVNET.HostAdapter = objNICs(0)
  WScript.Echo "Success: Created Virtual network: " & strVNETName & _
    " at " & strVNETPath
  WScript.Echo "Connected to:" & objVNET.HostAdapter
End If
```

Registering Existing Virtual Networks

Registering existing virtual networks is an infrequent task. Registering a virtual network assumes that the virtual network was originally created on the server. Each virtual network configuration file has a gateway value that maps to a *virtual_gateway* entry in the options.xml file for a physical adapter. If upon registration there is an adapter with a *virtual_gateway.id* value in options.xml that matches the *setting.gateway* value in the vnc file, the virtual network is bound to that adapter. If there is no match, the virtual network is left in an unbound state with no network connectivity and the host adapter needs to be reassigned.

You normally need to register virtual network configurations only if you have a collection of custom virtual networks that need to be restored on a server because of a disaster or if you are deploying a new host using a standard hardware configuration. In either of these situations, you have more than one virtual network to register and using a script makes the process more efficient. The RegisterVNC.vbs sample script was created to demonstrate how to use the *RegisterVirtualNetwork* method to register vnc files based on a name and optional path to the file if it does not reside in the default location.

RegisterVNC.vbs requires two command-line parameters to operate: the name of the vnc file, and the path to where the vnc file resides. RegisterVNC.vbs performs the following steps during execution:

1. Verifies the command-line parameters
2. Connects to Virtual Server
3. Verifies, by using *FindVirtualNetwork*, that a virtual network with the name specified does not already exist
4. Registers the virtual network by using the *RegisterVirtualNetwork* method
5. Returns an object reference to the newly created virtual network

RegisterVNC.vbs

```
'=========================================================================
' RegisterVNC.vbs - Register an existing VNC file
'=========================================================================

Option Explicit

Dim objVS, objVNC, objArgs
Dim strVNCName, strVNCPath

set objArgs = WScript.Arguments

If objArgs.Count<> 2 Then
  WScript.Echo "Missing command line arguments"
  WScript.Echo "VMName PathtoVNC"
  WScript.Quit
End If

strVNCName = objArgs(0)
strVNCPath = objArgs(1)

On Error Resume Next
'=========================================================================
```

```
' Connect to Virtual Server
'=======================================================================

Set objVS = CreateObject("VirtualServer.Application")

If Err.number <> 0 Then
  WScript.Echo "Failed to connect to Virtual Server"
  WScript.Echo "Error Number=" & Err.Number & " Description=" & Err.Description
  WScript.Quit
Else
  WScript.Echo "Successfully connected to Virtual Server"
  Err.Clear
  On Error GoTo 0
End If


'=======================================================================
' Look for a Virtual Network with the same name
'=======================================================================

Set objVNC = objVS.FindVirtualNetwork(strVNCName)


'=======================================================================
' Verify that you did not find the Virtual Network
'=======================================================================
On Error Resume Next
If objVNC Is Nothing Then

  Set objVNC = objVS.RegisterVirtualNetwork(strVNCName, strVNCPath)

  If objVNC Is Nothing Then
    WScript.Echo "ERROR: Failure registering VNC named " & strVNCName
    WScript.Echo Err.Description
  Else
    WScript.Echo "VNC named " & strVNCName & " registered successfully"
  End If
  Err.Clear
  On Error Goto 0
Else
  WScript.Echo "VM named " & strVNCName & " already exists"
  Err.Clear
  WScript.Quit
End if
```

Managing a Virtual Server Configuration

Managing a Virtual Server configuration is not about managing virtual machines or virtual networks; it is about managing the security settings and configuration options of a Virtual Server host. Table 9-14 shows the *VMVirtualServer* methods that exist for managing configuration settings on a Virtual Server.

Table 9-14 *VMVirtualServer* Methods to Manage a Virtual Server Configuration

Method name	Description
GetConfigurationValue	Retrieves configuration values from the options.xml file based on a preference key
RemoveConfigurationValue	Removes configuration values from the options.xml file based on a preference key
SetConfigurationValue	Sets configuration values from the options.xml file based on a preference key

To use the methods shown in the preceding table, you must pass a key to the method. The key value is a string that references the XML hierarchy of the options.xml file to the level of the variable you would like to reference:

```
<preferences>
  <version type="string">2.0</version>
  <properties>
    <modifier>
      <build type="string">1.1.603.0 EE R2 SP1</build>
      <name type="string">Microsoft Virtual Server</name>
    </modifier>
  </properties>
  ...
</preferences>
```

To retrieve the version string by using *GetConfigurationValue* requires the key value to be *version*. If you want to retrieve the build number, the key value is *properties/modifier/build*.

Managing configuration settings in the options.xml file is a very powerful feature. What is even more powerful is how you use the methods. Using the *SetConfigurationValue* method, you can create your own configuration values to store information in options.xml. For example, to create a value for ResourceKit Book number, you can call *SetConfigurationValue* to write a value of 1 for the book number, using *ResourceKit/Book/number* for the key value:

```
objvs.SetConfigurationValue "ResourceKit/Book/number", 1
return = objvs.GetConfigurationValue("ResourceKit/Book/number")
WScript.Echo "return value" & return
```

Note *SetConfigurationValue* is a subroutine, and therefore any parameters that are passed are not enclosed in parentheses.

Although using the three methods to directly access the options.xml parameters is extremely powerful and offers the capability to store your own custom properties, you must know the exact hierarchy path to get access to any property. *VMVirtualServer* provides predefined properties and methods that provide access to obtain the same information without having to know the exact hierarchy path to a key. You should refer to the Virtual Servers Programmer's Guide help file installed by default with Virtual Server 2005 R2 to obtain a complete list.

In addition to properties stored in options.xml, there are other properties and methods that access other information. Two key properties covered in this section as examples are *VMVirtualServer.HostInfo* and *VMVirtualServer.Security*. *HostInfo* is an object reference to a set of methods and properties that provide information about the Virtual Server host hardware and configuration. Table 9-15 shows the *HostInfo* methods that exist for managing configuration settings on a Virtual Server.

Table 9-15   *VMVirtualServer* **Methods to Obtain Host Information**

Method name	Description
GetHostDriveSize	Retrieves the size of the host drive in megabytes
IsHostDriveMounted	Returns TRUE if the specified host drive is mounted

Table 9-16 shows the *VMVirtualServer.HostInfo* properties that exist for retrieving configuration settings on a Virtual Server host.

Table 9-16   *HostInfo* **Properties to Retrieve Host Configuration Information**

Property name	Description
DVDDrives	Contains an array of drive letters associated with host CD-ROM or DVD-ROM devices
FloppyDrives	Contains an array of drive letters associated with host floppy drives
HostDrives	Contains an array of drive letters associated with host hard drives
LogicalProcessorCount	Contains the number of logical processors in the host machine
Memory	Contains the total quantity of physical RAM (megabytes) in the host machine as a number
MemoryAvail	Contains the total quantity of available RAM (megabytes) in the host machine as a number
MemoryAvailString	Contains the total quantity of available RAM (megabytes) in the host machine as a string
MemoryTotalString	Contains the total quantity of physical RAM (megabytes) in the host machine as a string
MMX	Specifies whether the host processor supports the MMX instruction set
NetworkAdapters	Contains an enumerable collection of the network interface cards that are installed on the host machine
NetworkAddresses	Contains an array of TCP/IP addresses in the host computer
OperatingSystem	Contains the name of the operating system currently running on the host machine as a string

Table 9-16   *HostInfo* Properties to Retrieve Host Configuration Information

Property name	Description
OSMajorVersion	Contains the major operating system release version currently running on the host machine as a number
OSMinorVersion	Contains the minor operating system release version currently running on the host machine as a number
OSServicePackString	Contains the service pack version currently installed on the host machine as a string
OSVersionString	Contains the version of the operating system currently running on the host machine as a string
ParallelPort	Contains the name of the parallel port on the host computer
PhysicalProcessorCount	Contains the number of physical processors in the host machine
ProcessorFeaturesString	Contains a list of features supported by the host processor as a string
ProcessorManufacturerString	Contains the manufacturer of the host processor as a string
ProcessorSpeed	Contains the speed, in MHz, of the host processor as a number
ProcessorSpeedString	Contains the speed, in MHz, of the host processor as a string
ProcessorVersionString	Contains the version of the host processor
SerialPorts	Contains a list of serial ports on the host computer
SSE	Indicates whether the host processor supports the SSE instruction set
SSE2	Indicates whether the host processor supports the SSE2 instruction set
ThreeDNow	Indicates whether the host processor supports the 3DNow! instruction set
UTCTime	Contains the current UTC time on the host machine

Reporting Host Information

Using the *VMVirtualServer.HostInfo* property, you can gather and report on Virtual Server host information about processors, memory, the operating system, peripherals, drives, network adapters, and network addresses.

HostInfo.vbs is a sample script that uses the *HostInfo* property to retrieve key information about the current host. Although some properties contain numbers or strings and can be used directly in *WScript.Echo* statements, others require additional processing. For example, the *HostInfo.HostDrives* property returns a collection of host drives. Once you have the collection, you can enumerate through each drive in the collection and obtain the name of the drive and the size of the drive. To get the size in megabytes, you must use the current drive in the collection as input to the *HostInfo.GetHostDriveSize* method as shown here:

```
For Each drive In drives
  WScript.Echo "Host Physical Drive    : " & drive
  WScript.Echo "Host Drive Size        : " & _
             objVS.HostInfo.GetHostDriveSize(drive) & " MB"
next
```

The *NetworkAdapters* and *NetworkAddresses* properties also return collections that must be enumerated to obtain the correct information.

HostInfo.vbs

```
'----------------------------------------------------------------
' HostInfo.vbs
'----------------------------------------------------------------
Option Explicit

Dim objVS, objHost
Dim drives, drive, Nics, Nic, Addrs, Addr
Set objVS = CreateObject("VirtualServer.Application")

Set objHost = objVS.HostInfo
WScript.Echo "----------------------------------------------------------------"
WScript.Echo "Processor information"
WScript.Echo "----------------------------------------------------------------"
WScript.Echo "Logical processor count  : " & objHost.LogicalProcessorCount
WScript.Echo "Physical processor count : " & objHost.PhysicalProcessorCount
WScript.Echo "Processor features       : " & objHost.ProcessorFeaturesString
WScript.Echo "Processor manufacturer   : " & objHost.ProcessorManufacturerString
WScript.Echo "Processor speed          : " & objHost.ProcessorSpeedString
WScript.Echo "Processor version        : " & objHost.ProcessorVersionString
WScript.Echo "----------------------------------------------------------------"
WScript.Echo " Memory information"
WScript.Echo "----------------------------------------------------------------"
WScript.Echo "Memory available         : " & objHost.MemoryAvailString
WScript.Echo "Memory total             : " & objHost.MemoryTotalString
WScript.Echo "----------------------------------------------------------------"
WScript.Echo " OS information"
WScript.Echo "----------------------------------------------------------------"
WScript.Echo "Operating system         : " & objHost.OperatingSystem
WScript.Echo "OS service pack          : " & objHost.OSServicePackString
WScript.Echo "OS version               : " & objHost.OSVersionString
WScript.Echo "----------------------------------------------------------------"
WScript.Echo " Peripheral information"
WScript.Echo "----------------------------------------------------------------"
WScript.Echo "Parallel port            : " & objHost.parallelPort
WScript.Echo "Serial port              : " & objHost.SerialPorts
WScript.Echo "----------------------------------------------------------------"
```

```
WScript.Echo " Drive information"
WScript.Echo "------------------------------------------------------------------"
drives = objVS.HostInfo.HostDrives
For Each drive In drives
  WScript.Echo "Host Physical Drive       : " & drive
  WScript.Echo "Host Drive Size           : " & _
            objVS.HostInfo.GetHostDriveSize(drive) & " MB"
next
WScript.Echo "------------------------------------------------------------------"
WScript.Echo " Network Adapter information"
WScript.Echo "------------------------------------------------------------------"
Nics = objVS.HostInfo.NetworkAdapters
For Each Nic In Nics
  WScript.Echo "Network Adapter           : " & Nic
Next
WScript.Echo "------------------------------------------------------------------"
WScript.Echo " Network Address information"
WScript.Echo "------------------------------------------------------------------"
Addrs = objVS.HostInfo.NetworkAddresses
For Each addr In Addrs
  WScript.Echo "Host Address              : " & Addr
next
```

Security Entries

Security entries in Virtual Server control access to the Administrative Console, the configuration files, virtual network, and virtual machine files. Maintenance on the entries is a common occurrence. To perform maintenance, you need a baseline document to determine what modifications are required.

VS_Security.vbs is a sample script that documents the security entries on a remote Virtual Server host. The script connects to a remote Virtual Server host, retrieves the security access rights entries, and then writes them to an output file formatted as a .CSV file for import into Microsoft Office Excel.

To execute the script, you must provide the name of the remote server on the command line and have administrative rights on the remote server. Once VS_Security.vbs verifies that you have supplied the correct number of parameters, it makes a connection to the remote Virtual Server. Once it is connected, a *FileSystemObject* is created and used to determine whether the output file already exists. This is done so that the returned Boolean value can be used to conditionally write the header to the file. If the file already exists, it assumes that the header is already written to the file. The next step is to open the output file using the *OpenTextFile* method, specifying to open the file for appending records and to create the file if it does not already exist:

```
Set fileCSV = objFSO.OpenTextFile("c:\newVMs\VS_Security.csv", _
    ForAppending, True)
```

Once the output file is open, the script obtains access to the VMVirtual *Server.Security* property and uses that property to obtain a collection of access rights entries. The script then starts actually writing entries to the output file. It first conditionally writes the header and then loops through each access right entry in the collection and writes out all the properties of the access right entry on a single line.

You can use VS_Security.vbs to document all the security entries of all your hosts. You can use it in a simple batch file, or you can modify the script to read an input file of remote server names and process each one. If you want to fully automate the script, you can query Active Directory for all the service principal name (SPN) registrations for Virtual Servers and use that list and the VS_Security.vbs script to query every Virtual Server host. These are all left to the reader as exercises in scripting.

VS_Security.vbs

```
'----------------------------------------------------------------
' VS_security.vbs
'----------------------------------------------------------------
Option Explicit
Dim objVS, objArgs, objSecurity, objAccessRights, arProperty
Dim objFSO, fileCSV, writeHeader
Const ForReading = 1, ForWriting = 2, ForAppending = 8

Set objArgs = WScript.Arguments

If objArgs.count <> 1 then
   WScript.Echo " ERROR: Remote server not specified"
   WScript.Quit
End if

On Error Resume Next
Set objVS = CreateObject("VirtualServer.Application", objArgs(0))

If Err.number <> 0 Then
   WScript.Echo "Failed to connect to Virtual Server"
   WScript.Echo "Error Number=" & Err.Number & " Description=" & _
     Err.Description
   WScript.Quit
Else
   WScript.Echo "Successfully connected to Virtual Server: " & objArgs(0)
   Err.Clear
   On Error GoTo 0
End if

On Error Resume Next
Set objFSO = CreateObject("Scripting.FileSystemObject")
writeHeader = objFSO.FileExists("c:\newVMs\VS_Security.csv")

Set fileCSV = objFSO.OpenTextFile("c:\newVMs\VS_Security.csv", _
   ForAppending, True)

If Err.number <> 0 Then
```

```
    WScript.Echo "Failed to open output file"
    WScript.Echo "Error Number=" & Err.Number & " Description=" & _
      Err.Description
    WScript.Quit
End If


Set objSecurity = objVS.Security
Set objAccessRights = objSecurity.AccessRights


If writeHeader = False Then
  fileCSV.WriteLine("ServerName,Name,SID,ReadAccess,WriteAccess," & _
    "DeleteAccess,ExecuteAccess,SpecialAccess,Flags,Change,Read,Type")
End If


For Each arProperty In objAccessRights
  fileCSV.WriteLine(objArgs(0) & "," & arProperty.Name & "," & _
    arProperty.Sid & "," & arProperty.ReadAccess & "," & _
    arProperty.WriteAccess & "," & arProperty.DeleteAccess & "," & _
    arProperty.ExecuteAccess & "," & arProperty.SpecialAccess & "," & _
    arProperty.Flags & "," & arProperty.ChangePermissions & "," & _
    arProperty.ReadPermissions & "," &  arProperty.Type )
Next


fileCSV.Close


WScript.Echo "Security Entry dump complete for " & objArgs(0)
```

Advanced Example

This chapter has talked about many different scripting interfaces for Virtual Server and the generic capabilities of Visual Basic Script. ArchiveVM.vbs combines many of the capabilities of Visual Basic Script (file access, writing to an event log, network access, shell access) with the *VMVirtualServer* interfaces to produce a useful script for test and development environments. You should not use this script for production environments because the script does not meet proper backup requirements for services such as Active Directory.

ArchiveVM.vbs is designed to take command-line input specifying a virtual machine name, back up the virtual machine locally, and then archive those backup files to a remote archive server. The following steps are required to achieve that goal:

1. Establish links to the file system, the shell, and the network interfaces.

2. Map a drive to a remote archive server.

3. Verify that the virtual machine is registered on the host.

4. Determine the current state of the virtual machine, and use that to conditionally determine whether the virtual machine needs to be placed in a saved state or whether the backup process can even continue.

5. If that backup process can continue, each virtual hard disk is enumerated and copied to the backup folder.

6. Once all drives are copied, the saved state, undo disk, and virtual machine configuration files are copied to the backup folder. At this point, the backup is complete.

7. Restart the virtual machine so that it can resume operation.

8. Once the virtual machine is restarted, the archive process can begin. The backup folder is copied to a remote archive server to provide protection if the virtual machine's files are lost or corrupted.

ArchiveVM.vbs

```
'=====================================================================
' ArchiveVM.vbs - Archives VHD drives for a VM to provide disaster
'                 recovery capability
'=====================================================================
Option Explicit

Dim objVM1, objVS, objArgs, colHDs, objDrive, objHardDisk
Dim fso, WshShell
Dim strVMName, strVMPath, strVMNETPath, strBackupPath, strArchivePath
Dim strVHDName
Dim saveTask, startupTask
Dim MyDate, pathArray
Dim WshNetwork
Dim returnVal, SAVEVM, BACKUP

Const InvalidVM = 0, TurnedOff = 1, Saved= 2, TurningOn = 3, _
   Restoring = 4, Running = 5, Paused = 6, Saving= 7, TurningOff = 8,_
   MergingDrives = 9, DeleteMachine = 10


'=====================================================================
' Retrieve Command Line Arguments
'=====================================================================


set objArgs = WScript.Arguments

If objArgs.Count<> 1 Then
   WScript.Echo "Missing command line argument"
   WScript.Echo "VMName"
   WScript.Quit
End If

strVMName = objArgs(0)
'=====================================================================
' Get a connection to Virtual Server on local machine
'=====================================================================
On Error Resume Next
Set objVS = CreateObject("VirtualServer.Application")

If Err.number <> 0 Then
   WScript.Echo "Failed to connect to Virtual Server"
   WScript.Echo "Error Number=" & Err.Number & " Description=" & _
```

```
                    Err.Description
    WScript.Quit
  Else
    WScript.Echo "Successfully connected to Virtual Server"
    Err.Clear
  End if
  '=================================================================
  ' Get a connection to the File System
  '=================================================================
  Set fso = CreateObject("Scripting.FileSystemObject")


  '=================================================================
  ' Get a connection to the Windows Shell
  '=================================================================
  Set WshShell = WScript.CreateObject("WScript.Shell")


  '=================================================================
  ' Get a connection to the Windows Network Interface
  '=================================================================
  Set WshNetwork = WScript.CreateObject("WScript.Network")


  '=================================================================
  ' Get the Date
  '=================================================================
  MyDate = Month(Date) & Day(Date) & Year(Date)

  strVMNETPath = "\\SERVER1\SCRATCH"

  WshShell.LogEvent 0, "Starting Archive of Solution"


  '=================================================================
  ' Map the drive to ARCHIVESERVER
  '=================================================================

  returnVal = WshNetwork.MapNetworkDrive( "V:", strVMNETPath)

  If NOT returnVal then
    WshShell.LogEvent 0, "Mapped drive V: to " & strVMNETPath
  Else
    WshShell.LogEvent 1, "FAILURE to map drive V:"
    WScript.Quit
  End if


  '=================================================================
  ' Get an Object link to the specified virtual machine
  '=================================================================
  Set objVM1 = objVS.FindVirtualMachine(strVMName)

  If objVM1 Is Nothing then
    WshShell.LogEvent 1, "Unable to start Backup - " & strVMName & _
                      " not found"
    WScript.Quit
  End if
```

```
'======================================================================
' Save the state of the VM if running
'======================================================================
WshShell.LogEvent 4, "Starting" & strVMName & " Backup"

Select Case objVM1.State

Case TurnedOff
  SAVEVM=False
  WshShell.LogEvent 0, strVMName & " VM not running"
  BACKUP=True
Case Saved
  SAVEVM=False
  WshShell.LogEvent 0, strVMName & " VM already in Saved State"
  BACKUP=True
Case TurningOn
  SAVEVM=True
  BACKUP=True
Case Restoring
  SAVEVM=True
  BACKUP=True
Case Running
  SAVEVM=True
  BACKUP=True
Case Paused
  SAVEVM=False
  WshShell.LogEvent 0, strVMName & _
          " VM paused, cannot be placed in Saved State"
  BACKUP=False
Case Saving
  SAVEVM=False
  WScript.Sleep(10000)
  If objVM.State = Saved Then
     BACKUP=True
  Else
     BACKUP=False
  End If
Case TurningOff
  SAVEVM=False
  WshShell.LogEvent 0, strVMName & " VM is turning off"
  WScript.Sleep(10000)
  If objVM.State = TurnedOff Then
     BACKUP=True
  Else
     BACKUP=False
  End If
Case MergingDrives
  SAVEVM=False
  WshShell.LogEvent 0, strVMName & " VM is merging drives"
  BACKUP=False
Case DeleteMachine
  SAVEVM=False
  WshShell.LogEvent 0, strVMName & " VM is being deleted"
  BACKUP=False
```

```
Case Else
  SAVEVM=False
  WshShell.LogEvent 0, strVMName & " Unknown Error with VM State"
  BACKUP=False
end Select

If SAVEVM=True then
  Set saveTask = objvm1.Save()
  saveTask.WaitforCompletion(60000)
  If objVM1.State = Saved Then
    WshShell.LogEvent 0, strVMName & " Save State Successful"
  Else
    WshShell.LogEvent 1, "Unable to Save State of " & strVMName
    WScript.Quit
  End If
End If

If BACKUP=False Then
  WshShell.LogEvent 1, " Archive aborted due to VM state"
  WScript.Quit
End If


Set colHDs = objVM1.HardDiskConnections

If colHDs.Count > 0 Then
  WScript.Echo "Hard disk connections: " & colHDs.Count

  For Each objDrive in colHDs
      Set objHardDisk = objDrive.HardDisk
      pathArray = Split(objHardDisk.File, "\", -1, 1)
      strBackupPath = Left(objHardDisk.File, (Len(objHardDisk.File)_
                    - Len(pathArray(UBound(pathArray)))))
      strArchivePath = strBackupPath & "Backup " & MyDate
      strVHDName = pathArray(UBound(pathArray))

    ' Create Archive Folder

    If(NOT fso.FolderExists(strArchivePath)) then
      fso.CreateFolder(strArchivePath)
    Else  ' Folder Exists
      fso.DeleteFile strArchivePath & "\*"
    End If

      fso.CopyFile objHardDisk.File, strArchivePath & "\"
    Next
    ' Copy remaining files
    fso.CopyFile strBackupPath & "\*.vsv", strArchivePath & "\"
    fso.CopyFile strBackupPath & "\*.vmc", strArchivePath & "\"
    fso.CopyFile strBackupPath & "\*.vud", strArchivePath & "\"
Else
  WScript.Echo "Error: No Hard disk connections"
End If
```

```
'=========================================================================
' Restart the VM
'=========================================================================
If SAVEVM=True Then
  WshShell.LogEvent 0, " Restarting VM"
  Set startupTask = objVM1.Startup()
  startupTask.WaitforCompletion(60000)
  If objVM1.State = Running Then
    WshShell.LogEvent 0, strVMName & " Restart Complete"
  Else
    WshShell.LogEvent 1, "Unable to Restart " & strVMName
    WScript.Quit
  End If
End If
'=========================================================================
' Archive the Backup file folder to ArchiveServer
'=========================================================================
WshShell.LogEvent 0, " Starting Archive to ArchiveServer"

fso.CopyFolder strArchivePath , "v:\"

WshShell.LogEvent 0, " Archive to ArchiveServer Complete"


'=========================================================================
' Remove the Map drive to ArchiveServer
'=========================================================================

returnVal = WshNetwork.RemoveNetworkDrive ("V:")

If NOT returnVal then
  WshShell.LogEvent 0, "Removed Mapped drive V: to " & strVMNETPath
Else
  WshShell.LogEvent 1, "FAILURE to remove map drive V:"
  WScript.Quit
End if

WshShell.LogEvent 0, " Archive Complete"
```

 On the Companion Media   Additional scripts have been provided on the companion media in the \Bonus Materials\Scripts directory.

Summary

The approach of the chapter was to provide you with building blocks and sample Visual Basic scripts to help you quickly learn the Virtual Server COM API. You learned how to connect to the Virtual Server object locally and remotely, retrieve and display information on the screen and in the Windows Event log, and add error-handling code to improve the stability of your scripts. The chapter also covered advanced topics such as file and folder management, retrieving events from the event log, working with tasks to provide management of the script, and using the Virtual Server WMI interfaces to gather information.

You obtained detailed knowledge from sample scripts for managing virtual machines, virtual hard disks, virtual networks, and Virtual Server configuration settings. Combining the advanced topics with the Virtual Server COM API produced scripts such as VS_Security.vbs, to document the security entries for a Virtual Server host, and Archive.vbs, to back up and archive a copy of test and development virtual machines to a remote server for disaster recovery.

Additional Resources

The following resources contain additional information related to this chapter:

- VBScript Errors Reference, *http://msdn2.microsoft.com/en-us/library/5ta518cw.aspx*
- Virtual Server Script Repository, *http://www.microsoft.com/technet/scriptcenter/scripts /vs/default.mspx*
- *Scripting.FileSystemObject* interface reference, *http://msdn2.microsoft.com/en-us/library /6kxy1a51.aspx*
- Visual Basic Scripting Language Reference, *http://msdn2.microsoft.com/en-us/library /d1wf56tt.aspx*

Chapter 10
Virtual Machine Migration Process

In this chapter:

Assessing Physical Workload Virtualization Potential 281

Understanding the Physical to Virtual Workload Migration Process 289

Using Automated Deployment Services and the Virtual Server
    Migration Toolkit 299

Summary 310

Additional Resources 311

This chapter focuses on the physical-to-virtual (P2V) migration process using the Virtual Server Migration Toolkit (VSMT), a free downloadable software tool used with Microsoft Virtual Server 2005 Release 2 (R2) to convert physical workloads into virtual machines (VMs). You will learn how to determine which workloads are good candidates for migration to a virtual machine and discover important factors to consider when defining workload resource requirements. The VSMT requirements, features, and deployment procedures are presented in detail, followed by step-by-step instructions to perform a physical to virtual machine migration. Additionally, the sequence to complete a virtual-to-virtual (V2V) machine migration is described.

Whereas VSMT is a viable tool to use for personal and small test and development environments where only a select number of P2V migrations must be accomplished and budget is limited, more robust and automatable tools are required for larger scale departmental, branch office, and data center environments. Microsoft System Center Virtual Machine Manager (VMM) is an enterprise-level application that can perform individual wizard-based P2V migrations or PowerShell-based scripted migrations. If you are interested in learning about VMM, you should review Chapter 19, "System Center Virtual Machine Manager 2007." There are also Independent Software Vendor (ISV) applications that support physical to virtual workload migrations, and these are covered in Chapter 20, "Additional Management Tools."

Assessing Physical Workload Virtualization Potential

The first step in the process to virtualize a physical workload is the assessment of its virtualization potential. The virtualization potential is determined by considering two major categories: workload requirements and workload limitations. The workload requirements are defined by the physical memory, processor, network, and storage resources needed to achieve the required level of performance. The workload limitations include specific hardware or operational dependencies that could prevent workload execution in a constrained virtual machine environment. This section focuses on the assessment for a single workload. In Chapter 14, "Virtualization Project: Assessment Phase," the concept is extended to encompass workloads on an enterprise scale.

Defining the Workload Memory Requirement

To define the workload memory requirement for a virtual machine, you must identify peak memory usage on the physical system. The information should be distilled from performance data captured over a sufficiently long period of time to reflect an accurate workload memory usage profile. In computing environments that operate at a fairly constant level, data collection over a one- to two-week period might be sufficient. In other environments that experience regular periodic activity spikes (monthly, bi-monthly, and so on), data collection over a two- to four-week period might be necessary. Longer data collection periods might be required to capture activity spikes, if there are seasonal or other parameters that drive more irregular fluctuations.

Using the peak memory usage as the basis to calculate the required virtual machine memory allocation ensures that performance under peak load can be sustained. In fact, virtual machine memory allocation must also account for a 32-MB virtualization overhead that is a result of video random access memory (VRAM) emulation and code cache of recently translated nonvirtualizable instructions. Therefore, virtual machine memory allocation is calculated using the following formula:

VM Memory = Workload Peak Memory Usage + 32 MB

The Workload Peak Memory Usage is the value that you should allocate when you create a virtual machine. This value actually defines the maximum amount of memory that the virtual machine can use while it is running. If sufficient physical memory is not available during virtual machine start-up, an error is logged in the Virtual Server 2005 R2 event log and the virtual machine cannot start. Once a virtual machine is started, it remains loaded in memory until it is shut down.

> **Important**   If the virtual machine memory allocation calculation yields a result greater than 3.6 GB, you should perform a thorough review to determine if this peak value is sustained and disqualifies the workload or whether the peak value is of short enough span to qualify the workload as a viable virtualization candidate. Virtual Server 2005 R2 limits maximum memory allocation to 3.6 GB per virtual machine.

Once you have defined the virtual machine memory allocation requirement, you must determine the total amount of memory needed for the physical server host. Because Virtual Server 2005 R2 runs as an application above the host operating system, you must also consider the

Virtual Server host operating system memory requirements in addition to those of the virtual machine. Consequently, the total memory specification for the physical server is calculated as follows:

Server Memory = [Host Memory + VM Memory] × 1.25

> **Best Practices**   At minimum, you should add 25 percent to the server memory calculation for capacity planning. It is important for you to tune the percentage based on specific growth projections. Nonetheless, this approach provides a buffer to manage virtual machine memory growth requirements and handle additional virtual machines. For example, if a Microsoft Windows Server 2003 R2 host server running Virtual Server 2005 R2 requires 1 GB of memory and the virtual machine allocation was calculated as 3 GB, the formula yields the following:
>
> *Server Memory (rounded up to even number) = [1 GB (Host) + 3 GB (VM) + 32 MB (Overhead)] × 1.25*
>
> *Server Memory (rounded up to even number) = 6 GB*

Defining the Workload Processor Requirement

There are two factors to take into account when defining the workload processor requirement for a virtual machine: processor scaling and peak processor utilization. Understanding the processor scaling requirements for a specific workload is crucial to defining the workload virtualization potential. Although Virtual Server 2005 R2 can scale across multiple processors, a virtual machine can be allocated a maximum of only one processor core. Hence, a workload with symmetric multiprocessing (SMP) requirements might not be a good candidate for virtualization in a production environment. However, it might be acceptable to virtualize the workload for a test or training environment where performance is not the primary driver or the required performance can be achieved when running on a single, more powerful processor core.

The maximum sustained processor utilization is used to define the virtual machine processor allocation requirement. Maximum sustained processor utilization should be captured in the same set of performance data as the peak memory usage. Use the following formula to calculate the virtual machine processor requirement:

Processor Requirement = number of CPU Cores × CPU Speed × Utilization (maximum sustained)

For example, using a physical server with two single-core 2-GHz processors and a maximum sustained utilization of 10 percent, the formula yields:

Processor Requirement = 2 × 2000 MHz × 10% = 400 MHz

Caution   This calculation assumes that the source and target processor architectures are similar enough to provide a valid processor performance comparison. If this is not the case, you need to include a performance factor in the calculation that corrects for the processor performance differences. You should also consider using a tool like System Center Virtual Machine Manager or another third-party tool that considers processor differences when determining virtual machine processor requirements.

Once the virtual machine processor requirement is known, you can determine the virtual machine CPU resource allocation settings to configure in Virtual Server 2005 R2. You should adjust these settings in anticipation of hosting additional virtual machines on the Virtual Server host. For example, if the Virtual Server 2005 R2 physical server includes two single-core processors running at 3.0 GHz, the server processor capacity is as follows:

Server Processor Capacity = 2 × 3000 MHz = 6000 MHz = 6GHz

Of course, processor capacity for the host operating system must be taken into account. Consider reserving at least 25 percent of the server processor capacity (or at least a single processor core, whichever is less) to determine the processor capacity available for allocation to virtual machines:

Available Processor Capacity = Server Processor Capacity × 0.75

You should fine-tune the reserved processor capacity if you intend to run other applications on the host operating system in addition to Virtual Server 2005 R2.

Best Practices   The general recommendation is to dedicate a physical server as a Virtual Server host and to not run additional applications. There are scenarios, such as in branch offices, where only a single server can be deployed and must support multiple applications. However, you should only deploy this configuration in such instances and not as a broad virtualization solution.

For the dual-processor server with 6 GHz of processor capacity and a 25 percent host operating system processor capacity reservation, the available processor capacity to allocate to virtual machines is as follows:

Available Processor Capacity = 6000 MHz × 0.75 = 4500 MHz = 4.5 GHz

There is now sufficient information to define the virtual machine processor resource allocation relative weight, reserved capacity, and maximum capacity settings. Table 10-1 lists the basic definitions for each of these parameters. Chapter 2, "Virtual Server 2005 R2 SP1 Product Overview," contains more detailed information on the processor resource allocation settings available in Virtual Server 2005 R2. Chapter 15 contains in-depth configuration guidance on setting these parameters in a multiple workload environment.

Table 10-1 CPU Resource Allocation Parameter Definitions

Parameter	Description
Relative Weight	A value used to determine additional processor resource allocation for a virtual machine compared to all other virtual machines in execution. By default, the relative weight is set to a value of 100, making all virtual machine resource requirements equal to each other.
Reserved Capacity (% of one CPU)	A value used to define the capacity of a single processor reserved for a virtual machine. The processor capacity allocated to the virtual machine is never less than this value.
Maximum Capacity (% of one CPU)	The maximum processor capacity that can be used by a virtual machine.

Continuing with the example of the single workload requiring a 400-MHz processor peak utilization and available processor capacity of 4.5 GHz, the CPU resource allocation settings are as follows:

Relative Weight = 100 (default setting)

Reserved Capacity (rounded up) = 4500 MHz / 400 MHz = 12 percent

Maximum Capacity = 100 percent (default setting)

There is no need to modify the default settings for relative weight and maximum capacity in the case of a single virtual machine. These settings should be revised based on workload priorities if additional virtual machines are hosted on the Virtual Server 2005 R2 machine.

Caution   If you allocate processor resources that exceed available processor capacity, Virtual Server 2005 R2 will not turn on a virtual machine that would result in processor capacity over-allocation. An error with Event ID 1042, indicating an unexpected error occurred, will be recorded in the Virtual Server application log.

Defining the Workload Network Requirement

The workload network requirement is another essential component in the identification of virtual machine resource needs. Analogous to the memory and processor requirements, the virtual machine network requirement is based on peak network utilization data captured from the workload executing on the physical server. This data is fundamental to determining whether the virtual machine requires one or more dedicated network interface cards (NICs), or if it can achieve desired performance levels using a shared network interface card.

In the case of a single virtual machine, if the workload on the physical server requires one or more dedicated network interface cards, you can implement the same configuration for the virtual machine. Depending on the fine points of the configuration, one or more virtual networks should be defined and connected to the appropriate network interface card to provide the required connectivity.

> **Important**   As a general rule, use a dedicated network interface card for the host operating system. This will ensure consistent communication with Virtual Server 2005 R2 and other applications installed directly on the host operating system. Also, unbind the Virtual Machine Network Service from the network interface card dedicated to the host to prevent any association to a virtual network within Virtual Server 2005 R2.

If multiple workloads without dedicated network interface card requirements will be hosted in virtual machines, use the following formula to determine the total network bandwidth utilization:

Total Network Requirement = SUM (NIC Speed × Peak Network Utilization)

As indicated, the total network requirement is simply based on the sum of the peak network bandwidth utilization of each workload. For example, consider four workloads running on physical servers configured with 100-Mb-per-second (Mb/s) network interface cards, and peak network utilization of 50 percent. Using the formula, the total network requirement is as follows:

Total Network Requirement = 4 × (100 Mb/s × 0.5) = 200 Mb/s

The result indicates that the combined virtual machine network requirement for the four workloads can be met using a single gigabit network interface card. Because network interface cards do not operate at 100 percent of capacity, assuming 75 percent network interface card efficiency, the remaining network capacity is as follows:

Remaining Network Capacity = (1000 Mb/s × 0.75) − 200 Mb/s = 550 Mb/s

> **Note**   If needed, use the Microsoft Loopback Network Adapter to enable connectivity between the Virtual Server 2005 R2 host and virtual machines. This will create a purely internal, isolated network that does not require configuration of a physical network interface card. Ensure that only the Virtual Machine Network Service is bound to the Loopback Network Adapter to dedicate it to Virtual Server networking. For further details, read the Microsoft Loopback Network Adapter configuration section in Chapter 4, "Installing Virtual Server 2005 R2 SP1."

As new workloads are hosted on the Virtual Server 2005 R2 machine, you should consistently review each workload's network requirement to determine whether there is sufficient bandwidth capacity provided by existing network interface cards.

Defining the Workload Storage Requirements

Defining the virtual machine workload storage requirement depends on the specification of storage capacity and performance. To properly configure and size the storage capacity, a number of aspects need to be considered besides the physical disk space profile. The workload performance requirement determines whether shared or dedicated storage configuration is needed to attain disk throughput levels.

Virtual machine storage capacity planning must account for additional disk space to store a Save State file coupled with the disk space needed for differencing and undo disks, if they are to be used in conjunction with the virtual machine. The Save State file (.vsv) size is directly dependent on the virtual machine memory allocation. For example, if a virtual machine has a 3-GB memory allocation, the Save State file size allocation will be 3 GB. In actuality, Virtual Server compresses the virtual machine memory content prior to saving it to the .vsv file; therefore, the size of the data saved to the .vsv file should always be smaller than the virtual machine memory allocation.

Note   In Virtual Server 2005 R2 SP1, a blank save state file is created when you start a virtual machine. The file size is based on the virtual machine memory allocation. The file is deleted when the virtual machine is turned off. This feature prevents data loss in a scenario where a virtual machine runs out of space on the physical hard disk where its VHD is located. Basically, Virtual Server 2005 R2 SP1 pre-allocates a large enough save state file for each running VM such that it can perform a save state for each affected running virtual machine.

Defining additional disk space to account for differencing and undo disks is a little more complex. Differencing disks and undo disks are special-purpose dynamically expanding virtual hard disks that allow virtual machine state changes to be saved in files that are separate from a base virtual hard disk. Differencing disks and undo disks both have the ability to grow as large as the base virtual hard disk. If a differencing or undo disk attempts to expand and causes the underlying physical drive to run out of disk space, Virtual Server 2005 R2 will suspend the virtual machine and place it in a saved state. Hence, to avoid virtual machine downtime, make sure to size storage capacity taking into account the size of each differencing and undo disk that will be used with the virtual machine.

Allowing for these factors, the virtual machine workload storage capacity requirement is defined as the aggregate of the following:

- Disk space used by the virtual machine VHDs on the physical server environment

- Disk space to be used by a Save State file, equivalent to the virtual machine memory allocation

- Disk space to be used by all differencing disks and undo disks associated with the virtual machine

- Disk space overhead no less than 25 percent of the total to provide additional storage and defragmentation capacity

In conjunction with storage capacity, you must also consider the workload storage performance requirement. The peak disk utilization for the physical workload and throughput attributes for the physical storage system are the key characteristics to consider when designing the physical storage environment to host virtual hard disks. Keep the following items in mind throughout the process:

- Use a fast access disk subsystem or storage area network (SAN).

- Use RAID 1+ 0 for the best disk performance or RAID 5 as an alternative in terms to support virtual hard disk storage.

- Dedicate disks and I/O channels for applications with very high throughput requirements.

- Dedicate disks for the host operating system and page file.

- Perform regular disk defragmentation.

As you add new virtual machines to Virtual Server 2005 R2, you must reassess whether the storage configuration and performance is sufficient to host additional workloads. If it is not, determine whether additional or dedicated disk resources are required and configure the storage environment to meet the new requirements.

 Important   To achieve the highest performance within the virtual machine, use fixed-size virtual hard disks connected to virtual SCSI adapters. Fixed-size virtual hard disks support up to 2 terabytes of data and will have less fragmentation than dynamically expanding disks. The SCSI protocol allows for multiple simultaneous operations, leading to higher throughput than IDE-connected virtual hard disks.

Defining the Workload Hardware Limitations

Because virtual machines execute within a constrained emulated hardware environment, some physical server workloads are precluded from a physical to virtual machine migration. In particular, disqualify any workloads that require the following items:

- USB devices (other than a keyboard and mouse)

- IEEE 1394 devices

- Non-Ethernet network interface cards

- Specialized SCSI adapters

- Specialized video or audio adapters

- Hardware dongles

The list is not exhaustive. However, it is evident that if a workload requires a specialized hardware device, it is not a suitable candidate for migration to Virtual Server 2005 R2.

Defining the Workload Operational Limitations

Finally, you must also consider any workload operational limitations in the assessment of a physical workload's suitability for migration to a virtual machine. For example, the following Microsoft server applications are not supported in a Virtual Server 2005 R2 production environment:

- Microsoft Speech Server

- Microsoft ISA Server 2000

- Microsoft ISA Server 2004

- Microsoft SharePoint Portal Server 2003

- Microsoft Identity Integration Server 2003

- Microsoft Identity Integration Feature Pack

If an application vendor does not support deployment of an application in a Virtual Server 2005 R2 production environment, it is not recommended that you do so. However, you can still leverage Virtual Server 2005 R2 to deploy the application in a testing or training environment.

Understanding the Physical to Virtual Workload Migration Process

The migration of a physical workload to a virtual machine consists of the three main phases described in Table 10-2. These phases are common to most migration tools available on the market, including the free, downloadable VSMT mentioned earlier in the chapter.

Table 10-2   **Physical-to-Virtual Workload Migration Phases**

Migration phase	Description
System Preparation	In the first phase, the source system is prepared for the migration process. If needed, the target system configuration is modified to comply with migration tool prerequisites and settings.
Workload Image Capture	In the second phase, migration tools collect source system configuration data, validate that the source system configuration is suitable for migration, and complete the workload image capture.
Virtual Machine Creation and Deployment	In the last phase, the migration tool creates, configures, and deploys a new virtual machine using the captured workload image.

The details of each phase presented in this section describe the process specifically implemented by VSMT to perform a physical-to-virtual workload migration. VSMT is a set of tools and customizable scripts used to collectively complete the migration process.

To use VSMT, you must be proficient with the Dynamic Host Configuration Protocol (DHCP), Pre-boot Execution Environment (PXE), and Windows Server 2003 Automated Deployment Services (ADS). If you are unfamiliar with one or more of these technologies, training material suggestions are provided at the end of this chapter in the "Additional Resources" section.

System Preparation Phase

Before using VSMT to perform a workload migration, the source system configuration must be evaluated to ensure compliance with the prerequisites listed in Table 10-3. These requirements specify not only the infrastructure protocols that the source system must support, but also characteristics—such as the operating system and file system type—that are driven by the boundaries of applicability of ADS and VSMT.

Table 10-3   **Virtual Server Migration Toolkit Prerequisites**

Prerequisite	Description
Pre-boot Execution Environment	The source system primary network interface card must support the PXE 0.99c protocol and allow a PXE boot from ROM or using a Remote Boot Disk Generator (RBFG) disk.
Dynamic Host Configuration Protocol	The source system must be able to obtain a network address and network configuration parameters from a DHCP server.

Table 10-3   Virtual Server Migration Toolkit Prerequisites

Prerequisite	Description
Hardware Abstraction Layer (HAL)	The source system must use one of the following hardware abstraction layer types: ■ Advanced Configuration and Power Interface (ACPI) PC - ACPI, PIC ■ ACPI Uniprocessor PC ■ ACPI Multiprocessor PC ■ Standard PC ■ MPS Uniprocessor PC - APIC, Non-ACPI ■ MPS Multiprocessor PC - APIC, Non-ACPI
Operating System	The source system must be running one of the following operating systems: ■ Microsoft Window NT Server 4.0, Service Pack 6a ■ Microsoft Windows 2000 Server, Service Pack 4 ■ Microsoft Windows 2000 Advanced Server, Service Pack 4 ■ Microsoft Windows Server 2003, Standard Edition ■ Microsoft Windows Server 2003, Enterprise Edition
Memory	The source system must have a minimum of 96 MB of physical memory.
Network Adapter	The MAC address of the primary network interface card that will be used during the migration must be identified. VSMT requires specification of the network interface card MAC address when multiple devices are present.
Disk Type	The source system must use basic disks. Dynamic disks cannot be migrated using VSMT.
File System	The source system drives must use NTFS. File allocation table (FAT) partitions cannot be migrated using VSMT.
Storage Area Network (SAN)	The source system must not have any SAN connections to migrate. If any such connections exist, the data must be copied to a virtual hard disk using either a backup and restore procedure or standard file copy process.
Windows Management Instrumentation (WMI)	The source system must have Windows Management Instrumentation installed and functional.
Security Account	An account with local Administrator rights on the source system must be used to execute the various VSMT utilities and scripts.

If the source system boot partition profile does not conform to the requirements, the discrepancies must be fixed prior to starting the actual migration process. Otherwise, the migration procedure will not be successful. Data partitions can be migrated separately to individual VHD files using a file copy or disk imaging tool.

Workload Image Capture Phase

The next phase of the migration process consists of several tasks that conclude with the workload image capture. VSMT uses a set of tools and scripts to complete this objective. Following are the four key actions taken during this phase of the migration process:

1. Inventory source system configuration

2. Validate source system configuration

3. Generate migration scripts

4. Capture source system image

Inventory Source System Configuration

The first step in this phase is accomplished by running the GatherHW.exe utility, included in VSMT, on the source system. GatherHW.exe conducts an inventory of the source system configuration and stores it in an XML file. GatherHW.exe collects the following type of information:

- Operating system configuration (version, language, service packs, HAL, and so on)

- General system configuration (BIOS, processors, memory, and so on)

- Storage configuration (controllers, physical disks, logical drives, and so on)

- Network configuration (adapters, TCP/IP settings, MAC address, and so on)

- Secondary hardware configuration (video, audio, serial port, CDROM, and so on)

- Software configuration (services, drivers, updates, and so on)

The GatherHW.exe utility uses the Windows Management Instrumentation interface to collect system configuration information.

Validate Source System Configuration

The second step in the workload capture phase uses VMScript, which is a VSMT script, to analyze the XML configuration file created by the GatherHW.exe utility and report on issues that could cause a migration failure. In fact, VMScript is a dual-purpose tool used not only to validate the source system configuration information prior to migration, but also to generate necessary migration scripts and files, as you will see in the next step.

In this step, VMScript is invoked to parse the XML file, determine whether any component or setting incompatibilities exist, and create a report similar to the following example:

```
Microsoft Virtual Server Migration Toolkit - VmScript Tool ver.5.2.5149.0
Copyright (C) 2004 Microsoft Corporation. All rights reserved.
Parsing System Configuration
        Name:           CONTOSO-ADS
        Memory:         1015MB
        Processors:     1
        HAL type:       acpipic_up
        OS Version:     5.2.3790 Service Pack 1
Parsing Network Configuration
        Network Card[0]
                MACAddress:  000AE45A7D1B
                DHCPEnabled:  True
                PrimaryNic : True
Parsing Storage Controller Configuration
        Controller ide[0]: PCI\VEN_8025&REV_03\3&61AAA01&0&F9
Parsing Logical Drive Configuration
        Found 1 logical disk drives
                Logical Drive[C:]
                        Size:                   12584644608
                        Hosts Windows Partition: True
Parsing Hard Disk Configuration
        Found 1 disk drives
        Disk Drive[0]: (\\.\PHYSICALDRIVE0)
                Size:       100027630080
                Partitions found: 1
                Partition[1]
                        Primary:                True
                        Bootable:               True
                        Hosts Windows Partition: True
                        Able to Capture:        True
                        Extended Partition:     False
                        BootIni:                True
                        Logical Drives:         C:
Parsing CDROM Configuration
        Found 1 cdrom drives
        CDROM Drive[0]: (IDE\CDROMPIONEER_DVD-RW_DVR-K13RA02020202)
Parsing Services Configuration
        Found 88 services
Parsing Drivers Configuration
        Found 174 drivers
Parsing Auto Run Programs Configuration
        Found 2 auto run programs
Parsing System File information
        Found 11 system files
Parsing Hotfix information
        Found 56 hotfixes
Parsing MountedDevices information
        Found 6 mounted device entries
Mapping Storage Devices
Using Windows Partition: \device\harddisk0\partition1 Disk:0 Partition:1
Using MAC[1]=000AE45A7D1B for PXE (Admin)
Checking configuration for incompatibilities.
No incompatibilities found.
Success.
```

VMScript also checks for problematic services or drivers, auto-run programs, key system files, and missing patches. The script then determines the primary operating system partition and MAC address of the network interface card that it should use for the workload image capture.

Direct from the Source: Identify and Load Missing System Files, Service Packs, and Updates

In the course of the source system configuration validation, VMScript reports whether any required system files are missing. The report includes the name of operating system files, service packs, or updates that contain system files that VSMT will need to perform a successful migration. VMScript uses an XML-based file, PatchFiles.xml, that is included with VSMT to determine which files are missing.

For English-language versions of supported operating systems, only files with updates and service packs available prior to the VSMT release are included with the toolkit. Equivalent files for non-English operating systems are not included by default. If you perform an operating system migration that requires an update or system file that was not included with VSMT, you must load the system files prior to initiating the migration.

To update the VSMT system file cache, use the Vmpatch.exe utility that comes with the toolkit. Vmpatch.exe loads required system files from the operating system driver cache or any folder where the source files are stored.

Because Vmpatch.exe is unable to directly copy service pack or updated binary files into the file system cache, begin by extracting the service pack or update file from the binaries and placing them into a folder. Then use Vmpatch.exe to load the required files into the VSMT system file cache.

Once all missing files have been loaded, you should run VMScript again to verify that you remedied all file issues and that no other incompatibilities exist. If the VMScript reports no further issues, you can proceed with generating migration scripts.

Eric Winner
Lead Program Manager, System Center Virtual Machine Manager

Generate Migration Scripts

Once VMScript has validated the source system configuration, the next step is to generate the scripts and files needed to capture the workload image and complete the migration. Table 10-4 lists the predefined scripts and task sequence files generated by VMScript based on the XML configuration file created by the GatherHW.exe utility.

Table 10-4   Migration Scripts and Task Sequence Files

Script/File	Description
*Source*_commonInit.cmd	Sets common environment variables.
*Source*_capture.cmd	Calls *Source*_commoninit.cmd to set common environment variables.
	Adds the source computer as a device in the ADS database.
	Initiates the ADS task sequences in capture-disk.xml to capture an image for each hard disk partition on the source system.
	Releases control of the device, and removes it from the ADS database when the capture is complete.
	Fixes certain system files on the captured images to make them compatible with the virtual machine environment.
*Source*_CreateVM.cmd	Creates a virtual machine on Virtual Server.
	Removes all network adapters from the virtual machine.
	Adds network adapters, the last one is the network adapter that will be used for PXE.
	Connects the Remote Installation Services (RIS) virtual floppy disk.
	Creates virtual hard disks, and attaches them to the virtual machine.
	Adds CD-ROM and DVD.
	Adds SCSI controllers, as required.
	Adds the virtual machine as a device in the ADS database.
	Creates a series of ADS actions to set a number of variables.
	Uses discovery to get information from the virtual machine.
	Opens the Virtual Server Administration Website.

Table 10-4   Migration Scripts and Task Sequence Files

Script/File	Description
*Source*_DeployVM.cmd	Calls *Source*_commoninit.cmd to set common environment variables.
	Connects the RIS boot floppy.
	Starts the virtual machine.
	Boots the virtual machine into the ADS Deployment Agent, runs the ADS deployment disk sequence in DeployVM.xml, and deploys the images to the virtual machine.
	Updates storage drivers.
	Runs the ADS task sequences, HAL.xml and Uniproc.xml, as needed to update the HAL and NTOSKRNL to single-processor versions compatible with the virtual machine environment.
	Runs the ADS service task sequence, *Source*_ServiceDriver.xml, to set the start state of devices and services in the virtual machine.
*Source*_PostDeploy.cmd	Resets attributes of the boot.ini file to System, Hidden, and Read-Only.
	For a source Windows NT 4.0 Server SP6a, the following tasks are also performed:
	■ Runs fixsetup.cmd to update the Setup.log file in the winnt\repair directory to reflect that the operating system is running on a single-processor computer.
	■ Service packs and hotfixes use the information in the Setup.log file to install the appropriate components.
*Source*_CleanupVM.cmd	Invokes only in the case of a failed migration attempt.
	Calls *Source*_Commoninit.cmd to set common environment variables.
	Stops running jobs, and turns off the virtual machine.
	Removes the virtual machine from Virtual Server.
	Releases control of the device in ADS.
	Removes the device from ADS.
	Deletes the virtual machine configuration file, as well as any virtual hard disk files associated with the virtual machine.

Table 10-4   Migration Scripts and Task Sequence Files

Script/File	Description
*Source*_captureDisk.xml	Boots the source system to the ADS Deployment Agent.
	Gets disk geometry (cylinders, heads, and sectors) for each disk.
	Captures an image for each partition.
	Shuts down the source system.
*Source*_DeployVM.xml	Obtains disk geometry (cylinders, heads, and sectors) for each physical hard disk.
	Initializes virtual hard disks.
	Creates disk partitions for the virtual hard disks.
	Obtains geometry for disk partitions.
	Deploys ADS images to the virtual machine.
*Source*_internalState.xml	Captures the state of internal hardware for each device.
*Source*_ServiceDriver.xml	Configures the starting state of services and devices in a virtual machine.

By default, the scripts are configured to create an unencrypted workload image. When migrating a physical system that stores sensitive or protected data, edit *Source*_captureDisk.xml and *Source*_DeployVM.xml and remove all instances of the following statement:

```
<parameter>-nonetencrypt</parameter>
```

Doing so will cause workload images to be encrypted when captured and deployed using VSMT.

Capture Source System Image

The last step in this phase is to capture the workload image from the source system. The process starts by executing the *Source*_capture.cmd script. This script invokes ADS, and by using the *Source*_capturedisk.xml sequence file, it completes four basic tasks.

The first task adds the source system to the device database controlled by ADS. Second, the source system is booted using PXE and ADS uploads the Deployment Agent to the source system. The Deployment Agent is a small-footprint, memory-resident operating system that provides an execution shell that can run additional commands to capture and deploy system images to ADS-controlled devices. The third task consists of retrieving source system disk information and capturing an image of each disk. Finally, once an image has been captured for each disk, ADS initiates a shutdown of the source system, releases control of it, and removes it from the device database.

Additionally, the attribute settings of specific system files in the captured images are modified to ensure compatibility with the virtual machine environment.

> **Note**   The time required for the image capture process varies, ranging anywhere from 0.5 to 1.5 GB per minute. For source systems with large disks, use a conservative transfer rate to estimate planned downtime and user impact as well as the number of concurrent migrations that can be supported by your network.

Virtual Machine Creation and Deployment

In the last phase of the migration process, a new virtual machine is created and then deployed after the source system disk images are restored to attached virtual hard disks. The process begins with the execution of the *Source*_CreateVM.cmd script to check the status of the target system in the ADS database. To perform the virtual machine creation tasks, the *Source*_CreateVM.cmd invokes the VMClient.exe utility from VSMT. VMClient.exe creates and configures virtual machines on Microsoft Virtual Server 2005 R2 through the Virtual Server Component Object Model (COM) interface.

VMClient uses a multistep procedure to create a virtual machine on Microsoft Virtual Server 2005 R2. First, VMClient constructs and registers a virtual machine configuration file (.vmc) to create a new virtual machine. When the new virtual machine is registered with Virtual Server, VMClient adds virtual network adaptors with corresponding source system MAC addresses to the new virtual machine and connects them to a pre-created virtual network. Finally, a Remote Installation Services (RIS) floppy disk image is assigned to the virtual machine, the virtual hard disks are created and initialized, and a virtual CD drive is attached to the virtual machine.

The virtual machine is created using the memory, disk size, network adapters, and MAC address information collected from the source system configuration file. By default, the processor allocation is 100 percent of a single CPU. Unless otherwise specified, virtual hard disks are created as fixed-size disks. Because the virtual hard disks are created sequentially, the disk initialization period can be quite long.

> **Important**   Modifications to the virtual machine creation options and resource allocations are made by updating the appropriate VMClient command lines in the *Source*_CreateVM.cmd script. For complete details on the VMClient.exe options and parameters, review the Microsoft Virtual Server 2005 Migration Toolkit help file, VSMT.chm, which can be found in %systemdrive%\Program Files\Microsoft VSMT\Help.

The *Source*_CreateVM.cmd script completes after adding the new virtual machine to the ADS database, ensuring it is ready for deployment.

Virtual machine deployment is controlled by the *Source*_DeployVM.cmd script and the task sequence file, *Source*_DeployVM.xml. The *Source*_DeployVM.cmd script invokes the VMClient utility to start the virtual machine from the RIS virtual floppy disk. The virtual machine acquires an IP address, and PXE boots into the ADS Deployment Agent. Once the virtual machine is booted, source system disk images are restored sequentially to the virtual hard disks. After the image restore procedure completes, the hardware-dependent system files are swapped for virtual machine–compatible versions and the virtual machine is powered off. At this point, the workload migration from source system to virtual machine is complete.

Using Automated Deployment Services and the Virtual Server Migration Toolkit

In this section, you will learn how to install ADS and VSMT to perform a physical to virtual machine migration. A full installation of ADS is described, including all the tools, samples, and templates needed to manage devices, capture disk images, and deploy disk images. As described in the previous section, VSMT leverages ADS to capture source system disk images, create virtual machines, and deploy source system disk images to virtual machines.

The following procedures are based on the assumption that ADS, VSMT, and Microsoft Virtual Server 2005 R2 SP1 are installed on a single physical server, referred to as the *Controller server*. This is not a requirement, but it is recommended as the quickest way to deploy and familiarize yourself with the tools and migration steps using a small footprint test environment. You will also need a second physical machine running the Windows Server 2003 operating system to represent a source system workload that will be migrated to a virtual machine.

Installing Automated Deployment Services

ADS is a Windows Server 2003 add-on that is available as a free download from the Microsoft Web site. The installation is straightforward with minimal requirements, as shown in Table 10-5.

Table 10-5   Automated Deployment Services Prerequisites

Requirement	Specification
Operating System	Windows Server 2003, Enterprise Edition.
DHCP Server	Any existing DHCP server that can provide TCP/IP network configuration settings to devices on the same network as the ADS server.
	Alternatively, install DHCP on the ADS server.
Database	Access to an existing Microsoft SQL Server to host the managed device database.
	Alternatively, install the Microsoft SQL Server Desktop Engine using the Automated Deployment Services Setup Wizard.
Storage	Size the disk space allocated to store source system images based on the physical disks that will be imaged.

The ADS installation includes the Controller Service, Image Distribution Service, and Network Boot Services. Once the installation package is downloaded, run the self-extracting executable and ensure that all the files are successfully extracted and placed into a new directory. To complete a full installation of ADS, follow these steps:

1. On the Controller server, use Windows Explorer to navigate to the directory that contains the extracted Automated Deployment Services installation files.

2. To begin the installation, locate and double-click the ADSSetup.exe file.

3. In the Welcome To Microsoft Windows Server 2003 Automated Deployment Services dialog box, click Install Microsoft SQL Server Desktop Engine (MSDE) SP4 (Windows) to create the Automated Deployment Services device database.

4. Once MSDE is installed, click Install Automated Deployment Services to start the Automated Deployment Services Setup Wizard.

5. In the Welcome To The Automated Deployment Services Setup Wizard dialog box, click Next.

6. In the License Agreement dialog box, review the license agreement. If you agree to the terms of the license, click I Accept The Terms Of The License Agreement and then click Next.

7. In the Setup Type dialog box, select Full Installation and then click Next.

8. In the Installing PXE dialog box, click OK.

9. In the Setup Type dialog box, click Next.

10. In the Configure The ADS Controller dialog box, use the default settings and click Next.

11. In the Network Boot Service Settings dialog box, select Prompt For The Path When Required and then click Next.

12. In the Windows PE Repository dialog box, click Do Not Create A Windows PE Repository and then click Next.

13. In the Image Location dialog box, use the default path or type a new path in the Path To Folder box, and then click Next.

14. If ADS Setup detects more than one network adapter in your computer, it displays the Network Settings For ADS Services dialog box. In the Bind To This IP Address text box, specify the IP address to bind the services and click Next.

15. In the Installation Confirmation dialog box, click Install.

16. In the Installing ADS dialog box, a progress bar appears to indicate the status of the installation.

17. When the Completing The Automated Deployment Services Setup Wizard dialog appears, click Finish.

18. During the installation process, a certificate is created to authenticate devices that interface with Automated Deployment Services. After the installation is complete, create a shared folder and copy %systemdrive%\Program Files\Microsoft ADS\Certificate \adsroot.cer into the shared folder.

19. Using Windows Explorer, navigate to %systemdrive%\Program Files\Microsoft ADS \Samples\Sequences and double-click on create-templates.bat. This will install sample job templates that are available to run and test the services.

To verify that the ADS installation was successful, use the Microsoft Management Console (MMC) snap-in to check whether the services are in the Connected state as shown in Figure 10-1.

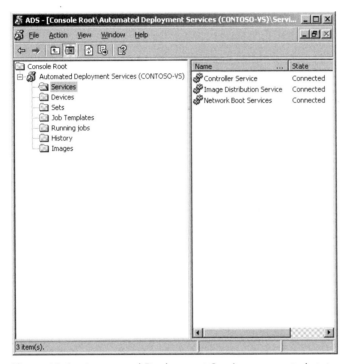

Figure 10-1   Automated Deployment Services connected state

To use the Automated Deployment Services MMC snap-in, follow these steps:

1. Click Start, click Run, in the Run dialog box, type **ads.msc**, and then click OK.

2. In the ADS-[Console-Root], click Automated Deployment Services in the left-hand pane to expand the tree structure, and then click the Services entry.

If all the service bindings were successful, the Controller Service, Image Distribution Service, and Network Boot Services states should display "Connected."

Installing the Virtual Server Migration Toolkit

VSMT is included in the Automated Deployment Services 1.1 installation package. Prior to installing the toolkit, ensure that you have already installed Microsoft Virtual Server 2005 R2 SP1 and ADS on the physical server.

To complete a full installation of VSMT, follow these steps:

1. On the Controller server, use Windows Explorer to navigate to the directory that contains the extracted Automated Deployment Services installation files.

2. To begin the installation, locate and double-click the ADSSetup.exe file.

3. In the Welcome To Microsoft Windows Server 2003 Automated Deployment Services dialog box, click Install Virtual Server Migration Toolkit.

4. In the Welcome To The Microsoft Virtual Server 2005 Migration Toolkit Setup Wizard dialog box, click Next.

5. In the License Agreement dialog box, review the license agreement. If you agree to the terms of the license, click I Accept The Terms Of The License Agreement and then click Next.

6. In the Setup Type dialog box, select Full Installation and then click Next.

7. In the Installation Confirmation dialog box, click Install.

8. In the Installing VSMT dialog box, a progress bar appears to indicate the status of the installation.

9. When the Completing The Microsoft Virtual Server 2005 Migration Toolkit Setup Wizard dialog box appears, click Finish.

At this time, you should also pre-create the default virtual network (VM0) that the *Source*_CreateVM.cmd script attaches to a new virtual machine. The virtual network is not created by default during the VSMT installation because the setup process does not assume that it is installed on the same physical system as Microsoft Virtual Server 2005 R2.

A script is provided with VSMT to automatically create the default virtual network. If the default virtual network does not exist, the virtual machine deployment will fail. To create the default virtual network using the script, follow these steps:

1. Using Windows Explorer, navigate to %systemdrive%\Program Files\Microsoft VSMT \Samples.

2. Locate and double-click the CreateVirtualNetwork.vbs file.

3. Open the Microsoft Virtual Server 2005 R2 Administration Website in your browser.

4. In the Virtual Networks pane, click Configure and verify that there is an entry for VM0 in the list of virtual networks.

Alternatively, you can execute the script by opening a command window and typing the following:

```
Cscript "%systemdrive%\Program Files\Microsoft VSMT\Samples\createvirtualnetwork.vbs"
```

> **Note**   You can also use a VMScript command-line option called /vsHostNet when generating the migration scripts to specify a different virtual network to use during the migration.

Performing a Physical to Virtual Machine Migration

Once the ADS and VSMT installations are completed, you are ready to begin the physical-to-virtual machine migration. The migration procedure consists of ten steps:

1. Preparing the source system.
2. Gathering the source system configuration information.
3. Validating the source system configuration information.
4. Generating the migration scripts.
5. Reviewing the migration scripts.
6. Loading drivers into ADS.
7. Capturing the source system disk images.
8. Creating the virtual machine.
9. Deploying the source system disk images to the virtual machine.
10. Completing the migration process.

To prevent any loss of data during the migration process, make a backup of the source system prior to starting the migration process. This step is particularly critical if you intend to migrate Windows NT 4.0 servers because the NTFS file system will be upgraded during the migration procedures.

Preparing the Source System

As part of the source system preparation, use the requirements list in Table 10-3 and Table 10-5 to ensure that the source system satisfies the conditions imposed by ADS and the VSMT for a successful migration. In addition, use the Chkdsk.exe utility to verify and resolve any disk errors, delete irrelevant or outdated files, and defragment the disks prior to the migration.

> **Note**   On a system running Windows NT Server 4.0, Service Pack 6a, you must install hotfix 872952 to ensure that the Chkdsk.exe utility still functions after the physical to virtual machine migration. Hotfix 872952 is available at *http://support.microsoft.com/kb/872952*.

If for any reason you intend to perform a migration from a source system configured with hardware drivers or services that are incompatible with the virtual machine environment, change the startup state to Disabled before starting the migration. Leaving incompatible drivers or services in an automatic startup state can cause the virtual machine to function improperly or fail to start.

> **Important**   If you use ADS to manage the source system, release control of the source system and delete the source system record prior to initiating the migration.

Gathering the Source System Configuration Information

When the system preparation is complete and the source system meets all the defined requirements, the next step is to run the GatherHW.exe tool from the VSMT. GatherHW.exe collects the source system information and creates an XML file that contains the system configuration data. Follow these steps to run GatherHW.exe on the source system:

1. Log on to the source system running Windows Server 2003.

2. Map a network drive to the root of the system drive on the Controller server.

3. Navigate to the Virtual Server Migration Toolkit installation folder, which is by default %systemdrive%\Program Files\Microsoft VSMT.

4. Copy GatherHW.exe to a directory on the source system.

5. Double-click GatherHW.exe on the source system to collect the configuration information.

6. GatherHW.exe creates an XML file with the name of the source system (*Source*.xml) in the directory from which GatherHW.exe was executed.

7. Copy *Source*.xml to the Controller server. If you followed the recommended procedure, Microsoft Virtual Server 2005 R2, VSMT, and ADS are installed on the Controller server.

Validating the Source System Configuration Information

After executing GatherHW.exe to collect the source system configuration information, you need to validate the data using the VMScript.exe utility. When VMScript.exe completes the configuration information analysis, it will indicate whether any errors or issues were encountered. Follow these steps to run VMScript.exe on the source system:

1. Log on to the Controller server and open a command window.

2. In the command window, change the directory to the Virtual Server Migration Toolkit installation folder, which by default is %systemdrive%\Program Files\Microsoft VSMT.

3. In the command window, start the VMScript execution by typing the following:

    ```
    VMScript.exe /hwvalidate /hwinfofile:"path\Source.xml"
    ```

    where *path\Source.xml* is the full path to the XML file.

Examine the VMScript output for any flagged issues, warnings, or errors. Correct any system discrepancies, and copy any missing system files, service packs, or hotfix files using VMPatch.exe before continuing to the next step.

> **Note**   For complete details on the VMPatch.exe options and parameters, review the Microsoft Virtual Server 2005 Migration Toolkit help file, VSMT.chm, located in %systemdrive%\Program Files\Microsoft VSMT\Help.

Generating the Migration Scripts

Once VMScript.exe has validated the source system configuration information, the next step is to execute VMScript.exe with a different set of options that generate the migration scripts that control disk image capture, virtual machine creation, and disk image deployment to the virtual machine. Follow these steps to generate the migration scripts using VMScript.exe:

1. Log on to the Controller server and open a command window.

2. In the command window, change the directory to the Virtual Server Migration Toolkit installation folder, which by default is %systemdrive%\Program Files\Microsoft VSMT.

3. In the command window, start the VMScript execution by typing the following text:

    ```
    VMScript /hwgeneratep2v /hwinfofile:"path\Source.xml" /name:vm_name /vmconfigpath:"vm path" /virtualDiskPath:"vm path" /hwdestvs:controller_server
    ```

    where *path\Source.xml* is the full path to the XML file, *vm_name* is the name to assign to the virtual machine, *vm path* is %systemdrive%\Program Files\Microsoft VSMT\VMs, and *controller_server* is the name of the Controller server.

> **Important**   By default, the migration scripts are configured to create fixed-size virtual hard disks. If the physical disks on the source system have an extensive amount of unallocated free space or you do not want to use fixed-size virtual hard disks, execute VMScript with the /virtualDiskDynamic option. This option directs VMScript to generate migration scripts that create dynamically expanding virtual hard disks. Forcing the migration scripts to create dynamically expanding virtual hard disks also reduces the total time to complete the migration by minimizing the virtual hard disk initialization process.

VMScript.exe generates the migration scripts in a subdirectory of %systemdrive%\Program Files\Microsoft VSMT\p2v. The subdirectory is given the same name assigned to the virtual machine. For example, if you provide *TestMigration* as the parameter to the VMScript /name option, the migration scripts are created in %systemdrive%\Program Files\Microsoft VSMT\p2v\TestMigration. All the generated migration files are also prefixed with the name of the virtual machine. Before moving to the next step, verify that the VMScript.exe output indicates that the migration files were created successfully.

Reviewing the Migration Scripts

Once the migration scripts are generated, you should familiarize yourself with each script and XML task sequence file. If any problems arise during the remaining migration tasks, it will be more difficult to troubleshoot issues if you are unfamiliar with the contents and actions contained within the generated migration scripts and files.

Loading Drivers into Automated Deployment Services

Even if VMScript successfully validates the source system configuration information, you must determine whether the network interface card installed in the source system is directly supported by ADS. If you had to load external network interface card drivers when you installed the operating system on the source system, you will most likely have to copy the same driver files into the Automated Deployment Services file cache before you can proceed and capture the source system disk image.

Follow these steps to copy and process the network interface card drivers into the Automated Deployment Services file cache:

1. Log on to the Controller server.

2. Download the latest network interface card drivers for the source system to a temporary directory.

3. Copy the driver files into %systemdrive%\Program Files\Microsoft ADS\NBS \Repository\User\PreSystem.

4. Open a command window.

5. In the command window, type **net stop adsbuilder** and then press Enter.

6. In the command window, type **net start adsbuilder** and then press Enter.

When you copy the network interface card driver files into the Automated Deployment Services file cache, do not create any subdirectories or include Txtsetup.oem files.

> **Note**   For more details on the issues that you can encounter when ADS lacks network interface card drivers for the source system, review Microsoft Knowledge Base article 841550 at *http://support.microsoft.com/kb/841550*.

Capturing the Source System Disk Image

At this stage, you are ready to capture the source system disk images. The *Source_*Capture.cmd migration script executes and leverages ADS to capture each source system disk image sequentially.

Follow these steps to start the source system disk image capture process:

1. Log on to the Controller server and open a command window.

2. In the command window, change directory to the Virtual Server Migration Toolkit subdirectory where the generated migration files are stored.

3. In the command window, execute the *Source_*capture.cmd script.

4. When prompted, log on to the source system, restart it, and PXE boot it.

ADS takes control of the source system and boots it into the Deployment Agent to initiate the disk image capture. You can follow the progress of each disk image capture using the Automated Deployment Service MMC snap-in on the Controller server. In the MMC snap-in, explore Devices and Running Jobs to view the status of the capture tasks.

When the image captures are complete, ADS shuts down and removes the source system from the device database. The last task before the script terminates is changing system file attributes, as shown in Figure 10-2.

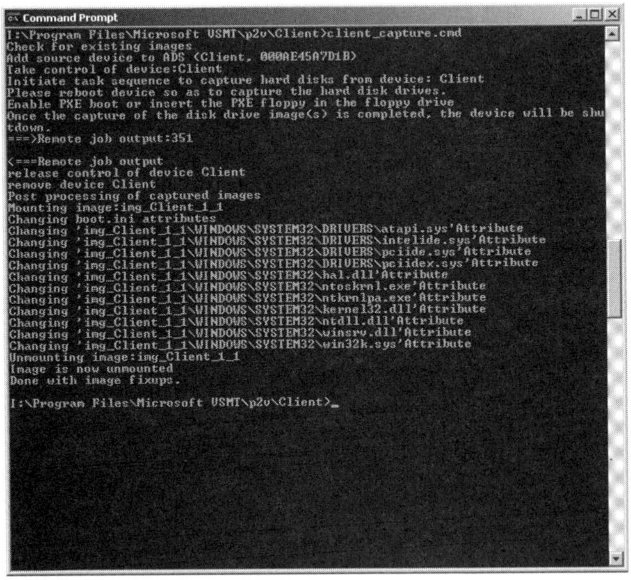

Figure 10-2 Sample output from the Source_capture.cmd script

Creating the Virtual Machine

The next step in the migration procedure is to execute the *Source*_CreateVM.cmd script and start the creation of the virtual machine in Virtual Server 2005 R2. Follow these steps to start the virtual machine creation:

1. Log on to the Controller server and open a command window.

2. In the command window, change the directory to the Virtual Server Migration Toolkit subdirectory where the generated migration files are stored.

3. In the command window, execute the *Source*_CreateVM.cmd script.

You can follow the progress of the virtual machine creation using the Virtual Server 2005 R2 Administration Website on the Controller server. You will see the creation of a new virtual machine configuration file, virtual machine creation, connection of the virtual machine to the default virtual network, creation and connection of the virtual hard disks to the virtual machine, and configuration of the virtual machine to attach an RIS virtual floppy drive.

When all these tasks are complete, check the ADS device database using the MMC snap-in. The virtual machine should have been added to the ADS device database and prepped for source system disk deployment. The script terminates after opening a browser window to the Virtual Server 2005 R2 Administration Website.

Deploying the Source System Disk Images to the Virtual Machine

After the virtual machine is created, the source system disk images must be restored to the attached virtual hard disks. The Source_DeployVM.cmd controls this part of the migration procedure. Follow these steps to restore the source system disk images and deploy the virtual machine:

1. Log on to the Controller server and open a command window.

2. In the command window, change the directory to the Virtual Server Migration Toolkit subdirectory where the generated migration files are stored.

3. In the command window, execute the Source_DeployVM.cmd script.

You can follow the progress of the virtual machine deployment using the Virtual Server 2005 R2 Administration Website on the Controller server. You will see the virtual machine boot into the Deployment Agent and the disk images restore to the virtual hard disks. The hardware-dependent system files are then swapped for virtual machine–compatible versions, and required operating system configuration settings are applied.

If you check the ADS device database using the MMC snap-in, you will see that the virtual machine is still in the device database. The script terminates after removing the RIS virtual floppy disk from the virtual machine. The virtual machine remains booted in the Deployment Agent.

Note   You can specify the state of the virtual machine after deployment is complete by using the VMScript /postDeployAction parameter when generating the migration scripts. In this manner, you can choose to leave the virtual machine device in the Deployment Agent, restart the virtual machine, or shut down the virtual machine. If you decide to bring the virtual machine online, you will have to ensure that the physical server remains offline. Since both the physical server and virtual machine utilize the same SID, active directory computer account, and so on, conflicts arise if both machines are online simultaneously.

Completing the Migration Process

To complete the source system to virtual machine migration process, there are a few final tasks to perform:

1. Open the Virtual Server 2005 R2 Administration Website, and verify that the Event Viewer does not report any errors.

2. Open the Automated Deployment Services MMC snap-in, and send a reboot command to the virtual machine.

3. In the Automated Deployment Services MMC snap-in, release control and delete the virtual machine from the device database.

4. Log on to the virtual machine, and install the Virtual Machine Additions.

5. Complete any remaining virtual machine configuration modifications.

6. Test the virtual machine connectivity and performance to ensure that it is running as expected.

Important   Once the virtual machine testing is complete, you can back up and delete the source system disk images from the Automated Deployment Services image store.

Performing a Virtual Machine to Virtual Machine Migration

You can use VSMT to migrate a VMware virtual machine to Virtual Server 2005 R2, provided that the VMware virtual machine is running one of the operating systems supported for migration. The migration procedure is the same as in the physical to virtual machine scenario. However, there are a couple of matters to consider prior to performing a VMware to Virtual Server virtual machine migration.

If the VMware virtual machine uses SCSI disks, you must copy the VMware SCSI drivers into the Automated Deployment Services file cache. Once you obtain the VMware SCSI drivers from the VMware Web site, follow the instructions in the "Loading Drivers into Automated Deployment Services" section earlier in this chapter.

> **Important**   If you encounter problems with the VMware SCSI drivers not loading correctly, there are two ADS hotfixes that you might have to apply to your installation. Review Microsoft Knowledge Base articles 829053 and 830413 found at *http://support.microsoft.com/kb/829053* and *http://support.microsoft.com/kb/830413*, respectively, for details.

In addition, you have to change the startup state of the VMware Tools Service to Disabled in the migrated virtual machine. Follow these steps to ensure that the VMware Tools Service is disabled automatically after the migration to Virtual Server 2005 R2:

1. Log on to the Controller server.

2. Using Windows Explorer, navigate to %systemdrive%\Program Files\Microsoft VSMT\Patches.

3. Right-click P2Vdrivers.xml and choose Edit.

4. Verify that the VMware Tools Service startup state is set to Disable.

The default P2Vdrivers.xml file specifies the startup state of drivers and services following the migration procedure. When generating the migration scripts, the VMScript.exe utility reads P2Vdrivers.xml and adds an entry in the generated task sequence that changes the start mode of the service or driver in the deployed virtual machine.

Summary

Before migrating a physical workload to a virtual machine, evaluate the workload memory, processor, network, and storage requirements to determine whether it is a good candidate for virtualization. To properly size the Virtual Server 2005 R2 physical host, consider the resource requirements of the host operating system in combination with the resource requirements of all the virtual machines that the system must support. A good rule of thumb is to add a 25-percent supplemental resource capacity to account for workload growth and additional virtual machines. Hardware and operational limitations must also be taken into account to ensure successful workload virtualization.

To understand the basic physical-to-virtual machine migration process, learn and use the free, downloadable VSMT in conjunction with ADS. Prior to starting the migration procedure, verify that the physical system configuration meets the requirements imposed by the tools. It is critical to review and understand the tools and scripts that are provided and created using the VSMT.

Once a migration procedure is complete, make sure to test the virtual machine under load to validate that performance and functionality meet production requirements. Finally, use VSMT to test the migration of virtual machines from VMware to Virtual Server 2005 R2.

Additional Resources

The following resources contain additional information related to the topics in this chapter:

- Knowledge Base article 829053, "Vendor-supplied drivers that you add to the ADS Deployment Agent Builder service repository are not installed," at *http://support.microsoft.com/kb/829053*

- Knowledge Base article 872952, "You cannot run the Chkdsk.exe program on NTFS file system volumes on a Windows NT 4.0 Service Pack 4-based computer," at *http://support.microsoft.com/kb/872952*

- Knowledge Base article 897614, "Windows Server System software not supported within a Microsoft Virtual Server environment," at *http://support.microsoft.com/kb/897614*

- Knowledge Base article 888794, "Considerations when hosting Active Directory domain controller in virtual hosting environments," at *http://support.microsoft.com/kb/888794*

- Knowledge Base article 830413, "The ADS Deployment Agent Builder Service does not correctly parse the latest .inf file formats," at *http://support.microsoft.com/kb/830413*

- Knowledge Base article 841550, "You receive an error message when you start a Windows Server 2003-based computer by using the ADS Deployment Agent," at *http://support.microsoft.com/kb/841550*

- Whitepaper, "Solution Accelerator for Consolidating and Migrating LOB Applications," at *http://www.microsoft.com/technet/solutionaccelerators/ucs/lob/lobsa/lobsaimg.mspx*

- Whitepaper, "Automated Deployment Services Technical Overview," at *http://www.microsoft.com/windowsserver2003/techinfo/overview/ads.mspx*

- Whitepaper, "Server Consolidation and Migration with VSMT," at *http://www.microsoft.com/windowsserversystem/virtualserver/overview/vsmtwhitepaper.mspx*

- ADS and VSMT Download, "Automated Deployment Services (ADS) 1.1," at *http://www.microsoft.com/downloads/details.aspx?FamilyID=d99a89c9-4321-4bf6-91f9-9ca0ded26734&DisplayLang=en*

Chapter 11
Troubleshooting Common Virtual Server Issues

In this chapter:

Common Setup and Installation Issues 313

Common Administration Website Issues................................ 316

Common Virtual Hard Disk Issues....................................... 320

Common Virtual Network Issues... 323

Common Virtual Machine Issues... 326

Summary.. 329

Additional Resources.. 330

The focus of this chapter is the resolution of common issues encountered when using Microsoft Virtual Server 2005 R2. The major areas that are covered include setup and installation, Web-based administration, virtual hard disk, virtual network, and virtual machines.

Common Setup and Installation Issues

Although there is not a great deal of complexity involved in the setup and installation of Virtual Server 2005 R2, there are a few basic issues that might occur. Problems encountered during this phase are usually resolved by properly configuring the host operating system to support the Virtual Server components selected during the setup.

Missing or Incompatible IIS Configuration

One of the most common issues that occurs during installation of Virtual Server 2005 R2 is shown in Figure 11-1. The dialog box indicates that the Virtual Server Administration Website installation requires Internet Information Services (IIS) to be configured and running on the host operating system.

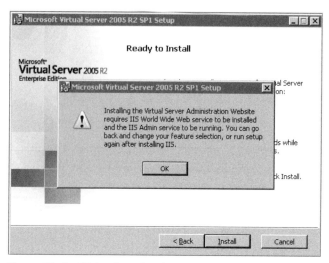

Figure 11-1   Dialog box showing IIS as a prerequisite for Administration Website installation

Resolution

There are two basic ways to address this issue. If you do not intend to manage any Virtual Server hosts from the physical server, go back and deselect the installation of the Administration Website. If you do plan to use the Administration Website to manage Virtual Server hosts from the physical server, you must cancel the Virtual Server 2005 R2 installation and install Internet Information Services (IIS) on the host operating system. Once the IIS installation is complete, you can restart the Virtual Server 2005 R2 setup. In Virtual Server 2005 R2 SP1, the setup process will make modifications to the IIS configuration required to properly integrate with the Virtual Server Administration Website.

Service Principal Name Registration Failures

A service principal name (SPN) allows Kerberos authentication to be used for services running on servers distributed across an Active Directory domain. An SPN is stored in a multivalued attribute, called *servicePrincipalName*, of an Active Directory computer account. At minimum, the information encapsulated in a registered SPN is the service name and the NetBIOS name, fully qualified domain name, or alias assigned to the computer that hosts the service. An SPN can also explicitly define the port number for the service and the account name under which the service runs, if it is different from the Local System or Network Service accounts. A separate SPN must be set for each host name by which the computer can be referenced. For a client machine to identify, mutually authenticate, and connect to a service, the service must have properly registered SPNs in Active Directory.

During Virtual Server 2005 R2 installation on a host that is a member of an Active Directory domain, the following SPN registrations are attempted:

- vmrc/*hostname:VMRC Port*
- vmrc/*fully qualified hostname:VMRC Port*
- vssrvc/*hostname*
- vssrvc/*fully qualified hostname*

If a Virtual Server host is unable to successfully register its SPNs in Active Directory, you will experience connection failures to the VMRC server and Administration Website on that host. When the Administration Website application attempts to connect to the Virtual Server service on another physical host, user credentials must be passed from the Administration Website to the remote Virtual Server service. This depends on the proper configuration and function of constrained delegation. Constrained delegation is the mechanism that enables an Active Directory computer or service account to perform Kerberos delegation to a well-defined and limited set of services. Because constrained delegation depends on access to properly registered SPNs in Active Directory, successful authentication to the remote Virtual Server service will fail if the SPNs are not registered. In addition, you might also encounter denied access to virtual machine resource files stored on a separate file server, since this access also depends on constrained delegation.

Resolution

If Virtual Server SPNs are not successfully registered in Active Directory, you can manually register the missing SPNs with Setspn.exe, a free utility available from Microsoft. Using Setspn.exe, you can manually add, delete, or view SPNs stored in Active Directory. Table 11-1 contains the basic Setspn.exe commands that you can use to configure the Virtual Server SPNs in Active Directory.

Table 11-1   Basic Setspn.exe Commands for Virtual Server Services

Action	Commands
View registered SPNs	**setspn -L** *hostname*
Add Virtual Server SPNs	**setspn -A** vmrc/*hostname*:5900
	setspn -A vmrc/*fully qualified hostname*:5900
	setspn -A vssrvc/*hostname*
	setspn -A vssrvc/*fully qualified hostname*
	Note: If you have changed the default VMRC Server port, replace *5900* with the new port number.

Table 11-1   Basic Setspn.exe Commands for Virtual Server Services

Action	Commands
Delete Virtual Server SPNs	**setspn -D** vmrc/*hostname*:5900
	setspn -D vmrc/*fully qualified hostname*:5900
	setspn -D vssrvc/*hostname*
	setspn -D vssrvc/*fully qualified hostname*
	Note: If you have changed the default VMRC Server port, replace *5900* with the new port number.

Note   The Setspn command-line tool is included in the Microsoft Windows Server 2003 Support Tools that can be found on the product CD or downloaded from *http://www.microsoft.com/downloads*. For more information on installing Windows Support Tools, see "Install Windows Support Tools" at *http://go.microsoft.com/fwlink/?LinkId=62270*.

Stop Error on x64 Windows Operating System with AMD-V

If you are installing Virtual Server 2005 R2 SP1 on a computer with AMD-V, AMD's hardware-assisted virtualization, which uses an x64 version of Windows Server 2003 or Windows XP as the host operating system, you will experience a stop error and restart of the host operating system. This occurs because the x64 versions of these Windows operating systems protect a critical system register that Virtual Server 2005 R2 SP1 attempts to modify during installation to enable hardware-assisted virtualization support.

Resolution

This issue is resolved by installing a hotfix prior to beginning the setup procedure for Virtual Server 2005 R2 SP1. A link to download the hotfix can be found at *http://support.microsoft.com/kb/924131*.

Common Administration Website Issues

One of the problems often encountered after installation of Virtual Server 2005 R2 is denied access to the Administration Website. Most common issues are easily resolved by modifying Internet Explorer options or security settings.

Blank Screen Display

One of the common issues encountered when you launch the Administration Website using the fully qualified domain name (FQDN) of the Virtual Server host (for example, *http://hostname.domain.com:1024*) and enter your credentials at the prompt is that only a blank screen is displayed. The FQDN is the format used in the Virtual Server Administration

Website Uniform Resource Locator (URL) shortcut created under Microsoft Virtual Server in the All Programs menu. When the FQDN of the Virtual Server host name is used, Internet Explorer interprets the destination as being outside of the local intranet and does not load the page.

Resolution

This problem can be easily resolved by adding the Virtual Server Administration Website URL to the Trusted Sites zone in the Internet Explorer configuration settings. Follow these steps to modify the Internet Explorer settings:

1. Open Internet Explorer and on the Tools menu, click Internet Options.

2. Click the Security tab, and then click the Sites button.

3. In the Add This Website To The Zone text box, type (or cut and paste) the Virtual Server Administration Website URL and then click Add.

4. If it is selected, deselect the Require Server Verification (https:) For All Sites In This Zone check box.

5. Click Close, and then click OK.

Always Prompted for Credentials

Another common problem is that you are prompted to enter your credentials every time you access the Administration Website using the FQDN of the Virtual Server host, even after it has been added as a trusted site. This is another issue that is related to the baseline configuration of Internet Explorer. By default, user credentials are automatically submitted for authentication only to sites that are interpreted to be in the Intranet zone. For all other zones, including Trusted Sites, the user authentication dialog box is displayed and credentials must be entered manually.

Resolution

To resolve this problem on Windows Server 2003, you can modify the Internet Explorer configuration to automatically submit user credentials for authentication regardless of the zone. Follow these steps to change the Internet Explorer user authentication settings:

1. Open Internet Explorer and on the Tools menu, click Internet Options.

2. Click the Security tab, and then click the Custom Level button.

3. Scroll down to the User Authentication section, and click the Automatic Logon With Current User Name And Password option button.

4. Click OK twice.

The drawback of this method is that you might encounter authentication failures if you have configured other trusted sites for which you need to present a separate set of user credentials.

Alternatively, if you are accessing a local instance of the Administration Website (running on the computer that you are logged in on), you can use a non-FQDN for the Virtual Server host in the URL (for example, http://*localhost:1024*).

When you are running Windows Vista, you have the added complexity of having to run the Administration Website in Internet Explorer as administrator when User Account Control (UAC) is enabled. If you are running in an isolated test environment, you can avoid this additional step by disabling UAC. Otherwise, follow these steps to grant your user account full administrative privilege in Virtual Server and eliminate the need for UAC:

1. Right-click the Internet Explorer icon in the Quick Launch section of the taskbar, and choose Run As Administrator from the menu.

2. In the User Access Control dialog box, click Allow.

3. In the Internet Explorer address bar, type in the URL to the Administration Website.

4. In the Virtual Server navigation menu, click Server Properties.

5. Click the Add Entry button.

6. In the new Permission Entry, type in your account name in the User Or Group text box.

7. In Permissions, select the Full check box to give your account full control.

8. Click OK.

> **Important**   In Internet Explorer 7, you must also ensure that the Enable Protected Mode option remains disabled for Trusted Sites. If Protected Mode is enabled, you will receive the following error when you attempt to access the Administration Website: "Could not connect to Virtual Server. Please add the Virtual Server administration Website to the Internet Explorer trusted sites list. You can specify an alternate Virtual Server below." To learn more about Internet Explorer 7 Protected Mode, review the blog entry written by a member of the Internet Explorer security team at *http://blogs.msdn.com/ie/archive/2006/02/09/528963.aspx*.

If you plan to use the Remote Desktop Protocol (RDP) to connect to a remote Virtual Server host, you must use the /console switch. Otherwise, when you launch the Administration Website site on the remote machine, you might be presented with "The Parameter is incorrect." Use one of the following methods to launch an RDP connection to a remote Virtual Server host console session:

■ Create a shortcut on your desktop and modify the shortcut target entry to reflect %systemroot%\system32\mstsc.exe /console.

■ Launch the RDP connection from the Start menu and specify "mstsc /console".

Access Is Denied Using Virtual Server Manager

When you use Virtual Server Manager from a centralized Administration Website to attempt to manage a remote Virtual Server that is a member of a different Active Directory domain, forest, or workgroup, you might receive an "Access was denied" error message when using the Switch Virtual Server option to connect to the remote Virtual Server. During the connection attempt, the local Administration Website application passes the account credentials of the context under which it is running to the remote Virtual Server. If authentication is successful, the Virtual Server target is added to the Virtual Server Manager list. If authentication fails, the error shown in Figure 11-2 is returned.

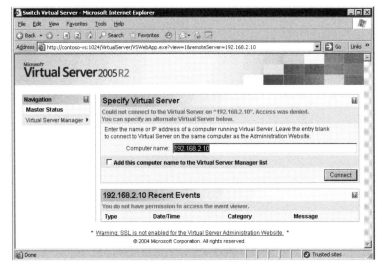

Figure 11-2 "Access was denied" error received when using the Administration Website Virtual Server Manager

Resolution

If you need to manage Virtual Server hosts across domain or forest boundaries using Virtual Server Manager from a centralized Administration Website, you must configure domain-level or forest-level trusts, and then grant permissions to manage each Virtual Server host to the user account under which context the Administration Website application will run.

If you must manage Virtual Server hosts across workgroups using Virtual Server Manager, you have to create a local user account on each Virtual Server host with the same user name and password to allow successful authentication during the connection process. You must also grant permissions to manage the Virtual Server host to the local user account on each server and use this "common" user account to run the centralized Administration Website. Although this solution works, it is not recommended because of user account management and security implications. If possible, you should deploy Virtual Server hosts within more secure and manageable Active Directory domains.

> **Note**   Review the Virtual Server management roles described in Chapter 6, "Security in Depth," to determine the appropriate set of permissions needed to manage Virtual Server.

Common Virtual Hard Disk Issues

The virtual hard disk (VHD) architecture is stable and mature, so you will probably seldom stumble into any major technical issues with a root cause related to a virtual hard disk. However, you might come across the following issues, which are common in the early stages of deploying Virtual Server hosts and ramping up the use of virtual machines in your environment.

Stop 0x7B Error Booting from a Virtual SCSI Disk

If you reconfigure a virtual machine VHD that contains a bootable guest operating system from a virtual IDE controller to a virtual SCSI controller, you will experience a blue screen when trying to start the guest operating system. Basically, if you simply just change the virtual machine configuration by switching the VHD from IDE to SCSI-attached, the guest operating system cannot find a valid SCSI controller driver during boot. This results in a STOP: 0x0000007B error message, followed by a virtual machine restart.

Resolution

Before you can switch a bootable VHD from virtual IDE to virtual SCSI, you have to first load the SCSI controller drivers in the guest operating system. Once the guest operating system is properly configured, you can shut down the virtual machine and reconfigure the VHD to attach to a virtual SCSI controller. The following procedure assumes the Virtual Machine Additions are installed in a Windows Server 2003 guest operating system prior to performing the installation of the SCSI controller drivers:

1. Open the Virtual Server Administration Website.

2. In the Master Status pane, click the icon to connect to the target virtual machine.

3. Once you are logged in, shut down the guest operating system and return to the Virtual Server Administration Website.

4. Under Virtual Machines, click Configure and select the new target virtual machine.

5. In the Virtual Machine Configuration pane, click SCSI adapters.

6. Click Add SCSI Adapter (ID 7), and then click OK.

7. Do not change the configuration of the bootable VHD; leave it as a virtual IDE disk.

8. In the virtual machine Status pane, point to the virtual machine name and select Turn On.

9. Click the icon to connect to the virtual machine and log in to the guest operating system.

10. The "Found new hardware: Adaptec AIC-7870 PCI SCSI Adapter" message will display. Windows Server 2003 comes packaged with a driver for the emulated Adaptec 7870 SCSI controller, so you will need a CD or ISO to load the aic78xx.sys driver file.

11. When the driver is installed, the virtual machine is configured to boot from SCSI, but the driver is a *slow* SCSI driver.

12. To load an accelerated SCSI controller driver, open Device Manager in the guest operating system.

13. Expand the SCSI and RAID controllers section.

14. Right-click the SCSI Controller and choose Update Driver.

15. On the Welcome To The Hardware Update Wizard page, click No, Not This Time and then click Next.

16. On the next page, select Install From A List Or Specific Location (Advanced) and then click Next.

17. Select Don't Search, I Will Choose The Driver To Install, and then click Next.

18. Click Have Disk.

19. Browse to C:\Program Files\Virtual Machine Additions, click Open, and then click OK.

20. Under Model, highlight the Microsoft Virtual Machine PCI SCSI Controller driver and then click Next to install the optimized SCSI controller driver.

21. On the Completing The Hardware Update Wizard page, click Finish.

22. Shut down the guest operating system.

23. Back in the virtual machine configuration pane, click Hard Disks.

24. In the Attachment drop-down list, select SCSI 0 ID 0 and then click OK.

25. Turn on the virtual machine.

> **Note**   A virtual machine can boot only from a VHD attached to the first virtual SCSI adapter. This adapter is identified as SCSI 0.

Broken Differencing Disk After Parent VHD Is Moved or Renamed

A differencing disk uses file path and name information stored in its dynamic disk header to locate and open its parent VHD. If the parent VHD is renamed or moved, the file path and name reference stored in the differencing disk header becomes invalid. This causes any virtual machine that uses a VHD in the differencing disk chain to fail at startup. Figure 11-3 shows the error (in bold text) that is captured in the Virtual Server Event Viewer log when a virtual machine is started after the differencing disk parent VHD is moved.

Figure 11-3   Error generated when a virtual machine is started after the differencing disk parent VHD is moved

> **Note**   Detailed information on the format and use of differencing disks can be found in Chapter 5, "Virtual Server 2005 R2 Advanced Features."

Resolution

To resolve this issue, you simply have to update the parent VHD path and file name reference in the differencing disk. You can accomplish this through the Administration Website or using a script. Follow these steps to inspect and modify the differencing disk through the Administration Website:

1. Open the Virtual Server Administration Website.

2. In the Virtual Disks navigation menu, click Inspect.

3. In Inspect Virtual Hard Disk, select the differencing disk from the Known Virtual Hard Disks pull-down menu. If the differencing disk does not appear in the list, enter the fully qualified path in the Fully Qualified Path To File text box.

4. Click Inspect.

5. Under the differencing disk Virtual Hard Disk Properties, click the link to the right of Parent Virtual Hard Disk(s).

6. Select the parent VHD from the Parent Virtual Hard Disk Path pull-down menu. If the parent VHD does not appear in the list, enter the fully qualified path to the parent VHD in the text box.

7. Click Update Parent Path.

> **On the Companion Media**   The companion media contains a Virtual Basic script named FixDiffDisk.vbs in the \Chapter Materials\Scripts directory. You can run (and customize) the script to update the parent VHD reference in the differencing disk. The script takes as input command-line parameters that define the fully qualified paths to the differencing disk and the parent VHD.

Common Virtual Network Issues

Virtual Server 2005 R2 provides the ability to very easily create flexible internal and external network configurations that allow seamless virtual machine connectivity to other networked components. The issues discussed in this section represent the common problems that you can encounter configuring virtual networks.

Problems Connecting a Virtual Network to a Physical Network Adapter

After completing an installation of Virtual Server 2005 R2, you might find that your physical network adapter is not available within Virtual Server to connect to a virtual network. If the Virtual Machine Network Services driver is not installed or bound to the network adapter on the physical host, it will not appear as an available network adapter within Virtual Server. Figure 11-4 shows the error that is generated if the Virtual Machine Network Services driver is not installed and properly configured in the physical network adapter properties.

Figure 11-4   Error generated when the Virtual Machine Network Services driver is missing or misconfigured

Resolution

To resolve this issue, you must install the Virtual Machine Services driver, if it is missing, and bind it to the physical network adapter. Follow these steps if you are running either Windows XP or Windows Server 2003:

1. Click Start, and then click Control Panel.

2. With Control Panel configured in classic view, click Network Connections.

3. Right-click the target network adapter, and then select Properties.

4. If Virtual Machine Network Services appears in the items list but is not selected, choose the associated check box to bind the driver to the network adapter and then click OK.

5. If Virtual Machine Network Services does not appear in the items list, click Install.

6. In Select Network Component Type, click Service and then click Add.

7. In Select Network Service, click Virtual Machine Network Services and then click OK.

8. Ensure that Virtual Machine Network Services is selected, and then click Close.

Follow these steps to install and bind the Virtual Machine Network Services driver to a network adapter in Windows Vista:

1. Click Start, and then click Control Panel.

2. Double-click Network And Sharing Center.

3. In the Task menu, click Manage Network Connections.

4. Right-click the target network adapter, and select Properties. If UAC is enabled, click Continue when the dialog box appears.

5. If Virtual Machine Network Services appears in the items list but is not selected, choose the associated check box to bind the driver to the network adapter and then click OK.

6. If Virtual Machine Network Services does not appear in the items list, click Install.

7. In Select Network Component Type, click Service and then click Add.

8. In Select Network Service, click Virtual Machine Network Services and then click OK.

9. Ensure that Virtual Machine Network Services is selected, and then click Close.

Duplicate MAC Addresses

Figures 11-5 and 11-6 show the errors generated when you configure and start two virtual machines with identical static media access control (MAC) addresses on the same Virtual Server host and virtual network.

contoso-vs Recent Events			
Type	Date/Time	Category	Message
⚠	4/15/2007 11:22:50 PM	Virtual Server	The static MAC address on "JSCTEST2" (00:03:FF:40:32:68) conflicts with the MAC address on "jsc-winxp". MAC address conflicts on the same virtual network may result in a loss of network connectivity.
⚠	4/15/2007 11:22:50 PM	Virtual Server	The static MAC address for "JSCTEST2" was changed. Multiple virtual machines using identical MAC addresses on the same virtual network may result in a loss of network connectivity.
⚠	4/15/2007 11:22:39 PM	Virtual Server	The static MAC address on "jsc-winxp" (00:03:FF:40:32:68) conflicts with the MAC address on "JSCTEST2". MAC address conflicts on the same virtual network may result in a loss of network connectivity.
⚠	4/15/2007 11:22:39 PM	Virtual Server	The static MAC address for "jsc-winxp" was changed. Multiple virtual machines using identical MAC addresses on the same virtual network may result in a loss of network connectivity.
ⓘ	4/15/2007 11:22:39 PM	Setting Change	The setting "hardware/pci_bus/ethernet_adapter/ethernet_controller [@id=0]/ethernet_card_address" for the virtual machine configuration "jsc-winxp" was changed.

Figure 11-5   Error generated when virtual machines with duplicate MAC addresses are registered on the same virtual server host

contoso-vs Recent Events			
Type	Date/Time	Category	Message
ⓘ	4/15/2007 11:25:40 PM	Virtual Machine	"JSCTEST2" was started.
ⓘ	4/15/2007 11:25:40 PM	Setting Change	The setting "settings/shutdown/quit/was_running" for the virtual machine configuration "JSCTEST2" was changed from false to true.
✖	4/15/2007 11:25:40 PM	Virtual Machine	The virtual machine "JSCTEST2" cannot connect virtual network adapter 1 because another virtual machine with the MAC address 00:03:FF:40:32:68 is already running. This virtual network adapter will be left disconnected.
ⓘ	4/15/2007 11:25:39 PM	Setting Change	The setting "virtual_machines/hw_assist/is_enabled_hw_assist" for the virtual machine activation "JSCTEST2" was changed from NULL to true.
ⓘ	4/15/2007 11:25:36 PM	Virtual Machine	"jsc-winxp" was started.
ⓘ	4/15/2007 11:25:36 PM	Setting Change	The setting "settings/shutdown/quit/was_running" for the virtual machine configuration "jsc-winxp" was changed from false to true.
✖	4/15/2007 11:25:36 PM	Virtual Server	Virtual Server could not open its emulated Ethernet switch driver. Access to the external network and host will be unavailable to all guests using the "NVIDIA nForce Networking Controller" adapter. Guests using Virtual Switch will still be able to access other guests using Virtual Switch.

Figure 11-6   Error generated when virtual machines with duplicate MAC addresses are started on the same virtual server host

If you use a single staging server to build a large number of virtual machines and change the MAC address configuration to static from dynamic for tracking purposes, the dynamic MAC address allocation system could generate a duplicate MAC address. If the Virtual Server host contains only a single physical network adapter, Virtual Server 2005 R2 assigns MAC addresses to virtual network adapters in the 00-03-FF-xx-xx-xx range, where the last two octets match the last two octets of the physical network adapter MAC address. For example, if the MAC address of the physical network card on your staging server is 00-16-31-53-32-68, Virtual Server will assign virtual network adapters a MAC address in the range 00-03-FF-xx-32-68.

If there are multiple network adapters in the physical server, the first 256 MAC addresses are allocated using the primary network adapter octet values, the next 256 MAC addresses are allocated from the second network adapter octet values, and this process continues until Virtual Server 2005 R2 has iterated through all the physical network adapters. If all network adapter octet values are exhausted, Virtual Server re-uses the first network adapter octet values.

Resolution

In general, there is no guarantee that dynamic MAC address allocation will be unique, even across multiple Virtual Server hosts. If you use a single staging server to generate virtual machines configured with static MAC address, you must institute a process to ensure that duplicate MAC addresses are identified and reconfigured prior to deployment. If you copy a virtual machine with a static MAC address to another computer that already has a virtual machine with an identical static MAC address, you must either manually or programmatically change the static MAC address of one of the virtual machines, or configure one or more of the virtual machines to use a dynamic MAC address. Virtual Server allocates a new dynamic MAC address in the following circumstances:

- A virtual machine is created.
- A virtual machine MAC address conflict is detected.
- A virtual machine is registered on a Virtual Server host.

Follow these steps to modify the virtual machine configuration to use a dynamic MAC address:

1. Open the Virtual Server Administration Website.
2. In Virtual Machines, click Configure and select the virtual machine from the list.
3. In the virtual machine Configuration pane, click Network Adapters.
4. In Ethernet (MAC) Address, select Dynamic.
5. Click OK.

> **More Info**   For additional information regarding the Virtual Server dynamic MAC address allocation algorithm, refer to *http://support.microsoft.com/default.aspx/kb/888030*.

Common Virtual Machine Issues

Chances are that creating, configuring, running, and managing virtual machines are the tasks that will encompass the bulk of your time in a Virtual Server infrastructure. In this section, you can review common virtual machine issues that you might encounter while performing these activities.

Guest Operating System Installation Is Slow

When you install Windows Server 2003, Windows 2000 Server, or Windows XP Professional as a guest operating system in a virtual machine, the installation process can take several hours to complete if the virtual hard disk is attached to a virtual SCSI adapter and the default Adaptec driver (aic78xx.sys) is installed in the guest operating system.

Resolution

Virtual Server 2005 R2 includes a virtual floppy disk image file named SCSI Shunt Driver.vfd that can be used to load the optimized Microsoft Virtual Machine PCI SCSI Controller driver (also referred to as the *accelerated SCSI driver*) when you are prompted to hit F6 during the guest operating system installation. Using the accelerated SCSI driver can significantly increase the speed of the guest operation system installation.

Follow these steps to load the accelerated SCSI driver using the SCSI Shunt Driver.vfd floppy disk image:

1. Open the Virtual Server Administration Website.

2. In the Master Status pane, click the virtual machine thumbnail to start the guest operating system installation.

3. Click the virtual machine thumbnail again to connect using the VMRC ActiveX client.

4. When the guest operating system installation prompts you to load a third-party SCSI or RAID driver, press F6. The F6 prompt displays at the bottom of the Setup screen.

5. When the guest operating system Setup screen displays a message indicating that Windows could not determine the type of mass storage device on your system, click Master Status in the navigation pane below the virtual machine VMRC display.

6. In Virtual Machines, click Configure and then select the virtual machine from the list.

7. In Configuration, click Floppy Drive.

8. In Floppy Drive Properties, click Known Floppy Disks, select the SCSI Shunt Driver.vfd floppy disk image file, and click OK.

9. In Status, click the virtual machine thumbnail to reconnect to it.

10. In the guest operating system Setup screen, type **S** and then press Enter.

11. Scroll to and select the accelerated SCSI driver entry that matches the guest operating system that is being installed, and then press Enter.

12. Press Enter to continue, and complete the guest operating system installation.

> **Note**   The SCSI Shunt Driver.vfd does not include an accelerated SCSI driver for Windows NT 4.0 Server. If your installation of Windows NT 4.0 Server on a VHD that is connected to a virtual SCSI adapter is progressing slowly, terminate the installation and connect the VHD to a virtual IDE adapter. Restart and complete the Windows NT 4.0 guest operating system using this configuration before reconnecting the VHD back to a virtual SCSI adapter.

Virtual Machine in Saved State Fails to Restart After a Change in Hardware-Assisted Virtualization State

If you enable hardware-assisted virtualization in your computer BIOS and try to start a virtual machine that was previously in a saved state, the virtual machine will not start up. Figure 11-7 shows the error that is logged in the event viewer when this situation occurs.

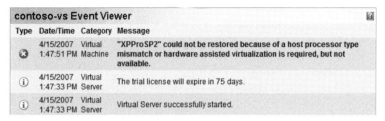

Figure 11-7   Error received when starting a saved state virtual machine after changing the hardware-assisted virtualization BIOS setting

When hardware-assisted virtualization is enabled, Virtual Server internal data structures differ. Therefore, saved state files that are created when hardware-assisted virtualization is disabled cannot be used to restore a virtual machine after hardware-assisted virtualization is enabled.

Resolution

In this case, the only solution is to ensure that you shut down all virtual machines prior to switching the hardware-assisted virtualization setting in your computer BIOS.

Virtual Machine in Saved State Fails During Start Up on a Different Virtual Server Host

If you move a virtual machine that is in a saved state to another Virtual Server host, your virtual machine might fail at startup. Saved state files are not compatible when moving between different processor brands (Intel, AMD) or processor steppings (Intel Northwood, Intel Prescott).

Resolution

If you need to move a virtual machine to a Virtual Server host whose motherboard contains a different processor manufacturer or processor stepping than the originating Virtual Server host, you must completely shut down the virtual machine prior to moving the files.

Virtual Machine Registration Fails After Previous Removal

If you remove a virtual machine through the Virtual Server Administration Website, and you later attempt to create or add a virtual machine of the same name, an error is generated stating that the virtual machine configuration file (.vmc) already exists. When you use the "remove" option, none of the virtual machine files is deleted off the server—only the shortcut entry that points to the location of the virtual machine configuration file is deleted.

Resolution

If you need to "remove" and "re-create" a virtual machine during testing or other activity, you have to either manually or programmatically delete all the virtual machine files. Once these files are deleted, you can create or add a virtual machine using the same name.

> **Note**   Step-by-step instructions on how to manually or programmatically delete virtual machine files can be found in Chapter 8, "Virtual Machine Creation Process."

Disabling Virtual Machine Hardware-Assisted Virtualization

By default, hardware-assisted virtualization is enabled in Virtual Server 2005 R2 SP1 if the feature is supported by the physical server. Using the Virtual Server Administration Website, you can disable this feature only for a single virtual machine at a time by configuring the Enable Hardware-Assisted Virtualization If Available option on the virtual machine configuration page.

Resolution

If you need to disable hardware-assisted virtualization for all virtual machines at once, you can modify the Options.xml file. To accomplish this, the value of the *enable_hw_assist* key in the Options.xml file must be set to false, as shown in the following example.

```
<preferences>
   <virtual_server>
        <hw_assist>
               <enable_hw_assist type="boolean">false</enable_hw_assist>
        </hw_assist>
   </virtual_server>
</preferences>
```

Summary

This chapter provides a reference of common Virtual Server issues that you might encounter during day-to-day operations. Remember that the first step in troubleshooting any issue should be to review event logs and gather as much corollary information as possible to better define the problem and possible causes. If your problem is not addressed in this chapter, use the Microsoft Knowledge Base and online search to determine whether the problem you are experiencing is documented and whether a workaround or hotfix was issued to resolve the problem. If you have exhausted your local and online resources, are still experiencing the problem, and need assistance to find a solution, consider engaging Microsoft Support Services or Microsoft Partner organizations that offers support services.

Additional Resources

The following resources contain additional information related to the topics in this chapter:

- Whitepaper, "Virtual Server 2005 – IDE to SCSI Virtual Machine Migration," at *http://www.microsoft.com/downloads/details.aspx?FamilyId=8D71F23D-0380-4C2F-81DF-6F96ABE05493&displaylang=en*

- Microsoft Help and Support Web site at *http://support.microsoft.com*

- Microsoft Windows Hardware Developer Central, "Debugging Tools for Windows – Overview," at *http://www.microsoft.com/whdc/devtools/debugging/default.mspx*

- Microsoft Program Manager, Ben Armstrong, Virtual PC Guy WebLog, at *http://blogs.msdn.com/virtual_pc_guy*

Part III
Virtualization Project Methodology

In this part:

Chapter 12: Virtualization Project: Envisioning Phase 333

Chapter 13: Virtualization Project: Discovery Phase 347

Chapter 14: Virtualization Project: Assessment Phase 361

Chapter 15: Virtualization Project: Planning and Design Phase 373

Chapter 16: Virtualization Project: Pilot Phase. 389

Chapter 12

Virtualization Project: Envisioning Phase

In this chapter:

What Is Envisioning?...333

Defining the Problem Statements......................................334

Establishing a Vision 336

Assembling a Project Team 336

Determining Project Scope 341

Identifying Risks...342

Creating a Project Budget 344

Summary...344

Additional Resources...345

What Is Envisioning?

Envisioning is the first step of a successful virtualization project. During envisioning, you should focus on defining the problems you are trying to solve with virtualization; obtaining consensus for the vision behind the project; establishing the scope of the project; establishing the project team, roles, and responsibilities; and determining project risks. Your goal for the envisioning phase is to produce a set of deliverables that define the project, help justify the project, and establish a preliminary budget for labor and resources. The deliverables will typically be used to determine if the project will be approved and continue to the next phase.

Envisioning is not about developing the solution. Many projects fail because the project team starts the project with a solution plan without really defining the scope or the problems they are trying to solve. This results in typically one of two consequences:

1. The solution is inadequate and increases the project costs to redesign the solution to meet the complete project requirements.

2. The solution is overdesigned and budget is wasted on a solution for a problem that does not exist.

The remaining phases of the project—Discovery, Assessment, Planning and Design, and Pilot—are designed to help the virtualization project be a success. Envisioning will be the shortest phase of the entire project, but it will ultimately define the project's success or failure.

Defining the Problem Statements

Defining the problems you are trying to solve with your virtualization project can help bring clarity to the vision and scope for the project. The problem statements should include both technical and business problems that you are experiencing within your company. By including both types of problems, you will ensure that all aspects of your business are considered during the planning and design phase.

Problem statements should include a description that identifies the problem in a quantitative manner if possible. This helps determine if the proposed solution solves the problem. Instead of stating the problem as "Rack space is at a premium in the data center," you should define a measurable component that the problem statement can be evaluated against, such as "There is currently only 10 percent of available rack space in the data center." If the virtualization project increases the available rack space in the data center above 10 percent, you have addressed the problem. There is still one component missing to determine if you have really met expectations—a project goal. In addition to stating the problem, you need to state a measurable goal for the problem resolution. A measurable goal in this example could be "Increase the available rack space to 25 percent."

Table 12-1 provides a collection of sample technical problem statements and goals.

Table 12-1   Technical Problem Statements

Problem statement	Goal
Short on available power—Data center has only 2-percent capacity remaining.	Increase the power capacity in the data center to 25 percent.
Short on available rack space—Data center has only 2,000 square feet of rack space remaining.	Increase the available rack space in the data center to 20,000 square feet.
Low server utilization—Average server utilization is 15 percent.	Combine workloads on servers to increase the average server utilization to 75 percent.
Legacy application compatibility—50 percent of legacy applications require an operating system that will not run on the latest hardware, requiring older hardware to be maintained.	Virtualize the workloads to eliminate the legacy hardware and support contracts.
Each standard physical server requires 2U of rack space.	Achieve a guest to host consolidation ratio of 16:1 for test/development servers and 10:1 for production servers to reduce rack space requirements.

Table 12-2 provides a collection of sample business problem statements and goals.

Table 12-2   **Business Problem Statements**

Problem statement	Goal
Average life-cycle time to procure and deploy a new server is two weeks. This delay results in lost return on investment.	Reduce the life-cycle time for a new server to 24 hours.
Business continuity using physical servers results in twice the hardware costs of using virtual servers.	Reduce the hardware costs for business continuity to a maximum of 25 percent of the total hardware costs by using virtualized servers instead of physical servers
Rebuilding servers during test and development requires on average two hours when using automated deployment techniques.	Reduce the rebuild time to less than 10 minutes.

Process for Defining Problem Statements

To assist in the definition of the technical problem statements for the virtualization project, solicit input from different information technology teams across different geographies within your company. Remember that potentially different problems exist at every data center location and remote office, so do not overlook any part of your company. Remember that you are looking for problems that should be in scope for the virtualization project.

Your internal customers are another source of problem statements. Talk to your business units or department heads to determine any business or technical problems they might be experiencing. Discuss issues that the development or testing teams are having with their environments. Talk to your operations teams to determine the top ten operational problems they experience.

There are also different ways to collect problem statements. You can send direct e-mail messages to individuals, gather input during team meetings, use electronic surveys, or use combinations of methods. The goal is to collect as many problem statements as possible so that you can ensure that you are addressing the key problems in the environment.

Setting Priorities

Once you have all the problem statements collected and the goals defined, you need to determine which problems should be included in the scope and which problems should be dealt with at a later time. To assist in that categorization, you should define a set of priorities and use that definition to assign a priority to each problem statement. The simplest set of priorities includes High, Normal, and Low.

Hold a priority-setting meeting with the project team, and reach an agreement on what priority should be assigned to each problem statement. Group the problem statements from High to Low. If you find that you have a long list of problem statements, you can use the three levels of priority to divide the project into three different phases to make it more manageable.

> **On the Companion Media**   To assist in collecting problem statements, you will find a Microsoft Office Excel spreadsheet in the \Job Aids folder called Problem Statement JobAid.xls on the companion media. This spreadsheet has a single worksheet that contains the recommended information to collect.

Establishing a Vision

A vision statement defines the desired end state of your environment once the project is complete. Vision statements should be concise—typically, a single sentence—and never more than two paragraphs long. All team members should be involved when developing the vision statement to ensure that it is a shared vision and covers the intended goals. A good vision statement builds trust and focus within the team and executive sponsors. Vision statements should also attempt to be motivational to the team and provide context for decision making. Table 12-3 provides some sample vision statements.

Table 12-3   Sample Vision Statements

Adopt leading-edge virtualization technology that allows the business to be more agile, bring new products to the market faster, and increase revenue.
Build a more efficient data center that provides higher availability, lower energy consumption, and more efficient use of resources while reducing capital expenditures.

Assembling a Project Team

Every successful project can be attributed to having a great team of people performing the correct roles by working from a concise list of requirements and project scope. Defining a project team consists of establishing the required project roles and identifying the number of project team members needed for each role. Once the requirements and scope are defined, a project plan can be created during the planning phase that defines when the project team roles are required in relation to the project timeline. You will typically find that some roles are not required throughout the project or that a single person can perform multiple roles.

Defining the Required Project Teams and Roles

Each virtualization project is different, but typically a defined set of project teams and team roles are required in every virtualization project. Project teams and roles vary by the project phase. Every project needs a project manager for the entire length of the project, but a tester is not required until the design is completed and the solution is ready to be tested against the requirements.

Table 12-4 provides a list of the recommended project teams and the team description for the roles that need to exist in the team for a virtualization project.

Table 12-4   Project Teams

Team	Description
Steering Committee	Provides project direction and integration between the project teams, the stakeholders, and the executive sponsor.
Project Management Team	Manages the overall project, project schedule, project requirements, project budget, and project communications. Also manages expectations.
Architecture Design Team	Provides overall project subject matter expertise, manages project specification, manages project risk, defines and supervises building of project features, estimates the time and effort to complete each feature, and manages the subject matter experts.
Subject Matter Expert Team	Technical, business, and application experts who help define the project requirements and specifications, build project features, and define the test requirements.
Test Team	Develops testing strategy, plans, and procedures; manages the project issues; and conducts the testing.
Operational Management Team	Defines the disaster recovery strategy, tests the disaster recovery procedures, defines operational requirements and procedures, and provides operational training.

Identifying Team Roles

Each project team has a set of roles and responsibilities within the project. Teams can vary in size from a single person performing multiple roles to a team member assigned a single role in a team. Different people in your organization or people outside your organization can fill roles in a team. The key action is to find the right person to fill the role, ensuring the project success.

Steering Committee

The steering committee is the bridge between the executive sponsor, stakeholders, and the project management team. The steering committee helps set project direction, scope, and budgetary requirements. Financial and business decisions are brought to the steering committee for review and approval.

The committee membership usually contains the project manager, budget manager, business stakeholders, and the executive sponsor. While the committee will meet regularly at the start of the project, typically once a week, once the project has met the first milestone, the committee meetings are reduced in frequency to once a month.

During the steering committee meetings, the project manager provides project status, milestone status, and project risks. The budget manager provides the status on the project budget, ROI, and potential cost savings. The business stakeholders and executive sponsor provide updates on any business issues that could impact the project.

Project Management Team

The project management team manages the entire project and is the main public face of the project. There are four primary roles in the project management team:

1. Project manager

2. Project scheduler

3. Budget manager

4. Communications manager

The key role within the project management team is the project manager. This individual is ultimately responsible for the project being completed on time and on budget. The project manager is directly responsible for managing the expectations of the project team, executive sponsor, and customer regarding project scope or requirements. This role also involves providing an overall project status report to management, managing any scope change requests, and approving any communications outside the team. The project manager also maintains the issue management system, where project issues are tracked and reported.

The project scheduler maintains the project plan, provides status reports on project milestones to the project manager, manages any changes to the work tasks in the schedule, and manages the resource scheduling and resource requests. The project scheduler takes any approved scope changes from the project manager, modifies the project plan, and documents for the team any impact such changes have on the plan. In addition, the project scheduler is responsible for communicating any work tasks to team members and informing any new team members of their project commitments.

The budget manager creates and maintains the project budget for resources and labor, manages requests for any hardware or software, and provides the interface to the procurement department to approve any project invoices. The budget manager is in the approval workflow process for any project scope additions to address budget concerns and obtain budget approval before the additional scope is forwarded to the project scheduler.

The communications manager manages all project communications and satisfaction surveys, and collects and distributes any reported issues. This role provides a single point of communication for the project team to increase efficiency. The communications manager works with business units and end users to inform them when servers will be unavailable during migration based on the schedule that the project scheduler has negotiated. During larger projects, the communications manager distributes and compiles results from satisfaction surveys with customers and within the project team.

Architecture Design Team

The architecture design team provides the core subject matter expertise, produces the functional specifications, identifies project risks, defines any features of the project, translates the functional specification into a list of work tasks, and calls upon application and business subject matter experts from the organization to assist when required. There are three primary roles in the architecture design team:

1. Lead project architect
2. Functional architects
3. Risk manager

The lead project architect participates in the virtualization project from start to finish. The person in this role provides the overall technical leadership and calls upon functional architects and subject matter experts on an as-needed basis. The lead project architect is ultimately responsible for the technical solution developed for the virtualization project. Lead architects also define the overall project requirements and specifications. They merge specific functional requirements and specifications from the functional architects and subject matter experts to create the complete requirements and functional specification document deliverables.

Functional architects provide technical expertise for virtualization aspects of the project. Functional architects include, at a minimum, the following technical areas: networking, servers, storage, client, and security. These architects are the subject matter experts for these technical areas within the company, and they know the currently implemented architecture and undocumented customizations. Functional architects are responsible for developing the functional specifications for their areas of expertise, assisting in the estimation of time to completion of project features and in the assembly of a test and pilot environment.

The risk manager maintains the solution used to manage risks during the project, enters identified risks, provides status reports on the state of identified risks, and closes risks that have been mitigated. Risk management solutions can vary from a simple Microsoft Office Excel spreadsheet to a complicated risk-management system with workflow and automated status-report generation.

Subject Matter Expert Team

The subject matter expert team is assembled from application and business experts specific to the servers that are considered in scope for the project. The subject matter experts have specific knowledge about application daily operations, unique server configuration, application and business dependencies, and business operations. This information is required during specification creation, project feature definition, and testing. This unique knowledge is also used to make decisions such as workload placement and server consolidation.

Test Team

The test team manages everything related to testing the proposed migration approach for the virtualization project. They develop testing strategy, write the procedures, assemble the testing schedule and plans, and conduct the testing. There are three primary roles within the test team:

1. Test manager

2. Test engineer

3. Subject matter expert

The test manager supervises the testing strategy, the testing schedule, and the test engineers. The test manager's primary responsibility is to ensure that the testing methodology has a minimal impact on the testing schedule. The test engineers are responsible for creating the test procedures, building the test environment, and performing the testing tasks. The subject matter experts are responsible for testing applications that require unique business and technical skills. This level of testing minimizes any application-specific issues.

Operational Management Team

The operational management team focuses on the post-migration management strategy for the new environment. Some customers falsely believe that managing a group of virtual machines will be the same as managing the physical machines. Virtual machine management involves dependencies that do not exist with individual physical machines. For example, a physical server can be updated and rebooted with minimal to no impact on other physical machines. Updating a Microsoft Virtual Server 2005 R2 SP1 host and requiring a reboot will affect every running virtual machine on the host. Managing farms of Virtual Server hosts requires proper planning and risk mitigation.

There are three primary roles within the operational management team:

1. Operations manager

2. Operations engineer

3. Training manager

The operations manager oversees the entire operational management team, defines the operational and disaster recovery strategy, defines the operational requirements, and assists in the creation of the disaster recovery plans. The operations engineers are responsible for defining, creating, and testing the operational and disaster recovery plans and procedures. And the training manager defines, creates, and delivers operational training.

> **Note**   The teams described in this section should vary in size based on the project size. Team members can perform multiple roles and some members might be only temporary. It is a best practice not to have the same members on both the architecture team and the test team, if possible. This provides an independent, unbiased evaluation of the solution.

Determining Project Scope

Defining the scope of the project is key to establishing a common understanding of what problem statements will be addressed and which ones will be postponed. This is defined as what is *in scope* and *out of scope*. Every time you add an item to the in-scope list, you increase the required project budget and add new work items to the project schedule. Every time you define an item as out of scope, you are potentially reducing the return on investment and not addressing a stated requirement. Establishing scope becomes a balancing act of trying to limit the project scope to increase the chances of success without placing too many requirements on hold.

Approach to Defining Scope

Defining scope is a three-step process: the first step involves deciding which of the collected problem statements will be addressed by the project, the second step involves deciding the scope limits required to solve those problems, and the third step involved determining if the project scope needs a phased approach. For example, the following generic problem statement does not provide enough detail to establish project scope: "Only 2000 square feet of data center rack space remains." This statement does not establish whether there are one or more data centers affected, does not specify which data center has remaining space, and does not provide information regarding any desire to consolidate data centers. If you modify that statement to obtain a scope definition for the project, you might obtain a statement such as this: "Existing physical servers in the Houston data center will be analyzed to determine the number of virtualization candidates and the amount of square feet of rack space that would be recovered to support additional server projects." This improved scope statement limits the scope to only the Houston data center, focuses the effort to recovering rack space using virtualization, and defines how the scope will be measured.

Defining What Is Out of Scope

Defining what problems are considered out of scope can be just as important to the project as defining what problems are considered in scope. Defining out-of-scope items allows you to eliminate project assumptions and clarify exactly what the project team is focused on. This helps prevent scope creep and establish a solid project plan. Out-of-scope items can include the following items:

- Location exclusions
- Server workload exclusions
- Applications exclusions
- Operating system exclusions
- Hardware exclusions

Determining Project Phases

Most virtualization projects should have different deployment phases to allow for different types of deployments. For example, the deployment and migration of servers in the data center should be completed in a different phase than deployment and migration of branch offices. Example reasons for separating a deployment into different phases are shown below.

- **Address low-hanging fruit first**   The first phase would focus on the servers that could be migrated quickly and with minimal planning.
- **Minimize travel disruptions**   If you combine data center migrations and branch office migrations in the same phase you will cause inefficiencies in the migration process resulting from travel disruptions.
- **Business unit at a time**   You might want to migrate a business unit at a time to reduce support issues and minimize the number of business units that are affected in the event of a deployment issue.
- **Hardware reuse**   If you are going to reuse hardware, you must migrate the servers that will provide the reusable hardware before you can migrate any server that will be hosted on the reused hardware.

Identifying Risks

Risks cannot be avoided, but they can be mitigated. Before you can mitigate a risk, you have to identify it, assign a likelihood and impact, and document it. Once you understand the risk, you can develop an approach to mitigating the risk. Identifying risks is a team event, so every member of the team should attend a risk identification brainstorming session. The brainstorming session focus should be on identifying any risk that might affect the virtualization project. You should collect both technical and business risks to ensure that you have identified all potential risks to the project. Business risks should include budgetary risks, project schedule risks, personnel risks, and other nontechnical risks. Technical risks should include resource risks, design risks, and assumption risks.

Some common risks that most projects share are as follows:

- **Changing scope**   Scope changes have an impact on project schedule and budget.

- **Loss of key project team members**   Project members get reassigned to other projects, change jobs within the company, or leave the company to seek new employment.

- **Poor communication**   Poor project communications increase the possibility that incorrect assumptions will be made, resulting in customer satisfaction issues.

- **Impact on security**   Network security (blocked ports on routers and firewalls) can affect the automated discovery on the servers, resulting in servers being inventoried by hand.

- **Insufficient funding**   Lack of funding can affect the scope and return on investment of the project.

Common risks that are specific to virtualization projects are as follows:

- **Change in operation processes**   Virtualization will affect existing processes and potentially increase operational costs.

- **"My server" syndrome**   Business units that refuse to combine their servers with other business units, reducing the consolidation ratio that could be achieved.

- **Chargeback**   Anability to obtain an agreement on how to chargeback business units for virtualized servers, delaying the adoption of virtualization.

- **Poor Consolidation Planning**   Not establishing a baseline performance for the host hardware and using that during consolidation planning. This can result in overutilization of the host hardware from using theoretical performance numbers instead of actual performance numbers.

Table 12-5 shows the list of attributes that should be collected for every risk that is documented.

Table 12-5   Risk Attributes

Attribute	Description
Risk ID	Numeric value that uniquely identifies a risk.
Probability	Likelihood that the risk will happen. It's specified as a numeric value from 1 through 100, where 100 is the highest probability.
Description	Description of the risk.
Consequence	Result if the risk scenario occurs. This could include the financial consequence if one exists.
Mitigation Plan	Description of how to stop the risk scenario from occurring.
Impact	What is the effect the risk will have. It's specified as a numeric value from 1 through 10, where 10 has the highest impact.
Owner	The individual who owns the risk and the mitigation plan.

On the Companion Media   To assist in collecting and tracking risks, you will find an Excel spreadsheet in the \Chapter Materials\Job Aids folder called Risk Management JobAid.xls on the companion media. This spreadsheet has a single worksheet that contains columns to collect the recommended risk attributes.

Direct from the Source: Ranking the Risks

Once you have identified the risks, you should rank them to determine the level of importance to the project. To do this, you take the probability (1 through 100) that you assigned the risk and multiply by the defined impact (1 through 10). This will give you a number between 1 and 1,000. Once you have the ranking, you can determine the order of importance for mitigation efforts.

Mike Williams
Senior Consultant, Microsoft Consulting Services

Creating a Project Budget

Once you have established a project scope, you can produce a preliminary project budget for the next two phases of the project: discovery and assessment. The data from these two phases is required before a detailed project budget and schedule is created. The preliminary project budget includes the following items:

- Labor budget for the envisioning, discovery, and assessment phases.
- Hardware and software budget required to perform the discovery and assessment.

The labor budget should include funding for the project manager, the lead architect, the project scheduler, the budget manager, and one functional architect. The hardware and software budget should include a minimum of one physical server with the required specifications to perform the discovery, the discovery software tools, the server operating system, and potentially a database license for storing the collected data.

Summary

This chapter outlines the first phase of a virtualization project: the envisioning phase. Envisioning is not about developing the solution, but about understanding the environment and the current problems that exist. During the envisioning phase, you assemble a list of the problems in the environment and prioritize them, assemble the project team, decide what problems are in scope and out of scope, identify and rank the project risks, and define a preliminary budget to complete the discovery and assessment phases.

Additional Resources

The following resource contains additional information related to this chapter:

- Microsoft Solution Framework, *http://www.microsoft.com/msf*

Chapter 13

Virtualization Project: Discovery Phase

In this chapter:

Collecting Active Directory Information 348

Inventory. 350

Performance Monitoring 355

Environmental Information 357

Tools. 358

Summary. 358

Additional Resources. 359

During the discovery phase of a virtualization project, you are focused on collecting all the required information to support the next project phase—assessment. You now have an approved project scope that defines the range of information that you need to discover. The challenge is determining exactly what information you need for assessing which servers are good virtualization candidates and how to best consolidate them. Discovering the information requires manual and automated methods. Sample scripts are provided in some sections of this chapter to assist in collecting the required information. The sample scripts are very basic, but they allow you to get started if there are no other tools available. At the end of the chapter, you will find a section on more advanced tools that can help you discover the required information in a more efficient manner.

To find and discover all the servers in your environment, you need to gather the following information:

- Active Directory information
- Hardware and software inventory
- Performance history
- Environmental information

This information is used in the assessment project phase to identify candidates for virtualization, group the virtualization candidates by different parameters (application, location, hardware attributes, and so on), decide how best to combine the candidates based on workload, and produce a cost-saving report detailing the savings in rack space, power, and cooling.

Collecting Active Directory Information

Active Directory is a building block of the information that you will gather during the discovery phase. To collect proper server information, you need to know all of the available Active Directory forests and domains in the enterprise. It is much easier to use a script that can point to an entire domain or forest, enumerate all the servers, and then collect required information.

You should collect information about every Active Directory forest and domain that is within the scope of the project. This information will help you determine which forests or domains are actively being used and which are dormant. Once you have all the forests identified, you need to identify or establish a valid administrator-level account so that you can use that account to collect information using scripts.

Collecting Domain Information

Collecting a list of Active Directory domains contained in every forest that is within the scope allows you to verify the current documented state. You should use an automated script or a specialized tool to collect all the domains.

Some inventory tools allow you to specify an Active Directory domain and a set of domain administrator credentials to use to query Active Directory and enumerate all computers. This simplifies the data collection process but creates a dependency for the known list of domains. If you miss a domain, critical servers can be overlooked in the data collection and planning phases.

> **On the Companion Media**   The companion media contains a Virtual Basic script named GetDomains.vbs in the \Chapter Materials\Scripts directory that you can run within your environment to collect a list of domains within a forest. If you have multiple forests, you need to run it in each forest with domain administrator–level credentials. You must modify the script before you use it to change the default domain from contoso.com.

Collecting Active Directory Site Information

Active Directory site information for a server provides a way to map a server to a network or physical location. Although site information typically is documented, it can become outdated quickly. In addition, most documented site information does not provide a mapping between the server and the site it belongs in. Therefore, you need to discover the server-to-site mapping.

> **On the Companion Media**   The companion media contains a Visual Basic script named GetSites.vbs in the \Chapter Materials\Scripts directory that you can run within your environment to collect the server-to-site mapping. You will be required to log on to a domain controller in the forest with administrator credentials and run GetSites.vbs. The GetSites.vbs script produces a .csv with a line for each server containing the site name and the server name.

Collecting Subnets-Per-Site Information

After you have all the site names, you must match them to subnets and physical locations in the environment. You will need this information to group servers together by physical location for consolidation planning or to obtain a filtered list of servers that you are targeting for inventory based on location.

Once you have collected the subnet-to-site mapping, you need to add the physical location information to the collected data. The network administrator within a company typically has this information documented in a company-wide network map or in a spreadsheet.

On the Companion Media   The companion media contains a Visual Basic script named GetSubnets.vbs in the \Chapter Materials\Scripts directory that you can run within your environment to collect a list of subnets assigned to each Active Directory site. The script requires domain administrator–level credentials to operate. The GetSubnets.vbs script produces a .csv with a line for each site containing the site name and the assigned subnets.

Collecting Server Information

Depending on the tool that you use to gather hardware and software inventory, you might need to know every server in the domain. Therefore, you might need to create an input file listing every server you want to inventory. One way to gather this information is to query Active Directory for every computer account in the domain. As you query for each computer name, you can retrieve additional information—such as the operating system, service pack, and distinguished name—in case you need to perform other Lightweight Directory Access Protocol (LDAP) queries. You can then use the operating system information to determine which machines are running a server operating system. With a little work, you can come up with a list of servers by domain.

There are a few issues with this approach, depending on how well you maintain your domains. Many domains have disabled computer accounts or dormant computer accounts still resident. You need a way to know how to distinguish an active computer account from a nonactive one. One way to do this is to retrieve the *whenchanged* parameter that tells you the last date and time that the computer changed its secure channel password. Because the maximum time between computer account password changes is 30 days, if the *whenchanged* parameter is over 30 days old and the operating system is a server version, you can deduce that this server is not active anymore.

On the Companion Media   The companion media contains a Visual Basic script named GetComputers.vbs in the \Chapter Materials\Scripts directory that you can run within your environment to collect a list of computer accounts in the domain. The script requires domain administrator–level credentials to run and must be run in each domain. The GetComputers.vbs script produces a .csv with a line for each computer containing the domain name, computer name, operating system, service pack version, and date when the computer account password was changed. You must modify the script before you use it to change the default domain from contoso.com.

Inventory

To perform an assessment of what machines are good candidates for virtualization, you must collect hardware and software information on every server. Hardware information includes processor, memory, network adapters, disk subsystem, USB connected devices, and parallel port connected devices. Software information includes a list of applications and any updates, hotfixes, or service packs installed on the server. In addition, you need to inventory all the services running on each server. You will use this information with a set of rules or thresholds—discussed in Chapter 14, "Virtualization Project: Assessment Phase"—to decide which servers should be virtualized.

Hardware Inventory

Table 13-1 provides a list of hardware devices and settings that you should collect during a hardware inventory of your servers. The major categories are BIOS, operating system, processor, memory, hard disk, network interface card, removable devices connected to USB interfaces, and devices connected to parallel ports. This information is used mainly to exclude a server from the virtualization candidate pool.

Table 13-1   Recommended Information to Collect During Hardware Inventory

Hardware category	Inventory information
BIOS	Server manufacturer
	Model number
	Serial number
Operating System	Operating system
	Service pack
	Domain
	Server name

Table 13-1   Recommended Information to Collect During Hardware Inventory

Hardware category	Inventory information
Processor	Processor manufacturer (Intel, AMD)
	Processor model (Pentium IV, Opteron)
	Processor speed (in MHz)
	Number of processors
	Number of cores
Memory	Amount of physical memory
	Total number of memory sockets*
	Size of memory sticks*
	Number of free memory sockets*
Hard Disk	Number of hard disks
	Total capacity of each disk
	File system (FAT, NTFS)
	Partitions
	Basic or Dynamic disk
	State (Active or Disabled)
Network Adapters	Number of cards
	Maximum speed of each card
	Current speed of each card
	Manufacturer
	Special configurations (teaming, VLAN)
	Network settings
USB Devices	Any devices connected via USB
Parallel Port Devices	Any devices connected to the parallel port

*Optional information

BIOS information is required to identify the manufacturer and model of the server hardware. This information will be used later in the process to collect environmental information, such as the number of rack units (Us) the server required in the data center, the power-consumption rating, and the heat-dissipation rating.

Operating system information is required to group virtualization candidates by operating system release and service pack version. You can also use this as a validation of the operating system value that was published in Active Directory. In addition, collecting the domain and server name provide additional unique values that will be needed when combining data from the different sample scripts.

Processor information is required to understand how the existing server compares to the capabilities of a Virtual Server 2005 R2 SP1 virtual machine. Key information needed for the comparison includes the number of processors (sockets), number of processor cores, and the speed of the processor in MHz. The processor manufacturer and model information are used to identify processor types in case the server is a candidate for reuse as a Virtual Server host but needs additional processors. The manufacturer and model information is also key to identifying unsupported processors like Intel Itanium.

Memory information is required to understand whether the current amount of memory in the physical server is the same as or lower than the 3.6-GB limit of a Virtual Server 2005 R2 SP1 virtual machine. Collect optional information to identify the number of free memory sockets in the server and the capacity of the existing memory sticks. This information is needed to determine the maximum amount of memory that the server can support without discarding any memory chips. The memory information is used to identify memory expansion capabilities in case the server is a candidate for reuse as a Virtual Server host but needs additional memory.

Hard-disk information is required to understand the disk space requirements and issues when performing a migration from a physical server to a virtual machine. Virtual Server 2005 R2 SP1 integrated development environment (IDE) connected virtual hard disks are limited to 127 GB in size and Small Computer System Interface (SCSI) connected virtual hard disks are limited to 2.04 terabytes in size for a single disk. Collecting the number of disks in the physical server and the size of each one allows you to determine whether any size limits have been exceeded. Collecting information about the partitions, file system type, and active state—and whether the disk is a dynamic disk or not—assists with understanding issues related to physical-to-virtual (P2V) machine migration. For example, many P2V tools support the migration of basic disks, but some do not support the migration of dynamic disks.

Network adapter information is required to compare the existing server adapter configuration to the capabilities of a Virtual Server 2005 R2 SP1 virtual machine. Virtual machines can have a maximum of four virtual Ethernet NICs installed at once, and they do not support advanced features such as TCP/IP offloading and NIC teaming. Physical Ethernet NICs can also support multiple speeds (10/100/1,000/10,000 Mb/s), so you need to document what speed the NIC is currently configured for to ensure that the Virtual Server environment can support that mode. Therefore, you must collect information such as the number of NICs in the server, the current and maximum interface speed of each adapter, the adapter manufacturer, and any details on special adapter modes such as teaming and Virtual Local Area Network (VLAN). You must also collect the TCP/IP settings from each adapter to understand what network connections exist so that you can determine whether the Virtual Server host machines will have virtual networks connected to the same physical networks.

USB-connected devices on physical servers are typically special devices that applications require. For example, a USB smart-card reader for increased security or a USB flash key to store an encryption key. Virtual Server 2005 R2 SP1 virtual machines support only keyboard and mouse USB-connected devices in pass-through mode. Therefore, collecting information on all USB-connected devices on a server will assist you in determining whether a server is a candidate for virtualization.

Parallel port devices on physical servers are not common because most server manufacturers have stopped including parallel ports. When you do find parallel ports, you might find a hardware key that software applications use as a method of combating application piracy. Virtual Server 2005 R2 SP1 does support a single virtual parallel port per virtual machine that can be directly mapped to a server's parallel port. Therefore, collecting information about any devices found to be connected through a parallel port will raise a flag that the physical server might have a hardware key.

Software Inventory

The goal of the software inventory is to provide you a list of all the applications installed on the servers, the version of the applications, and a list of the currently loaded updates or hotfixes installed. Knowing what applications are loaded on the servers allows you to make decisions on which machines should not be virtualized. In addition, knowing the application version and update-level information will help you group excluded servers into pools for homogeneous consolidation.

Table 13-2 provides a list of the software inventory information that you should collect from each server.

Table 13-2   Software Inventory Information

Software category	Inventory information
Application	Name
	Vendor
	Version
Updates	Name
	Version
	Application the update is for

The application name tells you the recognizable name of the application or application suite. The application vendor provides you with the company that publishes the application. The application version provides you with information on the version of the application installed and lets you compare how many versions of an application you have installed in your environment. The updates information tells you what updates or hotfixes have been installed on the server.

On the Companion Media   The companion media contains a Visual Basic script named GetSoftware.vbs in the \Chapter Materials\Scripts directory that you can run within your environment to collect a list of installed software. The script requires local administrator–level credentials to run and must be run on each server. The GetSoftware.vbs script produces a .csv with a line for each application containing the computer name, software application name, application publisher, and application version.

Services

Collecting the list of services on each computer provides information on the services installed versus those that are actively using resources. Table 13-3 provides a listing of the information that should be collected for each service on a server. The key values are the service name, startup mode, current state, and display name.

Table 13-3   Services Inventory Information

Service category	Inventory information
Service	Name
	Service type
	State
	Caption*
	Description*
	Display name
	Path
	Started
	Start mode
	Account name

*Optional information

On the Companion Media The companion media contains a Visual Basic script named GetServices.vbs in the \Chapter Materials\Scripts directory that you can run within your environment to collect a list of installed services. The script requires local administrator–level credentials to run and must be run on each server. The GetServices.vbs script produces a .csv with a line for each service containing the computer name, the service name, the type of service, the current service state, the defined caption, the defined description, the display name, the path to the service executable, whether the service is started, the startup mode, and the name of the account that the service runs under.

Performance Monitoring

Monitoring the performance of your servers provides critical information about the workload performance that the physical server is experiencing and provides insight into what performance issues might exist if the physical server is virtualized. Performance monitoring is the most time-intensive data collection task. To ensure that you have captured the peaks and lows of the performance signature for a server, you need to capture a representative sample of data.

When monitoring performance, you want to ensure that you capture data long enough so that it can capture events such as an end-of-the-month finance process, backup processes, any impacts on performance from scheduled tasks, and any other impacts on performance. Performance data should be captured for a minimum of one month so that all the monthly cycles of performance are captured. To minimize the impact of collecting performance data, the data should be collected on a set interval, measured in seconds. For example, if you use Perfmon to collect the data, using a five-second interval reduces the data collected and the impact on the server over the default value of one second.

Table 13-4 shows the major categories of performance parameters that should be monitored: processor, memory, network, and disk. Many of these performance parameters are performance counters in the operating system and can have multiple instances to collect. For example, on a multiprocessor server, you should monitor all processor or core instances.

Table 13-4 Performance Monitoring Information

Performance category	Monitoring parameters
Processor	Total percent of processor time
	Percent of processor time for each processor instance
	Percent interrupt time
Memory	Available bytes of memory
	Pages per second

Table 13-4   Performance Monitoring Information

Performance category	Monitoring parameters
Network (for each adapter instance)	Total bytes per second
	Bytes received per second
	Bytes sent per second
Disk	Disk read bytes per second
	Disk write bytes per second
	Average disk bytes read per second
	Average disk bytes written per second

Processor monitoring is focused on the utilized percent of the processors in the server and the percent interrupt time. The percent of processor time tells you how much processing power the workloads on the server require over time. This information is collected for each processor or core instance. The percent of interrupt time tells you how much time the processor is spending processing interrupts from devices and peripherals.

Memory performance monitoring gathers information on the available bytes and pages per second. Available memory bytes is the amount of physical memory in bytes that are available for a process to request for allocation, or the amount of free physical memory. Pages per second is the rate at which pages are read from or written to the hard disk to address page faults. Because disk I/O is one of the slowest components in the system, understanding the level of pages/sec that is causing disk I/O is important to the assessment of how well a server will perform in a virtual machine.

Network performance monitoring gathers information on the total bytes that are sent and received per second on each network adapter. If you are consolidating physical servers on the same Virtual Server host, you need to be concerned about how the network throughput of the two servers consolidates as a function of time. This information drives decisions to spread the virtual machines across virtual networks to balance the network workload across multiple host adapters.

Disk performance monitoring gathers information on the amount of data flowing between the memory and the disk subsystem. This is accomplished by using counters that provide real-time and average values for read and write operations to the physical disk. You must collect this information for each physical disk in the physical server.

Note   Because of the volume of information that needs to be collected and the number of servers you need to collect this data on during the discovery phase of a virtualization project, it is not recommended to use a script to collect this data. Therefore, no sample scripts are provided.

Environmental Information

When collecting information during the discovery phase, one area usually overlooked is the environmental information. Although it's not used in any decision making during the assessment or planning phases for virtualizing a server, it can be critical information for justifying the project and demonstrating the cost benefits.

As you virtualize a physical server, you are enabling that physical server hardware to be repurposed or retired. If your data center or remote office locations are low on rack or floor space, or if the current level of power consumption is preventing the expansion of servers at the rate that is required by your business growth, being able to retire or repurpose servers can be a huge benefit.

During the discovery process, you should identify all the different server manufacturers and models in addition to their quantity. Each rack-based server requires a certain amount of vertical space in the rack called a *Unit*, or *U*. The manufacturer product specifications should indicate how many Us a server requires in a rack. This can range from a 1-U server to as big as 10 Us. For server blades, you need to know how much rack space the enclosure requires in the rack and how many blades a rack typically holds. You need to take this into account in the calculation during the assessment phase to ensure that you are properly accounting for the rack space of blade servers.

In addition to collecting rack space information, you also need to collect the power consumption information for each server model. Each server typically has a power supply rated to handle the load of a server that is fully expanded. The larger servers also have redundant power supplies. The manufacturer product specification should have the power-consumption rating listed in watts or kilowatts.

Rack-based servers have supporting peripherals such as disk storage cabinets, KVMs, network switches, and other rack-mounted devices that are no longer needed when the server is virtualized. Collecting this information helps you estimate the complete picture of how much rack space or power consumption would be eliminated if the virtualization project goals were fully realized. Unfortunately, collecting information about a supporting peripheral in an automated fashion is not a trivial task.

On the Companion Media   To assist you in collecting environmental information, you will find an Microsoft Office Excel spreadsheet named Potential Cost Savings JobAid.xls in the \Chapter Materials\Job Aids folder. This spreadsheet has a worksheet called "Cost Savings Details" that contains the recommended environmental information to collect and some predefined calculations to assist in producing a cost savings summary.

Tools

The scripts provided on the companion media are a basic way of collecting the information you need during the discovery phase. Much better tools are available from Microsoft and independent software vendors (ISVs) that manufacture tools compatible with Microsoft products. Microsoft provides advanced tools such as Systems Management Server 2003 or System Center Configuration Manager 2007 for performing hardware and software inventory, and Operations Manager 2005 or 2007 for performance-monitoring information.

ISVs have produced tools that can assist in the discovery and assessment project phases also. PlateSpin, Ltd (*www.platespin.com*) produces a product called PowerRecon that is available in different versions, depending on what you want to accomplish. There is a PowerRecon for Inventory version that performs the hardware and software inventory functions, a Power-Recon for Monitoring that adds performance monitoring to the inventory capability, and a PowerRecon for Planning that adds consolidation assessment and planning to the Monitoring version.

SystemTools Software (*www.systemtools.com*) produces a nice tool for collecting a long list of information about Active Directory, servers, workstations, users, and much more. The tool is called Exporter Pro.

A free tool from Microsoft—Active Directory Topology Diagrammer (ADTD)—collects information about Active Directory forests and Microsoft Exchange environments. ADTD can optionally produce Microsoft Visio diagrams of Active Directory forest domain relationships in addition to Microsoft Exchange architectures.

 More Info   For more information on these tools and others, refer to Chapter 20, "Additional Management Tools." You will also find links to tools included on the companion media.

Summary

This chapter outlines the second step of a virtualization project, the discovery phase. The discovery phase focuses on collecting all the data required for the next phase of the virtualization project, the assessment phase. The data that you collect will be used to make decisions about which servers are candidates for virtualization, and when virtualized, which host these servers should be placed on for optimum use of host resources.

During the discovery phase, you collect information on the Active Directory forests, domains, sites, and subnets, and you match that information to physical locations. You collect a list of servers that are within the scope of the project. You also collect hardware and software inventory information for each server and performance counter information over a minimum of a one-month period so that you can analyze peak, minimum, and average values for processor, memory, network, and disk usage. You can leverage the hardware inventory data during the assessment to determine how many servers that are virtualization candidates have hardware specifications that would allow them to be reused and to offset any capital investment. From the environmental information that you collect, you will be able to produce a benefits analysis report in the assessment phase that details the amount of rack space, power consumption, and heat dissipation that can possibly be eliminated if the servers were virtualized.

Additional Resources

The following resources contain additional information related to this chapter:

- Microsoft Script Center. This is a resource for knowledge on writing scripts to collect information locally or remotely from Windows machines. Use the following link to access this site: *http://www.microsoft.com/technet/scriptcenter/default.mspx.*

- Connecting to WMI on a Remote Computer. Go to the following site for instructions on how to connect to the WMI provider on a remote computer and query any WMI interface available: *http://msdn2.microsoft.com/en-us/library/aa389290.aspx.*

- WMI Tasks for Scripts and Applications. The following site provides sample scripts for collecting data in different scenarios:*http://msdn2.microsoft.com/en-us/library /aa394585.aspx.*

Chapter 14
Virtualization Project: Assessment Phase

In this chapter:

Identifying a Virtualization Candidate 361
Capital Cost Savings 368
Environmental Savings 369
Summary 372
Additional Resources 372

The Assessment phase of a virtualization project focuses on using the collected information from the Discovery phase to determine which machines are good candidates for virtualization. Determining which servers are good candidates involves analyzing the hardware, software, and performance data on a per-server basis using a set of thresholds. Thresholds are defined by the limits of the virtual hardware and performance limits that you define for a virtual machine. Software does not define limits from a performance perspective, but it does define limitations on application support in virtual environments from the manufacturer.

Identifying a Virtualization Candidate

Identifying virtualization candidates starts with a list of physical servers that are in-scope for the virtualization project. Using a set of hardware-and-performance based thresholds, a physical server is then placed into the virtualization candidate list or excluded from that list. Hardware thresholds are defined by the virtual hardware limits of a Microsoft Virtual Server 2005 R2 SP1 virtual machine and physical hardware used for the Virtual Server host. These limits include the amount of memory, the number of processors, the maximum disk space, the number of network adapters required, and other special hardware requirements. Performance-based thresholds are specified as part of the assessment process and define limitations such as the average processor consumption in MHz and the network throughput in bytes per second (bytes/sec).

Identifying a virtualization candidate is really more about identifying physical servers that should be excluded from the virtualization candidate pool. The assumption is that any physical server remaining in the pool after the exclusions have been processed is a candidate for virtualization. This is a phased approach where you first determine exclusions based on hardware limits, then you determine exclusions based on performance thresholds, and finally you determine exclusions based on software application support. An exclusion triggered at any phase of the assessment immediately excludes a candidate from the pool.

Virtual Machine Hardware Limits

Virtual Server 2005 R2 SP1 virtual machines have a predefined set of hardware limitations. The only piece of hardware that can change based on the host that the virtual machine is running is the processor. This is because of the architecture of Virtual Server and the fact that the processor is not emulated but exposed directly through to the virtual machine. Therefore, the virtual machine hardware will see the same processor that the host has installed. If the host has a 3.0-GHz physical processor, the virtual machine will have a 3.0-GHz virtual processor. Table 14-1 provides the hardware limits of the virtual machine.

Table 14-1   Virtual Machine Hardware Limits

Hardware feature	Maximum limit
Number of processors	1
Processor speed (MHz)	Host processor speed
Memory	3.6 gigabytes
Number of network adapters	4
Number of hard disk drives	28 – SCSI
	4 - IDE
Hard disk drive size (per drive)	2 terabytes – SCSI
	127 gigabytes – IDE
Total disk space	56.51 terabytes
Number of serial ports	2
Number of parallel ports	1

Setting Performance Thresholds

During the Discovery phase, you collected performance data for memory, processor, disk, and network adapters. To use this data to determine whether a physical server is a candidate for virtualization, you must determine a performance threshold for these components to be evaluated against. This threshold defines the performance limits that a virtual machine should experience on average. If the physical server's average performance exceeds the thresholds that you set, the physical server should not be placed in the virtualization candidate pool.

The performance thresholds for virtualization candidates can be defined as a percentage of the available resources in a virtual machine or as the actual threshold value. If a percentage is specified, you must convert it to a value for use in the formulas. Thresholds such as processor speed and memory can be easily defined because they are fixed values. Thresholds for disk throughput are not as simple to define because there are so many variations based on how you configure the disk subsystem. Thresholds for network throughput are affected by the number of network adapters in the system. Table 14-2 provides some sample threshold percentages and respective values.

Table 14-2   Sample Virtual Machine Performance Thresholds

Hardware feature	Maximum limit	Threshold percentage	Threshold value
Processor speed (MHz)	Host processor speed (for example, 3000 MHz)	80	2400 MHz
Memory	3.6 gigabytes	80	2.9 gigabytes
Disk I/O	Host disk limit (for example, 200 MB/ second)	25	50 MB/second
Network speed (per adapter)	240 Mbits/second	80	192 Mbits/second

Note   Thresholds are the combined values for certain hardware features that have multiple instances on the physical server but only a single instance in the virtual machine. For example, the physical server could have multiple processors. The multiple processors' utilization summed together should be used as the total server processor utilization. You should also use the processor frequency rating and not the name for the AMD processor family, since the name of the AMD processor does not reflect the actual speed of the processor in MHz.

Assessing Hardware Limits

Hardware limits are used as the first layer of determining whether in-scope physical servers should be excluded from the virtualization candidate pool. Hardware limits include basic components such as memory, disk space, processor, and network. More advanced or special-ized limits include serial or parallel ports.

When performing the assessment process, you must evaluate the physical server against each hardware limit. If the physical server fails any of the hardware limit tests, it is immediately excluded from the virtualization candidate pool and the assessment process should proceed with the next physical server. If the physical server passes all hardware limit tests, it should proceed to the next phase of assessment, performance limits.

Processor Hardware Limits

A Virtual Server 2005 R2 SP1 virtual machine has a processor virtual hardware limit of one processor. Although this is a hardware limit, it is not a valid assessment to say that any physi-cal server that has more than one processor should be immediately excluded from the virtu-alization candidate pool. Processor consumption should be the driving assessment criterion for a physical server. It is possible to have a two- or four-processor server that has low proces-sor consumption that falls under the performance threshold. Therefore, you should defer any assessment of processor limits until the performance threshold assessment.

Memory Hardware Limits

A Virtual Server 2005 R2 SP1 virtual machine has a memory virtual hardware limit of 3.6 gigabytes of memory. When assessing hardware limits for memory, you can follow one of two approaches as the deciding factor:

1. Amount of physical memory installed
2. Physical memory consumption peak

The amount physical memory installed approach ignores how much memory the server is actually consuming and assesses the physical server based on how much memory is installed. This approach requires only that you have the hardware inventory information for the physical server to make a decision. Using this approach, if the physical server has more than 3.6 gigabytes of memory installed, it is excluded from the virtualization candidate pool.

The physical memory consumption approach uses the actual consumption of memory in the physical server as the deciding factor. This approach focuses on detecting physical servers that have more physical memory than they require. This approach requires the hardware inventory and performance data for available bytes of memory. Using this approach, if the physical server's peak memory consumption exceeds 3.6 gigabytes of memory, it is excluded from the virtualization candidate pool.

Network Adapter Hardware Limits

A Virtual Server 2005 R2 SP1 virtual machine has a virtual hardware limit of four active Ethernet network adapters. If the physical server requires more than four active network adapters or if it requires network adapters that are not Ethernet (for example, Token ring or other technology), the physical server should be excluded from the virtualization candidate pool.

Disk Hardware Limits

A Virtual Server 2005 R2 SP1 virtual machine has two virtual hardware limits for hard disks that must be assessed. The first is the size of a single disk partition. A virtual hard disk attached to a virtual IDE controller has a maximum partition size of 127 gigabytes, and a virtual hard disk attached to a virtual SCSI controller has a maximum partition size of 2 terabytes. Therefore, if any single hard disk partition on the physical server is larger than 2 terabytes, the server cannot be virtualized.

The second is the total amount of disk space attached to the physical server. A virtual machine has a limit of 56.51 terabytes of disk space that can be attached. Therefore, if the physical server has more than 56.51 terabytes of disk space, the server cannot be virtualized.

You might be asking yourself, "What about the disk controller?" The virtual machine hardware has only an IDE controller and up to four optional SCSI controllers. There is a high probability that the physical server's disk controllers do not match the SCSI controllers available in the virtual hardware. Fortunately, this issue is addressed during the physical-to-virtual server migration. Any existing hard disk is connected to one of the virtual SCSI or IDE controllers, and the system configuration is updated during the migration process.

Note   Virtual disk controllers do not have features like RAID. If the source host has RAID config-ured controllers, they will be seen as the partitions and volumes exposed to the operating system and attached to SCSI or IDE controllers as appropriate. If you want the performance from RAID, then you must ensure that the host disk subsystem where the VHD files are stored has RAID.

Peripheral Port Hardware Limits

A Virtual Server 2005 R2 SP1 virtual machine has a virtual hardware limit of two serial com-munication ports and one parallel communication port. The ports are pass-through connec-tions to the physical ports on the Virtual Server host. If the physical server has more than two *active* serial ports or one active parallel port, the server should be excluded from the virtual-ization candidate pool.

Note   Because the virtual peripheral ports are pass-through connections to the physical ports on the server, you cannot share these ports while they are in use. During the Planning and Design phase, you need to pay close attention to this limitation to ensure that as you com-bine the virtualization candidates together, you are not exceeding the number of available ports on the host.

Assessing Performance Limits

Performance limits for the processor, disk, and network are used as the second layer of deter-mining whether in-scope physical servers should be excluded from the virtualization candi-date pool. The following sections for the processor, disk, and network provide guidance on how to assess performance limits and exclude servers that exceed the performance limit.

Processor Performance Assessment

When assessing a physical server to determine whether the processor requirements will exclude a physical server from the virtualization candidate pool, you must look at the average processor utilization across the entire data collection window. Using the average value allows you to ignore peak values while making the virtualization candidate decision. Peak values become very important during the Planning and Design phase, as you combine workloads to determine the optimized placement of virtual machines on a host.

Note   Today's processors come with multiple cores and hyperthreading capabilities. Refer-ence to a *processor* refers to a physical processor that has a single core, or it refers to the core of a multiple core processor. Hyperthreaded logical processors are not considered a separate processor for performance planning.

To determine the average processor consumption in MHz for each processor in the physical server, you need to know the average processor utilization and the speed of the physical server's processor. Once you have the average processor utilization for each processor in the physical server, you can sum the values to obtain the total average processor consumption:

Total Average Processor Consumption = Sum (physical server processor speed × each processor's average processor utilization)(MHz)

Once you have the total average processor consumption for the physical server, you need to compute the virtual machine threshold processor consumption. The virtual machine threshold processor consumption is the amount of MHz that an individual virtual machine can consume from the host:

VM Threshold Processor consumption = Virtual Server host processor speed (MHz) × processor threshold percentage

Once you have the virtual machine threshold processor consumption, you can compare values to determine whether the processor threshold has been exceeded. If the total average processor consumption is less than or equal to the defined virtual machine threshold processor consumption, the physical server is a candidate for virtualization. If the total average processor consumption is greater than the virtual machine threshold processor consumption, the physical server is exceeding the defined threshold and should not be added to the pool of virtualization candidates.

The following scenario provides an example: You have an older server running Windows NT 4.0 on a dual processor, 200-MHz Intel Pentium III server. Processor 1 has an average utilization of 24 percent, and processor 2 has an average utilization of 29 percent. The total average processor consumption would be the sum of 24 percent multiplied by 200 (24% × 200 MHz) and 29 percent multiplied by 200 (29% × 200 MHz), which equals a total average processor consumption of 106 MHz. Your new Virtual Server host is using 3.0-GHz (3000 MHz) processors. You have established a threshold percentage of 80 percent, so your virtual machine threshold processor consumption equals 2400 Mhz. Using the defined logic, the total average processor consumption for the physical server (106 MHz) is less than the virtual machine threshold processor consumption, so based only on processor performance consumption, this server would be added to the virtualization candidate pool.

Disk Performance Assessment

Hard disk performance is a key concern when assessing a virtualization candidate. Combining multiple disk workloads onto a single machine can have a great impact on disk performance. Proper planning of the disk subsystem and workload optimization is extremely important and will be covered in Chapter 15, "Virtualization Project: Planning and Design Phase."

Disk performance is measured in reads and writes (bytes per second). As part of the Discovery phase, you collected the actual and average values for these two counters. For assessing the performance of a server for exclusion from the virtualization candidate pool, you should use the average read and write values in bytes per second. Using peak values would potentially exclude too many servers based on a disk performance anomaly that occurred during the discovered data timeline.

When assessing the disk performance, you should be conservative to ensure that no one candidate can saturate the disk subsystem on the host and to account for the overhead of disk operations in a virtualized environment. Therefore, the recommended threshold is set at a conservative number of 50 megabytes per second for both reads and writes. Determining whether a server should be excluded from the virtualization candidate pool becomes a simple comparison of the average values for read and write operations against the 50 MB/second threshold. If either read or write operations exceed the threshold, exclude the server from the candidate pool.

Network Performance Assessment

During the Discovery phase, you collected network performance data for send and receive operations in bytes per second for each network adapter. Assessing a physical server for exclusion from the virtualization candidate pool is based on the approach for assigning network resources and the speed of the network adapters in the Virtual Server host. A virtual machine connects to a virtual network, which is bound to a physical network adapter on the host. Because you can have one or more virtual machines connected to a virtual network, you can have one or more machines sharing a single network adapter on the host. Gigabit Ethernet network adapters are the recommended standard for the host.

In Chapter 3, "Virtual Server Architecure," you learned that a virtual network adapter has no coded performance limit. The practical limit for a single virtual network adapter is 550 megabits per second. Assuming that the Virtual Server host has gigabit Ethernet adapters, the recommended performance threshold for a candidate server is 80 percent of that value, or 440 megabits per second for a single virtual network adapter.

Assessing the physical server involves comparing the send and receive bytes/second of each adapter to determine whether the threshold value of 440 megabits per second has been exceeded for a sustained period of time. If the value has been exceeded for a sustained period on a single network adapter, you should exclude the server from the virtualization candidate pool.

> **Note**   During the planning process you will need to identify all candidates that have high network utilization and potentially dedicate a physical adapter and virtual network for their use. This can reduce the number of candidates that can be placed on a host depending on the number of network adapters available.

Assessing Application Support Limits

Application support limits are used as the third layer of determining whether in-scope physical servers should be excluded from the virtualization candidate pool. Not all applications are supported in a virtual machine environment. Some vendors might support their application in a virtual machine environment, but support only a specific vendor's implementation because of virtual hardware, performance, or other limitations.

During the Discovery phase, software inventory information was collected for every server. This information is the base for you to work from to determine any application support issues.

You first need to produce a list of unique software applications across the entire in-scope server list. This list should contain an entry for each different version or service pack revision of an application, because vendors might require a certain version or service pack for virtualization support. Once you have the list of unique software applications, applications can be eliminated from the list by determining whether they are not supported by the vendor if used in a virtual environment.

Microsoft applications are the best place to start to reduce the list. Microsoft understood that application support would be a huge issue for virtualization technology and early on placed requirements in its Windows Server System Common Engineering Criteria requirements that all new server-based applications that ship must be supported in a Virtual Server environment unless a waiver is granted.

Microsoft created Knowledge Base article 897614, "Windows Server System software not supported within a Microsoft Virtual Server environment," that is used to list all the latest Microsoft applications that are not currently supported in Virtual Server 2005 R2. Currently, that list includes the following shipping products:

- Microsoft Speech Server

- Microsoft Internet Server and Acceleration (ISA) Server 2004

- Microsoft SharePoint Portal Server 2003

- Microsoft Identity Integration Server (MIIS) 2003

- Microsoft Identity Integration Feature Pack

All other Microsoft server applications are supported in virtual machines running on Virtual Server 2005 R2 and later versions. Determining the support for the remaining third-party applications in the list requires you to visit the support Web sites for each product or to directly contact the vendor. Be sure to verify the version of the application supported and compare it to the inventory list.

Once you have a list of applications not supported in Virtual Server 2005 R2 or later, you can exclude any server that is running those applications in production.

Capital Cost Savings

After you have completed assessing which physical servers are candidates for virtualization, you can calculate the potential savings in capital costs. Capital costs include the cost of physical components like servers, switches, routers, racks, keyboard-video-mouse (KVM) devices, and disk systems. The major component in capital cost savings is the number of physical servers that will not have to be purchased in the future. When you virtualize existing physical servers you obtain cost savings in two ways. The first is the elimination of the need to refresh that physical server at a future date. The second is the potential offset of purchasing physical servers for Virtual Server hosts based on reusing existing equipment.

To calculate the future cost savings of not having to refresh a server, you need to know when that server was planned for refresh and the predicted cost for the refresh hardware. Companies generally vary from a two to five year refresh plan for servers. Create a spreadsheet that has columns for the next two to five years, based on your server refresh cycle, and a row for each virtualization candidate server. Place the cost savings for each virtualization candidate in the appropriate year. Now sum the columns to obtain an annual capital cost savings analysis for the next two to five years.

For virtualization projects where you are not virtualizing existing physical servers but are looking to create new servers using virtualization, the calculation is slightly different. In this case, you would first determine the number of physical servers that you would be deploying and the cost for those servers; this will be the capital cost for physical deployment. Next you would determine the number of Virtual Server hosts that you would need to host those same servers. If you have not done the planning yet for those servers, you can assume a consolidation ratio to determine the number of required hosts. Multiply the number of required hosts by the cost for a standard Virtual Server host to obtain the virtualization deployment capital cost. Subtract the virtualization deployment capital cost from physical deployment capital cost to obtain the potential virtualization capital cost savings.

Environmental Savings

Assessing the positive environmental impact of virtualizing servers by calculating the potential savings is a task that you do not want to overlook during the Assessment phase. Every server you virtualize is a server available for a repurposed workload or for retiring to save on power, cooling, and space. This information can be used to justify the project and demonstrate the cost benefits.

During the Discovery phase you should have identified all the different server manufacturers and models. If you did not collect rack space usage and power consumption information for each server, you need to go to the manufacturer's Web site and obtain that information at this point. Once you have all this information for each different server manufacturer and model, you can calculate the environmental savings.

For a complete estimate, you actually need to take into account not just the servers, but the supporting peripherals, such as disk cabinets, KVMs, network switches, and other rack-mounted devices that might be connected to the servers that would no longer be needed when the server was virtualized. Unfortunately, collecting that information in an automated fashion is not a trivial task because these devices do not typically run an operating system, nor are they listed as objects in Active Directory.

If you want to include this information, you can take one of two approaches. The first approach is to make an estimate based on the number of servers that you are virtualizing. For KVM switches, if the standard KVM switch used in the data center is an eight-port model, assume that you will eliminate a KVM switch for every eight servers virtualized. You can use the same approach for network switches, using the number of switch ports in the calculation. Disk cabinet estimates in this approach are more problematic unless there are standards for server deployments—so that you know that every server model *X* was deployed with disk cabinet *Y*. Without this knowledge, the second approach is the only way to gather this information for disk cabinets. An additional problem with the first approach is you will not know the location where you will be eliminating a device.

The second approach requires you to perform a physical inventory for every server in the virtualization candidate pool to identify the attached peripherals that would be eliminated. The second option is more accurate and provides location information, but it takes longer and costs more.

Rack Space Savings

The standard data center server rack is a 42U (Unit) high rack. Servers range anywhere from 1U to 10U of rack space each. Therefore, the number of servers per rack will vary, but the number of Us per rack is constant. For the rack savings calculation, you can assume that all rack space is used in every rack. If the racks are not all completely full, your calculation for the number of racks that you will empty by virtualizing all the servers will actually be on the low side.

To determine the amount of rack space saved, just determine how many servers of each manufacturer you will virtualize, multiple that number by the rack space used by the servers, and then sum those values. To determine the number of actual racks that you would free up in the data center, assuming the standard 42U rack, take the Total Rack Space Saved and divide by 42.

Power Consumption

Every server requires power to operate, and most servers operate on a 24 × 7 hourly basis 365 days a year (or you hope they do). Most servers are designed with a power supply that can provide power to the system if it is fully populated, and the power supply runs at only around 75-percent efficiency. It is usually a safe assumption to use the power supply rating in watts in your calculations.

To calculate the power consumption of each server, you also need to know the cost of a kilowatt-hour of electricity. Each location that you have servers at probably has a different cost for kilowatt-hour, so you need to make sure and collect those different values. In the sample calculations provided, an average value is used.

Once you have the power consumption of each server's power supply, the number of servers, and the cost per kilowatt-hour for electricity, you can use a series of formulas to determine the total cost saved from virtualizing your candidate servers. The first formula is the total power consumed by a certain model server in a year (in kilowatt-hours) assuming continuous operation:

Power consumption per server per year (kilowatts) = (watt rating of power supply × 365 × 24)/1000

Once you have the consumption determined by server model, you can determine the total consumption by multiplying by the number of servers of that model that you are virtualizing and sum those amounts:

Total Power consumption per year (kilowatts) = Sum (Power consumption per
   server model × quantity of servers)

Now you have the total power consumption per year for the virtualization candidates in kilowatt-hours. To obtain the power consumption cost, multiply the total power consumption per year by the average cost per kilowatt-hour:

Total Savings per year = Total power consumption per year × average $cost per kilowatt-hour

To provide an example of the potential power savings, we can assume that there are 500 servers in the virtualization candidate pool, each server has a power supply rating of 750 watts, and the cost per kilowatt hour is $.10:

Power consumption per server per year (kilowatts) = (750 × 365 × 24)/1000 = 6570
Total Power consumption per year (kilowatts) = 6570 × 500 = 3,285,000
Total Savings per year = 3,285,000 × $.10 = $385,000

Cooling Costs

In addition to the power consumption of the servers during normal operations, servers also generate heat that must be dissipated. Because the servers run continuously, they generate heat continuously and therefore the cooling must be provided continuously. For simplicity in calculating cooling costs, you can assume that every watt of power consumed by a server generates one watt of heat that needs dissipating.

Engineers and scientists have not been able to design and produce a cooling system that is 100-percent efficient, so you should assume an efficiency percentage in the 60 to 70 percent range to be conservative. This means that if you need to dissipate 1,000,000 kilowatts of heat and your cooling system is 65-percent efficient, it will require 1,000,000/.65 or 1,538,461 watts of power to cool.

Using the numbers from the previous 500 server example (3,285,000 kilowatts of annual power consumption and assuming one watt of power equals one watt of heat), there would be 3,285,000 watts of heat to dissipate. Assuming 65-percent efficiency for the cooling system, 5,053,846 watts of power would be required annually to cool the servers. At a cost of $.10 per kilowatt-hour, the savings would be $505,385 in cooling costs.

Important   Do not forget to subtract the space, power, and cooling requirements of the Virtual Server hosts from the potential savings numbers to obtain a more accurate prediction of real savings.

On the Companion Media   To assist you in collecting cost savings information and producing a potential cost savings summary, you will find an Microsoft Office Excel spreadsheet named Potential Cost Savings JobAid.xls in the \Chapter Materials\Job Aids folder. This spreadsheet has a single worksheet that contains the recommended information to collect and some predefined calculations to assist in producing a potential cost savings for servers and environmental items like power, cooling, and space. The spreadsheet does not take into account the space, power, and cooling of the new hosts.

Summary

This chapter described how to approach the third phase of a virtualization project, the Assessment phase. Assessment focuses on taking a list of potential virtualization server candidates and determining which servers should be removed from the candidates list based on hardware, performance, and supported software limitations. You learned how to set performance thresholds, and how to use those thresholds to make exclusion decisions. You also learned that one of the largest challenges to virtualization is vendor support. Once you have processed all the servers, the remaining pool of virtualization candidates will be used in the next phase of the virtualization project, Planning and Design.

In addition to learning how to assess a server for virtualization, you also learned how to use the virtualization and environmental information to calculate the savings in servers, space, power, and cooling. Using a sample scenario of 500 servers that use 750 watts of energy per hour at a cost of $.10 per kilowatt-hour, you determined that the combined power and cooling savings would result in a total cost savings of $833,885 per year.

Additional Resources

The following resources contain additional information related to this chapter:

- Windows Server System common engineering criteria, *http://www.microsoft.com /windowsserversystem/cer/default.mspx*

- Windows Server System software not supported within a Microsoft Virtual Server environment, *http://support.microsoft.com/kb/897614*

Chapter 15

Virtualization Project: Planning and Design Phase

In this chapter:

Defining Virtual Server Host Configurations................................374

Consolidation Planning..377

Solution Planning 385

Summary..388

Additional Resources..388

The Planning and Designing phase of a virtualization project involves three main tasks: determining the physical requirements of the Virtual Servers that will host the migrated virtualization candidates, determining how to best consolidate the workloads of the virtualization candidates to maximize the number of virtual machines per host, and designing the overall solution requirements of the virtualization environment. One of the main goals of consolidation planning is to achieve the highest number of virtual machines per host. This is referred to as the *consolidation ratio*. The higher the consolidation ratio, the lower the capital cost of the virtualization infrastructure.

Consolidation planning can be performed using two approaches: defining the hardware specifications and then determining the consolidation ratio that can be achieved, or defining the consolidation ratio and then determining the required hardware specifications. Table 15-1 identifies the key pros and cons for each approach.

Table 15-1   Consolidation Planning Approaches

Consolidation planning approach	Pros	Cons
Define hardware specifications, and obtain the consolidation ratio.	■ Ability to define standard configurations ■ Lower support costs	■ Lower workload optimization ■ Requires additional hardware
Define the consolidation ratio, and obtain the hardware requirements.	■ Higher consolidation ratio ■ Higher workload optimization	■ Each host has a custom configuration ■ Higher support costs ■ More complicated planning process

The first approach simplifies the planning process by defining the host hardware requirements: the number of CPUs, amount of memory, amount of disk space, number of disks used, number of network adapters, and speed of the network adapters. This provides a set of limits that you can use to perform workload optimization. Workload optimization then becomes a matter of determining the combination of virtualization candidate workloads that comes the closest to the defined thresholds without exceeding them. This approach of defining the hardware limits and attempting to combine the workloads together rarely results in a combined workload that matches the thresholds on every Virtual Server host. This results in nonoptimum use of resources.

The second approach removes the limits of predefined hardware specification and allows you to combine workloads that will then define the required hardware specification. This is accomplished by predefining a consolidation ratio target—for example, 20 virtual machines per host or a ratio of 20 to 1. During consolidation planning, you determine the 20 virtualization candidates that provide the lowest resource utilization when their workloads are combined. The resulting hardware requirements for processor, memory, disk, and network adapters then define the host hardware that is required to host the 20 virtualization candidates. This approach of letting the combined workloads define the hardware requirement results in a varied number of host hardware configurations that are tuned to match the required workload.

There are tradeoffs to each approach. Predefining standard hardware configurations streamlines the configuration process and increases the ability to obtain discounts on the configurations, but it does not always provide the optimum consolidation ratio and might waste resources. Predefining the consolidation ratio ensures that the hardware optimally matches the workload requirements, but it results in increased capital and management costs. This chapter focuses on the first approach by establishing the Virtual Server host hardware specifications and performing consolidation planning to maximize the consolidation ratio on those configurations.

Defining Virtual Server Host Configurations

Before you start the consolidation planning process, you should define Virtual Server host configurations. The configurations provide the limits used when you combine the virtualization candidates together to determine the optimal workload. During the project, you will be virtualizing physical servers in multiple locations with varying numbers of virtual machines per host. To provide for variance in the number of virtual machines based on location, you should establish a minimum of three configurations of Virtual Server hosts: a smaller host for locations such as branch offices, a medium-sized host for medium office locations or small data centers, and a larger host for large data center locations. Most smaller locations such as branch offices typically have four virtual machines or less, a medium-sized office or small data center location could have 20 virtualization candidates, while a large data center could have hundreds or thousands of virtualization candidates.

Physical Requirements

The Virtual Server host specification can vary widely because Microsoft Virtual Server 2005 R2 SP1 now supports a maximum of 512 virtual machines per host. With the availability of quad-core 64-bit processors from Intel and AMD, storage area networks (SANs), 10,000 and 15,000 RPM Serial Attached SCSI (SAS) hard disk drives, and gigabit Ethernet, many different configurations are possible.

> **Note**   Virtual Server 2005 R2 SP1 supports the Intel and AMD x64 line of processors, but not the Intel Itanium line of processors.

Even with the latest advances in server technology, processor or memory configurations of modern servers will limit consolidation planning. Most back-office-class servers range from single-processor to four-processor configurations with single, dual, or quad cores. This provides for a typical ceiling of 16 processor cores. Memory on modern servers is dependent on the speed selected. Slower memory allows you to have larger quantity. The typical memory ceiling is 128 gigabytes (GB), with a few systems able to achieve 256 GB of memory.

Table 15-2 provides the recommended minimum configuration for small, medium, and large categories of Virtual Server hosts. The configurations assume that virtual machines have a minimum of 1 GB of memory each with 1 GB of memory reserved for the host, a minimum of 1 processor core reserved for the host, and 1 network adapter dedicated for host communications. Small category hosts are recommended to have direct-attached storage (DAS) because of cost and management complexity. Medium and large category hosts are assumed to be located in facilities that would benefit from shared storage capability of storage area networks.

Table 15-2   Recommended Minimum Host Hardware Configurations

Host category	Processor	Memory	Disk	Network adapter
Small	1 dual- or quad-core	8 GB	DAS	2 x 1 gigabit Ethernet
Medium	2 quad-core	32 GB	SAN	5 x 1 gigabit Ethernet
Large	4 quad-core	64 GB	SAN	8 x 1 gigabit Ethernet

High-Availability Hardware Requirements

Consolidating multiple physical machines by migrating them to virtual machines and combining them on a single server can cause concern and raise the following questions: How do you handle a hardware failure? How do you update the Virtual Server host when virtual machines are running?

You need a solution that allows you to handle both of these situations. Virtual Server 2005 R2 SP1 provides support for a high-availability solution using Microsoft Cluster Service (MSCS) to cluster Virtual Server hosts or virtual machines. Either approach can support up to eight nodes in the cluster.

Virtual Server host clustering provides failover support on a virtual-machine or entire-host basis. Host clustering requires a minimum of two cluster nodes. Each node must be installed with Microsoft Windows Server 2003 R2 Enterprise edition or higher and be running MSCS. Once the nodes are installed and configured, one or more virtual machines can be manually or automatically failed across nodes. Using three or more nodes allows MSCS to fail virtual machines in a load-balanced approach to ensure that a single cluster node does not become overburdened with workloads. Virtual Server host clustering can take advantage of the MSCS clustering limit of up to eight nodes.

> **Note**   For more information on host clustering capabilities and installation, refer to Chapter 5, "Virtual Server 2005 R2 Advanced Features," and the detailed white paper installed with Virtual Server 2005 R2 SP1. You will find the detailed white paper on host clustering installed in the C:\Program Files\Microsoft Virtual Server\Host Clustering\ directory.

Planning for Virtual Server host clustering hardware and clustering configuration differs from a standard cluster planning in two primary ways:

1.   Installation of a special high-availability failover script that manages virtual machine failover requirements and mapping

2.   Shared-disk logical unit number (LUN) configuration

The high-availability failover script manages the virtual machine registration and power-on process as machines fail over from one node to another. The shared-disk LUN configuration determines the granularity of virtual machine failover. To be able to failover a single virtual machine between hosts, each virtual machine must be stored on a separate LUN. Shared disks can be stored on SAN-based or iSCSI-based shared disk systems.

Direct from the Source: Solving Drive Letter Restrictions with Mountpoints

Host clustering is a great solution for scheduled downtime where you want to quickly migrate a virtual machine from one node to another to service the underlying hardware like applying a BIOS update or adding memory or storage. Host clustering is also a great solution for unscheduled downtime, when a hardware failure occurs and you want the virtual machines to *automatically* failover over to another node.

When the migration or failure occurs, the entire drive or LUN moves to the recovery node. For a single virtual machine to migrate to another cluster node, the drive or LUN can contain only the files of that virtual machine. Typical installations of MSCS assign a drive letter to each LUN, but with only 26 letters in the English alphabet, this can be limiting. The solution is to place more than one virtual machine on a drive or find a way to have more LUNs accessible in cluster server via mountpoints. Mountpoints allow you to create an unlimited number of LUNs and provide a way for MSCS to access them. Refer to *http://support.microsoft.com/kb/280297* for details on how to create mountpoints to physical disks and use configure them as disk resources in MSCS.

Jeff Woolsey
Senior Program Manager, Windows Virtualization

When designing your host-clustering solution, the number of nodes in the cluster and the failure scenario can affect the required hardware configurations. With a two-node cluster configuration, you must design a single node to handle the workload of both servers in the event of failure. To do this, you must determine the hardware requirements for the workload of a single node and double it. For example, if a single node workload for running 20 virtual machines requires two quad-core processors and 24 GBs of memory, the hardware requirements for the node should be doubled to four quad-core processors and 48 GBs of memory to support the failure of the second node.

As you add nodes to the cluster, the workload of the failed node can be distributed across other nodes and the hardware requirement of each node decreases from the two-node scenario. Alternatively, you can plan for a warm standby node in the cluster running no workload. When a node fails, all the workload from that node resumes on the standby node. Using a warm standby node simplifies the design process, reduces the hardware requirements of each node (therefore reducing the cost of each node), and ensures that the failover process does not affect the workloads on the remaining nodes in the cluster.

Consolidation Planning

Consolidation planning involves determining the number of Virtual Server hosts required to virtualize all the candidate servers. The number of Virtual Server hosts is affected by how the virtualization candidates will be grouped. Grouping requires you to take requirements such as separate locations, management approach, and security into account. Once you have the virtualization candidates grouped, you can then start the workload analysis process to determine the optimal way to combine the candidates to achieve the highest consolidation ratio per host. Once you have completed the workload analysis, you can investigate the possibilities of reusing the virtualization candidate hardware to fill the Virtual Server host requirements.

Grouping the Candidates

You should have a list of virtualization candidates established as part of the Assessment phase of the virtualization project. Before you can start the workload analysis phase of consolidation planning, you must determine any grouping restrictions that you will need to place on the candidate pool. Sample grouping approaches you might consider include the following ones:

- Location
- Administration team
- Application

Location grouping is required for planning the number of Virtual Server hosts per location. Unless you consolidate sites together as part of a virtualization project, you cannot combine those workloads on the same host. Therefore, before you perform location-based grouping, make sure that you take into account any planned site consolidation. Because you will be using location information from the server data collection, any site consolidation needs to be reflected in the location data values for proper grouping to occur.

Administration team grouping might be required if you want to use a server-based security approach instead of a per-virtual-machine security approach. Server-based security means that you create a global group in Active Directory for an administrative team, place that group in the local administrators group of the Virtual Server host, and then place only virtual machines on that host that the administrative group has the rights to administer. The default security configuration of Virtual Server gives members of the local administrators group full control over all virtual machines. Although administration grouping is technically feasible and customers use it, this approach does not provide flexible use of the Virtual Server host resources and generally increases the number of required Virtual Server hosts. This approach also precludes clustering the Virtual Server host with another Virtual Server host managed by a different administration team.

A per-virtual-machine approach provides the most flexible use of the Virtual Server resources, but it requires complex configuration and management processes. By default, the security interface on the Administration Website assumes that the security settings apply to all virtual machines on the host. If you give a user or group full control rights, they have full control over all virtual machines. To establish the security on a per-virtual-machine basis, you are required to use file access control lists (ACLs) to secure each virtual machine.

 More Info   Refer to Chapter 6, "Security in Depth," for a detailed discussion on how to secure access to Virtual Server hosts and virtual machines.

Application-based grouping allows you to place servers running the same applications on the same Virtual Server host or allows you to define applications that should not be grouped on the same host for security or performance reasons. Application grouping can also be applied in two different approaches: dedicated or shared. The dedicated approach allows only virtual machines running a single application to be placed on a host. The shared approach allows for a combination of virtual machines running different applications to be placed on a single host. The shared approach normally defines a limit to the number of combined applications.

Performing Workload Analysis

Workload analysis is the process of combining hardware and performance information of multiple virtualization candidates together to come as close as possible to the desired hardware and performance thresholds for a Virtual Server host. To accomplish this, you must define thresholds for the Virtual Server host hardware configurations, collect the data for each grouping of candidates, and perform the calculations to obtain the optimal combinations of candidates.

Establishing Thresholds

During the Discovery phase of the virtualization project, you established a set of thresholds for determining whether a physical server was a good candidate for virtualization. The focus was to ensure that a virtualization candidate could have acceptable performance when migrated to a virtualized environment. During workload analysis, you need to set the thresholds for the entire Virtual Server host. These thresholds define the amount of server resources that will be reserved. The reserved resources will be used by the Virtual Server host to service local resource needs and as additional capacity for spikes in resource utilization.

The thresholds are defined for the four major components of a Virtual Server host: processor, memory, disk, and network. Table 15-3 provides a set of sample thresholds. For hardware components that can have multiple instances (processor, disk, and network), the values shown are for a single instance. Disk I/O is limited by the disk performance and the disk controller performance. The network interface performance is limited by the collision rate on the network and the driver configuration options.

Table 15-3   Sample Virtual Server Host Performance Thresholds

Hardware feature	Threshold
Processor utilization	80% of maximum processing power
Physical Memory utilization	80% of maximum physical memory
Disk I/O	75% of maximum disk controller throughput
Network I/O	80% of the maximum network adapter throughput

Direct from the Source: Benchmark Your Virtual Server Hosts

The maximum values for disk and network throughput can vary widely, depending on manufacturer, driver quality, configuration, and type of technology. You should not perform any workload analysis based on assumed performance levels. It is a best practice to perform baseline benchmarks on the proposed hardware for Virtual Server hosts to obtain realistic performance values. Using those values will provide a much better capacity planning capability than theoretical maximums.

Ken Durigan
Architect, Microsoft Consulting Services

Now that you have established the thresholds for the Virtual Server hosts, you must determine the thresholds for each category of server that you are using. Table 15-4 provides an example of possible thresholds for a small host category server. The assumption for the hardware configuration of a small host is a single quad-core processor, 8 GB of memory, a single disk controller with a maximum throughput of 320 MB/second, and a single dedicated gigabit Ethernet adapter for virtual machine usage with a maximum throughput of 550 Mbits/second. Threshold values are calculated using the following formula:

Threshold Value= (Maximum Value × Quantity × Threshold Percentage) / 100

Maximum Value is the maximum performance value for a single instance of a feature—for example, a 3-GHz processor. *Quantity* is the number of instances of a feature that are available for virtual machine use—for example, the small category server has four processor cores, but one is reserved for host processing, so three remain available for virtual machine use. *Threshold Percentage* is the performance threshold established to ensure that the host has reserved capacity.

Table 15-4 Sample Small Host Category Threshold Values

| Threshold | Threshold percentage | Small Host Category | | |
		Maximum value	Quantity for virtual machine use	Threshold value
Processor	80	3000 MHz	3	7200 MHz
Memory	80	8 GB	1	6.4 GB
Disk	75	320 MB/s	1	240 MB/s
Network	80	550 Mb/s	1	440 Mb/s

Table 15-5 provides an example of possible thresholds for a medium host category server. The assumption for the hardware configuration of a medium host is two quad-core processors (one core reserved for the host), 32 GB of memory, two disk controllers with a maximum throughput of 320 MB/second each, and four dedicated gigabit Ethernet adapters for virtual machine usage with a maximum throughput of 550 Mb/second each.

Table 15-5 Sample Medium Host Category Threshold Values

| Threshold | Threshold percentage | Medium Host Category | | |
		Maximum value	Quantity for virtual machine use	Threshold value
Processor	80	3000 MHz	7	16,800 MHz
Memory	80	32 GB	1	25.6 GB
Disk	75	320 MB/s	2	480 MB/s
Network	80	550 Mb/s	4	1,760 Mb/s

Table 15-6 provides an example of possible thresholds for a large host category server. The assumption for the hardware configuration of a large host is four quad-core processors (two cores reserved for the host), 64 GB of memory, four disk controllers with a maximum throughput of 320 MB/second each, and seven dedicated gigabit Ethernet adapters for virtual machine usage with a maximum throughput of 550 Mbits/second each.

Table 15-6   Example Large Host Category Threshold Values

Threshold	Threshold percentage	Large Host Category		
		Maximum value	Quantity for virtual machine use	Threshold value
Processor	80	3000 MHz	14	33,600 MHz
Memory	80	64 GB	1	51.2 GB
Disk	75	320 MB/s	4	960 MB/s
Network	80	550 Mb/s	7	3,080 Mb/s

Data Preprocessing

Once you have determined the threshold values for each host category and the grouping of candidates is completed, you can gather the required inventory and performance information and preprocess the data before workload analysis begins. Table 15-7 lists all the values that need to be assembled from the data collected during the Discovery phase. Both inventory and performance data are required in order to calculate a comparison value to the threshold value. For example, processor performance counter data was collected as a percentage of processor time for each processor in the system. To transform that into a value that can be compared against the threshold, you must multiply the percentage of processor time for each processor by the processor speed in megahertz to obtain the actual megahertz consumed by each processor. Then you must sum all processor values to obtain the total processor megahertz consumed.

Table 15-7   Performance Information

Performance category	Parameters
Processor	Processor speed in MHz
	Percent of processor time for each processor instance
Memory	Available bytes of memory
	Total physical memory
Network (for each adapter instance)	Total bytes per second
Disk (for each physical disk)	Disk read bytes per second
	Disk write bytes per second

Recommended performance data values collection intervals are every five minutes over a 30-day period. Although you could use all 8640 values during workload analysis, it would lengthen the analysis time greatly. To simplify the analysis process and reduce the time it will take to perform a what-if analysis, you should average the data values. You can average the values over different time periods, but the recommended minimum is hourly and the recommended maximum is daily.

Workload Analysis Calculations

Workload analysis is performed separately for each grouping of virtualization candidates. The process involves combining workloads of multiple servers and comparing that combined workload to the established threshold. The threshold you use is based on the server category that you need for the virtualization group you are analyzing. The workloads analyzed are processor, memory, disk, and network. The easiest way to combine workloads and compare them to the threshold value is to use the Microsoft Office Excel 2007 charting functionality or a custom SQL Reporting Services report, depending on how the data is stored.

Using Microsoft Excel, you can create charts that graph performance over time of each workload using the stacked area chart type. Stacked area charts allow you to combine data from multiple series in an additive manner. This data is graphed against the reference threshold value to determine whether the combined workload exceeds the threshold. Figure 15-1 shows an example of a 2-D stacked area chart of processor workload over a 30-day period. In this example, the processor workload has been combined for four servers on a host in the small host category. The chart shows that the threshold of 7400 MHz has not been exceeded by the combined workload.

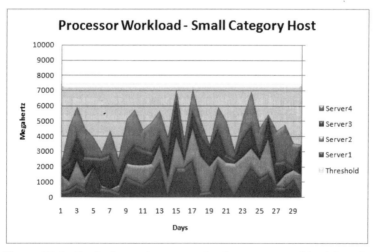

Figure 15-1   Stacked area chart example of processor workload from four servers

The workload analysis process involves selecting one server at a time and adding it to the proposed workload for a host. The data is added to each workload graph. As additional servers are selected and added to the workload graph, the performance trend will show how these servers' workloads would combine. As you add servers to the proposed workload, each graph should be analyzed to determine whether the threshold has been exceeded.

Figures 15-2, 15-3, and 15-4 show the memory, disk, and network workload charts, respectively, for the same four servers. If you analyze each of these charts, you can see that the disk and memory workloads have exceeded the threshold values, but the network workload has not.

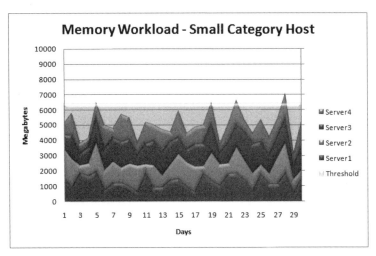

Figure 15-2   Stacked area chart example of memory workload from four servers

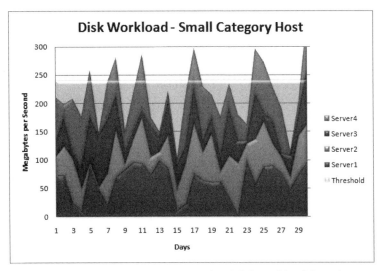

Figure 15-3   Stacked area chart example of disk workload from four servers

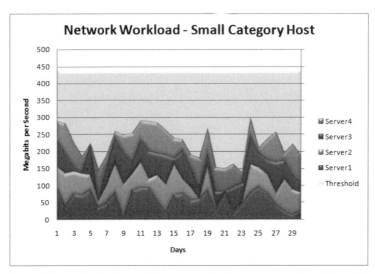

Figure 15-4   Stacked area chart example of network workload from four servers

If a performance threshold is exceeded, you have two options:

1.   Remove a server from the list to reduce the workload below the threshold and establish that set of servers as a finished scenario.

2.   Modify the selected servers to determine whether a different set of servers would combine workloads in a more efficient manner.

To maximize the consolidation ratio for each host and obtain the optimal workload deployment, the second option should be done for every possible combination of server workloads. Once you have determined the combination of servers that comes the closest to each combined workload category threshold without exceeding the threshold, that set of servers should be removed from the pool of servers to analyze and assigned to a host. The analysis is then repeated for the remaining pool of servers until every server has been assigned to a host.

Once you have completed a workload analysis on every server in every group of virtualization candidates, you can determine the number of host servers in each category that the virtualization project will require. This information will provide you with the ability to determine a preliminary host hardware budget estimate.

On the Companion Media   To assist you in performing workload analysis, you will find an Excel spreadsheet in the \Chapter Materials\Job Aids folder named Workload Analysis JobAid.xls. This spreadsheet has multiple preformatted worksheets and stacked area graphs that allow you to enter server data averaged over a daily basis for processor, memory, disk, and network workloads. Each worksheet has a row for the threshold values and a row for each set of server data. You must edit the source data area for each chart once you enter the server data on each worksheet. Microsoft Excel 2007 allows you to select individual rows of data to chart. This allows you to easily select servers for combined analysis.

Equipment Reuse

Virtualizing servers provides a large quantity of server hardware that can be repurposed in your environment. Depending on your server refresh life cycle, the reuse potential of the server hardware can vary. To determine the reuse potential of the hardware, you should perform an analysis of the inventory data collected during the Discovery phase. Using the server host category standards that you defined, analyze the inventory of hardware, looking for servers that could be reused for Virtual Server hosts. A determination needs to be made if you want to use only matching manufacturer models from the server host category specifications or if a server with a similar configuration would be acceptable.

When analyzing the inventory data, you should first look for models of servers that match the models you plan to purchase. The servers in the reuse inventory will probably not have all the required levels of components, but the server can be easily upgraded for less than the cost of purchasing a new server. Once you have identified the reuse candidates by matching manufacturer model, you should analyze the inventory for servers that have or could have the equivalent or better hardware specifications as the different category of Virtual Server hosts.

Once you have identified all possible reuse candidates, you can perform a cost savings analysis. Determine the number of Virtual Server hosts that you would not have to purchase as a result of reuse and then subtract the cost of upgrades required. That provides you with an estimate of the cost savings that you would achieve with equipment reuse.

Solution Planning

Virtualization projects tend to focus on the virtualization assessment and planning and ignore the operational changes and impacts that virtualization will introduce into an environment. Virtualization requires more than the virtualization host. It requires a complete solution that can manage the Virtual Servers and virtual machines, monitor the health of the virtual environment, and deal with special patch management issues.

Management

Virtual Server 2005 R2 SP1 includes a Web-based administration tool to administer the Virtual Server host and the virtual machines. The interface is designed to manage the local Virtual Server, or it can be designed to be centrally hosted and manage a group of Virtual Servers. In any configuration, it will allow you to manage only a single Virtual Server at a time. In most environments, using the included administration site is acceptable for up to about 10 hosts. If your virtualization project will have more than 10 hosts or if you require advanced features such as a virtual machine library or advanced management features, you should investigate Microsoft System Center Virtual Machine Manager (VMM).

For more detailed information on using the included Web administration site to manage a Virtual Server environment, refer to Chapter 17, "Managing a Virtual Server Infrastructure." For detailed information on System Center Virtual Machine Manager, installation instructions, and usage scenarios, refer to Chapter 19, "System Center Virtual Machine Manager 2007."

Monitoring

Virtual Server 2005 R2 SP1 contains a set of performance counters that you can use to monitor Virtual Server and virtual machine performance using the Windows Server 2003 Performance Monitor tool. Using this approach allows you to monitor a single Virtual Server, but it does not provide a robust monitoring, reporting, and alerting solution.

Microsoft Operations Manager (MOM) 2005 or 2007 provides a central console and an agent-based approach to monitoring, reporting, and alerting for Virtual Servers and virtual machines. In addition, MOM will monitor all the physical servers in your environment, allowing you to have a single console for both your physical and virtual environments. MOM uses management packs to provide modular application-specific monitoring functionality. Microsoft provides a free management pack for Virtual Server 2005 R2 for monitoring the virtual environment.

For more detailed information on Microsoft Operations Manager 2005 and the Virtual Server 2005 R2 management pack installation and operations, refer to Chapter 18, "Using the MOM 2005 Virtual Server Management Pack."

Patch Management

Microsoft Systems Management Server 2003, Windows Software Update Service (WSUS), and System Center Configuration Manager (SCCM) 2007 are Microsoft's premier solutions for patch management. Although WSUS is a patch management–only solution, SMS and SCCM provide additional features such as asset inventory and tracking, and software deployment.

Designing a patch management solution for a virtual environment has more issues and dependencies to consider. A patch management solution for a virtual environment needs to take into account the relationship between the Virtual Server host and the virtual machines running in it. This knowledge will assist in deployment planning so that an update to the Virtual Server host does not cause an unnecessary reboot and down time for the virtual machines. Technologies such as undo disk introduce additional challenges for tracking the correct status of installed updates.

For more detailed information on how to modify your current patch management solution for a Virtual Server environment and understanding key issues, refer to Chapter 17.

Backup Requirements

Backing up a virtual machine environment is slightly more complicated than backing up a physical environment. You must be able to back up the Virtual Server host and each virtual machine. Because you might be backing up a virtual machine while other virtual machines are providing production services, you must attempt to minimize the performance impact on the running virtual machines.

When performing a backup of a Virtual Server host, you need to ensure that you back up the following information:

- Virtual Server host configuration settings
- Virtual Server host system state
- Virtual Server host file system

When performing a backup of a virtual machine, you need to ensure that you back up the following information:

- Virtual machine configuration settings
- Virtual machine system state
- Virtual machine volumes
- Virtual machine undo disks
- Virtual machine difference disk hierarchy

Backup Approaches

You have three primary choices for backing up a Virtual Server and virtual machines:

1. Place a file-based backup agent on each computer (virtual machine and host), and back up across the network.

2. Shut down or save the state of the virtual machines, and back up the files on the host.

3. Perform a Volume Shadow Copy Service (VSS) snapshot of the host and virtual machines.

Using a local agent allows you to back up virtual machines as you do physical machines, but it places a performance overhead on the host while the backups are in progress and there is generally no knowledge that the machine is a virtual machine. Backing up the powered off or saved state files of the virtual machines provides a simple process, but it is not supported for some server roles such as Active Directory domain controllers. Virtual Server 2005 R2 SP1 introduces a new capability for the backup of Virtual Server hosts and virtual machines: the Volume Shadow Copy Service (VSS) writer. The Virtual Server VSS writer allows you to back up the host and all virtual machines from a single agent running on the host. The Virtual Server VSS writer backup approach provides the best features of the other two approaches in one solution and is the preferred backup method.

Backup Applications

To use the VSS backup approach, your backup software must understand and use the Virtual Server VSS writer to take data-consistent backups with the Volume Shadow Copy Service. You need to update your existing backup software to obtain this new capability or possibly change backup software vendors to obtain this capability.

Note   Refer to Chapter 17 for more detailed information on the backup process and the VSS architecture.

Summary

This chapter discussed the Planning and Design phase of a virtualization project and its four major parts: the consolidation planning approach, defining Virtual Server hardware configurations, consolidation planning, and solution planning. Based on the pros and cons of the two approaches for consolidation planning, the better approach was determined to be the following: define the hardware configurations first and then determine the consolidation ratio that could be achieved.

You learned why and how to establish different host configurations to match the workload scale your environment requires. An approach based on tested performance thresholds, appropriate grouping of candidates, and simple formulas demonstrates that consolidation planning is an achievable goal. You learned that once consolidation planning is complete, proper solution planning can help reduce the operational costs of a virtualized environment and that you must adapt your current processes for management and operations.

Additional Resources

The following resources contain additional information related to this chapter:

- System Center Virtual Machine Manager, *http://www.microsoft.com/systemcenter/scvmm/default.mspx*

- Microsoft Operations Manager 2005, *http://www.microsoft.com/mom/default.mspx*

- Windows Server System Reference Architecture (WSSRA) Virtual Environments for Development and Test, *http://www.microsoft.com/downloads/details.aspx?FamilyID=5ce8f01d-a421-4da8-9144-fbaf44e62c34&DisplayLang=en*

Chapter 16

Virtualization Project: Pilot Phase

In this chapter:

Pilot Objectives 389
Pilot Scope 390
Pilot Architecture. 391
Planning the Pilot 390
Implementing the Pilot. 399
Measuring Project Success 399
Incorporating Lessons Learned 400
Summary. 400
Additional Resources. 400

The Pilot phase of a virtualization project focuses on verifying the project planning and design. To accomplish this, you need to develop the pilot objectives, identify the pilot scope, design the pilot architecture, develop a pilot plan, implement the pilot, and then evaluate its success.

Pilot Objectives

Defining the pilot objectives allows you to identify the key aspects of the project plan and design that should be validated. From a high level, the pilot should focus on validating the migration, administration, management processes, and performance of the virtualized environment. Key aspects of the validation process for any virtualization project should include the following:

- Validating the Virtual Server environment configuration

- Validating the physical to virtual machine migration process

- Validating the virtual machine provisioning process

- Validating the administrative security model

- Validating the patch management process

- Validating the backup and restore process

- Validating the performance of the Virtual Server host design

Depending on the virtualization project scenario, there might be additional objectives. If your scenario involves creating a test and development environment, you should also validate aspects such as the ability to deploy multiple virtual machines in a single test case, perform the test, and then store the test case back into the library. If your scenario involves the virtualization of a branch office environment, you should validate security settings that protect a virtual domain controller. For a business continuity scenario, you should validate the failover and failback processes of the disaster recovery solution. Validating these core aspects of the project ensures that the resulting environment will be ready to support migration and operations.

Pilot Scope

A pilot must ensure that all aspects of the design are validated without requiring the entire project scope to be completed. To accomplish this, the pilot scope should limit the locations and virtualization candidates to the minimum set that is required to validate the objectives and the usage scenarios. All aspects of the design should be implemented (management, backup, administration, and so on), but the implementation does not have to include the full scale of the design. For example, to validate the physical to virtual machine migration process you need to perform only a representative set of migrations—you are not required to migrate every server in scope during the pilot.

Selecting Pilot Locations

During consolidation planning, virtualization candidates were grouped by location to ensure the proper number of Virtual Server hosts were identified. One way to reduce the scope from all virtualization candidates is to include only a subset of locations during the pilot. By doing this, you can select the locations based on priority, complexity, size, proximity, or supportability. If the virtualization project involves central data center and remote office locations, the pilot scope should include one data center location and one remote location at a minimum.

Selecting which locations to include depends on the testing approach followed. One approach is to identify the worst-case locations for the pilot scope. The worst case can be defined, for example, as the location with the slowest wide area network link, the location with no local technical support team, or possibly the location that is logistically the hardest to reach. The worst-case scenario assumes that the locations selected will provide the toughest challenge during the pilot and prepare the deployment team for the highest risk situations. The worst-case scenario also typically lengthens the pilot timeline or increases the required number of resources and the pilot cost.

An alternate approach is to focus on locations that minimize the pilot timeline and costs, reduce the logistics, and identify common issues. Therefore, you might select locations where technical support exists, smaller locations that can be fully migrated during the pilot, locations at which hardware already exists that can be used for Virtual Server hosts, or remote locations that are close in proximity to a central location to reduce travel time and cost.

Selecting Virtualization Candidates

Once you have identified the locations to use during the pilot, you need to analyze the consolidation plan for each location to identify the virtualization candidates you will migrate. Each location will have one or more Virtual Server hosts with an assigned group of virtualization candidates. Selection of candidates can be done at the host level or at the individual candidate level. Selecting a host selects all candidates assigned to that host. Selecting individual candidates might result in multiple Virtual Server hosts needing to be deployed to maintain the design workload optimization assignments.

If selecting individual virtualization candidates, focus on the unique pilot value of the candidates. Select servers with different types of applications, source hardware types (hardware manufacturer and configurations), and performance characteristics so that more potential issues can be identified during the pilot.

Pilot Architecture

Implementing the pilot requires the deployment of the basic architecture layers: virtualization, administration, management, backup, fault tolerance, and monitoring. Microsoft has a product solution for each layer:

- Virtual Server 2005 R2 SP1 provides virtualization and basic administration layers.
- System Center Virtual Machine Manager (VMM) provides the advanced administration and management layer.
- Data Protection Manager 2007 (DPM) provides the backup layer.
- Microsoft Cluster Services (MSCS) provides the fault tolerance layer.
- Operations Manager 2007 (MOM) provides the monitoring layer.

These layers integrate into the existing Active Directory domain and server deployment infrastructure. Figure 16-1 provides an architecture diagram view of a data center implementation showing all layers.

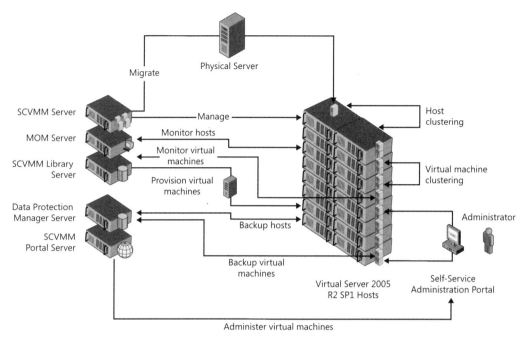

Figure 16-1 Pilot architecture

Planning the Pilot

A successful pilot project requires proper deployment, migration, and operational planning; communications within the project team and with the user community; an established project schedule with milestones, documented risks, and potential mitigations; and success criteria that will enable the pilot to evaluate whether the design meets the objectives.

Creating a Deployment Plan

A deployment plan is the road map for deploying the pilot architecture. The pilot deployment plan focuses on deploying the required architecture for the pilot scope. As shown in Figure 16-1, the central data center architecture should include one or more Virtual Server 2005 R2 SP1 hosts, at least one System Center Virtual Machine Manager server, at least one System Center Virtual Machine Manager library server, at least one System Center Virtual Machine Manager self-service portal server, a Microsoft Operations Manager 2007 monitoring console, and at least one System Center Data Protection Manager 2007 backup server. This provides the core Microsoft-supported architecture to host, provision, migrate, manage, monitor, and back up the pilot environment in the data center. Taking into account the pilot scope, you need to identify any additional data center or remote locations that need additional Virtual Server hosts or other architecture services.

To ensure proper architecture installation, create a set of deployment procedures for verification during the pilot. The procedures should include the step-by-step instructions to install the basic architecture services and verify that they are operating correctly. Ensure that the instructions cover items such as service accounts, hardware and software system requirements, and operating system configuration information for each server.

Creating a Support Plan

While the deployment plan focuses on the architecture that should be deployed for the pilot, the support plan focuses on the approach and team that will support the pilot while it is in operation. The support plan should answer the following questions at a minimum:

- Will there be a separate team and special support phone number or process?

- Will support be limited to certain hours of the day or days of the week?

- How will global support be provided?

- Will the pilot support team provide native-language speakers?

- What is the expected service-level agreement for response from the pilot support team?

- What is the escalation process if the pilot support team cannot resolve an issue?

The support plan should be integrated into the development of success criteria. Pilot support data can be analyzed to determine how service levels compare to historical operations on the migrated virtualization candidates. Data from pilot support cases can also be used to identify top issues.

Creating an Issue Tracking Plan

The pilot support team will be the primary interface for support calls. During a support case, an issue might be identified with a phase of the pilot. An issue tracking solution needs to be created and used to track issues and status throughout the pilot. You can use a Microsoft Office Excel spreadsheet, an Issues Log Web part on a Microsoft Office SharePoint Server 2007 portal, Microsoft Visual Studio Team System, or a dedicated tool for tracking issues. Table 16-1 provides a list of items the issue tracking system should collect.

Table 16-1   Issue Tracking Items

Item name	Item description
Issue Number	Unique number to track issue
Pilot Phase	The phase of the project in which the issue appeared
Date Issue Raised	The date the issue was submitted
Originator	The name or e-mail address of the issue originator
Issue Description	Detailed description of the issue
Pilot impact	How the issue affects the pilot (resources, time, efficiency, scope, and so on)

Table 16-1   Issue Tracking Items

Item name	Item description
Action	The actions that should be taken to resolve the issue
Action Owner	Identifies who will be performing the recommended action
Due Date	Specifies when the action is due to resolve the issue
Status	Status of the issue (such as not started, under review, action in progress, and issue resolved)

In addition to collecting the issues, you should produce weekly reports that provide the status of the number of issues in each status category. You should also establish a set of thresholds and an alerting process for issues that have exceeded thresholds for remaining in a single category. For example, if an issue remains at *not started* for more than 10 days, it should generate an alert to the pilot project manager.

On the Companion Media To assist in collecting and tracking issues, you will find an Excel spreadsheet in the \Chapter Materials\Job Aids folder called Issue Tracking JobAid.xls on the companion media. This spreadsheet has a single worksheet that contains columns to collect the recommended issue tracking attributes.

Direct from the Source: Using Office SharePoint Server 2007 to Track Virtualization Pilot Success

A good way to provide project visibility to management and the project team is to use Microsoft Office SharePoint Server (MOSS) 2007 during the pilot phase of the project to track issues and provide a dashboard for the pilot status. MOSS uses Web components called Web parts. Web parts are predefined modular Web interfaces that provide functionality such as document management, lists of information, calendars, task lists, and many more features. MOSS can be used to create a project portal providing document management for project documents, project task tracking, and metric reporting using scorecards.

Using the Document Library Web part, you can store, track versions of, and categorize project documents. Using the Project Tasks Web part, you can create a project plan complete with tasks, resource tracking, and Gantt charts. Using an Issue Tracking Web part, you can create a list to track issues throughout the project. By combining data from the Issue Tracking Web part and a Key Performance Indicator (KPI) List Web part, you can build a scorecard that contains a KPI status of the number of project issues categorized by the values in the issue status column (which include not started, under review, action in progress, and issue resolved).

Refer to the following video on Channel 9 on creating KPIs from SharePoint lists for more information: *http://channel9.msdn.com/Screencasts/214755_Dashboards.wmv.*

Dave Hamilton
Architect, Microsoft Consulting Services

Developing a Migration Plan

The migration plan focuses on how you will take a physical server and migrate it to a virtual machine with minimal effects on users and the server. The migration of physical machines to virtual machines has been greatly simplified with the introduction of tools that perform the physical to virtual (P2V) conversion in an automated fashion. Microsoft provides two tools for this process: Virtual Server Migration Tool (VSMT) and System Center Virtual Machine Manager (VMM). In addition to Microsoft's tools, there are many third-party vendors that provide similar tools. PlateSpin, LeoStream, and Hewlett-Packard are a few, but others exist.

A migration plan should address the following questions at a minimum:

- Can a live migration of the server be performed, or does the process require downtime?
- How will the final cutover of the server be handled?
- Will any special permissions be required to migrate a server?
- Will a new software license be required?
- Will the migrations be done manually or automated using scripts?
- What notifications are required to migrate a server?
- In what order will the physical servers be migrated?
- What are the migration dependencies?
- How will the migration process be monitored?
- What is the rollback process if a migration fails?

In addition to the migration plan, a set of migration procedures should be developed for the migration process for verification during the pilot. The procedures should include the step-by-step instructions to migrate the physical servers to virtual machines and verify that they are operating correctly after migration.

Developing an Operations Plan

An operations plan provides the road map to process change by addressing the changes in processes and procedures that will occur for the new virtualized environment. Changes will occur in administration, patch management, backup, disaster recovery, provisioning, and other areas. The operations plan should identify all the areas that change, outline the new processes, and provide detailed step-by-step procedures for verification during the pilot.

Developing a Training Plan

A training plan for a virtualization pilot will not focus on end users, but on administrators of the physical servers that are virtualized. The training plan should identify the users and processes that are affected. Ensure that both information technology department and business unit administrators are taken into account, especially if the business unit is managing the line of business (LOB) applications on the servers. Operation and management processes will generally be different for a virtualized server, and that information should be the primary focus of the training.

The method you select for remote management of virtualized servers will affect the scope of the training plan. If the server administrator uses Remote Desktop to remotely manage the server, managing a virtualized server will be no different. If the Virtual Server Virtual Machine Remote Control (VMRC) Client or System Center Virtual Machine Manager self-service portal interface is used, training needs to be provided.

Following is a list of common areas focused on in a training plan:

- Patch management
- Remote management tools and processes
- Backup tools and processes
- Disaster recovery processes
- New server provisioning process
- Application installation process

Creating a Communications Plan

A communications plan can be one of the most important aspects of a pilot program. The plan focuses on how to communicate, whom to communicate with, when to communicate, and what should be communicated. Communications need to be tailored to the target group.

Communicating to the pilot users or users who will be affected by the pilot is very important. You should not rely on a single communication method because users have different preferred ways of communicating. Combining e-mail messages, Web site postings, team meeting announcements, and other forms of communications ensures that the message will get timely delivery regardless of the end user's preferred method of communicating.

Targeting communications to the correct group of individuals helps the credibility of the project. A balance must be achieved between ensuring that users and administrators receive communications and avoiding over-communicating, which can result in the user ignoring communications. Categorize each communication, and ensure that only the users in that category receive the communication.

Ensure that the communications happen in a timely manner. If possible, notices should be communicated at a minimum of one week in advance. For example, users and administrators need a minimum of a week's notice of a physical server being migrated. LOB application administrators should be scheduled at a minimum of two weeks in advance for operations verification following the migration of a server.

Direct from the Source: Targeting Your Communications

Users have different e-mail habits. Some diligently read every message received, others create rules to categorize their inbox, while others do not read anything unless it is directly addressed to them. There is no way to prevent a user from creating an inbox rule to delete any pilot communications, but there are ways to increase the potential for the message to be read.

Instead of sending a message to a distribution list that can be easily filtered in a rule, send all communications directly to each user. This approach personalizes the message and increases the potential for the message to get past any inbox filtering rule.

To accomplish this in Microsoft Outlook, you could write a Visual Basic for Applications script that uses the *ExchangeDistributionList* object to enumerate a distribution list, create a new message to each member of the distribution list, attach a standard rich text message, and then automatically send the message. An example you can build from is provided:

```
Dim oDL As Outlook.ExchangeDistributionList
Dim oEU As Outlook.ExchangeUser
Dim oAE As Outlook.AddressEntry
Dim oAEs As Outlook.AddressEntries
Set oDL As <address entry for the DL - can be passed to this routine as a parameter>
Set oAEs = oDL.GetExchangeDistributionListMembers
For Each oAE in oAEs
   If oAE.AddressEntryType <> olExchangeDistributionListAddressEntry then
        Set oEU - oAE.GetExchangeUser
        <Script for sending email to the user goes here>
   Else
        <Recurse to run this script for embedded DLs>
   End If
Next
```

Another option is to use the Mail Merge feature of Microsoft Word 2007 to send to the individuals in the address list. You can personalize your e-mail so that individual addresses and names are included in your message. For more help on using *Exchange-DistributionList*, go to MSDN Outlook 2007 developer's reference at *http://msdn2.microsoft.com/en-us/library/bb176360.aspx*. For more help on using the Mail Merge feature of Microsoft Word 2007, search the Microsoft Word 2007 Help system for "Mail Merge."

Will Martin
Senior Consultant, Microsoft Consulting Services

Documenting Risks

Evaluating and documenting pilot project risks allows you to develop mitigation plans and processes to increase the success potential of the project. Business, technical, and resource risks should be captured at a minimum. A project risk list should be maintained and available to the entire pilot project team. Team members should be encouraged to raise new risks and assist in developing creative ways to mitigate risks.

Table 16-2 provides a list of the minimum items that a project risk list should contain.

Table 16-2   Project Risk Items

Item	Description
Risk Title	Descriptive title for the risk.
Risk Description	Description of the risk.
Probability	Measure of the likelihood that the risk will occur. Typically provided as a percentage or as a value from 1 through 10.
Impact	Estimate of the adverse effects or magnitude of loss if the risk occurs. Typically provided as a value from 1 through 10.
Mitigation Plan	Description of how to minimize or eliminate the risk with a series of tasks. If a mitigation plan is enacted, the project plan should be updated to reflect the tasks involved.
Owner	The owner of the mitigation plan.

Project risks should be maintained and updated in a manner that provides all project members and stakeholders easy access to the risk information. This can be accomplished with a posted Excel spreadsheet or a Web interface.

On the Companion Media To assist in collecting and tracking risks, you will find an Excel spreadsheet in the \Chapter Materials\Job Aids folder called Risk Management JobAid.xls on the companion media. This spreadsheet has a single worksheet that contains columns to collect the recommended risk attributes.

Establishing Project Milestones

Project milestones provide a reality check during the life of the project. Milestones help you answer the question, "How is the project doing?" Milestones vary by project, but they should always be used to measure progress. Milestones should also be considered a validation step in the project. At a minimum, every phase of a virtualization pilot project should have a milestone. You should not proceed to the next phase in a project if the previous phase milestone has not been reached (assuming the project phases are serial in nature). In addition, you cannot proceed to a new project task until a dependency has been met. For example, if you are reusing physical hosts for Virtual Server hosts, you have a dependency on the successful migration of the physical server before you can rebuild it and repurpose it as a Virtual Server host. You could define a milestone as the point in time when the last repurposed physical server has been successfully migrated.

In addition to project phase milestones, validation milestones should be implemented at other key points within a project phase. For example, during the migration phase of the pilot project, you could have a validation milestone after the first 10 percent of the migrations have been completed, to verify that the processes and procedures are working properly.

Establishing Success Criteria

Many projects are completed and considered a success without anyone ever really defining what success is. Success criteria (sometimes called *conditions of satisfaction*) are measurable events or outcomes that the project can be evaluated against. Success criteria should be defined and agreed upon by the executive sponsor before the project begins. This ensures that you are gathering the information required to evaluate the success criteria throughout the project.

Measurability is the key aspect of establishing success criteria. For example, stating the project is a success if *the Virtual Server host has higher utilization* is not measurable. Restated to create a measurable success criteria, the requirement would specify that the project is a success if *the Virtual Server host has an average utilization of 50 percent or higher.*

Success criteria for a virtualization pilot project should include criteria for different phases of the project. You should also have success criteria for project objectives and goals. For example, if you have a goal defined that states "Reduce physical server capital costs by 20 percent," you will have to perform the calculation to determine whether the savings met that goal.

Implementing the Pilot

Implementing the pilot allows you to verify all virtualization project plans and designs while you are accomplishing a subset of the overall project scope. The pilot should be implemented as a scaled version of the overall project to ensure dependencies and potential issues will be identified.

A pilot implementation is also a training opportunity for the production implementation team. If possible, staff the pilot implementation team with the identified key production implementation team members. This approach ensures that when the production begins the key members of the implementation team have experience.

Ensure that the pilot implementation is using the same hardware as the planned production implementation will use. This allows identification of issues and validation of procedures using the production hardware systems.

Measuring Project Success

Based on the defined success criteria, during the pilot you must collect the data that allows you to evaluate the project's success. This task involves both qualitative and quantitative data collection. Quantitative data requires data collection using tools such as VMM and MOM. By creating a report for each quantitative success criterion, you can quickly evaluate the project success and the trending. This helps you identify potential trends of decreasing success, and it helps you to respond to decreasing success by performing a root case analysis to determine how to correct the trend.

Qualitative data requires data collection using tools such as SharePoint surveys to examine the user feedback about how the pilot went. Make sure to survey not only the direct pilot users, but also any user who might have been affected by the pilot project because of things like server downtime or help desk response time. Also, survey the pilot team to determine if they felt the project went smoothly or if they have any suggestions to improve processes, procedures, or methods used in the pilot project.

Incorporating Lessons Learned

Inevitably, something will not go as planned during a pilot project and either a risk mitigation plan is put into action or another action is taken to resolve the problem. The project team analyzes the experience, learns from it, and then modifies the project plans to prevent it from happening in the production implementation. Modifications can take the form of task modification of the project schedule, additional project resources, changes to a process or procedure, or modifying the scope or objectives.

Summary

A pilot virtualization project is a scaled-down version of the production virtualization project. Before the pilot can begin, objectives must be developed, scope must be defined, and pilot architecture must be installed and validated. Planning for a pilot requires the creation of individual plans and procedures for deployment, support, migration, operations, and communications. During planning, you are also increasing project success by creating an issue tracking process, developing a training plan, documenting project risks and mitigations, establishing project milestones, and defining success criteria.

Once you are ready, you can implement the defined plans by establishing the architecture and support processes, migrating the virtualization candidates, and collecting quantitative and qualitative data. Once you have evaluated all the project success criteria against the collected data and all the success criteria have been met or exceeded, you can declare the pilot project a success. Before you implement the production project, you should benefit from the lessons learned during the pilot and modify the processes, procedures, and objectives.

Additional Resources

The following resources contain additional information related to this chapter:

- Microsoft Outlook 2007 Developers Reference, *http://msdn2.microsoft.com/en-us /library/bb177050.aspx*

- Windows Server System Reference Architecture (WSSRA) Virtual Environments for Development and Test *http://www.microsoft.com/downloads /details.aspx?FamilyID=5ce8f01d-a421-4da8-9144-fbaf44e62c34&DisplayLang=en*

- Solution Accelerator for Consolidating and Migrating LOB Applications, *http://www.microsoft.com/technet/solutionaccelerators/ucs/lob/lobsa/default.mspx*

Part IV
Virtual Server Infrastructure Management

In this part:

Chapter 17: Managing a Virtual Server Infrastructure 403

Chapter 18: Using the MOM 2005 Virtual Server 2005 R2
Management Pack 427

Chapter 19: Microsoft System Center Virtual Machine
Manager 2007 451

Chapter 20: Additional Management Tools 481

Chapter 17

Managing a Virtual Server Infrastructure

In this chapter:

Configuring a Centralized Administration Website 403
Managing Virtual Server and Virtual Machine Backups 410
Managing Virtual Server and Virtual Machine Patch Management 418
Monitoring Virtual Server and Virtual Machines 423
Summary 425
Additional Resources 426

In this chapter, you will review core aspects related to the management of a Microsoft Virtual Server 2005 R2 infrastructure. In particular, you will learn how to configure a centralized Virtual Server Administration Website within an Active Directory environment to manage large numbers of Virtual Server hosts. Backup and patch management strategies for both Virtual Server and virtual machines are also covered, with emphasis on special considerations related to a virtualized infrastructure. Additionally, you will gain an understanding of the Windows Management Instrumentation (WMI) objects and counters that can be used to monitor the performance of the Virtual Server host operating system as well as virtual machine guest operating systems.

The material covered in this chapter is focused on using management resources that are either built directly into Virtual Server 2005 R2 or provided by the host operating system. Chapter 18, "Using the MOM 2005 Virtual Server 2005 R2 Management Pack," and Chapter 19, "System Center Virtual Machine Manager 2007," cover additional Microsoft application solutions that integrate into and present significant advantages in the management of an enterprise-class Virtual Server infrastructure.

Configuring a Centralized Administration Website

Any Virtual Server deployment that is composed of multiple hosts controlled by a central administrative team can be managed using a centralized Virtual Server Administration Website. In this configuration, Internet Information Services (IIS) and the Virtual Server Administration Website application (VSWebApp.exe) are installed only on the central management platform. Virtual Server hosts do not install these components; their installation includes only the core Virtual Server services and drivers needed to run virtual machines.

To deploy this configuration in the most secure way using constrained delegation, you must install the Virtual Server Administration Website and Virtual Server hosts in the same Active Directory domain, or in a trusted domain or forest. Several benefits result from this implementation for the Virtual Server hosts:

1. Smaller attack surface, because fewer services are installed

2. Higher performance without the IIS and VSWebApp.exe application overhead

3. Fewer number of updates to install, because of fewer running services

Choosing a Deployment Topology

There are two supported centralized management deployment topologies that provide virtual machine resource file (.vhd, .vmc, .iso, and so on) storage flexibility, each with slightly different configuration options. The first option, shown in Figure 17-1, is to configure a centralized Virtual Server Administration Website, and multiple Virtual Server hosts that store virtual machine resource files on direct-attached storage (DAS), a storage area network (SAN), or other supported storage device.

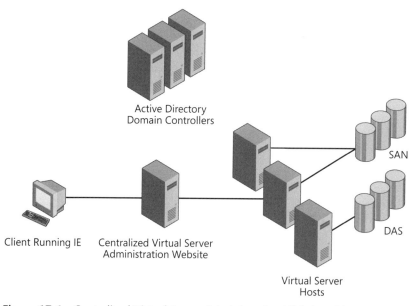

Figure 17-1   Centralized Virtual Server Administration Website with separate Virtual Server hosts topology

In this topology, you can use one of the following options to enable successful authentication and access to distributed Virtual Server resources:

■ Constrained delegation in the Active Directory domain

■ Basic authentication for the Virtual Server Administration Website

By default, the Virtual Server Administration Website is configured to use integrated Windows authentication. If you use basic authentication, you should use it in combination with the Secure Sockets Layer (SSL) protocol to encrypt the authentication data transmitted between the Virtual Server Administration Website and Virtual Server hosts. Otherwise, user names and passwords are transmitted in plain text, creating a serious security risk.

> **Note** For more information on how to configure SSL in IIS, see "How to Implement SSL in IIS" at *http://support.microsoft.com/kb/299875*.

The second option, shown in Figure 17-2, is to configure a centralized Virtual Server Administration Website, multiple Virtual Server hosts, and one or more file servers to store virtual machine resource files. In this case, constrained delegation must be implemented to enable authentication and access to distributed Virtual Server resources.

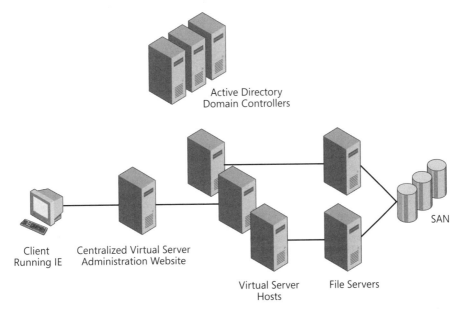

Figure 17-2 Centralized Virtual Server Administration Website with separate Virtual Server hosts and file servers topology

> **Important** Microsoft Windows Vista and Windows XP do not support constrained delegation. Therefore, you cannot use these as host platforms for a centralized Virtual Server Administration Website.

For both topologies, when using constrained delegation, the Virtual Server Administration Website application (VSWebApp.exe) must be configured to execute under the context of the Local System. Figure 17-3 shows the option presented during the Virtual Server Administration Website application installation on Windows Server 2003. This option is not presented when you install on Windows XP or Windows Vista because neither platform supports constrained delegation.

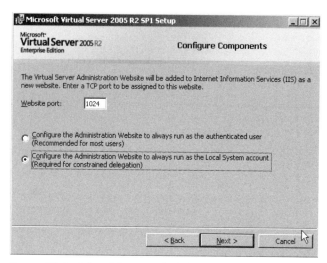

Figure 17-3   Virtual Server Administration Website application installation under the Local System account context

Configuring Constrained Delegation

With constrained delegation, you can configure computer or service accounts to perform Kerberos delegation to a limited set of services running on remote servers. Windows Server 2003 implements the Allowed-to-Delegate-to (A2D2) Active Directory attribute for service accounts to enforce constrained delegation. The A2D2 attribute contains a list of service principal names (SPNs) to which a given service account can perform delegation. When a Windows Server 2003 Kerberos Key Distribution Center (KDC) processes a service ticket request using constrained delegation, the KDC verifies that the target SPN is listed in the A2D2 attribute before issuing the service ticket to the requesting server.

In a Virtual Server infrastructure, as shown in Figure 17-4, this process allows user credentials to be passed from the Administration Website to a Virtual Server host and, if necessary, to a file server hosting the virtual machine resource files. It also allows access to remote Virtual Server services and files.

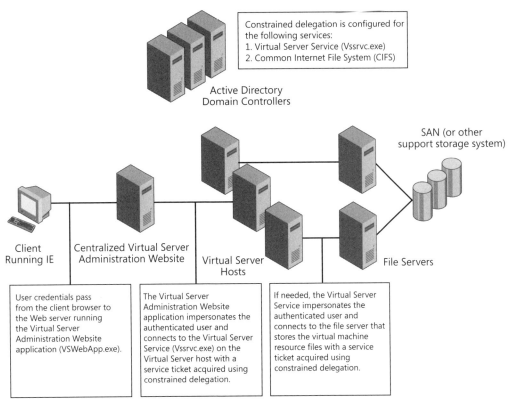

Constrained delegation is configured for
the following services:
1. Virtual Server Service (Vssrvc.exe)
2. Common Internet File System (CIFS)

Active Directory
Domain Controllers

SAN (or other
support storage system)

Client
Running IE

Centralized Virtual Server
Administration Website

Virtual Server
Hosts

File Servers

User credentials pass
from the client browser to
the Web server running
the Virtual Server
Administration Website
application (VSWebApp.exe).

The Virtual Server
Administration Website
application impersonates the
authenticated user and
connects to the Virtual Server
Service (Vssrvc.exe) on the
Virtual Server host with a
service ticket acquired using
constrained delegation.

If needed, the Virtual Server
Service impersonates the
authenticated user and
connects to the file server that
stores the virtual machine
resource files with a service
ticket acquired using
constrained delegation.

Figure 17-4   Using constrained delegation in a Virtual Server infrastructure

Because constrained delegation is a feature that was first introduced in Windows Server 2003,
it is available only if the Active Directory domain is in Windows Server 2003 functional level.
If you have pre-Windows Server 2003 domain controllers deployed, you will not be able to
raise the functional level of your Active Directory domain to Windows Server 2003 until these
legacy domain controllers are upgraded to Windows Server 2003. Once your domain is raised
to the Windows Server 2003 functional level, you can proceed with the constrained delegation configuration.

Figure 17-5 shows constrained delegation enabled for the Common Internet File System
(CIFS) service and the Virtual Server service (Vssrvc.exe) between a centralized Virtual Server
Administration Website server and a Virtual Server host.

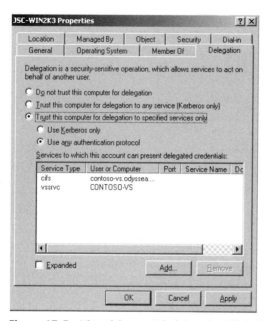

Figure 17-5 Virtual Server Administration Website constrained delegation configuration

Follow these steps to configure constrained delegation on the Virtual Server Administration Website server:

1. On a domain controller, open Active Directory Users And Computers.

2. In the console tree, under the domain name, click Computers.

3. Right-click the server running the Virtual Server Administration Website, and then click Properties.

4. On the Delegation tab, select the Trust This Computer For Delegation To Specified Services Only option.

5. Select the Use Any Authentication Protocol option.

6. Click Add, and then click Users And Computers.

7. Type the name of the Virtual Server host that is running the Virtual Server service, and then click OK.

8. From the list of available services, select cifs and vssrvc and then click OK.

9. Repeat steps 7 and 8 to enable delegation to additional Virtual Server hosts.

If you store virtual machine resource files on one or more separate file servers, you also need to enable constrained delegation for the CIFS service between Virtual Server hosts and file servers, as shown in Figure 17-6.

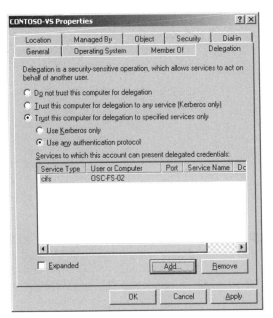

Figure 17-6   Virtual Server host constrained delegation configuration

Follow these steps to configure constrained delegation on the Administration Website server:

1.   On a domain controller, open Active Directory Users and Computers.

2.   In the console tree, under the domain name, click Computers

3.   Right-click the Virtual Server host, and then click Properties.

4.   On the Delegation tab, select the Trust This Computer For Delegation To Specified Services Only option.

5.   Select the Use Any Authentication Protocol option.

6.   Click Add, and then click Users And Computers.

7.   Type the name of the file server on which the virtual machine resources files are stored, and then click OK.

8.   From the list of available services, select cifs and then click OK.

9.   Repeat steps 7 and 8 to enable delegation to additional file servers.

Configuring the Virtual Server Manager Search Paths

When you have completed the constrained delegation configuration for each Virtual Server host that you want to manage, you can add each one into the Virtual Server Manager search paths. This will create a list of Virtual Server hosts that you can select to manage from the Virtual Server Manager link in the navigation pane of the Administration Website.

Follow these steps to configure the Virtual Server Manager search paths:

1. Open the Virtual Server Administration Website.

2. In the Virtual Server navigation pane, select Website Properties.

3. In the Virtual Server Manager Search Paths section, type in the fully qualified name or IP address for each Virtual Server host on a separate line.

4. Click OK.

Because these settings are client specific, they are stored in a cookie on the client computer. Therefore, if you access the Administration Website from multiple client computers, you will have to repeat the Virtual Server Manager search paths configuration on each of them.

Managing Virtual Server and Virtual Machine Backups

A virtualization environment requires the same attention to backup planning as a physical environment, with additional focus on dependencies related to the virtualization layer. As opposed to a physical server whose internal system resource usage does not directly affect the performance of another physical server workload, a virtual machine shares a single set of physical hardware with other virtual machines, creating the potential for virtual machines to affect the performance and workloads of one another. Therefore, a Virtual Server backup strategy must emphasize a virtual machine backup schedule that minimizes the impact on performance and application availability.

In addition, when dealing with a single physical server, backup scope involves only the individual server. In a virtualized environment, the backup scope might include the Virtual Server host as well as virtual machines. Therefore, a Virtual Server backup strategy has to further balance the backup schedule for the virtual machines with that of the Virtual Server host.

In reality, the backup method is paramount to developing a successful strategy for a virtualized environment. If you can leverage the Volume Shadow Copy Service (VSS) and the new Virtual Server VSS writer interface to perform Virtual Server and virtual machine backups, you can implement a fairly straightforward backup strategy. However, if you have to use traditional backup methods for your virtualized environment, you significantly increase the complexity of your backup strategy.

Understanding the Virtual Server VSS Writer

Virtual Server 2005 R2 SP1 enables a new backup method using the included Virtual Server VSS writer interface. Generically, a VSS writer is an interface provided by an application to manage data and state information, ensuring that pending data is flushed to disk and the application is quiescent prior to initializing a volume shadow copy. An application is quiescent after it commits buffers or data held in memory to disk, and ensures that no further data can be written to a volume until the volume shadow copy is complete. This procedure is necessary to provide a consistent application state prior to performing the backup.

Without a VSS writer interface, an application can still be backed up using VSS. However, application state consistency cannot be guaranteed, and therefore, neither can the backup. This is the case for versions of Virtual Server prior to SP1. Virtual machines can be backed up using VSS, but restoring a VSS snapshot is equivalent to turning off a virtual machine and then turning the machine back on, losing all state information for applications and services, and losing all data stored in memory.

The Virtual Server VSS writer, which is implemented within the Virtual Machine Helper service, is provided with both 32-bit and 64-bit versions of Virtual Server 2005 R2 SP1. The Virtual Server VSS writer offers the following functionality:

- Backup and recovery of Virtual Server 2005 R2 SP1 and all configuration settings

- Online backup of Windows Server 2003 or later version virtual machines when Virtual Server 2005 R2 SP1 virtual machine additions are installed

- Offline backup for all supported virtual machine guest operating systems if Virtual Server 2005 R2 SP1 virtual machine additions are not installed

- Recovery of individual virtual machines to the same Virtual Server host or different Virtual Server host

The Virtual Server VSS writer does not provide the following functionality:

- Online backup of Windows Server 2003 or later versions if Virtual Server 2005 R2 SP1 virtual machine additions are not installed

- Online backup of virtual machines running operating systems other than Windows

- Online backup of virtual machines with FAT or FAT32 volumes

- Incremental backups (only full backups are supported)

- Backup of virtual machines with remotely stored virtual hard disks

- Backup of virtual machines with an iSCSI provider loaded in the guest operating system and connected to iSCSI disks

Direct from the Source: Virtual Server VSS Writer Tools

To use the Virtual Server VSS writer, a VSS requestor is required. The Volume Shadow Copy Service SDK, available for free from the Microsoft Download Center, contains two test applications that implement a VSS requestor interface. BETest and VShadow are excellent applications to highlight the functionality of the Virtual Server VSS writer and perform backup and recovery in a test environment. Windows Server 2008 will include a command-line tool called DiskShadow, an application that uses the VSS API to perform backups and shadow copies. DiskShadow is a complete VSS requestor that allows a user to enumerate all active VSS writers and their components, VSS providers, and shadow copies, or perform a VSS writer-based shadow copy of a set of volumes. To use DiskShadow, you can execute a script or use a command-line interface. DiskShadow also has some advanced features like exposing a shadow copy to the local file system and reverting a volume to a shadow copy.

Michael Michael
Senior Software Design Engineer, Windows Server Division

Using VSS to Back Up Virtual Server and Virtual Machines

Using the new Virtual Server VSS writer interface, backing up a Virtual Server environment becomes a much more straightforward process than in the past. However, before implementing a VSS-based backup strategy, you must ensure that your environment meets the requirements presented in Table 17-1, which are dependent on the target VSS backup scenario. The available VSS backup scenarios include the following:

- Virtual Server backup (including configuration information)
- Virtual machine online backup
- Virtual machine offline backup

Note   Backing up the Virtual Server configuration information is of particular importance because it stores data such as the registration of all the virtual machines and virtual networks, and licensing information. Without this information, Virtual Server cannot operate and neither can the virtual machines.

Table 17-1 Requirements and Affected VSS Backup Scenario

Requirement	Description	Scenario
Windows Server 2003 SP1 and later	Virtual Server host operating system needed to support VSS backup operations using the Virtual Server VSS writer.	All
Virtual Server 2005 R2 SP1	Virtual Server version that includes the Virtual Server VSS writer.	All
A backup application (VSS requestor) with knowledge of the Virtual Server VSS writer	The backup application must have been developed to interface with the Virtual Server VSS writer.	All
Virtual machines resource files on local storage	VSS functions only with locally stored data.	Virtual machine online and offline backups
Windows Server 2003 with Virtual Server 2005 R2 SP1 virtual machine additions	Virtual machine guest operating system configuration.	Virtual machine online backup

Virtual Server VSS Backup Process

Figure 17-7 shows the components involved in the Virtual Server VSS backup process. Overall, the VSS service is the communications broker between the VSS requester, VSS writer, and VSS provider. The VSS requestor makes requests to the VSS service to enumerate available VSS writers and requests shadow copies. The VSS provider creates and maintains volume shadow copies.

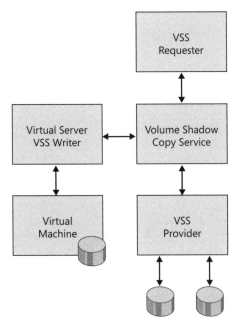

Figure 17-7   Volume shadow copy process components

The following is a step-by-step description of how the components pictured in Figure 17-7 interface to perform a Virtual Server VSS-based volume shadow copy:

1. The VSS requestor (backup application) requests a list of VSS writers from VSS.

2. The VSS requestor selects the Virtual Server VSS writer and requests backup metadata that lists the configuration and volume information.

3. The Virtual Server VSS writer gathers the metadata information and sends the information to VSS to provide to the VSS requestor.

4. The VSS requestor uses the metadata to select the configuration information, volumes, and virtual machines to back up.

5. VSS notifies the Virtual Server VSS writer to initiate preparation for shadow copy execution.

6. The Virtual Server VSS writer notifies all running virtual machines to flush all buffers and caches. When this has been completed, the Virtual Server VSS writer informs VSS that it is ready.

7. VSS notifies the Virtual Server VSS writer to proceed into the commit shadow copy phase.

8. The Virtual Server VSS writer informs the virtual machines to quiesce all data, buffers, and caches and then temporarily freezes all write requests. (Reads are still valid.)

9. VSS flushes the file system–level buffer and freezes the file system.

10. VSS informs the VSS provider to create the shadow copy (which takes only a few seconds).

11. The VSS provider responds to VSS that it successfully created the shadow copy.

12. VSS unfreezes the file system and informs the Virtual Server VSS writer to also unfreeze.

13. The Virtual Server VSS writer re-enables writes, and all pending write I/Os are performed.

14. VSS verifies that all queued writes from all writers were successful.

15. If everything is nominal, VSS provides a shadow copy pointer to the VSS requestor.

16. The VSS requestor backs up the configuration and virtual machines from the shadow copy.

17. The VSS requestor saves a copy of the Virtual Server VSS writer metadata in an XML file for future restore operations.

Virtual Server VSS Writer Metadata Document

In order for the VSS requestor to use the VSS application programming interface (API) to accomplish a valid shadow copy, it requires detailed information concerning what should be included in the shadow copy, where the information is currently stored, and the volumes on which it resides. The mechanism for this information to be transferred from the VSS writers to the VSS requestor is the metadata document.

The Virtual Server VSS writer metadata document includes the following information:

- Virtual Server VSS writer GUID and friendly name
- Virtual Server configuration file information
- Virtual machine configuration and component file information
- Backup scenario supported for each virtual machine (online or offline)

The metadata document is actually a set of information gathered using the VSS and VSS writer APIs, and stored by the VSS requestor as an XML document for use in future restore operations. The XML document includes the following information:

- Identification section to identify the VSS writer that provided the metadata
- Restore method section that details how the restore should be performed and if a reboot will be required
- Online backup section that details all virtual machines that can be backed up in the online scenario
- Offline backup section that details all virtual machines that can be backed up in the offline scenario
- Virtual Server configuration section that details all the configuration files that should be backed up to restore the Virtual Server configuration

Note   The backup application, not the Virtual Server VSS writer, provides the backup granularity, whether it includes the entire volume on which virtual machines are stored or just the actual virtual machine files. The metadata document provides all required configuration and path information.

Using Traditional Methods to Back Up Virtual Server and Virtual Machines

If a VSS-based backup cannot be implemented in your environment, you can still use traditional backup methods to ensure that you can recover from a Virtual Server host or virtual machine failure. In addition to backing up the Virtual Server host, you must back up the files that make up each virtual machine configuration. A virtual machine consists of a configuration file and one or more data files. Some of them are permanent—such as virtual hard disks (VHDs) and the virtual machine configuration file (.vmc), which maintains the virtual environment settings, resource allocation, and special features configuration—and some of them are transient, such as undo disks.

A traditional backup method for a physical server is to use a backup application that installs an agent in the operating system. Agent-based backup applications typically provide extensive granularity in choosing the backup set and allow backing up data across the network. This backup method can also be used for a virtual machine by installing the agent in the guest operating system. An important benefit is the ability to perform a backup while the virtual machine is online.

Because a virtual machine consists of a portable set of files that can easily be moved between servers, another option is to perform a file-based backup that includes all associated virtual machine files: the virtual machine configuration file (.vmc), the virtual hard disks (.vhd), the save state file (.vsv), and any undo disk file (.vud). This backup method does not require the installation of any additional software. However, a virtual machine backup can be performed only while the virtual machine is powered off or in a saved state. If a backup was attempted while the virtual machine remained powered on and the virtual machine files were in an open state, some files might fail to be captured while others might be corrupted.

Table 17-2 provides a comparison of the agent-based and file-based backup methods. If your environment supports a regular schedule to take virtual machines offline to perform faster virtual machine backups, you can implement a file-based backup method. If your environment requires maximum virtual machine uptime, you can implement an agent-based backup method.

Table 17-2   Backup Methods Comparison

Consideration	File-Based Backup	Agent-Based Backup
Virtual machine state	Offline—powered off or in a saved state.	Online.
Backup speed	Faster—Fewer larger files.	Slower—More smaller files.
Backup of special files	More flexible—This method can capture all virtual machine–related files (.vhd, .vmc, .vsv, .vud).	Less flexible—The agent installed inside the virtual machine is unaware of other virtual machine files.
Backup overhead	Lower—The backup runs at the Virtual Server host operating system level with the virtual machine offline.	Higher—The agent is installed and runs inside each virtual machine. Therefore, there is an impact on virtualization.
Restore speed	Slower—If the virtual machine uses only 10 GB of a 100-GB VHD, the entire 100 GB is restored.	Faster—If the virtual machine uses only 10 GB of a 100-GB VHD, only 10 GB is restored.
Restore options	Less flexible—This method can restore only entire files.	More flexible—This method can restore partitions, directories, or individual files.

Table 17-2 **Backup Methods Comparison**

Consideration	File-Based Backup	Agent-Based Backup
Automation	More flexible—Backup automation can be easily scripted and modified using the Virtual Server COM API.	Less flexible—Backup automation is controlled by the application.

More Info   System Center Data Protection Manager 2007 (DPM) includes support for host-based backup of virtual machines running on Virtual Server 2005 R2. DPM uses a single host-based agent to provide application-consistent backups of virtual machine guests on a Virtual Server host. DPM can be used to back up virtual machines running any operating system or applications.

Backing Up an Active Directory Domain Controller Virtual Machine

There are special considerations to take into account when defining a backup strategy for an Active Directory domain controller running in a virtual machine. Basically, Active Directory domain controllers should be backed up only using an application that properly interfaces with Active Directory during backup and restore operations. Because Active Directory is transactional in nature, the backup application must ensure that the data backup represents a consistent database state. By default, when restoring a domain controller, the backup application must modify the Active Directory database version to indicate that it was restored from backup and that it must acquire the latest updates from its replication partners.

In particular, Windows 2000 Server and Windows Server 2003 domain controllers use update sequence numbers (USNs) to track updates originating from the local domain controller. Each domain controller uses USNs to track the latest originating update it has received from each source replication partner, as well as the status of every other domain controller that stores a replica of the directory partition. When a domain controller is restored following a failure, it queries its replication partners for updates with USNs larger than the USNs in its records.

In addition to using USNs for tracking, domain controllers keep track of source replication partner directory database identities through the *invocationID* attribute of the NTDS Settings object. When a domain controller is properly restored, the *invocationID* is reset and replicated to all domain controllers in the forest. Domain controllers in the forest also update their USNs to match the highest USNs of the restored domain controller. The combination of the new *invocationID* and the USN updates allows replication to properly originate from the restored domain controller.

Both the Virtual Server VSS writer and agent-based backup applications developed to support Active Directory can be used to perform backup and restore operations of domain controllers. When the Active Directory VSS writer is triggered before a VSS shadow copy is made, a flag is set in the Active Directory database to indicate that it is in a backup state. The Active Directory database quiesces, disk write operations are frozen, and the VSS shadow copy completes. Subsequently, the flag setting is changed to indicate that the Active Directory database is in a running state. Starting with Windows Server 2003, an Active Directory database restored in a backup state resets the *invocationID* to allow proper replication to take place.

In contrast, virtual machine file-based backup and restore operations do not take into consideration the USN and *invocationID* updates that must be propagated to the domain controller replication partners to maintain a consistent Active Directory environment.

Important For the reasons just listed, the virtual machine file-based backup method should *never* be used for backup and restore operations associated with *production* Active Directory domain controllers.

However, in a test and development environment, where you want to maintain a specific configuration of an Active Directory environment, the file-based backup method can be used to accomplish this goal. The key is that you must "freeze" the environment (suspend Active Directory changes) and perform a file-based backup of all domain controller virtual machines at the same time to maintain the integrity of the test scenario. Consequently, you must restore all domain controller virtual machine backups from the same backup data set to set up a new consistent Active Directory environment.

Note The details of the way the replication system tracks directory changes, the process of recovery following a restore procedure, and the operating system changes that protect against inappropriate replication are described in the "Running a Domain Controller in Virtual Server 2005" white paper, available at *http://www.microsoft.com/downloads/details.aspx?FamilyID= 64DB845D-F7A3-4209-8ED2-E261A117FC6B&displaylang=en*.

Managing Virtual Server and Virtual Machine Patch Management

Patch management is a crucial component to enhance the security and performance of physical and virtual machine environments. Although you can use Microsoft Software Update Service (SUS), Microsoft Systems Management Server (SMS), Microsoft System Center Configuration Manager (SCCM), or other third-party applications to perform patch management in both physical and virtualized environments, standard procedures must be adapted to perform patch management for a virtualized infrastructure.

Extending a Patch Management Strategy for Virtualized Environments

Extending a patch management strategy to include a virtualized environment requires adapting structured plans and processes to mitigate the risk and downtime associated with the installation of updates on Virtual Server hosts and virtual machines. Following are the two major steps that you need to undertake:

- Identify key issues and challenges that affect existing procedures.

- Define patch management procedures for Virtual Server hosts and virtual machines.

Identifying Key Issues and Challenges

In most instances, Virtual Server hosts and virtual machines can be treated much the same way as their physical counterparts. However, Table 17-3 provides a list of common issues and challenges that must be accounted for when defining patch management procedures in a virtualized environment. This list does not cover issues and challenges related to any specific patch management solution; rather, these items are intrinsic to virtualized environments. You should perform a thorough assessment of deployed Virtual Server hosts and virtual machines, identify any additional problems inherent to your specific environment, and address them in your patch management procedures.

Table 17-3   Common Patch Management Issues and Challenges

Issue/Challenge	Description
Virtual Server host updates	A Virtual Server host that requires a reboot after installation of an update affects the availability and downtime of virtual machines running on that host.
Virtual machine is connected to internal virtual network	A virtual machine can be executing but connected only to an internal virtual network.
Virtual machine is powered off	A virtual machine used for test and development or other purposes might be powered off for long periods of time.
Undo disks	A virtual machine can be configured with undo disks enabled, and updates can be lost if undo disks are discarded.
Test environment	A test environment might require that updates not be installed on certain virtual machines to maintain a specific functionality or configuration state.
Impact on performance	Virtual machines on the same host can have a significant impact on performance if updated concurrently.

Addressing Key Issues and Challenges

Before you can define robust patch management procedures for your virtualized environment, you must determine how to mitigate or resolve the issues and challenges previously identified. Here are recommendations on addressing the common issues and challenges presented in Table 17-3.

Virtual Server Host Updates   If an update or service pack is installed on a Virtual Server host, there is a possibility that a reboot will be required to complete the update of affected files. If the updates are not critical, you can delay the reboot, but eventually the Virtual Server host will need to be restarted. During this time, applications running in virtual machines will be unavailable and end users will be affected.

Coordinating the timing of updates to the virtual machines and Virtual Server host is critical to reducing downtime. When scheduling common updates that require a reboot, you should first update all affected virtual machines, shut down all virtual machines, update the Virtual Server host, and then reboot the Virtual Server host and power on all the virtual machines.

Virtual Machine Is Connected to Internal Virtual Network   A virtual machine that has limited or no connectivity to the production network cannot be updated using a standard solution. There are two options to resolve this issue. The first option involves using the physical server CD or DVD to copy the required updates onto the virtual machine and executing the updates. The second approach involves installing a patch management solution such as SUS in a virtual machine that is connected to both the internal virtual network and the production network. The SUS application can download new updates using the production network and distribute them to the isolated virtual machine using the internal virtual network.

Virtual Machine Is Powered Off   At this point in time, there is no way to update a virtual machine while it is powered off or in a saved state. Although it is possible to use VHDMount to mount a virtual machine VHD on the Virtual Server host while it is powered off to obtain access to the directory structure, current Microsoft update technology requires a running virtual machine.

To update a virtual machine that is powered off or in a saved state, you must be able to identify it from an inventory of virtual machines maintained using an application such as Microsoft Systems Management Server (SMS) 2003 SP1 (or later), or any other tool or script that can compile a list of registered virtual machines and identify those that are powered off. Once you have a list of virtual machines that are powered off, you can use another custom script to power on the virtual machine, initiate updates, and power off the virtual machine when the process completes.

Undo Disks   A virtual machine with undo disks enabled allows you to commit or discard changes that occur between power-on and power-off states. If you apply updates while the virtual machine is running and then discard the changes, all installed updates will be lost.

Installing updates in this type of scenario requires committing the updates to the VHDs. The best process to do this is to start from a fresh power-on session, immediately install the required updates, and then commit the changes to the virtual hard disk. Once you follow these procedures, the updates are integrated into the virtual machine and will be present for all future sessions.

Test Environment   A test environment is generally designed to verify application functionality, compatibility, performance, and scalability. This usually means that different versions of a service pack or hotfix might be required on multiple test machines. To maintain various revisions of updates and service packs that are applied to a common baseline configuration, use differencing drives. The baseline configuration can be created in a read-only VHD that is used as the parent VHD to one or more child differencing drives attached to new virtual machines. Each virtual machine can then be updated to the individually required level, with the changes affecting only the associated differencing drive.

In addition, a test environment usually supports update verification and validation prior to deployment in production environments. This typically requires the implementation of a separate patch management solution for the test lab or a set of dedicated machines that are isolated from the production patch management solution.

Impact on Performance   Updating multiple virtual machines on a single host machine concurrently can have an impact on performance. This performance impact can affect the machines being updated, lengthening the time it takes to install updates and affecting available resources for unrelated production workloads. To prevent updates from having a negative impact on performance, the distribution of updates to virtual machines running on the same Virtual Server host should be performed serially.

Defining Patch Management Procedures

When deploying updates in a virtualized environment, you must address the issues discussed in the previous section with the objective to reduce risks and effects that could result in unnecessary downtime. Figure 17-8 shows a diagram view of the recommended update deployment process for a Virtual Server host and virtual machines.

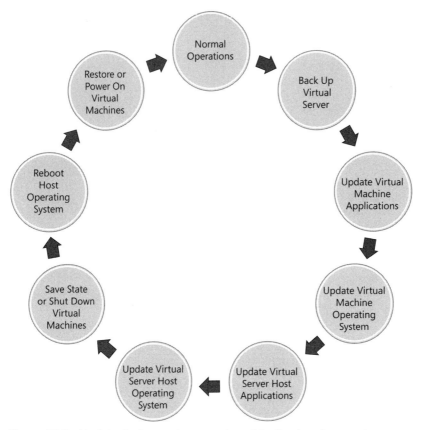

Figure 17-8   Update deployment process in a virtualized environment

The following deployment process provides a step-by-step process for deploying a set of updates to a Virtual Server host and associated virtual machines:

1. Install updates on the applications running in virtual machines.

2. Install updates on the virtual machine operating system that do not require the system to reboot.

3. Install updates on the virtual machine operating system that require reboot, but defer the reboot.

4. Install updates on the applications running on the Virtual Server Host.

5. Install updates on the Virtual Server host operating system that do not require the system to reboot.

6. Install updates on the Virtual Server host operating system that require the system to reboot, but defer the reboot.

7. Power down all virtual machines that have a pending reboot.

8. Save the state of all remaining virtual machines.

9. Reboot the Virtual Server host.

10. Power on all the virtual machines in a staged manner. First restore the virtual machines that are in a saved state, and then start up the virtual machines that are powered off.

Monitoring Virtual Server and Virtual Machines

Monitoring the performance of Virtual Server, virtual machines, and virtual machine workloads is another crucial aspect of maintaining your virtualized infrastructure. Monitoring performance data helps to do the following:

- Understand workload profiles and resource usage trends so that you can perform capacity planning.

- Determine how to tune resources to achieve better workload performance.

- Diagnose issues and identify problem components.

Standard performance tools, such as the Windows Server 2003 System Monitor or Performance Logs and Alerts, and more sophisticated third-party applications developed to monitor a traditional physical infrastructure are just as applicable to monitoring the performance of a Virtual Server host operating system and virtual machine guest operating systems.

To specifically monitor the performance of virtual machines and virtual networks, Virtual Server 2005 R2 provides the Virtual Server Windows Management Instrumentation (WMI) class. The Virtual Server WMI class exposes two objects, *VirtualMachine* and *VirtualNetwork*, each with their own set of counters. Table 17-4 lists the *VirtualMachine* WMI object counters that allow you to monitor processor, disk, memory, network, heartbeat, and uptime characteristics.

Table 17-4 *VirtualMachine* WMI Object Counters

Counter	Description
CpuUtilization	Percentage of processor resources allocated to a virtual machine that are currently in use. A zero indicates that a virtual machine might not be running. A 100 indicates that a virtual machine is consuming all currently allocated processor resources.
DiskBytesRead	Number of bytes read by all virtual hard disks attached to a virtual machine since the virtual machine was last powered on.
DiskSpaceUsed	Total disk space used by all virtual hard disks attached to a virtual machine.
DiskBytesWritten	Number of bytes written by all virtual hard disks attached to a virtual machine.

Table 17-4   *VirtualMachine* **WMI Object Counters**

Counter	Description
HeartbeatCount	Number of heartbeats received since the virtual machine was last powered on.
HeartbeatInterval	The heartbeat interval period in seconds.
HeartbeatPercentage	Percentage of total expected heartbeats received during the last heartbeat interval. A HeartbeatPercentage of zero might indicate a problem with the guest operating system. A number greater than zero but less than 100 might indicate that a heavy input/output (I/O) load is causing the heartbeat not to transmit.
HeartbeatRate	The number of heartbeats expected per heartbeat interval.
NetworkBytesSent	Total bytes transmitted through all virtual networks connected to a virtual machine since the virtual machine was last powered on.
NetworkBytesReceived	Total bytes received through all virtual networks connected to a virtual machine since the virtual machine was last powered on.
PhysicalMemoryAllocated	The physical memory allocated to a virtual machine. The allocation includes 4 MB of video RAM (VRAM), but it does not include the additional 32 MB of "overhead" memory used by each virtual machine. If a virtual machine is performing poorly or "swapping" and additional RAM is available, increase the physical memory allocation.
Uptime	Number of seconds that a virtual machine has been running since it was last powered on.

Because the *VirtualMachine* WMI object counters do not provide cumulative totals for all running virtual machines, you have to use a monitoring tool that can compile the data, manually compile the data, or script the capture and compilation of the desired cumulative data.

Table 17-5 lists the *VirtualNetwork* WMI object counters that allow you to monitor the transmission characteristics of a virtual network that is connected to a physical network adapter and has one or more active virtual machine connections.

Table 17-5   *VirtualNetwork* **WMI Object Counters**

Counter	Description
Name	Name of the physical network adapter attached to a virtual network.
BytesDropped	Number of bytes dropped by a virtual network. Any number above zero indicates a virtual network issue.

Table 17-5 *VirtualNetwork* WMI Object Counters

Counter	Description
BytesReceived	Total bytes received by a virtual network since the first connected virtual machine was powered on.
BytesSent	Total bytes sent by a virtual network since the first connected virtual machine was powered on.
PacketsDropped	Number of data packets dropped by a virtual network. Any number above zero indicates a virtual network issue.
PacketsReceived	Total number of data packets received by a virtual network since the first connected virtual machine was powered on.
PacketsSent	Total number of data packets sent by a virtual network since the first connected virtual machine was powered on.

You should monitor your virtualized infrastructure using the same methods and procedures as you do in your physical environment. You can use the physical workload performance baseline captured prior to the virtual machine migration to evaluate the performance delta. With this data, you can determine whether additional resources must be allocated to the virtual machine workload; whether it must be moved to a Virtual Server host with a more powerful processor, more memory, and larger storage systems; and in very rare cases, whether the workload should be migrated back out of a virtual machine and onto a physical server.

Summary

Secure, centralized management of a Virtual Server infrastructure in an Active Directory domain using the Administration Website requires using constrained delegation. Constrained delegation supports virtual machine resource file storage on the Virtual Server host where the virtual machine is registered, as well as on one or more separate file servers.

With the introduction of the Virtual Server VSS writer in Virtual Server 2005 R2 SP1, VSS-based backup applications can be used to greatly simplify and reduce the time needed to back up Virtual Server hosts and virtual machines. If VSS-based backups are not possible, traditional backup methods (using either an agent-based application or file-based method) can still be used. Remember to never use file-based backups for Active Directory domain controllers. A rigorous procedure must be followed to back up and restore Active Directory domain controllers in order to avoid collapsing the replication topology and corrupting the Active Directory database.

Standard patch management procedures must be modified to support a virtualized environment. Because of the high degree of linkage between Virtual Server hosts and virtual machines, patch management procedures must be properly scheduled to minimize risk and downtime. In addition, updates that require a reboot must be installed using a very structured method to avoid performing multiple reboots.

Finally, performance monitoring differs little between a physical and virtualized infrastructure. However, specific Virtual Server WMI counters are required to capture the performance of virtual machines and virtual networks. Performance monitoring is critical to establish Virtual Server host and virtual machine performance baselines, to perform capacity planning, and to assist in performance tuning and troubleshooting.

Additional Resources

The following resources contain additional information related to the topics in this chapter:

- Microsoft Virtual Server Partners Web site at *http://go.microsoft.com/fwlink /?LinkId=83112*

- VSS backup process overview at *http://msdn2.microsoft.com/en-us/library /aa384589.aspx*

- Running a Domain Controller in Virtual Server 2005 at *http://www.microsoft.com/downloads /details.aspx?FamilyID=64DB845D-F7A3-4209-8ED2-E261A117FC6B&displaylang=en*

- System Center Configuration Manager Web site, *http://www.microsoft.com/smserver /default.mspx*

- Volume Shadow Copy Service SDK at *http://www.microsoft.com/downloads /details.aspx?FamilyID=0b4f56e4-0ccc-4626-826a-ed2c4c95c871&DisplayLang=en*

Chapter 18

Using the MOM 2005 Virtual Server 2005 R2 Management Pack

In this chapter:

Understanding the Virtual Server 2005 R2 Management Pack 427

Installing the Virtual Server 2005 R2 Management Pack 433

Monitoring Virtual Server Hosts and Virtual Machines. 436

Summary. 450

Additional Resources. 450

This chapter contains the information you need to install, manage, and monitor a Virtual Server infrastructure using the Microsoft Operations Manager (MOM) 2005 Virtual Server 2005 R2 Management Pack. You will learn how the Microsoft Virtual Server 2005 R2 Management Pack can assist you to centrally monitor the performance and health of your Virtual Server infrastructure. In addition, you will discover how to use Virtual Server 2005 R2 Management Pack reports to identify physical servers that are candidates for migration to a virtual machine and which Virtual Server hosts have the resources to meet the performance requirements to deploy a new virtual machine. Finally, you will learn how the Virtual Server 2005 R2 Management Pack can assist you in planning to rebalance virtual machine workloads across Virtual Server hosts to optimize performance.

Understanding the Virtual Server 2005 R2 Management Pack

The Virtual Server 2005 R2 Management Pack is an optional component that is imported onto a MOM Management Server. A MOM Management Server controls access to the MOM database; manages the installation, configuration, and data collection for MOM agents; and commits MOM agent data to the MOM database. The MOM Management Server provides a central management point that allows MOM configuration tasks (deploy agents, create new tasks, and so on) to be managed separately from the operations tasks (review and resolve alerts, control virtual machine state, and so on).

MOM configuration tasks are performed using the Administrator Console shown in Figure 18-1. The Administrator Console is the primary user interface to configure and administer the MOM environment. Actions performed using the Administrator Console include deploying MOM agents, creating logical computer monitoring groups, creating new tasks, and importing new Management Packs and reports onto the MOM Management Server, to name just a few.

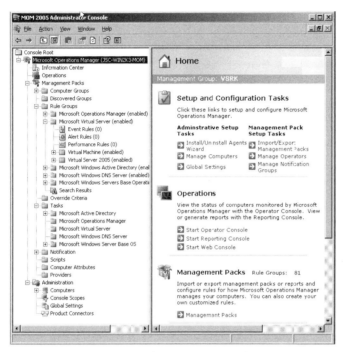

Figure 18-1   MOM 2005 Administrator Console

In contrast, MOM operations tasks are performed using the Operator Console shown in Figure 18-2. The MOM Operator Console is the primary user interface to view and manipulate monitoring data. The data collected through MOM agents is compiled and processed to present state, alerts, events, performance data, and machine relationship diagrams. The Operator Console also provides an interface to run predefined tasks against specified machines.

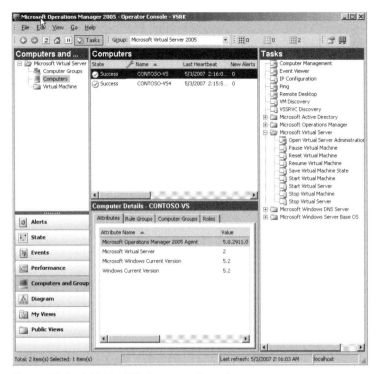

Figure 18-2   MOM 2005 Operator Console

MOM 2005 basic monitoring features are enhanced by importing application-specific Management Packs that define how a MOM Management Server collects, handles, and responds to data gathered from application instances. Some key items that a Management Pack defines are entities to manage (and their relationships), management rules, scripts, groups, data views, tasks, and a knowledge base that assists you to correct known application issues.

More Info   Microsoft System Center Operations Manager (SCOM) 2007, the latest version of the management application, was released in March 2007. You can import the Microsoft Virtual Server 2005 R2 Management Pack into SCOM 2007 after installing the MOM 2005 Backward Compatibility Management Pack. A new Server Virtualization Management Pack is also planned for release in the same timeframe as System Center Virtual Machine Manager.

Microsoft Virtual Server 2005 R2 Management Pack Features

The Virtual Server 2005 R2 Management Pack supports Virtual Server 2005 and Virtual Server 2005 R2 hosts, as well as their virtual machines. Once you import and configure the Virtual Server 2005 R2 Management Pack on a MOM Management Server, you can use it to monitor the Virtual Server hosts and virtual machine parameters listed in Table 18-1.

Table 18-1   Virtual Server 2005 R2 Management Pack Monitoring

Component	Description
Virtual Server State	■ Monitors Virtual Server state using the Virtual Server service status, virtual machines state, and unresolved error and warning alerts generated by the Virtual Server service. ■ Detects configuration errors. ■ Detects critical error conditions.
Virtual Machine State	■ Monitors virtual machine state (if Virtual Machine Additions are installed) using the percentage of expected heartbeats, the status last reported in Virtual Server, and the presence of unresolved error and warning alerts. ■ Detects start and restore failures. ■ Detects save failures. ■ Detects critical error conditions.
Virtual Machine Performance	■ Monitors processor usage. ■ Monitors memory usage. ■ Monitors disk space usage.

The Virtual Server 2005 R2 Management Pack includes the feature improvements listed in Table 18-2.

Table 18-2   Virtual Server 2005 R2 Management Pack Improvements

Feature	Description
Launch Virtual Server Administration Website	The Virtual Server Administration Website for a selected Virtual Server host is directly launched from within the MOM 2005 Operator Console using the Open Virtual Server Administration Website task. *Note: This functionality requires access to TCP port 1024 on the target Virtual Server hosts, which might require you to configure a firewall rule.*
Virtual machine power state alerts	The virtual machine power state (running, saved state, paused, powered off) is tracked, and the following alerts are recorded: ■ Service Unavailable—If the virtual machine is in a saved state or powered off. ■ Warning—If the virtual machine is paused.

Table 18-2   Virtual Server 2005 R2 Management Pack Improvements

Feature	Description
Virtual machine name mismatch alert	The virtual machine guest operating system computer name is compared to the virtual machine name registered in Virtual Server. If the names do not match, an alert is recorded.
	Note: This functionality requires that both Virtual Machine Additions and a MOM agent are installed in the guest operating system.
Virtual machine guest operating system and Virtual Server host	The virtual machine guest operating system computer name is identified as well as the name of the hosting Virtual Server. These names are identified using the registry keys (HostName, PhysicalHostName, PhysicalHostNameFullyQualified, VirtualMachineName) that are added to the guest operating system when Virtual Machine Additions are installed.
	The Virtual Server 2005 R2 Management Pack adds four computer attributes to capture this data:
	■ *VirtualMachineName*
	■ *VSHostName*
	■ *VSPhysicalHostName*
	■ *VSPhysicalHostNameFullyQualified*
	Note: This functionality requires that both Virtual Machine Additions and a MOM agent are installed in the guest operating system.
Notification group for Virtual Server 2005 R2 Management Pack alerts	The Virtualization Administrators group is a notification group that is created by the Virtual Server 2005 R2 Management Pack to receive e-mail messages or pages in response to Critical Error and Service Unavailable alerts.
Virtual Server Diagram View	The diagram is a graphical representation that shows the association between virtual machines and Virtual Server hosts.

Table 18-2 Virtual Server 2005 R2 Management Pack Improvements

Feature	Description
Virtual Server reports	The Virtualization Candidates report helps to identify physical machines that are good candidates for migration to a virtual machine. The report contains performance counter data (processor, memory, disk) and hardware configuration parameters (number of processors, processor speed, memory) for a defined set of physical machines.
	The Performance History report provides trend data for processor use, available memory, disk performance, and network traffic over a defined period of time for one or more virtual machines.

> **Note** For more information on the virtual machine registry keys that specify the guest operating system and host name information, refer to Chapter 8, "Virtual Machine Creation Process."

MOM Agent Requirements

A MOM agent must be deployed to the Virtual Server host to monitor the Virtual Server service and partially monitor virtual machines. A MOM agent must also be deployed to each virtual machine running a Microsoft Windows guest operating system to enable the following Management Pack monitoring features:

- Guest operating system computer name
- Mismatch between a virtual machine name and guest operating system computer name
- Guest operating system performance and health data
- Application performance and health data
- Virtual Machine Details report
- Performance History report
- Virtualization Candidates report

With a MOM agent, virtual machine Windows guest operating system performance and health data is gathered through the Windows Servers Base Operating System Management Pack. In addition, application performance and health data, such as for Microsoft Exchange, can also be monitored using additional Management Packs. If you do not install a MOM agent in a virtual machine guest operating system, the performance and health data that is collected is restricted to the information that is gathered from the Virtual Server host. Also, applications running in a virtual machine guest operating system cannot be monitored.

Installing the Virtual Server 2005 R2 Management Pack

In preparation for the installation of the Virtual Server 2005 R2 Management Pack, you must verify that the prerequisites listed in Table 18-3 are completed in your environment.

Table 18-3   Virtual Server 2005 R2 Management Pack Prerequisites

Prerequisite	Description
Install Microsoft Operations Manager 2005	At minimum, you must install one MOM Management Server before you can import and use the Virtual Server 2005 R2 Management Pack.
Import Microsoft Windows Servers Base Operating System Management Pack	Three reports defined in the Virtual Server 2005 R2 Management Pack (Virtualization Candidates, Performance History, and Virtual Machine Details) use data that is collected based on the configuration defined in this Management Pack. *Note: Import version 05.0.2803.0000 or later.*
Install Virtual Machine Additions on every virtual machine	If Virtual Machine Additions are not installed, MOM 2005 cannot monitor the heartbeat of the virtual machine and cannot accurately report the state of the virtual machine.

Executing the Microsoft Virtual Server 2005 R2 Management Pack Installer Package

The files needed to import the Microsoft Virtual Server 2005 R2 Management Pack onto the MOM Management Server are contained in an installer package (Microsoft Virtual Server 2005 R2 MOM 2005 MP.msi). You must execute the installer package to extract its contents onto the file system before you can import the Management Pack.

> **Note**   The latest Virtual Server 2005 R2 Management Pack installer package can be downloaded from the Management Pack and Product Connector Catalog Web site at *http://www.microsoft.com/technet/prodtechnol/mom/catalog/catalog.aspx?vs=2005*.

Follow these steps to run and complete the Virtual Server 2005 R2 Management Pack installer package:

1. On the MOM Management Server, open Windows Explorer and then select the folder that contains the Microsoft Virtual Server 2005 R2 Management Pack installer package (Microsoft Virtual Server 2005 R2 MOM 2005 MP.msi).

2. Double-click the Microsoft Virtual Server 2005 R2 Management Pack installer to begin the installation of the Management Pack files.

3. If a security dialog box is displayed, click Run.

4. In the License Agreement dialog box, select I Agree and then click Next.

5. In the Select Installation Folder dialog box, click Next.

6. In the Confirm Installation dialog box, click Next.

7. In the Installation Complete dialog box, click Close.

Importing the Microsoft Virtual Server 2005 R2 Management Pack

After successful execution of the Virtual Server 2005 R2 Management Pack installer package, you can use the MOM 2005 Administrator Console to import the Management Pack onto your MOM Management Server.

Follow these steps to import the Virtual Server 2005 R2 Management Pack onto your MOM Management Server:

1. From the MOM Management Server, open the MOM 2005 Administrator Console.

2. In the left pane, under the Console Root, expand Microsoft Operations Manager.

3. Right-click Management Packs, and then select Import/Export Management Pack.

4. In the Welcome To The Management Pack Import/Export Wizard dialog box, click Next.

5. In the Import Or Export Management Packs dialog box, select Import Management Packs And/Or Reports and then click Next.

6. In the Select A Folder And Choose Import Type dialog box, click Browse and select the folder that was created during the installer package execution to contain the Management Pack files.

7. In the Type Of Import section, select Import Management Packs And Reports (you must have SQL Server Reporting Services installed to import reports) and then click Next.

8. In the Select Management Packs dialog box, select the Microsoft Virtual Server 2005 R2 Management Pack entry and then click Next. For example, the English version of the pack is named MicrosoftVirtualServer2005R2_ENU.akm.

9. In the Select Reports dialog box, select the Microsoft Virtual Server 2005 R2 report entry and then click Next. For example, the English version of the report file is named MicrosoftVirtualServerReportsR2.xml.

10. If Secure Sockets Layer (SSL) is not configured for access to the reporting Web site, you might see a Secure Sockets Layer Confirmation dialog box. If this is the case, click Continue.

11. In the Completing The Management Pack Import/Export Wizard dialog box, click Finish.

12. In the Import Status dialog box, review the status of the import operations and then click Close.

Verifying the Microsoft Virtual Server 2005 R2 Management Pack Version

Because Management Pack updates are released from time to time to include patches or provide enhancements, you might need to verify the version of the Virtual Server 2005 R2 Management Pack imported into the MOM Management Server. Follow these steps to verify the Management Pack version information:

1. From the MOM Management Server, open the MOM 2005 Administrator Console.

2. In the left-hand pane, under the Console Root, expand Microsoft Operations Manager.

3. Expand Management Packs, and then expand Rule Groups.

4. Under Rule Groups, right-click Microsoft Virtual Server (enabled) and then select Properties.

5. In the Rule Group Properties dialog box, on the General tab, verify the version number displayed in the Version field.

 Note   One way that you can receive information about new Management Pack releases is to subscribe to the Microsoft Operations Manager RSS catalog feed by clicking the Subscribe To This Feed link located at *http://www.microsoft.com/windowsserver2003/evaluation/rss /momrss.aspx*. Once you subscribe, you will receive e-mail notification when a Management Pack update is available.

Installing a MOM Agent

As described earlier, a MOM agent must be installed on Virtual Server hosts and virtual machines to fully monitor the performance and health of the infrastructure. MOM 2005 provides an automated installation procedure to deploy agents to physical and virtual machines. Follow these steps to deploy MOM agents to Virtual Server hosts and virtual machines:

1. From the MOM Management Server, open the MOM 2005 Administrator Console.

2. In the left pane, click Microsoft Operations Manager to display the Home page in the right pane.

3. Under Setup And Configuration Tasks, Administrative Setup Tasks, select Install /Uninstall Agents Wizard.

4. In the Welcome To The Install/Uninstall Agents Wizard dialog box, click Next.

5. In the Install Or Uninstall Agents dialog box, select Install Agents and then click Next.

6. In the Method For Discovering Computers And Installing Agents dialog box, select Browse For Or Type In Specific Computer Names and then click Next.

7. In the Computer Names dialog box, enter the NetBIOS or fully qualified domain name of the machine to which you want to deploy a MOM agent. Alternatively, click Browse to find the machine names. When you have entered all target machine names, click Next.

8. In the Agent Installation Permissions dialog box, click Next to use the default Management Server Action Account. Otherwise, select Other and enter a domain account with sufficient privileges, and then click Next.

9. In the Agent Action Account dialog box, click Next to use the default Local System account. Otherwise, select Other and enter a domain account with sufficient privileges, and then click Next.

10. In the Agent Installation Directory, click Next to use the default local directory for the MOM agent installation. Otherwise, type in the path to the desired directory and then click Next.

11. In the Completing The Install/Uninstall Agents Wizard dialog box, review the MOM agent installation selections and then click Finish.

12. A Microsoft Operations Manager Task Progress dialog box will appear and provide the status of the MOM agent installation procedure. You can click Details to see more information. Click Close when the installation procedure is complete.

> **Important** By default, the Local System account is used as the agent Action Account. However, you can specify credentials for a domain or local account if you need to define a lower-privilege account to meet security policy requirements. Although this is possible, you must be mindful of two tasks (Start Virtual Server and Stop Virtual Server) that cannot be executed using a low-privilege account, but instead require that the agent Action Account have administrative rights on the target Virtual Server host. To learn more about modifying the agent Action Account, review the information in the Microsoft Operations Manager 2005 Security Guide at *http://go.microsoft.com/fwlink/?linkid=63717*.

Monitoring Virtual Server Hosts and Virtual Machines

Using MOM 2005, the Virtual Server 2005 R2 Management Pack, and MOM agents deployed on each Virtual Server host and virtual machine, you can leverage the MOM Management Server—and specifically, the Operator Console—to centrally monitor your Virtual Server infrastructure. However, before Virtual Server 2005 R2 Management Pack features are applied to collect performance and health monitoring data, a service discovery must occur. Service discovery is a per-application process that is defined in a Management Pack and that identifies data collection parameters, software component survey requirements, and the roles and relationships between monitored components.

Virtual Server Service Discovery

The Virtual Server 2005 R2 Management Pack service discovery uses a VBScript (Virtual Server – Services) to gather information about Virtual Server hosts, virtual machines, and virtual networks. Virtual Server service discovery is scheduled to automatically occur every four hours. However, this parameter is configurable. During service discovery, Virtual Server host information such as the machine name, disk size, memory allocation, and registered virtual machines is collected. By default, service discovery also checks the state of a virtual machine based on a configurable heartbeat threshold and status listed in the Virtual Server host, and whether Virtual Machine Additions are installed in a virtual machine. Table 18-4 lists the three configurable parameters that the script takes as input. The heartbeat thresholds determine when the state of a virtual machine is changed from Green (Success) to Yellow (Warning) to Red (Critical Error).

Table 18-4   Virtual Server 2005 R2 Service Discovery Script Parameters

Parameter	Description
HeartbeatPercentCriticalThreshold	Sets the percentage of expected heartbeats below which the virtual machine state turns Red and a Critical Error alert is generated. The default threshold is 15 percent.
HeartbeatPercentWarningThreshold	Sets the lower threshold of expected heartbeats for which the virtual machine state turns Yellow and a Warning alert is generated. The default threshold of 50 percent generates a Warning alert when the virtual machine reports only 15 percent through 49 percent of expected heartbeats.
AlertOnNoAdditions	Specifies whether an Error alert is generated when Virtual Machine Additions are not installed on a virtual machine. In this case, the virtual machine state turns to Red. The default value for this parameter is True (enabled).

To change the service discovery script parameter values, follow these steps:

1. From the MOM Management Server, open the MOM 2005 Administrator Console.

2. In the left pane, expand Microsoft Operations Manager and then expand Management Packs.

3. Click Scripts, and then scroll down in the right pane until you find the Virtual Server – Service Discovery entry.

4. Right-click the Virtual Server – Service Discovery entry and select Properties.

5. In the Script Properties dialog box, click the Parameters tab.

6. In the Parameters tab, highlight the parameter that you want to change and then click Edit.

7. In the Script Parameter dialog box, type the new value in the Value text box and then click OK.

8. Repeat steps 6 and 7 to modify any other parameters.

9. In the Script Properties dialog box, click Apply and then click OK.

If after you update the script parameters, you want to deploy the changes immediately, you must commit the Virtual Server 2005 R2 Management Pack configuration changes manually. Otherwise, to commit the configuration changes, follow these steps:

1. From the MOM Management Server, open the MOM 2005 Administrator Console.

2. In the left pane, expand Microsoft Operations Manager.

3. Right-click Management Packs and select Commit Configuration Change.

Operator Console Views

The Operator Console provides several views to review and analyze performance and health monitoring data. Table 18-5 lists the various views and provides a description of the type of data presented in the view.

Table 18-5   Operator Console Views

Type	Description
Alerts	This view displays the following items: ■ Virtual Server Error, Critical Error, and Service Unavailable alerts. ■ Virtual Server 2005 R2 Management Pack alerts. ■ Virtual Server and virtual machine MOM 2005 alerts.
State	This view displays the following items: ■ Virtual Server service state. ■ Virtual machine state.
Events	This view displays the following items: ■ Virtual Server host events. ■ Virtual machine events.
Performance	This view allows you to select Virtual Server host and virtual machine performance counters to display in a graph.

Table 18-5   Operator Console Views

Type	Description
Computers and Groups	This view displays the machine attributes, rule groups, computer groups, and roles details for Virtual Server hosts and virtual machines.
Diagram	This view displays a diagram of the relationships between Virtual Server hosts and virtual machines.
My Views	This allows you to build customized views using existing views as building blocks.

Virtual Server and Virtual Machine State

The Virtual Server 2005 R2 Management Pack provides state information for Virtual Server hosts and virtual machines. The state reported for Virtual Server hosts, reflects the health of the Virtual Server service as well as the factors described in Table 18-6.

Table 18-6   Virtual Server State

State	Description
Green	A Green state indicates the following conditions: ■ The Virtual Server service is running. ■ No unresolved error or warning alerts exist for the Virtual Server service, virtual hard disks, or the Virtual Machine Remote Control client (VMRC).
Yellow	A Yellow state indicates that the virtual machine host is not a member of an Active Directory domain, so the Kerberos protocol cannot be used for users accessing virtual machines by using VMRC.

Table 18-6   Virtual Server State

State	Description
Red	A Red state indicates one or more of the following conditions: ■ The Virtual Server service is not running, suffered a fatal error, or raised a service-level exception. ■ The Virtual Server installation is corrupted or expired. ■ Physical disk space or memory on the host computer is critically low. ■ A user is unable to access a resource because of insufficient permissions. ■ Virtual Server is unable to create, compact, convert, or merge a virtual hard disk or to expand a virtual hard disk on a FAT volume. ■ Virtual Server cannot access or update files or disks for a virtual machine on the host. ■ Virtual machines cannot access networks because the physical network adapter could not be found. ■ Users cannot access virtual machines remotely by using VMRC.

The state reported for virtual machines is based on the heartbeat threshold settings, the status reflected in Virtual Server (running, paused, and so on), and the additional factors described in Table 18-7.

Table 18-7   Virtual Machine State

State	Description
Green	A Green state indicates the following condition: ■ The virtual machine is running and returning 50 percent or more of expected heartbeats, based on the default threshold.
Yellow	A Yellow state indicates: ■ The virtual machine is returning between 15 percent and 49 percent of expected heartbeats, based on the default threshold. ■ The virtual machine is paused.

Table 18-7   Virtual Machine State

State	Description
Red	A Red state indicates one or more of the following conditions:

- Virtual Machine Additions are either not installed on a virtual machine or the installed version is out of date. As a result, the heartbeat of the virtual machine is not monitored and it is not possible to accurately report the state of the virtual machine.

- A running virtual machine is returning 14 percent or fewer of expected heartbeats (based on default thresholds).

- A virtual machine is powered off, in a saved state, or has been reset.

- A virtual machine is low on physical disk space.

- A virtual machine cannot be started, saved, or restored because of insufficient memory on the host, a shortage of disk space, or other problem.

- A user on a virtual machine cannot access network resources or a local device.

- A user cannot connect to a virtual machine using VMRC.

- Disk access problems are causing a virtual machine to function improperly.

- The name assigned to a virtual machine does not match the computer name of the guest operating system.

Figure 18-3 shows the Operator Console view of Virtual Server and virtual machine state. In this view, state information is displayed for two Virtual Server hosts, CONTOSO-VS and CONTOSO-VS4.

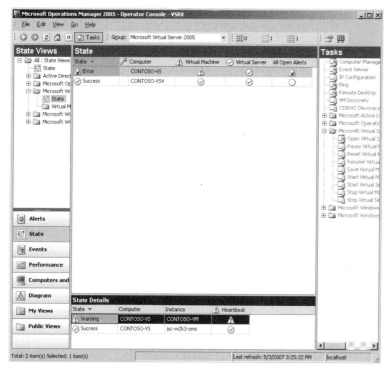

Figure 18-3 MOM 2005 Operator Console state display

Each Virtual Server host supports two virtual machines. The State pane in the middle of the display reflects a Yellow state for the CONTOSO-VS Virtual Server, and a warning indicator in the Virtual Machine column. In the State Details pane below, you can see that the CONTOSO-VM virtual machine Heartbeat column also contains a warning indicator. Figure 18-4 shows the Operator Console alert view for the CONTOSO-VS Virtual Server host that shows the warning indicator was set in response to the virtual machine being paused.

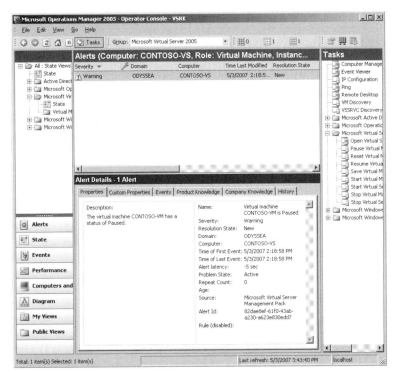

Figure 18-4   MOM 2005 Operator Console virtual machine alert display

Virtual Server and Virtual Machine Rules

The alert shown in Figure 18-4 is generated in response to the virtual machine pause event. Responses in the form of alerts are defined in rules. Rules define the events and performance data that is collected, how the data is processed, and the response that is generated when a rule match occurs. Alerts are one form of response to a rule match. Rule groups are a hierarchical way to collect and apply a set of multiple rules (event, alerts, performance data) to a focused group of machines.

The Virtual Server 2005 R2 Management Pack includes the rule groups listed in Table 18-8. Appendix B contains a detailed list of event, alert, and performance data rules included in the Virtual Server 2005 R2 Management Pack.

Table 18-8   Virtual Server 2005 R2 Management Pack Rule Groups

Rule group	Description
Microsoft Virtual Server/Virtual Machine	The Virtual Machine rule group contains one event rule targeted to identifying name mismatches between a virtual machine and the guest operating system.
Microsoft Virtual Server/Virtual Server 2005/ Core Service	The Core Service rule group contains 42 event rules, one alert rule, and three performance rules targeted to identifying Virtual Server host and virtual machine resource issues; notifying Virtualization Administrators of alerts with a minimum Critical Error severity; and capturing virtual machine disk space, memory, and processor usage.
Microsoft Virtual Server/Virtual Server 2005/ State Monitoring and Service Discovery	The State Monitoring and Service Discovery rule group contains two event rules and one alert rule targeted to performing service discovery of Virtual Server hosts, virtual machines, and virtual networks to determine whether the Virtual Server service stops, as well as to notify Virtualization Administrators when alerts with a minimum Critical Error or Service Unavailable severity are generated.

Virtual Server and Virtual Machine Tasks

When a rule results in generating an alert or condition indicating a Virtual Server or virtual machine problem occurred that requires a response, tasks are the mechanisms that allow performing an action to resolve the problem. In particular, the Virtual Server 2005 R2 Management Pack defines the tasks listed in Table 18-9.

Table 18-9   Virtual Server 2005 R2 Management Pack Tasks

Task	Description
Start Virtual Machine	The task starts a virtual machine.
Save Virtual Machine State	The task saves the state of a virtual machine.
Pause Virtual Machine	The task pauses a virtual machine.
Resume Virtual Machine	The task resumes a virtual machine.
Reset Virtual Machine	The task resets a virtual machine.
Stop Virtual Machine	The task stops a virtual machine.
Start Virtual Server	The task starts the Virtual Server service on a selected Virtual Server host.
Stop Virtual Server	The task stops the Virtual Server service on the selected Virtual Server host.
Open Virtual Server Administration Website	The task launches the Virtual Server Administration Website for the selected Virtual Server host.

These tasks are implemented as VBScripts that leverage the Virtual Server Component Object Model (COM) application programming interface (API) to perform the stated action on the selected Virtual Server host. For example, to resolve the warning shown in Figure 18-4, which resulted when the CONTOSO-VM virtual machine was paused, you can use the Resume Virtual Machine task to start the virtual machine back up. In the center pane shown in Figure 18-5, a diagram view of a Virtual Server infrastructure reflects the relationships between Virtual Server hosts and virtual machines. In the right pane, the Tasks view lists all the base tasks provided with MOM 2005, as well as additional tasks grouped by the Management Pack that provides them.

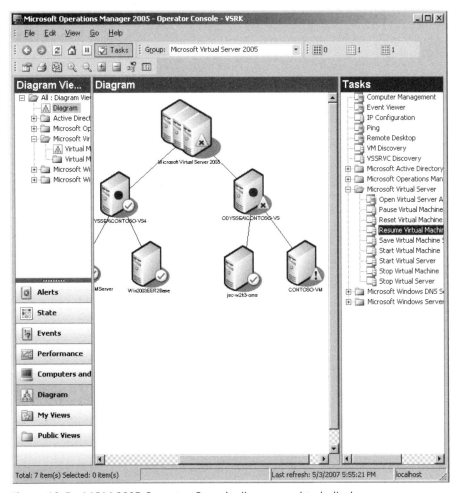

Figure 18-5   MOM 2005 Operator Console diagram and task display

To execute a task on a Virtual Server host or virtual machine, follow these steps:

1. From the MOM Management Server, open the Operator Console.

2. In the left pane, select Diagram.

3. In the Diagram, select the Virtual Server host or the virtual machine that is the target for the task execution.

4. In Tasks, select the target task.

5. Use the Launch Task Wizard to select or set input parameters and launch the task.

Virtual Server and Virtual Machine Reports

The Virtual Server 2005 R2 Management Pack provides reports that you can use to assess the performance of your Virtual Server infrastructure, as well as to identify good virtualization candidates and determine how to rebalance virtual machines across Virtual Server hosts to optimize the infrastructure. Both SQL Server Reporting services and MOM Reporting are required to generate and view the reports. There is no special configuration required other than selecting the reports when importing the Virtual Server 2005 R2 Management Pack onto the MOM Management Server. MOM Reporting relies on a nightly scheduled Data Transformation Services (DTS) job to transfer data from the MOM database to the MOM Reporting database. This ensures that reporting tasks do not affect and degrade the MOM 2005 performance during peak monitoring periods.

Note   If you want to force DTS replication of all existing data to the MOM Reporting database, you can execute the DTS package manually. The DTS package is located at %ProgramFiles% \Microsoft System Center Reporting\Reporting\MOM.Datawarehousing.DTSPackageGenerator.exe. The process will take a few minutes to complete, but no user interface is presented as the task runs in the background.

MOM Reporting is accessible from either the Administrator Console or the Operator Console. To launch the MOM Reporting console, follow these steps:

1. From the MOM Management Server, open the Operator Console.

2. From the Go menu, select Open Reporting Console.

Figure 18-6 shows the MOM Reporting console home page that is loaded in your browser. To access the Virtual Server 2005 R2 Management Pack report, just click the Microsoft Virtual Server link.

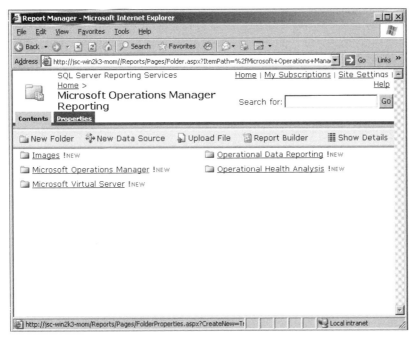

Figure 18-6   MOM Reporting console home page

In Figure 18-7, you can see the Virtual Server reports that are available through MOM Reporting.

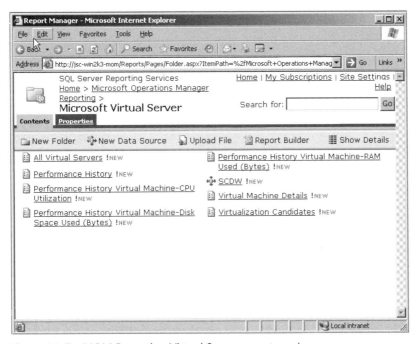

Figure 18-7   MOM Reporting Virtual Server reports main page

All Virtual Servers Report

The All Virtual Servers report can help you identify underutilized and highly utilized Virtual Server hosts, and it provides crucial information needed to develop a workload rebalancing plan to optimize performance across a Virtual Server infrastructure. At the top of the report, graphs identify the five Virtual Server hosts with the most available processor, memory, and disk space, as well as the five Virtual Server hosts with the least amount of available processor, memory, and disk space. A listing of Virtual Server hosts and associated virtual machines follows the graphical data. For each Virtual Server host, the listing includes the name of the physical machine, uptime, the IP address and port used for the VMRC client, the number of virtual machines hosted, and the Virtual Server default search paths. For each virtual machine, the listing includes the machine NetBIOS name, guest operating system, state, size of the virtual hard disk (.vhd), memory used, and Virtual Machine Additions version. Although the report defaults to include all Virtual Server hosts in the report, you can narrow the scope of the report by selecting to generate it for only a specific server.

Performance History Report

The Performance History report displays graphical Virtual Server host trends for processor utilization, available memory, disk performance, and network performance during a specified time period. The Performance History report is dependent on the following MOM 2005 performance rules for data collection:

- Performance\Performance Measuring: Processor\% Processor Time_Total
- Performance\Performance Measuring: Memory\Available Mbytes
- Performance\Performance Measuring: Network Interface\Bytes Total/sec
- Storage\Performance Measuring: PhysicalDisk\Disk Bytes/sec_Total

Although the report defaults to include all Virtual Server hosts in the report, you can narrow the scope of the report by selecting to generate it for only a specific server. You can use this report to determine if any physical Virtual Server host resources are being stressed, which resources need to be upgraded, and if virtual machines need to be rebalanced to other Virtual Server hosts.

Performance History Virtual Machine—CPU Utilization Report

The Performance History Virtual Machine–CPU Utilization report displays a graph showing the CPU utilization for one or more selected virtual machines hosted on one or more Virtual Server hosts during a specified time period. You can narrow the scope of the report by selecting to generate it for only a specific server and a specific virtual machine. The data collection for this report is based on queries to the VirtualMachine WMI object CpuUtilization counter.

 Note   Details on the VirtualMachine WMI object can be found in Chapter 17, "Managing a Virtual Server Infrastructure."

Performance History Virtual Machine—Disk Space Used (Bytes) Report

The Performance History Virtual Machine–Disk Space Used (Bytes) report displays a graph showing the disk space used by a selected virtual machine during a specified time period. The data collection for this report is based on queries to the VirtualMachine WMI object DiskSpaceUsed counter.

Performance History Virtual Machine—RAM Used (Bytes) Report

The Performance History Virtual Machine–RAM Used (Bytes) report displays a graph showing the physical memory used by a selected virtual machine during a specified time period. The data collection for this report is based on queries to the VirtualMachine WMI object PhysicalMemoryAllocated counter.

Virtual Machine Details Report

The Virtual Machine Details report displays the virtual machine NetBIOS name, virtual machine name, network configuration, and total disk space used (with specific information about the save state disk size, undo disk size, maximum virtual hard disk size, and location of VHD files). You can generate a report that includes details for all virtual machines running on all Virtual Server hosts, or you can limit the report to the virtual machines on a specific Virtual Server host. You will not see the NetBIOS name and network card details for virtual machines unless the Windows Servers Base Operating System Management Pack is imported onto the MOM Management Server. This report is a good, quick source to capture virtual machine configuration information.

Virtualization Candidates Report

The Virtualization Candidates report displays average values for a set of performance counters that include processor, memory, and disk utilization, over a specified period of time, in addition to hardware configuration (processor speed, number of processors including hyperthreading, and total memory). The data in this report can be directly leveraged to identify physical computers that are good candidates for migration to a virtual machine. You can limit the report to include only information for machines that meet a specific profile by adjusting the following report parameters:

- Max CPU Usage (%) <=
- Total RAM (MB) <=
- Number of Processors <=
- Avg CPU Usage (%) <=
- Avg Memory Usage (%) <=

The Virtualization Candidates report is dependent on the following MOM 2005 performance rules for data collection:

- Performance\Performance Measuring: Processor\% Processor Time_Total

- Performance\Performance Measuring: Memory\Available Mbytes

- Performance\Performance Measuring: Network Interface\Bytes Total/sec

- Storage\Performance Measuring: PhysicalDisk\Disk Bytes/sec_Total

- Storage\Performance Measuring: LogicalDisk\% Free Space

> **Best Practices**   For all reports that require specification of a time period to generate graphical data, you should limit the time period to a reasonable span. The processing time needed for data-intensive reports depends on many factors, including MOM database size, MOM Management Servers, and the selected time period. If you must analyze large amounts of data, you might have to adjust report execution timeout values.

Summary

MOM 2005 and the Virtual Server 2005 R2 Management Pack provide a centralized monitoring solution for a Virtual Server infrastructure. Virtual Server hosts and virtual machine state, alerts, events, performance data, and machine relationship diagrams can all be monitored using the MOM Operator Console. The Virtual Server 2005 R2 Management Pack also provides a set of tasks that allows manipulation and control of the Virtual Server service and virtual machine state (running, paused, saved state, and so on) through the MOM Operator Console. In addition, the Virtual Server 2005 R2 Management Pack defines several reports that allow evaluation of the performance of your Virtual Server infrastructure, as well as identification of virtualization candidates, and opportunities to rebalance virtual machine workloads to optimize performance.

Additional Resources

The following resources contain additional information related to the topics in this chapter:

- "MOM 2005 Conceptual Guide" at *http://www.microsoft.com/technet/prodtechnol /mom/mom2005/Library/ed4712c6-96b5-4241-a2b5-0dfaed30619c.mspx?mfr=true*

- "MOM Management Pack Catalog" at *http://www.microsoft.com/technet/prodtechnol /mom/catalog/catalog.aspx?vs=2005*

Chapter 19

Microsoft System Center Virtual Machine Manager 2007

In this chapter:

Understanding System Center Virtual Machine Manager 2007 451

Deploying System Center Virtual Machine Manager 2007 470

Using System Center Virtual Machine Manager 2007 473

Summary 479

Additional Resources 480

This chapter introduces Microsoft System Center Virtual Machine Manager 2007 (VMM), a server-based application that allows centralized management of a virtualized infrastructure built on Microsoft Virtual Server 2005 R2 and Windows Server Virtualization. The information contained in this chapter is based on VMM Beta 2, a pre-release version of the software.

Understanding System Center Virtual Machine Manager 2007

System Center Virtual Machine Manager 2007 (VMM) facilitates the management of Virtual Server 2005 R2 hosts and virtual machines in small and enterprise-wide deployments. Table 19-1 provides a list of the major features included in VMM.

Table 19-1   System Center Virtual Machine Manager 2007 Features

Feature	Description
Physical-to-virtual (P2V) machine conversions	VMM provides a wizard-based P2V machine conversion procedure that supports the following operating systems: ■ Windows 2000 Server with Service Pack 4 (SP4) ■ Windows Server 2003 with Service Pack 1 (SP1) ■ Windows Server 2003 R2 The P2V conversion procedure requires the installation of a software agent on the physical server to gather configuration information. The software agent is removed at the end of the conversion procedure.
Virtual-to-virtual (V2V) machine conversions	VMM provides a V2V machine conversion procedure to migrate VMware virtual machines to Virtual Server virtual machines by using a Windows PowerShell command-line interface.
Virtual Server host grouping	VMM provides the ability to organize Virtual Server hosts into groups that facilitate administration, monitoring, and access to virtual machines.
Virtual Server configuration	VMM provides the ability to install and configure Virtual Server on a physical server running Windows Server 2003 with Service Pack 1 (SP1). VMM can also modify Virtual Server settings such as Virtual Machine Remote Control (VMRC) access to hosted virtual machines, Virtual Server search paths, virtual networks, and so on.
Virtual Server ratings	VMM provides a Virtual Server host rating system that assists in deploying new virtual machines to the most suitable host.
Virtual machine and template creation	VMM provides the ability to create new virtual machines from blank virtual hard disks (VHDs) or by using templates. Virtual machine templates include a guest operating system profile, a hardware profile, and at least one VHD for which the System Preparation tool (Sysprep.exe) has been applied to remove computer identity information from the guest operating system.
Virtual machine configuration and management	VMM provides the ability to modify properties of virtual machines and manage the state of virtual machines (start, stop, pause, save state, and so on).

Table 19-1   System Center Virtual Machine Manager 2007 Features

Feature	Description
Virtual machine checkpoints	VMM provides the ability to create multiple virtual machine checkpoints using differencing disks. Checkpoints are managed through VMM and enable rollback of a virtual machine to a previous state.
Virtual machine migration	VMM provides the ability to move virtual machines through a drag-and-drop interface to a specific Virtual Server host or the most suitable host in a Virtual Server host group.
Virtual machine self-service	VMM provides the ability for administrators to create self-service policies that define the access and control rights of users and groups to virtual machines. Through self-service policies, virtual machines can be shared, viewed, and controlled by any group member.
Virtual component library	VMM provides the ability to create a repository of components (VHDs, templates, ISO images, and so on) used to quickly create and configure new virtual machines.
Virtual infrastructure reporting	VMM allows viewing reports defined in the Server Virtualization Management Pack for System Center Operations Manager 2007 from within the VMM administrator console.
Windows PowerShell interface	VMM leverages the Windows PowerShell, and each action that can be performed in the Administrator Console is mapped to a Windows PowerShell cmdlet. This allows administrators the choice of managing their Virtual Server infrastructure using the Administrator Console, using a graphical user interface management tool, or through a command-line interface.

Figure 19-1 shows the major components that make up the VMM architecture and how VMM integrates with Virtual Server 2005 R2, Microsoft SQL Server 2005, and Microsoft System Center Operations Manager 2007.

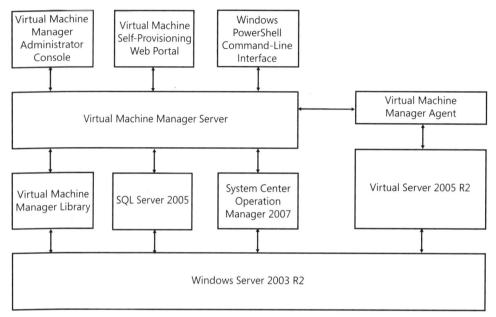

Figure 19-1   Virtual Machine Manager architecture

Virtual Machine Manager Server

The VMM server (VMMService.exe) is the service that implements and controls management of Virtual Server hosts and virtual machines. You can access VMM server management features through the VMM Administrator Console, the Windows PowerShell command line, and the virtual machine self-provisioning Web portal. The VMM server also manages VMM library shares that store the components needed to quickly create and deploy new virtual machines.

VMM server stores Virtual Server host and virtual machine configuration information in a Microsoft SQL Server 2005 database. The database can be created using Microsoft SQL Server 2005 Express edition for small or test deployments, or you can use Microsoft SQL Server 2005 Enterprise edition for large, distributed implementations. The VMM server communicates with managed Virtual Server hosts and virtual machines through the Virtual Machine Manager agent.

Virtual Machine Manager Agent

The VMM server deploys a Virtual Machine Manager agent to every Virtual Server host and VMM library server. The VMM agent allows the VMM server to monitor and manage Virtual Server hosts, VMM library servers, and virtual machines. By default, a VMM agent is also installed on the VMM physical server during the installation process to enable the server to function as a VMM library server for virtual machine resources.

Important   Before a VMM agent is deployed, Windows Remote Management (WinRM) must be installed on the targeted server. Microsoft developed WinRM as an implementation of the WS-Management Protocol, which provides standardized methods to manipulate management information across heterogeneous systems. For more details on WinRM, refer to *http://msdn2.microsoft.com/en-us/library/aa384426.aspx.*

Virtual Machine Manager Library

A VMM library is a repository of resources, managed by the VMM server that is used to create and manage virtual machine components. The VMM server maintains a catalog of resources for each VMM library that can be viewed through the VMM Administrator Console. A VMM library consists essentially of files stored in a standard file share monitored and controlled by the VMM server through the VMM agent, as well as configuration settings stored in the VMM database. Table 19-2 provides a list of the resources managed within a VMM library and indicates whether they are stored in a library share or VMM database.

Table 19-2   Virtual Machine Manager Library Server Resources

Feature	Description
Virtual machine template	A virtual machine template defines a guest operating system profile, a hardware profile, and one or more virtual hard disks (.vhd files), which can be used to create a new virtual machine. Computer identity information must have been removed from the VHD file that contains the operating system files by using the System Preparation tool (Sysprep.exe). **Storage Location: VMM Database**
Guest operating system profile	A guest operating system profile is a collection of configuration parameters that provide operating system settings for a virtual machine. Guest operating system profiles ensure consistent operating system configuration when creating virtual machines from a template. A guest operating system profile contains information such as the following: ■ Computer name ■ Administrator password ■ Product key ■ Time zone ■ Domain or workgroup details ■ Sysprep answer file name ■ GUI Run Once commands **Storage Location: VMM Database**

Table 19-2   Virtual Machine Manager Library Server Resources

Feature	Description
Hardware profile	A hardware profile is a collection of hardware configuration parameters that can be imported into a new virtual machine or a new virtual machine template. Hardware profiles ensure consistent hardware settings when creating virtual machines from a template. A hardware profile contains information such as the following: ■ Processor type requirement ■ Processor resource allocation ■ Memory allocation ■ Floppy drive settings ■ IDE and SCSI adapter settings ■ Virtual network adapter settings ■ MAC address setting ■ Virtual machine relative weight **Storage Location: VMM Database**
ISO image	An ISO image is a disk image (.iso) of an ISO 9960 file system. ISO images can be used instead of a physical CD or DVD to install an operating system in a virtual machine, or any additional software application or utilities such as Virtual Machine Additions. **Storage Location: File share**
Virtual hard disk	A virtual hard disk resource is a VHD file that stores guest operating system and application data. **Storage Location: File share**
Virtual machine	A virtual machine resource consists of the set of files (.vhd, .vmc, and so on) for an inactive virtual machine. The individual files cannot be used to create or configure new virtual machines. **Storage Location: File share**
Scripts	Any file containing commands and actions that can be applied to the configuration of a virtual machine, including Sysprep answer files (.inf) and Windows PowerShell scripts. **Storage Location: File share**

During VMM installation, a default library share is created (\\%*ComputerName*% \MSSCVMMLibrary) on the server hosting the VMM server service. The default library share contains two blank virtual hard disks. You can create additional VMM libraries that are geographically distributed to support local virtual machine creation and deployment, such as in branch offices.

When you add a new VMM library, the VMM server deploys a VMM agent to the physical server hosting the file share. The VMM agent collects and transfers data about the files located in the library file share to the VMM server, enabling it to build a resource catalog for each VMM library. The VMM agent also controls the transfer of files between a library file share and a Virtual Server host when a new virtual machine is deployed or stored in the library.

The VMM server periodically updates the resource catalog it maintains for each VMM library from information provided by the VMM agent. During the updates, the VMM agent discovers new files added to the library file share and transmits data concerning the files to the VMM server. The VMM server uses the information to create a new object in the appropriate VMM library resource catalog. The VMM agent discovers the following files:

- ISO images (.iso)
- Sysprep.exe answer files (.inf)
- Virtual hard disks (.vhd)
- Virtual floppy disks (.vfd)
- Windows PowerShell scripts (.ps1)
- Virtual machine configuration files created in VMware (.vmx)

By default, the VMM server receives VMM library updates based on one-hour intervals. However, the VMM library update frequency can be adjusted from one hour to 336 hours (14 days), in hourly increments. You can also disable automatic library updates or perform the updates manually.

Virtual Machine Manager Administrator Console

The VMM Administrator Console is a graphical user interface (GUI) that allows you to centrally manage Virtual Server hosts, virtual machines, and VMM libraries. It also enables you to view reports generated by the Microsoft System Center Operations Manager 2007 Server Virtualization Management Pack. The VMM Administrator Console actions are performed using defined Windows PowerShell cmdlets, and any action that is available through the console can also be performed using the Windows PowerShell command-line interface.

Figure 19-2 shows the basic layout of the VMM Administrator Console. By default, there are five main views among which you can alternate:

- Hosts view
- Virtual Machines view
- Library view
- Jobs view
- Administration view

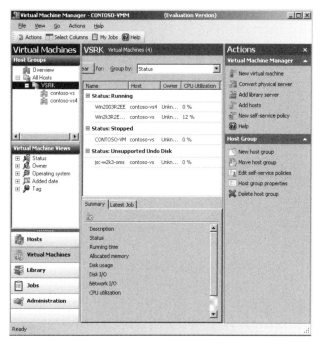

Figure 19-2   Virtual Machine Manager Administrator Console layout

There is a sixth view, the Reporting view, which is enabled when the VMM server is configured to integrate with and display System Center Operations Manager 2007 reports.

Hosts View

As shown in Figure 19-3, the Hosts Overview provides a display with graphical summary information about VMM-managed Virtual Server hosts, including their status (Responding, Not Responding, or Transitioning) and cumulative processor utilization. Although they are not shown in the figure, to the right of the graph there are links that allow you to add new hosts to be managed by VMM, as well as links to learn more on how to add new Virtual Server hosts to VMM.

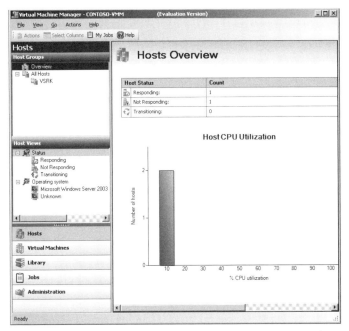

Figure 19-3   Virtual Machine Manager Administrator Console Hosts Overview

Figure 19-4 shows the Hosts detail view with customizable columns that can report additional information about VMM-managed Virtual Server hosts.

Figure 19-4   Virtual Machine Manager Administrator Console Hosts detail view

Specifically, VMM can report the following Virtual Server host information:

- Host name

- Processor utilization

- Operating system

- Virtualization software (Virtual Server 2005 R2, Virtual Server 2005 R2 SP1, and so on)

- Description

- Processor speed

- Physical server total memory

- Physical server available memory

- VMM agent version

- Number of processors

- Number of virtual machines registered

- Maintenance mode (describes whether the Virtual Server host is a staging server)

- Placement availability (describes the Virtual Server as available or unavailable for virtual machine placement)

- Host group (a Virtual Server host organizational container)

- Host group path (location of the host group in the hierarchy)

- VMRC server status (on or off)

- Virtual Server host status

- Virtual Server version

> **Important**   In VMM, the process of selecting the most suitable host for a virtual machine deployment is known as *Intelligent Placement*. To optimize placement, hosts are rated based on virtual machine hardware and resource requirements, as well as anticipated resource use. Host ratings also depend on the placement goal, which is either maximum resource utilization or load balancing among Virtual Server hosts.

From within the Hosts view, you can create new host groups that allow you to organize Virtual Server hosts into logical monitoring and management units. Host groups are also used to define and apply virtual machine self-service policies. By default, an All Hosts group is created when the VMM server is installed, and unless you define and use other host groups, all new managed Virtual Server hosts are added to it. Virtual Server hosts can be moved between host groups using a drag-and-drop operation from the Hosts view or the Move To Host Group action menu selection.

In the Hosts view, you can also quickly filter the information displayed in the host group pane by selecting one of the options listed under Status (Responding, Not Responding, or Transitioning) or Operating System from within the Host Views pane. This provides a quick way to view only the subset of objects that meet a particular condition or characteristic.

Virtual Machines View

In Figure 19-5, you can see the Virtual Machines Overview, which provides both tabular and graphical summary information about the status of VMM-managed virtual machines. In particular, status information is provided for recently created (or added) virtual machines.

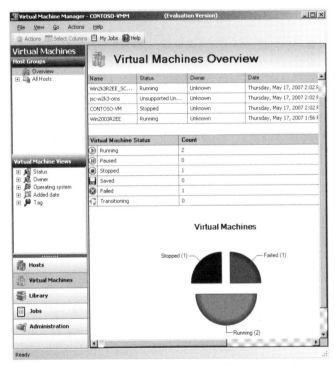

Figure 19-5   Virtual Machine Manager Administrator Console Virtual Machines Overview

There is also a table that summarizes the number of virtual machines in each of the following states:

- Running
- Paused
- Stopped
- Saved
- Failed
- Transitioning

Although they are not shown in the figure, to the right of the table, there are links that allow you to create a new virtual machine or convert a physical server to a virtual machine.

Figure 19-6 shows the Virtual Machines detail view with customizable columns that can report additional information about VMM-managed virtual machines.

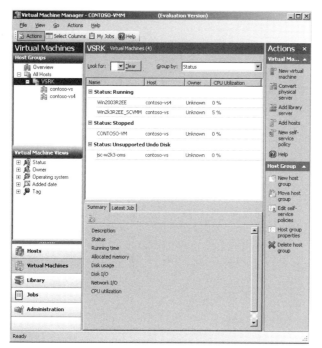

Figure 19-6 Virtual Machine Manager Administrator Console Virtual Machines detail view

Specifically, VMM can report the following virtual machine information:

- State
- Virtual Server host
- Virtual machine owner
- Processor utilization
- Job status
- Guest operating system
- Description
- Virtual Machine Additions version
- Creation date
- Modification date
- Memory allocation
- Disk input/output
- Network input/output

- Disk allocation

- Tag

- Cost center

- Quota points

- Self-service policy

- Custom fields (there are 10 of these)

From within the Virtual Machines view, you can create new virtual machines or choose to convert a physical server to a virtual machine. You can also change the state of a virtual machine, view virtual machine properties, create and manage checkpoints, disable undo disks, move a virtual machine to another Virtual Server host (if it is stopped or stored in a VMM library), connect to a virtual machine using VMRC, store a virtual machine in a VMM library, clone an existing virtual machine, or remove a virtual machine.

In the Virtual Machines view, you can quickly filter the information displayed in the virtual machines pane by selecting one of the options listed under Status, Owner, Operating System, Added Date, or Tab in the Virtual Machine Views pane. If you highlight a virtual machine, a thumbnail is displayed in the Summary tab as shown in Figure 19-7. You can connect to the virtual machine using VMRC by double-clicking the thumbnail.

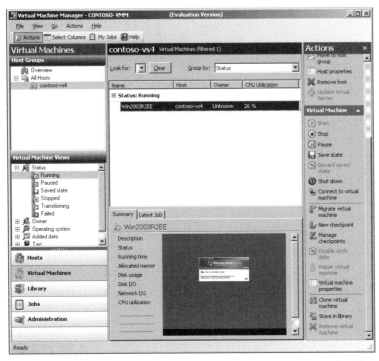

Figure 19-7   Virtual Machine Manager Administrator Console Virtual Machine thumbnail

Library View

As shown in Figure 19-8, the Library Overview provides both tabular and graphical summary information about VMM library servers and their stored resources, including the number of VMM-managed library servers as well as the number and kind of managed resources. Although they are not shown in the figure, to the right of the graph, there are links that allow you to add a new library server, a new virtual machine, or a new template.

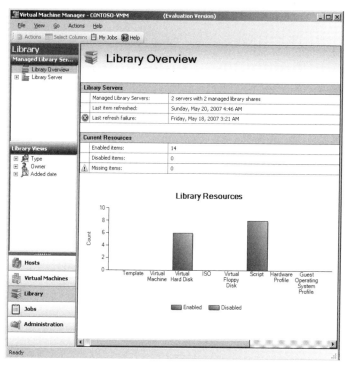

Figure 19-8 Virtual Machine Manager Administrator Console Library Overview

Figure 19-9 shows the Library view with customizable columns that can report additional information about VMM-managed library resources.

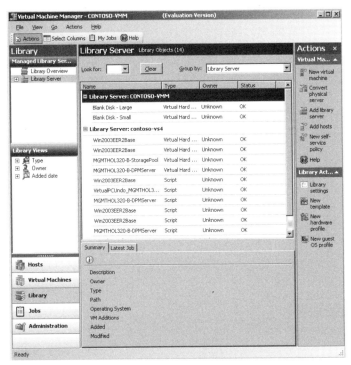

Figure 19-9 Virtual Machine Manager Administrator Console Library detail view

Specifically, VMM can report the following library resource information:

- Library server
- Type (VHD, script, and so on)
- Operating system (if applicable)
- Owner
- Status
- Added date
- Modification date
- Path (VMM library share relative path where the resource is stored)
- Cost center
- Self-service policy
- Quota points
- Tag
- Custom fields (there are 10 of these)

From within the Library view, you can add new library servers and create new virtual machine templates, hardware profiles, or guest operating system profiles. You can also view the properties of stored scripts, remove them from the VMM library, and enable or disable them to control whether they can be accessed and executed when creating new virtual machines.

In the Library view, you can also quickly filter the information displayed in the library server pane by selecting one of the options listed under Type, Owner, or, Added Date in the Library Views pane.

Jobs View

The Jobs Overview, shown in Figure 19-10, provides both tabular and graphical summary information about the most recently run and failed jobs executed on the VMM server, the context in which the job was executed, and the resulting target of the actions completed during the job.

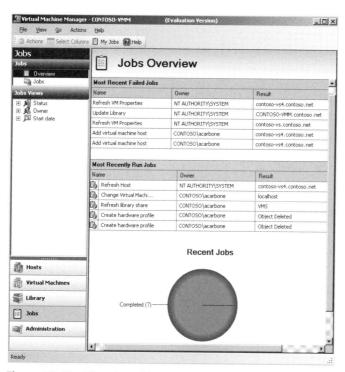

Figure 19-10   Virtual Machine Manager Administrator Console Jobs Overview

Figure 19-11 shows the Jobs view with customizable columns that can report additional information about the jobs executed on the VMM server.

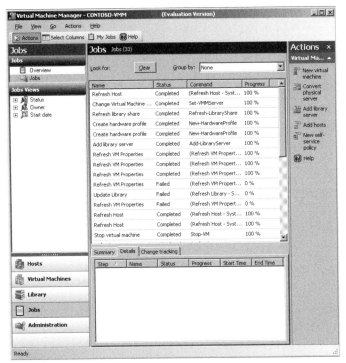

Figure 19-11   Virtual Machine Manager Administrator Console Jobs detail view

Specifically, VMM can report the following jobs information:

- Status
- PowerShell command
- Start date
- End time
- Progress
- Result name
- Result type
- Owner

From within the Jobs view, you can cancel or restart jobs. You can also quickly filter the information displayed in the jobs pane by selecting one of the options listed under Status, Owner, or Start Date in the Jobs Views pane.

Administration View

The Administration view, shown in Figure 19-12, provides access to create and manage virtual machine self-service policies, VMM agent updates, and settings for library refresh period, virtual machine placement goal and resource importance, reporting activation, self-service administrative contact, and VMRC port and account access.

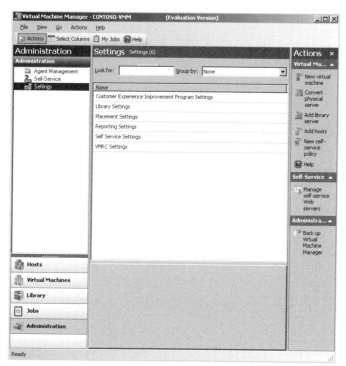

Figure 19-12   Virtual Machine Manager Administrator Console Administration view

Self-service policies allow a VMM administrator to grant permissions to users so that they can create and operate their own virtual machines within a specific host group. Through self-service policies, a VMM administrator defines the scope of actions permitted to manage virtual machines. Self-service users manage virtual machines by using the VMM self-provisioning Web portal.

The VMM administrator can set a quota on the virtual machines that self-service users can deploy. Quota points are assigned to the templates that self-service users use to create their virtual machines. When the self-service quota is reached, a user cannot create any new virtual machines until an existing virtual machine is removed or stored in the library. Quota points apply only to virtual machines that are deployed on a Virtual Server host. If a self-service user is allowed to store virtual machines, the quota does not apply to virtual machines stored in the library.

Self-service policies are created either for a user or a group. A group self-service policy can be configured for shared ownership or per-user ownership. In shared ownership, all members of the group own all virtual machines that are created for the group, and the self-service policy applies a single quota to all group members. For per-user ownership, a separate quota applies to each individual user.

Windows PowerShell Command-Line Interface

VMM provides the Windows PowerShell command-line interface to use in addition to or instead of the VMM Administrator Console for centralized management of your Virtual Server infrastructure. All administrative functions performed through the VMM Administrator Console can also be performed using the Windows PowerShell, including adding new VMM-managed Virtual Server hosts, creating new virtual machines, and adding new resources to a library server. Windows PowerShell is a command-line shell and scripting language that is available as a free download for Windows XP SP2, Windows Server 2003 SP1 and SP2, Windows Server 2003 R2, and Windows Vista. The Windows PowerShell is also integrated into Windows Server 2008. Windows PowerShell and VMM each provide commands (cmdlets in Windows PowerShell) that you can use individually to perform simple tasks or in combination with other cmdlets to perform complex tasks.

> **More Info**   For additional information on the Windows PowerShell, refer to *http://www.microsoft.com/windowsserver2003/technologies/management/powershell/default.mspx.*

Virtual Machine Manager Self-Provisioning Web Portal

When one or more self-service policies are defined, users granted permissions in the self-service policies can use the VMM self-provisioning Web portal, through which they can create and manage their own virtual machines. During a session, self-service users see only the virtual machines that they own and the actions based on permissions granted to them. The permissions that can be granted to a self-service user are as follows:

- Full Control
- Start Virtual Machine
- Stop Virtual Machine
- Remove Virtual Machine
- Pause and Resume Virtual Machine
- Shut Down Virtual Machine
- Local Administrator on Virtual Machine
- VMRC Access to Virtual Machine
- Create and Merge Checkpoints on Virtual Machine

> **Important**   VMM administrators can access the VMM self-provisioning Web portal only in troubleshooting mode. The troubleshooting mode allows a VMM administrator to log on as a user with view-only access to the user session.

Deploying System Center Virtual Machine Manager 2007

System Center Virtual Machine Manager can be deployed to manage a range of virtual environments that extends from a single-server, multiple virtual machine test environment to a multiple-server, multiple virtual machine enterprise environment. VMM can manage Virtual Server hosts joined to the same Active Directory domain, trusted domains, and on perimeter networks (behind a firewall). Virtual Server hosts that are not in the same domain as the VMM server, must either be in a domain that has a two-way trust relationship with the domain that contains the VMM server, in a forest that has a cross-forest trust relationship with the forest that contains the Virtual VMM server, or if on a perimeter network or in a domain that does not have a trust relationship with the VMM server domain, must have a VMM agent installed locally on the Virtual Server hosts before they can be managed by VMM.

Hardware Requirements

Before you install VMM, you must verify that the physical servers that will host the application components meet the recommended hardware requirements to operate them.

The minimum recommended hardware requirements for the VMM server are listed in Table 19-3.

Table 19-3   VMM Server Minimum Recommended Hardware Requirements

Hardware Component	Minimum Recommendation
Processor	Intel Pentium 4, 2.8 GHz
Memory	2 GB
Hard drive space	■ 7 GB (using a local default installation of Microsoft SQL Server 2005 Express Edition) ■ 1 GB (using a remote SQL Server 2005 database) ■ 80 GB (using the VMM server as a library server)
Network	100-Mb Ethernet

The minimum recommended hardware requirements for the VMM Administrator Console are listed in Table 19-4.

Table 19-4   VMM Administrator Console Minimum Recommended Hardware Requirements

Hardware Component	Minimum Recommendation
Processor	Intel Pentium III, 500 MHz
Memory	256 MB
Hard drive space	512 MB
Network	100-Mb Ethernet

The minimum recommended hardware requirements for the VMM self-provisioning Web portal are listed in Table 19-5.

Table 19-5   VMM Self-Provisioning Web Portal Minimum Recommended Hardware Requirements

Hardware Component	Minimum Recommendation
Processor	Intel Pentium III, 500 MHz
Memory	256 MB
Hard drive space	512 MB
Network	100-Mb Ethernet

As you define the actual hardware requirements to support management of your environment, consider the following factors:

- Number of managed Virtual Server hosts

- Number of managed virtual machines

- Number of managed library servers

- Number and size of stored library resources

- Number of virtual machines provisioned, the size of associated VHDs, and frequency of moves between Virtual Server hosts, VMM library servers, or both

- Number of self-service users with concurrent access needs to the Web portal and library servers

- Number of P2V and V2V conversions

> **Important**   Provisioning and moving virtual machines with large VHDs between Virtual Server hosts or VMM library servers that are not connected to a shared storage system such as a storage area network (SAN) require that you configure each system with at least a 100-Mb network connection. However, you will need gigabit network connections in each server to minimize the time required to copy VHDs between storage systems in a production environment.

Software Requirements

Deploying VMM in your environment also requires that the following software requirements are met prior to installation of the application.

Table 19-6 lists the software prerequisites for the VMM server installation.

Table 19-6   VMM Server Software Prerequisites

Component	Prerequisite
Operating system	Microsoft Windows Server 2003 SP1 or later
Microsoft .NET version	■ Microsoft .NET Framework 2.0 ■ Microsoft .NET Framework 3.0
Microsoft SQL Server version	Any one of the following Microsoft SQL Server editions can support VMM: ■ Microsoft SQL Server 2005 Express Edition SP1 or later ■ Microsoft SQL Server 2005 Standard Edition SP1 or later ■ Microsoft SQL Server 2005 Enterprise Edition SP1 or later
Management interface	Windows Remote Management (WinRM)
Microsoft Core XML Services	MXSML 6.0

Table 19-7 lists the software prerequisites for the VMM Administrator Console installation.

Table 19-7   VMM Administrator Console Software Prerequisites

Component	Prerequisite
Operating system	Microsoft Windows Server 2003 SP1 or later
Microsoft .NET version	■ Microsoft .NET Framework 2.0 ■ Microsoft .NET Framework 3.0
Scripting interface	Microsoft Windows PowerShell 1.0

Table 19-8 lists the software prerequisites for the VMM self-provisioning Web portal installation.

Table 19-8   VMM Self-Provisioning Web Portal Software Prerequisites

Component	Prerequisite
Operating system	Microsoft Windows Server 2003 SP1 or later
Microsoft .NET version	■ Microsoft .NET Framework 2.0 ■ Microsoft .NET Framework 3.0
Scripting interface	Microsoft Windows PowerShell 1.0
Web server	Microsoft Internet Information Services (IIS)

Table 19-9 lists the software prerequisites for the VMM agent installation.

Table 19-9   VMM Agent Software Prerequisites

Component	Prerequisite
Operating system	Microsoft Windows Server 2003 SP1 or later
Microsoft Virtual Server version	Microsoft Virtual Server 2005 R2 or later (32-bit or 64-bit)
Management interface	Windows Remote Management (WinRM)
Web server	Microsoft Internet Information Services (IIS)

Important   If you plan to enable and use the VMM reporting features, you must deploy System Center Operations Manager 2007, System Center Operations Manager 2007 Reporting Server, and the Virtualization Management Pack for System Center Operations Manager 2007.

Single-Server Configuration

In a single-server configuration, all VMM components are installed and run on the Virtual Server host. This scenario is suitable for small test and development teams that don't require an extensive virtual infrastructure but can benefit from the ability to create and manage several virtual machines, virtual machine checkpoints, and library servers to store virtual machine components.

Multiple-Server Configuration

In a branch office, corporate data center, or enterprise-wide scenario, VMM components might be distributed among multiple servers to accommodate remote management of Virtual Server hosts and virtual machines. In these configurations, the centralized VMM server and administration console can still be leveraged, but distributed VMM library servers and self-provisioning Web portals can also be used to co-locate the library resources with the Virtual Server hosts, resulting in the transfer of large VHDs across a local area network (LAN) instead of a wide area network (WAN) during the creation and deployment of new virtual machines.

Using System Center Virtual Machine Manager 2007

VMM combines in one application the major virtualization tasks that previously required multiple tools. Specifically, VMM allows an administrator to perform P2V and V2V conversions; create templates for faster provisioning of virtual machines; create self-service policies to allow users and groups to create, share, and manage their virtual machines; and place virtual machines on Virtual Server hosts based on maximizing or balancing physical server resource utilization. VMM also provides the flexibility for novice administrators to perform tasks using the VMM Administrator Console graphical user interface and task wizards, while allowing experienced VMM administrators to use Windows PowerShell cmdlets.

Physical-to-Virtual Machine Conversion

Using the VMM Administrator Console, you can convert a physical server to a virtual server using a task-based wizard. If you use Windows PowerShell cmdlets, the entire migration process can be scripted and performed in phases (imaging, system file updates, virtual machine creation, and so on). Unlike the Virtual Server Migration Toolkit (VSMT), no additional PXE or ADS infrastructure is required when performing P2V conversions using VMM. In addition, Windows Server 2003 and Windows Server 2003 R2 servers can even be migrated without downtime using the Volume Shadow Copy Service (VSS). Because Windows 2000 and Windows XP machines do not support VSS, P2V conversions from these operating systems require taking the machine offline during the conversion process.

VMM uses "smart" disk copy algorithms to reduce the time needed to perform a conversion. This is accomplished by transferring only allocated disk blocks from the source volume to the target VHD. During the conversion process, you also have the option of expanding the VHD size and selecting a dynamically expanding or fixed VHD. To preserve the identity of the source physical server, all network settings are preserved, including the MAC address.

The following steps represent how to perform a P2V conversion using the Convert Physical Server Wizard within the VMM Administrator Console:

1. Open the VMM Administrator Console.

2. In the Actions pane, click Convert Physical Server.

3. On the Select Source Wizard page, enter the computer name of the physical server, specify a user account that has local administrator rights and permissions on the physical server, and then click Next.

4. On the Virtual Machine Identity Wizard page, enter a virtual machine name, specify a domain account that will be the owner of the virtual machine, and then click Next.

5. On the Gather Information Wizard page, click Gather System Information to begin a hardware and software survey of the physical server and to identify any missing components that are required for the P2V conversion. The wizard installs a software agent on the physical server to gather the data and removes it when the conversion is complete.

6. The Conversion Information Wizard page reports any issues to resolve before the conversion can be performed. Each issue provides information to resolve the problem. After resolving all issues, click Check Again to check for additional issues. When no additional issues are detected, click Next.

7. On the Volume Configuration Wizard page, choose the volumes that you want to associate with the new virtual machine. The new virtual machine must contain the system volume and the boot volume from the physical server, but you can remove other volumes if you do not want to associate them with the new virtual machine.

8. If required, adjust the VHD size, VHD type (Dynamic or Fixed), and the disk adapter channel for each selected volume, and then click Next.

9. On the Select Virtual Machine Host Wizard page, select a Virtual Server host to deploy the new virtual machine and then click Next.

10. On the Select Path Wizard page, select the path to the folder that will store the configuration files for the virtual machine and then click Next.

11. On the Additional Properties Wizard page, select actions that will be performed when the Virtual Server service starts and stops.

12. If hardware-assisted virtualization is supported on the Virtual Server host, select the Use Hardware-Assisted Virtualization check box and then click Next.

13. On the Summary Wizard page, review the settings and click Create.

> **Note**   You can click the View Script button to display the Windows PowerShell cmdlets that will be used to perform the P2V conversion.

Virtual-to-Virtual Machine Conversion

In addition to enabling you to perform P2V conversions, VMM also provides the ability to convert a VMware disk or VMware virtual machine to Virtual Server equivalents. The conversion process supports four types of VMware virtual disks: flat, sparse, full, and 2-GB split. During the conversion process, one or more VHDs and a virtual machine configuration file are created. If the operating system in the VMware virtual machine is Windows 2000 Server or Windows Server 2003, the conversion process performs driver and system file updates to ensure that the operating system can boot in a Virtual Server–based virtual machine.

Virtual Machine Templates

A virtual machine template is the combination of a hardware profile, guest operating system profile, and one or more VHDs used to define a new virtual machine. Templates are used by the VMM administrator or VMM self-service users to create new virtual machines. Only templates assigned to a self-service policy can be used by self-service users to create new virtual machines.

Templates are created using a template wizard. As you build a new template, you specify the primary virtual hard disk; assign the template name, owner, and description; select an existing hardware profile; and then select a guest operating system profile. When the template settings are complete, you save the template in the VMM database for future assignment to a self-service policy or to create new virtual machines at a later point in time.

The following steps represent how to create a new virtual machine template from an existing VHD stored in a VMM library using the New Template Wizard within the VMM Administrator Console:

1. Open the VMM Administrator Console, and click Library in the navigation pane.

2. In the Library Actions pane, click New Template.

3. On the Select Source Wizard page, click Use An Existing Template Or Virtual Hard Disk Stored In The Library, and then click Select.

4. In the Select Library Resource dialog box, select a virtual hard disk and then click OK.

5. On the Select Source Wizard page, click Next.

6. On the Template Identity Wizard page, enter a template name and description, specify the template owner, and then click Next.

7. On the Configure Hardware Wizard page, customize the disk adapter, DVD, network adapter, processor, and memory hardware settings.

8. When you finish configuring hardware requirements, click Next.

9. On the Guest Operating System Wizard page, select each of the options listed under General Settings, Networking, and Scripts and configure them according to your requirements.

10. When you finish configuring the guest operating system requirements, click Next.

11. On the Summary Wizard page, click Create.

The template creation process might take some time to complete. If you want to review the progress of the template creation job, the My Jobs Status Tracking window is opened by default when the wizard closes.

Virtual Machine Provisioning

VMM allows administrators and users to provision new virtual machines. VMM administrators can provision virtual machines from the VMM Administrator Console using a task-based wizard or a Windows PowerShell script. Self-service users can provision virtual machines only from the self-provisioning Web portal using virtual machine templates that they have been assigned in applied self-service policies.

VMM administrators can provision virtual machines from virtual machine templates, virtual hard disks, existing virtual machines, or physical servers. Table 19-10 shows the requirements to provision a virtual machine from these various sources.

Table 19-10   Virtual Machine Provisioning Requirements

Source	Requirements	Results
Virtual machine template	Virtual hard disk must have the Windows 2000 Server, Windows Server 2003 SP1, or Windows Server 2003 R2 operating system installed.	Task fails if all requirements are not met.
	Virtual Machine Additions must be installed.	
	Virtual hard disk must have been prepared using the System Preparation tool (SysPrep.exe).	
	Local Administrator password must be blank.	
Virtual hard disk	None	Guest operating system cannot be customized.
Virtual machine	None	Guest operating system cannot be customized.
		Virtual machine must be powered down.
Physical server	Windows Server 2003 SP1, or Windows Server 2003 R2 operating system	Virtual machine has the same identity as the source computer.

The self-provisioning Web portal is a key feature for test and development environments that require rapid provisioning and tearing down of test virtual machines. VMM administrators can create a set of templates for predefined server roles or scenarios, place those templates in the library, and assign the templates to the users or groups through a self-service policy.

Virtual Machine Placement

Virtual machine placement is the process of determining the most suitable host on which to deploy a virtual machine, and is referred to as Intelligent Placement within VMM. To determine which host is the most suitable, VMM uses the performance history of the source machine and the target Virtual Server host. Virtual machine placement occurs during a P2V conversion, the provisioning of a new virtual machine, or when migrating a virtual machine between Virtual Server hosts.

Each VMM server has a set of placement settings divided into two areas, placement goals and resource importance. Figure 19-13 displays the placement settings available in the VMM Administrator Console.

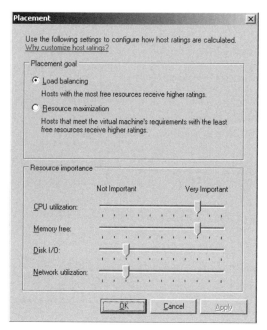

Figure 19-13   Virtual Machine Manager Administrator Console placement settings

VMM also defines two virtual machine placement goals: maximize resource utilization on individual Virtual Server hosts, and maximize load balancing between Virtual Server hosts. Virtual machine placement to maximize the resource utilization of Virtual Server hosts focuses on maximizing the consolidation ratio for Virtual Server hosts by placing as many virtual machines as possible on each Virtual Server host. Use of this placement method requires establishing the capacity limits of each Virtual Server host and placing virtual machines on it until the capacity has been reached. Virtual machine placement to maximize load balancing between Virtual Server hosts focuses on minimizing the processor load on each Virtual Server host by placing virtual machines where there are the most available processor resources.

The requirements for a virtual machine are established by collecting performance information on processor, memory, disk, and network interface resources. Resource importance establishes the weighted importance of a resource to use during placement. Figure 19-13 also displays the four resource importance settings: processor utilization, free memory, disk utilization, and network utilization. The default settings place more importance on processor utilization and available memory than on disk or network utilization. However, you can adjust these settings to reflect the Virtual Server resource profile that meets your environment needs.

When a virtual machine is deployed, VMM analyzes the Virtual Server hosts and assigns a rating that ranges between 0 (zero) and 5. The Virtual Server host rating reflects the suitability to host a virtual machine with the defined hardware and software requirements, resource usage history, as well as the Virtual Server host resource usage history. Host ratings also factor in the virtual machine placement goals and resource importance settings.

When presented with a rating selection screen, note that higher ratings indicate better Virtual Server host suitability based on the defined settings. However, you are not forced to select the highest ranked host in the list. You can prevent a Virtual Server host from consideration for any virtual machine placements by deselecting the This Host Is Available For Placement check box, which is shown in Figure 19-14 in the Virtual Server Host Properties dialog box.

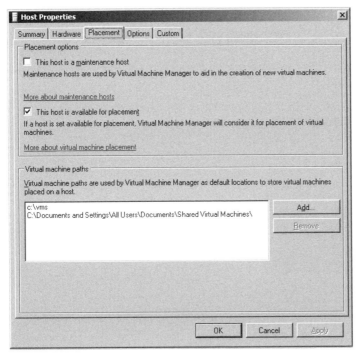

Figure 19-14   Virtual Machine Manager Administrator Console Host Properties Placement tab

Summary

System Center Virtual Machine Manager provides a centralized management solution for a Virtual Server infrastructure. Virtual Server hosts and virtual machines can be managed and operated using the VMM Administrator Console. The VMM Administrator Console provides well-defined and separate views to manage Virtual Server hosts within host groups, virtual machines, library servers and resources, running and completed jobs, and administrative settings. The VMM self-provisioning Web portal allows users and groups with appropriate permissions granted by the VMM administrator to create and manage their own virtual machines. The VMM library server provides a distributed repository to store building blocks for new virtual machines, as well as to store existing inactive virtual machines. VMM can manage a wide range of Virtual Server environments, from a single-server local installation to a multiple-server enterprise-wide deployment. In addition, VMM can integrate with System Center Operations Manager 2007 to assist you in planning physical server consolidation by identifying machines that are good virtualization candidates. VMM also directly supports P2V and V2V conversions and templates that can be used to create standardized virtual machines. Finally, VMM provides the ability to distribute virtual machine workloads to maximize Virtual Server host utilization or load-balance resource utilization.

Additional Resources

The following resources contain additional information related to the topics in this chapter:

- "Microsoft System Center Virtual Machine Manager, General Overview White Paper" at *http://go.microsoft.com/fwlink/?LinkID=89130*

- "System Requirements for Deploying Virtual Machine Manager (VMM)" at *http://go.microsoft.com/fwlink/?LinkID=89173*

- System Center Virtual Machine Manager download at *http://connect.microsoft.com*

Chapter 20
Additional Management Tools

In this chapter:

Analysis and Planning Tools 481

Conversion Tools 488

VHD Tools 493

Administration Tools 495

Summary 498

Additional Resources 498

This chapter presents an overview of additional software tools that are useful to manage a virtualized infrastructure based on Microsoft Virtual Server 2005 R2. The list of tools is not all-inclusive. However, it is representative of tools that are commonly used to analyze, plan, and manage a Virtual Server 2005 R2 environment. You should evaluate these tools against your project requirements and budget to determine which ones support your management strategy and complement your administrative tool set. You should also thoroughly test any tools that are of interest to ensure compatibility and performance of the tool prior to deployment and operation in a production environment.

Analysis and Planning Tools

Analysis and planning tools are used to inventory, evaluate, and define the set of physical servers in your environment that can be successfully converted to virtual machines. Successful server consolidation and virtualization projects require careful planning, which depends on having the right set of tools to gather, analyze, and present hardware, software, and services inventory and utilization data in a manner that is easily applicable to project planning.

Microsoft Active Directory Topology Diagrammer

The Active Directory Topology Diagrammer (ADTD), formerly named ADMAP, is a free tool (included on the companion media) that you can use to document various aspects of an Active Directory infrastructure. ADTD retrieves information from Active Directory using the Lightweight Directory Access Protocol (LDAP), Active Directory Services Interface (ADSI), and ActiveX Data Objects (ADO). Table 20-1 lists the Active Directory information that is captured with ADTD.

Table 20-1   ADTD Component Documentation List

Active Directory Component	Documentation
Domain	■ Domain name
	■ Domain functional level
	■ Number of domain controllers
	■ Domain controller details
	■ Name
	■ Operating system
	■ Service pack level
	■ Global catalog servers
	■ Number and types of trusts
	■ Number of user accounts
	■ Operations master role owners
	■ Schema version
Organizational Unit (OU)	■ OU hierarchy
	■ OU name
	■ Group Policy Object (GPO) links
Site	■ Site name
	■ Inter-site topology generator (ISTG)
	■ Total number of domain controllers in each site
	■ Total number of subnets in each site
	■ Domain controllers in each site
	■ Global catalog servers in each site
	■ Subnets in each site
	■ Internet Protocol (IP) and Simple Mail Transfer Protocol (SMTP) site links
	■ Replication connections within a site
	■ Replication connections between sites
Application Partition	■ Application partition name
	■ Total number of domain controllers that host the application partition
	■ Domain controllers that host the application partition

In addition to capturing Active Directory component information, ADTD can also capture basic information for Microsoft Exchange Server. Table 20-2 lists the Exchange organization information that is captured with ADTD.

Table 20-2   Exchange Information Captured by ADTD

Microsoft Exchange Server	■ Routing groups
	■ Administrative groups
	■ Routing group master
	■ Message connectors
	■ Replication connectors
	■ SMTP connectors
	■ Total number of Microsoft Exchange servers
	■ Total number of mailboxes
	■ Exchange server details
	■ Name
	■ Exchange version
	■ Service pack level
	■ Number of hosted mailboxes
	■ Microsoft Exchange schema version

To use the tool, you need only to provide the name of a global catalog server in an Active Directory domain, choose the level of information desired, and enter the account name and password of an account with administrator credentials, if so prompted. By default, the information that ADTD gathers is logged to a file (ADTD.csv). However, a main benefit of this tool is that you can choose to have ADTD create Microsoft Visio 2003 (or later) diagrams of the data, including the Active Directory domain structure; OU hierarchy; application partitions; and site topology, links, and replication connections.

> **On the Companion Media**   You can find the single ADTD installation file, ADTD.Net Setup.msi, in the \Chapter Materials\Tools\Microsoft\ADTD directory on the companion media. The installation procedure creates a directory to hold the ADTD binaries and documentation. An entry for ADTD is also created in the Programs menu.

Microsoft Windows Server System Virtualization Calculators

Microsoft has created two Web-based Windows Server System Virtualization Calculators, Calculator 1 and Calculator 2, to help you estimate the cost and number of Windows Server 2003 R2 licenses needed to implement your virtualization scenario. In particular, Calculator 1 allows you to compare the number and cost of Windows Server 2003 R2 licenses (by operating system editions, Datacenter, Enterprise, and Standard) and other Microsoft server applications (such as Microsoft SQL Server and Microsoft Exchange Server) on a single physical server hosting multiple virtual machines. Additionally, Calculator 2 allows you to estimate the number and cost of only Windows Server 2003 R2 licenses based on the number of physical servers and virtual machines that you define for your virtualization scenario.

Calculator 1

By default, Calculator 1 uses a nonclustered server with two processors running Virtual Server 2005 R2 as the standard platform for the Windows Server (and applications) licensing and cost estimates. However, the standard platform can be modified to select the following configurations:

- 1, 2, 4, 8, or 16 processors
- Cluster support (limits the estimates to Windows Server Enterprise and Datacenter Editions)
- Virtualization technology
    - Microsoft Virtual Server 2005 running on Windows Server
    - Third-party virtualization solution running on Windows Server
    - Third-party virtualization solution as host operating system

Once the standard platform is defined, you configure the number of virtual machines and applications that will be hosted on the server. Every virtual machine is configured with a single instance of Windows Server as the guest operating system, and allocated a single virtual processor. Calculator 1 allows you to choose the following Microsoft Server Standard Edition (SE) or Enterprise Edition (EE) applications for each virtual machine:

- BizTalk (SE, EE)
- Exchange (SE, EE)
- Host Integration Server (SE)
- Internet Security and Acceleration Server (SE, EE)
- Live Communication (SE, EE)
- Microsoft Operations Manager (EE)
- Microsoft Operations Manager Workgroup Edition
- SharePoint and SharePoint Internet
- SharePoint Search (SE, EE)
- Systems Management Server (EE)
- SQL Server (SE, EE)
- SQL Server Workgroup Edition

You can also configure a virtual machine with only Windows Server to simulate hosting a third-party application or Windows Server–based service such as Active Directory, Domain Name System (DNS), or Dynamic Host Configuration Protocol (DHCP). When you complete the definition of the virtual machine configuration running on the standard platform, Calculator 1 displays an estimate of the number of licenses and cost to implement the standard platform on Windows Server 2003 R2 Datacenter, Enterprise, and Standard Editions. The estimated license cost supports only the following currencies: the United States dollar, the Japanese yen, the British pound, and the euro.

Calculator 2

Calculator 2 provides two options to estimate the number of Windows Server licenses and cost to support your virtualization scenario. Option A allows you to enter the number of servers by processor count (single processor, dual processor, and so on) and the average number of Windows Server–based virtual machines that you plan to run on each of them. Option B allows you to define the processor configuration of each individual server and the number of Windows Server–based virtual machines that you plan to run on each server.

When you complete the definition of the servers and virtual machine configuration, Calculator 2 displays an estimate of the total number and cost of Window Server licenses needed (by edition). This allows you to determine whether it might be more cost-effective to implement your virtualization scenario using Windows Server 2003 R2 Standard, Enterprise, or Datacenter Edition. The estimates that Calculator 2 provides are limited geographically to the United States and the United States dollar.

Note The Windows Server Virtualization Calculators are available online at *http://www.microsoft.com/windowsserver2003/howtobuy/licensing/calculator.mspx*. You should thoroughly review the pricing information details that accompany the calculators to understand the applicability of the estimates to your environment.

PlateSpin PowerRecon

PlateSpin PowerRecon is a sophisticated tool that provides an end-to-end analysis and planning software solution for server consolidation and virtualization projects. Specifically, PowerRecon offers the following key features:

- Hardware, software, and services inventory collection and reports
- Server and workload resource utilization collection and reports
- Workload consolidation and distribution planning and modeling

PowerRecon supports inventory and utilization data collection for Windows, Novell SuSE, RedHat, and Sun Solaris SPARC and x86 operating systems.

Hardware, Software, and Services Inventory Collection and Reporting

PowerRecon can be deployed in a single instance or multi-instance configuration that supports inventory data collection ranging from small-scale, single-location scenarios to enterprise-wide, geographically distributed scenarios. Each instance of PowerRecon can support up to 1500 servers, with the ability to aggregate the data collected by each PowerRecon server to a single, master location for centralized analysis and planning.

PowerRecon collects inventory data without requiring the installation of a software agent, instead gathering data through instrumentation that is built in the supported operating system platforms. Hardware inventory data for each targeted server includes processor, memory, network, and disk resources. Software inventory data includes host operating system, installed and running applications and services, and installed service packs and updates.

Server and Workload Resource Utilization Collection and Reporting

PowerRecon can collect server and workload utilization information for any and all machines in its inventory. Utilization information is available to create charts and reports that allow analysis of server processor, memory, network, and disk space resource usage. PlateSpin provides a management pack to configure Microsoft Operations Manager (MOM) 2005 to integrate with PowerRecon. The management pack activates all the data counters required by PowerRecon and configures a five-minute monitoring interval.

PowerRecon comes with many predefined but customizable reports that document static hardware inventory data, deployed software and services, utilization metrics, and consolidation planning. Filters are also available to produce reports focused on specific server groupings and constrained resource utilization time periods.

Workload Consolidation and Distribution Planning and Modeling

PowerRecon includes a consolidation planning module that provides the ability to create consolidation scenarios with candidate workloads based on the server and workload utilization data gathered using PowerRecon. Consolidation scenarios can be constrained to include only specific workload types and resource utilization time periods for modeling purposes. Projected workload growth and variations can also be factored into consolidation scenarios.

PowerRecon consolidation scenarios allow you to determine the minimum number of servers needed to consolidate a defined set of workloads, or consolidation workload candidates and distribution across a defined set of servers. Server templates are defined for use in consolidation scenarios and model target virtualization hosts for workload distribution. PowerRecon provides several predefined server templates, or you can define new server templates configured to meet the standards defined in your environment. The information provided to define a server template includes the following general data:

- Server name, make, and model

- Total cost of ownership, rack unit requirements, and power consumption characteristics

- Host virtualization software (used to define the overhead associated with the virtualization host operating system)

The following hardware configuration parameters and resource utilization limitations are also defined for each server template:

- Number of processors and speed

- Memory allocation

- Disk space allocation

- Total processor, memory, and disk space percentage thresholds

- Total disk operations and network bandwidth thresholds

You can configure server templates with different processor, memory, disk, and network bandwidth allocations and apply them to consolidation scenarios to determine the most cost-effective architecture that can support a defined workload set.

PowerRecon can generate summary and workload reports that contain the results from the consolidation scenarios, including comparisons of pre-consolidation utilization with post-consolidation projections, and workload distribution recommendations. PowerConvert, the PlateSpin tool that is used for physical-to-virtual machine conversions, integrates with PowerRecon to implement server consolidation plans and workload distribution recommendations. (PowerConvert is described in more detail later in this chapter in the "Conversion Tools" section.)

Note   More information on PlateSpin PowerRecon is available online at *http://www.platespin.com/products/powerrecon*.

SystemTools Exporter Pro

SystemTools Exporter Pro is a tool that you can use to document the configuration of Active Directory and Windows Servers deployed in small to medium-size environments. Exporter Pro is designed to capture a wide range of information that includes the following:

- Active Directory objects (OUs, groups, computer accounts, and so on)

- Machine software configuration (operating system, services, applications, and so on)

- Machine hardware configuration (processors, memory, network, disk space, and so on)

- Machine network configuration (TCP/IP, MAC address, and so on)

- Machine processes

- Machine applications

- Machine shares

- Machine local users and groups

- Security settings for files, shares, printers, services, and the registry

- Files and directories

- Scheduled tasks

- User rights

- Account and audit policies

- Logged-on users

In fact, Exporter Pro can collect this data for any server or workstation in your environment, provided that you are running the tool in the context of an account with sufficient permissions and access rights to the data sources.

Once you define the component data that you want to collect, Exporter Pro uses a combination of methods and protocols to retrieve information from Active Directory and directly from targeted machines, including registry, WMI, and Active Directory queries. Exporter Pro provides predefined registry templates to capture installed software and updates information and predefined WMI queries to capture machine-specific information, including hardware, operating system, processes, event log information, and more. Exporter Pro also supports user-defined Active Directory queries. Exporter Pro saves the collected data into delimited output text files for export into any database or spreadsheet program to perform data analysis and produce reports.

Note More information on SystemTools Exporter Pro can be obtained online at *http:// www.systemtools.com/exporter/index.html*. A 30-day trial version is also available for download from the site.

Conversion Tools

Every project that involves the migration of one or more physical server workloads into virtual machines requires a physical-to-virtual machine (P2V) conversion tool. Conversion tools can also help to migrate virtual machines between virtualization platforms by supporting virtual-to-virtual machine (V2V) conversions, a process that generally involves translating the virtual hard disks to a format that is compatible with the new virtualization host platform. In Chapter 19, "Microsoft System Center Virtual Machine Manager 2007," you learned about System Center Virtual Machine Manager (VMM), a Microsoft enterprise-level management tool that provides P2V and V2V conversion capabilities. The tools described in this section are additional enterprise-class applications that enable you to perform P2V and V2V conversions.

Invirtus Enterprise VM Converter 2007

Invirtus Enterprise VM Converter 2007 provides P2V and V2V conversion of servers running 32-bit versions of Microsoft Windows XP, Windows 2000 Server, and Windows Server 2003 to the following virtualization platforms:

- Microsoft Virtual PC 2004, Virtual PC 2007, Virtual Server, Virtual Server 2005, and Virtual Server 2005 R2 (including SP1)

- VMware ESX Server 3.x/2.x, VMware Workstation, VMware ACE, VMware GSX Server, VMware Server, and VMware Player

- Virtual Iron

Enterprise VM Converter 2007 does not require deployment of a software agent. However, it uses a proprietary remote launch tool and protocol, along with the source server administrative credentials that you provide, to connect to and launch the conversion tool on the source server. Nonetheless, there is no downtime requirement for the source server during the conversion process.

Enterprise VM Converter 2007 P2V and V2V conversions are supported in manual mode or batch mode. In manual mode, only a single conversion can be performed at a time. In batch mode, multiple conversions can be performed simultaneously, staggered, or as scheduled tasks.

The Enterprise VM Converter 2007 conversion process consists of a sector-by-sector copy of the source server disks to the .VHD or .VMDK virtual hard disk format (based on the choice of target virtualization platform), and modifications to the operating system kernel and driver files needed to run in a virtual machine. If the source server has multiple partitions, you can select the conversion of specific partitions or all partitions. You can also choose to create a larger target virtual hard disk if the source disk is undersized. When the conversion process is complete, you can define a new virtual machine using the new virtual hard disk files.

P2V and V2V conversions can be performed between source servers and target virtualization hosts that are members of different Active Directory domains. However, you must provide administrator credentials for the target virtualization host before the conversion process can be started.

On the Companion Media   Additional details on Invirtus Enterprise VM Converter 2007 are available online at *http://www.invirtus.com/content/view/806/393/*. A trial version of the software can be found on the companion media in \Chapter Materials\Tools\Invirtus\Enterprise VM Converter 2007.

Leostream P>V Direct 3.0

Leostream P>V Direct 3.0 provides single and repeated P2V conversions of servers running 32-bit versions of Microsoft Windows NT 4.0 SP6a, Windows XP, Windows 2000 Server, and Windows Server 2003 to the following virtualization platforms:

- Virtual Server 2005 R2 (including SP1)

- VMware ESX Server 3.0/2.5.x, VMware GSX Server 3.x, VMware Server, and VMware Workstation 5.x

Repeated conversions allow you to periodically resynchronize the latest source server data to the virtual hard disks after the initial P2V conversion. This feature supports creating virtual machines that are used in backup or disaster recovery scenarios. Because initial conversion settings can be saved and used during subsequent synchronization sessions, repeated conversions can be scheduled and do not require manual interaction.

Leostream P>V Direct 3.0 consists of three main components: the Leostream P>V Direct Wizard, the Leostream Host Agent, and the Leostream Converter. The Leostream P>V Direct Wizard installs and runs on the source server. It allows you to configure the P2V conversion by specifying the following parameters:

- Target virtualization host

- Target virtualization platform

- Virtual machine memory allocation

- Drives and partitions to convert to virtual hard drives (includes dynamic disks if they are contained within a single physical disk)

The Leostream P>V Direct Wizard provides the option to convert all source server drives and partitions, or you can select only specific ones for conversion. You can also indicate whether to resize the disks and partitions created within the virtual hard drives. Additionally, you must define network parameters (IP address, subnet mask, default gateway) that are used by the Leostream Converter during the initial boot of the new virtual machine.

The Leostream Host Agent installs and runs on the target virtualization host. It communicates with the Leostream P>V Direct Wizard and uses the configuration information that it receives to create and configure a new virtual machine on the virtualization host. The Leostream Host Agent initially configures the new virtual machine to boot into the Leostream Converter.

The Leostream Converter is an embedded operating system contained in a virtual floppy disk image that is attached to a new virtual machine prior to the initial boot. After a new virtual machine is created and boots into the Leostream Converter, the Leostream P>V Direct Wizard communicates with the Leostream Converter to image the selected source server drives to new virtual hard drives. When the imaging process is complete, the virtual machine reboots and the Leostream Converter virtual floppy disk image is detached.

After the virtual machine reboots, modifications are made to the guest operating system to allow it to run within the virtual environment. Leostream P>V Direct 3.0 does not require any downtime or reboots of the source server during the conversion process. In addition, multiple conversions can be performed simultaneously.

On the Companion Media   Additional details on Leostream P>V Direct 3.0 are available online at *http://www.leostream.com/productPV.html*. A trial version of the software can be found on the companion media in the \Chapter Materials\Tools\Leostream directory.

PlateSpin PowerConvert

PlateSpin PowerConvert provides P2V and V2V conversion of servers running 32-bit versions of Microsoft Windows NT 4.0 (SP4 and SP6a), Windows XP SP2, Windows 2000 Server, and Windows Server 2003 to the following virtualization platforms:

- Virtual Server 2005 and Virtual Server 2005 R2 (including SP1)

- VMware Infrastructure 3, VMware ESX Server 2.1 and later, and VMware Server

- Virtual Iron 3.1

- XenSource 3.1

Note   PlateSpin PowerConvert also supports several Red Hat Linux and SuSE Linux operating system releases. More information on supported Linux distributions can be found online at *http://www.platespin.com/products/powerconvert/requirements.aspx*.

Besides P2V and V2V conversions, PowerConvert supports physical-to-physical (P2P), virtual-to-physical (V2P), physical-to-image (P2I), image-to-physical (I2P), virtual-to-image (V2I), and image-to-virtual (I2V) conversions for a full mesh migration of workloads between physical machines, virtual machines, and stored images. PowerConvert supports multiple imaging technologies, including Acronis True Image, Symantec LiveState, and Symantec Ghost, as well as the PlateSpin proprietary Flexible Image format. In addition, PowerConvert also supports several backup formats, including those produced by Double-Take, Veritas Backup Exec, and CA BrightStor ArcServe.

PowerConvert includes the ability to convert physical and virtual machine workloads into the Flexible Image format and maintain hardware-independent images that are available for subsequent deployment to new physical or virtual machines. This feature allows PowerConvert to decouple the workload conversion process from the deployment process, removing the requirement for a target virtualization (or physical) host during conversion. For example, if your organization decided to reduce the number of managed data centers and needed to consolidate and convert physical servers into virtual machines hosted in a central data center, you could use PowerConvert to convert the physical server workloads deployed in the remote data center into Flexible Image files, and redeploy the server workloads in the central data center by converting the Flexible Image files to virtual machine workloads without regard to hardware dependencies on the virtualization hosts.

Although PowerConvert supports single P2P, P2V, and V2P conversions, it can also be configured to perform manual or scheduled incremental synchronizations between source and target systems. This allows PlateSpin PowerConvert to support backup and disaster recovery scenarios, as well as duplication and synchronization of physical production environments with counterpart virtualized testing environments. PowerConvert supports block-level and file-level data replication. Block-level data replication transfers only data that has changed since the last full synchronization between the source and target servers, allowing incremental updates of workload data. File-level data replication transfers all the data, regardless of the amount of file data that has changed since the last full synchronization between the source and target servers.

PowerConvert offers two methods to perform P2V, V2V, V2P, and P2P conversions: Live Transfer, and Take Control Transfer. The Live Transfer method does not require any downtime for the source server. The Take Control Transfer method requires taking the source server offline and booting it into an alternate execution environment to perform the conversion. The choice of method depends on operating system characteristics, as well as the applications and services running on the source server. For example, source servers that are Active Directory domain controllers or DNS servers cannot be converted using a Live Transfer method. These server workloads require you to use the Take Control Transfer conversion method.

PowerConvert allows single or concurrent P2V and V2V conversion tasks. For P2V conversions, the conversion process parameters that you can modify include the following:

- Target virtualization host
- Target virtualization platform
- Virtual machine memory allocation
- Virtual machine network settings
- Virtual machine processor allocation
- Physical disks to convert to virtual hard drives
- Windows services to disable during conversion (original settings can be automatically reapplied after the conversion process completes)
- Conversion task scheduling

PowerConvert provides the option to convert all source server drives, or you can select only specific ones for conversion. You can also indicate whether to resize the target virtual hard drives. Additionally, you can set the initial state of the new virtual machine once the conversion process completes to come online or stay powered off. When the virtual machine initially comes online, PowerConvert automatically configures the server workload to operate on the target environment, making driver, kernel, and other necessary changes to the guest operating system to allow it to run within the virtual environment.

> **Note**   PowerConvert is a full-featured toolkit of which only a broad overview was given in this section. More details are available online at *http://www.platespin.com/products/powerconvert/*.

VHD Tools

In Chapter 5, "Virtual Server 2005 R2 Advanced Features," you learned how to reduce the size of existing virtual hard disks (VHDs) using the Virtual Server 2005 R2 precompaction and compaction utilities. Although these utilities are very useful, the tools presented in this section can assist you to optimize virtual machine performance and resize VHD files.

Invirtus VM Optimizer 3.0

Invirtus VM Optimizer 3.0 reduces the size of virtual hard disk files and can improve the performance of virtual machines running Microsoft Windows guest operating systems. VM Optimizer 3.0 supports the optimization of the following virtual machine guest operating systems:

- Microsoft Windows XP Professional and Windows XP Home
- Microsoft Windows 2000 Professional and Windows 2000 Server
- Microsoft Windows Server 2003 Standard and Enterprise Editions
- Microsoft Windows Vista

The following virtualization platforms are supported:

- Microsoft Virtual PC 2004, Virtual PC 2007, Virtual Server, Virtual Server 2005, and Virtual Server 2005 R2 (including SP1)
- VMware GSX Server, VMware Server, and VMware Workstation

VM Optimizer 3.0 can assist you to reduce the size of a virtual hard disk in the following example scenarios:

- Virtual hard disk archival to disk-based storage
- Virtual hard disk network transfer
- Virtual hard disk copy to removable media, such as a CD or DVD
- Virtual hard disk growth projected beyond physical disk partition size
- Virtual hard disk preparation prior to virtual machine imaging

In all these cases, reducing the size of the virtual hard disk decreases the amount of disk storage space required to store, transfer, or capture the virtual machine VHDs. In addition, optimizing the virtual machine guest operating system leads to faster boot time and increased overall performance.

VM Optimizer 3.0 installs on the virtualization host operating system. During the installation process, InvirtusVMOptimizer.iso is copied to the virtualization host. To begin the virtual machine optimization and VHD file-size reduction process, the InvirtusVMOptimizer.iso file is attached to the virtual CD or DVD drive of the target virtual machine. If the target virtual machine is shut down, start the virtual machine, log in, and VM Optimizer 3.0 will launch automatically.

After VM Optimizer 3.0 starts to run in the virtual machine, you can configure the optimization options that you want to apply, including the following ones:

- Registry modifications

- Removal of unneeded software (games, accessories, and so on)

- Removal of unneeded log, backup, temporary, autorecovery, installer, and service pack cache files

- Clear local profiles, system volume information folder, Recycle Bin, and temporary Windows Update folders

- Removal or resizing of the pagefile

- Disk defragmentation

You can also select to run InvirtusFreeSpace, a tool that is included with VM Optimizer 3.0 and that automatically traverses and zeroes out all virtual hard disk unused sectors. You can select specific virtual hard disks to process using InvirtusFreeSpace, or you can choose to process all virtual hard disks.

Once all the configuration options are defined, VM Optimizer 3.0 gathers information from the virtual machine guest operating system, generates an optimization plan, and prepares the virtual machine for the optimization. The virtual machine reboots, and then the virtual machine optimization and VHD resize operations begin. When the process completes, VM Optimizer 3.0 generates a report detailing the status of the optimization and the amount of recovered disk space.

On the Companion Media   Additional details on Invirtus Enterprise VM Optimizer 3.0 are available online at *http://www.invirtus.com/content/view/16/387/*. A trial version of the software can be found on the companion media in \Chapter Materials\Tools\Invirtus\Enterprise VM Optimizer 3.0.

xcarab VHD Resizer

xcarab VHD Resizer is a tool that allows you to quickly clone, resize, and convert VHD files between fixed and dynamic file types. VHD Resizer creates a new VHD file based on the file size that you specify. A sector-by-sector copy is performed to move the data from the source VHD to the new target VHD. No modifications are made to the source VHD.

On the Companion Media   Additional details on xcarab VHD Resizer are available online at *http://vmtoolkit.com/files/folders/converters/entry87.aspx/*. A trial version of the software can be found on the companion media in \Chapter Materials\Tools\xcarab.

Xtralogic VHD Utility

The Xtralogic VHD Utility provides the ability to expand the size of fixed and dynamic VHDs and increase their storage capacity. VHD Utility is a 32-bit application that runs on Microsoft Windows 2000, Windows XP, or Windows Server 2003 operating systems. VHD Utility includes a graphical user interface (GUI) integrated into Windows Explorer, and a command-line interface called VHDU. VHDU provides the same functionality as the GUI-based version.

When you use VHD Utility to resize a VHD file, you can select to expand the source VHD file, or you can choose to create a new, expanded VHD file and copy the data from the source VHD into the new file. Prior to resizing a VHD file, undo disks must be disabled.

To expand a VHD using the Windows Explorer GUI, you right-click the VHD file and select the Expand VHD option from the menu. This action launches the Disk Expansion Wizard, which provides you with the option to expand and replace the source VHD or create a new VHD file. You are then prompted to enter the new size for the VHD file, followed by dialog box that contains a summary of actions that the tool will perform.

Because VHD Utility resizes only the VHD file, not the operating system partitions that it contains, you must manually run a utility such as the Microsoft DiskPart utility to extend the operating system partition to the new maximum size.

Note   Additional details concerning the Xtralogic VHD Utility are available online at *http://www.xtralogic.com/products_vhd_utility.shtml*. You can download a 30-day free trial of Xtralogic VHD Utility at *http://www.xtralogic.com/products_vhd_utility_download.shtml*.

Administration Tools

The tools covered in this section provide alternatives to using the Virtual Server 2005 R2 Administration Website to manage Virtual Server hosts, configure virtual machines, or connect to a virtual machine guest operating system. For enterprise-class management of an infrastructure based on Virtual Server 2005 R2, you should consider using Microsoft System Center Virtual Machine Manager, as described in Chapter 19. However, the following tools allow administrators to quickly view and manage virtual machines and Virtual Server hosts.

HyperAdmin

HyperAdmin is a Web-based application for Virtual Server 2005 R2 that allows you to configure and use a single administration interface to manage virtual machines distributed across multiple Virtual Server hosts. Even though HyperAdmin is not a complete replacement for the Virtual Server Administration Website, it provides the ability to create and maintain logical collections of virtual machines that are physically distributed across multiple Virtual Server hosts, and quickly access and connect to the virtual machines without first having to switch the focus to the Virtual Server host, as is the case with the Virtual Server Administration Website.

Because HyperAdmin is a Web-based application, it requires the configuration of Internet Information Services 6.0 (IIS 6.0). HyperAdmin also requires access to a local or remote Microsoft SQL Server database to store configuration information.

HyperAdmin uses a proxy account to connect to a Virtual Server host. All administration tasks performed on the Virtual Server host are executed in the context of the proxy account. Before HyperAdmin can connect to a Virtual Server host and manage a virtual machine, the proxy account must be added to the local administrators group, or a new Virtual Server permission entry must be created for the proxy account with Full Control permissions.

HyperAdmin requires registration of Virtual Server hosts and virtual machines in the Web-based interface before they can be managed through the interface. The HyperAdmin Discovery Wizard assists you in connecting to a remote Virtual Server host and enumerating all registered virtual machines. As a Virtual Server host is discovered, it is added to the navigation tree, and all virtual machines are enumerated and automatically added as child nodes below it. HyperAdmin also includes a rescan feature that detects any new virtual machines that have been added to a Virtual Server host. You can also manually rescan for new virtual machines if needed.

Once virtual machines are registered in the HyperAdmin console, you can manage the state of a virtual machine (Power On/Off, Save State, Pause, and Reset) or connect to the virtual machine guest operating system. HyperAdmin leverages the VMRC ActiveX control to connect to running virtual machines. By creating logical collections of virtual machines running on different Virtual Server hosts, you can define administrative groups and easily switch between virtual machines to manage them.

Through the HyperAdmin interface, you can also mount and unmount ISO images to virtual machines. In addition, HyperAdmin supports the configuration of search paths for ISO image files that it applies to all Virtual Server hosts registered in its interface.

Note   Additional details on HyperAdmin are available online at *http://www.hyperadmin.com/*. The HyperAdmin software can be downloaded from *http://www.hyperadmin.com/download/*.

Microsoft Virtual Machine Remote Control Plus

Virtual Machine Remote Control Plus (VMRCplus) is a free, Windows forms-based application developed to work with Virtual Server 2005 R2 and Virtual Server 2005 R2 SP1. VMRCplus provides a graphical user interface (GUI) that offers an alternative to the Virtual Server 2005 R2 Administration Website. In contrast to the Virtual Server 2005 R2 Administration Website, which can manage and display information only for a single Virtual Server host at a time, VMRCplus allows you to connect to and manage multiple Virtual Server hosts and associated virtual machines. Nearly all of the functionality provided by the Administration Website is duplicated in VMRCplus, and it is complemented with some new features not supported in the Administration Website.

The VMRCplus application consists of four main dialog boxes: the Guest Manager, the Virtual Disks Manager, the Virtual Networks Manager, and the Console Manager. From the Guest Manager dialog box, you can connect to multiple Virtual Server hosts and display virtual machine information for each selected host. The Guest Manager dialog box allows you to quickly switch between Virtual Server hosts by clicking a tab created for the Virtual Server host when it first establishes a session with VMRCplus. The virtual machine list for each Virtual Server host is updated periodically based on a user-configurable refresh interval. The Guest Manager dialog box also supports the configuration of Virtual Server host properties, including the following ones:

- VMRC settings
- Security settings
- Default virtual machine configuration folder

In addition, the Guest Manager dialog box supports both the creation and configuration of a single virtual machine or multiple virtual machines at one time. If the option to create multiple virtual machines is selected, VMRCplus names the additional virtual machines by adding a hyphen and sequential number to the original virtual machine name. Furthermore, VMRCplus supports cloning of an existing virtual machine (prepared with Sysprep) to create one or more new virtual machines. All the virtual machine configuration options provided by the Virtual Server 2005 R2 Administration Website application are also configurable in VMRCplus. Departing from the process followed by the Virtual Server 2005 R2 Administration Website application, VMRCplus creates two VHD files for each new virtual machine and attaches them to virtual SCSI adapters.

The Virtual Disks Manager dialog box has a tabbed interface that allows you to quickly switch between and create the different virtual disk types supported in Virtual Server. Within this dialog box, you can also inspect VHDs and create virtual floppy disks. One of the nice features in this dialog box is the availability of a display that reflects the parent-child hierarchy for a differencing disk. This information is gathered when you inspect a differencing disk.

The Virtual Networks Manager dialog box provides the ability to create and add virtual networks to the Virtual Server host configuration. Within this dialog box, you can attach a physical host network adapter to the virtual network, as well as configure the virtual DHCP settings.

Lastly, the Console Manager dialog box displays the VMRC sessions that are established with virtual machines. The Console Manager allows you to create a connection to a single virtual machine or multiple, concurrent connections, each to an individual virtual machine. As with the Guest Manager dialog box, you can quickly switch between VMRC sessions by clicking the tab created for each established VMRC session.

On the Companion Media   Additional details on VMRCplus and copies (x86, x64) of the software are available on the companion media in \Chapter Materials\Tools\Microsoft\VMRCplus.

Summary

In this chapter, you learned about additional management tools that can complement an administration toolkit used in a Virtual Server–based environment. Tools were presented in four major categories: analysis and planning tools, conversion tools, VHD tools, and administration tools. Remember that you should always thoroughly evaluate tools against your project requirements and budget to determine which ones support your management strategy. You should also thoroughly test any new tools to ensure software compatibility and performance prior to deployment and operation in a production environment.

Additional Resources

The following resources contain additional information related to the topics in this chapter:

- "Licensing Microsoft Windows Server 2003 R2 to Run with Virtualization Technologies" at *http://download.microsoft.com/download/7/a/a/7aa89a8b-bf4d-446b-a50c-c9b00024df33/Windows_Server_2003_R2.docx*

- Active Directory Topology Diagrammer (ADTD), on the companion media in \Chapter Materials\Tools\Microsoft\ADTD

- Windows Server Virtualization Calculators, at *http://www.microsoft.com/windowsserver2003/howtobuy/licensing/calculator.mspx*

- PlateSpin PowerRecon, at *http://www.platespin.com/products/powerrecon*

- SystemTools Exporter Pro, at *http://www.systemtools.com/exporter/index.html*

- Invirtus Enterprise VM Converter 2007, on the companion media in \Chapter Materials \Tools\Invirtus\Enterprise VM Converter 2007

- Leostream P>V Direct 3.0, on the companion media in \Chapter Materials\Tools \Leostream

- PlateSpin PowerConvert, at *http://www.platespin.com/products/powerconvert*

- Invirtus Enterprise Optimizer 3.0, on the companion media in \Chapter Materials \Tools\Invirtus\Enterprise VM Optimizer 3.0

- xcarab VHD Resizer, on the companion media in \Chapter Materials\Tools\xcarab

- Xtralogic VHD Utility, at *http://www.xtralogic.com/products_vhd_utility.shtml*

- HyperAdmin, at *http://www.hyperadmin.com/*

- VMRCplus, on the companion media in \Chapter Materials\Tools\Microsoft\VMRCplus

Part V
Appendices

In this part:

Appendix A: Virtual Server 2005 R2 Event Codes 503

Appendix B: Virtual Server 2005 R2 Management Pack Rules 521

Appendix A
Virtual Server 2005 R2 Event Codes

These are the event codes that can be generated by Microsoft Virtual Server 2005 R2, including those for the Virtual Machine Additions.

Table A-1   Virtual Server Networking Event Codes

Event	Description
5	A client application registered to receive Ethernet frames directed to the MAC address
6	A new MAC address was generated for a client application. It will receive Ethernet frames directed to the MAC address
7	A request to register in order to receive Ethernet frames directed to the MAC Address
8	A request to create a new MAC address failed
9	A request to register in order to receive Ethernet frames directed to the MAC address %2 failed. The client application is not allowed to register using a NULL address, multicast address or the Host adapter's MAC address
10	A client application unregistered and will no longer receive Ethernet frames directed to the MAC address
11	The attempt to unregister the MAC address failed
12	A client application enabled packet reception using the filter
13	A client application disabled packet reception
14	A client application attempted to specify an invalid packet filter

Table A-2   Virtual Server VSS Writer Event Codes

Event	Description
1024	The VSS writer for Virtual Server failed to start. Close and then restart the Virtual Server and Virtual Machine Helper services.%0
1025	The VSS writer for Virtual Server failed during the Identify phase, and would not show up in the list of writers on the machine. Close and then restart the Virtual Server and Virtual Machine Helper services.%0
1026	The VSS writer for Virtual Server failed during the PrepareBackup phase, since the backup of virtual machine %1 failed. Retry the operation.%0
1027	The VSS writer for Virtual Server failed during the PrepareBackup phase, since the backup of virtual machine %1 did not complete in time. Check if the virtual machine %1 is running and then retry the operation. Note that the backup of the virtual machine might eventually succeed and stale shadow copies might be left behind.%0

Table A-2   Virtual Server VSS Writer Event Codes

Event	Description
1028	The VSS writer failed to get the properties of the virtual machine %1. The virtual machine is allowed for Offline backup only.%0
1029	The VSS writer failed to get the properties of the virtual machine %1, since the operation did not complete in maximum allowed time. The virtual machine is allowed for Offline backup only. Check if the virtual machine %1 is running and then retry the operation, if needed to be backed Online.%0
1030	The VSS writer for Virtual Server failed during the PostBackup phase, during the mounting of disk %1 for virtual machine %2. Confirm that the vhd mount driver in installed correctly and is able to mount virtual hard disks.%0
1031	The VSS writer for Virtual Server failed during the PostBackup phase, during the mounting of disk %1 for virtual machine %2. Some of the volumes on the disk failed to mount on the host file system.%0
1032	The VSS writer for Virtual Server failed during the PostBackup phase, during the mounting of disk %1 for virtual machine %2. The disk was a foreign/offline disk and the writer failed to make it Online, in order to access volumes on the disk.%0
1033	The VSS writer for Virtual Server failed during the PostBackup phase, during the mounting of disk %1 for virtual machine %2. The disk was a foreign/offline disk and the writer failed to make it Online, in order to access volumes on the disk.%0
1034	The VSS writer for Virtual Server failed during the PostBackup phase. The guest shadow copies did not get exposed on the host machine, after mounting all the virtual hard disks of the virtual machine %1.%0
1035	The VSS writer for Virtual Server failed during the PreRestore phase, since it was unable to stop and unregister the already existing virtual machine %1.%0
1036	The VSS writer for Virtual Server failed during the PreRestore phase, since it was unable to stop and unregister the already existing virtual machine %1.%0
1037	The VSS writer for Virtual Server encountered some errors during the PostRestore phase, while fixing alternate restore locations in the virtual machine configuration for the virtual machine %1. You may need to change some of the file locations manually through Virtual Server Administration Website.%0
1038	The VSS writer for Virtual Server failed unexpectedly. Close and restart the Virtual Server and Virtual Machine Helper services.%0
1039	The VSS writer for Virtual Server does not support backing up of virtual machine %1. The virtual machine contains iSCSI disks or files on a remote machine. Remove them to be able to backup the virtual machine.%0
1040	The VSS writer for Virtual Server does not support Online Backup of running virtual machine %1. The virtual machine contains volume(s) that do not support shadow copies; or have volumes whose shadow copy areas exist on a different volume. Remove them to be able to take an online backup of the virtual machine.%0
1041	The VSS writer for Virtual Server does not support Online Backup of running virtual machines on this computer. Online backup is only supported on virtual server hosts running Windows Server 2003 SP1 and above.%0

Table A-2   Virtual Server VSS Writer Event Codes

Event	Description
1042	The VSS writer for Virtual Server does not support Online Backup of running virtual machines on this computer. The vhd mount driver is not installed. Confirm that the vhd mount driver in installed correctly and is able to mount virtual hard disks.%0
1043	The VSS writer for Virtual Server does not support Online Backup of running virtual machine %1. The operating system on the virtual machine should be Windows Server 2003 and above, with the latest Virtual Machine Additions installed.%0
1044	The VSS writer for Virtual Server failed during PostBackup phase, since configuration of the virtual machine %1 changed during the backup.%0

Table A-3   Virtual Server Disk Operations Event Codes

Event	Description
1024	The virtual hard disk "%1" was created.
1025	The virtual hard disk "%1" was compacted
1026	The virtual hard disk "%1" was converted to "%2"
1027	The virtual hard disk "%1" was merged to "%2"
1028	The virtual hard disk "%1" was merged with its parent
1029	The virtual hard disk "%1" could not be created.
1030	The virtual hard disk "%1" could not be compacted.
1031	The virtual hard disk "%1" could not be converted
1032	The virtual hard disk "%1" could not be merged
1033	The virtual floppy disk "%1" was created.
1034	The volume "%1" only has %2 MB of space left. The virtual hard disk "%3" has been expanded, and very little space remains. You may wish to free some additional space.%0
1035	The volume "%1" only has %2 MB of space left. The virtual hard disk "%3" has been expanded, and very little space remains. Disk-related operations may fail if additional space is not made immediately.%0
1036	%1 supports using virtual disk images only on NTFS volumes.
1037	%1 supports using virtual disk images only on NTFS volumes.The disk operation will abort now

Table A-4   Virtual Server Virtual Machine Event Codes

Event	Description
1024	%1 was paused.%0
1025	%1 was resumed.%0
1026	The saved state for "%1" was discarded.%0
1027	The undo disks for "%1" were discarded.%0
1028	%1 was turned off without saving state.%0
1029	%1 was turned off by shutting down the guest operating system.%0
1030	%1 was reset.%0
1031	%1 may be crashed as it has not responded recently.%0

Table A-4   Virtual Server Virtual Machine Event Codes

Event	Description
1032	%1 was started with no boot disk specified.%0
1033	The virtual machine "%1" was not started because the trial period has expired.%0
1034	%1 was unable to write to one of its virtual hard disks.%0
1035	Virtual Server was unable to create an undo disk for "%1".%0
1036	%1encountered an error when attempting to use one of its virtual hard disks.%0
1037	%1 could not initialize the emulated Ethernet controller because the controller's address is in use by another copy of Virtual Server running on this computer.%0
1038	%1 could not initialize the emulated Ethernet controller.%0
1039	%1 could not find the virtual network attached to virtual NIC %2. This virtual NIC has been reattached to the "%3" virtual network.%0
1040	The virtual hard disk "%1" for the %2 device of IDE bus %3 of "%4" could not opened with read-write access. You need read-write access to the virtual hard disk to boot a virtual machine.Another virtual machine or the Virtual Disk Manager might be using this disk right now.%0
1041	The virtual hard disk "%1" for a device on SCSI bus %2 of "%3" could not opened with read-write access. You need read-write access to the virtual hard disk to boot a virtual machine.Another virtual machine or the Virtual Disk Manager might be using this disk right now.%0
1042	%1 is being restored on a system whose host processor differs from the processor at the time it was saved. This may result in guest OS instabilities.
1043	The virtual hard disk "%1" which is connected to "%2" is already in a saved state. Running the virtual machine with this virtual hard disk will cause the previous saved state to become invalid.
1044	The new virtual floppy disk "%1" could not be mounted by "%2". The new virtual floppy disk does not exist, it may be in use, or you may not have the proper access privileges.%0
1045	%1 could not mount the host floppy drive. Make sure the host floppy drive isn't being used by another virtual machine or by the host.%0
1046	%2 could not mount the floppy image. This file "%1" does not appear to be a floppy image. Floppy image files must be of the correct size (either 720K or 1.4MB).%0
1047	Virtual Server was unable to commit the changes made during the current session of "%1". A likely cause of this problem is lack of free hard drive space, the virtual hard disk file being marked read-only, or the virtual hard disk file is currently in use. The data in the undo disk is retained.%0
1048	Virtual Server was unable to commit the changes made during the current session of "%1". The cause of this problem is that the parent disk is read-only. The data in the undo disk is retained.%0
1049	Virtual Server has disabled live resolution switching for "%1" because the guest OS has switched the resolution. Some programs require specific resolutions to run properly. In order to maintain compatibility, Virtual Server has disabled live resizing of the Guest window until the virtual machine restarts.%0

Table A-4   Virtual Server Virtual Machine Event Codes

Event	Description
1050	There was an error trying to open the following port "%1" on your host machine. Before this port can be connected to "%2", you must verify that a device is attached to the port, and that it is not being used by another process.%0
1051	%1 experienced a fatal processor error and has been reset.%0
1052	%1 is using an invalid differencing virtual hard disk.%0
1053	%1 is using a differencing virtual hard disk with an invalid parent virtual hard disk.%0
1054	%1 has encountered a fatal error. Details have been logged to "%2".%0
1055	%1 cannot start the terminal server because port %2 is already in use.%0
1056	The virtual machine "%1" cannot connect virtual network adapter %2 because either the virtual network is invalid or access was denied. This virtual network adapter will be left disconnected.%0
1057	The saved state for "%1" cannot be found.%0
1058	%1 could not be started because there is not enough physical memory or system resources available.%0
1059	%1 could not be started because a disk-related error occurred.%0
1060	%1 could not be started because access was denied to one of the virtual hard disks.%0
1061	%1 could not be started because an unexpected error occurred.%0
1062	%1 could not be started because one of its virtual hard disks could not be located.%0
1063	%1 could not be started because one of its virtual hard disks is already in use by another running virtual machine.%0
1064	%1 could not be started because it is being used by another program, or marked as read-only. %0
1065	%1 could not be started because "Virtual Hardware Standard" version "%2" is not supported.%0
1066	The "Virtual Hardware Standard" (%2) in the configuration .vmc file for "%1" was not created by Virtual Server. "%1" can start, but some settings may be changed and some settings may not be used.%0
1067	%1 could not be saved because there is not enough physical memory or system resources available.%0
1068	%1 could not be saved because a disk-related error occurred. Make sure you have sufficient free space and write access to the directory that contains the virtual machine configuration file.%0
1069	%1 could not be saved because an unexpected error occurred.%0
1070	%1 could not be saved because an operation is pending. Try saving again in a little while.%0
1071	%1 could not be restored because there is not enough physical memory or system resources available.%0
1072	%1 could not be restored because a disk-related error occurred.%0
1073	%1 could not be restored because an unexpected error occurred.%0
1074	%1 could not be restored because the saved state was either corrupt or incompatible with this version of Virtual Server.%0

Table A-4   Virtual Server Virtual Machine Event Codes

Event	Description
1075	%1 could not be restored because of a host processor type mismatch or hardware assisted virtualization is required, but not available.%0
1076	%1 could not be restored because one of its virtual hard disks could not be located.%0
1077	%1 could not be restored because an error occurred when attempting to use one of its virtual hard disks.%0
1078	%1 could not be restored because the Ethernet controller address is in use by another copy of Virtual Server running on this computer.%0
1079	%1 could not be restored because the emulated Ethernet controller could not be initialized.%0
1080	The script could not be attached because the maximum number of scripts has been reached. Remove a different script before attaching the new one.%0
1081	The thread "%1" was forcibly terminated because it did not exit after a waiting period.%0
1082	Virtual Machine Additions were installed into "%1".%0
1083	Virtual Machine Additions were removed from "%1".%0
1084	Virtual Server was unable to find an undoable hard disk file for "%1". Disconnecting the parent drive from the PC, or "Discard Undo Drives" may fix this issue.%0
1085	The virtual hard disk for "%1" was created by the trial edition of Virtual Server, and the trial period has expired. To continue using this virtual hard disk, upgrade to the full version.%0
1086	Failed to delete the following file : %1.%0
1087	The memory for "%1" could not be allocated entirely within one node. The performance of this virtual machine may be degraded.%0
1088	The memory for "%1" was allocated in node %2.%0
1089	The virtual hard disk "%1" of "%2" is connected to a physical drive that has volumes mounted on the host. You need to unmount these volumes from the host to use this physical drive with a virtual machine.%0
1090	Virtual Machine Additions on "%1" is out of date. Please update to the latest version of Virtual Machine Additions.%0
1091	The volume "%1" only has %2 MB of space left. The virtual hard disk "%3" associated with the virtual machine "%4" has been expanded, and relatively little space remains. You may wish to free some additional space.%0
1092	The volume "%1" only has %2 MB of space left. The virtual hard disk "%3" associated with the virtual machine "%4" has been expanded, and very little space remains. The virtual machine will be paused.%0
1093	The virtual machine "%1" cannot connect virtual network adapter %2 because you do not have sufficient access rights to the virtual network. This virtual network adapter will be left disconnected.%0
1094	The virtual machine "%1" cannot connect virtual network adapter %2 because of the following error: %3. This virtual network adapter will be left disconnected.%0
1095	The serial port output text file "%2" for virtual machine "%1" cannot be created or opened because "%3" does not have sufficient access rights. All output to this serial port will be lost.%0

Table A-4   Virtual Server Virtual Machine Event Codes

Event	Description
1096	The serial port output text file "%2" for virtual machine "%1" cannot be created or opened because an unexpected error occurred. All output to this serial port will be lost.%0
1097	Running the script "%2" for an action by the virtual machine "%1".%0
1098	Running the script "%2" for an action by the virtual machine "%1".%0
1099	Virtual Server was unable to commit the changes made during the current session of "%1". The cause of this problem is that the parent virtual hard disk is a part of a saved state. The data in the undo disk is retained.%0
1100	The virtual hard disk "%1" for the %2 device of IDE bus %3 of "%4" could not opened.
1101	Virtual disk images upto 127.5 GB can only be attached to the IDE bus of a virtual machine.%0
1102	%1 supports using virtual disk images only on NTFS volumes.
1103	The virtual hard disk "%2" associated with the virtual machine "%3" will not be expanded beyond %4 GB. Please move this disk image to an NTFS volume.%0
1104	%1 supports using virtual disk images only on NTFS volumes.The virtual hard disk "%2" associated with the virtual machine "%3" has been nearly expanded to %4 GB.Due to the limitation of the file system, the file will not be expanded beyond %4 GB. The virtual machine will be paused.%0
1105	The virtual hard disk "%1" for a device on SCSI bus %2 of "%3" is not a fixed hard disk image. Sharing of SCSI hard disks in a cluster environment is supported only with fixed hard disk images.Please attach a fixed hard disk image.%0
1106	The virtual hard disk "%1" of "%2" is either a linked virtual hard disk, or a differencing virtual hard disk to a linked virtual hard disk. A virtual machine cannot use these type of virtual hard disks. Please use virtual hard disk images that are not connected to the host disk.%0
1107	The virtual hard disk "%1" for a device on SCSI bus %2 of "%3" is either a linked virtual hard disk, or a differencing virtual hard disk to a linked virtual hard disk.
1108	A virtual machine cannot use these type of virtual hard disks. Please use virtual hard disk images that are not connected to the host disk.%0
1109	Running the script "%2" because the virtual machine "%1" was turned on.%0
1110	Running the script "%2" because the virtual machine "%1" was restored from saved state.%0
1111	Running the script "%2" because the virtual machine "%1" was saved.%0
1112	Running the script "%2" because the virtual machine "%1" was turned off without being saved.%0
1113	Running the script "%2" because the virtual machine "%1" was turned off by shutting down the guest operating system.%0
1114	Running the script "%2" because the virtual machine "%1" was reset.%0
1115	Running the script "%2" because the virtual machine "%1" experienced a guest processor error.%0
1116	Running the script "%2" because the virtual machine "%1" has no heartbeat.%0
1117	Running the script "%2" because the virtual machine "%1" received a warning due to low disk space.%0

Table A-4   Virtual Server Virtual Machine Event Codes

Event	Description
1118	Running the script "%2" because the virtual machine "%1" received an error due to low disk space.%0
1119	The ISO Image "%1" has an unrecognized Volume Descriptor. Guest CD/DVD mount operation may fail.%0
1120	The ISO Image "%1" does not have a Primary Volume Descriptor. Guest CD/DVD mount operation may fail.%0
1121	The ISO Image "%1" does not have a Volume Terminator Descriptor. Guest CD/DVD mount operation may fail.%0
1122	The ISO Image "%1" Volume Descriptor has invalid Sector Size. Guest CD/DVD mount operation may fail.%0
1123	The ISO Image "%1" file is too small. Guest CD/DVD mount operation may fail.%0
1124	I/O Error while reading ISO Image "%1". Guest CD/DVD mount operation may fail.%0
1125	The ISO Image "%1" actual file size does not match the size in the ISO Volume Descriptor. Guest CD/DVD mount operation may fail.%0
1126	The virtual machine "%1" could not be started because there is not enough free space remaining to save state on %2. There is only %3 MB available. Virtual Server needs approximately %4 MB to save this virtual machine.%0
1127	The virtual hard disk "%1" attached to %3 (%2) of "%4" could not opened with read-write access. You need read-write access to the virtual hard disk to boot a virtual machine. Another virtual machine or the Virtual Disk Manager might be using this disk right now.%0
1128	The virtual hard disk "%1" attached to %3 (%2) of "%4" could not opened.
1129	Virtual disk images upto 127.5 GB can only be attached to the IDE bus of a virtual machine.%0
1130	The memory for "%1" could not be allocated in the preferred node. The performance of this virtual machine may be degraded.%0
1131	The virtual machine "%1" cannot connect virtual network adapter %2 because another virtual machine with the MAC address %3 is already running. This virtual network adapter will be left disconnected.%0
1132	Virtual Server was unable to commit the changes made during the current session of "%1". A likely cause of this problem is the undo drive cannot be opened for read/write or it might be in use or the user has no read/write/modify permissions. The data in the undo disk is retained.%0
1133	Virtual Server was unable to commit the changes made during the current session of "%1". A likely cause of this problem is the parent virtual hard disk cannot be opened for read/write or it might be in use or the user has no read/write/modify permissions. The data in the undo disk is retained.%0
1134	Virtual Server was unable to commit the changes made during the current session of "%1". A likely cause of this problem is the user may not have permissions to read/write/modify undo disk or parent virtual hard disk.%0

Table A-5   Virtual Server Preference Change Event Codes

Event	Description
1024	The setting "%1" for the virtual machine configuration "%4" was changed from %2 to %3.
1025	The setting "%1" for the virtual machine configuration "%4" was changed.%2%3
1026	The setting "%1" for the virtual machine activation "%4" was changed from %2 to %3
1027	The setting "%1" for the virtual machine activation "%4" was changed.%2%3
1028	The setting "%1" for the virtual network configuration "%4" was changed from %2 to %3
1029	The setting "%1" for the virtual network configuration "%4" was changed.%2%3
1030	The Virtual Server setting "%1" was changed from %2 to %3
1031	The Virtual Server setting "%1" was changed
1032	The setting "%1" for the virtual machine configuration "%2" was removed
1033	The setting "%1" for the virtual machine activation "%2" was removed
1034	The setting "%1" for the virtual network configuration "%2" was removed
1035	The Virtual Server setting "%1" was removed
1036	The security settings for the virtual machine configuration path "%1" cannot be synchronized with the Virtual Server security settings. You will need to adjust the security settings manually.%0
1037	The security settings for the default virtual machine configuration path cannot be synchronized with the Virtual Server security settings. You will need to adjust the security settings manually.%0
1038	The security settings for the virtual network configuration path "%1" cannot be synchronized with the Virtual Server security settings. You will need to adjust the security settings manually.%0
1039	The security settings for the default virtual network configuration path cannot be synchronized with the Virtual Server security settings. You will need to adjust the security settings manually.%0
1040	The security settings for the Virtual Server event log cannot be synchronized with the Virtual Server security settings. See Virtual Server Help for more information.%0
1041	The security settings for "%1" were changed
1042	The security settings for the Virtual Server event log were changed.

Table A-6   Virtual Server VMRC Event Codes

Event	Description
1024	The user "%2" at Internet address %1 established a new connection to the VMRC server using %3 authentication. The administration display is currently displayed.%0
1025	The user "%2" at Internet address %1 failed to authenticate a new connection to the VMRC server
1026	The user "%2" at Internet address %1 has disconnected from the VMRC server
1027	The user "%2" at Internet address %1 switched the VMRC display to "%3"
1028	The user "%2" at Internet address %1 switched the VMRC display to the administration display

Table A-6   Virtual Server VMRC Event Codes

Event	Description
1029	The user "%2" at Internet address %1 was idle too long and has been disconnected from the "%3" VMRC server
1030	The user "%2" at Internet address %1 was idle too long and has been disconnected from the administrator VMRC server
1031	The service principal name for the VMRC server could not be registered. Automatic authentication will always use NTLM authentication.
1032	The VMRC server cannot start because the service principal name required for Kerberos authentication could not be registered.
1033	Virtual Server could not start the VMRC server. Another server may be using the selected TCP/IP port.%0
1034	This computer does not belong to an Active Directory domain. Automatic authentication will always use NTLM authentication.
1035	The VMRC server cannot start because Kerberos authentication requires that the computer belong to an Active Directory domain. Use NTLM authentication instead.%0
1036	The user "%2" at Internet address %1 has been disconnected from the VMRC server as multiple connections are disabled.%0

Table A-7   Virtual Server Main Event Codes

Event	Description
1024	Debug Assertion Event
1025	Virtual Server successfully started
1026	Virtual Server is attempting to stop
1027	Virtual Server successfully stopped
1028	The configuration file "%1" was created
1029	The configuration file "%1" was deleted
1030	The configuration file "%1" was added
1031	The configuration file "%1" was removed
1032	The configuration file "%1" was renamed to "%2"
1033	A valid Virtual Server license file was installed
1034	Virtual Server is running low on memory
1035	Virtual Server recommends upgrading to Windows 2000 Service Pack 3
1036	Unable to launch the script "%1" because of the following error: %2
1037	Unable to use the linked virtual hard disk. The host partition or volume has changed since the virtual hard disk was first created
1038	The file you have selected is not the parent of the differencing virtual hard disk
1039	The parent virtual hard disk appears to have been modified without using the differencing virtual hard disk located at "%1". Modifying the parent virtual hard disk may result in data corruption. It is strongly recommended that you lock the parent virtual hard disk to prevent this in the future. If you recently changed time zones on your computer, you can safely continue using this virtual hard disk

Table A-7   Virtual Server Main Event Codes

Event	Description
1040	The virtual hard disk's parent appears to have been modified without using the differencing virtual hard disk located at "%1". Modifying the parent virtual hard disk may result in data corruption. It is strongly recommended that you lock the parent virtual hard disk to prevent this in the future. Currently, we do not have write access to your differencing virtual hard disk. It may be marked as a read-only file, or you may not have the proper privileges to access it. Due to this we cannot make the appropriate modifications to your differencing virtual hard disk
1041	%1 is not the correct parent virtual hard disk for the differencing virtual hard disk "%2"
1042	VM Startup Failed
1043	Virtual Server could not open its emulated Ethernet switch driver. Access to the external network and host will be unavailable to all guests using Virtual Switch Networking. Guests using Virtual Switch will still be able to access other guests using Virtual Switch
1044	Virtual Server could not open its emulated Ethernet switch driver. To fix this problem, re-enable the Virtual Server Emulated Ethernet Switch service on one or more Ethernet adapters or reinstall Virtual Server.
1045	The Virtual Server Emulated Ethernet Switch driver version installed is incorrect. To fix this problem, reinstall Virtual Server
1046	No network adapter was found on the host machine. To fix this problem, re-enable the Virtual Server Emulated Ethernet Switch service on one or more network adapters or re-install Virtual Server.%0
1047	Virtual Server could not open its emulated Ethernet switch driver. Access to the external network and host will be unavailable to all guests using the "%1" adapter. Guests using Virtual Switch will still be able to access other guests using Virtual Switch.%0
1048	Virtual Server could not open its emulated Ethernet switch driver. To fix this problem, re-enable the Virtual Server Emulated Ethernet Switch service on the "%1" adapter or reinstall Virtual Server.%0
1049	Virtual Server was unable to open the file or device "%1" because you do not have sufficient privileges
1050	Virtual Server suffered a fatal error
1051	Virtual Server could not be launched because it has not been configured with a valid serial number
1052	An error occurred when attempting to load configuration or preferences information from the file named "%1"
1053	An error occurred when attempting to save configuration or preferences information to the file named "%1"
1054	Error retrieving value for "%1" from configuration "%2". The value "%3" is invalid for this configuration key.
1055	%1 is not the correct parent virtual hard disk for the differencing virtual hard disk "%2"
1056	Virtual Server is unable to start because it failed to initialize COM security
1057	Virtual Server has encountered a fatal exception. Details have been logged to "%2"
1058	Virtual Server has encountered a non-fatal exception. Details have been logged to "%2"
1059	An invalid Virtual Server license file was installed

Table A-7   Virtual Server Main Event Codes

Event	Description
1060	The parent virtual hard disk "%1" for the differencing virtual hard disk "%2" does not exist. Please reconnect the differencing virtual hard disk to the correct parent virtual hard disk
1061	The parent virtual hard disk "%1" for the undo virtual hard disk "%2" does not exists
1062	A COM object could not be instantiated because the maximum allowable number of COM objects already exists. There may be too many scripts running
1063	Virtual Server has canceled a COM call (an event fired) to a script because the script event handler took too long to return.
1064	Virtual Server can not find the installed license file. Virtual machines will not be bootable until another license file is installed.
1065	Virtual Server can not find the certificate file. Virtual machines will not be bootable until another certificate is installed.
1066	Virtual Server encountered an unexpected error, %1
1067	Virtual Server ran out of memory. Please free up memory resources before running Virtual Server again
1068	Virtual Server ran out of disk space. Please free up some disk space before running Virtual Server again
1069	Virtual Server is incompatible with the host operating system. This version of Virtual Server requires Windows 2000
1070	Windows Application Compatibility Mode detected. Virtual Server cannot be run under Windows Application Compatibility Mode settings. Please turn off these settings before running Virtual Server again.%0
1071	Virtual Server is incompatible with the host processor in this machine. Virtual Server requires at least a Pentium II (or equivalent) processor.
1072	Virtual Server is already running. Only one copy of Virtual Server can be executing at a time.
1073	One or more files from the Virtual Server installation are missing. Please reinstall Virtual Server and try again.
1074	Virtual Server did not properly exit last time. On multiprocessor systems, this can lead to system instability. Please restart your machine before running Virtual Server again
1075	One or more files from the Virtual Server installation are out of date. Please reinstall Virtual Server and try again
1076	One or more files from the Virtual Server installation are out of date. Please reinstall Virtual Server and try again
1077	The administration terminal server cannot start because port %1 is already in use.
1078	The configuration file referenced by the configuration "%1" could not be found. The configuration has been removed.
1079	The virtual machine "%1" could not be used because its .vmc file (%2) contains invalid or malformed XML data. UTF-16 formatted data is required. The virtual machine has been removed
1080	The virtual network "%1" could not be used because its .vnc file (%2) contains invalid or malformed XML data. UTF-16 formatted data is required. The virtual network has been removed.

Table A-7   Virtual Server Main Event Codes

Event	Description
1081	OBSOLETE
1082	OBSOLETE
1083	The virtual server service configuration file "%1" could not be used because it contains invalid or malformed XML data. UTF-16 formatted data is required. The invalid file has been replaced and default settings are being used.
1084	The trial license will start in %1 %2
1085	The trial license will begin in less than one day
1086	The trial license will expire in %1 %2
1087	The trial license will expire in less than one day
1088	The trial license expired %1 %2 ago
1089	The trial license expired less than one day ago
1090	The trial license has expired. Virtual Server has started successfully, but virtual machines will fail to start.
1091	The network adapter with address "%1" of virtual machine "%2" failed to initialize because the address is a null address
1092	The network adapter with address "%1" of virtual machine "%2" failed to initialize because the address is a multicast address.
1093	The network adapter with address "%1" of virtual machine "%2" failed to initialize because the address is in use by another virtual machine.
1094	The virtual DHCP server of virtual network "%1" failed to initialize because an internal error occurred.%0
1095	%1 is being registered with a static MAC address. Multiple virtual machines using identical MAC addresses on the same virtual network may result in a loss of network connectivity.%0
1096	The static MAC address on "%1" (%2) conflicts with the MAC address on "%3". MAC address conflicts on the same virtual network may result in a loss of network connectivity.%0
1097	The static MAC address for "%1" was changed. Multiple virtual machines using identical MAC addresses on the same virtual network may result in a loss of network connectivity.%0
1098	The static MAC address on "%1" (%2) conflicts with the MAC address on "%3". MAC address conflicts on the same virtual network may result in a loss of network connectivity.%0
1099	The host machine has multiple NUMA nodes
1100	Node %1 has %2 megabytes of available memory
1101	Some nodes on this machine do not have local memory. This can cause virtual machines to run with degraded performance
1102	Some nodes on this machine do not have local memory. This can cause virtual machines to run with degraded performance
1103	The Virtual Machine Helper backing store file was corrupt. All virtual machine credentials will need to be reentered.

Table A-7   Virtual Server Main Event Codes

Event	Description
1104	Launched Script Success
1105	Launched Script Success Unknown
1106	The configuration value for automatically starting the virtual machine "%1" cannot be read because the defined user account does not have access to the configuration file.
1107	There was an error while processing the XML data in file "%1". Error code: %2, Line: %3, Pos: %4, Reason: %5, Text: %6.%0
1108	Exceeded the maximum size for XML %2 node "%3" while reading file "%1". Maximum size for this node type is %4, got %5 UTF-16 characters instead. Using first %4 characters.%0
1109	Exceeded the maximum size for XML %2 node "%3" while writing file "%1". Maximum size for this node type is %4, got %5 UTF-16 characters instead. Writing first %4 characters.%0
1110	Read invalid characters for XML %2 node "%3" while reading file "%1". If possible, using default value instead.%0
1111	%1 does not support accessing split virtual disk images
1112	%1 is being registered with a saved state and a dynamic MAC address. Multiple virtual machines using identical MAC addresses on the same virtual network may result in a loss of network connectivity.%0
1113	The dynamic MAC address on "%1" (%2) conflicts with the MAC address on "%3". MAC address conflicts on the same virtual network may result in a loss of network connectivity.%0
1114	Virtual Machine "%1" could not be registered because the contents of the configuration XML file "%2" are not supported. Only Microsoft Virtual Machine Configuration XML files, version "2.0", can be registered.%0
1115	Virtual Machine "%1" could not be registered because its "Virtual Hardware Standard" version is not supported. Only Microsoft Virtual Machine Configuration XML files which contain "Virtual Hardware Standard" version "0001" can be registered.%0
1116	Running script "%1" because Virtual Server started.%0
1117	Running script "%1" because Virtual Server stopped
1118	Running script "%1" because a virtual machine was turned on
1119	Running script "%1" because a virtual machine was restored from saved state
1120	Running script "%1" because a virtual machine was saved
1121	Running script "%1" because a virtual machine was turned off without saving state.
1122	Running script "%1" because a virtual machine was turned off by shutting down the guest operating system
1123	Running script "%1" because a virtual machine was reset
1124	Running script "%1" because a virtual machine experienced a guest processor error
1125	Running script "%1" because no heartbeat was detected for a virtual machine
1126	Running script "%1" because a virtual machine received a warning due to low disk space
1127	Running script "%1" because a virtual machine received an error due to low disk space
1128	The configuration file (%1) referenced by the configuration link "%2" could not be found

Table A-7   Virtual Server Main Event Codes

Event	Description
1129	The service principal names for Virtual Server could not be registered. Constrained delegation cannot be used until the SPNs have been registered manually.
1130	The event (category="%1", id="%2") has been suspended for user "%3" until %4 because it has occurred over its allowable limit.%0
1131	Host processor affinity for %1 physical processors and %2 logical processors: 0x%3.%0
1132	The host network adapter "%1" is invalid or missing
1133	This version of Virtual Server is designed for 32-bit operating systems, and cannot run within the WOW64 emulation layer.%0
1134	A connection couldn't be established between the Virtual Machine Helper service and the Virtual Server service. Virtual Server cannot run without this connection.%0
1135	An error has occured during the creation of Service Connection points for Virtual Server in Active Directory. Either a domain controller is not available to complete the operation or there is a security problem accessing the domain. This operation will be retried the next time the service starts.

Table A-8   Virtual Server VHDSTOR Driver Event Codes

Event	Description
1	%2 device has started
2	%2 device has been removed
3	Unable to start %2 device. Failed to initialize the device
4	PnP manager is unable to start the device
5	Unable to start %2 device. Failed to create the device
6	Unable to start %2 device. Failed to register the device
7	The device has been stopped
8	Unable to start %2 device. Failed to allocate device extension
9	Unable to start %2 device. Failed to initialize configuration object
10	%2 is unable to initialize WMI for the device
11	Checksum error occurred while verifying the VHD footer
12	Signature in the VHD file footer is invalid
13	The given file is not a valid VHD
13	The header of the given Dynamic VHD is not valid
14	The Parent VHD of the given Differencing disk could not be found
15	The Parent UniqueId specified in the Differencing disk %2 does not match that of the Parent
16	VHD opened successfully
17	Access denied to VHD
18	Could not allocate required resources

Table A-8   Virtual Server VHDSTOR Driver Event Codes

Event	Description
19	The parent virtual hard disk appears to have been modified without using the differencing virtual hard disk located at %2. Modifying the parent virtual hard disk may result in data corruption. It is strongly recommended that you lock the parent virtual hard disk to prevent this in the future. If you recently changed time zones on your computer, you can safely continue using this virtual hard disk.

Table A-9   Windows 2000 Virtual Machine Additions i8042 Mouse and Keyboard Driver Event Codes

Event	Description
0x0001	Not enough memory was available to allocate internal storage needed for the device %1
0x0002	Not enough memory was available to allocate the ring buffer that holds incoming data for %1
0x0003	The hardware locations for %1 could not be translated to something the memory management system understands
0x0004	The hardware resources for %1 are already in use by another device
0x0005	Some firmware configuration information was incomplete, so defaults were used.
0x0006	User configuration data is overriding firmware configuration data
0x0007	Unable to create the device map entry for %1
0x0008	Unable to create the device map entry for %1
0x0009	Could not connect the interrupt for %1
0x000A	The ISR has detected an internal state error in the driver for %1
0x000B	The ring buffer that stores incoming keyboard data has overflowed (buffer size is configurable via the registry)
0x000C	The ring buffer that stores incoming mouse data has overflowed (buffer size is configurable via the registry)
0x000D	The ring buffer that stores incoming mouse data has overflowed (buffer size is configurable via the registry)
0x000E	The Initiate I/O procedure has detected an internal state error in the driver for %1.
0x000F	The keyboard reset failed
0x0010	The mouse reset failed
0x0011	The device sent an incorrect response(s) following a keyboard reset
0x0012	The device sent an incorrect response(s) following a keyboard reset
0x0013	Could not set the keyboard typematic rate and delay
0x0014	Could not set the keyboard typematic rate and delay
0x0015	Could not tell the hardware to send keyboard scan codes in the set expected by the driver
0x0016	Could not set the mouse sample rate
0x0017	Could not set the mouse resolution
0x0018	Could not enable transmissions from the mouse
0x0019	Unable to create the symbolic link for %1
0x001A	Exceeded the allowable number of retries (configurable via the registry) on device %1

Table A-9   Windows 2000 Virtual Machine Additions i8042 Mouse and Keyboard Driver Event Codes

Event	Description
0x001B	The operation on %1 timed out (time out is configurable via the registry).
0x001C	Could not successfully write the Controller Command Byte for the i8042
0x001D	An unexpected ACKNOWLEDGE was received from the device.
0x001E	An unexpected RESEND was received from the device.
0x001F	No mouse port ("PS/2 compatible") mouse device was detected on the i8042 auxiliary port (not a problem unless this type of mouse really is connected)
0x0020	No mouse port ("PS/2 compatible") mouse device was detected on the i8042 auxiliary port (not a problem unless this type of mouse really is connected)
0x0021	The keyboard and mouse devices do not exist or were not detected.
0x0022	An error occurred while trying to determine the number of mouse buttons.
0x0023	An unexpected RESET was detected from the mouse device.
0x0024	An unexpected RESET was detected from the mouse device. The wheel has been deactivated.
0x0025	A bogus RESET was detected from the mouse device.
0x0026	A wheel mouse was detected after a device reset. The wheel has been reactivated.
0x0027	A protocol error has occured. Resetting the mouse to known state.
0x0028	An error occurred while trying to acquire the device ID of the mouse
0x0029	An error occurred while enabling the mouse to transmit information. The device has been reset in an attempt to make the device functional

Table A-10   Windows NT Virtual Machine Additions i8042 Mouse and Keyboard Driver Event Codes

Event	Description
0x0001	Not enough memory was available to allocate internal storage needed for the device %1
0x0002	Not enough memory was available to allocate the ring buffer that holds incoming data for %1
0x0003	The hardware locations for %1 could not be translated to something the memory management system understands
0x0004	The hardware resources for %1 are already in use by another device
0x0005	Some firmware configuration information was incomplete, so defaults were used.
0x0006	User configuration data is overriding firmware configuration data
0x0007	Unable to create the device map entry for %1
0x0008	Unable to create the device map entry for %1
0x0009	Could not connect the interrupt for %1
0x000A	The ISR has detected an internal state error in the driver for %1
0x000B	The ring buffer that stores incoming keyboard data has overflowed (buffer size is configurable via the registry)
0x000C	The ring buffer that stores incoming mouse data has overflowed (buffer size is configurable via the registry)

Table A-10   Windows NT Virtual Machine Additions i8042 Mouse and Keyboard Driver Event Codes

Event	Description
0x000D	The ring buffer that stores incoming mouse data has overflowed (buffer size is configurable via the registry)
0x000E	The Initiate I/O procedure has detected an internal state error in the driver for %1.
0x000F	The keyboard reset failed
0x0010	The mouse reset failed
0x0011	The device sent an incorrect response(s) following a keyboard reset
0x0012	The device sent an incorrect response(s) following a keyboard reset
0x0013	Could not set the keyboard typematic rate and delay
0x0014	Could not set the keyboard typematic rate and delay
0x0015	Could not tell the hardware to send keyboard scan codes in the set expected by the driver
0x0016	Could not set the mouse sample rate
0x0017	Could not set the mouse resolution
0x0018	Could not enable transmissions from the mouse
0x0019	Unable to create the symbolic link for %1
0x001A	Exceeded the allowable number of retries (configurable via the registry) on device %1
0x001B	The operation on %1 timed out (time out is configurable via the registry).
0x001C	Could not successfully write the Controller Command Byte for the i8042
0x001D	An unexpected ACKNOWLEDGE was received from the device.
0x001E	An unexpected RESEND was received from the device.
0x001F	No mouse port ("PS/2 compatible") mouse device was detected on the i8042 auxiliary port (not a problem unless this type of mouse really is connected)
0x0020	No mouse port ("PS/2 compatible") mouse device was detected on the i8042 auxiliary port (not a problem unless this type of mouse really is connected)
0x0021	The keyboard and mouse devices do not exist or were not detected.
0x0022	An error occurred while trying to determine the number of mouse buttons.
0x0023	An unexpected RESET was detected from the mouse device.
0x0024	An unexpected RESET was detected from the mouse device. The wheel has been deactivated.

Table A-11   Windows NT Virtual Machine Additions S3 Video Driver Event Codes

Event	Description
1	An S3 adapter was detected but can not be used by the system due to a limitation in the driver: The S3 ROM could not be found

Appendix B

Virtual Server 2005 R2 Management Pack Rules

The Virtual Server 2005 R2 Management Pack includes the following rule groups and rules. All rules are enabled by default.

Table B-1 Virtual Machine Rules

Rule	Definition	Type	Severity
Virtual Machine: Virtual machine name does not match computer name	This rule generates an Error alert if the name assigned to a virtual machine in Virtual Server does not match the computer name of the guest operating system. This alert is generated only if the guest operating system has both Virtual Machine Additions and a MOM agent installed.	Event	Error

Table B-2 Core Service Rules

Rule	Type	Severity
Virtual Hard Disk: Low disk space	Event	Error
Virtual Hard Disk: NTFS file system is required	Event	Error
Virtual Hard Disk: Unable to access or write to disk	Event	Error
Virtual Machine: Administrator needs to check virtual machine	Event	Critical Error
Virtual Machine: Cannot mount virtual floppy disk	Event	Error
Virtual Machine: Device is not available	Event	Error
Virtual Machine: Duplicate MAC address	Event	Error
Virtual Machine: Fatal error - parent differencing disk is invalid	Event	Error
Virtual Machine: IDE disk error	Event	Error
Virtual Machine: Incompatible saved state	Event	Service Unavailable
Virtual Machine: Linked disk error	Event	Error
Virtual Machine: Low disk space	Event	Error
Virtual Machine: NTFS file system is required	Event	Error
Virtual Machine: The Virtual Server 2005 Evaluation Kit license has expired	Event	Service Unavailable

Table B-2   Core Service Rules

Rule	Type	Severity
Virtual Machine: Unable to access or write to disk	Event	Critical Error
Virtual Machine: Virtual Machine Additions is out of date	Event	Error
Virtual Machine: Virtual machine could not be started	Event	Error
Virtual Machine: Virtual machine has experienced a fatal error	Event	Critical Error
Virtual Machine: Virtual machine has insufficient memory	Event	Critical Error
Virtual Machine: Virtual machine improperly configured	Event	Error
Virtual Machine: Virtual network could not be found	Event	Error
Virtual Machine: Virtual Network Services driver error	Event	Error
Virtual Server configuration: Cannot access or write to file	Event	Error
Virtual Server: Cannot save changes to the virtual machine configuration file	Event	Error
Virtual Server: Fatal error	Event	Service Unavailable
Virtual Server: Invalid entry in virtual machine configuration file	Event	Error
Virtual Server: Invalid parent disk	Event	Critical Error
Virtual Server: Invalid XML configuration file	Event	Error
Virtual Server: Low disk space	Event	Critical Error
Virtual Server: Low memory	Event	Error
Virtual Server: No physical network adapter was found	Event	Error
Virtual Server: Non-fatal exception	Event	Critical Error
Virtual Server: The Virtual Server 2005 Evaluation Kit license has expired	Event	Service Unavailable
Virtual Server: The Virtual Server installation has become corrupted	Event	Critical Error
Virtual Server: User has insufficient permissions	Event	Error
Virtual Server: Virtual machine configuration file is corrupt	Event	Error
Virtual Server: Virtual Machine Helper service error	Event	Error
Virtual Server: Virtual Machine Network Services driver error	Event	Error
VMRC: Port in use	Event	Critical Error
VMRC: Server not a domain member	Event	Warning
VMRC: Service principal name (SPN) could not be registered	Event	Critical Error
VMRC: User could not connect	Event	Error
Notify Virtualization Administrators of alerts with severity of Critical Error or greater	Notification	Not applicable
VM Disk Space Used	Performance Measuring	None
VM RAM Used	Performance Measuring	None
VM CPU Utilization	Performance Measuring	None

Table B-3   State Monitoring and Service Discovery Rules

Rule	Definition	Type
Virtual Server Service Discovery	This rule performs service discovery for Virtual Server hosts, virtual machines, and virtual networks. By default, a service discovery is performed every 4 hours.	Event
	This rule generates several types of alert. The rule changes the state of a virtual machine in the Operator Console based on the number of expected heartbeats received since the previous service discovery or based on virtual machine status in Virtual Server.	
	By default, if 50 percent or more of expected heartbeats are reported, virtual machine state is set to Green (Running), 15 percent through 49 percent of expected heartbeats sets the state to Yellow (Warning), and 14 percent or fewer of expected heartbeats sets the state to Red (Critical Error).	
	If Virtual Machine Additions are not installed on a virtual machine (and the heartbeat cannot be monitored), an error is generated and the virtual machine state is set to Red.	
Virtual Server Service Health Check	If the Virtual Server service is in a Stopped state, this rule generates a Service Unavailable alert and sets the state of the Virtual Server host to Red.	Event
Notify Virtualization Administrators of Critical Error or greater	This rule notifies members of the Virtualization Administrators notification group (using e-mail message or a pager response) when a rule in the State Monitoring and Service Discovery rule group generates an alert with a severity of Critical Error or Service Unavailable.	Notification

Glossary

A

ACPI   Advanced Configuration and Power Interface; an open specification that defines common interfaces for hardware recognition, power management, and hardware configuration.

ADS   Automated Deployment Services; a service that runs on Windows Server 2003 and provides network-based deployment of server images to physical or virtual hardware.

agent   A software application that provides remote functions and interfaces for another application.

Allowed-to-Delegate-to (A2D2)   An attribute for service accounts that contains a list of service principal names to which a service account can perform delegation.

AMD-V   AMD's virtualization technology that provides hardware virtualization features, which can be leveraged by software vendors to extend their virtualization solution architectures.

application-level virtualization   Virtualization approach that partitions and isolates applications from each other to prevent interaction or incompatibilities from occurring.

B

BAT   Block allocation table; a table of absolute sector offsets to the data blocks in the virtual hard disk header.

binary translation   The emulation of one instruction set by another.

business continuity   The approach of defining and implementing a server and application solution that will resume services in a minimum amount of time in the event of a major disaster.

C

checkpoint   The creation of a differencing disk as a way to provide rollback to a previous state of a virtual machine.

clustering   Using two or more servers connected to a shared disk system as a single logical system for failure recovery.

Cmdlet   A command implemented by deriving a class from one of two specialized Windows PowerShell base classes.

CMS   A single-user operating system, developed by IBM for the System/360 Model 67. It ran inside a virtual machine to deliver access to underlying system resources to each user .

collection   An array of object references that can be enumerated.

COM   Component Object Model; a programming interface that allows interprocess communication and dynamic object creation.

commit   Process that modifies the parent virtual hard disk by merging the contents of an undo disk (.vud) file to the virtual hard disk.

Common Internet File System (CIFS)   An Application-layer network protocol that allows access to shared files, printers, and serial ports between nodes on a network.

compact   Process of removing empty sectors from a dynamically expanding virtual hard disk to reduce space used on the host.

COM port   Communications Port; the serial ports of the computer.

conditions of satisfaction   Measurable events or outcomes that a project can be evaluated against to determine success.

constrained delegation   The ability to specify that a computer or service account can perform Kerberos delegation to a limited set of services.

CScript   The command prompt-based VBScript processing engine.

D

DACL   Discretionary access control list; contains allow and deny access control entries for an object.

defragmentation   The process that a hard disk is put through to ensure that files are stored as contiguous blocks in the hard disk, improving performance.

differencing disk   A virtual hard disk that is an overlay to another virtual hard disk called a "parent" and that stores the disk writes. Differencing disks can have many overlay layers and a parent can have many "children" differencing disks.

disk geometry   The combination of cylinders, heads, and sectors that define the capacity and configuration of a hard disk.

E

emulation   The process whereby a virtual computer system or component performs in the same way as a physical computer system or component.

F

fully qualified domain name (FQDN)   The combination of the server name and the domain where it resides. For example, a server named *server1* in a domain *contoso.com*, the FQDN would be *server1.contoso.com*.

G

Gb/s   Gigabit per second

GB   Gigabyte

GHz   Gigahertz

Globally Unique Identifier (GUID)   A type of identifier used in software applications to provide a unique reference number to an object.

Guest   The virtual machine being hosted by Virtual Server that is made up of the virtual hardware, operating system, and installed applications.

guest operating system   The operating system that executes in the virtual machine.

H

HAL   Hardware Abstraction Layer; a layer that is implemented in software to provide a standard interface to the hardware and hide differences to the operating system and applications.

HBA   Host Bus Adapters; specialized disk controllers that provide high-speed connections between the host machine and the disk system.

heartbeat   A signal emitted at regular intervals by a virtual machine to indicate that it is still running.

heterogeneous consolidation   Combining different application workloads from multiple servers on a single server.

homogeneous consolidation   Combining multiple server workloads for the same application on a single server.

host   Physical server that is running Virtual Server 2005 R2.

host group   A collection of Virtual Server hosts that are grouped together for administration, management, or security reasons.

host key   The key (right ALT key, by default) that must be pressed within Virtual Server to move keyboard and mouse focus from a guest operating system back to the host operating system.

Hosted Virtualization   Virtualization application that requires an underlying host operating system like Windows Server to run.

hotfix   A software update that addresses a specific problem.

hypercall   A special interface that provides access to computer instructions to an operating system running in a virtual machine. The operating system must be modified to use the hypercall instead of the standard interface.

hypervisor   A virtual machine monitor implemented in software that can run directory on hardware or as a layer of an operating system.

I

IDE   Integrated Drive Electronics; the hard and floppy disk interface that comes with almost every personal computer. The controller electronics are implemented on the hard disk itself.

in-scope   A task, action, or object that is considered part of a project.

Intel VT   Intel's virtualization technology that provides hardware virtualization features, which can be leveraged by software vendors to extend their virtualization solution architectures.

iSCSI   Internet SCSI; (1) SCSI protocols over IP networks; (2) Technology that allows a remote server to serve out a chunk of its storage space and have it look like a local SCSI disk.

.iso   ISO files are images of CD or DVD disks that can be connected to the virtual CD/DVD drive of a virtual machine.

K

KB   Kilobyte or Knowledge Base

Kb/s   Kilobit per second

KVM   A device that allows you to share a keyboard, video, and mouse between multiple computers.

L

Lightweight Directory Access Protocol (LDAP)   Application protocol for querying and modifying directory services over TCP/IP. Standard defined by the Internet Engineering Task Force and defined in RFC 4510.

LUN   Logical Unit Number; an address to a partition of a set of hard disks. The partition size can be any percentage of the disk array.

M

Management Pack   An extension to Microsoft Operations Manager that predefines rules, filters, performance counters, and alerts that should be monitored for a specific application or hardware.

maximum capacity   The maximum percentage of a single processor (or core if multicore) that can be consumed by a virtual machine.

maximum system capacity   The maximum percentage of the host's resources that a virtual machine can consume. This is 1 divided by the number of processors (or cores if multicore) in the host.

Mb/s   Megabits per second

MB   Megabytes

MB/s   Megabytes per second

media access control (MAC)   Unique, 6-byte hardware address assigned to a network adapter so that any packet it sends can be returned. Virtual Server-assigned MAC addresses are in the 00-03-FF-xx-xx-xx range.

merge   The process of combining sectors from multiple differencing virtual hard disks to produce a single virtual hard disk with all changes.

MHz   Megahertz

N

NAS   Network Attached Storage; a technology that allows disk systems to be directly attached to an IP network and accessed like a local disk.

native virtualization   Virtualization approach that requires a processor to support virtualization aware instructions to offload software processing.

NUMA   Non-Uniform Memory Access; a processor architecture feature that provides faster access to memory that is locally attached to the processor so that it is tuned for performance.

O

operating system–level virtualization   Virtualization approach where a single operating system is abstracted to provide multiple isolated virtualized copies of the kernel, memory, and configuration. Only one copy of the operating system is ever running.

Options.xml   Configuration file that contains the Virtual Server host configuration information, administration console settings, and binding information for physical network adapters.

out-of-scope   A task, action, or object that is not considered part of a project.

P

P2V   Process of migrating a physical machine to a virtual machine.

paravirtualization   Virtualization approach where the operating system requires modification to handle nonvirtualizable x86 instructions being supported between the virtual machine and the hypervisor via custom APIs called hypercalls.

PerfMon   A performance monitoring application included with Windows 2000 and newer operating systems.

PowerShell   A new scripting language and command line interface shell from Microsoft.

PreCompaction   The process of running a tool that will clear any unused sectors in a virtual hard disk by writing zeros to the sectors.

PXE   Pre-boot Execution Environment; a BIOS-enabled option to boot the computer from a network boot server. Typically enabled by pressing F12.

Q

quiesce   The process of flushing all memory and disk buffers to ensure that all transactions are complete before attempting a backup.

quorum disk   The shared cluster disk on which configuration data is maintained in the quorum log, cluster database checkpoint, and resource checkpoints.

R

RAID   Redundant Array of Inexpensive Disks; a technology for combining hard disks together in a logical unit. There are different types of RAID that focus on availability and speed.

relative weight   A numeric value assigned to a virtual machine that defines the importance of the virtual machine's access to resources versus another virtual machine. Virtual machines with higher relative weights obtain higher priority on resources.

reserved capacity   The percentage of a single processor (or core, if multicore) that is reserved for the virtual machine's use.

reserved system capacity   The percentage of a total host processor (or core, if multicore) capacity that is reserved for the virtual machine's use. This value cannot be larger than the maximum system capacity.

ring compression   The process of executing multiple ring modes for a virtual processor in a single ring mode of the physical processor.

RIS   Remote Installation Service; a Windows application that provides remote boot and operating system installation across the network.

ROI   Return on Investment; the cost savings experienced from deploying a technology. The return is the total savings minus the cost of deploying and operating the new technology. Total savings would include capital, power, space, cooling, manpower, and time cost savings.

rule   Microsoft Operations Manager feature that define events, alerts, and performance data to collect and what to do with the information after it is collected.

S

SAN Storage Area Network, a technology to allow one or more computers to attach to a large array of disk drives and access defined chunks in independent or shared mode.

save state The process of saving the current memory, process, and disk configuration to a file called a save state file (.vsv) so that the machine can be quickly resumed. Similar to the concept of hibernating a computer.

SCP Service Connection Point; a feature that allows a service to register itself in Active Directory tied to the host that it is running on.

SCVMM Microsoft's server application to manage one or more Virtual Server hosts.

search paths Paths to directories that should be included in the search scope when populating selection boxes in the administration console.

server consolidation The process of reducing the number of physical servers that are required to run a set of workloads by combining workloads on fewer servers.

side-by-side execution The ability for two applications to execute at the same time, referencing different versions of the same dynamic link library (DLL).

SLA Service Level Agreement; a written definition of the expected service level that an organization managing a server would provide to the users. The agreement normally defines the levels and types of support and communications that are expected as well as any impacts that will result if the levels are not reached or maintained.

snapshot Copy of the current hardware, software, process, memory, and disk state of a virtual machine that can be quickly restored.

SP1 Service Pack 1

SPN Service Principle Name; the information stored in Active Directory that defines a service running on a server and allows Kerberos authentication to the service.

support level An expected performance for support of a service, server, or application defined as a percentage value.

SysPrep A process and tool that allows you to remove the unique identity of a computer and reset it at next boot.

T

TB Terabytes

teaming The ability to have multiple network adapters act as one to provide higher throughput and failover. This is a network adapter manufacturer feature.

threshold A value selected to be a maximum or minimum limit target value. Usually, the objective is to get as close to the threshold value as possible without exceeding it.

U

undo disk A virtual hard disk that stores all the writes to virtual hard disk so that the original disk is not modified. When the virtual machine is powered off, you have the choice of committing all the writes in the undo disk to the original or discarding the writes and returning the original back to the state at power on.

unit (U) A standard for measuring the height of a rack mount device and the rack it is installed.

update sequence number (USN) A number assigned to an object in Active Directory that is used to track updates originating from a domain controller.

User Account Control (UAC) Feature of Windows Vista that forces all processes to run at a lower level of privilege by default and requires any action needing a higher level of privilege be approved before it will be executed. This feature is available to users with administrative privileges.

UUID An identifier that is used to provide a unique tracking number for an object.

V

virtual-to-virtual (V2V)   The process of migrating a virtual machine of one format to another format.

virtualization   The abstraction of physical systems resources such that multiple logical partitions can be created to host a heterogeneous set of operating systems, each running simultaneously on a single server.

virtualization candidate   A physical server that meets all the requirements to be migrated to a virtual server.

.vfd   Virtual Floppy Disk; the file-based representation of a virtual floppy disk with full disk header and data storage.

.vhd   Virtual Hard Disk; a portable, file-based representation of a physical hard disk with complete replication of disk header structure.

VHDMount   Utility that allows a host to mount a VHD file as a local disk for read and write operations.

VLAN   Virtual Local Area Network; a technology to provide multiple logical networks on a single physical cable.

VM   A virtual machine monitor developed by IBM for the System/360 Model 67. It created and controlled virtual machines.

.vmc   Virtual Machine Configuration; the file that holds the configuration information of the virtual machine (memory, hard disk, network adapters, BIOS settings, etc.).

VMM   Virtual Machine Monitor; responsible for the creation, isolation, and preservation of virtual machine state, as well as the orchestration of access to system resources.

VMNS   Virtual Machine Network Service; the service that binds the virtual network to the physical network adapter in the host and allows traffic from the virtual machines to share the physical network adapter.

VMRC   Virtual Machine Remote Control, a protocol that was developed to provide remote control of a virtual machine from the moment it boots.

VMRC Client   A Windows forms-based application that utilizes the VMRC protocol to remotely manage running virtual machines.

VNC   Virtual Network Configuration; the file that holds the virtual network configuration information (network bindings, DHCP settings, etc.).

virtual machine   A computer that exists only in software and has virtual hardware components like a motherboard, hard disks, memory, video, network adapters, and SCSI adapters.

virtual floppy drive   A software-based emulation of a 1.44MB floppy 3.5" floppy drive.

virtual floppy disk   A software-based representation of a 1.44MB floppy disk.

Virtual Machine Additions   A set of drivers and services that are installed in a virtual machine to provide better performance and enhanced user experience.

virtual machine library   Collection of pre-built virtual machines accessible for modification and rapid deployment.

virtual machine memory   The memory currently reserved for the virtual machine. Virtual memory can only be allocated from the host's available physical memory.

virtual network   A network switch implemented in software that provides an unlimited number of ports for virtual machines to connect and a single uplink port that can be bound to a physical network adapter in the host.

VSMT   Virtual Server Migration Toolkit; an application that allows you to migrate a physical server to a virtual machine.

VSS   Volume ShadowCopy Service; the service available in Windows Server 2003 or newer operating systems that allows the server and any VSS-compatible applications to be quickly backed up without data loss.

.vsv   Virtual Saved State; the file-based storage of the current memory, process, and configuration of the virtual machine.

.vud   Virtual Undo Disk; the file-based storage of delta changes to a virtual machine that can be merged to the original VHD or discarded. If undo disks are enabled, all virtual hard disks attached to the virtual machine will have a VUD.

W

Windows Remote Management (WinRM)

Microsoft implementation of WS-Management Protocol, a standard Simple Object Access Protocol (SOAP)-based, firewall-friendly protocol that allows hardware and operating systems, from different vendors, to interoperate.

WMI   Windows Management Instrumentation; the set of interfaces that allow you to obtain hardware and software information about the local server. Virtual Server 2005 R2 provides WMI interfaces.

WScript   The Windows form-based VBScript processing engine.

X

XML   Extensible Markup Language; a general purpose structured data format that facilitates the sharing of data across different information systems or applications.

Z

z/VM   A current IBM virtualization product.

About the Authors

Janique Carbone has developed Virtual PC and Virtual Server training for customer events such as TechEd, authored whitepapers for the Microsoft Windows Storage team, delivered customer and partner-focused Windows Server training, and assisted customers in planning, maintaining, and optimizing business critical Windows Server infrastructures, including Microsoft Virtual Server 2005 deployments. She has been working in IT for over 14 years on projects ranging from application development to enterprise infrastructure design. In May 2006, after 7 years at Microsoft, she founded the Infrastructor Group, whose charter is to deliver in-depth training, consulting, and community management encompassing the entire virtualization project lifecycle. While at Microsoft, Janique worked as a Senior Consultant in Microsoft Consulting Services, specializing in the architecture and deployment of Active Directory for large enterprises. During her tenure in Microsoft Premier Support, she focused on operational management for medium-size enterprises. Janique is an MCSE, and holds a B.S. and M.S. in Aerospace Engineering as well as an M.S. in Computer Science. She currently lives in Texas and shares life with her great husband, two wonderful children, and four lively dogs.

Robert Larson is an Architect with Microsoft Consulting Services (MCS) and a subject matter expert on virtualization technologies. Robert is a regular speaker at TechEd and ITForum conferences on virtualization topics and has delivered multiple TechNet webcasts on Virtual Server 2005 clustering and COM API. He has authored or helped develop whitepapers for Microsoft on building clusters using Virtual Server 2005 and best practices around using virtualization with Active Directory. Robert also writes articles for Windows IT Pro magazine on virtualization topics. Robert has worked in the IT industry for over 17 years as engineer, outsourcer, and consultant. As an Architect for MCS, he assists customers and partners to plan and design data center and server consolidation projects involving virtualization. Robert has a master's degree in Computer Science. Robert lives with his lovely wife and two active children outside Houston, Texas, where he enjoys basketball, scuba diving, and cooking.

Index

A

accelerated SCSI driver, 327
Acceleration (ISA) Server 2004, 368
access control lists (ACLs), 75, 170
ACPI. *See* Advanced Configuration and Power Interface (ACPI)
ACS. *See* Audit Collection Systems (ACS)
Active Directory, 159
  collecting Active Directory Site information, 348
  collecting domain information, 348
  collecting server information, 349–350
  collecting subnets-per site information, 349
Active Directory domain controller virtual machine, backing up, 417–418
Active Directory Service
  constrained delegation supported in, 78
  requirements for installing Virtual Server 2005 R2 with SP1, 75–76
  virtual machine server publication using connection points, 21
Active Directory site information, collecting, 348
Active Directory Topology Generator (ADTD), 358
Active Directory Users, 78–79
ActiveX control, 171
ActiveX Data Objects (ADO), 481
Adaptec SCSI driver, 59, 326
AddHardDiskConnection method, 246, 254
Add/Remove Windows Components, 85
AddSCSIController method, 251
AddVHD.vbs, 251–253
administration team grouping, 377–378
administration tools
  HyperAdmin, 496–497
  Microsoft Virtual Machine Remote Control Plus (VMRCplus), 497–498
  overview, 495–496
Administration Website, 32, 76
  access denied using Virtual Server Manager, 319
  always prompted for credentials, 317–318
  application, 165
  blank screen display, 316–317
  configuring, 167–173
  configuring centralized, 403–410
  and configuring constrained delegation, 78k
  configuring default virtual machine configuration folder, 169–170
  configuring search paths, 167–169
  and constrained delegation, 163
  enabling reduced colors from, 178–179
  enabling Virtual Machine Remote Control (VMRC), 170–173

  inspecting Virtual Server Event Viewer, 52
  installing, on Central Server, 94
  installing Virtual Server host server with no local, 96–97
  managing with
    Master Status page, 35–36
    multiple virtual server hosts, 36–37
    virtual hard disks, 40–41
    virtual machine resource allocation, 51–52
    virtual machines, 37–40
    virtual networks, 42–44
    virtual server properties, 44–49
    Website Properties, 49–51
  securing remote, 164
  server farm with, and remote resources, 93–97
  uninstalling Virtual Server 2005 R2 SP1, 101
  user interface (UI), 148
Administration Website Properties, 49–50, 153
Administrative Console, 248, 250–253
Administrators Permission Entry, 148–149
ADO. *See* ActiveX Data Objects (ADO)
ADS. *See* Automated Deployment Services (ADS)
ADTD. *See* Microsoft Active Directory Topology Diagrammer (ADTD)
Advanced Configuration and Power Interface (ACPI), 291
agent-based backup application, 416–417
AlertOnNoAdditions, 437
alerts, 438, 443
All parameter, 122
All Virtual Server report, 448
Allowed-to-be Delegate (A2D2) Active Directory attribute, 406
AMD Virtualization (AMD-V)
  defined, 4
  stop error on x64 Windows operating system with, 316
  to support native virtualization, 6, 19–20
  and Windows Server 2008, 26
  See also performance
AMD-V. *See* AMD Virtualization (AMD-V)
analysis and planning tools
  Microsoft Active Directory Topology Diagrammer (ADTD), 481–483
  Microsoft Windows Server System Virtualization Calculators, 483–485
  overview, 481
  PlateSpin PowerRecon, 485–487
  SystemTools Exporter Pro, 487–488
antivirus software, 180
application folders, 146–148

application information, collecting, 353–354
application programming interface (API), 445
application programming interface (API). *See*
    Component Object Model (COM) application
    programming interface (API)
application support limits, assessing, 367–368
application support policy, 24–25
application-based grouping, 377–378
application-level virtualization, 9–10
architecture
    hardware assisted virtualization and, 61
    pilot, 391–392
    product, 55–57
    save state file, 57, 69
    virtual floppy disks, 57, 69
    virtual hard disks, 57, 64–68
    Virtual Machine Additions, 57–59
    Virtual Machine Helper service, 57–58
    Virtual Machine Monitor (VMM), 57–58
    virtual memory, 57, 61–64
    virtual networks, 57, 61–64
    virtual processors, 57, 59–61
    Virtual Server service, 57–58
architecture design team, 337, 339, 341
Assessment phase, of virtualization project
    capital cost savings, 368–369
    environmental savings, 369–371
    identifying virtualization candidate, 361–368
AttachVirtualNetwork method, 254
Audit Collection Systems (ACS), 154
Automated Deployment Service MMC snap-in, 307–308
Automated Deployment Services (ADS)
    capturing source system image, 297
    function of, 17
    installing, 299–301
    prerequisites, 299
    and virtual network adapters, 34

B
backup
    Active Directory domain controller virtual machine,
        417–418
    agent-based applications, 416–417
    applications for, 387
    file-based, 416–418
    management of, 14
    requirements, 386–387
    system, 193
    using traditional methods to, Virtual Server and
        virtual machines, 415–417
    using VSS to, Virtual Server and virtual machines,
        412–415
backup driver, 59
bare metal virtualization, 8
basic input/output system (BIOS)
    collecting information about, 350–351
    configuring virtual machine settings for, 211
    installing guest operating system, 213–215
    and Intel support, 20
    as virtualized hardware component, 30
BETest, 412
BIOS. *See* basic input/output system (BIOS)
BIOS Power-on Self Test (POST), 35
BIOS Setup Utility Main screen, 212
blank screen display, 316–317
block allocation table (BAT), 65, 68
block size field name, 67, 112
blue screen, 320
branch office, consolidating, 15–16
budget, creating project, 344
budget manager, 338
builder role, 221–222
business problem statements, 335
Bypass Traverse Checking, 153
BytesDropped counter, 243, 424
BytesReceived counter, 244, 425
BytesSent counter, 244, 425

C
Calculator 1, 483–485
Calculator 2, 483, 485
Cancel method, 240
candidates, grouping virtualization, 377–378
capital cost savings, 368–369
capture source system image, 297–298
CD/DVD, 39, 203–204
CEC. *See* Windows Server System Common Engineering
    Criteria (CEC)
central server, installing Administration Website on,
    93–97
centralized Administration Website
    choosing deployment topology, 404–406
    configuring constrained delegation, 406–409
    configuring Virtual Server Manager search paths,
        409–410
    overview, 403–404
    with separate Virtual Server hosts, 404
    with separate Virtual Server hosts and file servers
        topology, 405
chain, 110
Change permission, 150
checksum field name, 66–67, 112
Chkdsk.exe utility, 303
CIFS. *See* Common Internet File System (CIFS) service
CIPS service, 91
Clear method, 231
Cluster Configuration Wizard, 133
clustering
    configurations, 130
    host, 20–21, 376–377

Microsoft Cluster Server (MSCS), 130–131
using advanced features, 130–142
Virtual Machine Cluster using iSCSI, 130–135
Virtual Server Host Cluster, 130–131
CMS. *See* Conversational Monitor System (CMS)
Collection.count property, 230
colors
enabling reduced, from Administration Website, 178–179
enabling reduced, from VRMC Windows Client, 179
COM+ interface, 58. *See also* Virtual Server service
COM port settings, changing virtual, 207–208
COM ports, 40
command queuing, 181–182
command-line
examples of, 106–107
installing, 102–107
options for, 103–106
performing installation scenarios using, 107
uninstalling work, 107
commercial-grade virtualization, 4
Commit Undo Disks option, 117
Common Internet File System (CIFS) service, 407–408
communications manager, 338–339
communications plan, creating, 396–397
compaction
defragmenting virtual hard disk file, 123–124
precompaction of virtual hard disk file, 124–125
virtual hard disk file, 125–126
Component Object Model (COM) application, 76, 298
Component Object Model (COM) application
programming interface (API)
adding VHDs to virtual machine, 250–253
advanced example, 274–279
advanced scripting, 236–253
connecting to remote Virtual Server, 233–234
connecting to Virtual Server object, 228–229
creating virtual hard disks, 248–250
error handling, 230–233
file and folder management, 237–238
logging events, 238–240
managing virtual machines, 253–262
managing virtual networks, 262–267
managing Virtual Server configurations, 267–274
obtaining virtual hard disk information, 246–248
retrieving and displaying information, 229–230
scripting with, 227–234
using , with Visual Basic Script, 227–279
using tasks, 240–241
using Virtual Server CVMI namespace, 242–246
VHMount functions, 235
VMGuestOS properties and methods, 235–236
VMRCClient Control property, 236
VMTask properties, 235
computer groups, 439

computing resources, increasing availability of, 13
conditions of satisfaction, 399
configuration file, add virtual network, 43
Configure Components dialog box, 95
Configure Your Server Wizard, 85–86
Connectix Virtual PC product, 17
ConnectToVS.vbs script, 231–232
Console Manager, 497–498
consolidation planning approaches
equipment reuse, 385
grouping virtualization candidates, 377–378
performing workload analysis, 379–384
consolidation ratio, 373–374
constrained delegation
choosing deployment topology, 405–406
configuring, 78–80, 406–409
defined, 78, 315
enabling, 163
content refresh, and virtual machine library, 225
Control Panel, 82–86
Control permission, 150
Controller server, 299–300
Conversational Monitor System (CMS), 4
Conversion Information Wizard page, 474
conversion tools
Invirtus Enterprise VM Converter 2007, 489
Leostream P V Direct 3.0, 490
overview, 488
PlateSpin PowerConvert, 491–493
cookie field name, 66–67, 112–113
cooling costs, 371
CopyFile method, 237
CopyFolder method, 237
Core Service rules, 521–522
costs
capital cost savings, 368–369
cooling, 371
environmental savings, 369–371
reducing capital and operating, 11–12
Count property, 230
CPU Resource Allocation
form for, 51–52
parameter definition, 285
CpuUtilization counter, 242, 423
Create Virtual Machine form, 37–38
CreateDifferencingVirtualHardDisk method, 245, 249
CreateDynamicVirtualHardDisk, 245, 249
CreateFixedVirtualHardDisk method, 245, 249
CreateFolder method, 237
CreateHostDriveVirtualHardDisk method, 245
CreateObject command, 232–233
CreateObject() method, 228
CreateVirtualMachine method, 253–254
CreateVirtualNetwork method, 263–264
CreateVM.vbs, 255–257

CreateVNET.vbs, 264–265
creator application field name, 66
creator host OS field name, 66
creator version field name, 66
credentials, always prompted for, 317–318
CScript, 229
current size field name, 66
Custom Setup dialog box, 96
Customer Service and Support (CSS), 25

D

DACL. *See* discretionary access control list (DACL)
data blocks, 65
data center, 15
data offset field name, 66–67, 112
data processing, 381–382
Data Protection Manager 2007, 391–392
Data Transformation Services (DTS), 446
Debug Assertion Event, 512
debugging scripts, 232–233
default virtual network (VM0), 302
defragmentation, 123–1124
DeleteFile method, 237
DeleteFolder method, 237
DeleteVirtualMachine method, 253, 257–259, 263
DeleteVM.vbs, 258–259
deployment topology, 404–406
Description method, 240
Description property, 231
DHCP. *See* Dynamic Host Configuration Protocol (DHCP)
DHCP Server Properties form, 44
diagram, 439
differencing virtual hard disk
    broken, after parent virtual hard disk is moved or
        renamed, 321–323
    and compaction, 123
    creating, 111–112
    defined, 32, 65, 109–110, 287
    examining parent-child differencing disk
        relationships, 112–114
    inspecting virtual hard disks, 41
    merging, 114–115
    multilevel, 110–111
    overview, 110–111
    and undo disks, 116
    using, 115–116
    using, to create guest VMs for concurrent testing,
        115–116
Discard Saved State registry key, 218
Discard Undo Disks option, 117
Discovery phase, of virtualization project
    collecting Active Directory information, 348–350
    defined, 347
    environmental information, 357

inventory, 350–355
    performance monitoring, 355–356
    tools, 358
discretionary access control list (DACL), 149–151
disk access, measurement of, 175. *See also* memory
        performance
disk array, creating, 182
disk drive configuration, 182–183
Disk Expansion Wizard, 495
disk geometry field name, 66
disk hardware limits, 364–365
disk monitoring, 356
disk performance assessment, 366–367
disk resources, configuring, 140
disk subsystem, scalable and high-performance, 221
disk type, 291
disk type field name, 66
DiskBytesRead counter, 242, 423
DiskBytesWritten counter, 242, 423
DiskShadow, 412
DiskSpaceUsed counter, 242
display graphics performance, increasing, 177–178
DNS. *See* Domain Name Server (DNS)
Document Library Web page, 394
documentation and developer resources, 97–98, 107
Domain Administrators group, 75
domain controller manager, 223
domain controller user, 223
domain controllers, 417–418
domain information, collecting, 348
Domain Name Server (DNS), 159
DOS Virtual Machine Additions.vfd, 206
drive letter restrictions, solving with mountpoints,
        376–377
DriveLetter, 122
driver updates, 184
drivers, loading, into Automated Deployment Services
        (ADS), 306
DTS. *See* Data Transformation Services (DTS)
DVDDrives property, 269
dynamic disk header, 65, 67–68, 112
Dynamic Host Configuration Protocol (DHCP), 159,
        290
dynamic virtual hard disk (VHD), 23
dynamically expanding hard disk, 31, 41, 65, 188–189

E

Echo command, 229
emulated SCSI bus, 23
Enable Virtual Server extensions in Windows Firewall,
        89–90
Enhanced SCSI driver, 59
enlightenments, 7
environmental cost savings, 369–371
environmental information, collecting, 357

Envisioning, phase of virtualization project
   assembling project team, 336–341
   creating project budget, 344
   defined, 333–334
   defining problem statements, 334–336
   establishing vision statement, 336
   identifying risks, 342–344
equipment reuse, 385
Err object, 230–232
Error handling, 230–233
Error property, 241
ErrorDescription method, 241
Ethernet network adapter, 204
event codes
   Virtual Server Main Event, 512–517
   Virtual Server Networking, 503
   Virtual Server Preferences Change, 511
   Virtual Server VHDSTOR Driver, 517–518
   Virtual Server Virtual Machine, 505–510
   Virtual Server VMRC, 511–512
   Virtual Server VSS Writer, 503–505
   Windows 2000 Virtual Machine Additions i8042
      mouse and keyboard driver, 518–520
   Windows NT Virtual Machine Additions i8042
      mouse and keyboard driver, 519–520
   Windows NT Virtual Machine Additions S3 video
      driver, 520
Event Viewer, 52
event viewer properties, 51
events, 438
exchange server manager, 223
exchange server user, 223
ExecQuery method, 239
External Network, 33
external virtual network, 204

F

FAT. *See* file allocation table (FAT)
features field name, 66
fiber channel, 182
file allocation table (FAT), 291
file and folder management, 237–238
file format version field name, 66
file system, 291
file-based backup, 416–418
FileExists method, 237
FileSystemObject, 237, 272
FindVirtualMachine method, 253–254, 257, 261
FindVirtualNetwork method, 263
fixed virtual hard disk, 31, 41, 65
fixed-size virtual hard disk, 188–189
floppy disk drive
   changing settings for virtual, 206–207
   virtual machine configuration option, 40–41, 57, 69
   virtualized hardware component, 30

floppy disk image, 298
FloppyDrives property, 269
FolderExists method, 237
For Next loop, 230
FQDN. *See* fully qualified domain name (FQDN)
Full permission, 149
full virtualization, 5–6
fully qualified domain name (FQDN), 316–317
functional architect, 339

G

Gather Information Wizard page, 474
GatherHW.exe utility, 292, 295–297, 304
General Properties configuration, 163
general system configuration, 292
GetConfigurationValue method, 268
GetHardDiskInfo.vbs, 246–248
GetHostDriveSize method, 268
GetObject function, 239
GetSCSIAddress function, 235
GetVirtualMachineFiles method, 253
GetVirtualNetworkFiles method, 263
Gigabit Ethernet network adapter, 367
graphics performance
   increasing display, 177–178
   understanding, 187–188
green state, 439–440
group self-service policy, 468
grouping, of virtualization candidates, 377–378
guest kernal patches, 34
Guest Manager, 497
guest operating system
   installing, 213–215
   overview, 20, 22–23
   and product architecture, 55
   slow installation, 326–327
guest operating system profile, 455
guest virtual machine capacity, 23

H

hard disk footer, 65–67
hard disk information, collecting, 351–352
hard disk performance
   assessment of, 366–367
   disk drive configuration, 182–183
   evaluating applications affecting, 180
   how disks types affect performance, 181–182
   optimizing, 179–180
   understanding, 180–181
hard disk platters, 180
hard disks, 39. *See also* virtual hard disk (VHD); *and
   entries for specific types of hard disks*
HardDiskConnections, 246
Hardware Abstraction Layer (HAL), 291

hardware components, virtualized, 30–31
hardware configuration, secondary, 292
hardware inventory information, collecting, 350–353
hardware limits, virtual machine, 362–365
hardware performance thresholds, 379
hardware profile, 456–457
hardware requirements
    defining, 288–289
        high availability, 375–377
    for installing Virtual Server 2005 R2 SP1, 74
    for VMM Administrator Console, 470
    for VMM self-provisioning Web portal, 471
    for VMM server, 470
hardware-assisted virtualization state, 327–329
havm.vbs script, configuring, 140
HBAs. *See* Host bus adapters (HBAs)
header version field name, 67, 112
heartbeat generator, 34
heartbeat thresholds, 437
HeartbeatCount counter, 242, 424
HeartbeatInterval counter, 242, 424
HeartbeatPercentage counter, 242, 424
HeartbeatPercentCriticalThreshold, 437
HeartbeatRate counter, 242, 424
HeartbestPercentWarningThreshold, 437
HelpContext property, 231
HelpFile property, 231
hierarchies
    multilevel differencing disk, 110–111
    parent-child, 110–114
high-speed network interface, 220
Host bus adapters (HBAs), 182
host clustering, 20–21, 376–377
host information
    HostInfo properties to retrieve, 269–270
    reporting, 270–272
    VMVirtualServer methods to obtain, 269
host operating system, 5–7, 20–22
host performance
    increasing display graphics performance, 177–178
    increasing VMRC performance, 178–179
    maximizing memory performance, 174–176
    maximizing processor performance, 173–174
    thresholds, 379
HostDrives property, 269
Hosted machine model, 55–56
hosted virtualization solution, 8–9
HostInfo properties, 270–271
HostName registry key, 215
Hosts Overview, 458–459
host-to-guest networking
    creating virtual network for, 128
    defined, 126
    enabling Virtual DHCP Server on Virtual Network,
        128–129

implement, 128
HTTP. *See* Hypertext Transfer Protocol (HTTP)
HyperAdmin, 496–497
hypercall, 7–8
Hypertext Transfer Protocol (HTTP), 164
hyperthreaded logical processors, 173–174, 365
Hypervisor, 5–9

I
ID method, 241
IDE. *See* Integrated Drive Electronics (IDE)
IDE protocol, 201–202
IDE/ATAPI storage, 31
Image Distribution Service, 300–301
Imaging Tool installation setting, 213
independent software vendors (ISVs), 76
initiation, 183
installation
    of guest operating system, 213–215
    Internet Information Services (IIS), 81–86
    scenarios, 76–77
    slow, of guest operating system, 326–327
    troubleshooting issues, 313–316
    Virtual Server 2005 R2 Management Pack, 433–436
    of Virtual Server 2005 R2 SP1, 74–107
Integrated Drive Electronics (IDE), 32, 189, 320–321,
        364–365. *See also* virtual IDE interface
Integrated Windows authentication, 78
Intel Virtualization Technology (VT), 4, 19–20, 173–174
Intelligent Placement, 460, 477. *See also* virtual machine
        placement
interface
    high-speed network, 220
    and optimizing network performance, 183–184
Internal Network, 33
internal virtual network, 204
Internet connection sharing (ICS), 126, 129–130
Internet Information Services (IIS), 403
    installing, 81–86
    missing or incompatible configurations, 313–314
    Windows Server 2003, 85–86
    Windows Vista, 82–85
    Windows XP, 81–82
Internet SCSI (iSCSI)
    defined, 182–183
    implement Virtual Server Host Cluster using, 135–
        142
    initiator service, 132
    requirements for, 136–137
    requirements for Virtual Machine Cluster, 130–132
    Virtual Machine Cluster using, 130–135
inventory information, collecting
    hardware, 350–353
    services, 354–355
    software, 353–354

inventory source system configuration, 292
Invirtus Enterprise VM Converter 2007, 489
Invirtus VM Optimizer 3.0, 493–494
invocationID attribute, 417
ISA. *See* Acceleration (ISA) Server 2004
IsCancelable method, 240
IsComplete method, 241
iSCSI. *See* Internet SCSI (iSCSI)
iSCSI shared disk, configuring, 132–133, 138
IsHostDriveMounted method, 269
ISO Image, 456–457
ISO Image installation setting, 214
isolated physical network, 204
Issue Tracking Web part, 394
issues on tracking plan, creating, 395–396
ISVs. *See* independent software vendors (ISVs)

J

Jobs Overview, 466–467

K

KDC. *See* Windows Server 2003 Kerberos Key Distribu-
tion Center (KDC)
Keep Undo Disks option, 117
Kerberos, 35
Kerberos delegator, 78, 406
Key Performance Indicators (KPI) List Web part, 394
keyboard, 30, 34
Knowledge Base articles, 24
KVM switch, 369

L

LDAP. *See* Lightweight Directory Access Protocol
(LDAP)
lead project architect, 339
Leostream Converter, 490
Leostream Host Agent, 490
Leostream P V Direct 3.0, 490–491
Leostream P V Direct Wizard, 490
library of virtual machines, 192–193
Library Overview, 464–466
Lightweight Directory Access Protocol (LDAP), 21, 349,
481
linked virtual hard disk, 31
creating, 119
defined, 110, 118–119
requirements for using, 118–119
using, to convert physical disk, 119–120
Linux Guest Virtual Machine SCSI Emulation fix, 23
Linux virtual machine, 7, 20
Live Transfer method, 492
Local Administration Website, 107
Local Service account, 164

location grouping, and consolidation planning,
377–378
LogEvent method, 238–240
logfile parameter, 103
logging events, 238–240
logical partition, 4
logical unit numbers (LUNs), 182, 376–377
LogicalProcessorCount property, 269
Loopback Network Adapter, 126–129, 286
looping, 230
LPT port, 40, 209
LUNs. *See* logical unit numbers (LUNs)

M

MAC address(es)
changing virtual network adapter setting, 204
duplicate, 324–326
specific, when multiple devices are present, 291
virtual networking, 64
machine script settings, changing, 205–206
machine-level virtualization, 5–8
Mail Merge feature, 397
Managed Virtual Machines storage locations, 223
management tools
administrative tools, 495–498
analysis and planning tools, 481–488
conversion tools, 488–493
VHD tools, 493–495
manager role, 221–222
Master Status page, 35–36, 38
master status view, 50, 153
max table entries field name, 67, 112
maximum capacity allocation, 185–187, 285
MCSC. *See* Microsoft Cluster Server (MSCS)
memory, 31
allocation of, 196
defining workload requirements, 282–283
hardware components, 39
prerequisite for source system, 291
memory configurations, 175
memory hardware limits, 364
memory information, collecting, 351–352
memory monitoring, 355–356
memory performance, maximizing, 174–176
Memory Properties page, 201
Memory property, 269
memory setting, 201
memory types, 174
MemoryAvail property, 269
MemoryAvailString property, 269
MemoryTotalString property, 269
metadata document, 414–415
Microsoft Active Directory Topology Diagrammer
(ADTD), 358
documentation list, 482

exchange information captured by, 483
Microsoft Cluster Server (MSCS)
  configuring, on first virtual machine, 133–134
  configuring, on first virtual server host, 138–139
  configuring, on second virtual machine, 134–135
  configuring, on second virtual server host, 139
  and load-balanced approach, 376–377
  in pilot architecture, 391–392
  and unplanned cluster failure events, 136
  virtual machine cluster using iSCSI, 130–131
Microsoft Customer Service and Support (CSS). *See*
    Customer Service and Support (CSS)
Microsoft Exchange Server, 483
Microsoft Identity Integration Feature Pack, 24, 368
Microsoft Identity Integration Server (MIIS) 2003, 24,
    368
Microsoft Installer (MSI) package, 77
Microsoft Internet Server, 368
Microsoft ISA Server 2000, 24
Microsoft ISA Server 2004, 24
Microsoft iSCSI Software Initiator, 132
Microsoft Loopback Adapter
  configuring, 127–128
  defined, 126
  installing, 127
Microsoft Loopback Network Adapter. *See* Loopback
    Network Adapter
Microsoft Management Console (MMC), 78, 119
Microsoft Office SharePoint Server (MOSS) 2007, 394
Microsoft Operations Manager (MOM) 2005, 386
  agent requirements, 432
  Operator Console, 445
  overview, 427–429
Microsoft Operations Manager (MOM) 2007, 386
Microsoft Operations Manager (MOM) 2005 Operator
    Console
  tasks performed in, 428–429
  views, 438–439, 441–442
Microsoft Operations Manager (MOM) 2005 Virtual
    Server 2005 R2 Management Pack, 427–450
Microsoft Outlook, 397
Microsoft PS/2 mouse driver, 59
Microsoft Server Virtual Storage DeviceXX, 121
Microsoft SharePoint Portal Server 2003, 24, 368
Microsoft Software Updated Service (MSUS), 224
Microsoft Speech Server, 24, 368
Microsoft Support Lifecycle policy, 24
Microsoft System Center Operations Manager 2007
    Audit Collection Services (ACS), 154
Microsoft System Center Virtual Machine Manager
    (SCVMM), 385
Microsoft Systems Management Server 2003, 386
Microsoft Virtual Disk Service (VDS). *See* Virtual Disk
    Service (VDS)

Microsoft Virtual Machine PCI SCSI Controller driver,
    326–327
Microsoft Virtual Machine Remote Control Plus
    (VMRCplus), 497–498
Microsoft Virtual Server 2005. *See* Virtual Server 2005
Microsoft Virtual Server 2005 R2 SP2. *See* Virtual Server
    2005 R2 SP2
Microsoft Window NT Server 4.0, 291
Microsoft Windows 2000 Advanced Server, 291
Microsoft Windows 2000 Server, 291
Microsoft Windows Server 2003, 85–86, 147–148
  Datacenter Edition with SP1, 74–75
  Enterprise Edition with SP1, 23, 74–75, 291
  Enterprise Edition with SP2, 23, 75
  Standard Edition with SP1, 22, 74, 291
  Standard Edition with SP2, 23
Microsoft Windows Server 2003 R2
  Datacenter Edition, 74–75
  Enterprise Edition, 23, 74–75
  Standard Edition, 22, 74–75
Microsoft Windows Server System (WSS). *See* Windows
    Server System
Microsoft Windows Server System Virtualization Calcu-
    lators, 483–485
Microsoft Windows Small Business Server 2003 R2, 74
Microsoft Windows Small Business Server 2003 with
    SP1, 74
Microsoft Windows Vista applications folders, 146–148
Microsoft Windows Vista Business, 23, 74–75, 82–85
Microsoft Windows Vista Enterprise, 23, 74–75
Microsoft Windows Vista Ultimate, 23, 74–75
Microsoft Windows XP, 81, 146–148
Microsoft Windows XP Professional with SP2, 23, 74–
    75, 81–82
Microsoft Word 2007, 397
migration process. *See* physical-to-virtual (P2V) migra-
    tion process; virtual-to-virtual (V2V) machine
    migration
migration scripts, generate, 295–297. *See also entries for
    individual scripts*
MMC. *See* Microsoft Management Console (MMC)
MMX property, 269
Modify permission, 150
MOM configuration tasks, 427–428
MOM Management Server, 446
MOM Reporting, 446–450
MOSS. *See* Microsoft Office SharePoint Server (MOSS)
    2007
mountpoints, solving drive letter restrictions with, 376–
    377
MountVHD function, 235
mouse, 30, 34, 59
MoveFile method, 237
MoveFolder method, 237
MPS Multiprocessor PC, 291

MPS Uniprocessor PC, 291
MS Virtual Server SCSI Disk Device, 120
MSI. *See* Microsoft Installer (MSI) package
MSIFILE parameter, 103
MSUS. *See* Microsoft Software Updated Service (MSUS)
multilevel differencing disk hierarchy, 110–111
multiple core processor, 365
multiple virtual server hosts, managing, 36–37
multiple-sever configuration, 473
Multiport DEC 21140 network adapter, 34
My Views, 439

N

Name counter, 242–243, 424
named pipe setting, 208
naming standard, 190–192
NAS. *See* Network-Attached Storage (NAS)
NAT. *See* Network Address Translation (NAT)
Native Command Queuing (NCQ), 181
native virtualization, 5–7
NCQ. *See* Native Command Queuing (NCQ)
NDIS. *See* Network Driver Interface Specification (NDIS)
network adapter, 40
    changing settings, 204–205
    multifunction, 30, 291
network adapter hardware limits, 364
Network Address Translation (NAT), 126, 129–130
Network Boot Service, 300–301
network configuration, 292
Network Driver Interface Specification (NDIS), 56–57
network (for each NIC instance) monitoring, 356
network interface, high-speed, 220
network interface card information, collecting, 351–353
network interface card teaming, 34
Network Monitor, 64
network performance, 183–184, 367
network ports, 165
Network Properties form, 42–43
network requirement, defining workload, 285–287
Network Service account, 164
NetworkAdapters property, 269, 271
NetworkAddresses property, 269, 271
Network-Attached Storage (NAS), 32
NetworkBytesReceived counter, 242, 424
NetworkBytesSent counter, 242, 424
Non-Uniform Memory Access (NUMA), 175–176
Notify Virtualization Administrators of Critical Error or Greater rule, 523
NT4 Network Driver.vfd, 206
NTBackup, 193
NTFS settings changes, 155–157
NTLM, 35
NUMA. *See* Non-Uniform Memory Access (NUMA)
Number property, 231

O

object counters, 423–425
objVM variable, 257
On Error statement, 231
OpenTextFile method, 272
Operating System, 291
operating system
    collecting information about, 350, 352
    configuration of, 292
    requirements for installing Virtual Server 2005 R2 SP1, 74
OperatingSystem property, 269
operating-system virtualization, 8–9
operation tasks, 427–428
operational limitations, defining workload, 289
operational management team, 337, 340–341
operations engineer, 340
operations manager, 340
Operations Manager 2007, 391–392
operations plan, developing, 395
Operator Console
    tasks performed in, 428–429
    views, 438–439, 441–442
Original Media installation setting, 213
original size field name, 66
OSMajorVersion property, 270
OSMinorVersion property, 270
OSServicePackString property, 270
OSVersionString property, 270

P

PacketsDropped counter, 244, 425
PacketsReceived counter, 425
PacketsSent counter, 244, 425
Parallel Advanced Technology Attachment (PATA), 181
parallel port devices information, collecting, 351, 353
ParallelPort property, 270
paravirtualization, 5, 7–8
parent disk, read-only, 114
parent locator entries, 68, 113
parent time setup, 68
parent time stamp, 112
parent unicode name, 68, 112
parent unique ID, 68
parent UUID, 112
parent-child hierarchies, 110–114
PATA. *See* Parallel Advanced Technology Attachment (PATA)
patch management, 386
    defined, 224
    defining procedures, 421–423
    extending strategy for virtualized environments, 419
    identifying key issues and challenges, 419–421

managing Virtual Server and virtual machine, 418–423

Pause registry key, 217

peak processor utilization, 283–285

PercentCompleted method, 240

performance

assessing limits of, 365–367

monitoring, 355–356

Operator Console views, 438

optimizing virtual machine, 184–189

setting thresholds for, 362–363

See also entries for different types of performance

Performance History report, 448

Performance History Virtual Machine–CPU Utilization report, 448

Performance History Virtual Machine–Disk Space Used (Bytes) report, 449

Performance History Virtual Machine–RAM Used (Bytes) report, 449

Performance Logs and Alerts, 423

Performance Monitor Tool, 386

performance-tuned SCSI controller driver, 34

performance-tuned video driver, 34

peripheral port hardware limits, 365

permission entries, security, 46

physical adapter, 204

mapping virtual network adapter to, 190–191

problems connecting virtual network to, 323–324

physical computer serial port setting, 208

physical disk, using linked disk to convert, 119–120

physical workload virtualization potential, assessing, 281–289

PhysicalHostName registry key, 215

PhysicalHostNameFullyQualified registry key, 216

PhysicalMemoryAllocated counter, 424

PhysicalProcessorCount property, 270

physical-to-virtual (P2V) machine conversion, 452, 474–475, 488. *See also* conversion tools

physical-to-virtual (P2V) migration process

assessing physical workload virtualization potential, 281–289

capturing source system disk image, 307

completing migration process, 309

creating virtual machine, 308

defining workload hardware limitations, 288–289

defining workload memory requirements, 282–293

defining workload network requirement, 285–287

defining workload operational limitations, 289

defining workload processor requirement, 282–285

defining workload storage requirements, 287–288

deploying source system disk image to virtual machine, 308–309

gathering source system configuration information, 304

generating migration scripts, 305–306

loading drivers into Automated Deployment Services (ADS), 306

performing migration, 303–309

phases of, 289–299

validating source system configuration information, 304–305

PhysicaMemotyAllocated counter, 242

Pilot phase of virtualization project, 304

creating communications plan, 396–397

creating issues on tracking plan, 395–396

creating support plan, 395

deployment plan, 392–393

developing migration plan, 395

developing training plan, 395–396

documenting risks, 398

establishing project milestones, 398

establishing success criteria, 399

implementing pilot, 399

incorporating lessons learned, 400

measuring project success, 399–400

objectives, 389–390

operations plan, 395

pilot architecture, 391–392

selecting pilot locations, 390

selecting virtualization candidates, 391

Planning and Designing phase, of virtualization project

consolidation planning approaches, 373–374, 377–385

defined, 373

defining Virtual Server host configurations, 374–377

solution planning, 385–387

PlateSpin, Ltd, 358

PlateSpin PowerConvert, 491–493

PlateSpin PowerRecon, 485–487

Plug and Play Manager, 120

ports, Virtual Server network, 165. *See also entries for individual ports*

POST. *See* BIOS Power-on Self Test (POST)

power consumption information, collecting, 357, 370–371

PowerConvert, 491–493

PowerRecon, 358

Pre-boot Execution Environment protocol (PXE), 34, 290, 297, 299

precompaction, 123–125

printer (LPT) port, 30

problem statements

defining, 334–336

setting priorities, 335–336

processor, 31

assessing performance, 365–366

collecting information about, 351–352

defining workload requirement, 283–285

hardware limits, 363

maximizing performance, 173–174

monitoring, 355–356

and resource allocation, 185
See also entries for individual processor types
processor scaling, 283–285
ProcessorFeaturesString property, 270
ProcessorManufacturerString property, 270
ProcessorSpeed property, 270
ProcessorSpeedString property, 270
ProcessorVersionString property, 270
Product support policy, 24
project budget, creating, 344
project management team, 337–339
project manager, 338
project scheduler, 338
Project Tasks Web part, 394
project team, assembling
  defining out-of-scope, 341–342
  defining required teams and roles, 336–337
  defining scope approach, 341
  determining project phases, 342
  identifying roles, 337–3341
project-managed virtual machine security, 161–162
Property variables, 229
Protected Mode, 318
P2V. *See* physical-to-virtual (P2V) migration process
PXE. *See* Pre-boot Execution Environment protocol (PXE)
PXE-based installation, 214

Q
queuing, command, 181–182
quota points, 468

R
rack space information, collecting, 357, 370
RAID. *See* Redundant Array of Inexpensive Disks (RAID)
Raise method, 231
RBFG. *See* Remote Boot Disk Generator (RBFG)
RDP. *See* Remote Desktop Protocol (RDP)
read-only parent disk, 114
recent event properties, configuring, 50
Recovery plans, implementation of, 15–17
Red Hat Enterprise Linux 4, 23
Red Hat Enterprise Linux 2.1 (Update 6), 23
Red Hat Enterprise Linux 3 (Update 6), 23
Red Hat Enterprise Server 9, 23
Red Hat Linux 7.3, 23
Red Hat Linux 9.0, 23
red state, 440–441
Redundant Array of Inexpensive Disks (RAID), 182–183
RegisterVirtualMachine method, 253, 259–260, 265–267
RegisterVirtualNetwork method, 263
RegisterVM.vbs, 259–260
RegisterVNC.vbs, 266–267

registry keys, virtual machine additions, 215–216
relative weight allocation, 185–186, 285
Remote Boot Disk Generator (RBFG), 290
Remote Desktop Protocol (RDP), 35, 318
Remote Installation Services (RIS), 34, 214, 298
remote resources, 91–97
remote Virtual Server, connecting to, 233–234
Remove permission, 150
*RemoveConfiguration*Value method, 268
RemoveHardDiskConnection method, 246
reserved capacity allocation, 185–187, 285
reserved field name, 67–68, 112–113
Reset registry key, 218
resource allocation management page, 185–187
resources group, configuring, 140
Restore From Saved State registry key, 218
Result method, 240
Resume registry key, 217
ring compression, 6–8, 60–61
RIS. *See* Remote Installation Services (RIS)
risk manager, 339
risks
  attributes of, 343
  common, 342–343
  documenting, 398
  identifying, 342–344
  ranking, 344
rules, 443. *See also* Virtual Server 2005 R2 Management Pack

S
SAN. *See* storage area network (SAN)
SAS. *See* Serial Attached SCSI (SAS)
SATA. *See* Serial Advanced Technology Attachment (SATA)
Save State and Commit Undo Disks registry key, 217
Save State and Keep Undo Disks registry key, 217
Save State file, 57, 69, 287
Save State registry key, 217
saved state
  file compatibility, 209–210
  virtual machine in, fails during start up on different Virtual Server host, 328
  virtual machine in, fails to restart after change in hardware-assisted virtualization state, 327–328
saved state field name, 67
scalable and high-performance disk subsystem, 221
SCCM. *See* Systems Center Configuration Manager (SCCM) 2007
SCOM. *See* Microsoft System Center Operations Manager (SCOM) 2007
SCP. *See* Service connection point (SCP)
script debugger, 232–233
Script Settings form, 47–48
scripting

adding virtual hard disks (VHDs) to virtual machine, 250–253
advanced concepts, 236–253
with Component Object Model (COM) application programming interface (API), 227–234
creating virtual hard disk (VHDs), 248–250
debugging, 232–233
file and folder management, 237–238
logging events, 238–240
obtaining virtual hard disk information, 246–248
using tasks, 240–241
using Virtual Server WMI namespace, 242–246
Scriptomatic 2.0, 245
scripts
feature of Virtual Machine Manager Library Server resources, 456–457
generating migration, 295–297, 305–306
virtual machine configuration option, 40, 47–48
See also entries for individual scripts
SCSI. *See* Small Computer System Interface (SCSI)
SCSI adapters, 40, 189
SCSI controller driver, 203
adding virtual hard disks to virtual machine, 251
disk hardware limits, 364–365
STOP: Ox7B Error, 320–321
SCSI protocol, 202–203
SCSI Shunt Driver.vfd, 206, 326–327
SCSI storage, 31
SCVMM. *See* System Center Virtual Machine Manager (SCVMM)
search paths, configuring, 167–169, 409–410
secondary hardware configuration, 292
Secure Sockets Layer (SSL) protocol, 164, 405
security
application folders, 146–148
configuring Virtual Network Manager role, 156–157
configuring Virtual Server Manager role, 157–158
configuring Virtual Server View Only role, 152–153
configuring VMRC client role, 158–159
of remote Administration Website, 164
virtual machine access, 159–164
and virtual machine library, 224
Virtual Machine Manager role, 154–156
of Virtual Server 2005 R2, 145–151
Virtual Server configuration, 272–274
Virtual Server network ports, 165
Virtual Server Security Manager role, 153–154
Virtual Server Services security, 164–165
Windows Server 2003 application folders, 146
security entries, 272
security group, 220, 222–223
Security Properties form, 45
self-provisioning Web portal. *See* Virtual Machine Manager self-provisioning Web portal
self-service policies, 467–468

Serial Advanced Technology Attachment (SATA), 181–183
Serial Attached SCSI (SAS), 181–183
serial (COM) port, 30
SerialPorts property, 270
Server Core role, 26
server farm, 93–94
server information, collecting, 349–350
service connection point (SCP), 21, 76
service discovery, 436–438
service principal name (SPN), register, 75
service principal name (SPN) registration failures, 314–316
servicePrincipalName, 314
services, 13–14, 75–76. *See also entries for individual services*
services information, collecting, 354–355
Set command, 228–229
SetConfigurationValue method, 268
Setspn.exe, 315–316
setup and installation troubleshooting issues
missing or incompatible IIS configuration, 313–314
service principal name (SPN) registration failures, 314–316
stop error on x64 Windows operating system with AMD-V, 316
Setup Type dialog box, 94
Share Virtual Machines folder, 159
Shared Folders features, 128
ShrinkEnabled, 236. *See also* VMRCClientControl property
Shut Down Guest OS and Commit Undo Disks registry key, 217
Shut Down Guest OS and Keep Undo Disks registry key, 217
Shut Down Guest OS registry key, 217
shutdown script, 140, 200
single-server configuration, 89–91, 473
single-server installation, 107
64-bit host operating system, 74–75
Small Computer System Interface (SCSI), 32, 181, 320–321. *See also* virtual SCSI interface
"smart" disk copy algorithm, 474
Snapshot technology, 14
Snare, 315
SoftGrid products, 10
Softricity, 10
software configuration, 292
software inventory information, collecting, 353
software requirements, System Center Virtual Machine Manager, 471–473
software virtualization
application-level virtualization, 9–10
defined, 4
machine-level virtualization, 5–8
operating system-level, 8–9
sound card, 31

Source property, 231
source system configuration, 292–295, 303–304
source system disk image
    capturing, 307
    deploying, to virtual machine, 308–309
Source_Capture.cmd, 307–308
Source_captureDisk.xml, 297
Source_CleanupVM.cmd, 296
Source_commonlnit.cmd, 295
Source_CreateVM.cmd, 295, 298, 302
Source_DeployVM.cmd, 296, 298
Source_DeployVM.xml, 297
Source_internalState.xml, 297
Source_PostDeploy.cmd, 296
Source_ServiceDriver.xml, 297
Special Permission, 150
Specify Virtual Server form, 36–37
SPN. *See* Service principal name (SPN)
SQL Server 2005, 454
SSE property, 270
SSE2 property, 270
stacked area chart, 382–384
standards, establishing, 189–192
startup, automating, 200
state, 438
State Monitoring and Service Discover rules, 523
steering committee, 337–338
stop error, 316
storage area network (SAN), 32
storage configuration, 292
storage locations, Virtual Machines, 223
storage requirements, defining workload, 287–288
subject matter expert team, 337, 339–340
subnets-per-site information, collecting, 349
Support policies, 24–25
SuSE Linux 9.2, 23
SuSE Linux 9.3, 23
SuSE Linux 10.0, 23
SuSE Linux Enterprise Server 9, 23
SWSoft, 9
system backup, 193
System Center Operations Manager (SCOM) 2007, 429, 454
System Center Virtual Machine Manager (SCVMM)
    defined, 451
    deploying, 470–473
    developing migration plan, 395–396
    features, 452–453
    hardware requirements, 470–471
    overview, 25–26, 451
    physical-to-virtual machine conversion, 474–475
    pilot architecture, 391–392
    software requirements, 471–473
    using, 473–479

Virtual Machine Manager Administrator Console, 457–468
Virtual Machine Manager agent, 454–455
Virtual Machine Manager library, 455–457
Virtual Machine Manager self-provisioning Web portal, 469
virtual machine manager server (VVM server), 454
virtual machine placement, 477–479
virtual machine provisioning requirements, 476–477
virtual machine templates, 475–476
virtual-to-virtual machine conversion, 475
Windows PowerShell command-line interface, 469
System Preparation tool, 213, 290
Systems Center Configuration Manager (SCCM) 2007, 386
Systems Management Server, 224
SystemTools Exporter Pro, 487–488
SystemTools Software, 358

T
table offset field name, 67, 112
Tagged Command Queuing (TCQ), 181
Take Control Transfer conversion method, 492
target, 183
task sequence files, 295–297
Tasks. *See* VMTask methods
TCP Port 135, 165
TCP Port 1024, 165
TCQ. *See* Tagged Command Queuing (TCQ)
team roles
    architecture design team, 337, 339, 341
    operational management, 337, 340–341
    project management team, 337–339
    steering committee, 337–338
    subject matter expert team, 337, 339–340
    test team, 337, 340
technical problem statements, 334
template creation, 452
test engineer, 340
test manager, 3404
test team, 337, 340
testing
    using differencing disks to create guest VMs for concurrent, 115–116
    virtualization of, 15–16
text file setting, 208
32-bit host operating system, 74–75
ThreeDNow property, 270
time setup field name, 66
time synchronization with physical host, 34
tools, for collecting information, 358. *See also* management tools; *and entries for specific tools*
tracks, 180
training manager, 340–341
training plan, developing, 395–396

Traverse Folder/Execute File permission, 153
troubleshooting
  Administration Website issues, 316–320
  setup and installation issues, 313–316
  virtual hard disk (VHD) issues, 320–323
  virtual machine issues, 326–329
  virtual network issues, 323–326
Turn Off registry key, 217
Turn Off Virtual Machine and Commit Undo Disks
  registry key, 218
Turn Off Virtual Machine and Discard Undo Disks
  registry key, 218
Turn Off Virtual Machine and Keep Undo Disk registry
  key, 218
Turn On registry key, 217

U

UAC. *See* User Account Control (UAC)
undo hard disk, 65, 287
  and compaction, 123
  configuring, 116–117
  defined, 109, 116, 419
  managing, 117
  using, 118
unique ID field name, 67
UnMountVHD function, 235
UnregisterVirtualMachine method, 257, 261
UnregisterVM.vbs, 261–262
update sequence numbers (USNs), 417
updates information, collecting, 353–354
uplink port, 62
Uptime counter, 242, 424
USB devices information, collecting, 351, 353
user account, configuring virtual machine, 163–164
User Account Control (UAC), 318
user role, 221–222
UTCTime property, 270

V

Validated Write To Service Principal Name permission,
  75
VBScript, 437
VE. *See* virtual environments (VE)
Version property, 229
VHD. *See* virtual hard disk (VHD)
VHD compaction, 110, 123–126
.vhd file name extension, 116
VHD Mount tool, 77, 99–100, 107
VHDFileName, 121
VHDMount command-line tool
  defined, 20–21, 110, 120–121
  defining options, 121
  to determine virtual hard disk name, 122–123
  to mount virtual hard disk (VHD) file, 123

  to plug in and mount virtual hard disk file, 122
  to plug in virtual hard disk file, 121
  to unmount virtual hard disk file, 122
VHDMount functions, 235
video card, 31
video driver, 34, 59
View permission, 150
Virtual Administration Website application
  (VSWebApp.exe), 403
virtual COM port settings, changing, 207–208
virtual component library, 453
Virtual DHCP server, 33
Virtual DHCP Server, enabling, on Virtual Network,
  128–129
Virtual Disk Precompactor tool, 124
Virtual Disk Service (VDS) API, 21, 120
Virtual Disks Manager, 497–498
Virtual Disks menu Create option, 40–41
virtual environments (VE), 8–9
Virtual Floppy Disk form, 41
virtual floppy disks, 57, 69
virtual floppy drive, changing drive settings, 206–207
virtual hard disk (VHD)
  advanced features, 109
  broken differencing disk after parent VHD is moved
    or renamed, 321–323
  changing settings, 201–203
  compacting, 125–126
  create, 40–41
  default size for dynamic, 23
  defined, 456–457
  defragmenting, 123–124
  description, 196
  differencing disks, 109–116
  and disaster recovery plans, 17
  hardware required, 64–65
  inspecting, 41
  linked disks, 110
  managing, 40–41
  obtaining information about, 246–248
  overview, 57, 64–68
  performance of, 188–189
  STOP: 0x7B error booting from Virtual SCSI disk,
    320–321
  structure of, 65–68
  types, 31–32, 65
  undo disks, 109
  VHD compaction, 110
  VHDMount command-line tool, 110
  VMVirtualMachine methods to add or remove, 246
  VMVirtualServer methods to create, 245–246
  See also entries for specific types
virtual hard disk (VHD) file, 121, 456–457
virtual hard disk (VHD) name, 122–123
virtual hard disk (VHD) tools

Invirtus VM Optimizer 3.0, 493–494
xcarab VHD Resizer, 495
Xtralogic VHD Utility, 495
virtual hard drive naming standard, 191
virtual IDE interface, 32
virtual infrastructure reporting, 453
Virtual Local Area Networks (VLANS), 34
virtual LPT port settings, 209
virtual machine
 operational considerations, 189–193
 performance, 430
 setting thresholds, 362–363
Virtual Machine Additions
 configuration option, 39
 defined, 34
 installing, 215–216
 optimizing virtual machine performance, 184–185
 overview, 56–59
 registry keys, 215–216
virtual machine and template creation, 452
virtual machine checkpoints, 453
virtual machine cluster
 two-node, using iSCSI, 132
 using iSCI, 130–135
virtual machine configuration file (.vmc), 38
virtual machine configuration folder, configuring
 default, 169–170
Virtual Machine Configuration pane, 38–40
virtual machine configuration (.vmc) file name,
 190–191
virtual machine creation and deployment phase, 290,
 298–299
Virtual Machine Details report, 449
virtual machine folder, 164
virtual machine guest operating system, 55
Virtual Machine Helper service, 57–58, 200
virtual machine library
 capacity planning, 223–224
 centralized storage, 220–221
 components of, 219–220
 content refresh, 225
 defined, 192–193
 features and benefits of, 218–219
 patch management, 224
 security, 220, 222–224
 structured roles, 220–223
Virtual Machine Manage self-provisioning Web portal,
 469
Virtual Machine Manager Administrator Console, 454,
 474
 Administration view, 467–468
 defined, 457–458
 hardware requirement for, 470
 host information, 460
 Hosts detail view, 459

Hosts Overview, 458–461
Jobs Overview, 466–467
layout, 458
Library Overview, 464–466
placement settings, 478
Placement tab, 479
software prerequisites, 472
virtual machines view, 461–463
Virtual Machine Manager agent, 454–455, 457, 473
Virtual Machine Manager architecture, 453–454
Virtual Machine Manager kernal, 56–58
Virtual Machine Manager library, 454–457
Virtual Machine Manager role, 154–156
Virtual Machine Manager self-provisioning Web portal,
 469, 476–477
 hardware requirements for, 471
 physical-to-virtual machine conversion, 474–475
 software prerequisites, 472
Virtual Machine Manager Server, 454, 472
virtual machine memory allocation, calculation for,
 282–283
virtual machine migration process, 281–310, 453
Virtual Machine Monitor (VMM)
 architecture, 57–58
 full virtualization, 5–6
 implementation, 5
 native virtualization, 5–7
virtual machine name, 196
Virtual Machine Network Services (VMNS), 42, 62–64,
 77, 183, 323–324
virtual machine operating system installation options,
 213–215
virtual machine patch management, 418–423
virtual machine placement, 477–479
virtual machine provisioning requirements, 476–477
Virtual Machine Remote Control (VMRC), 396
 configuration options, 171–172
 configuring, 46–47
 configuring properties, 51
 defined, 35, 58, 77
 enabling, 170–173
 event codes, 511–512
 installing, 98–99
Virtual Machine Resource Allocation, managing, 51–52
virtual machine rules, 521
virtual machine scripts, 47–48, 205–206
virtual machine security
 configuring centrally managed, 159–160
 configuring organizationally managed, 160–161
 configuring project-managed, 161–162
virtual machine self-provisioning Web portal, 454
virtual machine self-service, 453
virtual machine server publication, 20–21
virtual machine state, 217–218, 430, 440–443
Virtual Machine Status page, 38

virtual machine template, 455, 475–476
virtual machine user account, 163–164
virtual machine (VM), 456–457
  access
    configuring centrally managed virtual machine
      security, 159–160
    configuring organizationally managed virtual
      machine security, 160–161
    configuring project-managed virtual machine
      security, 161–162
    configuring virtual machine user account, 163–164
    enabling constrained delegation, 163
    rules, 443–444
  adding, 209–210
  adding pre-existing, 38
  adding virtual hard disks (VHDs) to, 250–253
  basic configuration parameters, 196
  configuration
    automating startup and shutdown, 200
    changing CD/DVD drive settings, 203–204
    changing virtual COM port settings, 207–208
    changing virtual floppy drive settings, 206–207
    changing virtual hard disk settings, 201–203
    changing virtual LPT port setting, 209
    changing virtual machine name, 199
    changing virtual network adapter settings,
      204–205
    completing, on second virtual server host, 141–142
    and management, 452
    memory settings, 201
    tuning, settings, 198–209
    virtual machine script settings, 205–206
  configuring Microsoft Cluster Server on first, 133–134
  configuring Microsoft Cluster Server on second,
    134–135
  create, 197–198
  creating, 37–38, 253–257, 308
  creating, on first virtual server host, 141
  creation process, 196–225
    adding virtual machine, 209–210
    benefits of virtual machine library, 218–219
    configuring virtual machine BIOS settings, 211–213
    controlling virtual machine state, 217–218
    creating virtual machine library, 220–223
    installing virtual machine additions, 215–216
    removing virtual machine, 211
  defined, 4
  delete, 257–259
  deploying source system disk image, 308–309
  disabling hardware-assisted virtualization, 329
  hardware environment, 30–31
  hardware limits, 362
  managing, 37–40, 253–262
  managing configurations, 38–40
  monitoring, 423–425, 436–450

  optimizing performance, 184–189
  register, 259–260
  registration fails after previous removal, 328–329
  removing, 211
  reports from, 446–450
  in saved state fails during start up on different Virtual
    Server host, 328
  in saved state fails to restart after change in hardware-
    assisted virtualization state, 327–328
  slow guest operating system installation, 326–327
  tasks of Virtual Server 2005 R2 Management Pack,
    444–446
  understanding graphics performance, 187–188
  unregistering, 261–262
  using traditional methods to back up, 415–417
  using VSS to back up, 412–415
  VMVirtualServer methods to create, delete, and
    register, 253
  See also library of virtual machines
Virtual Manager Machine Administrator Console,
  457–468
Virtual Manager Server, hardware requirements for, 470
virtual memory, 57, 61–64
virtual network adapter, 34
  description, 196
  mapping, to physical adapter, 190–191
Virtual Network Computing (VNC), 35
virtual network configuration folder, 164
Virtual Network Manager role, 156–157
virtual network naming standard, 191
Virtual Network Properties pane, 43
virtual network (VM0), default, 302
virtual network(s)
  add configuration file, 43
  advanced network features, 126–130
  configure, 43–44
  creating, 42, 128, 263–265
  defined, 33, 57, 61–64
  duplicate MAC addresses, 324–326
  host-to-guest networking, 126
  Internet connection sharing with Network Address
    Translation, 126, 129–130
  managing, 42–44, 262–267
  Microsoft Loopback Adapter, 126–128
  and optimizing performance, 183–184
  problems connecting virtual network to physical
    network adapter, 323–324
  register existing, 265–267
Virtual Networks Manager, 497–498
Virtual PC 2004, 17, 26
Virtual PC 2007, 26, 58, 128
virtual processors, 57, 59–61
virtual SCSI interface, 32–33
Virtual Security Manager role, 153–154
Virtual Server 2005

documentation and developer resources, 76
feature evolution, 18–19
monitoring, 423–424
patch management, 418–423
reports from, 446–450
rules, 443–444
tasks of Virtual Server 2005 R2 Management Pack, 444–446
using traditional methods to back up, 415–417
using VSS to back up, 412–415
Virtual Server 2005 R2, 454
advanced features, 109–142
event codes, 503–520
features, 19
infrastructure of, 403–425
security, 145–151
service discovery, 436–438
Virtual Server 2005 R2 COM API, outlining, 53
Virtual Server 2005 R2 Management Pack
executing installer package, 433–434
features, 429–432
importing, 434
improvements, 430–432
installing, 433–436
installing MOM agent, 435–436
monitoring, 430
overview, 427–429
prerequisites for installation, 433
rule groups, 443–444
rules, 521–523
tasks, 444–446
verifying version of, 435
Virtual Server 2005 R2 SP1, 58, 391–392
benefits, 17–19
features, 19
installing, 74–107
Knowledge Base articles, 24
Local Administration Web site, 91–93
new in, 235–236
product overview, 29–53
single-server configuration, 89–91
support policies, 24–25
uninstalling, 101–102
upgrading, 87–89
VHDMount, 235
VMGuestOS properties and methods, 235–236
VMRCClientControl property, 236
VMTask properties, 235
Virtual Server 2005 R2 SP2, 19–23
Virtual Server architecture, 55–69
Virtual Server COM API, 32
Virtual Server compaction tool, 125
Virtual Server Component Object Model (COM) application programming interface (API), 445

Virtual Server Component Object Model (COM) interface, 298
Virtual Server configuration, 452
managing, 267–274
reporting host information, 270–272
security entries, 272–274
VMVirtualServer methods to manage, 268–269
Virtual Server Event Viewer, 52
Virtual Server host applications, 180
Virtual Server Host Cluster, 130–131
scenarios, 135–136
using iSCSI, 135–142
Virtual Server Host cluster nodes, 140
Virtual Server host clustering, 20–21
Virtual Server host configurations
defining, 374–377
high-availability hardware requirements, 375–377
physical requirements, 375
Virtual Server host grouping, 452
Virtual Server host performance thresholds, 379
Virtual Server host server, installing, 96–97
Virtual Server host(s), 328, 454
completing virtual machine configuration on second, 141–142
configuring Microsoft Cluster Server on first, 138–139
configuring Microsoft Cluster Server on second, 139
creating virtual machine on first, 141
managing multiple, 36–37, 436–450
Virtual Server Information and Properties pane, 44–45
Virtual Server Main Event codes, 512–517
Virtual Server Manager role, 157–158, 319
Virtual Server manager search paths, configuring, 51
Virtual Server methods, 268–269
Virtual Server Migration Toolkit (VSMT), 17, 281, 395, 474
installing, 302–303
physical-to-virtual (P2V) migration phases, 290–299
prerequisites, 290–291
workload image capture migration phase, 292–295
See also physical-to-virtual (P2V) migration process
Virtual server network ports, 165
Virtual Server Networking event codes, 503
Virtual Server object, connecting to, 228–229
Virtual Server Preference Change event codes, 511
Virtual Server Properties
configuring
Virtual Machine Remote Control Server Properties, 46–47
Virtual Server Script Settings, 47–48
Virtual Server Search Paths, 49
Virtual Server Security Properties, 45–46
managing, 44–49
permission entries, 46
Virtual Server ratings, 452
Virtual Server Script Settings, configuring, 47–48

Virtual Server search paths, configuring, 49, 409–410
Virtual Server Security Permissions, 149–150
Virtual Server Security Properties, 45–46, 148, 151
Virtual Server Service Directory rule, 523
Virtual Server Service Health Check rule, 523
Virtual Server service (VSSRVC), 57–58, 75–76, 79, 93
Virtual Server Services security, 164–165
Virtual Server state, 430, 439–440, 442–443
Virtual Server VHDSTOR Driver event code, 517–518
Virtual Server View Only role, configuring, 152–153
Virtual Server Virtual Machine event codes, 505–510
Virtual Server VSS Writer, 410–412
Virtual Server VSS Writer event codes, 503–505
Virtual Server VSS Writer metadata document, 414–415
Virtual Server Web application, disabling, 96
Virtual Server Windows Management Instrumentation (WMI). *See* Windows Management Instrumentation (WMI)
Virtual Server WMI namespace, 242–246
Virtual Studio, 97
virtualization
    bare metal, 8
    consolidating branch office, 15–16
    data center consolidation, 15
    decreasing management complexity, 14
    decreasing time to provision or distribute services, 13–14
    defined, 4
    defining scenarios, 15–17
    full, 5–6
    hardware-assisted, 61, 327–329
    implementation of business continuity and recovery plans, 15–17
    implementing simple, flexible, and dynamic infrastructure, 12–13
    increasing availability of computing resources, 13
    machine-level, 5–8
    native, 5–7
    operating system-level, 8–9
    reducing capital and operating cost, 11–12
    software, 4–5
    of test and development infrastructure, 15–16
virtualization candidate
    assessing application support limits, 367–368
    assessing hardware limits, 363–365
    assessing performance limits, 365–367
    grouping, 377–378
    overview, 361–362
    selecting, 391
    setting performance thresholds, 362–363
    virtual machine hardware limits, 362
Virtualization Candidates report, 449–450
virtualization product roadmap, 25–26
virtualization project
    Assessment phase, 361–371

Discovery phase, 347–358
Envisioning phase, 333–344
Pilot phase, 389–400
Planning and Designing phase, 373–387
VirtualMachine object counter, 423–424
VirtualMachine WMI class property, 242–246
VirtualMachineName registry key, 216
VirtualMachines property, 230
VirtualNetwork object counter, 423–425
virtual-to-virtual (V2V) machine conversion, 452, 475, 488. *See also* conversion tools
virtual-to-virtual (V2V) machine migration, 281, 309–310
Virtuozzo, 9
vision statement, establishing, 336
Visual Basic for Applications script, 397
Visual Basic Script, 227
    connecting to Virtual Server object, 228–229
    file and folder management, 237–238
    See also Component Object Model (COM) application programming interface (API)
Visual Effects Performance Options dialog box, 187–188
VLANS. *See* Virtual Local Area Networks (VLANS)
VM. *See* virtual machine
VM Optimizer 3.0, 493–494
.vmc file name extension, 116
VMClient.exe utility, 298
VMGuestOS properties and methods, 235–236
VMI. *See* Windows Management Instrumentation (WMI)
VMM. *See* Virtual Machine Monitor (VMM)
VMM.SYS driver, 56–57
VMNS. *See* Virtual Machine Network Services (VMNS)
Vmpatch.exe utility, 294
VMRC. *See* Virtual Machine Remote Control (VMRC)
VMRC client role, configuring, 158–159
VMRC performance, increasing, 178–179
VMRCClientControl property, 236
VMRCplus. *See* Microsoft Virtual Machine Remote Control Plus (VMRCplus)
VMScript, 292–297
VMScript.exe utility, 304–306
VMTask methods, 240–241
VMTask properties, 235
VMVirtualMachine methods, to add or remove virtual hard disks (VHDs), 246
VMVirtualMachine.AddHardDiskConnection method, 251
VMVirtualMachine.SCSIControllers, 251
VMVirtualServer interface, 228
VMVirtualServer methods, 267–268
    to create, delete, and register virtual machines, 253
    to create, register, and remove, 263
    to create virtual hard disks (VHDs), 245–246
    to object host information, 269
VMVirtualServer.GetHardDisk method, 245

VMware Tools Service, 310
VMware virtual machine, 309–310
VM_WMI_Properties.vbs script, 242–243
VNC. *See* Virtual Network Computing (VNC)
VNET_WMI_Properties.vbs script, 244
Volume Configuration Wizard page, 474
Volume Shadow Copy Service support, 19–21, 77
Volume Shadow Copy Service (VSS)
    back up scenarios, 413–414
    defined, 387, 410–412
    physical-to-virtual machine conversion and, 474
    using, to back up Virtual Server and virtual machines, 412–415
    VSS backup writer for, 59
Volume Shadow Copy Service (VSS) writer, 193
VRMC Windows Client, enabling reduced colors from, 179
VShadow, 412
VSMT. *See* Virtual Server Migration Toolkit (VSMT)
VSS. *See* Volume Shadow Copy Service (VSS)
VSS backup writer, 59
VS_Security.vb, 273–274
VT. *See* Intel Virtualization Technology (VT)
.vud file name extension, 116
V2V. *See* virtual-to-virtual (V2V) machine migration

W

WaitForCompletion method, 240–241
WDM. *See* Windows Driver Model (WDM)
Website Properties
    configuring event viewer properties, 51
    configuring master status view, 50
    configuring recent event properties, 50
    configuring Virtual Server manager search paths, 51
    configuring VMRC properties, 51
    managing, 49–51
whenchanged parameter, 349
Windows 2000 Server, 417, 474
Windows 2000 Virtual Machine Additions i8042 mouse and keyboard driver event codes, 518–520
Windows Component Wizard, 81
Windows Defrag utility, 124
Windows Driver Model (WDM), 62
Windows Feature dialog box, 83–84
Windows Firewall, 62, 89–90, 95
Windows Management Instrumentation (WMI), 58
Windows Management interface (WMI), 242–246, 423
Windows NT Virtual Machine Additions i8042 mouse and keyboard driver event codes, 519–520
Windows NT Virtual Machine Additions S3 video driver event codes, 520
Windows PowerShell command line, 453–454, 469, 474
Windows PowerShell command line interface, 469
Windows Server 2003, 17, 417–418, 474

Windows Server 2008, 26
Windows Server 2003 Kerberos Key Distribution Center (KDC), 406
Windows Server 2003 Performance Monitor Tool, 386
Windows Server 2003 R2, 454, 474
Windows Server 2003 System Monitor, 423
Windows Server Automated Deployment Services (ADS). *See* Automated Deployment Services (ADS)
Windows Server Base Operating System Management Pack, 432
Windows Server Catalog, 135
Windows Server System Common Engineering Criteria (CEC), 24, 368
Windows Server System (WSS), 24
Windows Server Virtualization, 6–8, 25–26
Windows Software Update Service (WSUS), 386
Windows user interface, configuring, 187–188
Windows VMRC Client, 171
Windows XP, 474
WMI. *See* Windows Management Instrumentation (WMI)
WMI namespace, 242–246
workload analysis, performing
    calculations for, 382–384
    data processing, 381–382
    establishing thresholds, 379–381
workload hardware limitations, 288–289
workload image capture, 290
    capture source system image, 297–298
    generate migration scripts, 295–297
    inventory source system configuration, 292
    validate source system configuration, 292–295
workload memory requirements, defining, 282–283
workload network requirement, defining, 285–287
workload operational limitations, defining, 289
workload processor requirement, defining, 283–285
workload storage requirements, defining, 287–288
WScript.Arguments, 233
WScript.Echo command, 229, 232
WSUS. *See* Windows Software Update Service (WSUS)

X

x64 Intel Virtualization Technology (VT), 26
x86 Intel Virtualization Technology (VT), 6
x86 processor platform, 4, 21–23
x64 version, of Windows Server 2005 R2 SP1, 22–23, 316
xcarab VHD Resizer, 495
Xen, 7
XenSource, 7
Xtralogic VHD Utility, 495

Y

yellow state, 439–440

Windows Vista™ Resources for Administrators

Windows Vista Administrator's Pocket Consultant
William Stanek
ISBN 9780735622968

Portable and precise, this pocket-sized guide delivers immediate answers for the day-to-day administration of Windows Vista. Featuring easy-to-scan tables, step-by-step instructions, and handy lists, this book offers the straightforward information you need to solve problems and get the job done—whether you're at your desk or in the field!

Windows Vista Resource Kit
Mitch Tulloch, Tony Northrup, Jerry Honeycutt, Ed Wilson, Ralph Ramos, and the Windows Vista Team
ISBN 9780735622838

Get the definitive reference for deploying, configuring, and supporting Windows Vista—from the experts who know the technology best. This guide offers in-depth, comprehensive technical guidance on automating deployment; implementing security enhancements; administering group policy, files folders, and programs; and troubleshooting. Includes an essential toolkit of resources on DVD.

MCTS Self-Paced Training Kit (Exam 70-620): Configuring Windows Vista Client
Ian McLean and Orin Thomas
ISBN 9780735623903

Get in-depth preparation plus practice for Exam 70-620, the required exam for the new Microsoft Certified Technology Specialist (MCTS): Windows Vista Client certification. This 2-in-1 kit focuses on installing client software and configuring system settings, security features, network connectivity, media applications, and mobile devices. Ace your exam prep—and build real-world job skills—with lessons, practice tests, evaluation software, and more.

MCITP Self-Paced Training Kit (Exam 70-622): Installing, Maintaining, Supporting, and Troubleshooting Applications on the Windows Vista Client – Enterprise
Tony Northrup and J.C. Mackin
ISBN 9780735624085

Maximize your performance on Exam 70-622, the required exam for the new Microsoft® Certified IT Professional (MCITP): Enterprise Support Technician certification. Comprehensive and in-depth, this 2-in-1 kit covers managing security, configuring networking, and optimizing performance for Windows Vista clients in an enterprise environment. Ace your exam prep—and build real-world job skills—with lessons, practice tests, evaluation software, and more.

MCITP Self-Paced Training Kit (Exam 70-623): Installing, Maintaining, Supporting, and Troubleshooting Applications on the Windows Vista Client – Consumer
Anil Desai with Chris McCain of GrandMasters
ISBN 9780735624238

Get the 2-in-1 training kit for Exam 70-623, the required exam for the new Microsoft Certified IT Professional (MCITP): Consumer Support Technician certification. This comprehensive kit focuses on supporting Windows Vista clients for consumer PCs and devices, including configuring security settings, networking, troubleshooting, and removing malware. Ace your exam prep—and build real-world job skills—with lessons, practice tests, evaluation software, and more.

See more resources at **microsoft.com/mspress**
and **microsoft.com/learning**

Microsoft Press® products are available worldwide wherever quality computer books are sold. For more information, contact your bookseller, computer retailer, software reseller, or local Microsoft Sales Office, or visit our Web site at **microsoft.com/mspress**. To locate a source near you, or to order directly, call 1-800-MSPRESS in the United States. (In Canada, call **1-800-268-2222**.)

2007 Microsoft® Office System Resources for Developers and Administrators

Microsoft Office SharePoint® Server 2007 Administrator's Companion

Bill English with the Microsoft SharePoint Community Experts
ISBN 9780735622821

Get your mission-critical collaboration and information management systems up and running. This comprehensive, single-volume reference details features and capabilities of SharePoint Server 2007. It delivers easy-to-follow procedures, practical workarounds, and key troubleshooting tactics—for on-the-job results.

Microsoft Windows SharePoint Services Version 3.0 Inside Out

Errin O'Connor
ISBN 9780735623231

Conquer Microsoft Windows SharePoint Services— from the inside out! This ultimate, in-depth reference packs hundreds of time-saving solutions, troubleshooting tips, and workarounds. You're beyond the basics, so now learn how the experts tackle information sharing and team collaboration— and challenge yourself to new levels of mastery!

Microsoft SharePoint Products and Technologies Administrator's Pocket Consultant

Ben Curry
ISBN 9780735623828

Portable and precise, this pocket-sized guide delivers immediate answers for the day-to-day administration of Sharepoint Products and Technologies. Featuring easy-to-scan tables, step-by-step instructions, and handy lists, this book offers the straightforward information you need to get the job done—whether you're at your desk or in the field!

Inside Microsoft Windows® SharePoint Services Version 3

Ted Pattison and Daniel Larson
ISBN 9780735623200

Get in-depth insights on Microsoft Windows SharePoint Services with this hands-on guide. You get a bottom-up view of the platform architecture, code samples, and task-oriented guidance for developing custom applications with Microsoft Visual Studio® 2005 and Collaborative Application Markup Language (CAML).

Inside Microsoft Office SharePoint Server 2007

Patrick Tisseghem
ISBN 9780735623682

Dig deep—and master the intricacies of Office SharePoint Server 2007. A bottom-up view of the platform architecture shows you how to manage and customize key components and how to integrate with Office programs—helping you create custom enterprise content management solutions.

Microsoft Office Communications Server 2007 Resource Kit

Microsoft Office Communications Server Team
ISBN 9780735624061

Your definitive reference to Office Communications Server 2007—direct from the experts who know the technology best. This comprehensive guide offers in-depth technical information and best practices for planning, designing, deploying, managing, and optimizing your systems. Includes a toolkit of valuable resources on CD.

Programming Applications for Microsoft Office Outlook® 2007
Randy Byrne and Ryan Gregg
ISBN 9780735622494

Microsoft Office Visio® 2007 Programming Step by Step
David A. Edson
ISBN 9780735623798

See more resources at **microsoft.com/mspress**
and **microsoft.com/learning**

Additional SQL Server Resources for Administrators

Published and Forthcoming Titles from Microsoft Press

Microsoft® SQL Server™ 2005 Reporting Services *Step by Step*
Hitachi Consulting Services ● ISBN 0-7356-2250-7

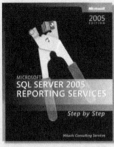

SQL Server Reporting Services (SRS) is Microsoft's customizable reporting solution for business data analysis. It is one of the key value features of SQL Server 2005: functionality more advanced and much less expensive than its competition. SRS is powerful, so an understanding of how to architect a report, as well as how to install and program SRS, is key to harnessing the full functionality of SQL Server. This procedural tutorial shows how to use the Report Project Wizard, how to think about and access data, and how to build queries. It also walks the reader through the creation of charts and visual layouts to enable maximum visual understanding of the data analysis. Interactivity (enhanced in SQL Server 2005) and security are also covered in detail.

Microsoft SQL Server 2005 Administrator's Pocket Consultant
William R. Stanek ● ISBN 0-7356-2107-1

Here's the utterly practical, pocket-sized reference for IT professionals who need to administer, optimize, and maintain SQL Server 2005 in their organizations. This unique guide provides essential details for using SQL Server 2005 to help protect and manage your company's data—whether automating tasks; creating indexes and views; performing backups and recovery; replicating transactions; tuning performance; managing server activity; importing and exporting data; or performing other key tasks. Featuring quick-reference tables, lists, and step-by-step instructions, this handy, one-stop guide provides fast, accurate answers on the spot, whether you're at your desk or in the field!

Microsoft SQL Server 2005 Administrator's Companion
Marci Frohock Garcia, Edward Whalen, and Mitchell Schroeter ● ISBN 0-7356-2198-5

Microsoft SQL Server 2005 Administrator's Companion is the comprehensive, in-depth guide that saves time by providing all the technical information you need to deploy, administer, optimize, and support SQL Server 2005. Using a hands-on, example-rich approach, this authoritative, one-volume reference book provides expert advice, product information, detailed solutions, procedures, and real-world troubleshooting tips from experienced SQL Server 2005 professionals. This expert guide shows you how to design high-availability database systems, prepare for installation, install and configure SQL Server 2005, administer services and features, and maintain and troubleshoot your database system. It covers how to configure your system for your I/O system and model and optimize system capacity. The expert authors provide details on how to create and use defaults, constraints, rules, indexes, views, functions, stored procedures, and triggers. This guide shows you how to administer reporting services, analysis services, notification services, and integration services. It also provides a wealth of information on replication and the specifics of snapshot, transactional, and merge replication. Finally, there is expansive coverage of how to manage and tune your SQL Server system, including automating tasks, backup and restoration of databases, and management of users and security.

Microsoft SQL Server 2005 Analysis Services *Step by Step*
Hitachi Consulting Services ● ISBN 0-7356-2199-3

One of the key features of SQL Server 2005 is SQL Server Analysis Services—Microsoft's customizable analysis solution for business data modeling and interpretation. Just compare SQL Server Analysis Services to its competition to understand/grasp the great value of its enhanced features. One of the keys to harnessing the full functionality of SQL Server will be leveraging Analysis Services for the powerful tool that it is—including creating a cube, and deploying, customizing, and extending the basic calculations. This step-by-step tutorial discusses how to get started, how to build scalable analytical applications, and how to use and administer advanced features. Interactivity (which is enhanced in SQL Server 2005), data translation, and security are also covered in detail.

Microsoft SQL Server 2005 Express Edition
Step by Step
Jackie Goldstein ● ISBN 0-7356-2184-5

Inside Microsoft SQL Server 2005:
The Storage Engine
Kalen Delaney ● ISBN 0-7356-2105-5

Inside Microsoft SQL Server 2005:
T-SQL Programming
Itzik Ben-Gan ● ISBN 0-7356-2197-7

Inside Microsoft SQL Server 2005:
Query Processing and Optimization
Kalen Delaney ● ISBN 0-7356-2196-9

For more information about Microsoft Press® books and other learning products,
visit: **www.microsoft.com/mspress** *and* **www.microsoft.com/learning**

Microsoft Press products are available worldwide wherever quality computer books are sold. For more information, contact your book or computer retailer, software reseller, or local Microsoft Sales Office, or visit our Web site at **www.microsoft.com/mspress**. To locate your nearest source for Microsoft Press products, or to order directly, call 1-800-MSPRESS in the United States. (In Canada, call **1-800-268-2222**.)

What do you think of this book?

We want to hear from you!

Do you have a few minutes to participate in a brief online survey?

Microsoft is interested in hearing your feedback so we can continually improve our books and learning resources for you.

To participate in our survey, please visit:

www.microsoft.com/learning/booksurvey/

...and enter this book's ISBN-10 number (appears above barcode on back cover*). As a thank-you to survey participants in the United States and Canada, each month we'll randomly select five respondents to win one of five $100 gift certificates from a leading online merchant. At the conclusion of the survey, you can enter the drawing by providing your e-mail address, which will be used for prize notification only.

Thanks in advance for your input. Your opinion counts!

* Where to find the ISBN-10 on back cover

Example only. Each book has unique ISBN.